Thoughts for Festive Foods

COMPANION VOLUMES

Thoughts for Food
Thoughts for Buffets

Decorations by Hilary Wills

Thoughts
for
Festive Foods

HOUGHTON MIFFLIN COMPANY BOSTON

Acknowledgments

GREAT cookbooks are rare; they come only out of long experience in entertaining and good cooking.

We are grateful to all our hostesses, who have devoted their time and recipes in helping to bring our *Thoughts for Festive Foods* to you.

We wish especially to acknowledge the selfless contribution of time, skill, and experience of Elaine Frank and Florence Hirschfeld, without which *Thoughts for Festive Foods* would not exist.

We are pleased that it is now available and can take its rightful place beside its sister books, *Thoughts for Food* and *Thoughts for Buffets*, in the libraries of hostesses everywhere.

INSTITUTE PUBLISHING COMPANY

Preface

AGAIN, we carry the culinary torch.

It is a paradox that in this era of change the centuries-old interest in food has become more intensified. Once again the magic carpet of cooking has brought us together.

Basically, recipes are not so very different, and we might well ask, why so many cookbooks?

The answer? Perhaps they offer the provocative challenge which each potential cook can attempt to meet.

The same recipes? Yes. But the good cook adds her imaginative creativity and daring, and presents an entirely new gourmet façade.

As hostesses, we present our contemporary version of eye-catching, taste-provoking, and interesting foods. Our earliest book, *Thoughts for Food* (1938), now actually a classic, presented menus for an era with expert professional assistance in the home.

In 1958, we followed with *Thoughts for Buffets,* designed for the "help-less" housewife, both the young and the experienced, who accomplished the myriad household tasks often alone and unaided. In the tradition of fine dining, we all recognize the limitations of the day by utilizing a growing range of the expedient new mixes, frozen foods, and other available preparations.

The importance of dining in its relationship to good living has swung the gastronomic pendulum back to enjoyment of time-consuming preparation and traditional foods. In this volume, *Thoughts for Festive Foods,* we offer you the delicacies of past and present without eliminating too many of our modern time-savers.

Dining is an art which provides a pleasant background for the sharing of interests with appreciative guests. We give you cooking today, circa 1964, retaining the bond with the past, when in 500 B.C. Aeschylus said that "the pleasantest of ties is that of host and guest."

THE AUTHORS

Contents

List
of Menus

Thoughts for
Festive Foods

Introduction

THIS COOKBOOK is designed to suggest and help you to organize your menu plans for special events.

The 175 menus represent, by name, those many occasions which are typical of today's living. The title "Symphony Luncheon" is only an idea. Your imagination will dictate that this menu will serve you better for your "Cousins Club," or perhaps that the "Bowling Award Dinner" will be perfect for entertaining your college roommate.

As carefully as we have planned these menus, we urge you to make those substitutions which better serve your particular purpose. Within these names are many hundreds of recipes, which we hope you will interchange in this same fashion. For example, don't hesitate to take Escalopes de Veau out of the "Teacher Comes to Dinner" menu and substitute Ginger Baked Chicken from the "Spinster Dinner" menu.

It is important to note that the number of servings per recipe is indicated under the title of the menu. Most of the recipes can be increased or reduced.

The Advance Preparation Schedule, which accompanies each menu, has been carefully planned to help you avoid as much last-minute cooking as possible. Here again you may prefer to prepare a "deep freeze" recipe suggestion the day before and refrigerate it overnight or to make a "previous day" preparation and assemble it the same day.

As in our *Thoughts for Buffets* we have included some marvelously handy Hints to the Help-Less Housewives, a simple glossary of terms, a table of measurements and weights, and recipes for leftovers.

We think you will appreciate our new suggested Pantry and Wine lists, and find Pots, Pans, and Gadgets an intriguing aid to your cooking.

For easy and complete reference, we hope you will find our newly designed index completely encompassing.

As a last and most important suggestion, we urge you to read our chapter entitled "How to Fully Enjoy Using This Cookbook."

In 1796, Yan Mei, a Chinese poet who wrote a cookbook said, "So much planning and hard thinking go with the preparation of every dish that one might well say 'I serve it with my whole soul.'"

How to Fully Enjoy
Using This Cookbook

THERE ARE two styles of reading and cooking the same recipe. The "hit or miss" style is one—quick and casual, producing a few successful results but many more failures.

The second is the meticulous and careful observation of the ingredients and method which a good recipe merits. This second style, the "read and cook method," may seem obvious and disarmingly simple, but is well worth the extra few minutes which can make every dish a triumph.

We recommend these "read and cook" habits, as described, to the new and older cooks alike, as the only device worthy of the hundreds of superb recipes contained in our book. The following rules are offered as a guide for careful procedure and method so that you may "Fully Enjoy Using This Cookbook."

1. Select a Menu Several Days Prior to the Occasion

A. Use the recipes with the menus, if appropriate, or
B. Find fitting substitutions.
C. Note the approximate serving yield.

2. Check Individual Recipes at Least a Day in Advance

A. Read recipe through very carefully, including method and helpful notes.
B. Determine your needs to increase or decrease quantities.
C. Do you have proper size cooking, baking, and serving containers?

    D. Do you have necessary ingredients on hand?

3. Try Menus and Recipes Unfamiliar to You

    A. Be adventuresome with these foods; this is a wonderful way to enjoy new taste thrills.

    B. All are tested for flavor, texture, color, and garnish and have been proven delectable.

4. Refer to the Advance Preparation Schedule

    A. Is it necessary or suggested that your recipe be frozen or prepared in advance?

    B. Have you noted those foods which require last-minute cooking and serving?

5. Assemble Ingredients, Equipment and Suitable Serving Pieces

    A. Which ingredients should be at room temperature?

    B. Grease or line molds and pans.

    C. Prepare and make ready garnishes.

6. Reread the Recipe; Follow the Instructions Meticulously

    A. Measure ingredients with great care. All measurements are dead level.

    B. Use preparation method precisely in the order indicated.

    C. Preheat oven when necessary.

7. Read "Hints to the Help-Less Housewife" Now and Again

    A. As a reminder of convenient tricks which many cooks forget periodically.

    B. To give you new ideas on timesaving methods and preparation.

8. Concentrate Completely on What You Are Preparing

    A. Relax as you develop the engrossing mystery of a new recipe; enjoy the complete release and freedom this concentration offers.

Though we encourage you to be creative or imaginative in altering some recipes, we stress the importance of accuracy. Your experience may warrant your making changes to suit your individual taste. However, we feel that each cook will find in almost all instances these recipes are delicious, interesting and varied enough to follow exactly.

Holidays

WE MOVE through the calendar to the days where we join heart and hands to celebrate those festivities which belong to each and every one of us. We wave a flag; we say a prayer; we sing together, and offer thanks.

What better way to share than at a bountiful board?

The world goes around, bringing celebrations, holidays, and events that mark the passing years. For each celebration there is traditional feasting. We have planned the menus for many, hoping to lighten your responsibilities and to heighten your enjoyment of each day.

New Year's Eve

(SERVES 6)

Nova Scotia Mold   Eggs à la Russe

Cherry Chicken

Finocchio Salad

Profiterole Pyramid — Raspberry Sauce

Coffee   Brandy

Suggested wine: Champagne

ADVANCE PREPARATION SCHEDULE

Deep Freeze	Previous Day	Early Morning
Profiteroles	*Nova Scotia Mold*	*Chicken*
		Cook eggs
		Dressing
		Sauces

NOVA SCOTIA MOLD

1 envelope (1 tablespoon) unflavored gelatin
¼ cup cold water
½ cup hot cream
1 8-ounce package cream cheese, softened
1 cup dairy sour cream
1 teaspoon Worcestershire
Dash Tabasco
2 tablespoons chopped green onions *or* chives
1 teaspoon lemon juice
1 tablespoon chopped parsley
1 tablespoon prepared horseradish
½ pound Nova Scotia *or* smoked salmon; coarsely chopped (1 cup)
4 ounces red caviar
Lettuce

Soak gelatin in cold water; dissolve thoroughly in hot cream; cool. Mash cheese until smooth; blend with sour cream, Worcestershire, Tabasco, and onion or chives; stir into dissolved gelatin; add lemon juice, parsley, horseradish, and salmon. Fold caviar in very carefully, so as not to break the globules. Pour into well-greased 3-cup mold. Refrigerate until congealed. To serve, turn onto lettuce-lined platter.

Garnish with watercress and cherry tomatoes. Circle with icebox rye bread, sliced thin.

EGGS A LA RUSSE

6 hard-cooked eggs, peeled and halved   1 head iceberg lettuce, shredded

Place eggs, cut side down, on a platter solidly covered with shredded lettuce. Pour Russian Dressing generously over eggs. Chill before serving. Eggs may be served individually, two halves to a person.

Russian Dressing:

1 tablespoon grated onion
1 tablespoon chopped chives
1 tablespoon chopped parsley
1 tablespoon chopped pimiento-stuffed green olives
1 cup mayonnaise
3 tablespoons chili sauce

Combine ingredients and blend well.

CHERRY CHICKEN

½ cup all-purpose flour
1 tablespoon salt
2 medium-size frying chickens, quartered
½ cup (¼ pound) butter *or* margarine
1 medium onion, minced
¼ cup (⅛ pound) butter *or* margarine
¼ cup cornstarch
½ teaspoon salt
1 1-pound, 14-ounce can pitted Bing cherries
2 cups chicken broth
½ cup port
½ teaspoon rosemary, crushed
½ cup toasted, slivered almonds (optional)
¼ teaspoon pepper

Combine flour, 1 tablespoon salt, and pepper in paper bag; shake chicken pieces in mixture to coat thoroughly. Heat ½ cup butter in skillet and brown chicken thoroughly; cover. Cook slowly for 40 minutes or until tender. Sauté minced onion in ¼ cup butter for 5 minutes. Blend cornstarch and ½ teaspoon salt with ½ cup juice from Bing cherries. Add sautéed onions and stir in chicken broth. Simmer until thickened and smooth, stirring constantly. Strain, to remove onion pieces. Add drained cherries and port. Sprinkle with rosemary, heat thoroughly. To serve, arrange chicken pieces on a heated serving platter. Pour part of hot cherry sauce over chicken and serve remainder of sauce separately. Sprinkle with almonds. Serve with Fluffy Rice (see Index).

FINOCCHIO SALAD

1 cup diced finocchio
1 tablespoon butter, melted
2 chicken livers
1 cup French Dressing
½ teaspoon garlic salt (optional)
2 quarts mixed salad greens

Peel finocchio and let stand in ice water to become crisp, as for celery. Dice when ready to serve. Heat butter and sauté chicken livers for 5 minutes; press through sieve and add to French Dressing. Add garlic salt and chill. Toss greens with finocchio. Pour just enough dressing to moisten greens well, but not enough to collect in the bottom of the bowl. Serve very cold. This delicious anise-flavored vegetable is a gourmet change, also called fennel; may be cooked like celery.

French Dressing:

¼ cup vinegar	1 teaspoon salt
¾ cup salad oil	1 teaspoon sugar
½ teaspoon paprika	¼ teaspoon dry mustard
Dash freshly ground pepper	

Combine all ingredients in a glass jar; cover tightly and shake until thoroughly blended. Chill. Shake dressing each time before using.

PROFITEROLE PYRAMID

1 cup boiling water	4 eggs
½ cup shortening	2 quarts ice cream
½ teaspoon salt	¼ cup raspberry brandy *or*
1 cup sifted all-purpose flour	Curaçao (optional)

Combine water, shortening, and salt in saucepan; bring to a rolling boil. Add flour all at once; stir vigorously over low heat 1 minute or until mixture leaves sides of pan and forms a compact ball. Remove from heat and continue beating; cool mixture slightly, about 2 minutes. Add eggs, one at a time, beating after each addition; beat until mixture has a satinlike sheen. Drop from tablespoon onto ungreased baking sheet about 2 inches apart to allow for spreading; make 16 mounds, swirling each as it is dropped from spoon. Place in a preheated 375° oven; bake 50 minutes or until browned and puffy. Remove from heat; with a knife, make a small slit in each puff. Cool on cake rack. Split cream puffs through the side; fill each cream puff with ice cream. If made in advance, place in freezer until ready to serve.

Just before serving, remove from freezer and pile in pyramid fashion on serving platter. Pour Raspberry Sauce over profiteroles; warm brandy, flame, and pour over pyramid.

RASPBERRY SAUCE

2 10-ounce packages frozen raspberries   2 tablespoons sugar
2 tablespoons cornstarch

Thaw berries; place in saucepan. Combine sugar and cornstarch with ¼ cup of the juice; blend and return to saucepan. Simmer for 10 minutes; cool and refrigerate.

New Year's Day Dinner

(SERVES 8)

New Year's Punch
Deviled Crab Shells
Veal Roulet   Cinnamon Apples
Poppy-Seed Noodle Ring   Mushrooms Chablis
Tomato à l'Oignon
Butterflake Snails
Apricot Queen Cake
Coffee

ADVANCE PREPARATION SCHEDULE

Deep Freeze	Previous Day	Early Morning
Snails	*Cinnamon apples*	*Marinate meat*
Cake	*Deviled Crab*	*Prepare mushrooms*
	Onion sauce	*Frost cake*

NEW YEAR'S PUNCH

3 oranges   ⅘ quart port
6 whole cloves   1 tablespoon honey
½ cup brandy

Stud 2 oranges with cloves; roast over a fire or in a preheated 350° oven for 20 minutes, until oranges are soft and begin to brown. Place 1 roasted orange in pan, add port and honey; simmer over low heat 15 minutes. Pour port mixture into warm punch bowl. Set second orange in large ladle; pour warmed brandy over orange and flame it. Lower blazing orange into hot punch. Slice remaining orange and use to garnish punch. Serve in warm mugs.

Double or triple recipe as needed.

DEVILED CRAB SHELLS

½ cup minced onion
¼ cup minced celery
1½ cups minced green pepper
1 garlic clove, minced
1 tablespoon chopped parsley
½ cup (¼ pound) butter
2 cups soft bread crumbs
½ cup heavy cream

2 eggs, beaten
2 hard-cooked eggs, chopped
1 tablespoon white wine vinegar
1 teaspoon Worcestershire
¼ teaspoon thyme
2 drops Tabasco
1 teaspoon salt
1½ pounds lump crabmeat

Sauté onion, celery, green pepper, garlic, and parsley in 6 table-spoons butter for 10 minutes; cool. Add 1 cup bread crumbs, cream, raw and cooked eggs, vinegar, Worcestershire, thyme, Tabasco, and salt to sautéed vegetables. Add crabmeat and toss lightly to mix. Spoon into 12 scallop shells or individual baking dishes. Melt remaining 2 tablespoons butter and toss with remaining bread crumbs; top crab mixture with buttered crumbs. Place shells in shallow baking pan. Pour ¼ inch water in bottom of pan. Bake in preheated 450° oven for 10 minutes or until browned and hot.

VEAL ROULET

1 6-pound leg of veal
2 teaspoons seasoned salt
1 teaspoon ground coarse pepper
½ teaspoon thyme
1 cup white wine
2 cups canned tomatoes
1 onion, sliced fine

3 tablespoons flour
2 tablespoons shortening
½ cup minced onion
1 cup chopped celery
2 small garlic cloves, sliced fine
1 bay leaf
1 cup beef bouillon

Place roast in pan, coat with seasoned salt, pepper, and thyme. Combine ¼ cup wine, 1 cup tomatoes, 1 sliced onion; pour over meat. Let stand 2 hours in refrigerator turning meat frequently. Remove and drain. Dust with flour. Heat shortening in large saucepan, add onion and celery; sauté lightly. Add roast to pan with vegetables and brown lightly. Place rack in roasting pan; make small slits in roast and insert slivers of sliced garlic. Add bay leaf; cover. Pour remaining wine, tomatoes, and bouillon into pan and roast in a preheated 325° oven, allowing 30 minutes per pound. When almost tender, remove cover and roast until nicely browned. To serve, slice roast, arrange on platter, cover with sauce and garnish with Cinnamon Apples.

CINNAMON APPLES

8 small uniform-sized apples	6 large marshmallows
½ cup sugar	1 cup water
¼ cup cinnamon drops	

Pare apples without removing stems. Combine sugar, water, marshmallows and cinnamon drops in large saucepan and bring to a boil. Add apples. Cook gently until apples are tender; test with a straw. Remove to platter. Boil syrup until thick and pour over apples. Place in refrigerator to chill.

Note: Marshmallows will foam and act as a self-baster for apples.

POPPY-SEED NOODLE RING

1 8-ounce box wide noodles, boiled and drained	1 cup chicken *or* beef bouillon
¼ cup poppy seeds	1½ cups dried chipped beef, chopped
2 tablespoons minced onion	
2 tablespoons butter	

Combine noodles, poppy seeds, minced onion, bouillon, and 1 cup chopped beef. Pour into well greased 5-cup ring mold. Cover with remaining beef; bake ½ hour in a preheated 325° oven. Turn out on platter. Fill center with Mushrooms Chablis.

MUSHROOMS CHABLIS

1½ pounds fresh mushrooms	¼ teaspoon freshly ground black pepper
½ cup (¼ pound) butter, melted	1 cup chicken bouillon
1 tablespoon chopped marjoram	¼ cup Chablis *or* other dry white wine
1 teaspoon minced chives	
1 teaspoon salt	

Wash mushrooms and place in buttered casserole. Combine butter with marjoram, chives, salt, and pepper. Add bouillon and wine. Stir well and pour over mushrooms. Cover and bake in a preheated 350° oven for 20 minutes.

TOMATO A L'OIGNON

Sliced ripe tomatoes. Allow 3 slices per serving.

Onion Sauce:

3 large Bermuda onions	½ cup vinegar
1 2-ounce can pimientos	1 cup salad oil
3 tablespoons sugar	1½ tablespoons salt
	½ cup water

Grind onions and pimiento in meat grinder and place in quart jar; add sugar, vinegar, salad oil, salt, and water. Refrigerate a few hours to blend flavors. Peel and slice tomatoes; arrange overlapping slices on a bed of romaine or leaf lettuce. Cover with sauce.

Variation:

Slice beefsteak tomatoes to top tossed salad. Serve with Onion Sauce.

BUTTERFLAKE SNAILS

2 cakes compressed yeast (*or* 2 packages active dry yeast)	¼ cup sugar
¾ cup lukewarm water	1 teaspoon salt
¼ cup sugar	6 egg yolks, beaten
4 cups sifted all-purpose flour	1 cup (½ pound) butter, softened (to spread on dough)
½ cup (¼ pound) butter, softened	

Dissolve compressed yeast in lukewarm water (dry yeast in warm water); add ¼ cup sugar and stir until dissolved. Blend in 1 cup flour. Cover and let rise in warm place (85° to 90°) until light and bubbly, about 20 to 30 minutes. Cream ½ cup butter, gradually add ¼ cup sugar, salt and egg yolks, creaming well. Add raised yeast mixture; mix well. Beat in 3 cups flour, one cup at a time; knead on floured board about 30 strokes; place in greased bowl and cover. Let rise in warm place free from drafts until almost double in bulk, about 1½ hours. Divide dough in half. Roll each half of dough separately on lightly floured board to an 18″ x 6″ rectangle. Spread ¼ cup butter on center third of one rectangle. Fold one side of dough to overlap center. Spread again with ¼ cup butter. Fold opposite side to overlap. Repeat with second rectangle. Again roll each half to another 18″ x 6″ rectangle. Cut into 1-inch strips. Coil each strip loosely on well-greased baking sheets to form a "snail." Let rise in warm place until double in bulk. Bake in a preheated 375° oven 12 to 15 minutes. Makes 36 Snails.

APRICOT QUEEN CAKE

2½ cups sifted cake flour	2 eggs
2½ teaspoons baking powder	2 egg yolks
1 teaspoon salt	¼ cup milk
⅔ cup shortening	1 cup apricot nectar
1¾ cups sugar	½ teaspoon lemon extract

Sift together flour, baking powder, and salt. Add shortening gradually to sugar, creaming well. Blend in 2 eggs; then blend in egg yolks, one at a time, and beat for 1 minute. Add ¼ of the dry ingredients; mix well. Blend in milk. Combine mixture with apricot nectar; add lemon extract alternately with remaining dry ingredients to creamed mixture, beginning and ending with dry ingredients. Blend thoroughly after each addition. Pour into 3 well-greased and lightly floured 9-inch round layer cake pans. Bake in a preheated 350° oven 25 to 30 minutes. Cool; spread Apricot Filling between layers. Frost top and sides with white frosting.

Apricot Filling:

¼ cup cornstarch   2 cups apricot nectar
2 teaspoons lemon juice

Combine cornstarch and ¼ cup apricot nectar; blend well. Add remaining apricot nectar; mix until smooth. Cook over direct heat until thick, about 5 minutes, stirring constantly. Add lemon juice; cool.

White Frosting:

2 egg whites	2 tablespoons water
¾ cup sugar	¼ teaspoon salt
⅓ cup light corn syrup	¼ teaspoon cream of tartar
1 teaspoon vanilla	

Combine all ingredients, except vanilla, in top of double boiler. Cook over rapidly boiling water, beating with rotary beater or electric mixer about 7 minutes or until mixture stands in peaks. Remove from heat. Add vanilla; continue beating until thick enough to spread.

New Year's Day Supper

(SERVES 12)

Herring William Tell   Cocktail Rye Bread

Avocado Spread   Cheese Potato Chips

Broiled Shrimp

Herbed Eggs   Cauliflower Aurore

Veal Mozzarella Sandwiches

Chicken Legs Vermouth

Ringos   Fruit Torte

Chocolate Meringue Vienna

Coffee

Suggested wine: Valpolicella or Chianti

ADVANCE PREPARATION SCHEDULE

Deep Freeze	Previous Day	Early Morning
Ringos	*Cook shrimp*	*Avocado spread*
Fruit Torte	*Herring*	*Marinate chicken*
	Potato Chips	*Eggs*
	Cauliflower Aurore	*Arrange cauliflower*

Each country has its own good-luck food, but herring is generally accepted by all. We give you our simple version of Herring in Sour Cream with our good wishes all through the years.

2 12-ounce jars wine herring	1 teaspoon sugar
1 large onion, sliced	1½ cups dairy sour cream
2 medium red apples, unpeeled, sliced thin	

Remove herring fillets and drain. Place in bowl in alternate layers with onion, apple, sugar, and sour cream, with additional layer of sour cream on top. Cover and refrigerate several hours or overnight.

Note: To ascertain the accurate amount to be served in a menu for a group is always a hostess's problem. The considerations are the guests' tastes and appetites.

AVOCADO SPREAD

3 avocados	1 clove garlic, mashed
½ cup mayonnaise	½ teaspoon freshly ground black
3 tablespoons lemon juice	pepper
1 teaspoon chili powder	

Peel avocados and mash pulp; add remaining ingredients and mix well. Cover and let stand for at least 1 hour. Serve with Cheese Potato Chips. Makes 3 cups.

CHEESE POTATO CHIPS

Potato chips   Grated Parmesan cheese

Spread potato chips on baking sheet and sprinkle with Parmesan cheese. Bake in a preheated 400° oven for 5 minutes or until very hot.

BROILED SHRIMP

2 pounds jumbo shrimp, cooked (about 40 shrimp)	¼ cup olive oil
	¼ cup butter, melted
¼ cup flour	1 tablespoon minced garlic
¼ cup minced parsley	

Shell and devein shrimp. Do not remove tail. Dry; dust with flour. Stir oil and butter into flat baking dish. Place shrimp in dish; broil at medium heat 8 minutes. Add garlic and parsley to Drawn Butter Sauce. Pour over shrimp; stir until shrimp are coated. Broil for 2 minutes. Serve immediately.

Drawn Butter Sauce:

2 tablespoons butter	Dash freshly ground black pepper
2 tablespoons flour	1 cup hot water
⅛ teaspoon salt	½ teaspoon lemon juice

Melt butter in saucepan. Add flour, salt, and pepper; blend until smooth. Add water, stirring constantly; boil 5 minutes. Combine with lemon juice.

The shrimp may be served in a dish with a warmer, or broiled as needed. These should be piping hot.

HERBED EGGS

12 eggs	2 tablespoons lemon juice
2 tablespoons minced chives	1 teaspoon curry powder
2 tablespoons minced parsley	Salt and freshly ground black
½ cup dairy sour cream	pepper to taste
Dash cayenne pepper (optional)	

Hard-cook eggs, plunge in cold water, and shell immediately. Cut eggs in half lengthwise, forming a shell. Remove and mash yolks. Add remaining ingredients to the yolks and mix well. Spoon yolk mixture into egg white shells. Chill at least 1 hour. Serve around platter with Cauliflower Aurore and Tomato Rose Garnish.

CAULIFLOWER AURORE

1 cooked firm cauliflower	Watercress
(1 large or 2 or 3 small)	Paprika

Remove outer stalks of cauliflower, leaving a few of light green as a frame. Place in 1 inch of boiling water, using ½ teaspoon salt per cup. Cover and boil about 20 minutes. Do not let it cook too long as it will fall apart.

To serve, chill thoroughly, place on serving platter with base of watercress, mask with Sauce Aurore and dust with paprika. Garnish with arrangement of Herbed Eggs and Tomato Roses.

Tomato Roses: A decorative garnish

Peel tomatoes with vegetable peeler, starting at top and peeling around and around to bottom of tomatoes. Roll peeling around itself into rose shapes. Use pulp for Sauce Aurore.

Sauce Aurore:

2 tomatoes	⅛ teaspoon sweet basil
2 cups mayonnaise	⅛ teaspoon ground pepper

Peel tomatoes and mash; blend with mayonnaise, basil and pepper.

VEAL MOZZARELLA SANDWICHES

1 cup (½ pound) butter, softened	1 teaspoon oregano
1 teaspoon anchovy paste	12 slices white bread, toasted
1 teaspoon dry mustard	12 thin slices cooked veal
12 thin slices Mozzarella cheese	

Cream butter with anchovy paste, mustard, and oregano. Spread on toast. Top with veal and cheese. Broil under low heat until cheese melts.

To allow more time for the enjoyment of your New Year's Day, correlated planning of the menu is suggested. Increase required quantity of New Year's Day Dinner roast so a sufficient amount remains for these sandwiches.

CHICKEN LEGS VERMOUTH

24 chicken legs	2 garlic cloves, minced
24 chicken thighs	1 teaspoon chopped tarragon
1 cup dry vermouth	1 teaspoon chopped basil
1 cup oil	1 teaspoon salt
1 tablespoon lemon juice	10 peppercorns, crushed
3 shallots *or* 1 medium onion, chopped	

Marinate chicken in remaining ingredients, which have been well blended. Let stand at room temperature for at least 4 hours. Turn chicken pieces once or twice and spoon marinade over. Broil chicken for about 30 minutes, turning frequently and basting with marinade. To serve, place in chafing dish or heated container.

RINGOS

2 cakes compressed yeast	⅓ cup sugar
¼ cup lukewarm water	2 teaspoons salt
or	2 teaspoons grated orange rind
2 packages dry yeast	2 eggs unbeaten
¼ cup warm water	4 to 4½ cups sifted all-purpose
⅓ cup butter *or* margarine	flour
¾ cup milk, scalded	¼ cup orange juice
3 tablespoons sugar	

Soften compressed yeast in lukewarm water; dry yeast in warm water. Combine butter and hot scalded milk in large bowl; stir until butter melts. Cool to lukewarm. Add ⅓ cup sugar, salt, orange rind, eggs, and yeast mixture. Gradually add flour to form a stiff dough; mix thoroughly and cover. Let stand 30 minutes, while preparing Nut Filling. Roll out dough to a 22" x 12" rectangle on floured board. Spread half of dough along 22-inch side with filling. Fold uncovered dough over filling. Cut into 1-inch strips crosswise. Twist each strip 4 or 5 times. Then hold one end down on greased baking sheet for center of roll (ringo); curl strip around center, tucking other end under. Cover with waxed paper or towel. Let rise in warm place (85° to 90°) until light and doubled in size, 45 to 60 minutes. Bake in a preheated 375° oven 15 minutes until light golden brown. Meanwhile combine orange juice and 3 tablespoons sugar for glaze. Brush tops of rolls with this glaze and bake 5 minutes longer until deep golden brown. Remove from baking sheet immediately.

Nut Filling:

⅓ cup butter *or* margarine	1 cup nutmeats (filberts *or*
1 cup sifted confectioners' sugar	hazelnuts suggested), ground
	or chopped

Cream butter; blend in sugar thoroughly; add nuts.

FRUIT TORTE

1 cake compressed yeast
½ cup lukewarm water
1½ cups (¾ pound) butter, softened

4 cups sifted all-purpose flour
4 egg yolks
½ cup dairy sour cream

Dissolve yeast in water. Cream butter and 1 cup flour until blended; add egg yolks and beat thoroughly. Add yeast and sour cream; beat remaining flour in gradually. Turn out onto floured pastry cloth; knead until smooth. Divide dough into 3 parts. Roll 1 part to fit in 13" x 9" x 2" pan.

Filling:

1½ cups chopped walnuts *or* pecans
¾ cup sugar
1 teaspoon cinnamon
½ cup sugar

¼ cup margarine, softened
1 cup (12 ounces) fruit filling (apricot, plum, prune, etc.)
4 egg whites

Blend 1 cup nuts with sugar, cinnamon, and margarine until crumbly. Sprinkle over dough. Roll second part same size and place over nut mixture. Gently spread fruit filling over dough. Roll third part same size and place over fruit. Bake in a preheated 350° oven for 45 minutes. Remove from oven. Beat egg whites until stiff but not dry; beat in ½ cup sugar gradually. Spread over top layer and sprinkle with remaining ½ cup nuts. Return to oven and bake at 350° for 15 minutes longer.

CHOCOLATE MERINGUE VIENNA

Shell:

3 egg whites
¼ teaspoon cream of tartar

Dash salt
¾ cup sugar

Grease bottom and sides of an 8-inch pie pan. Beat egg whites until they stand in soft peaks, sprinkle in cream of tartar and salt. Add sugar gradually and continue beating until stiff, and points form when beaters are lifted. Spread about ⅔ of meringue on bottom of pie pan. Use remaining mixture to cover sides evenly and form mound around rim of pan. Bake 1 hour in a preheated 275° oven until shell is a delicate gold. Cool.

Chocolate Filling:

12 ounces semi-sweet chocolate bits	1 cup heavy cream, whipped
	1 teaspoon vanilla extract

Melt chocolate pieces in top of double boiler over hot, not boiling water. Beat with wooden spoon, as you would fudge, until very creamy and slightly cool. Fold cream into chocolate mixture gently; add vanilla extract and pour into cool shell. Chill in refrigerator for 2 hours.

Variation — Mocha Viennese:

1 tablespoon instant coffee	¼ cup boiling water

Combine instant coffee and boiling water and add to melted chocolate.

For Angel Pie refrigerate Chocolate or Mocha Viennese overnight.

Valentine Dinner Party

(SERVES 6 TO 8)

Lobster Mousse   Jellied Caviar Heart Garni

Tomato Velvet   Crouton Hearts   Sesame Crackers

Fillet of Beef Flambé

Beet Valentines   Crisp Rolls

Cherry Tart   Coffee

Suggested wine: red Burgundy or Bordeaux

ADVANCE PREPARATION SCHEDULE

Previous Day

Lobster Mousse and Aspic
Tomato Velvet
Cherry Tart
Beets in oil and vinegar
Crouton Hearts

Early Morning

Season beef

LOBSTER MOUSSE

1 tablespoon butter *or* margarine
4 teaspoons all-purpose flour
Dash pepper
½ teaspoon salt
Dash paprika
⅛ teaspoon dried tarragon
⅔ cup milk

1 5½-ounce can lobster *or*
½ pound fresh cooked lobster
1 cup canned condensed beef
broth, undiluted
1 envelope unflavored gelatin
2 tablespoons sherry
1 egg white

1 cup heavy cream, beaten stiff

Melt butter in medium saucepan over low heat; stir in flour, pepper, salt, paprika, and tarragon until blended smoothly. Slowly add milk, stirring constantly over fire until smooth and thickened. Remove from heat; cool. Cut lobster meat in bite-size chunks into a 2-quart bowl. Pour beef broth into small saucepan; sprinkle gelatin over, then stir over low heat until it is dissolved; remove from heat, blend in the sherry. Stir into cooled white sauce, then pour over lobster. Refrigerate until slightly thickened. Beat egg white until stiff, not dry. Fold egg white and cream into cooled lobster mixture. Pour into 2-quart soufflé dish. Refrigerate for at least 6 hours.

Sherry Aspic:

1 10½-ounce can condensed beef
consommé, undiluted

2 teaspoons unflavored gelatin
¼ cup sherry

Pour beef consommé, undiluted, into small saucepan. Sprinkle gelatin over; stir over low heat until gelatin is dissolved. Remove from heat; stir in sherry. Reserve ½ cup gelatin mixture in a small bowl; pour remainder into a 9″ x 5″ x 3″ loaf pan. Refrigerate. To garnish, cut aspic into ½-inch cubes and arrange as directed in method "To Assemble."

JELLIED CAVIAR HEART GARNI

½ cup gelatin mixture
(reserved from sherry aspic)

1 2-ounce can red caviar

Refrigerate gelatin until of jellylike consistency. Add red caviar and pour into well-oiled 4-ounce heart-shaped mold.

To Assemble:

Cubed aspic ¼ cup snipped parsley
Lettuce

Place lobster mousse in soufflé dish on platter. Unmold jellied caviar heart and center it on top of the lobster mousse as a garnish. Circle the heart mold with cubed aspic. Sprinkle lobster with parsley. Arrange lettuce cups on platter around mousse and let each guest spoon individual servings into lettuce cups.

TOMATO VELVET

1 #2½ can tomatoes	5 stalks celery
1 #2½ can water	Salt, pepper, 1 bay leaf
1 onion, sliced	1½ cups thick white sauce

Place tomatoes, water, onion, celery, salt, pepper and bay leaf in saucepan; cook until celery is soft, about 30 minutes. Strain through food mill or sieve. Heat white sauce and add slowly to hot tomato mixture; mix well. Serve very hot with Crouton Hearts. To reheat, bring to boiling point but do not boil.

White Sauce:

3 tablespoons butter	¼ teaspoon paprika
¾ teaspoon salt	1 cup milk
3 tablespoons flour	Dash pepper

Melt butter in saucepan; add flour and stir well until smooth and bubbly. Blend milk slowly, stirring until heated; add salt, paprika, and pepper.

Crouton Hearts:

6 or 8 slices bread   2 tablespoons butter

With a cooky cutter, cut a heart from center of bread slices. Melt butter in a saucepan and sauté hearts until lightly browned. Dry thoroughly.

Note: This recipe may be used for small crouton cubes, also.

FILLET OF BEEF FLAMBE

1 cup (½ pound) butter	4-pound beef fillet
2 2-ounce cans pâté de foie gras	Pepper, salt
1 clove garlic, crushed	½ cup claret
¼ cup brandy, warmed	

Mash together butter, pâté de foie gras, and crushed garlic; spread on fillet and place in refrigerator for 2 hours or more. Grind fresh black pepper over beef; place under preheated broiler for 5 minutes; dust with salt and turn, adding claret, and broil another 5 minutes. Pour off juices and set aside. Continue broiling and turning for another 30 minutes or until of desired doneness. Add warmed brandy to these juices and flame. Pour sauce over beef. Serve in slices, being certain to spoon this savory sauce over each portion. Garnish with Bouquet of Carrot Daisies (see Index) and parsley.

BEET VALENTINES

5 tablespoons salad oil	2 cups diced celery
3 tablespoons wine vinegar	½ teaspoon salt
1 #2½ can sliced beets	⅛ teaspoon pepper
3 hard-cooked egg yolks	2 teaspoons finely chopped
1 raw egg yolk	chives

Leaf lettuce

Combine oil and vinegar; drain beets and cut each slice heart-shaped, using a small heart-shaped cooky cutter. Place in oil-vinegar mixture; moisten thoroughly, drain, and set in refrigerator. To oil and vinegar liquid add egg yolks, raw egg, celery, salt, pepper, and chives. Make a bed of lettuce on each salad plate. Mound celery mixture on each serving and circle with sliced beet hearts. If needed, add more oil and vinegar.

CHERRY TART

Crust:

1¼ cups sifted all-purpose flour	½ cup (¼ pound) butter
¼ cup sugar	2 egg yolks, beaten
¼ teaspoon salt	1 teaspoon vanilla

Sift flour with sugar and salt. Cut in butter with pastry blender or knives until mixture is like coarse meal. Add egg yolks and vanilla; mix just until a soft dough is formed. Press over bottom and up 1 inch on sides of a 9-inch spring form pan. Bake in a preheated 350° oven about 25 minutes. While still hot loosen crust from side of pan with knife; then cool in pan. Spread Filling over bottom of crust. Chill. Spoon Cherry Topping over Filling. Sprinkle with almonds. Chill until ready to serve.

Filling:

1 8-ounce package cream cheese, 1 teaspoon lemon juice
  softened   2 tablespoons milk
½ cup sifted confectioners' sugar

Beat cheese until smooth. Mix in sugar, lemon juice and milk; continue beating until smooth and fluffy.

Cherry Topping:

1 can (1 pound, 4 ounces) frozen ¼ teaspoon almond extract
  sweetened pitted cherries,   ⅛ teaspoon ground cloves
  thawed   2 tablespoons toasted, slivered
⅓ cup sugar   almonds
2 tablespoons cornstarch

Drain juice from cherries adding enough water to make 1 cup of liquid. Place in saucepan. Combine sugar and cornstarch and blend into juice. Cook, stirring constantly, until clear and thickened. Stir in cherries, almond extract, and cloves; cool. Pour over filling in Tarts as directed; sprinkle with almonds.

Mother's Day Patio Party

DAD — CHIEF COOK

(SERVES 4)

Lazy Day Clam Dip   Sister's Cheese Wafers
Grilled Steak Mon Père
Noodle Pudding — Queen's Taste   Chick Pea Salad
Apricot Torte   Festive Fruitcake
Brother Elmer's Sundae
Coffee   Tea   Milk

Suggested wine: Rosé

ADVANCE PREPARATION SCHEDULE

Deep Freeze	Previous Day	Early Morning
Wafers, unbaked, frozen	*Marinate steaks*	*Chick Pea Salad*
Elmer's Sundae	*Boil noodles*	*Clam Dip*
	Fruitcake	*Bake wafers*
		Noodle Pudding
		Torte

LAZY DAY CLAM DIP

2 10½-ounce cans minced clams, drained
2 tablespoons clam juice
1 8-ounce package cream cheese, softened
1 teaspoon onion juice
Juice of 2 lemons
Dash Tabasco
1 teaspoon prepared horseradish
¼ teaspoon salt

Drain clams thoroughly, reserving the 2 tablespoons clam juice. Moisten cream cheese with clam juice, onion juice, lemon juice, Tabasco, horseradish, drained clams, and salt. Blend well; place in small bowl on serving plate. Border with assorted crackers and potato chips.

SISTER'S CHEESE WAFERS

1 cup (½ pound) butter
½ pound process American cheese, shredded
½ teaspoon dry mustard
Dash cayenne
½ teaspoon smoked salt
2⅔ cups sifted all-purpose flour
Caraway *or* poppy seed
½ teaspoon steak sauce

Have butter and cheese at room temperature. Cream butter; gradually add and beat in cheese, mustard, cayenne, smoked salt, and steak sauce. Gradually blend in flour; chill. Shape into four 6-inch rolls about 1½ inches round. Wrap in waxed paper and refrigerate several hours. To bake, cut slices ½ inch thick. Sprinkle with caraway or poppy seeds. Place on ungreased cooky sheets and bake in a preheated 350° oven 10 to 12 minutes. Serve warm. Makes about 8 dozen; bake quantity desired, freeze balance for other menus.

GRILLED STEAK MON PERE

1 chuck roast 2 to 3 inches thick,
or 2 chuck steaks 1 inch thick
1 onion, minced
2 cloves garlic, minced
¼ cup olive oil
¼ teaspoon dry mustard

1 teaspoon seasoned salt
1 teaspoon soy sauce
2 tablespoons wine vinegar
4 tablespoons red wine
4 tablespoons catsup
⅛ teaspoon thyme

Place onion, garlic, olive oil, mustard, seasoned salt, soy sauce, vinegar, wine, and catsup into a blender; blend for 2 minutes. Add thyme; mix well. Place meat in a bowl and pour sauce over it. Marinate for 24 hours, turning frequently. Barbecue roast for 40 minutes over white-hot charcoals, basting often with mixture and turning, or cook steaks for 10 minutes on each side, basting frequently.

NOODLE PUDDING — QUEEN'S TASTE

1 8-ounce package noodles
1 cup dairy sour cream
1 cup cottage cheese, small curd
½ cup milk
2 teaspoons Worcestershire
1 small onion, grated

1 garlic clove, minced (optional)
1 teaspoon salt
⅛ teaspoon pepper
Dash cayenne
Coarse bread crumbs
3 tablespoons butter

Cook noodles until tender; then drain. Combine with sour cream, cottage cheese, milk, Worcestershire, onion, garlic clove, salt, pepper, cayenne. Turn into flat baking dish. Sprinkle bread crumbs on top and dot generously with butter. Cover dish and bake for 15 minutes in a preheated 350° oven; remove cover and bake about 10 minutes longer, or until browned lightly on top. Serve from baking dish.

CHICK PEA SALAD

1 #2 can chick peas, drained
2 tablespoons French dressing
½ cup chopped green pepper
¼ cup chopped pimiento

1 cup chopped celery
1 teaspoon salt
½ teaspoon ground black pepper
½ cup mayonnaise

½ tablespoon prepared horseradish

Marinate chick peas with French dressing; add green pepper,

pimiento, celery, salt, pepper, and toss lightly. Add mayonnaise and horseradish, and blend. Serve on crisp lettuce cups.

APRICOT TORTE

1 cup (½ pound) butter	1 teaspoon vanilla
½ cup sugar	2 cups all-purpose flour
2 egg yolks	1 cup apricot jam

Cream butter and sugar; add egg yolks, vanilla, and flour. Press into bottom of 10½-inch spring form to ¼-inch thickness. Extend dough to form a 1-inch gallery edge. Spread apricot jam over top. Bake 45 minutes in a preheated 350° oven. For added ornamentation reserve part of batter for lattice top over jam. Use a cooky press or pastry bag or roll dough with hands into 10-inch pencil-like strips and crisscross them over jam topping, 1 inch apart.

FESTIVE FRUITCAKE

1 cup evaporated milk	½ teaspoon nutmeg
32 large marshmallows, finely cut (or 4 cups miniatures)	¼ teaspoon ground cloves
6 tablespoons orange juice	2 cups seedless raisins (preferably half golden, half dark)
8 cups fine graham cracker crumbs (about 8 dozen, 2½ inch size, crushed)	1 cup pitted dates, finely cut
½ teaspoon cinnamon	1½ cups nuts, broken
	1½ cups chopped, mixed candied fruit

Place evaporated milk, marshmallows, and orange juice into 3-quart bowl. Into larger bowl measure graham cracker crumbs, cinnamon, nutmeg, cloves, raisins, dates, nuts, and candied fruit. Work in milk mixture with spoon, then with hands until crumbs are moist. Press mixture firmly into wax-paper-lined 10-inch spring form. Place in refrigerator two days to blend flavors and set. Remove and drizzle thin confectioners' sugar frosting over top. Decorate with candied fruit, if desired.

BROTHER ELMER'S SUNDAE

The sauce for Elmer's Sundae may be purchased commercially.

Make ice cream balls, six to 1 quart; cover with chocolate sauce and place in freezer. For a patio party do not remove in advance, but serve as they are taken from freezer.

Easter Brunch

(SERVES 6)

Avocado Orange Salad

Risotto of Chicken Livers and Lamb Kidneys

Apricot Nut Bread — Cream Cheese Spread

Coffee Toffee Bars   Delcal

Coffee   Tea

ADVANCE PREPARATION SCHEDULE

Deep Freeze	Previous Day	Early Morning
Apricot bread	*French dressing*	*Peel and slice oranges*
Toffee bars		*Cook livers and kidneys*
Delcal		*Cream Cheese Spread*

AVOCADO ORANGE SALAD

3 oranges, peeled and sliced
1 Italian onion (sweet), sliced fine
½ cup French dressing

2 large avocados
2 tablespoons lemon juice
Boston *or* Bibb lettuce

Place oranges and onion in bowl and pour French dressing over. Chill in refrigerator for several hours, to marinate. Peel avocados, slice; sprinkle with lemon juice to prevent discoloration. For individual service, form bed of lettuce on each of 6 plates. Drain oranges and onion, reserving dressing, and alternate orange, onion, and avocado slices on lettuce. Serve with drained French dressing. This arrangement is also attractive when used for platter service.

RISOTTO OF CHICKEN LIVERS
AND LAMB KIDNEYS

½ pound chicken livers	1 tablespoon tomato paste
6 lamb kidneys	1½ cups raw rice
2 tablespoons butter	2 cups beef stock
1 large onion, sliced	4 tomatoes, skinned and sliced
6 fresh mushrooms, sliced	¼ cup grated cheese
Butter for topping	

Slice livers and halve kidneys, heat butter in saucepan and brown quickly. Remove and add onion to butter. Brown slowly, add mushrooms. Simmer for 5 minutes; add tomato paste and rice and sufficient stock to cover. Simmer until rice is cooked, about 20 minutes, adding more stock as needed. Dice livers and kidneys and add to mixture with the tomatoes. Place in well-greased 6-cup casserole, sprinkle with cheese, dot with butter, and bake in a preheated 250° oven 15 minutes. Place casserole in holder or wrap it in a folded napkin, then set on a platter and serve piping hot.

APRICOT NUT BREAD

1 cup dried apricots (half of 11-ounce package)	2 tablespoons soft butter *or* shortening
2 cups sifted all-purpose flour	1 egg
2 teaspoons baking powder	¼ cup water
½ teaspoon soda	½ cup orange juice
1 teaspoon salt	½ cup chopped pecans *or*
1 cup granulated sugar	walnuts

Soak apricots for 30 minutes in enough warm water to cover. If apricots are unusually dry, it may be necessary to soak longer. Measure sifted flour and sift again with baking powder, soda, and salt. Mix together sugar, butter, and egg. Stir in water and orange juice and sifted dry ingredients. Drain apricots and cut into ¼ inch pieces. Blend apricots and nuts into flour mixture. Grease 9½″ x 5¼″ x 2″ loaf pan. Line bottom of pan with wax paper and grease paper. Pour in batter; let stand 20 minutes to allow loaf to rise slowly. Bake in a preheated 350° oven for 45 to 65 minutes, until done when tested with a straw. Remove from pan and take paper off immediately; cool on rack. Especially good with Cream Cheese Spread.

CREAM CHEESE SPREAD

1 3-ounce package cream cheese 1 tablespoon cream
⅛ teaspoon salt

Soften cheese. Mash with fork, add cream and salt; beat with rotary beater until smooth.

COFFEE TOFFEE BARS

1 cup (½ pound) butter
1 cup dark brown sugar
 firmly packed
2 eggs
2½ cups sifted all-purpose flour
½ teaspoon baking powder
¼ teaspoon salt

1 teaspoon vanilla *or* almond
 extract
2 teaspoons instant coffee
½ cup nuts
1 6-ounce bar semi-sweet chocolate, melted

Cream butter; add sugar and cream together; add eggs, flour, baking powder, salt, vanilla, coffee, nuts, and chocolate; press dough into well-greased 15″ x 10″ x 1″ pan. Bake in a preheated 350° oven 25 minutes. Cut into bars or squares. Makes 3 dozen.

DELCAL

½ pound (1 cup) butter
½ pound cream cheese

2 cups unsifted flour
¼ teaspoon salt

Cream butter, cream cheese, flour, and salt together with pastry blender, then using hands knead dough very thoroughly; chill dough a minimum of 2 hours; or it can be frozen for any length of time. Assort them as crescents, filled cookies, or just sugared for single cookies.

Meringue Filling:

½ cup sugar 3 egg whites 1 teaspoon cinnamon

Beat egg whites until stiff and gradually add sugar and cinnamon while beating. Prepare this before you roll out the dough (if eggs are small, use 4).

For crescents, roll the dough as for pie crust, about ¼-inch thick, spread with ¾ of the meringue, cut in 8 triangular pieces and roll from wide end to the point. Place on cooky sheet, then spread remainder of meringue over the Delcal. Bake in a preheated 375° oven 25 to 30 minutes until lightly browned.

Easter Dinner

(SERVES 8)

Lobster Amsterdam   Relishes

Tomato Soup Julienne   Caraway Rounds

Easter Ham

Spinach Ricotta Balls   Sweet Potatoes Royal

or

Sweet Potato Ring

Easter Egg Salad   Watermelon Preserves

Rolls

Chocolate Cheese Cake

Coffee

ADVANCE PREPARATION SCHEDULE

Deep Freeze	Previous Day	Early Morning
Rolls	*Cook lobster*	*Caraway Rounds*
	Soup	*Ham*
	Preserves	*Hard-cooked eggs*
	Sauces	
	Cook potatoes	
	Cheese Cake	

LOBSTER AMSTERDAM

8 small lobster tails, cooked, *or*
   3 cups fresh *or canned lobster*
2 grapefruit, sectioned (see Index)
1 cup mayonnaise
Juice of ½ lemon
1 tablespoon Worcestershire
½ cup catsup

1 cup cream
½ jigger cognac
½ jigger sherry
1 tablespoon chopped parsley
¼ teaspoon black pepper,
   freshly ground

Cut boiled lobster in bite-size pieces. Combine mayonnaise, lemon, Worcestershire, catsup, cream, cognac, sherry, parsley, and pepper. Add sections of 2 whole grapefruit and any juices; then add sauce. Chill and serve in cocktail glasses.

Variation:

Crabmeat may be substituted for lobster.

To Boil Lobster Tails:

For frozen unthawed, drop into boiling salted water (1 teaspoon salt to 1 quart water) to cover. Boil 3 minutes longer than ounce weight of largest lobster tail. For example, if largest tail weighs 7 ounces, boil 10 minutes. If thawed, boil 1 minute longer than ounce weight; 7 ounces, boil 8 minutes.

TOMATO SOUP JULIENNE

2 tablespoons butter
¼ cup celery, cut in ¼-inch slices
¼ cup carrots, cut in 1-inch slices
½ teaspoon sugar

½ teaspoon salt
1 tablespoon instant onion
1 #1 can stewed tomatoes
1 quart bouillon, beef or chicken

½ cup dry white wine

Heat butter in 2-quart saucepan; add celery, carrots and sugar, sauté 5 minutes, but do not brown. Add salt, instant onion, tomatoes, and bouillon; simmer 15 minutes. Blend in wine and heat to boiling point. Serve with croutons. If a clear soup is desired, strain before serving.

Note: Two 10-ounce cans bouillon and 1 can water may be used instead of home-prepared bouillon.

CARAWAY ROUNDS

3 tablespoons butter, softened   36 melba rye rounds
2 tablespoons caraway seed

Spread butter on rounds, sprinkle with caraway seed. Before serving, place in a preheated 350° oven for 8 minutes.

EASTER HAM

1 smoked whole tenderized ham
1½ cups brown sugar, firmly
   packed
2 tablespoons flour
1 teaspoon dry mustard

3 tablespoons pineapple juice
2 tablespoons whole cloves
1 #2½ can sliced pineapple,
   drained
Maraschino cherries

Bake a 10- to 12-pound ham 25 minutes per pound.
Bake a larger ham 20 minutes per pound.
Bake a half ham 30 minutes per pound.

Scrub ham well and place on a rack, fat side up, in a roasting pan; do not cover. Bake in a preheated 300° oven required amount of time. Forty-five minutes before ham is done, remove from oven and take off rind, all except a collar around the shank bone. Cut 1-inch diagonals across fat to form diamonds and place a clove in each cut intersection. Combine flour, sugar, and mustard; drain pineapple, reserve juice and make a paste of dry ingredients and 3 tablespoons of the drained pineapple juice. Layer 1 cup of paste on the ham ½ inch thick and place slices of pineapple over it, in conventional pattern. Baste frequently — every 10 minutes with remaining juice. Before last 10 minutes, layer ham with remaining paste, raise heat to 425°, and remove when glazed and brown. Decorate with cherries in center of each pineapple slice.

The preceding recipe is comparatively recent and excellent.

It is impossible to forego the mouth-watering recollection of a baked ham served many years ago. The files and memory restore it. Here is "Baked Ham" as Mother "babied" it:

Scrub ham well and place on rack in roasting pan, fat side up. Score fat, using care that meat is not touched; insert whole cloves at intersecting lines. Cover top surface with ¼-inch layer of smooth peanut butter, then with the brown sugar paste as directed in

Easter Ham. Place in preheated 300° oven, baste every 20 minutes with pineapple juice and ginger ale. Forty-five minutes before ham is done, prepare glaze as directed for Easter Ham: Combine flour, sugar and mustard; drain pineapple, reserve juice and make a paste of dry ingredients and 3 tablespoons of the drained pineapple juice. Layer 1 cup of paste on ham ½ inch thick and place slices of pineapple over it, in conventional pattern. Baste frequently, every 10 minutes, with remaining juice. Before last 10 minutes, layer with remaining paste, raise heat to 425° and remove when glazed and brown. Decorate with cherries in center of each pineapple slice.

Variation:

Instead of pineapple slices, decorate ham with four 5-petaled daisies. Cut 20 1-inch petals of candied orange peel and fasten each petal to ham with whole cloves. Center each "daisy" with a half of candied cherry.

The following sauces are choices as accompaniments to the ham. However, we suggest that if you wish to use the Apricot Sauce, the Sweet Potato Ring be substituted for the Sweet Potato Royal.

Baltimore Sauce:

> 1 10-ounce jar currant jelly   ½ cup coarsely chopped chutney
> 1 cup sherry

Melt currant jelly over low heat. Cool. Blend with chutney and sherry. Serve separately. Makes 2½ cups.

Variation:

Glaze with Apricot Sauce instead of pineapple juice, last 30 minutes of baking.

Apricot Sauce and Glaze:

> 1 tablespoon butter, melted   1 teaspoon dry mustard
> 1 tablespoon flour   ½ teaspoon cloves, ground
> 1½ cups apricot nectar   ¼ teaspoon nutmeg
> 1 beef bouillon cube   ½ cup currant jelly
> 1 tablespoon grated orange rind

Heat butter in saucepan. Blend in flour and stir until light brown and bubbly. Add apricot nectar, bouillon cube, mustard, cloves,

nutmeg, jelly, orange rind and simmer until slightly thick. Baste
ham every 10 minutes during last 45 minutes of baking. Serve remaining sauce with ham. Makes 2 cups.

SPINACH RICOTTA BALLS

2 packages frozen spinach,   ½ cup ricotta cheese
   chopped   2 tablespoons Parmesan cheese,
½ teaspoon salt   grated
Dash pepper   ¼ cup butter

Cook spinach according to package directions. Drain thoroughly
and squeeze out any excess liquid. Mix in salt, pepper, ricotta, and
Parmesan cheeses. Form into ping-pong size balls. Heat butter in
skillet and drop in the spinach balls. Sauté over low flame, basting
with butter until thoroughly hot. To serve, border Sweet Potato
Ring.

SWEET POTATO RING

12 small to medium sweet pota-   1 cup brown sugar, firmly packed
   toes, boiled and mashed   ¼ cup nutmeats, coarsely
½ cup (¼ pound) butter, melted   chopped

Scrub potatoes and boil in sufficient salted water (½ teaspoon salt to
1 cup water) to cover for 30 to 35 minutes. Peel cooked potatoes and
mash to a fine purée. Grease a 6-cup mold thoroughly. Pour in
melted butter and tilt pan so bottom and sides are thoroughly
covered. Add sugar evenly and cover with nuts. Place in refrigerator to set. When ready to bake, fill with mashed potatoes. Place in
a pan of hot water and bake in preheated 350° oven for 45 minutes.
To serve, turn out on platter as for an upside-down cake, so ring
will be caramel topped. Encircle with Spinach Balls. If using ring
mold place a small bowl of hot or cold Watermelon Preserves in
center. (See Index.)

SWEET POTATOES ROYAL

1 cup dried apricots   ¼ cup butter or margarine,
2 cups water   melted
1 cup brown sugar, firmly packed   ¾ cup almonds, sliced and
2 pounds sweet potatoes, cooked   blanched
   and peeled

Wash the apricots and soak in water 2 hours. Bring to a boil and cook over low heat 20 minutes or until tender. Stir in sugar. Slice the potatoes ½ inch thick and layer with undrained apricots in a well-greased 1½-quart casserole. Pour the butter over all. Bake in 375° oven 30 to 35 minutes, basting twice. Sprinkle with the almonds and bake 10 minutes longer.

Arrange on platter with Spinach Ricotta Balls.

EASTER EGG SALAD

2 heads escarole	4 hard-cooked eggs, halved
16 2-inch strips pimiento	lengthwise

Make a bed of escarole, place hard-cooked egg halves in center, crisscross with 2 pimiento strips and serve with Lemon French Dressing (see Index).

Note: The green of this salad will be interesting, and the eggs significant of the occasion.

CHOCOLATE CHEESE CAKE

Crust:

1 cup fine graham cracker crumbs	¼ cup sugar
¼ cup ground walnuts	¼ cup butter, melted
¼ teaspoon cinnamon	

Mix cracker crumbs, nuts, sugar, butter, and cinnamon. Press mixture into a 10-inch spring form to make a thin bottom layer and side crust. Set in refrigerator while preparing filling.

Filling:

1 pound cream cheese	½ cup sugar
3 egg yolks	3 tablespoons cocoa
1 teaspoon vanilla	3 egg whites, beaten stiff

Beat cheese, egg yolks, and vanilla with electric mixer until smooth. Sift sugar and cocoa and beat into cheese mixture until blended. Fold in egg whites. Turn into lined form. Bake in a preheated 375° oven 20 minutes. Remove from oven and cool.

Topping:

¼ cup sugar	1 teaspoon vanilla
2 tablespoons cocoa	2 cups dairy sour cream

Stir sifted sugar, cocoa, and vanilla into sour cream. Spoon mixture gently over top of filling. Return to 475° oven and bake 10 minutes. Cool. Store in refrigerator until serving time.

Passover Dinner

(SERVES APPROXIMATELY 8)

CEREMONIAL FOOD PLATE

Chorosis

Gefilte Fish

Chicken Consommé — Matzo Ball Float

Traditional Turkey

Honeyed Carrots   Tzimmes Medley

Spring Salad — Orange Dressing   Matzos

Almond Torte   Holiday Doughnuts

Tea with Lemon

Suggested wine: a traditional Passover wine

The Ceremonial Plate is set before the head of the family, who conducts the service.

ADVANCE PREPARATION SCHEDULE

Deep Freeze	**Early morning**
Fish	*Giblet dressing*
Consommé	*Carrots*
Matzo balls	*Turkey*
Tzimmes	
Salad dressing	
Torte	
Doughnuts	

CHOROSIS

The Passover Appetizer.

This is a recipe dating from the era when measurements were not needed and housewives were innately cooks, the day when you took a little of this and a bit more of that. We give you an approximation.

Apples	Cinnamon
Almonds, blanched and ground	Dash ground ginger
Grated lemon rind	Passover red wine
A little sugar	

Pare and chop apples. Add sugar, cinnamon, ginger, ground almonds, grated lemon rind, mix thoroughly and add wine to bind. Should have a strong taste of cinnamon. Serve in individual ramekins.

GEFILTE FISH

Prepare Court Bouillon for fish.

Court Bouillon:

2 quarts water	4 carrots, ¼-inch slices
Bones and skins of fish	2 teaspoons salt
2 onions, sliced	¾ teaspoon pepper
½ teaspoon sugar	

Combine all ingredients in a large, heavy kettle. Cook rapidly for 30 minutes.

Gefilte Fish:

3 pounds whitefish	2½ cups cold water
1½ pounds trout	3 large onions, ground with fish
1½ pounds pike	2 large onions, sliced in pot
3 eggs	Salt and pepper to taste
½ cup bread crumbs *or* matzo meal	4 carrots, sliced in pot

Grind raw fish and onions with fine blade of grinder and place in mixing or chopping bowl, add eggs, salt, pepper, sugar and matzo meal; blend thoroughly, mixing or chopping very well. Those cooks to whom the making of Gefilte Fish (literally Filled Fish) is an art insist that the important secret is long and thorough chopping. The younger generation claims that the slow and thorough addition of the ice water is the secret of fluffy, yet firm fish balls. What is your decision? Add ice water gradually, mixing constantly until water is absorbed and well blended. Remove skin, bones, onions, and carrots from court bouillon. Reserve carrot slices. Bring stock to a boil. The fish can now be rolled into balls. Moisten hands with cold water and shape mixture into 2-inch balls, or flatten them if you wish. Drop them into the boiling stock. Cover loosely, reduce heat, and simmer 2½ to 3 hours.

Cool slightly; then remove pieces carefully; place on platter; top each with a carrot slice. Strain stock into bowl, refrigerate. It will jell as an aspic. To serve, place fish on a bed of lettuce, garnish with cubed aspic, a sprig of parsley, and accompany with red horseradish.

CHICKEN CONSOMME

1 4-pound hen chicken	3 carrots
1½ pounds lean beef (optional)	3 stalks celery, with leaves
1 beef soup bone, with meat	1 parsley *or* celery root
4 quarts water	8 sprigs parsley
1 tablespoon salt	1 parsnip
2 dried, red onions	⅛ teaspoon nutmeg

1 teaspoon sugar

Select a young hen and place with beef and bone in water in a large kettle; add salt and onions. Cover and simmer very slowly for 1 hour. Add carrots, celery with leaves, parsley or celery root, parsley sprigs, parsnip, nutmeg, and sugar. Bring to a boil, cover, reduce heat and simmer for about 3 hours. Remove the chicken when tender (about 1½ hours). It is more convenient to remove vegetables if they have been tied together in a faggot. To heighten color of the consommé, add a few outside leaves of the dried red onion. Strain soup, cool and refrigerate overnight. When cold, remove fat. Reheat to serve.

MATZO BALL FLOAT

4 egg yolks, well beaten	Dash white pepper
½ cup cold water	Pinch nutmeg (optional)
⅓ cup chicken fat, softened	1 cup matzo meal
1 teaspoon salt	4 egg whites, stiffly beaten

2 quarts boiling salted water or consommé

Combine yolks, water, chicken fat, salt, pepper, and nutmeg. Beat in matzo meal gradually, blending well. Fold in beaten egg whites. Refrigerate a minimum of one hour. Shape into walnut-sized balls and drop into boiling water. Cover and simmer 28 minutes. Remove with slotted spoon. Makes about 20 balls. Place 2 or 3 in each plate and pour in hot soup.

TRADITIONAL TURKEY

3 teaspoons salt	1 clove garlic, minced
3 teaspoons freshly ground pepper	¼ cup melted shortening
2 teaspoons paprika	1 16-pound turkey

Blend together salt, pepper, paprika, garlic; rub into turkey, inside and out. Stuff turkey lightly with Giblet Dressing. Lace opening with skewers and thread. Truss legs together and tie wings closely to the body. Spread turkey well with shortening. Place turkey on its side on rack of roasting pan and place in a preheated 325° oven. When brown turn on other side, and then breast up, until done. Baste every 20 minutes of roasting time. Use shortening or combine shortening with giblet stock for basting. Roast about 4 hours. When leg joint moves readily, turkey is done. Poultry varies in age and tenderness, whether fresh or frozen, and roasting time therefore, must be an approximation.

Giblet Dressing:

1 cup boiling water	Liver, heart and gizzard, cooked
12 matzos, crumbled	and chopped
8 tablespoons shortening *or*	6 tablespoons chopped parsley
chicken fat	4 teaspoons salt
4 onions, chopped	1 teaspoon freshly ground black
6 stalks celery, chopped	pepper

4 eggs, beaten

Pour boiling water over matzos; soak for 5 minutes; drain. Melt shortening in skillet; add onions and celery; sauté for 5 minutes, stirring frequently. Add liver, heart, and gizzard and sauté for 10 minutes, stirring occasionally. Add parsley, salt, pepper, eggs, and matzos. Mix well, stuff turkey loosely and roast.

To cook giblets:

Wash giblets thoroughly in cold salted water. Remove any membrane or fat. Place a small onion and a stalk of celery in 3 cups of water. Add drained heart and gizzard, cover and simmer for about 1 hour or until both are tender. Then add liver and cook 15 minutes longer. Remove giblets and chop coarsely for dressing. Reserve the stock for basting.

HONEYED CARROTS

3 tablespoons shortening	1½ teaspoons salt
6 cups sliced carrots	¼ teaspoon dry ginger
3 tablespoons orange juice	4 tablespoons honey

Combine all ingredients in saucepan; cover and cook over low heat for 25 minutes, stirring occasionally.

TZIMMES MEDLEY

1½ pounds pitted prunes	¼ teaspoon pepper
3 cups boiling water	6 large sweet potatoes, peeled
1½ tablespoons chicken fat	and quartered
3 pounds brisket of beef	½ cup honey
2 onions, diced	2 whole cloves
1½ teaspoons salt	½ teaspoon cinnamon

Wash prunes and let soak in boiling water ½ hour. Melt fat in Dutch oven. Cut beef in 6 or 8 pieces; place in heated fat with onions and brown. Sprinkle with salt and pepper; cover with water and cook over low heat 1 hour. Add undrained prunes, sweet potatoes, honey, cloves, and cinnamon. Replace cover, leaving it ajar, and cook over low heat for 1½ hours.

SPRING SALAD

1 head Boston lettuce   1 #2 can asparagus
8 thick slices tomato   6 green pepper rings

Form cups of lettuce leaves, place tomato slice on each. Slip 3 or 4 stalks of asparagus through a ring of green pepper; place on tomato slice. Dust with paprika. Serve on chilled individual salad plates, with Orange Dressing.

Orange Dressing:

¼ cup olive oil   ½ teaspoon paprika
¼ cup orange juice   1 teaspoon sugar
½ teaspoon salt   ¼ cup lemon juice

Mix ingredients in order given. Chill and shake well before serving.

ALMOND TORTE

6 eggs, separated   ⅔ cup matzo cake meal
¾ cup sugar   1 tablespoon potato starch
2 cups finely chopped *or* ground   1 tablespoon grated lemon rind
   nutmeats   2 teaspoons brandy
⅛ teaspoon salt

Beat egg yolks with sugar until mixture is very light and fluffy. Beat in nutmeats, matzo cake meal and potato starch; add grated lemon rind and brandy. Add salt to egg whites and beat until stiff, but not dry. Fold yolk mixture into stiffly beaten whites, pour into unbuttered 9-inch spring form with tube center. Bake in a pre-heated 325° oven about 1 hour, or until cake springs back when dented with finger. Invert cake pan until cake is cool. Release by running a spatula around the cake in the pan. If cake rises above top of pan, raise the pan by placing center on a small can, or over the neck of a beverage bottle.

HOLIDAY DOUGHNUTS

⅓ cup shortening   1 cup matzo meal
⅔ cup water   3 eggs
¼ teaspoon salt   Confectioners' sugar

Combine shortening, water, salt and bring to a boil. Add matzo meal, stirring well. Let mixture come to a boil. Remove from heat and beat thoroughly. Add eggs, one at a time, beating well after each addition. Grease hands well and pinch off pieces of dough of a size to roll into balls 2 inches in diameter. Dip finger in water and pierce a hole through the center of each ball. Place on greased pan and bake in a preheated 375° oven 1 hour. Roll in confectioners' sugar while hot.

Decoration Day Picnic

(SERVES 6 TO 8)

Deviled Eggs (see Index)   Potato Chips   Cherry Tomatoes
Pickles   Cucumber Sticks
Barbecued Ribs   Broiled Picnic Chicken
Party Baked Beans
Fresh Fruits: Oranges, Watermelons, Fresh Pineapple Wedges
Pecan Coffee Cake   Chocolate Refreshers
Thermos of Fruit Punch
Cold Bottled Beverages

ADVANCE PREPARATION SCHEDULE

Previous Day

Broiled Picnic Chicken
Marinate ribs

BARBECUED RIBS

Marinade or Sauce for Ribs:

1½ cups wine vinegar	1 tablespoon salt
½ cup brown sugar	1 tablespoon dry mustard
¼ cup Worcestershire	1 tablespoon paprika
1½ cups catsup	¾ teaspoon garlic salt
3 cups pineapple juice	6 pounds ribs

Combine ingredients and simmer 15 minutes. Marinate ribs several hours or overnight. Drain, reserve marinade. Place ribs on rack in roasting pan. Bake uncovered, 15 minutes in a preheated 500° oven; baste twice with reserved marinade. Reduce heat to 325° and bake uncovered 1 hour, basting every 15 minutes with marinade and drippings. Remove from oven, separate ribs, using shears, cut in portions of 1 or 2 ribs. To serve, place in 325° oven for 30 minutes, basting every 10 minutes.

Variation:

Barbecued chickens may be prepared with the ribs. Disjoint them, marinate as for ribs, but do not place them in 500° oven. Start roasting when heat is reduced to 325° and proceed according to recipe.

Note: In this preparation ribs may be made in advance except for last half hour and are very good for outdoor follow-up cooking. For the picnic, cook ribs 1 hour and separate as above. To complete cooking at the picnic, heat the coals in a portable grill. Barbecue for about 30 minutes or until heat of coals is low. Baste ribs again. Place over coals 5 minutes on each side. Serve with remaining marinade for dipping. Any left over may be reserved and refrigerated for future use. It keeps well.

BROILED PICNIC CHICKEN

4 broilers, 1½ to 2 pounds each, halved	1 tablespoon salt
	1 teaspoon white pepper
8 tablespoons butter, melted	3 small garlic cloves, crushed

Clean, wash, and thoroughly dry chicken. Blend 4 tablespoons of the butter with salt, pepper, and garlic. Spread mixture evenly on all parts of chicken. Broil about 7 minutes on one side until light brown. Turn and broil other side the same way. Turn back again and baste first side with 2 tablespoons of remaining plain melted butter. Broil another 7 or 8 minutes until golden brown. Turn again and repeat process with balance of butter. Serve picnic-cold or broiler-hot as a dinner entrée.

Note: Broiling cannot brown chicken as evenly as frying, but frequent turning will produce an attractive color.

PARTY BAKED BEANS

¾ pound bacon
2 small onions, sliced thin
3 jumbo (1-pound, 10-ounce) cans baked beans

1 cup catsup
¾ cup dark brown sugar

Place bacon in large skillet and sauté partially; add onions and sauté until onions are brown and bacon is done. Remove to paper toweling, cool bacon and crumble. Mix gently with beans, catsup, and brown sugar. Place in bean pot or casserole and refrigerate overnight. Heat before leaving for picnic. An insulated bag will keep beans hot for 3 or 4 hours; a vacuum jug for an indefinite time. The portable grill is a convenient way to reheat foods.

FRESH FRUITS
(Pack in plastic containers)

Oranges: Cut in sections with peel and wrap in original shape in sheer plastic wrappings.
Melon: Cut in wedges, add a few slices of lemon.
Pineapple: Cut in fingers.
Include other preferred fruits.

PECAN COFFEE CAKE

½ cup coarsely chopped pecans
¾ cup butter
1½ cups sugar
3 cups all-purpose flour

3 teaspoons baking powder
3 eggs, beaten
1 cup milk
1 lemon, juice and grated rind

Prepare a 9-inch tube pan; grease it well and cover evenly with pecans. Cream butter, add sugar, and beat until fluffy; add eggs and beat well. Sift flour with baking powder and add alternately with milk to first mixture. Add the lemon juice and grated rind. Mix thoroughly; pour into prepared tube pan. Place in a preheated 350° oven and bake for 1 hour. Cool cake a few minutes and turn out of pan onto cake rack to cool completely. For the picnic, return cake to pan when cool. Wrap in wax paper, and cut cake as served.

CHOCOLATE REFRESHERS

1¼ cups dates, cut in pieces
¾ cup brown sugar, firmly packed
½ cup water
½ cup (¼ pound) butter *or* margarine
1 cup semi-sweet chocolate chips (6-ounce package)

2 eggs, unbeaten
1¼ cups sifted all-purpose flour
¾ teaspoon soda
½ teaspoon salt
½ cup orange juice
⅓ cup milk
1 cup chopped nutmeats (pecans or walnuts)

Combine dates, sugar, water, and butter in large saucepan. Cook over low heat, stirring constantly until dates soften. Remove from heat, stir in chocolate chips, beat in eggs, add dry ingredients alternately with orange juice and milk. Blend thoroughly after each addition, stir in nutmeats. Bake in well greased 15" x 10" x 1" jelly roll pan in a preheated 350° oven 25 to 30 minutes. Cool. Spread with Orange Glaze, cut into bars or small squares, and top each square with half a pecan.

Orange Glaze:

1½ cups confectioners' sugar
2 tablespoons butter, softened
2 teaspoons orange rind, grated

3 tablespoons cream (or orange juice)

Combine the above ingredients and spread glaze on Chocolate Refreshers.

Note: For the picnic, carry Chocolate Refreshers in pan in which they were baked and remove to serve.

FRUIT PUNCH

½ cup sugar
1 cup water
1 cup strong tea
1 cup pineapple juice

¾ cup lemon juice
⅓ cup orange juice
2 cups lime rickey
Orange and lemon slices

Boil sugar in water 5 minutes. Add other ingredients. Chill. Pour into thermos jug. Serve with lemon and orange slices.

Note: Fifteen times the above recipe serves 100 people amply.

COLD BOTTLED BEVERAGES

Serve other very cold soft drinks in their own bottles. Place them in a newspaper-lined bucket, and cover with newspapers. Bring along the opener and straws.

Father's Day Dinner

(SERVES 8)

Crabmeat and Salmon Mousse   Melba Toast Rounds
Citrus Lamb
Paprika Potatoes   Green Peas Sauterne
Mint Sherbet
Chocolate Angel Cake
Coffee

Suggested wine: red Bordeaux

ADVANCE PREPARATION SCHEDULE

Deep Freeze	**Previous Day**	**Early Morning**
Mint sherbet	*Crabmeat Mousse*	*Chocolate Angel Cake*
		Boil potatoes
		Lamb

CRABMEAT AND SALMON MOUSSE

¼ cup butter
¼ cup flour
1 cup canned chicken broth
1 cup milk
2 envelopes (2 tablespoons) unflavored gelatin
¼ cup water
1 6½-ounce can crabmeat, flaked and boned
1 7½-ounce can salmon, drained and flaked

½ cup celery, chopped
1 tablespoon Worcestershire
½ teaspoon salt
2 teaspoons grated onion
1 tablespoon lemon juice
½ teaspoon paprika
½ cup mayonnaise
1 cup cream, whipped

Melt butter in saucepan and add flour; stir until blended. Bring broth and milk to boil and add to flour, stirring vigorously. Soften gelatin in cold water and add to hot sauce, stirring until gelatin has dissolved. Blend in crabmeat and salmon, celery, Worcestershire, salt, onion, lemon juice, paprika, and mayonnaise, and refrigerate until mixture just begins to set; fold in whipped cream. Pour into oiled 6-cup ring mold and refrigerate until set. Unmold on platter rimmed with parsley and radish roses. Center with bowl of sauce.

Sauce:

1 cup mayonnaise
1 tablespoon prepared horseradish
½ teaspoon prepared mustard

1 tablespoon prepared barbecue sauce

CITRUS LAMB

1 5- to 6-pound leg of lamb
Salt, pepper, paprika
Juice of 1 lemon
2 cloves garlic (optional)
2 onions, sliced

2 stalks celery, sliced
½ cup water
3 tablespoons butter
2 tablespoons Worcestershire
½ cup chili sauce

½ cup lime *or* orange marmalade

Sprinkle lamb with salt, pepper, paprika, and lemon juice; rub with cut cloves of garlic. Place onions and celery in roaster without a rack, add water and butter, and set lamb on top of vegetables. Roast in a preheated 325° oven 30 minutes, then add Worcestershire and chili sauce. Baste frequently, adding water as needed, allowing 30 minutes to the pound for complete roasting time. Spread marmalade over lamb for glaze, and return to oven for last 30 minutes of cooking time, just before serving.

PAPRIKA POTATOES

6 potatoes, halved   ¼ teaspoon paprika
¼ cup vegetable shortening   ¼ teaspoon salt

Boil potatoes in salt water. Heat shortening, add paprika; place cooked potatoes in hot shortening, sauté until brown. Remove and sprinkle with salt and additional paprika.

GREEN PEAS SAUTERNE

3 cups fresh *or* 2 10-ounce   3 teaspoons cornstarch
packages frozen peas   1 tablespoon water
1½ cups thinly sliced celery   ⅓ cup sauterne *or* other white
1 teaspoon seasoned salt   dinner wine
1½ cups chicken broth   4 tablespoons butter
Pepper

Combine peas, celery, salt, and broth in saucepan. Cover and cook gently until peas are almost tender. Make paste of cornstarch and water. Blend with peas. Stir in wine, butter, pepper, and additional salt to taste. Continue cooking until liquid is clear and very hot.

MINT SHERBET

3 pints lemon sherbet   ⅓ cup Crème de Menthe *or*
3 to 4 drops green food   ¾ teaspoon mint flavoring
coloring

Soften sherbet in large bowl of electric mixer and beat quickly. Add Crème de Menthe and blend. If using mint flavoring, add coloring. Fill 8 individual sherbet glasses and store in freezer.

CHOCOLATE ANGEL FOOD CAKE

1 cup cake flour, sifted	1 teaspoon cream of tartar
4 tablespoons Dutch cocoa	1⅓ cups sugar
⅛ teaspoon salt	1 teaspoon vanilla
1⅓ cups egg whites (about 11 eggs)	

Sift flour and cocoa together 5 or 6 times. Add salt to egg whites and beat with wire whisk beater until foamy. Add cream of tartar and continue beating until eggs are stiff but not too dry. Fold in sugar, a tablespoon at a time. Sift flour and cocoa together and combine with whites. Add vanilla. Pour batter into ungreased angel food pan and cut through a few times with knife to eliminate air bubbles. Bake in a preheated 300° oven 1 hour, raising heat to 350° the last 15 to 20 minutes. Remove from oven. Invert pan and let stand about 1 hour or until cake is cold. Remove by cutting around cake with a spatula. Shake gently. Frost with Chocolate Marshmallow Butter Cream Frosting.

This recipe is larger than needed. Leftovers may be frozen for future use.

Chocolate Marshmallow Butter Cream Frosting:

2 egg whites	⅛ teaspoon salt
3 tablespoons water	1 cup granulated sugar
1 teaspoon vanilla	1 cup (½ pound) unsalted butter
¼ teaspoon cream of tartar	¼ cup Dutch cocoa, sifted

Combine egg whites, water, vanilla, cream of tartar, salt, and sugar in upper part of double boiler. Mix well. Beat over heat with rotary beater 6 or 7 minutes (electric mixer 2 minutes), or until mixture stands in peaks. If using electric beater bring water in lower part of double boiler to a rapid boil. Remove from stove and beat 3 or 4 minutes at high speed until it stands up in peaks. (Be careful not to scrape beaters against bottom of pan as it will darken marshmallow mixture.) Allow marshmallow to become cool, keeping it covered with damp towel, which prevents crust from forming.

Cream butter thoroughly and add cold marshmallow to it, a little at a time, beating thoroughly. Add Dutch cocoa. Use more cocoa if more intense flavor is desired. Have marshmallow and butter at about same temperature and consistency before combining them, otherwise frosting will have tendency to separate or curdle. Keep in cool, not cold, place until ready to be used.

Note: If frosting should curdle, add about 2 tablespoons hot melted butter and beat well.

Fourth of July Informal Dinner

(SERVES 8)

Gazpacho Majorca

Strip Steaks from the Grill — Soy Steak Sauce and/or

Beer Barbecue Sauce

Golden Corn Soufflé

Portuguese Salad

Iced Berries and Cream   Red and White Cake

Citrus Ice Tea

Suggested wine: a red Burgundy

ADVANCE PREPARATION SCHEDULE

Deep Freeze	Previous Day	Early Morning
Barbecue Sauce	*Steak Sauce*	*Gazpacho*
	Icing	*Salad Dressing*
		Berries
		Cake

GAZPACHO MAJORCA

1 #3 (46-ounce) can tomato juice	2 cups chopped green pepper
2 cups peeled and diced cucumber	2 cups croutons
1 cup chopped green onions	1 cup chopped parsley
2 cups diced celery	2 cups cubed tomatoes

Salt and pepper

Serve tomato juice in soup mugs. Arrange on serving tray, in separate bowls, the cucumbers, onions, celery, green pepper, croutons, parsley, tomatoes, and salt and pepper. Pass vegetables to each guest for his choice. Use at least four of the suggested vegetables.

STRIP STEAKS FROM THE GRILL

8 strip steaks

Flame coals and allow them to smolder. Place steaks on barbecue grill over smoldering coals; grill to individual taste and serve with sauce.

SOY STEAK SAUCE

2 tablespoons brown or white sugar	3 tablespoons soy sauce
⅛ teaspoon coarse black pepper	3 tablespoons bottled meat sauce
1 large clove garlic, mashed	½ cup catsup
1 teaspoon salt	1 tablespoon vinegar *or* lemon juice
3 tablespoons grated onion	3 dashes Tabasco

¼ cup butter

Combine ingredients and simmer for 30 minutes.

BEER BARBECUE SAUCE

2 14-ounce bottles catsup	1½ cups wine vinegar
1 12-ounce bottle chili sauce	1 cup fresh lemon juice
⅓ cup prepared mustard	½ cup bottled thick steak sauce
2 tablespoons dry mustard	¼ cup Worcestershire
1½ cups firmly packed brown sugar	1 tablespoon soy sauce
2 tablespoons coarse, freshly ground pepper	2 tablespoons salad oil
	1 12-ounce can beer
	1 garlic clove

Dash Tabasco

Combine all ingredients except garlic. Mix well. Add garlic clove and store this way. Makes about 3 quarts. Pour into sterilized jars. Will keep indefinitely. May be frozen.

GOLDEN CORN SOUFFLE

¼ cup butter
¼ cup flour
2 cups cream-style corn (16-ounce can)
⅓ cup milk
¼ teaspoon salt

⅛ teaspoon garlic salt
½ teaspoon Worcestershire
½ cup shredded Provolone cheese *or* Mozzarella cheese
1½ cups shredded Cheddar cheese
5 large egg yolks, slightly beaten

5 large egg whites

Place a shallow pan on oven rack. Set a 2-quart ungreased casserole in pan. Pour boiling water around casserole to depth of at least 1 inch. Preheat oven to 325°. While oven and casserole are preheating, melt butter in a saucepan and stir in flour until smooth. Add corn, milk, salt, garlic salt, and Worcestershire; blend well. Cook, stirring constantly, until mixture thickens. Add cheese and stir until melted. Blend sauce into beaten egg yolks. Cool slightly. Beat egg whites until stiff but not dry. Gently fold cheese mixture into beaten egg whites. Spoon into the ungreased 2-quart casserole. Using a spatula, make a groove around soufflé about 1 inch deep and 1 inch from edge of casserole. Return casserole to pan of hot water in oven. Bake in a preheated 325° oven 60 to 75 minutes or until knife inserted halfway between center and outer edge comes out clean.

PORTUGUESE SALAD

2½ quarts salad greens
1 cup pitted ripe olives
4 hard-cooked eggs, quartered
1 2-ounce can anchovies

½ cup salad oil
¼ cup vinegar
½ teaspoon salt
Cracked pepper

1 tablespoon chopped capers

Break salad greens into bite-sized pieces. Add olives and eggs. Drain anchovies and chop; add to salad. Put salad oil, vinegar, salt, pepper, and capers into a jar; cover and shake well. Pour over salad before serving.

ICED BERRIES AND CREAM
(A charming recipe with linear measures)

1 quart berries: raspberries, strawberries *or* blueberries	1 tablespoon Kirsch
1 quart heavy cream, whipped	3 tablespoons brandy
	1 cup brown sugar (about)

Cover bottom of 3-quart casserole or soufflé dish with berries, add Kirsch and brandy. The liquid should just cover fruit. Add more if needed but, to quote our Mexican hostess, "do not permit the berries to swim."

Add 4 inches of whipped cream, a 1-inch layer of brown sugar, and spread each evenly. Refrigerate 4 hours.

To serve, place under broiler to brown lightly and quickly, 1 to 1½ minutes.

RED AND WHITE CAKE

½ cup shortening	1 teaspoon salt
1½ cups sugar	1 cup buttermilk
2 eggs	2¼ cups all-purpose flour
2 ounces red food coloring (4 bottles)	1 teaspoon vanilla
	1 tablespoon white vinegar
2 tablespoons cocoa	1 teaspoon baking soda

Cream shortening, sugar, and eggs. Make a paste of food coloring and cocoa. Add to shortening mixture. Add salt, buttermilk, flour, and vanilla; beat well. Add (do not beat) vinegar and soda. Pour batter into two 8-inch cake pans. Bake in a preheated 350° oven for 30 minutes. Allow layers to cool before frosting.

Icing:

5 tablespoons flour	1 cup granulated sugar
1 cup milk	1 cup (½ pound) butter
1 teaspoon vanilla	

Combine flour and milk in saucepan. Cook mixture until thick. Allow to cool. Place in refrigerator to chill further. (This part of mixture can be made the night before and refrigerated.) Cream sugar, butter, and vanilla. Add to flour and milk mixture. Do not overbeat. Cut each layer in half. Frost top, sides and layers.

To serve, place cake on 12-inch circle of white Styrofoam, cut about 2 inches thick. Stick tiny American flags around it. If available, use sparklers instead, to be lighted at dessert time.

CITRUS ICE TEA

8 teaspoons tea	Juice of 5 oranges
Juice of 5 lemons	Bunch of mint

Steep tea in 1 pint boiling water for 15 minutes. Strain. Mix with fruit juice, 1 quart cold water, and ice; sugar to taste. Add mint.

Labor Day Brunch

(SERVES 6 OR 8)

Cointreau Strawberries   Grapefruit à l'Orange
Eggs Florentine   Quiche Lorraine
Mushroom Salad
Tea Rolls   Preserves
Coffee

Suggested wine: Graves

ADVANCE PREPARATION SCHEDULE

Deep Freeze	Previous Day	Early Morning
Tea Rolls	*Pastry shell*	*Strawberries*
	Salad dressing	*Cointreau sauce*
		Grapefruit
		Eggs Florentine
		Quiche
		Salad

COINTREAU STRAWBERRIES

6 eggs, separated	2 tablespoons chopped fresh mint
1 cup confectioners' sugar	2 ounces Cointreau
3 pints ripe strawberries	

Beat egg whites until very stiff, gradually adding sugar. Place egg yolks in another bowl, add mint and beat until smooth. Fold yolks into whites; add Cointreau. Chill mixture thoroughly. Rinse and dry strawberries, leaving stems on, and heap them on a platter surrounding a bowl of sauce. The quantity of sauce is more than generous but the berries are succulent bits when dipped. The Cointreau cream may be stored in the refrigerator several days.

GRAPEFRUIT A L'ORANGE

3 or 4 grapefruit
Dash salt
1 cup orange juice

2 tablespoons fresh *or* 2 teaspoons dried mint

Peel grapefruit over bowl to catch juice. Starting at stem end, peel grapefruit in spiral fashion, cutting through skin and membrane exposing pulp and thus removing all white substance. Slip a sharp knife between pulp and membrane in both sides of each section until all are released. Use care so they are not broken. Place in large bowl; stir salt into orange juice; pour over grapefruit and refrigerate about 1 hour, or longer, if convenient. Sprinkle with chopped mint.

Note: Oranges may be sectioned in same manner as grapefruit.

EGGS FLORENTINE

1 pound spinach, fresh *or* frozen
¼ cup (⅛ pound) butter
¼ cup flour
1 cup milk
1 cup half and half cream

½ teaspoon salt
⅛ teaspoon pepper
¼ teaspoon nutmeg
12 poached eggs
Grated Parmesan cheese

Wash and cook spinach. (Cook frozen spinach according to package directions.) Drain and chop very fine. Melt butter in saucepan; add flour, stirring until blended. Heat milk and cream; add to butter mixture, stirring constantly until thickened. Add salt and pepper. Combine spinach with half of sauce and add nutmeg. Pour spinach mixture into large shallow ovenproof casserole. Arrange poached eggs on top. Pour remaining sauce over the eggs. Sprinkle with Parmesan cheese. Bake in a preheated 400° oven until browned, about 10 minutes.

QUICHE LORRAINE

Pastry for 9-inch pie shell	1 teaspoon salt
½ pound bacon	Pinch white pepper
4 eggs	Pinch cayenne
1¾ cups light cream	½ pound Swiss cheese, grated
2 ounces Gruyère cheese, grated	

Line a 9-inch pie plate with pastry. Flute the edge for a standing rim. Chill while preparing filling. Cook bacon until crisp; drain on paper toweling and crumble into small pieces. Beat eggs slightly, add cream, salt, white pepper, and cayenne; mix well. Arrange crumbled bacon in pastry-lined pan; add Swiss and Gruyère cheese to form the next layer. Pour egg-cream mixture over cheese. Bake in a preheated 400° oven 35 to 45 minutes, or until a silver knife comes out clean from center of mixture. Remove from oven and allow to cool 7 to 10 minutes on a cake rack before cutting.

Prize Pie Crust:

½ cup (¼ pound) butter	Pinch salt
1 cup flour	2 tablespoons half and half cream

With pastry cutter cut butter into flour until dough is the size of small peas. Add salt, cream, and mix with fork until it forms a ball. Press into pie plate, lining it evenly, and prick bottom several times with fork.

MUSHROOM SALAD

2 pounds fresh mushrooms	½ cup Parsley French Dressing
2 bunches watercress	

Scrub mushrooms and slice thin; cover with Parsley French Dressing and marinate 2 hours in refrigerator. Turn once while marinating. Serve on a bed of watercress.

Parsley French Dressing:

1 teaspoon salt	2 tablespoons lemon juice
⅛ teaspoon pepper	¾ cup salad oil
2 tablespoons vinegar	2 tablespoons chopped parsley
½ teaspoon dill weed	

Blend together salt, pepper, vinegar, lemon juice, and oil; add parsley and dill. Mix thoroughly.

TEA ROLLS

2 cups all-purpose flour	1 teaspoon vanilla
2 teaspoons baking powder	¼ cup (⅛ pound) butter, melted
½ cup sugar	¼ cup sugar
½ teaspoon salt	¼ teaspoon cinnamon
½ cup (¼ pound) butter, softened	½ cup chopped nuts
	1 cup raisins, soaked until soft
2 eggs, well beaten	½ cup jelly (cherry *or* grape)

Combine flour, baking powder, sugar, and salt. Mix in butter until blended; stir eggs with vanilla and add to mixture. Texture will be crumbly. Mix this batter with a fork until dough forms a ball. Refrigerate overnight. Cut dough into three equal parts. Roll out each piece until quite thin; a little flour at a time may be added to keep dough from sticking. Spread each third with melted butter. Combine sugar and cinnamon and sprinkle the dough with this mixture, nuts, and raisins. Spoon on jelly in several places. Roll each into long roll and bake in a preheated 350° oven 30 minutes. Cool and cut into slices. Serve warm or cold.

Labor Day Supper

(SERVES 6)

Crab Avocado en Coquille
Assorted Crisp Relishes
Veal Blades
Orange Rice   Asparagus Gourmet
Mocha Chocolate Cake

ADVANCE PREPARATION SCHEDULE

Deep Freeze
Cake

Early Morning
Crab Coquille
Veal
Asparagus
Frost cake

CRAB AVOCADO EN COQUILLE

1 cup frozen crabmeat, thawed
1 tablespoon butter *or* margarine
1½ tablespoons flour
½ cup chicken stock *or* bouillon cube
⅛ teaspoon salt
Dash cayenne pepper
¾ teaspoon curry powder
3 tablespoons cream
1½ tablespoons lemon juice
1 avocado
¼ cup slivered almonds

Thaw frozen crabmeat; break into chunks. Melt butter in saucepan, blending in flour and chicken stock. (Chicken bouillon cube dissolved in 1 cup of hot water is fine.) Cook and stir until thickened. Add salt, pepper, curry powder, cream, lemon juice, and crabmeat. Peel and slice avocado; sprinkle with more salt and lemon juice. Layer crab and avocado in individual appetizer shells, ending with crab sauce; top with slivered almonds. Place under broiler until very hot and flecked with brown.

VEAL BLADES

2 pounds veal steak or cutlet, cut very thin
Cut clove of garlic, *or* garlic salt
Flour to coat veal
¼ cup (⅛ pound) butter
1 pound fresh mushrooms, sliced thin
½ teaspoon salt
⅛ teaspoon pepper
½ cup dry vermouth
1 teaspoon lemon juice
2 tablespoons chopped parsley

Pound veal extra-thin with wooden mallet, or with the edge of a saucer. This cut has become so popular that most markets now carry it, and they are called "veal thins." Rub veal with garlic. Dip in flour, coating each side well.

In heavy skillet, heat butter to bubbling; add veal and sauté until golden brown on both sides. Heap mushrooms on top. Sprinkle with salt, pepper, and vermouth. Cover and cook over low heat about 20 minutes, or until tender. As it cooks, be sure it is moist; if not, add a little water. Before serving, sprinkle with lemon juice, chopped parsley, and juices in pan.

ORANGE RICE

1 cup raw rice	¾ cup orange juice
⅔ cup diced celery	2 cups water
3 tablespoons butter	1 teaspoon soy sauce
2 tablespoons grated orange rind	1 teaspoon celery seed

1½ teaspoons salt

Butter a 2-quart baking dish or casserole with a tight-fitting cover. Combine ingredients in order listed, blend well, and place in dish. Bake in a preheated 350° oven 1 hour.

ASPARAGUS GOURMET

1 egg, beaten	3 pounds asparagus
2 tablespoons dry white wine	½ teaspoon garlic powder
1 cup potato chip crumbs, combined with	Dash freshly ground pepper
	½ cup flour
1 tablespoon grated Parmesan cheese	2 tablespoons olive oil

Beat egg with wine; combine potato chip crumbs with cheese. Wash asparagus thoroughly, breaking off tough ends of stalks. Dip into flour, then egg mixture, and into potato chip mixture, to which garlic and pepper have been added. Heat olive oil in saucepan, and sauté prepared asparagus over low heat for 10 minutes, or until tender.

Variation:

For canned asparagus, sauté for 3 minutes until browned.

MOCHA CHOCOLATE CAKE

3 cups sifted cake flour	¾ cup butter
¾ teaspoon soda	2¾ cups sugar
¾ teaspoon salt	¾ cup dairy sour cream
¾ cup Dutch cocoa	1½ teaspoon vanilla
1⅛ cup hot coffee	5 egg whites, beaten stiff

Combine flour, soda, and salt; sift 3 times. Combine cocoa and hot coffee; cool. Cream butter and sugar until light and fluffy. Add cocoa mixture, sour cream, vanilla, flour, soda, and salt, stirring until smooth. Fold in egg whites very carefully. Bake in 3 well-greased 9-inch pans in a preheated 350° oven for 30 minutes, or until cake draws away from sides of pan. Put layers together with Custard Filling and frost with Rich Chocolate Frosting.

Custard Filling:

½ cup flour	1⅓ cups hot milk
Dash salt	2 egg yolks
½ cup sugar	1 teaspoon vanilla
⅓ cup heavy cream, whipped	

Mix flour, salt, and ¼ cup sugar; stir in milk. Place in top of double boiler, over boiling water, and cook until smooth and thickened, stirring constantly. Combine yolks and remaining sugar and add, continuing to cook and stir for an additional 3 minutes. Cool; then fold in cream and vanilla.

Rich Chocolate Frosting:

1⅔ cups sifted confectioners' sugar	⅛ teaspoon salt
3 1-ounce squares unsweetened chocolate, melted	½ tablespoon hot coffee
	3 egg yolks
¼ cup butter, softened	

Sift sugar and add half to chocolate, mixing thoroughly. Add salt, coffee, remaining sugar, and beat well. Add yolks, one at a time, beating well after each addition. Add butter and again beat well. Spread over entire cake, top and sides.

Thanksgiving Dinner

(SERVES 8 OR 10)

Samplers

1. Artichoke Appetizers   2. Swiss Cheese Tarts
3. Pickled Carrot Strips   4. Sherried Mushrooms

Blushed Turkey   Forcemeat Dressing   Broiled Peach Garni
Brussels Sprouts Amandine   Squash Cornucopia
Sweet Potato Puffs
Parker House Rolls
Chocolate Cream Roll   Coffee

Suggested wine: Rhine or red Burgundy

ADVANCE PREPARATION SCHEDULE

Previous Day	Early Morning
Cheese tarts	*Artichoke appetizer*
Carrot strips	*Stuff turkey*
Mushrooms	*Cornucopias*
Dressing for Turkey	*Sweet Potatoes*
Mousse	*Dessert Sauce*
Cranberry glaze	

SAMPLER I — ARTICHOKE APPETIZER

1 7-ounce can artichoke hearts	½ cup mayonnaise
1 2-ounce can caviar	½ teaspoon paprika
4 hard-cooked eggs, chopped	1 tablespoon cream
6 sweet pickles, chopped	Sliced pimiento
6 large ripe olives, chopped	Stuffed green olives

Chop artichoke hearts coarsely and place small amount on platter; sprinkle alternately in layers with caviar, then eggs, pickles, and olives. Repeat until all are used. Pat into a mound. Beat mayonnaise with paprika and cream. Spread over mound and garnish with sliced pimiento and stuffed green olives.

SAMPLER II — SWISS CHEESE TARTS

1 cup sifted all-purpose flour   ⅓ cup shortening
½ teaspoon salt   2 tablespoons water
Swiss Cheese Filling

Mix flour and salt. Cut in shortening thoroughly. Sprinkle with water and mix with a fork to make dough form into a smooth ball. Roll out on a sheet of heavy duty aluminum foil to ⅛ inch thickness. Cut foil and pastry into 3-inch circles. Turn up sides of dough and foil to make tart shells. Prick bottom and rib edges with fork. Bake in a preheated 450° oven for 6 to 8 minutes until light brown. Fill with Swiss Cheese Filling. Reduce temperature to 350° and bake 20 to 25 minutes, or until filling is golden brown. Serve warm. Makes 12 to 15.

Swiss Cheese Filling:

1 tablespoon grated onion   1 cup light cream
2 tablespoons butter *or* margarine ½ teaspoon salt
1 cup Swiss cheese, grated   Dash dry mustard
2 eggs   Dash cayenne pepper
Dash black pepper

Sauté onion in butter until soft. Add to grated cheese; mix well. Beat eggs until foamy. Beat in remaining ingredients. Combine egg and cheese mixtures and fill tart shells. May be baked and reheated to serve.

SAMPLER III — PICKLED CARROT STRIPS

⅓ cup sugar   3 teaspoons mustard seed
1¼ cups white vinegar   4 cups carrots, scraped and cut
1¼ teaspoons salt   into strips
1½ teaspoons celery seed

Heat sugar, vinegar, salt, celery seed, and mustard to boiling point. Add carrot strips, cover and simmer, stirring frequently, until carrots are tender but still crisp. Chill and serve as a relish.

SAMPLER IV — SHERRIED MUSHROOMS

1 3-ounce jar button mushrooms   Sherry

Drain mushrooms; add sufficient sherry to cover. Marinate in refrigerator overnight. Keeps for several days.

Note: A sectional dish or a setting of similar dishes placed on a
tray is a convenient and simple way to serve these samplers.

BLUSHED TURKEY

Here are two versions of Thanksgiving turkey. The rotisserie
method for those who celebrate the holiday in the sunshine; the
oven preparation for those who are geographically cold. The same
ingredients are used.

Rotisserie Method:

1 18-pound turkey

Stuff turkey with forcemeat dressing. Place on barbecue rack, fasten
firmly with adjustable screws, and lock in revolving rotisserie.
Meanwhile charcoal fire has been reduced to medium heat and
there should be an auxiliary bed of coals from which to feed the
roasting fire during the cooking period. Baste with corn oil on
start but turkey will, for the most part, be self-basting as it re-
volves. Cook approximately 5 hours and keep fire constant by
adding from hot coal supply.

Forcemeat Dressing:

¾ pound beef stew meat	6 peppercorns
¾ pound veal stew meat	1 teaspoon salt
¾ pound lamb stew meat	1¼ pounds wild rice
Turkey liver and giblets	1 medium onion, minced
1 bay leaf	3 stalks celery, minced
1 medium onion studded with 6	1 6¼-ounce can water
cloves	chestnuts, quartered
1 teaspoon marjoram	2 small jars sliced
1 teaspoon oregano	mushrooms

Salt and pepper to taste

In 2 quarts water boil beef, veal, lamb and turkey giblets with bay
leaf, onion studded with cloves, marjoram, oregano, peppercorns,
and 1 teaspoon salt; boil slowly for approximately ¾ hour. Watch
the water line and be sure that there will be enough broth to cook
the rice. Remove meat; save the broth and run the meat repeatedly

through the food chopper until it is the consistency of a pâté. Cook wild rice in broth after following package instructions for washing and cooking time. When done, mix it thoroughly with the pate and then add minced onion, celery, water chestnuts, sliced mushrooms, and salt and pepper to taste. Mix well.

Oven Method:

Stuff turkey and proceed as for traditional turkey (see Index). One half hour before removing from oven, paint it repeatedly with Cranberry Glaze, until glowing and shiny.

Cranberry Glaze:

1 #2 can jellied cranberries	½ teaspoon dry ginger
½ cup dark brown sugar, firmly packed	½ teaspoon cinnamon

Heat and stir cranberries, brown sugar, ginger, and cinnamon until sugar is dissolved; one half hour before removing turkey from fire, paint with this glaze until desired amount has been applied.

Broiled Peach Garni:

2 #2½ cans peach halves, drained   Seeds of 1 pomegranate

Cover baking sheet with foil. Place peaches, cavity side up, on foil and broil for about 3 to 4 minutes until heated and lightly browned. Sprinkle with pomegranate seeds and place on platter around turkey. Intersperse peach halves with crisp watercress, if desired.

To serve, tuck parsley and carrot daisies about turkey and serve on convenient unadorned carving board. Retain a platter, garnished with broiled peach halves, for receiving turkey as it is sliced and portioned.

BRUSSELS SPROUTS AMANDINE

2 pounds brussels sprouts	2 tablespoons butter
¼ cup slivered almonds	Salt

Cook brussels sprouts covered in 1 inch of boiling water for 20 minutes, or until tender, using ½ teaspoon salt per cup of water. Place almonds in skillet with butter and brown lightly; watch carefully that they do not burn. To serve, drain brussels sprouts, blend with almonds and place in Squash Cornucopia.

SQUASH CORNUCOPIA

Select 2 winter squash, green in color and well shaped to resemble a cornucopia. Cut off large end of squash; remove pulp, leaving green shell; scallop cut edge in harlequin points. Place on serving platter with hollow ends at opposite sides. Fill with brussels sprouts. Decorate with sprigs of parsley and radish roses. Border with Sweet Potato Puffs.

SWEET POTATO PUFFS

3 cups mashed sweet potatoes
⅛ teaspoon white pepper
1 teaspoon grated orange rind
3 tablespoons butter, melted
½ teaspoon salt
2 tablespoons orange juice
1 cup cornflakes, crushed lightly
4 maraschino cherries

Combine all ingredients except cornflakes and cherries. Beat well; form into 8 balls. Roll each in cornflakes and top with ½ cherry. Place on a buttered baking sheet. To serve, heat in a preheated 350° oven 15 to 20 minutes. Arrange around Squash Cornucopia with parsley garnish.

CHOCOLATE CREAM ROLL

¾ cup sugar
½ cup sifted cake flour
¼ cup sifted cocoa
1 teaspoon vanilla
7 eggs, separated
⅛ teaspoon salt
¾ teaspoon cream of tartar

Sift sugar 3 times; sift combined flour and cocoa 3 times. Beat egg whites with rotary beater or electric mixer for 1 minute, add salt and beat until foamy, then add cream of tartar. Continue beating until whites cling to sides of bowl. Beat egg yolks until thick and lemon colored; fold into egg whites gently, but quickly. Fold in sugar and vanilla, then combined flour and cocoa; fold only until blended. Do not overmix.

Pour into greased and floured 12″ x 18″ jelly roll pan. Spread evenly from center to sides with a spatula. Cut through batter several times to break air bubbles. Bake in a preheated 400° oven on center rack 12 to 15 minutes. Remove when cake tests done. Loosen around edges with a knife, and turn out on dry towel. Cut off crisp edges and roll quickly in towel. Do not unroll until cold.

To fill, unroll carefully, place on wax paper, fill with peppermint ice cream, leaving 1 inch uncovered around all sides. Reroll tightly in wax paper; place in freezer. Remove from freezer about ½ hour to defrost. To serve, place on platter and cover with Chocolate Mallow Sauce or Sabayon Sauce.

Chocolate Mallow Sauce:

1 4-ounce package sweet cooking chocolate	10 large marshmallows
	4 tablespoons cream
Dash salt	

Combine ingredients in double boiler until melted and well blended. Serve hot or cold. Stores well in refrigerator. Reheat to serve. For yellow cake roll, use ¾ cup sifted cake flour and omit cocoa. Fill with Coffee Ice Cream; serve with Chocolate Mallow Sauce.

Sabayon Sauce:

1 tablespoon melted butter	1 lemon, juice and grated rind
1 tablespoon flour	½ cup sherry or Madeira
4 egg yolks	1 cup sugar
⅛ teaspoon salt	1 cup heavy cream, whipped

Melt butter in top of double boiler; blend in flour. Add eggs, salt, lemon juice and rind, sherry, and sugar; beat until light. Then place over hot water and cook until thickened, stirring constantly. Cool thoroughly; fold in whipped cream.

Variation:

Fill with 1 cup heavy whipped cream, combined with ⅓ cup crushed peppermint candy. Reroll and chill 1 hour before serving. Serve with Chocolate Mallow Sauce.

Thanksgiving Weekend Luncheon

(SERVES 6)

See Thanksgiving Dinner Menu for Leftovers

Turkey Pancakes (using turkey leftovers)

Salad Medley (using remaining marinated vegetables)

Grapefruit Meringue

Butter Chews   Coffee

Suggested wine: Liebfraumilch or a white Bordeaux

ADVANCE PREPARATION SCHEDULE

Deep Freeze	Early Morning
Butter Chews	*Pancakes*
	Filling
	Prepare grapefruit

TURKEY PANCAKES

1 cup flour	½ teaspoon salt
2 eggs	½ cup milk
½ cup cream	

Combine all ingredients and beat until light and fluffy. Let batter stand ½ hour before using. Grease heated 6-inch skillet lightly and pour just enough batter to cover with a very thin layer (about 2 tablespoons). Tilt pan quickly so mixture spreads to cover bottom of pan. Makes 18 very thin pancakes.

Filling:

4 tablespoons butter	⅓ cup sliced mushrooms, sautéed
2 tablespoons flour	2 cups diced cooked turkey
½ onion, finely chopped	½ teaspoon salt
1½ cups turkey stock *or* chicken consommé	½ teaspoon pepper
	½ cup warm cream

Melt butter in saucepan, add flour and onion, and sauté until onion is browned; add stock and cook until thickened and smooth. Add mushrooms, turkey, salt, and pepper; mix well. Remove mixture from heat; add cream and continue to stir until blended. Fill each pancake by placing a tablespoon or more creamed turkey in the center and roll pancake tubelike. Place on ovenware dish and keep warm to serve.

SALAD MEDLEY

Form a bed of curly endive on individual salad plates. Use remaining carrot sticks, sherried mushrooms, or artichoke hearts of appetizer. If the amount is insufficient, add sliced canned beets to the arrangement. Serve French Dressing (see Index) separately.

GRAPEFRUIT MERINGUE

3 medium grapefruit   ¼ teaspoon salt
4 egg whites   ⅓ cup granulated sugar
6 teaspoons sherry (optional)

Cut grapefruit in half; snip center core from each half, then cut around all sections. Arrange halves in shallow baking dish. In small bowl, beat egg whites with salt until stiff enough to hold their shape; gradually add sugar, while beating until stiff and glossy. Sprinkle 1 teaspoon sherry on each half grapefruit. Then pile meringue mixture on top of each and bake in a preheated 375° oven for 15 minutes.

BUTTER CHEWS

½ cup (¼ pound) butter   1½ cups brown sugar, firmly
2 tablespoons sugar   packed
1 cup all-purpose flour   ½ cup chopped nuts
2 eggs, separated   ½ cup coconut

Cream butter and 2 tablespoons sugar; add flour to creamed mixture and blend well. Press evenly into buttered 8″ x 12″ cake pan. Bake 15 minutes in a preheated 375° oven. Beat egg yolks well. Add brown sugar and mix thoroughly; add nuts and coconut. Beat egg whites until stiff and fold into mixture. Pour over the baked layer. Bake in 375° oven an additional 25 to 30 minutes. Cut into squares while warm. Makes about 12 squares.

Christmas Eve Supper

(SERVES 6)

Crabmeat Cheese Puffs

Celery Curls   Rose Radishes

Pepper Steak Del Prado

Pâté de Pommes de Terre   Brussels Sprouts Vineyard

Fresh Lemon Sherbet Cup   Florentines

Coffee

Suggested wine: dry Semillon

ADVANCE PREPARATION SCHEDULE

Deep Freeze	Previous Day	Early Morning
Sherbet	*Crabmeat filling*	*Prepare potato pie*
Puffs	*Pastry for potato pie*	*for baking*
		Salad

CRABMEAT CHEESE PUFFS

Puffs:

¼ cup water

¼ cup (⅛ pound) butter *or* margarine

⅛ teaspoon salt

½ cup sifted all-purpose flour

½ cup grated sharp Cheddar cheese

2 eggs

Place water, butter, and salt in heavy saucepan; heat to boiling. When water is boiling briskly, add flour all at once, stirring vigorously with wooden spoon. Add cheese, beating until mixture forms a smooth ball which leaves sides of pan. Remove from heat. Beat in eggs, one at a time. Continue beating until mixture is thick and smooth and breaks off when spoon is raised. Place in pastry bag, press out batter in 1¼-inch rounds on greased baking sheet, or drop from teaspoon. Bake in a preheated 450° oven 8 minutes; lower heat to 350° and bake 15 minutes longer. Cool; fill with Crabmeat Filling. Makes 30 puffs.

Note: Use these tiny round puff shells for dessert fillings as well. Form them into oblongs ½ by 1¼ inches for eclairs.

Crabmeat Filling:

1 6½-ounce can crabmeat	½ teaspoon salt
2 tablespoons butter *or* margarine	¼ teaspoon dry mustard
2 tablespoons flour	Dash cayenne
¾ cup milk	2 tablespoons white wine
½ teaspoon minced onion	¼ cup grated American cheese

Flake crabmeat, removing cartilage and bony tissue. Melt butter in a skillet; add flour, stirring until smooth. Add milk gradually. When thickened, add onion, salt, mustard, cayenne, wine, and cheese; blend well. Add crabmeat and heat thoroughly.

PEPPER STEAK DEL PRADO

2 tablespoons freshly ground pepper	¼ cup undiluted canned beef consommé
2 pounds raw beef tenderloin, cut in ¼-inch slices	1 teaspoon Worcestershire
2 tablespoons butter	1 beef bouillon cube, diluted in ½ cup boiling water
½ cup cognac	

Press pepper into steak with edge of saucer or with heel of the hand. Melt butter in large skillet and heat to chestnut brown; brown steak quickly on both sides. Add consommé, cognac, Worcestershire and cook slowly for 5 minutes.

Note: Tenderloin slices more easily when slightly frozen.

PATE DE POMMES DE TERRE
(Potato Pie)

Pastry:

2¼ cups sifted all-purpose flour	½ cup shortening
1¼ teaspoons salt	¼ cup (⅛ pound) butter *or*
1 tablespoon sugar	margarine

3½ tablespoons water (about)

Sift flour, salt, and sugar into medium bowl. Cut in shortening with two knives or pastry blender until mixture is as fine as cornmeal; cut in butter until of size of peas. Sprinkle water, a little at a time, over mixture, mixing thoroughly with a fork; blend until dough leaves sides of bowl clean and press gently into smooth ball. Wrap in wax paper and set aside.

Filling:

7 cups pared potatoes, sliced thin	1 large onion, sliced thin
2 teaspoons salt	1 tablespoon minced parsley
⅛ teaspoon pepper	2 tablespoons butter *or* margarine
	1 tablespoon milk

1 cup heavy cream

Toss potatoes with salt, pepper, onion, and parsley. Roll out half of pastry to extend 1½ inches over outer edge of 1½-quart shallow baking dish; fit pastry loosely into dish and fill with potato mixture; dot with butter, and trim pastry even with edge of dish. Roll out remainder of pastry and lay over potatoes. Trim top crust so it extends 1 inch beyond edge of dish; fold it under bottom crust; press edges firmly together in stand-up rim; make rope or fluted edge; cut few slits in top to release steam. Brush with milk. Bake 1 to 1¼ hours in a preheated 350° oven or until potatoes are tender when tested with knife. Remove from oven; make small hole in crust and pour in cream. A baster works well. Let stand 5 minutes before serving.

BRUSSELS SPROUTS VINEYARD

2 quarts fresh brussel sprouts *or* 2 10-ounce packages frozen	Freshly ground pepper
1½ teaspoons salt	¼ clove garlic, crushed (optional)
2 teaspoons sugar	1 cup halved seedless green grapes
¼ cup butter	2 teaspoons honey

Cook fresh sprouts in rapidly boiling water about 8 minutes, until just tender. (Cook frozen brussels sprouts 2 minutes less than package instructions.) Drain and add salt, sugar, and 1 tablespoon of butter, pepper, and garlic. Heat remaining butter gently in a skillet with grapes and honey. When bubbly add sprouts.

FLORENTINES

½ cup heavy cream	⅓ cup sifted all-purpose flour
3 tablespoons butter	¾ cup finely chopped candied
½ cup sugar	orange peel
1¼ cups finely chopped almonds	½ cup chocolate bits, melted

Combine cream, butter, and sugar; bring to a boil. Remove from heat and stir in almonds, flour, and orange peel. Drop by tablespoons on greased and floured cooky sheet, 3 inches apart. Bake in a preheated 350° oven about 10 minutes. Cool 5 minutes and remove with spatula to cake rack. Cool. Spiral melted chocolate over each cooky top. Multicolored decorettes may be sprinkled as well. Makes 2 dozen 3-inch cookies.

LEMON SHERBET

2 cups milk	Juice of 2 lemons plus 3
2 cups heavy cream	tablespoons
2 cups sugar	½ pound lemon drops, crushed
Rind of 2 lemons, grated	fine

Combine milk and cream, add sugar, stir until dissolved. Add lemon rind, lemon juice, crushed candy, and blend well. Pour into 2½-quart container and place in freezing compartment. Let stand in freezer 5 hours or more, or overnight. Stir occasionally as it chills, as crushed candy sinks to the bottom. Makes 1 quart. Serve in goblets over diced pineapple.

To prepare pineapple:

Fresh pineapple is preferable, though canned chunks may be used. Peel and quarter pineapple, remove core and dice in bite-sized pieces. Place in goblets, for variation, or in sherbet glasses.

Note: This recipe may be halved or increased. The latter is suggested so there will be sufficient for the requests for seconds.

Late Christmas Eve Refresher

THE TREE IS TRIMMED

(SERVES 8)

Wild Rice Casserole   Curried Eggs

Spinach Salad

Hard Rolls   Apple and Ginger Cheese

Chocolate Angel Food Torte

Blueberry Coffee Cake

Tea   Coffee

ADVANCE PREPARATION SCHEDULE

Deep Freeze	Previous Day	Early Morning
Rolls	*Bake cake*	*Rice casserole*
Coffee cake		*Ginger Cheese*
		Eggs
		Frost cake

WILD RICE CASSEROLE

1 pound pork sausage meat *or* link sausages
1 pound fresh mushrooms, sliced
1 cup chopped onion
2 cups wild rice
¼ cup all-purpose flour
½ cup heavy cream
2½ cups condensed chicken broth
1 teaspoon monosodium glutamate
Generous pinch oregano, thyme, and marjoram
1 tablespoon salt
⅛ teaspoon pepper
½ cup toasted, slivered, blanched almonds

Sauté sausage (see directions following); drain on paper toweling and break into small pieces. Sauté mushrooms and onions in sausage fat; add cooked sausage. Wash wild rice thoroughly, rinsing several times, and cook 10 to 12 minutes in boiling salted water; drain well. Add rice to sausage mixture. Cream flour and heavy cream together until smooth; add chicken broth and cook slowly until thickened. Season with monosodium glutamate, oregano, thyme, marjoram, salt, and pepper. Mix and toss together with wild rice and meat mixture. Place in 2-quart lightly greased casserole and bake in a preheated 350° oven 25 to 30 minutes until thoroughly heated.

Sprinkle almonds around rim of casserole before serving. If making in advance and rice absorbs liquid, add a little more chicken broth before baking.

To cook link pork sausage:

Separate sausages and place in skillet; add boiling water to about ½ inch in depth. Cover pan and cook gently for 10 minutes. Remove cover and if water has not been absorbed, drain it from sausages. Continue to sauté sausages over low heat until lightly browned. Move them gently while cooking to prevent sticking.

To cook pork sausage meat:

Form into patties about ½ inch thick. Place in cold, ungreased skillet. Cook slowly, turning occasionally, for 12 to 15 minutes or until lightly browned and pink color is completely eliminated. Pour off fat as it accumulates in pan, reserving it for use with Wild Rice Casserole.

Variation:

Use this recipe for lunch or brunch with other egg dishes.

CURRIED EGGS

8 eggs, hard-cooked	2 tablespoons butter
¾ teaspoon dry mustard	2 tablespoons flour
2 teaspoons white vinegar	1 teaspoon curry powder
2 teaspoons Worcestershire	1 teaspoon salt
3 tablespoons mayonnaise	1 cup milk

Cut eggs in half; remove yolks and mash. Add dry mustard, vinegar, Worcestershire, and mayonnaise. Mix well and stuff into egg whites. Place them in a shallow baking dish. Melt butter in a saucepan. Add flour, curry powder, and salt. Cook for 1 minute and stir milk in slowly. Continue cooking until thick and pour over stuffed egg whites; bake in a preheated 300° oven 20 minutes.

SPINACH SALAD

1 pound raw spinach	4 tomatoes, quartered
Oil and Vinegar Dressing	⅓ cup grated Parmesan cheese
6 slices crisp bacon, crumbled	

Wash spinach carefully; toss with dressing. Arrange on individual salad plates with 2 wedges of tomato on each plate. Sprinkle with cheese and bacon.

Oil and Vinegar Dressing:

¾ cup salad oil	½ teaspoon freshly ground pepper
½ cup vinegar	½ teaspoon dry mustard
1 teaspoon salt	¼ teaspoon basil

Combine all ingredients and mix well.

HARD ROLLS

1 package active dry yeast *or*	1½ teaspoons salt
1 cake compressed yeast	Yellow cornmeal
1¼ cups water	1 egg white, slightly beaten
3½ to 3¾ cups sifted all-purpose flour	

Soften dry yeast in warm water, or compressed yeast in lukewarm water. Add 1½ cups flour; beat well. Add salt and stir in about 1¾ cups of remaining flour. (Dough should be stiffer than for ordinary bread). Turn out on lightly floured surface; cover and let stand for 10 minutes. Knead 15 to 20 minutes or until very elastic, kneading in remaining flour. Place dough in lightly greased bowl, turning once to grease surface. Cover; let rise in warm place until double in bulk, about 1½ hours. Punch down; let rise again until double, about 1 hour. Turn out onto lightly floured surface. Cover and let stand 10 minutes. Divide dough in 12 parts. Grease cooky sheets and sprinkle with yellow cornmeal. Shape each part in oval or round roll; place about 2 inches apart on cooky sheet. Add 1 tablespoon water to egg white; brush over sides and top of rolls. Cover with damp cloth, which should not touch dough. Raise cloth by setting it on wineglasses (tall enough to clear rolls) on sheet. Let rise in warm place until double in bulk, about 1 to 1½ hours. Place large shallow pan of boiling water on lower rack of oven; bake rolls in a preheated 400° oven 15 minutes. Brush again with egg-white mixture. Bake 10 to 15 minutes longer or until browned and done. For crackly crust, cool in draft.

APPLE AND GINGER CHEESE

6 large Delicious apples
1 8-ounce package cream cheese
4 tablespoons finely diced candied ginger

Dash salt
Crisp crackers

Core apples but do not peel; cut into thick slices. For individual service, arrange slices in a fan shape on dessert plates. Whip cream cheese and blend in ginger; add salt. Heap cheese-ginger mixture in mound beside apple slices and serve with crisp crackers.

CHOCOLATE ANGEL FOOD TORTE

¾ cup sifted cake flour
¾ cup plus 2 tablespoons sugar
¼ cup cocoa
1½ cups egg whites (about 12 whites)

1½ teaspoons cream of tartar
¼ teaspoon salt
1½ teaspoons vanilla
¾ cup sugar

Have eggs at room temperature. Preheat oven to 375°. Sift cake flour, sugar, and cocoa together three times. Beat egg whites, cream of tartar, salt, and vanilla with wire whisk in large bowl until foamy throughout. Add 2 tablespoons of sugar at a time, beating about 10 seconds after each addition. Continue beating until meringue is firm and holds stiff straight peaks when whisk is gently removed; this requires considerable beating. Sift 3 tablespoons flour mixture over meringue; fold gently with wire whip 8 to 10 strokes until flour mixture disappears, turning bowl after each stroke. Repeat until all has been folded in. Scrape down sides of bowl with rubber scraper and fold 8 to 10 more strokes or until completely blended. Batter will be very thick. If using electric mixer, use medium speed until all sugar is added to egg whites. Then turn to highest speed until meringue holds stiff straight peaks. Scrape sides of bowl constantly. Complete cake by hand, bringing rubber scraper down through center of batter and up at side. For thorough blending, turn bowl each stroke. Carefully push batter into ungreased

10″ x 4″ tube pan; cut through batter 5 or 6 times with knife to eliminate air bubbles and level top. Bake 30 to 35 minutes in a preheated 375° oven or until top springs back when lightly touched. Remove and immediately turn upside down to cool. Allow to stand a minimum of 1 hour. Split cooled cake crosswise in 3 even layers. Spread layers, top and sides with Chocolate Fluff. Store finished cake in refrigerator. There will be cake leftovers.

Chocolate Fluff:

1 cup sugar	⅛ teaspoon salt
¾ cup cocoa	3 cups heavy cream

Combine and sift sugar, cocoa, and salt in chilled bowl. Stir in heavy cream. Whip to spreading consistency.

Note: Cut both Angel Food and Sunshine cakes with a sawing motion. Do not attempt to cut straight down as cake will become lumpy.

BLUEBERRY COFFEE CAKE

¼ cup (⅛ pound) butter, softened	2 cups all-purpose flour
¾ cup sugar	2 teaspoons baking powder
1 egg	½ teaspoon salt
½ cup milk	2 cups blueberries (fresh *or* frozen)

It is important that berries be thoroughly dried after washing. Cream butter and sugar; beat in egg and milk. Sift flour, baking powder, and salt together; combine with butter mixture. Add blueberries carefully. Pour into a greased 9-inch square cake pan. Sprinkle with topping.

Topping:

½ cup sugar	½ teaspoon cinnamon
⅓ cup flour	¼ cup butter

Combine sugar, flour, and cinnamon; cut in butter with pastry blender as for pie dough. Sprinkle topping over batter, place in a preheated 350° oven, and bake 35 minutes.

Christmas Brunch

(SERVES 4 TO 6)

Curried Tomato Juice ⋅ Petites Fish Fillets
Eggs Gaxton   Corn Puffs
Toasted English Muffins   Apricot Jam
Old-Fashioned Coffee Cake
Coffee

Suggested wine: Graves

ADVANCE PREPARATION SCHEDULE

Deep Freeze	Previous Day	Early Morning
Coffee Cake	*Apricot Jam*	*Tomato Juice*

CURRIED TOMATO JUICE

Juice of 1 lemon   1 teaspoon curry powder
1 18-ounce can tomato juice

Mix lemon juice and curry thoroughly; stir into tomato juice. Chill.

PETITES FISH FILLETS

1 pound fish fillets, perch *or*   ¼ teaspoon ginger
   flounder   2 tablespoons brown sugar
4 teaspoons soy sauce   6 tablespoons salad oil
½ cup bread crumbs

Wash fish; cut into 1½-inch pieces. Place in bowl, combine soy sauce, ginger, brown sugar, and 3 tablespoons salad oil. Pour over fish and marinate 2 hours in refrigerator. Drain; dip in bread crumbs. Heat remaining 3 tablespoons salad oil in skillet and sauté fish until evenly and lightly browned. Serve with tartar sauce or browned almonds. Makes 16 pieces.

Browned Almonds:

After removing fish from skillet, place ¼ cup slivered almonds in oil and brown quickly. Remove with slotted spoon to drain and spread over fillets. Serve at once, piping hot.

EGGS GAXTON

4 tablespoons butter
½ small green pepper, sliced
½ cup sliced medium-sized mushrooms
¼ cup shredded white meat of
chicken
¼ cup shredded boiled ham

¼ cup shredded beef tongue
½ shredded small pimiento
1 whole tomato, canned *or*
2 small fresh tomatoes
6 eggs slightly beaten
Salt and pepper
1 tablespoon chopped chives
Paprika

Melt 2 tablespoons of butter in serving skillet; add green pepper and mushrooms; simmer for 5 minutes. Then add other ingredients (all but last three) and simmer 3 minutes. Melt remaining butter in separate skillet; add eggs and scramble lightly. Then, combine with other ingredients. Season to taste. Heat thoroughly. Garnish with chopped chives and paprika. Attractive served in the popular cast-iron skillet.

CORN PUFFS

2 cups sifted all-purpose flour
3 teaspoons baking powder
2 teaspoons salt
1 cup whole kernel corn (canned
niblets can be used)

2 egg yolks
2 tablespoons butter, melted
⅔ cup milk
2 egg whites, beaten stiff

Sift flour, baking powder, and salt. Mix corn with egg yolks, melted butter, and milk; fold in egg whites. Add to sifted dry ingredients; blend well. Drop by teaspoonfuls into deep fat heated to 370°. Fry to golden brown. Puffs may be pan fried in small cakes.

Serve for luncheon or brunch with orange slices and strawberry preserves.

APRICOT JAM

4 cups diced ripe apricots   3 cups sugar
2 tablespoons lemon juice

Combine ingredients and let stand for 12 hours. Place mixture in

saucepan and bring to a rolling boil; cook until thickened. Stir occasionally to keep from sticking. Pour jam, while hot, into hot sterilized jelly glasses and seal at once. Makes approximately 8 glasses.

OLD-FASHIONED COFFEE CAKE

½ cup (¼ pound) butter	2 eggs
2 cups sifted cake flour	¾ cup milk
1 cup sugar	1 teaspoon vanilla
½ teaspoon salt	1 teaspoon cinnamon
1 tablespoon baking powder	½ cup chopped nuts
1 teaspoon grated lemon *or* orange rind	

Combine butter, flour, sugar, salt, baking powder, and grated rind with pastry blender or knives as for pie crust. Reserve ½ cup of mixture. To rest of mixture add the eggs, milk, vanilla, and beat well until smooth. Pour batter into a well-greased 8- or 9-inch pan, square or round, and 3 inches deep. Add cinnamon and nuts to ½ cup of reserved butter-flour mixture for topping (a streusel); sprinkle over batter. Bake in a preheated 350° oven 40 minutes, or until done.

Christmas Dinner

(SERVES 10)

Eggnog (optional)   Mushroom Turnovers
Hot Cheddar Marbles   Icicle Soup
Grape Wine Goose — Prune Dressing
Crabapple Ornaments
Dilled December Beans   Roquefort Mousse Salad
Pêches Flambées   Sherry Loaf
Coffee
Brandy

ADVANCE PREPARATION SCHEDULE

Deep Freeze	Previous Day	Early Morning
Mushroom Turnovers	*Hot Cheddar Marbles*	*Eggnog*
Sherry Loaf	*for baking*	*Grape Wine Goose*
	Icicle Soup, without	*Prune Dressing*
	cream	*Crabapples*
	Roquefort Mousse Salad	

EGGNOG

4 tablespoons sugar	1 cup half and half cream
3 egg yolks, well beaten	1 ounce rum
3 egg whites, beaten stiff	1 cup brandy
1 cup milk	Nutmeg

Add sugar to yolks and beat well. Fold whites and yolks together; add milk and cream. Blend in rum and brandy. Chill until very cold; pour into a large bowl and ladle into mugs. Serve with a dash of nutmeg.

MUSHROOM TURNOVERS

Delcal Dough (see Index). Flour surface of board lightly; roll dough to ⅛-inch thickness and cut into 3-inch rounds, or squares. Place 1 teaspoon filling on each; fold over and press edges together with tines of fork. Prick tops to allow steam to escape. Bake in a preheated 375° oven 12 to 15 minutes, or until golden brown.

Mushroom Filling:

3 tablespoons butter	⅛ teaspoon coarsely ground
1 onion, grated	pepper
½ pound mushrooms, ground	Pinch of dried tarragon
½ teaspoon salt	1 tablespoon flour

Heat butter in skillet; add onion and mushrooms; sauté 3 minutes. Add salt, pepper, tarragon, and sprinkle with flour. Blend well. Arrange on platter with Cheddar Marbles. Garnish with Sweet Pickle Fans and sprigs of holly.

Variation:

See Index for Piroschki meat filling.

HOT CHEDDAR MARBLES

¼ cup (⅛ pound) butter, softened
1½ cups grated sharp Cheddar cheese
1 teaspoon lemon juice
¾ cup all-purpose flour
1 teaspoon concentrated meat extract
1 6-ounce jar pimiento-stuffed olives

Cream butter and cheese; add lemon juice, flour, and meat extract; blend thoroughly. Grease cooky sheet. Pinch off small pieces of dough and roll into marbles. Place on pan; flatten slightly with fork to ridge top. Press small stuffed olive in center of each. Refrigerate until ready to bake. Place in a preheated 400° oven about 10 minutes. Do not overbake. Serve with Mushroom Turnovers.

ICICLE SOUP

1 quart bottled prepared beet borscht
2 eggs, well beaten
¼ cup lemon juice
2 tablespoons sugar
1 pint dairy sour cream
Chopped parsley

Strain borscht liquid into beaten eggs; mix thoroughly with lemon juice and sugar. Chill. Serve in iced bowls, topped with generous serving of sour cream. Use reserved beets at another time as salad or relish. The red soup must have a sprinkling of green parsley.

GRAPE WINE GOOSE

1 14-pound goose
1 tablespoon salt
½ teaspoon pepper
2 teaspoons paprika
½ teaspoon garlic salt
½ teaspoon dry ginger
1 teaspoon monosodium glutamate
3 stalks celery, cut
2 onions, sliced
1 carrot, quartered
1½ cups sweet grape wine
¾ cup water
1 8-ounce jar currant jelly
2 tablespoons flour

Wash goose thoroughly; dry. Combine seasonings and rub into the goose, outside and in cavity. Stuff with Prune Dressing at neck and in cavity. Skewer and lace openings. Preheat oven to 475°. Prick skin of the goose until it is well punctured and place on rack in roasting pan, then into the oven. Roast 15 minutes, remove and drain off the fat, return to oven for 15 minutes and repeat the draining twice. Reduce temperature to 325°. Add celery, onions, and carrot to pan; combine 1 cup wine and water; pour over goose and continue to roast, basting frequently. Allow 25 minutes per pound for total roasting. One hour before completion of roasting time, spread currant jelly on breast, add remaining ½ cup of wine and baste every 15 minutes with pan drippings until tender. When done, remove to platter, strain pan drippings. Smooth flour with a small amount of drippings and then return to pan with strained liquid. Heat, adding water until of correct consistency.

Decorate platter with crabapple ornaments and green-tinted canned pears, arranged on sprigs of parsley.

Prune Dressing:

1 pound dried prunes, pitted	1 cup dried bread crumbs
1 cup water	2 teaspoons lemon juice
4 cups peeled and sliced apples	1 tablespoon sugar
½ teaspoon cinnamon	

Place prunes in saucepan, add water, simmer for 10 minutes. Drain. Add apples, bread crumbs, lemon juice, sugar, and cinnamon. Toss lightly and stuff goose loosely, as dressing swells.

CRABAPPLE ORNAMENTS

1 14-ounce jar spiced crabapples	1 tablespoon butter
1 4-ounce package slivered almonds	

Drain apples. Heat butter in saucepan, add almonds, and brown lightly. Cool. Spear apples porcupine-like with slivered almonds, spaced about ½ inch apart. Chill.

DILLED DECEMBER BEANS

1 tablespoon butter	2 10-ounce packages frozen
1 tablespoon flour	Italian beans
1 cup hot milk	¼ cup coarsely chopped dill
½ teaspoon salt	pickles
Dash paprika	1 teaspoon dill weed

Melt butter in saucepan over low heat; add flour and mix until blended. Gradually add milk and stir until thickened and smooth;

add salt and paprika. Cook beans according to package directions, but be certain not to overcook. Drain and add to heated sauce; blend in chopped pickle and dill weed. Serve very hot.

ROQUEFORT MOUSSE SALAD

2 envelopes (2 tablespoons) unflavored gelatin	1 tablespoon capers
	1 teaspoon grated onion
¼ cup lemon juice	1 cup grated cucumber, drained
1 cup boiling water	½ teaspoon salt
4 tablespoons minced parsley	½ teaspoon pepper
2 tablespoons minced pimiento	½ pound blue cheese, mashed
1 cup heavy cream, whipped	

Soften gelatin in lemon juice; add boiling water and stir until gelatin mixture is dissolved. Cool. Combine parsley, pimiento, capers, onion, cucumber, salt, and pepper to mashed cheese; mix thoroughly. Combine with gelatin mixture. Chill about 30 minutes or until slightly thickened. Fold in whipped cream; pour into greased Christmas tree mold or other 4-ounce individual molds. Refrigerate several hours or until very firm. Molds can be greased with salad oil and drained of any excess oil by reversing several minutes before filling. Unmold on individual salad plates, lined with leaf or other very green lettuce.

PECHES FLAMBEES

1 #2½ can cling peach halves	1 orange rind, coarsely shredded
⅓ cup brandy	⅓ cup currant jelly
½ cup syrup from peaches	1 quart vanilla ice cream

Drain peaches, pour half of brandy over them, and allow to stand 1 hour. Heat syrup from peaches with orange rind in blazer or chafing dish, and boil until volume is reduced about half. Add currant jelly and stir until melted. Add peaches with brandy, and heat thoroughly. Pour remaining warmed brandy over hot peaches and ignite. Serve over very hard ice cream.

Peaches may be heated in saucepan, then flamed at the table in a shallow pan or heatproof dish.

SHERRY LOAF

½ cup hot water	1 egg
1 6½-ounce package dates, cut fine	1 teaspoon vanilla
	1⅔ cups sifted cake flour
½ cup sherry	1 scant teaspoon baking soda
¼ cup (⅛ pound) butter *or* margarine	½ teaspoon salt
	½ cup chopped nutmeats
1 cup sugar	Confectioners' sugar

Pour hot water over dates, let stand until cool, add sherry. Cream shortening, sugar, egg, and vanilla until fluffy. Sift flour, soda, and salt, mix alternately with date, water and sherry mixture. Stir in nuts. Pour into greased and floured 8-inch loaf tin. Bake in a preheated 350° oven 40 to 45 minutes. Dust with confectioners' sugar or ice with Confectioners' Sugar Icing.

Confectioners' Sugar Icing:

1 cup confectioners' sugar	1 tablespoon butter
3 tablespoons cream	1 tablespoon sherry

Combine above ingredients and frost Sherry Loaf.

Christmas Dinner

(SERVES 10 OR 12)

Shrimp in Aspic   Crabmeat Mushrooms
Salted Nuts   Relishes
Duckling aux Pêches   Wild Rice Cashews
Brussels Sprouts   Cranberry Candles
Baba au Rhum Aglow — Rhum Glaze — Pavillon Sauce
Filbert Holiday Mold   Coffee
Holiday Cookies

Suggested wine: Médoc or red Burgundy

Previous Day	Early Morning
Shrimp in Aspic	*Assemble mushrooms for baking*
Cranberry candles	*Partially roast ducks*
Filbert mold	*Partially cook rice*
	Babas
	Pavillon Sauce

SHRIMP IN ASPIC
(On holly)

1 10-ounce can tomato aspic	⅛ teaspoon celery salt
1 teaspoon lemon juice	1 pound shrimp, cooked
1 teaspoon Worcestershire	Melba toast rounds

Place tomato aspic in saucepan and heat slowly until melted; cool and add lemon juice, Worcestershire, and celery salt. Chill 2 plastic storage egg holders; pour 1 teaspoon of aspic mixture in each egg cup, set in refrigerator until of jelly-like consistency; remove and place 1 shrimp in each; if necessary add sufficient aspic to fill cup. To serve, remove by loosening with a knife and place each mold on toast round. Circle platter with holly and arrange aspic canapés attractively. Holly berries as a center would be a festive touch. Makes 24.

CRABMEAT MUSHROOMS

24 large fresh mushrooms	½ cup fresh crabmeat
¼ cup (⅛ pound) butter	1 tablespoon parsley, minced
1 clove garlic, minced	1 whole egg
Freshly ground pepper	1 tablespoon sherry
Salt	Cornflake crumbs
	Butter

Remove stems from mushrooms; chop very fine. Set whole mushroom caps aside. Sauté in ¼ cup of butter with garlic for about 5 minutes. Remove from heat. Add pepper, salt, crabmeat, parsley, egg, and sherry. Mix well. Fill mushroom caps with mixture; sprinkle with crumbs and dot with butter. Place on greased cooky sheet and bake in a preheated 350° oven about 20 minutes.

DUCKLING AUX PECHES

2 5- or 6-pound ducks	6 tablespoons sugar
2 teaspoons salt	4 teaspoons arrowroot,
1 teaspoon nutmeg	cornstarch, *or* flour
2 #2 cans peach halves	½ cup Grand Marnier *or* Curaçao
¼ cup butter, melted	Maraschino cherries

Sprigs of watercress

Season ducks with salt and nutmeg, inside and out. Place on rack in roasting pan in a preheated 400° oven. Drain peaches, combine half the juice with melted butter and reserve remaining half of peach juice. Baste ducks every 15 minutes with combined juice and butter. Roast 1 hour. Reduce heat to 325°; continue roasting 45 minutes longer. Remove ducks from pan and skim off all excess fat; reserve drippings. Place ¼ cup (4 tablespoons) of the sugar in a saucepan. Make a paste of ½ cup drippings, 2 teaspoons of arrowroot, ¼ cup Grand Marnier and add to the sugar. Cook until light caramel in color. Make a paste of remaining 2 teaspoons arrowroot and remaining drippings, and add to boiling sugar mixture. Strain through a fine sieve, add reserved peach juice, and set aside until serving time. To serve, pour peach sauce into roaster; reheat and add ducks; place in a preheated 325° oven about 15 minutes, or until ducks are hot. Sprinkle remaining sugar over peach halves and put under broiler until glazed. Place ducks on warm platter. Add remaining ¼ cup of Grand Marnier to sauce, reheat quickly and pour over ducks.

Garnish with peach halves, centered with maraschino cherries; set on clusters of watercress.

WILD RICE CASHEW

2 cups wild rice	⅓ cup butter *or* margarine
Salt	½ cup broken cashews (optional)
2 cups sliced fresh mushrooms	Chopped parsley

Wash rice thoroughly, place in saucepan; cover with cold water and bring to a boil. Drain. Repeat this procedure three times. The last time add salt to the water, ½ teaspoon for each cup, and cook until tender. Drain well. Sauté mushrooms in butter; pour over rice. Add cashews, toss and serve very hot, garnished with parsley.

BRUSSELS SPROUTS

3 pounds brussels sprouts, *or* 3 packages frozen brussels sprouts

Wash fresh sprouts; leave whole. Place in saucepan and add boiling water to cover. Cook rapidly for 12 minutes. Drain; serve with Drawn Butter Sauce. (If frozen sprouts are used, follow directions on package for cooking.)

Drawn Butter Sauce:

¼ cup (⅛ pound) butter *or* margarine	Dash paprika
2 tablespoons flour	½ teaspoon salt
Dash pepper	1 cup water
	1 teaspoon lemon juice

Melt butter; stir in flour, pepper, paprika, and salt. Add water slowly and cook until thickened and smooth. To serve, add lemon juice and pour over brussels sprouts.

CRANBERRY CANDLES

2 1-pound cans whole cranberry sauce	¼ teaspoon salt
1½ cups boiling water	1 tablespoon lemon juice
1 3-ounce package cherry-flavored gelatin	½ cup mayonnaise
	1 orange, peeled and diced
	¼ cup chopped walnuts

Plan for candles by collecting twelve 6-ounce empty fruit juice cans in advance. Heat cranberry sauce, strain, and set berries aside. Combine hot juice and water and add gelatin, stirring until dissolved. Add salt and lemon juice. Cool; place in refrigerator until thickened enough to mound slightly when dropped from a spoon. Beat in mayonnaise with rotary beater until light and fluffy. Fold in cranberries, fruit, and nuts. Divide mixture evenly into the fruit juice cans. Chill 4 hours or longer. Unmold on Christmas doilies. To flame, insert small wax birthday candles into tops of Cranberry Candles. Light and bring each guest the cheer of a flame.

· BABA AU RHUM AGLOW

1 ¼-ounce package dry yeast	1 tablespoon currants
¼ cup warm water	1 tablespoon raisins
1½ cups all-purpose flour	1 cup heavy cream, whipped
2 tablespoons sugar	Candied violets, crumbled
½ teaspoon salt	(optional)
2 large eggs (½ cup)	For flame (optional):
beaten slightly	12 sugar cubes
¼ cup milk	2 tablespoons lemon extract
⅔ cup shortening, softened	

Dissolve yeast in warm water. Combine flour, sugar, and salt in mixing bowl. Stir in yeast and eggs. Add milk and beat by hand until batter is smooth, about 2 minutes. Let stand, covered, away from drafts for about 40 minutes or until doubled in bulk. Blend in shortening, currants, and raisins; beat well. Grease 12 small custard cups and fill halfway. Let rise again, covered, in warm place (85°) for 1 hour or until almost doubled. Preheat oven to 400°. Bake 10 minutes; reduce heat to 350° and continue to bake an additional 10 to 12 minutes, or until lightly browned. Unmold babas into individual serving dishes; spoon Rhum Glaze over each. Let stand several hours. Just before serving, circle with whipped cream and crumbled violets; place a sugar cube dipped in lemon extract on each baba and light.

Note: Babas may be baked several hours before serving. Cool in custard cups on cake rack. Reheat at 400° for 8 to 10 minutes just before serving.

Too many lights? Perhaps, but so bright for a happy day! Freeze extras for New Year's.

Rhum Glaze:

1 12-ounce can apricot nectar	½ cup water
½ cup sugar	¼ cup rum

Combine apricot nectar, sugar, and water. Bring to rapid boil, remove from heat and add rum; pour over babas.

PAVILLON SAUCE

2 cups sugar	1 cup Grand Marnier Liqueur
1 cup very hot and strong coffee	1 teaspoon vanilla

Melt sugar in a heavy skillet over low heat until liquid becomes light brown in color. Remove from heat and add coffee slowly, stirring constantly. Then simmer, stirring until all caramel is dissolved. Stir in liqueur and vanilla. Continue cooking until slightly thickened. Serve warm or cool over babas. Can be served over any kind of ice cream.

FILBERT HOLIDAY MOLD

1 cup chopped filberts	¼ cup water
1 envelope (1 tablespoon) unflavored gelatin	3 egg yolks
	3 egg whites
¼ cup cold water	3 tablespoons sugar
¼ cup dark corn syrup	1 cup mincemeat
⅛ teaspoon cinnamon	1 cup heavy cream, whipped
½ teaspoon salt	Green and red maraschino cherries

Toast chopped filberts. Soak gelatin in ¼ cup water. Combine syrup, cinnamon, salt, and another ¼ cup of water in a saucepan. Beat egg yolks until light and add to syrup mixture. Cook over medium heat until thickened. Add softened gelatin, stirring until dissolved. Cool; chill in refrigerator until of jelly-like consistency. Beat egg whites until stiff; add sugar and continue beating until they will stand in peaks. Fold nuts and mincemeat into gelatin mixture; then fold in egg whites. Pour into a 5-cup mold and chill until firm. Unmold; garnish with whipped cream and cherries. (Serves approximately 8.)

Note: Using both desserts on this Christmas Dinner menu, this mold should be of sufficient quantity.

Holiday Cookies

THESE cookies and many of those in the other menus make a delicious assortment. Pack them for holiday gifts. With the rush of this busy season, serve as a "cooky break" with a glass of milk or a cup of coffee.

GINGER COOKIES

⅝ cup molasses
1¾ cups sugar
½ cup butter
½ cup dairy sour cream
2 tablespoons finely chopped orange peel
Colored sugar

2 teaspoons cinnamon
1 teaspoon each cloves, allspice, ginger
4 egg yolks
2 teaspoons soda
6 cups all-purpose flour (about)
1 egg yolk, slightly beaten

Heat molasses and sugar until dissolved; add butter and allow to cool before adding sour cream, chopped orange peel, and seasonings. Add 1 egg yolk at a time alternately with the flour sifted with soda. Cut out in Christmas shapes. Brush with beaten egg yolk and sprinkle with colored sugar. Bake in a preheated 350° oven about 15 minutes.

Variation:

Or frost with cream icing after baking.

Cream Icing:

¾ cup confectioners' sugar, sifted   ¼ teaspoon vanilla
1 tablespoon cream

Blend well.

FOUR-SQUARE COOKIES

1 cup (½ pound) butter
1 cup sugar
1 egg yolk

2 cups all-purpose flour
1 teaspoon cinnamon
1 teaspoon vanilla

½ cup ground pecans

Cream butter and sugar thoroughly; add egg yolk and beat in flour; blend in cinnamon and vanilla. Spread ¼ inch thick in buttered 11″ x 16″ tin and sprinkle evenly with pecans. Bake in a preheated 350° oven 20 to 25 minutes, until lightly browned. Cut in squares, about 1½ inches, while hot, and allow cookies to cool in pan.

CANDY FRUIT BARS

½ pound candied cherries, diced
½ pound candied pineapple, diced
1 pound dates, coarsely chopped
1 cup all-purpose flour

1 cup confectioners' sugar
1 teaspoon baking powder
¼ teaspoon salt
4 eggs, well beaten

To repeat, fruit should be cut in small pieces, placed in a bowl. Sift flour, sugar, baking powder, and salt together, then sift again over fruit, and mix well. Add eggs and blend thoroughly. Pour mixture into well-greased jelly roll or cooky pan and spread evenly. Bake no longer than 20 minutes in a preheated 350° oven; cake must be moist. Cut into squares while hot. Makes about 50 squares, depending on size.

Icing:

1 cup confectioners' sugar   3 tablespoons rum *or* whiskey
2 cups chopped candied fruit and nuts

Combine sugar with the rum. Icing should be thin and spreadable; apply to cake with pastry brush. Decorate with pieces of candied fruit or nuts. Freezes well.

PECANESQUES

1 cup (½ pound) butter
2 cups brown sugar, firmly packed
2 eggs

1½ cups cake flour
⅓ teaspoon soda
½ pound pecans, ground
1 teaspoon vanilla

Cream butter, sugar, and eggs. Add flour, soda, ground pecans, and vanilla. Mix well. Drop from teaspoon on buttered cooky sheet. Bake 10 minutes in a preheated 350° oven.

DATE SURPRISE COOKIES

½ cup (¼ pound) butter *or* margarine
½ cup sugar
2 eggs, well beaten
1 teaspoon vanilla
1½ cups flour

½ teaspoon soda
¼ cup half and half cream *or* top milk
1 pound dates, pitted
Nutmeats (optional)
Confectioners' sugar

Cream butter; add sugar, cream well. Add eggs and vanilla; beat well. Sift flour and soda, add alternately with cream. Stuff dates with nutmeats (optional). Dip into batter, cover thoroughly. Bake on greased cooky sheet in a preheated 375° oven 12 minutes. When cool, sprinkle with confectioners' sugar.

BIT COOKIES

6 ounces chocolate bits	1 can (6½-ounce) salted cashews
6 ounces butterscotch bits	1 can (5-ounce) Chinese noodles

Melt in double boiler the chocolate and butterscotch bits. Chop nuts slightly. Add nuts and noodles to melted bits. While warm, drop small amount of mixture on greased cooky sheet and place in refrigerator to cool. The cookies are ready to serve. Good, if you like this kind of cooky.

RUM BALLS

½ pound vanilla wafers, ground	1 cup ground walnuts
1 cup confectioners' sugar	½ cup light corn syrup
2 tablespoons cocoa	¼ cup rum

Blend vanilla wafers, sugar, cocoa, walnuts, syrup, and rum. Dip hands in confectioners' sugar and roll mixture into small balls. These do not require baking.

PEANUT BUTTER COOKIES

½ cup (¼ pound) butter *or* margarine	1 teaspoon vanilla
½ cup peanut butter	1¾ cups sifted all-purpose flour
½ cup sugar	1 teaspoon baking soda
½ cup brown sugar	½ teaspoon salt
1 egg	7 bars (⅞-ounce) milk chocolate

Cream butter, peanut butter, and sugar until light and fluffy. Combine with egg and vanilla; beat well. Add sifted dry ingredients thoroughly. Shape dough into balls about ½ inch in diameter. Roll in granulated sugar, and place on greased cooky sheets. Bake in a preheated 375° oven 10 minutes. While hot, top each cooky with one square chocolate candy and press in firmly until edges of cooky crack. Return to oven and bake 2 minutes longer.

LEMON COOKIES
(Sugar free)

½ cup shortening
1 tablespoon Sucaryl *or*
  24 tablets, crushed
1 egg
1 tablespoon water
1 tablespoon lemon juice

1 teaspoon grated lemon peel
1 teaspoon vanilla
½ cup shredded dry coconut
2 cups sifted all-purpose flour
1 teaspoon baking powder
½ teaspoon salt

Cream shortening in small mixer bowl on high speed. Add Sucaryl, egg, water, lemon juice, lemon peel, and vanilla. Beat until thoroughly blended. Mix in coconut. Sift dry ingredients together; add to creamed mixture, mixing thoroughly. Form dough into a roll 2 inches in diameter. Wrap in wax paper; chill until firm. Cut into thin slices and bake on an ungreased cooky sheet in a preheated 400° oven 10 to 15 minutes.

Through the Years

HERALDED by the arrival of the briefly clad New Year, our festive menus, too, announce the coming milestones. So do we welcome our newcomers with a cheer and a toast, to bless them through the years.

Circus Party for Pre-Schoolers

(SERVES 6)

Chicken à la King —
Croutons *or* Noodle Nests
Butterscotch Brownies   Gumdrop Cookies
Ice Cream Clowns
Cupcake Clowns
Chocolate Milk

ADVANCE PREPARATION SCHEDULE

Deep Freeze

Brownies
Gumdrop cookies
Ice cream balls
Cupcakes

Previous Day

Cook chicken

Early Morning

Chicken à la King

CHICKEN A LA KING

2 cups cooked chicken	Paprika
½ pound mushrooms	2 cups half and half cream
2 tablespoons butter	3 egg yolks
1 green pepper, diced	2 tablespoons cream
2 teaspoons salt	2 tablespoons sherry
¼ teaspoon white pepper	(for parents)

Cut chicken in bite-sized pieces. Wash mushrooms and slice lengthwise through stems. Melt butter in top of double boiler, directly over heat. Add mushrooms, sauté 5 minutes; add green pepper, cook additional 5 minutes, and combine with chicken, seasonings, half and half cream. Bring to a boil; remove from heat; stir rapidly. Beat egg yolks with additional 2 tablespoons of cream; stir into chicken mixture. Do not allow mixture to boil after adding eggs. Place over hot water in double boiler and heat until thick. Add a festive touch of sherry for the doting parents. Serve on ½-inch Croutons (see Index), or noodle nests, which may be purchased at your local market.

Small Croutons and small pieces of chicken make eating simpler for the little ones.

BUTTERSCOTCH BROWNIES

2 cups brown sugar	1 cup all-purpose flour
½ cup (¼ pound) butter, melted	1 teaspoon baking powder
2 eggs, beaten	1 teaspoon vanilla
½ teaspoon salt	1 cup chopped nuts

Cream brown sugar and butter until smooth. Add eggs and beat until fluffy. Sift salt, flour, and baking powder together. Add to first mixture and beat until very smooth. Add vanilla, nuts, and combine well. Grease 8" x 14" pan. Bake in a preheated 375° oven 20 to 25 minutes. Makes 40.

GUMDROP COOKIES

1 cup (½ pound) butter *or* margarine
1 cup white sugar
1 cup brown sugar
2 eggs
2 cups all-purpose flour

1 teaspoon soda
2 teaspoons baking powder
½ teaspoon salt
1 cup medium-size gumdrops, quartered
1½ cups quick-cooking oats

1 cup shredded coconut

Cream butter with sugars; add eggs and blend well. Sift flour, soda, baking powder, and salt. Add gumdrops, oats, and coconut to sugar mixture. Combine ingredients and make into balls; place on a greased cooky sheet. Bake in a preheated 350° oven 25 minutes. Makes 60 to 65.

Variations:

Substitute 1 cup chocolate bits instead of gumdrops, or make half of each; divide sugar mixture into two after adding oats and coconut. Now add ½ cup gumdrops to one, and ½ cup chocolate bits to the other.

ICE CREAM CLOWNS

1 quart vanilla ice cream
6 ice cream cones
12 chocolate bits for eyes

6 pink spice drops for nose
6 red finger gumdrops for mouth
6 lace paper doilies

Scoop 6 balls of ice cream. Wrap individually in wax paper and place in freezer. To serve, place doily on dessert plate and ice cream ball on each. Use listed ingredients for decorating faces as indicated. Place cone on top of ball for clown's hat. Packaged ice cream balls are usually available in the markets.

CUPCAKE CLOWNS

Use ½ recipe for Mock Sponge Cake (see Index). Line 3-inch muffin tins with paper baking cups. Fill half full with Sponge Cake batter. When baked, remove paper cups, cool and frost.

Frosting:

2 tablespoons butter	Dash salt
3½ cups sifted confectioners' sugar	⅛ teaspoon almond extract
	12 ice cream cones
¼ cup milk	Miniature gumdrops *or* raisins
	Aluminum foil

Beat butter until soft. Add sugar gradually, alternating with milk; beat well after each addition. Stir in salt and almond extract. Frost bottoms and sides of cupcakes. Place an ice cream cone on top of each frosted cupcake for clown's hat. Use gumdrops or raisins for faces. Place each cupcake on a collar of fluted aluminum foil. Makes 1 dozen large clowns.

Christening Luncheon

(SERVES 8)

Shrimp Glacée — Caviar Dressing

Chicken Breasts in Wine Sauce

Noodles Viennoise   Vegetable Trio   Cloverleaf Rolls

Bing Cherry Mold — Fruit Garni

Nut Torte

Coffee

Suggested wine: Muscadet

ADVANCE PREPARATION SCHEDULE

Deep Freeze	Previous Day	Early Morning
Rolls (*see Index*)	*Shrimp Glacée*	*Dressing*
	Torte	*Chickens for final heating*
	Frosting	*Noodles*
	Cherry Mold	

SHRIMP GLACE

½ 3-ounce package lemon-
flavored gelatin
1¾ cups hot water
2 pounds shrimp, cooked
and cleaned
1 envelope (1 tablespoon)
unflavored gelatin

¼ cup cold water
1 cup boiling water
1 pint mayonnaise
½ pint heavy cream, whipped
1½ tablespoons prepared mustard
¼ teaspoon salt
⅛ teaspoon pepper

2 ounces caviar

Dissolve lemon gelatin in hot water and pour half of this mixture
(making a thin layer) into an oiled 6-cup fish or melon mold. Place
in refrigerator. When jelly-like, arrange a layer of half the shrimp.
Space them evenly, all turned in the same fashion. When un-
molded they should form a pattern. Cover with remaining lemon
gelatin. Chill until firm. Soak unflavored gelatin in cold water, dissolve in boiling water; then cool. Blend with the mayonnaise,
whipped cream, mustard, and seasoning. Place in refrigerator until
slightly thickened. Fold in caviar. Mix carefully and pour over
congealed gelatin in ring. Space remaining shrimp in the mixture.
Chill until firm. Serve on lettuce leaves with Caviar Dressing.

CAVIAR DRESSING

1 cup mayonnaise
½ cup catsup
½ cup chili sauce
2 teaspoons pimiento, minced
2 tablespoons chives, chopped
1 tablespoon parsley, minced

1 chopped egg
1 tablespoon lemon juice
2 tablespoons caviar
Salt
Paprika
Dash of cayenne

Combine all ingredients; blend carefully and well.

If using domestic black caviar, drain it well as it tends to dis-
color lighter colored foods. The imported or red caviar will not.
Makes 2 cups, approximately.

CHICKEN BREASTS IN WINE SAUCE

¼ cup salad oil
8 chicken breasts
3 tablespoons butter
2 medium onions, sliced
1½ cups dairy sour cream

3 tablespoons prepared mustard
⅓ cup red wine
⅔ cup chicken broth
1 teaspoon salt
¼ teaspoon pepper

Dash nutmeg

Heat oil in skillet, add chicken breasts and brown evenly. Cover and continue cooking until tender, about 30 minutes. Heat butter in saucepan and sauté onion slices until soft but not too brown. Add sour cream, mustard, wine, broth, salt, pepper, and nutmeg; simmer 5 minutes. Remove cooked chicken from oil; place in sauce, cover and simmer gently for 15 minutes. Serve with hot boiled rice.

NOODLES VIENNOISE

1½ pounds ground beef
¼ cup minced onion
1½ teaspoons salt
¼ teaspoon monosodium glutamate
¼ teaspoon ground black pepper

24 giant fresh mushroom caps
½ pound medium noodles, cooked
¼ pound Swiss cheese, grated
1 quart Supreme Sauce
4 egg yolks, beaten
4 egg whites, beaten stiff

Combine beef with onion, salt, monosodium glutamate, and pepper. Blend well and place in large skillet. Heat and cook meat until red disappears. Wash mushroom caps and fill with beef mixture. Mix noodles and cheese; set aside. Heat Supreme Sauce and stir ¼ cup of sauce slowly into egg yolks; return to remaining sauce and blend well; cool. Fold beaten egg whites into yolk mixture. Place mushrooms in one layer in large buttered casserole; cover with noodle mixture and pour sauce over all. Bake for 30 minutes in preheated 350° oven; serve piping hot. Serves 6 to 8.

This is a superb dish! Leftovers are well worth freezing.

Supreme Sauce:

5 tablespoons butter
6 tablespoons flour
3 cups soup stock, heated
¾ cup half and half cream

1 teaspoon salt
1 tablespoon Worcestershire
1 teaspoon lemon juice
¼ teaspoon pepper

Melt butter; add flour to make a roux, cook until smooth and bubbly, but do not brown. Add preheated soup stock, stirring constantly until blended. Add cream, salt, Worcestershire, lemon juice, and pepper; bring to a boil. Makes 1 quart sauce.

VEGETABLE TRIO

1 large cooked cauliflower
2 cans extra-tiny sifted peas
2 jars baby carrots *or* 2 #2 cans whole baby beets

3 tablespoons melted butter
1 tablespoon chopped mint
Paprika
Watercress

Wash cauliflower, leaving it whole and with a few green leaves at the base. Cut base evenly so it will stand upright, and slash it once or twice up from bottom of stalk. Soak in ice water ½ hour. Drain. Cook in boiling salted water to cover about 12 minutes. Test for doneness, and do not permit it to cook too long as it will be served in one piece. Drain and place in center of warmed platter.

To assemble, place cauliflower in center of platter; place peas at the ends and beets or carrots at the sides. Pour butter over cauliflower and beets, sprinkle peas with chopped mint, and dust cauliflower with paprika.

Note: There are any number of variations; just use them with an eye for color as well as taste. The Index offers a large choice.

BING CHERRY MOLD—FRUIT GARNI

1 #2½ can pitted black cherries, drained
3½ cups liquid
2 3-ounce packages black cherry gelatin *or* 1 package black cherry and 1 package black raspberry

¼ cup port
2 oranges, sectioned
2 grapefruit, sectioned (see Index)
1 pint strawberries, not hulled
2 avocados, sliced

Reserve canned cherry liquid and add sufficient water to make 3½ cups liquid. Boil 1½ cups of liquid; add gelatin and dissolve. Add 2 cups cold liquid, wine, and blend. Refrigerate until of jelly-like consistency; stir in cherries and pour into individual 4-ounce oiled molds.

To serve, unmold on a bed of greens; leaf lettuce makes an attractive and flat surface. Garnish with the orange and grapefruit segments, strawberries, and avocado slices.

NUT TORTE

3 whole eggs	½ teaspoon grated orange rind
6 egg yolks	1 teaspoon lemon juice
1½ cups sugar	1 teaspoon orange juice
1 teaspoon baking powder	½ teaspoon vanilla
12 ounces nuts — pecans and walnuts mixed together and ground	⅛ teaspoon salt
	6 egg whites

Beat whole eggs and yolks together thoroughly; add sugar and beat well again. Mix baking powder, ground nuts, orange rind, lemon juice, and orange juice; blend into yolk mixture. Sprinkle salt on egg whites and beat until stiff enough to form peaks. Add vanilla and fold slowly and carefully into nut mixture. Pour into large ungreased 10-inch angel food pan. Bake in preheated 325° oven 1 hour and 15 minutes to 1 hour and 25 minutes. Invert cake to cool. Cake will drop in height when cool. Dust with confectioners' sugar or frost with Whipped Cream Frosting.

Whipped Cream Frosting:

1 cup heavy cream	2 tablespoons Dutch cocoa
1 cup half and half cream	½ cup confectioners' sugar

Mix together in bowl; do not beat. Refrigerate overnight. To serve, whip until very stiff and frost cake.

Tricks or Treats

(SERVES 8)

Pizzaburgers

Deviled Eggs   Potato Chips

Orange Frosted Doughnuts

Cinnamon Stars   Chocolate Tops

Apple Cider

ADVANCE PREPARATION SCHEDULE

Deep Freeze	Previous Day	Early Morning
Chocolate Tops	*Pizzaburgers*	*Deviled Eggs*
Cinnamon Stars	*Orange Frosted*	
	Doughnuts (packaged)	

PIZZABURGERS

1 pound ground beef, raw	¼ cup chopped ripe olives
⅓ cup Parmesan cheese	½ teaspoon oregano
¼ cup chopped onion *or* 1 table-	⅛ teaspoon ground pepper
spoon instant minced onion	1 loaf French bread, halved
1 6-ounce can tomato paste	lengthwise
1 teaspoon salt	

Combine beef, cheese, onion, salt, olives, oregano, and pepper; mix well. Spread equally on both halves of bread. Place on cooky sheet under broiler, 5 inches from heat, for 10 minutes. Arrange Topping of cheese and tomato slices alternately and return to broiler for 2 minutes. The Topping is optional, but good.

Topping:

6 slices tomato   6 slices Cheddar cheese

DEVILED EGGS

8 eggs, hard-cooked   1 teaspoon prepared mustard
¼ cup mayonnaise   ¼ teaspoon vinegar
½ teaspoon salt

Cut eggs carefully in halves lengthwise. Remove yolks and blend thoroughly with mayonnaise, mustard, vinegar, and salt. Fill egg-white shells. Sprinkle with paprika.

CINNAMON STARS

1 pound ground almonds   6 egg whites
1 pound confectioners' sugar   Rind of 1 lemon, grated
1 teaspoon cinnamon

Beat egg whites until stiff, adding sugar gradually. Blend in lemon rind. Set aside ¼ of mixture to use as frosting. To the balance, add cinnamon and almonds. Roll on well-floured board and cut into stars or other shapes. Place on buttered pans, frost, and bake until they turn golden in preheated 300° oven for about 15 to 20 minutes.

CHOCOLATE TOPS

1 cup (½ pound) butter *or* margarine	1 cup sifted all-purpose flour
½ cup brown sugar	1 cup rolled oats
½ cup sugar	6 1-ounce milk chocolate bars
2 egg yolks	2 tablespoons butter
	½ cup chopped nuts

Cream butter and sugar thoroughly. Beat in egg yolks. Add flour and rolled oats and mix well. Spread in a greased and floured 9″ x 13″ pan. Bake in a preheated 350° oven 20 minutes. Cool for 10 minutes.

Melt chocolate bars with butter. Spread over cooled cooky layer; sprinkle with nuts. Cut into 1½-inch squares. Makes 48 cookies.

Teen-Age Party

(SERVES 10 TO 12)

Hero Sandwich

Italian Spaghetti   Sour Cream Slaw

Ice Cream Balls

Fudge Sauce   Pineapple-Caramel Sauce

Butterscotch Cookies

Milk

ADVANCE PREPARATION SCHEDULE

Deep Freeze	Previous Day	Early Morning
Ice Cream Balls	*Cookies*	*Spaghetti Sauce*
	Fudge Sauce	*Slaw*
	Pineapple-Caramel Sauce	

HERO SANDWICH

1 loaf French bread, 2 feet long	6 tomato slices
¾ cup butter *or* margarine, softened	6 green pepper rings
	6 onion slices
½ pound salami *or* bologna, sliced	Mustard and catsup
½ pound brick *or* Muenster cheese, sliced	

Split bread in half lengthwise. Spread cut surface with butter. Place meat on bottom half of loaf, top with cheese slices, then tomatoes, green peppers, and onions. Replace top of loaf. When ready to serve, cut into 12 servings. Place on large platter, surrounded by parsley and assorted pickles. Serve with mustard and catsup.

ITALIAN SPAGHETTI

2 tablespoons imported olive oil	1 cup catsup
6 pork chops	4 tablespoons Worcestershire
2 Bermuda onions, cut up	2 cloves garlic, minced
1 large green pepper, cut up	1½ teaspoons salt
1 pound fresh mushrooms, sliced	1 teaspoon paprika
	2 teaspoons sugar
2 #2½ cans tomatoes (drain liquid from one)	2 1-pound packages spaghetti
	Parmesan cheese (optional)

Heat olive oil in a large iron skillet or Dutch oven. Cut the pork chops into cubes, and brown in olive oil, with the bones of the chops. Add onions, green pepper, mushrooms, and cook to a golden brown. Stir in tomatoes, catsup, Worcestershire, garlic, salt, paprika, and sugar; bring entire mixture to a boil. Cover and reduce heat; let simmer for 3 hours, stirring occasionally. Remove the bones of pork chops from sauce before serving. Cook spaghetti, according to directions on package; drain. Pour sauce over spaghetti and serve very hot with Parmesan cheese on the side.

SOUR CREAM SLAW

1½ cups dairy sour cream	¼ teaspoon pepper
½ cup mayonnaise	2 tablespoons vinegar
4 tablespoons sugar	4 tablespoons minced onion
1 teaspoon celery seed	Dash cayenne
2 teaspoons salt	8 cups shredded cabbage

Blend sour cream, mayonnaise, sugar, celery seed, salt, pepper, vinegar, onion, and cayenne. Pour over shredded cabbage and mix. Chill until ready to serve.

ICE CREAM BALLS WITH CHOPPED NUTS

2 quarts ice cream   1 cup coarsely chopped nuts

Make ice cream balls in advance, using a scoop. Coat with nuts and wrap individually in wax paper cups; store in freezer.

Note: A convenience is packaged chopped nuts.

Fudge Sauce:

2 1-ounce squares unsweetened chocolate	1 6-ounce can evaporated milk
½ cup (¼ pound) butter	2 cups sifted powdered sugar
	1 teaspoon vanilla

Melt chocolate and butter in top of a double boiler; add milk, powdered sugar, and vanilla. Mix well and cook for 10 minutes.

PINEAPPLE-CARAMEL SAUCE

¼ cup pineapple syrup (drained from canned pineapple tidbits)	1 cup well-drained pineapple tidbits
20 vanilla caramels	

Place pineapple syrup in top of double boiler; add caramels and heat over hot water, stirring occasionally until caramels are melted. Remove from heat and fold in pineapple tidbits.

BUTTERSCOTCH COOKIES

1½ cups (¾ pound) butter or margarine	1 teaspoon lemon juice
1 cup granulated sugar	2 tablespoons vinegar
1 cup light brown sugar	3 cups sifted all-purpose flour
2 eggs	½ teaspoon salt
1 teaspoon vanilla	2 teaspoons baking powder
	1 teaspoon baking soda
1 3½-ounce can flaked coconut	

Cream butter and sugars until light and fluffy. Add eggs, vanilla, lemon juice, vinegar and beat thoroughly. Add sifted dry ingredients and coconut and beat until well blended. Drop from a teaspoon on ungreased cooky sheet and bake in a preheated 375° oven 8 to 10 minutes or until delicately browned.

Teen-Age Party

(SERVES 12)

Chopped Steak à la Singapore   Chinese Hot Dogs
Double Bean Salad
Teen Tequila
Glazed Doughnut Balls

ADVANCE PREPARATION SCHEDULE

Early Morning

Prepare meat
Prepare hot dogs
Cook rice
Lemonade
Doughnuts

CHOPPED STEAK A LA SINGAPORE

3 pounds sirloin steak, ground
2 onions, chopped fine
2 teaspoons salt
½ teaspoon black pepper
3 eggs
3 green peppers, sliced
1 2-ounce jar pimiento strips
2 tablespoons butter
12 hamburger buns

Add onion, salt, black pepper, and eggs to ground sirloin. Mix thoroughly. Shape into 12 patties and broil. Sauté green peppers and pimiento in butter until tender and serve on top of cooked beef patties. Serve on buns.

Note: Freshly ground lean chuck is an inexpensive and excellent substitute for the sirloin.

CHINESE HOT DOGS

2 pounds hot dogs	4 tablespoons soy sauce
4 tablespoons butter	3 cups water
1 cup sweet mixed pickles	4 tablespoons cornstarch
1½ cups pineapple chunks	4 cups hot cooked rice
1 cup pineapple juice	2 5-ounce cans chow mein noodles

Slice hot dogs lengthwise and then in half; brown in butter. Add sweet pickles, pineapple chunks, pineapple juice, and soy sauce to water and bring to a boil. Blend in cornstarch, mixed with a little cold water. Cook until thickened, stirring constantly. Add browned hot dogs and serve over cooked rice, sprinkled with chow mein noodles.

DOUBLE BEAN SALAD

2 #2 cans kidney beans, drained	2 tablespoons minced parsley
2 10-ounce packages frozen baby lima beans	1 clove garlic, crushed (optional)
	6 strips crisp bacon, crumbled
1 cup minced celery	3 hard-cooked eggs, chopped fine
4 green onions and tops, minced	1 cup French dressing
¼ cup mayonnaise	

Place kidney beans in bowl. Cook lima beans as indicated on package and add to kidney beans. Mix with celery, onions, parsley, garlic. Toss with French Dressing, then mayonnaise. To serve, chill thoroughly and serve on lettuce leaves. Sprinkle with bacon and chopped eggs.

French Dressing:

1 teaspoon salt	¼ cup sugar
½ teaspoon black pepper	¼ cup wine vinegar
¼ teaspoon paprika	1 cup olive *or* salad oil

Combine salt, pepper, paprika, sugar. Mix well and blend well with vinegar and oils. Makes approximately 1¼ cups.

TEEN TEQUILA

3 cans frozen lemonade
9 cups water
3 teaspoons maraschino cherry juice
36 maraschino cherries

3 drops red coloring
12 large orange slices, slit in middle
12 slices cucumber
12 slices lemon
12 candy cinnamon sticks

Combine lemonade, water, cherry juice, cherries, and red coloring. Blend thoroughly. Serve ice-cold in individual tall glasses; decorate with a cinnamon stick speared through orange slice to use as sipper. Top each with cucumber and lemon slices.

GLAZED DOUGHNUT BALLS

2 eggs
½ cup sugar
1 tablespoon orange rind, grated
2 tablespoons soft shortening
2 cups sifted all-purpose flour
2 teaspoons baking powder

1 teaspoon salt
¼ cup sherry
¼ cup orange juice
Hot fat, 3 to 4 inches deep, for frying
1 cup sifted confectioners' sugar
2 tablespoons sherry

Beat eggs until light and foamy; add sugar, orange rind, and shortening; blend well. Sift flour, baking powder, and salt together and stir into egg mixture alternately with wine and orange juice; beat until batter is smooth. Drop by teaspoonfuls into hot fat (375°). Dip spoon in fat first, to allow dough to slide off easily. Fry about 2 minutes, turning to brown evenly. Drain on paper toweling. While doughnuts are still hot, dip them into glaze made of confectioners' frosting (see Index) or for the more sophisticated—

Sherry Frosting:

1 cup confectioners' sugar, blended with 2 tablespoons sherry.

Confirmation Reception Supper

(SERVES 12)

Fly-High Chicken Wings   Fish Soufflé ChaudFroid
Initialed Mints   Fondant-Dipped Nuts
Sherried Peach Mold   Roquefort Cream Ring
Blushed Turkey
Hot Roast Beef Sandwiches
Nasi Goreng   Hard Rolls
Burnt Sugar Cake   Devil's Food Torte   Gâteau au Grog
Coffee

Suggested Wine: Champagne

ADVANCE PREPARATION SCHEDULE

Deep Freeze	Previous Day	Early Morning
Cake	*Chicken Wings*	*Turkey (see Index)*
Torte	*Fish Soufflé*	
	Peach Mold	
	Roquefort Ring	
	Gâteau	

FLY-HIGH CHICKEN WINGS

24 chicken wings
½ teaspoon salt
1 cup chicken stock
1 clove garlic, crushed
¾ cup bourbon
1 tablespoon sugar
1 tablespoon green
   onions, minced
¼ teaspoon nutmeg
6 tablespoons soy sauce
Peanut oil
2 tablespoons cornstarch
¼ cup water
2 8-ounce cans whole mushrooms, drained

Rub chicken wings with salt. Combine chicken stock, garlic, bourbon, sugar, green onions, nutmeg, and soy sauce in a large bowl and marinate chicken in the mixture for 2 hours. Drain, reserving marinade. Brown wings in enough peanut oil to cover bottom of skillet to a depth of about ¼ inch. When wings are brown, remove oil and add marinade liquid to pan. Simmer over low heat for 20 to 25 minutes, or until meat is tender. Remove chicken to serving platter. Mix cornstarch and water until smooth; stir into drippings in skillet and cook, stirring until smooth and thickened. Add mushrooms, heat through. Serve in chafing dish.

Note: With this recipe, a casserole over heat or a chafing dish is needed as wings must be kept hot. For another day and a less pretentious dinner, serve the wings over fluffy rice and border platter with sliced tomatoes, sprinkled with chopped parsley.

FISH SOUFFLE CHAUDFROID

3 pounds fish, trout and pike *or*   4 egg yolks, slightly beaten
  whitefish   1 cup cream
1 large onion   Salt and pepper
             4 egg whites, beaten stiff

Prepare previous day. Have fish boned and salted in market. Wash and grind the raw fish with the onion. Add egg yolks, cream and seasoning. Fold in stiffly beaten egg whites. Grease a fish mold or ring mold thoroughly, pour in the mixture, and place in a pan of hot water; cover tightly with foil and bake 1 hour in a preheated 350° oven. Cool and place in refrigerator overnight. Garnish with half lemon cups filled with red beet horseradish, hard-cooked eggs, and asparagus.

If fish mold is used, decorate with black sliced olives for scales, slices of pimiento olives for eyes, etc.

Delicious as a luncheon entrée; add rolls and preserves, dessert and coffee.

SHERRIED PEACH MOLD
(Prepare 2 recipes for this menu)

1 #2½ can peach halves *or* 9 fresh peach halves, peeled
1 3-ounce package lemon-flavored gelatin

¾ cup sherry
2 tablespoons lemon juice
Dash of salt
Walnut halves *or* red cherries

Drain syrup from peach halves and heat. Add gelatin and dissolve, then wine, lemon juice, and salt. Cool and refrigerate until it begins to thicken. Pour over peach halves arranged round side up in an 8-inch square greased pan. Chill until firm. Cut into 9 squares and serve on lettuce, topped with Fluffy Dressing. Decorate with walnut halves or red cherries.

Fluffy Dressing:

2 3-ounce packages cream cheese, softened

5 tablespoons sherry

Whip cheese with a fork until fluffy, adding sherry slowly.

ROQUEFORT CREAM MOLD

12 ounces cream cheese, softened
1 cup Roquefort cheese
2 teaspoons Worcestershire
¼ cup parsley *or* watercress, finely chopped
1 teaspoon salt

1 teaspoon paprika
2 envelopes (2 tablespoons) unflavored gelatin
¼ cup cold water
1 cup hot water
2 cups heavy cream, whipped

Combine two cheeses and mix until well blended. Add Worcestershire, parsley or watercress, salt, and paprika. Soften gelatin in cold water. Add hot water and stir until gelatin is dissolved. Add cheese and chill in refrigerator until mixture is jelly-like in consistency. Fold cream into partially thickened mixture. Spoon into two 4-cup oiled ring molds or one 8-cup mold and refrigerate until firm. Serve with fresh fruit: strawberries, sliced pineapple fingers, avocado and grapefruit sections, on tossed greens.

Note: Mound whole stemmed strawberries in center, arrange sliced avocado and pineapple fingers spoke-like around the mold and add slices of other fruit in season.

Variation:

This mold may also be made with Cheddar cheese.

ROAST BEEF

1 standing rib roast of beef, about 8 pounds

Rub with salt, about 1 teaspoon per pound. Dust with pepper and garlic salt, if desired. Set in large pan on a rack, fat side up. Preheat oven to 325°. The following chart is for meat taken directly from the refrigerator. Roast as follows:

Rare — 26 minutes per pound	Do not add water
Medium — 30 minutes per pound	Do not baste
Well Done — 35 minutes per pound	Do not cover

For frozen meat, take meat directly from freezer and increase cooking time 15 minutes per pound.

HOT ROAST BEEF SANDWICHES

15-pound top quality round of beef, boned

Roast on a rack in a preheated 300° oven 3¼ to 3½ hours. Spoon some of the drippings over the meat every hour while roasting. To serve, place large end of meat flat on platter with smaller end up. Using long thin-bladed sharp knife, cut very thin slices. Dip each into a bowl of beef juices and serve 3 or 4 pieces in split hard roll or on rye, white or whole wheat bread. Have relishes and mustard at hand. (Serves 50.)

Note: This recipe is for your convenience when serving a large number of guests. Freezer storage always good for leftover meats.

NASI GORENG

½ cup butter	3 teaspoons salt
1 pound chicken livers, halved	6 cups water
½ cup celery, chopped	2 medium cucumbers, scored
½ cup onions, chopped	and sliced
½ teaspoon crushed red pepper	½ cup sliced zucchini
3 cups long-grained quick-cooking rice, raw	1 pound whole medium shrimp, cooked, shelled and deveined

½ cup salted dry peanuts

Melt butter in large saucepan, add livers and sauté 3 minutes; add celery and onions and cook slowly 3 more minutes. Mix in red pepper, rice, and salt; stir until rice has absorbed butter. Pour on water and bring to a boil. Cover, reduce heat to simmer and cook 15 minutes, until water is absorbed. Add cucumbers, shrimp, and zucchini and cook for 5 minutes, adding more water if needed. Sprinkle with peanuts, toss all together carefully, and let stand to blend flavors. To serve, heat slowly, stirring often to prevent scorching.

Note: Use more red pepper for a hotter version of this Indonesian recipe.

BURNT SUGAR CAKE

1½ cups sugar, sifted	2 cups sifted cake flour
½ cup (¼ pound) butter, softened	3 tablespoons burnt sugar
	2 teaspoons baking powder
3 egg yolks	1 teaspoon salt
3 egg whites, beaten stiff	1 cup cold water
1 teaspoon vanilla	

Cream sugar and butter until very light. Beat in egg yolks, one at a time; then Burnt Sugar. Resift flour with baking powder and salt. Add ½ cup of flour at a time, alternately with water, and ending with flour. Beat 5 minutes. Fold in egg whites and vanilla. Pour into two 8-inch layer cake pans; bake 25 to 30 minutes in a preheated 375° oven. Remove to cake rack to cool. Frost with Caramel Icing.

Burnt Sugar:

½ cup granulated sugar

Place sugar in a heavy saucepan over low heat; stir constantly until melted to a golden brown syrup.

Caramel Icing:

2 cups confectioners' sugar	2 tablespoons burnt sugar
1 teaspoon vanilla	3 tablespoons cream

Combine all ingredients and blend well, adding more cream if necessary.

DEVIL'S FOOD TORTE

2 1-ounce squares unsweetened chocolate
½ cup hot, freshly brewed coffee
1¾ cups sifted cake flour
1½ cups sugar

¾ teaspoon baking soda
¾ teaspoon salt
¾ teaspoon ground cloves
½ cup buttermilk
½ cup margarine, softened

2 eggs

Melt chocolate in double boiler over hot water; combine chocolate and hot coffee, stirring until smooth; cool. Sift flour with sugar, soda, salt, and cloves. Add buttermilk and margarine; beat 2 minutes. Add eggs and cooled chocolate mixture and beat another 2 minutes. Pour into two greased and floured 8-inch layer cake pans. Bake in a preheated 350° oven for 30 to 35 minutes. Cool. Cut layers crosswise in halves, then frost, put together and top with mocha frosting.

Mocha Frosting:

2 cups heavy cream
2 cups cold milk

1 tablespoon powdered instant coffee

2 3¾-ounce packages instant chocolate pudding

Pour cream and cold milk into mixing bowl. Add instant coffee and instant chocolate pudding. Beat with rotary beater until well mixed. Let stand until thickened to a spreadable consistency, then spread between layers and on top of cake. Refrigerate until serving time.

Note: For a simpler preparation, Devil's Food Cake Mix may be substituted.

1 package Devil's Food Cake Mix
¼ cup confectioners' sugar

1 pint heavy cream, whipped, *or* commercial canned whipped cream

1 teaspoon vanilla

Bake cake according to package directions; when cool, split the 2 layers to make 4 layers. Whip cream, fold in sugar and vanilla, use as filling between 1st and 3rd layers and to frost sides. Prepare date mixture and use as middle filling and to spread over top of cake.

Date Filling:

⅔ cup half and half cream
⅔ cup sugar
2 egg yolks, beaten

½ cup pitted, chopped dates
½ teaspoon vanilla
½ cup chopped nuts

Combine cream, sugar, egg yolks, and chopped dates; simmer slowly for 6 minutes. Add vanilla and chopped nuts. Cool.

GATEAU AU GROG

1 cup (½ pound) butter, softened
1½ cups confectioners' sugar
2 eggs, separated
Pinch of salt
¼ cup light rum
½ cup almonds, chopped

6 macaroons (soft, chewy kind)
1½ dozen large lady fingers
½ cup heavy cream
¼ cup dried macaroon crumbs
¼ cup maraschino cherries, chopped

Cream butter and sugar, add egg yolks. Add salt to whites and beat until very stiff. Fold into yolk mixture carefully. Add 3 tablespoons rum and nuts; cut the macaroons into small pieces and add to mixture. Line a 10-inch spring form or soufflé dish on sides and bottom with wax paper and then with 1 layer of lady fingers. Sprinkle base layer only of lady fingers with 1 teaspoon of remaining rum. Pour in ½ of macaroon mixture, cover with second layer of lady fingers, sprinkle with second teaspoon of rum; pour in remaining macaroon mixture; top with last layer of lady fingers, sprinkle with last teaspoon of rum. Let stand in refrigerator at least 3 hours. To serve, remove rim of spring form or unmold from dish. Top with whipped cream, dried macaroon crumbs and cherries.

Note: This is best when made one day in advance.

Sweet Sixteen Luncheon

(SERVES 8)

Hot Chicken Sandwiches

Rainbow Mold — Spectrum Garni — Whipped Fruit Dressing

Assorted Relishes — Olives — Pickles — Carrot Sticks

White Chocolate Cake   Baked Alaska Pie Flambé

Punch   Peanut Brittle

ADVANCE PREPARATION SCHEDULE

Deep Freeze	Previous Day	Early Morning
Chocolate Cake	*Prepare poultry*	*Cream Sauce*
Baked Alaska Pie	*Rainbow Mold*	*Bacon*
	Peanut Brittle	*Punch*
		Dressing

HOT CHICKEN SANDWICHES

½ cup grated American cheese
2 cups Cream Sauce (see Index)
8 slices baked chicken *or* turkey, cut ¼ inch thick

8 slices toast
16 strips bacon, partially cooked
8 tablespoons grated Parmesan cheese

Blend cheese with cream sauce until melted. Place chicken on each piece of toast and cover with ¼ cup of sauce. Cross 2 strips of half-cooked bacon on each sandwich and sprinkle with 1 tablespoon of grated Parmesan cheese. Place on baking sheet and broil until cheese melts and becomes light brown. Serve at once.

RAINBOW MOLD

1 package cherry-flavored gelatin
1 package lime-flavored gelatin
1 package orange-flavored gelatin

4½ cups liquid (fruit juice *or* water)
1½ cups dairy sour cream
1½ cups diced fruit (peaches, pears, pineapple, strawberries, etc.)

Pour each flavor into separate bowls. Add 1½ cups of hot liquid to each and dissolve. Blend ½ cup of sour cream with each gelatin mixture. Place in refrigerator and when of jelly-like consistency add ½ cup of diced fruit to each of the three bowls. Chill again until partially set. Rinse an 8-cup mold with cold water. Place large spoonfuls from each bowl of gelatin in rotation. When congealed, it has a marble-like effect. Surround the platter with Spectrum Garni and serve with Whipped Fruit Dressing.

SPECTRUM GARNI

Red — cherries
Orange — mandarin sections
Yellow — banana chunks

Green — honeydew balls
Blue — Italian plums, halved
Violet — candies

WHIPPED FRUIT DRESSING

2 tablespoons mayonnaise
2 tablespoons lemon juice
2 tablespoons honey
1 cup heavy cream, whipped
Paprika

Combine mayonnaise, lemon juice, and honey; fold in whipped cream. Pour into bowl and dust with paprika.

WHITE CHOCOLATE CAKE

1 package (6-ounce) semi-sweet chocolate pieces
½ cup boiling water
1 cup butter
2 cups sugar
4 eggs, separated

1 teaspoon vanilla
2½ cups sifted all-purpose flour
1 teaspoon soda
1 teaspoon salt
1 cup buttermilk

Melt semi-sweet chocolate pieces in boiling water. Cream together butter and sugar, and beat in egg yolks one at a time; then the melted chocolate and vanilla. Sift together flour, soda, and salt and add to chocolate mixture alternately with buttermilk. Beat egg whites until stiff but not dry; fold into batter and pour into a well-greased and floured 10-inch tube pan. Bake in a preheated 350° oven 1½ hours. Place on cake rack and cool 10 minutes before removing from pan. Frost with white icing (see Index) and bring it in with 17 candles. The extra one for good luck, of course.

Note: May be served in another menu with ice cream and butterscotch sauce (see Index). Excellent with frostings when baked in three 8-inch round layer cake pans 30 to 40 minutes.

BAKED ALASKA PIE FLAMBE

1 quart ice cream	4 egg whites
1 chilled Graham Cracker Pie	½ cup sugar
Crust (see Index)	2 tablespoons brandy, warmed

Allow ice cream to soften sufficiently to spread and fill pie crust. Place in freezer until solid. Beat egg whites very stiff; gradually add sugar, beating until thick and glossy. Spread over the ice cream pie, making certain that all the ice cream is completely covered and sealed. This may be made many days in advance and stored in freezer. Place pie in a preheated 450° oven for about 3 minutes or until meringue is just brown. Warm brandy in ladle, sprinkle over meringue, set aflame. The flaming dessert reflects the glow of this occasion.

PUNCH

2 cups water	1 cup fresh orange juice
2 cups sugar	½ cup fresh lemon juice
1 cup pineapple juice	Water
2 cups apricot nectar	Orange rind curls
3 pints ginger ale	

Boil water and sugar in a large saucepan for 5 minutes; cool. Mix pineapple juice, apricot nectar, orange juice, and lemon juice in a large bowl. Blend sugar syrup with fruit mixture and refrigerate until thoroughly chilled. Make an ice ring by filling a 1½-quart ring mold with water and freezing until solid. Remove from freezer and arrange orange rind curls over the top and add a little more water. Freeze until solid. Just before serving, remove cold fruit-juice mixture from refrigerator and stir in ginger ale. Pour into punch bowl. Remove ice ring mold from freezer and dip briefly in warm water to loosen. Unmold and float in punch. Makes about 3 quarts.

PEANUT BRITTLE

1 cup white sugar	1 pound salted redskin peanuts *or*
1 cup white corn syrup	1 pound mixed salted nuts
½ teaspoon baking soda	

Cook sugar and corn syrup together until it spins a thread when dropped from spoon. Add nuts. Cook together until syrup turns to medium butterscotch color. Remove from flame. Fold in baking soda. Grease one large cooky sheet, 11" x 17". Pour mixture onto sheet. Cool for 5 minutes. Then grease two more large cooky sheets or use a porcelain or formica area that would be equivalent. Use a greased spatula to lift a small portion of mixture. With greased hands spread as thin as desired. Do this until all the mixture is used up. Let set until completely cooled. Use spatula to lift off sheets, and break into desired size.

Do not make peanut brittle on a rainy day.

Graduation Party

(SERVES 8)

Onion and Sour Cream Dip Cheese Chutney Canapes
Shrimp Ramaki — Cocktail Sauce Cantonese Beef
Soft Rolls
Gourmet Salad Soy Fried Rice
Diploma Cake
Fruit Punch

ADVANCE PREPARATION SCHEDULE

Deep Freeze	Previous Day	Early Morning
Diploma Cake	*Marinate Ramaki*	*Onion Dip*
	Fruit Punch	*Wrap Ramaki*
	(see Index)	*Cheese mixture*
		Soy Fried Rice

ONION AND SOUR CREAM DIP

1 pint sour cream   1 package onion soup mix
Potato chips

Mix sour cream and onion soup mix well and refrigerate 4 to 5 hours before serving. Makes 2 cups. Serve with potato chips.

CHEESE CHUTNEY CANAPES

1 8-ounce package cream cheese   Pinch baking powder
½ cup grated Herkimer cheese   36 1½-inch rounds of bread
1 egg white, slightly beaten   3 tablespoons chutney

Mix cream cheese, Herkimer cheese, egg white, and baking powder. Toast rounds of bread on one side. Spread untoasted side with cheese mixture. Center with ¼ teaspoon chutney and toast in broiler just before serving. Makes 36 sandwiches.

SHRIMP RAMAKI

2 pounds shrimp   2 cups Cocktail Sauce
20 slices bacon, cut in half

Cook and clean shrimp. Marinate in Cocktail Sauce 1 to 6 hours. Drain, wrap in bacon, spear with a toothpick and broil just before serving. Makes approximately 40.

Cocktail Sauce:

1½ cups catsup   4 tablespoons lemon juice
½ cup chili sauce   2 teaspoons Worcestershire
3 tablespoons prepared   ¼ teaspoon salt
    horseradish

Combine catsup, chili sauce, horseradish, lemon juice, Worcestershire, and salt; blend well and refrigerate.

Note: A delicious sauce to serve with seafood cocktails. Makes 2 cups.

CANTONESE BEEF

4 tablespoons cooking oil
2 pounds trimmed beef tenderloin, sliced thin in 1" x 2" strips
2 1-pound, 3-ounce cans Chinese vegetables with liquid
2 4-ounce cans mushrooms (optional)
¼ teaspoon garlic salt
1 teaspoon salt
1 teaspoon sugar
1 teaspoon monosodium glutamate
3 tablespoons bead molasses
2 teaspoons soy sauce
3 tablespoons cornstarch
¼ cup water
3 1-pound cans Chinese fried noodles

Heat the oil in a 2-quart saucepan. Add the meat, stirring until coated with the oil. Add vegetables, liquid, and mushrooms; heat gently. Combine garlic salt, salt, sugar, monosodium glutumate, molasses, soy sauce, and stir into the meat mixture. Make a paste of cornstarch and water; add to the beef and heat over moderate flame for 2 or 3 minutes or until cornstarch has cleared.

Serve in casserole or chafing dish and accompany with a bowl of crisp Chinese noodles.

Note: Excellent recipe for leftover meats. Substitute 2 cups cooked beef or other meat for tenderloin.

SOY FRIED RICE

4 tablespoons peanut oil
3 eggs, beaten
1 bunch green onion tops, sliced
1 14-ounce box minute rice, cooked as directed
1 tablespoon soy sauce

Heat oil in skillet to frying temperature. Add eggs, mixing continuously, breaking up with fork. Sauté about 3 minutes until done. Add eggs and onions to cooked rice, with soy sauce to color rice brown. Blend well and serve very hot. To reheat, place in a preheated 350° oven for 30 minutes, stirring occasionally.

GOURMET SALAD

2 heads iceberg lettuce
½ head escarole
2 apples, peeled and chopped
2 tablespoons finely chopped onion
4 tablespoons olive or salad oil
¼ teaspoon salt
3 tablespoons cider vinegar
2 tablespoons chopped parsley
2 tablespoons lemon juice
½ teaspoon white pepper

Break up lettuce and escarole; add apple and onion; drizzle oil over all. Combine salt and vinegar; add while turning salad; add parsley. Sprinkle with lemon juice and pepper, and toss again.

DIPLOMA CAKE

18 lady fingers, split
2 quarts ice cream, assorted flavors
1 pint heavy cream
1 cup powdered sugar

½ cup cocoa
Green pistachio nuts, slivered almonds, or chocolate decorettes

Combine heavy cream, powdered sugar and cocoa and place in refrigerator overnight.

Next morning whip cream mixture until stiff. Line bottom and sides of well-greased 10-inch spring form with lady fingers. Place a layer of scooped ice cream of assorted flavors on the lady fingers, cover with half the whipped cream, and repeat the layer of ice cream and the whipped cream. Sprinkle with your choice of decoration and place in freezer. Remove about ½ hour before serving. As freezers vary in cold intensity the exact time of removal is left to your discretion.

Remove rim of spring form; serve on doily-covered serving plate.

Debut Tea

(SERVES APPROXIMATELY 8)

Sandwich Platter

Ribbon Sandwiches   Crabmeat Sandwiches
Pyramid Sandwiches   Olive and Nut Sandwiches

Spun Sugar Bowl

Strawberries and Grapes

Accompaniment of Brown Sugar and Sour Cream

Pineapple Angel Food   Almond Slices   Apricot Bars

Coffee   Tea

ADVANCE PREPARATION SCHEDULE

Deep Freeze	Previous Day	Early Morning
Apricot Bars	*Ribbon Sandwiches*	*Make Sandwiches*
Almond Slices	*Fillings for Sandwiches*	
	Sugar Bowl	
	Bake Angel Food	

RIBBON SANDWICHES

12 slices white bread
6 slices whole-wheat bread
1 3-ounce package cream cheese, softened
½ pound small-curd creamed cottage cheese
1 teaspoon prepared horseradish

½ teaspoon paprika
½ teaspoon poppy seeds
½ teaspoon dry mustard
2 tablespoons minced parsley
¼ teaspoon poultry seasoning
½ teaspoon salt
Watercress

Trim crusts from bread. Mash cream cheese and combine with cottage cheese to make a smooth mixture; beat in horseradish, paprika, poppy seeds, mustard, parsley, poultry seasoning, salt; blend thoroughly. Spread a slice of white bread with the cheese spread and cover with a slice of whole-wheat. Spread this whole-wheat bread with cheese spread and cover it with a white slice. Cut into 4 lengthwise strips and place cut side up on a serving plate. Repeat this with remaining 3 slices of bread. Wrap in moist towels to refrigerate for several hours or overnight. To serve, arrange on a platter and garnish with watercress. For variety, alternate whole-wheat bread with homemade apricot bread for the center slice. See Index for Apricot Bread. Makes 24 sandwiches.

CRABMEAT SANDWICHES

1 cup crabmeat, shredded
1 pimiento, minced
4 tablespoons mayonnaise
1 cup finely chopped tart apples

25 1½-inch bread rounds
Butter
Sprigs of parsley
Paprika

Mix crabmeat, pimiento, mayonnaise, and apples well. Toast bread rounds on one side; butter untoasted sides and spread with crabmeat mixture. Dip tiny sprigs of parsley in paprika and place on top. Makes 25 sandwiches.

PYRAMID SANDWICHES

8 3-inch rounds of bread	8 shrimps
8 2-inch rounds of bread	1 3-ounce package cream cheese
8 1-inch rounds of bread	¼ teaspoon seasoned salt
1 cup chicken salad	¼ cup currant jelly
Mayonnaise	8 slices pimiento-stuffed olives

8 capers (optional)

Spread 3-inch rounds of bread with cream cheese, softened and mixed with seasoned salt; spread jelly over this. Place 2-inch round on top; cover with 1½ tablespoons chicken salad. Place 1-inch round on top; spread with mayonnaise, and place shrimp and olive slice on top. Dot with capers. Serve with salad fork.

OLIVE AND NUT SANDWICHES

1 3-ounce package cream cheese	½ cup walnuts, chopped
½ cup pimiento-stuffed olives, chopped	2 tablespoons mayonnaise
	12 thin slices fresh sandwich bread

Blend cream cheese, olives, nuts, and mayonnaise; spread on 6 slices of bread. Cover with remaining 6 slices. Trim crusts and cut each sandwich in 3 to make 18 finger sandwiches.

SPUN SUGAR BOWL

2 cups sugar	Few drops food coloring to
½ cup water	suit decorations

Bring sugar and water to a boil and cook until it reaches 280° on a candy thermometer. Add coloring. Pour immediately on a lightly oiled marble slab. Let stand 1 to 1½ minutes; turn over onto oiled dish of whatever shape you wish. Flute sides as desired. Allow to cool and harden, approximately 3 minutes. Remove from mold and it is ready to be filled.

To serve:

2 quarts strawberries	1 cup light brown sugar
2 bunches white seedless grapes	2 cups dairy sour cream

Place spun sugar bowl on platter and fill with strawberries. Drape grapes artistically on sides of bowl; surround base of bowl with more grapes. Place twin bowls of brown sugar and sour cream to be used as accompaniment to strawberries and grapes. Dip fruit in each.

PINEAPPLE ANGEL FOOD

1¼ cups cake flour
1¼ cups granulated sugar
1 cup powdered sugar
1½ cups egg whites (12 eggs)
1 teaspoon cream of tartar

1 teaspoon vanilla
½ teaspoon almond flavoring
1 #2 can crushed pineapple
1 cup heavy cream, whipped
Pineapple chunks
Maraschino cherries

Sift flour before measuring; sift each dry ingredient 5 times, separately. Combine the sugars and sift 3 times. Beat egg whites in a large bowl. When they begin to get fluffy, add cream of tartar. Continue beating until stiff but not dry; fold in flour, sugars, vanilla, and almond. Pour into ungreased 10-inch tube pan and bake in a preheated 275° oven 1 hour. Invert to cool. When cool, remove cake from pan and cut in 3 layers. Spread each with drained crushed pineapple. Cover with whipped cream. Garnish with pineapple chunks and tiny maraschino cherries.

ALMOND SLICES

1½ cups flour
1½ teaspoons baking powder
1 pound light brown sugar, firmly packed

1 teaspoon cinnamon
¼ pound almonds, blanched and sliced
4 eggs beaten
1 teaspoon vanilla

Sift flour and baking powder together; combine with sugar, cinnamon, almonds, eggs, and vanilla. Pour into a well-greased cake pan 13″ x 9″ x 2″ and bake in a preheated 400° oven for 30 minutes. Cool and cut in 1″ x 3″ slices. Makes 20 slices.

APRICOT BARS

⅔ cup dried apricots
½ cup butter, softened
¼ cup sugar
1⅓ cups all-purpose flour, sifted
½ teaspoon baking powder
¼ teaspoon salt

1 cup light brown sugar, firmly packed
2 eggs, well beaten
½ teaspoon brandy flavoring (optional)
½ cup walnuts, chopped

Rinse apricots and cover with water; boil 10 minutes, drain, cool, and chop coarsely; mix butter with ¼ cup sugar and 1 cup of the flour until crumbly. Press mixture into bottom of greased 8-inch square pan. Bake in a preheated 350° oven for 25 minutes. Sift together the remaining ⅓ cup flour, baking powder, and salt. Beat brown sugar slowly into eggs, beating well after each addition. Stir in flour mixture, flavoring, nuts, and apricots. Spread over baked layer; return to oven and bake 30 minutes longer. Cool in pan. When cool, cut into 1" x 2" bars. Makes 32.

Engagement Announcement Formal Dinner

(SERVES 8)

Fish en Gelée Blanche — Elysée Sauce

Caraway Velouté   Cheese Crisps

Purple Plum Ducklings

Celery and Mushroom Amandine   Hard Rolls

Deep Green Salad — Mustard Dressing

Lemon Meringue Nests

Coffee

Suggested wine: Côte-Rôtie or other red Rhone

ADVANCE PREPARATION SCHEDULE

Deep Freeze	Previous Day	Early Morning
Meringues	*Fish en Gelée*	*Plum Sauce*
Cheese Crisps (see Index)	*Elysée Sauce*	*Bake ducks 1½ hours*
	Caraway Velouté	*Celery and mushrooms*
		Crisp greens
		Salad dressing
		Lemon custard

FISH EN GELEE BLANCHE

2 pounds fish — halibut, *or*
  1 pound pike and 1 pound
  whitefish
2 envelopes (2 tablespoons)
  unflavored gelatin
½ cup cold water
¾ cup hot water *or* fish stock
1 cup dairy sour cream
¼ cup mayonnaise
1 tablespoon grated onion *or*
  1 teaspoon onion flakes

1 cup finely chopped celery
2 tablespoons finely chopped
  green pepper
1 teaspoon salt
½ teaspoon white pepper
½ teaspoon dill weed
1 teaspoon oregano
2 teaspoons Worcestershire
¼ cup lemon juice

Poach fish; cool and flake carefully to remove all bones. Soak gelatin in cold water for 5 minutes, then dissolve in hot water or fish stock. Blend gelatin with sour cream, mayonnaise, onion, celery, green pepper, salt, white pepper, dill weed, oregano, and Worcestershire. Add flaked fish; blend well and pour into well-oiled 5-cup mold. Refrigerate several hours.

To serve, unmold on bed of endive and garnish with hard-cooked eggs, olives, pimiento, and green pepper; center the mold with bowl of Elysée Sauce.

Garnish:

Curly endive
Quartered hard-cooked
  eggs

Olives
Pimiento
Green pepper rings

Court Bouillon (*to poach fish*):

1 quart water
2 bay leaves
2 tablespoons vinegar
6 whole black peppercorns
  ½ teaspoon sugar

1 stalk celery, sliced
2 carrots, sliced
2 onions, sliced
2 teaspoons salt

To prepare stock (Court Bouillon) for poaching fish, pour water into 2-quart saucepan; add bay leaves, vinegar, peppercorns, celery, carrots, onions, salt, and sugar; bring to a boil. Place fish in stock carefully, and reduce to a simmer. Cook slowly for about 45 minutes, or until fish is firm and flakes easily when tested with a fork. Remove, drain, and cool. To poach a whole fish, wrap in cheesecloth, tie at each end so ends become handles to lift fish from bouillon.

ELYSEE SAUCE

1 cup dairy sour cream	½ teaspoon onion, grated
½ cup mayonnaise	1 2-ounce can black caviar,
½ cup chili sauce	imported (optional)
2 tablespoons lemon juice	1 hard-cooked egg, sieved

Combine sour cream, mayonnaise, chili sauce, lemon juice, onion, and chill very thoroughly. Top with caviar and egg. Makes 2 generous cups.

CARAWAY VELOUTE

2 tablespoons butter	3 stalks celery
2 tablespoons flour	2 egg yolks, beaten
1 tablespoon caraway seeds	1 teaspoon salt (optional)
½ teaspoon paprika	1 tablespoon chopped chives or
6 cups chicken soup	parsley
1 onion	

Melt butter in 2-quart saucepan and blend in flour, stirring until smooth; heat slowly until lightly browned. Add caraway seeds and paprika. Remove from heat. Pour in soup stock, stirring constantly. Be careful that flour does not lump. Place on heat and bring to a boil; reduce heat and simmer. Add onion and celery, cover tightly and continue to simmer ½ hour. Remove from heat; stir 2 tablespoons of soup into egg yolk, blend well and return slowly to soup. Season with salt and pepper and simmer 5 more minutes. Pour through a fine strainer. Reheat to serve. Garnish with Croutons (see Index) and sprinkle with parsley.

PURPLE PLUM DUCKLINGS

2 5- to 6-pound ducklings	2 teaspoons garlic salt
2 teaspoons minced onion	4 oranges, halved crosswise

Have ducklings quartered; season well with onion and garlic salt. Place oranges on rack, cut side up, in roasting pan and ¼ duckling over each half orange. Bake in a preheated 350° oven 1½ hours. Remove oranges and ducks from pan, drain off fat, and remove rack. Place ducklings and oranges side by side in bottom of roaster. Brush all generously with Plum Sauce and bake in 350° oven about

1 hour, or until ducklings and oranges are tender and glazed, basting with sauce every 10 minutes.

To serve, arrange ducklings and orange halves on platter and serve additional sauce separately. Garnish with sprigs of watercress.

Plum Sauce:

¼ cup (⅛ pound) butter *or* margarine
1 medium onion, chopped
1 #2½ can purple plums
1 6-ounce can frozen lemonade

⅓ cup chili sauce
¼ cup soy sauce
1 teaspoon Worcestershire
1 teaspoon dry ginger
2 teaspoons prepared mustard
2 drops Tabasco

Heat butter in large skillet, add onion, and cook until tender. Set food mill or sieve over a 4-cup bowl and pour in plums and juice; pit plums and purée them into juice in bowl. Add puréed plums and juice to onions in saucepan; blend in frozen lemonade, chili sauce, soy sauce, Worcestershire, ginger, mustard, and Tabasco; simmer 15 minutes. Serve with duckling.

Note: Do allow sufficient time for roasting, as poultry varies in age and texture. Use the Plum Sauce with other poultry or lamb as well. Deliciously different.

CELERY AND MUSHROOMS AMANDINE

4 cups celery, diced
1 cup chicken broth
¼ cup butter
½ pound fresh mushrooms, sliced, *or* 2 3-ounce cans mushrooms

⅛ teaspoon pepper, freshly ground
1 teaspoon soy sauce
½ cup slivered almonds, toasted
2 #2 cans pickled beets

Add celery to chicken broth in saucepan and simmer until barely tender, about 8 to 10 minutes. Heat butter in skillet, add mushrooms, and sauté for 5 minutes; add pepper and soy sauce. Drain celery, mix with mushrooms and almonds, and toss gently. Heat about 5 minutes. Place on platter, dust with paprika, and border with heated, drained beets.

DEEP GREEN SALAD

4 large heads Bibb lettuce   2 bunches watercress

Wash and separate sprigs of watercress, trim stems; wash lettuce, separate leaves and place all greens in refrigerator to crisp thoroughly. Arrange greens with lettuce leaves spread outward on salad plates. Center with watercress and serve with Mustard Dressing.

MUSTARD DRESSING

¼ cup wine vinegar	2 teaspoons dry mustard
½ teaspoon salt	½ cup salad oil
¼ teaspoon freshly ground pepper	2 tablespoons chopped parsley

Blend vinegar, salt, pepper and mustard. Gradually add salad oil, stirring until blended; add parsley. Makes 1 cup dressing.

LEMON MERINGUE NESTS

4 egg whites	1 cup sugar
¼ teaspoon cream of tartar	1 teaspoon vanilla
⅛ teaspoon salt	

Beat egg whites until foamy, sprinkle cream of tartar and continue beating until stiff. Gradually beat in ¾ cup of sugar, about 1 tablespoon at a time. When glossy and very stiff, fold in balance of sugar, vanilla and salt.

Grease and flour cooky sheet and drop by tablespoons into 12 mounds. Hollow centers and swirl to form nests. Place in a preheated 275° oven, reduce to 250° and bake for 50 minutes, or until dry. Turn off heat and allow to remain in oven until cool. Remove from pan. These may be made in advance, placed in a tin or plastic bag and kept a week or more. Fill with ice cream and serve with sauce, or fill with a custard and whipped cream.

LEMON CUSTARD
(Using the yolks remaining from meringues)

4 egg yolks	1 cup heavy cream, whipped
½ cup sugar	(for custard)
3 tablespoons lemon juice	1 cup heavy cream, whipped
2 teaspoons lemon rind, grated	(for topping)
Yellow sugar (optional)	

Place yolks in top of double boiler and beat until thick and lemon-colored; beat in sugar, lemon juice, and rind. Place over boiling water and cook for about 10 minutes, stirring constantly until thick.

When custard is cool, fold in 1 cup whipped cream. Pour into meringue shells; top each with whipped cream and sprinkle with colored sugar.

Variation:

This recipe becomes Angel Pie when assembled as directed and refrigerated 24 hours.

SHORTCUT LEMON CHIFFON FOR MERINGUES

1 3-ounce package lemon pie filling mix	1 teaspoon lemon juice
⅛ teaspoon salt	1 cup heavy cream, stiffly beaten

Prepare filling for lemon chiffon according to package directions; add salt and lemon juice. Pour into shells and refrigerate a minimum of 2 hours. Serve with dollop of whipped cream on each.

Pink Trousseau Luncheon

(SERVES 8)

Pink Champagne

Cheese Puffs Paprika   Anchoiade

Celery   Olives

Crab Louis Mold Garni — Pink Louis Dressing

Melon Platter   Refrigerator Rolls

Chocolate Ring   Peppermint Balls

Coffee

ADVANCE PREPARATION SCHEDULE

Deep Freeze	Previous Day	Early Morning
Peppermint Balls	*Crab Louis Mold*	*Louis Dressing*
	Refrigerator Rolls	*Cheese Puffs*
		Anchovy mixture
		Chocolate Ring

CHEESE PUFFS PAPRIKA

1 3-ounce package	1 egg yolk
cream cheese	Few dashes Worcestershire
1 teaspoon onion, grated	Paprika

Blend ingredients together until smooth. Spread on small crackers or rounds of bread, toasted on one side. Place under broiler until tops are browned. Watch closely as they brown quickly. Sprinkle heavily with paprika. Serve hot.

Variation:

Mix in 1 chicken bouillon cube, dissolved in 1 tablespoon boiling water. Anchovies, minced shrimp, or mashed sardines may be added. Top with button mushrooms. Makes 12 to 15.

ANCHOIADE
(Anchovy Canapés)

1 2-ounce tin anchovy fillets	⅛ teaspoon coarsely ground
2 shallots, finely chopped, *or* green onions	pepper
3 tablespoons parsley, finely chopped	4 thin slices day-old bread
	1 tablespoon butter *or* oil

Drain anchovy fillets, reserve oil; place fillets in strainer and let stand 30 minutes under cold running water. Drain. Crush with a fork and mix with shallots and parsley; season with a little pepper and beat in sufficient reserved oil to make a smooth mixture. Cut bread slices in half diagonally and sauté the triangles in butter or oil until golden brown. Spread each with the anchovy mixture and place in a preheated 400° oven for 5 to 10 minutes. Serve immediately.

CRAB LOUIS MOLD GARNI

2 envelopes (2 tablespoons) unflavored gelatin
1 cup cold water
⅔ cup chili sauce
½ cup Rosé wine
½ cup dairy sour cream
½ cup mayonnaise
½ cup tomato juice
1 tablespoon instant minced onion
1 tablespoon lemon juice
½ teaspoon salt
½ cup ripe olives
1½ cups crabmeat, fresh or frozen
Hard-cooked eggs, quartered
Salad greens
Quartered tomatoes
2 12-ounce packages frozen crab legs

Soften gelatin in ½ cup water. Heat remaining ½ cup water with chili sauce. Dissolve gelatin in hot mixture. Add wine, sour cream, mayonnaise, tomato juice, minced onion, lemon juice, and salt. Chill until partially set. Save a few olives for garnish, then cut remaining olives into slices or wedges. Fold crabmeat and olives into gelatin mixture. Turn into an oiled 6-cup mold. Chill until firm and unmold on salad greens. Garnish with hard-cooked eggs and quartered tomatoes interspersed with crab legs; add a few olives for contrast. Serve with Pink Louis Dressing.

PINK LOUIS DRESSING

⅓ cup mayonnaise
½ cup chili sauce
2 tablespoons French Dressing
¼ cup sweet cream
½ teaspoon minced onion
½ teaspoon Worcestershire
Salt and pepper

Combine mayonnaise and chili sauce. Blend in French Dressing (see Index); add remaining ingredients and mix until thoroughly blended. Makes 1 cup.

MELON PLATTER

¼ watermelon
2 avocados, sliced
1 honeydew melon, cut in balls
1 pound Tokay grapes
1 pint raspberries

Arrange a border of wedges of watermelon alternately with slices of avocado. Pile melon balls and small clusters of frosted grapes in the center. Sprinkle with raspberries.

REFRIGERATOR ROLLS

2 medium-size potatoes	1 cup milk, scalded
1 cake compressed yeast	3 eggs, beaten
½ cup lukewarm water	¾ cup sugar
½ cup shortening	2 teaspoons salt
5 cups sifted all-purpose flour	

Boil potatoes until tender. Press through a ricer or sieve and measure 1 cup. Dissolve yeast in water. Place shortening in a bowl and add milk, stirring until shortening is melted. Add potatoes and dissolved yeast. Blend in eggs, sugar, and salt; beat well. Add 4 cups of the flour, continuing to beat well. Knead or stir in remaining cup of flour. Grease top of dough lightly to prevent drying; cover bowl and place in the refrigerator for a minimum of 24 hours.

Remove quantity needed 2 hours before baking. Form into balls to fill greased muffin tins ⅓ full. Spread tops with soft butter. Let rise uncovered in a warm place, free from drafts, until doubled in bulk, about 2 hours. Bake in a preheated 425° oven 20 minutes or until lightly browned.

This dough will keep for a week and may be used for coffee cakes as well. Makes 40 2-inch rolls.

Note: If using dry yeast, use *warm* water.

CHOCOLATE RING

1 cup unsalted butter	2⅔ cups powdered sugar
8-ounce package chocolate bits	8 eggs, separated

Place butter and chocolate bits in a saucepan; stir over low heat until melted. Add sugar, blend until dissolved. Cool. Add egg yolks and beat thoroughly. Beat egg whites until very stiff; fold into mixture. Thoroughly grease a 6-cup ring mold and pour in chocolate batter. Place in a pan of boiling water and set in a preheated 350° oven. Bake 2½ hours. Remove to serving platter. Frost with Mocha Icing. To serve, fill center with peppermint ice cream balls and add a pink posy or two on the outer edge of the platter.

Mocha Icing:

⅓ cup unsalted butter	½ teaspoon salt
¼ cup cocoa	1 teaspoon vanilla
4 cups powdered sugar	⅓ cup strong brewed coffee

Cream butter until very smooth and soft. Sift together cocoa, sugar, and salt. Blend gradually with butter; add coffee until mixture reaches spreading consistency. Stir in vanilla.

Trousseau Tea

(SERVES APPROXIMATELY 8)

Cucumber Sandwiches

Hot Hors d'Oeuvres — Crabmeat Imperial   Soufflé Roll

Nut Tarts and Date Torte Cookies   Petits Fours

Chocolate Mocha Torte

Initial Mints   Walnut Prunes   Salted Nuts

Jamaican Punch

Tea   Coffee

ADVANCE PREPARATION SCHEDULE

Deep Freeze	Previous Day	Early Morning
Soufflé rolls	*Prepare crabmeat*	*Cucumber Sandwiches*
Date cookies	*Prepare Nut Tarts*	
Petits Fours	*Chocolate Torte*	
	Walnut Prunes	

CUCUMBER SANDWICHES

1 *or* 2 thin young cucumbers, as needed	1½ ounces blue cheese
8 slices thin-sliced bread	2 tablespoons cream
Mayonnaise	1 teaspoon anchovy paste
1½ ounces cream cheese	Parsley
	Paprika

Wash and score cucumber in length with cooky cutter or tines of

fork. (Do not peel.) Cut into ⅛-inch slices. Cut bread into 2-inch circles, 2 to a slice. Spread with mayonnaise and place slice of cucumber on each; combine cheeses, cream, anchovy paste and mound on each slice of cucumber. Garnish with tiny sprig of parsley dipped in paprika. Makes 16 sandwiches. Double or triple recipe as needed.
Simple and always delicious.

CRABMEAT IMPERIAL

1 green pepper, finely diced	1 cup mayonnaise
2 pimientos, finely diced	¼ teaspoon Worcestershire
1 tablespoon sharp prepared mustard	Dash Tabasco
	¼ teaspoon onion salt
1 teaspoon salt	3 pounds lump crabmeat, fresh
½ teaspoon white pepper	*or* frozen
2 whole eggs	Paprika

Combine green pepper, pimientos, mustard, salt, white pepper, eggs, mayonnaise, Worcestershire sauce, Tabasco, onion salt and blend well. Add crabmeat and mix carefully with fingers so the lumps are not broken. Divide mixture in 8 individual crab shells or casseroles, heaping it lightly. Top with a light coating of mayonnaise and dust with paprika. Bake in a preheated 350° oven 15 minutes. Serve hot or cold. (Serves 8; or with small shells, 16 may be served.)

SOUFFLE ROLL

4 tablespoons butter	4 egg yolks, beaten
½ cup flour	1 teaspoon sugar
⅛ teaspoon salt	⅛ teaspoon grated nutmeg
2 cups milk	(optional)

4 egg whites, beaten stiff

Prepare a roux: melt butter, add flour, salt and stir until smooth, about 1 minute. Heat milk and add gradually; cook for about 5 minutes, stirring constantly. Stir a small amount into the yolks, then return to heated sauce. Remove from heat; add sugar and nutmeg. Fold in beaten egg whites which should be stiff but not dry. Oil a 10″ x 15″ jelly roll pan, line with wax paper, and oil again. Spread batter evenly in pan and bake in a preheated 325° oven for 45 minutes or until golden. To remove, turn out onto two overlapping strips of wax paper, at least 16 inches long, lift off pan and gently remove wax paper.

Spread with a selected filling from following list and roll it gently, using the wax paper on which it is spread. Use salted sour cream or other sauces as accompaniment. This roll freezes well and if served with a hot filling may be reheated in a 300° oven. If served with a cold filling, just defrost.

A truly delicious hors d'oeuvre.

Mushroom Filling:

2 large onions, chopped	2 tablespoons lemon juice
4 tablespoons oil, olive *or* salad	¼ cup finely chopped green
¾ pound mushrooms, chopped	onions
4 tablespoons dairy sour cream	Salt and pepper to taste

Sauté onions in oil until soft and add mushrooms. Cook over low heat for 5 minutes. Add remaining ingredients, blending well. Serve hot.

Chicken Filling:

¼ pound mushrooms	4 tablespoons dairy sour cream
1 tablespoon butter	1 tablespoon chopped dill, fresh
1 cup finely diced chicken	*or* weed
3 hard-cooked eggs, finely chopped	Salt and pepper

Sauté mushrooms in butter for 4 minutes. Add chicken, eggs, sour cream, dill, and seasonings. Blend well and heat in top of double boiler. Serve hot.

Ham Filling:

1½ cups finely chopped cooked ham	1 teaspoon prepared horseradish
½ cup chopped chives *or* onions	½ teaspoon Dijon-type mustard
	1 cup cream, whipped

Combine ham with chives or onions, horseradish, mustard, and whipped cream. Serve cold.

Caviar Filling:

2 3-ounce packages cream cheese	¼ cup dairy sour cream
1 4-ounce jar red caviar	

Let cheese stand at room temperature and beat well with rotary beater. Add cream and fold in caviar gently. Serve hot or cold.

Shrimp Filling:

1 3-ounce package cream cheese
¼ cup sour cream
1 pound cleaned, deveined
    shrimp, chopped fine

3 tablespoons chopped chutney
3 tablespoons chopped preserved
    ginger
1 teaspoon curry powder

Have cheese at room temperature. Beat cheese and sour cream together; combine with remaining ingredients. Serve cold.

Though the soufflé appears an effort, it may be prepared in advance and frozen, and is truly party fare.

NUT TARTS

1 3-ounce package cream cheese
1 cup all-purpose flour
½ cup (¼ pound) butter
¾ cup dark brown sugar,
    firmly packed

1 egg
1 tablespoon melted butter
1 teaspoon vanilla
½ cup chopped nuts

Mix cream cheese, flour, and butter. Form into 24 balls. Refrigerate about an hour or two until firm. Mix brown sugar, egg, melted butter, and vanilla. Flatten balls of dough and fit into very small muffin tins which have been lined with wax paper cups. Pour brown sugar mixture over dough in each muffin cup; top with chopped nuts. Bake in a preheated 350° oven 15 minutes; reduce heat to 250° and bake 18 minutes. Makes 24 cooky tarts.

DATE TORTE COOKIES

2 eggs
1 cup sifted confectioners' sugar
2 tablespoons flour
½ teaspoon salt
1 teaspoon baking powder

1 cup pitted dates, cut up
    (do not pack dates too tightly)
1 cup broken nuts, pecans *or*
    walnuts
Confectioners' sugar

Beat eggs until light and fluffy. Gradually add sugar, beating until thick. Sift together flour, salt and baking powder. Add dates and nuts and fold into egg mixture. Spread in greased and floured 9″ x 9″ x 2″ pan. Bake in a preheated 350° oven 30 minutes or until lightly browned. Cool. Cut into 16 squares. Roll in confectioners' sugar.

Note: If dates have become dry, cover with ½ cup boiling water, let stand ½ hour; drain, then add to batter.

Old-fashioned, always popular.

PETITS FOURS

6 tablespoons butter	¼ teaspoon salt
1 cup sugar	½ cup milk
2 eggs, beaten	1 lemon rind, grated
1½ cups all-purpose flour, sifted	⅔ cup sugar
1½ teaspoons baking powder	Juice of 1 lemon

Cream butter with 1 cup of sugar. Beat in eggs, flour, baking powder, salt, milk, and lemon rind. Pour batter into a greased 13" x 9" x 2" baking pan and bake in a preheated 350° oven 25 minutes. Meanwhile mix ⅔ cup sugar with lemon juice. When cake has baked 25 minutes, carefully spoon lemon-sugar mixture over the top and bake 5 minutes more. Cut while still warm into 1-inch squares. Makes 117 tea-sized cakes. Extras will freeze well.

CHOCOLATE MOCHA TORTE

¾ cup sifted cake flour	5 eggs
½ teaspoon baking powder	¾ cup sugar
½ teaspoon salt	¼ cup cold water
2½ 1-ounce squares unsweetened chocolate	¼ teaspoon soda
	2 tablespoons sugar
Confectioners' sugar	

Measure sifted flour, add baking powder and salt; sift again. Melt chocolate over hot water. Beat eggs in a large bowl until thick and light in color; add sugar gradually, 1 tablespoon at a time, beating after each addition. Add flour mixture all at once and blend in with a wire whisk or rubber spatula. Remove chocolate from hot water and immediately add cold water, soda, and 2 tablespoons of sugar. Stir until thick and smooth. Fold easily and quickly into batter. Grease a 15½" x 10½" x 1" pan, cover with wax paper, and grease again. Pour batter into pan and bake in a preheated 350° oven 18 to 20 minutes.

Meanwhile, sprinkle confectioners' sugar on a clean towel. When cake is baked, turn immediately upside down on sugared towel.

Remove wax paper. Cool. Then cut each cake in 4 equal parts and split each quarter horizontally, making 8 thin layers.

Spread about 3 tablespoons Fluffy Mocha Frosting on a layer of cake, top with a second layer, and repeat until all 8 layers are frosted. Cover top and sides of layered cake with remaining frosting. Or use Chocolate Glaze (optional) as directed. Chill before serving. Makes 8 generous or 16 small slices.

Fluffy Mocha Frosting:

2 tablespoons instant coffee	⅔ cup butter
2 tablespoons hot milk	2 egg whites, unbeaten
1 pound confectioners' sugar, sifted	1 teaspoon vanilla

Dissolve coffee in hot milk. Cool slightly. Cream butter and blend with 1 cup of the sugar. Add dissolved coffee. Mix well. Add remaining sugar, egg whites and vanilla. Blend. Place in a bowl of ice water and beat with rotary beater until of spreading consistency.

Chocolate Glaze (optional, for glamour):

1 square unsweetened chocolate	5 tablespoons milk
1 tablespoon butter	Dash of salt
1½ cups sifted confectioners' sugar	

Melt combined chocolate and butter over hot water. Place sugar, milk, and salt in a small bowl. Add chocolate mixture slowly, blending well. While glaze is still warm spread with spatula over top of torte, allowing glaze to dribble down sides.

WALNUT PRUNES

1 pound large prunes	½ cup sugar
Sweet grape wine to cover prunes	¼ cup sweet grape wine
½ cup water	15 to 20 walnut halves

Wash prunes and remove pits. Cover with wine and refrigerate overnight. They will puff up. Combine water and sugar in a saucepan and simmer 10 minutes; add ¼ cup wine. Drain prunes, place in large skillet, add syrup and simmer, turning prunes frequently until prunes are well glazed and syrup completely reduced. Fill with walnut halves.

Variation:

For a traditional sweet, roll the stuffed prunes in ⅓ cup finely chopped walnuts.

JAMAICAN PUNCH

¾ cup sugar	⅘ quart Jamaica rum
1 quart club soda	1 pint cognac
1 pint lemon juice	2 ounces peach liqueur

Place sugar in a large bowl; add 1 cup soda to dissolve sugar. Add lemon juice, rum, cognac, and remaining 3 cups of soda. Stir, add peach liqueur, then a large block of ice. Let stand for 2 hours before serving, stirring occasionally.

Rum has quite a kick. Look out!

Bridal Shower Luncheon

(SERVES 8)

Tomato Caviar Canapés
Soft-Shell Crabs Amandine
Spinach Casserole
Hot Brandied Fruit
Bread Baskets — Shoestring Potatoes
White Cake Firenze
Coffee   Tea   Milk

ADVANCE PREPARATION SCHEDULE

Deep Freeze	Previous Day	Early Morning
Cake	*Spinach*	*Crabs*
	Bread basket	*Frost cake*
	Brandied fruit	

TOMATO CAVIAR CANAPES

8 slices white bread	1 head Boston lettuce
1 2-ounce package Roquefort cheese	4 tomatoes, cut in ½-inch slices
	1 2-ounce jar caviar
2 tablespoons cream	2 egg yolks, hard-cooked, sieved

Cut bread into 3-inch rounds; toast on one side. Mash cheese, blend with cream, and spread on untoasted side of bread. Make a lettuce cup on each salad plate; on it place the bread, cheese side up, then place tomato slice, spread with caviar, and sprinkle with sieved egg yolk.

SOFT-SHELL CRABS AMANDINE

16 cleaned soft-shell crabs	2 tablespoons chopped parsley
Salt and pepper	2 teaspoons fresh lemon juice
⅔ cup butter *or* margarine	1 teaspoon Worcestershire
½ cup almonds, blanched and slivered	

Season crabs with salt and pepper. Melt butter in skillet and sauté crabs, a few at a time, until just golden brown; approximately 3 minutes on each side. Remove crabs to serving platter and keep warm. Add almonds to butter left in skillet and brown lightly; add parsley, lemon juice, and Worcestershire. Blend and pour over crabs.

BREAD BASKETS — SHOESTRING POTATOES

1 round loaf white bread   ½ cup butter
2 4-ounce cans shoestring potatoes

Cut a large slice from top of loaf; remove bread from hollow to form a basket of the crust. Brush with melted butter and place in 450° oven for 15 minutes or until lightly browned. Use as a serving dish for shoestring potatoes.

SPINACH CASSEROLE

3 10-ounce packages frozen spinach
2 tablespoons butter
1 tablespoon grated onion
½ teaspoon salt
⅛ teaspoon pepper

3 3-ounce cans sliced broiled mushrooms
⅛ teaspoon garlic salt
¼ cup buttered cracker crumbs
2 tablespoons butter
2 cups White Cheese Sauce

Cook spinach according to package directions. Heat butter, add onion; sauté until soft, but not brown; add salt and pepper and combine with spinach. Butter 1½-quart casserole well, pour in half the spinach, layer of mushrooms, sprinkle with garlic salt, and cover with half the White Cheese Sauce. Layer remainder of spinach and sauce. Top with buttered crumbs and dot with butter. Bake in a preheated 350° oven 1 hour. May be prepared previous day and stored in refrigerator.

White Cheese Sauce:

2 tablespoons butter
3 tablespoons flour
1¾ cups milk

½ teaspoon salt
⅛ teaspoon pepper
¼ cup grated sharp cheese

Heat butter in saucepan. Add flour, stir until bubbly, but not brown. Heat milk, add, stirring into sauce. Cook until smooth. Add salt, pepper, and cheese. Heat until well blended.

BRANDIED FRUIT

1 1-pound 14-ounce can peaches, with juice
1 1-pound 14-ounce can pears, with juice

½ cup brandy
1 teaspoon apple pie spice
⅓ cup brown sugar
2 tablespoons butter

1 lemon, with rind, sliced

Combine all ingredients in saucepan, cover, simmer slowly 1 hour. Serve hot. This is a fine accompaniment for beef, as well.

WHITE CAKE FIRENZE

¾ cup butter
1½ cups sugar
2¾ cups cake flour
3 teaspoons baking powder

¼ teaspoon salt
1 cup milk
1½ teaspoons vanilla
6 egg whites, beaten stiff

Cream butter and sugar thoroughly. Sift flour once and measure; add baking powder and salt; sift together 5 times. Add alternately with the milk to the creamed butter and sugar. Blend in vanilla and fold in beaten egg whites. Bake in two greased 9-inch layer pans in a preheated 350° oven for 25 to 30 minutes. Fill with Pineapple Filling. Frost with whipped cream or white Seven-Minute Frosting, and sprinkle with grated coconut.

Pineapple Filling:

    1 #2 can crushed pineapple   3 tablespoons cornstarch

Pour pineapple and juice into saucepan, reserving about ½ cup of juice. Combine juice with cornstarch and mix to a smooth paste; return to pineapple in saucepan and cook, stirring constantly until clear and thickened. Cool.

Seven-Minute Frosting:

    ⅓ cup egg whites   ⅓ cup water
    1½ cups sugar   Dash salt
    ¼ teaspoon cream of tartar   1½ teaspoons vanilla
              1 cup grated coconut

Combine egg whites, sugar, cream of tartar, water, and salt in top of double boiler; beat with rotary beater until mixture holds its shape. When beaten stiff, add vanilla. Frost cake and sprinkle thickly with coconut.

Note: Hand beater takes about 7 minutes; electric beater about 2 minutes.

Variation:

A layer of Egg Custard (see Index) added to the pineapple layer.

Wedding Rehearsal Dinner Buffet Service

(SERVES 10)

Relish Tray

Crabmeat Dip — Chippers

Tureen of Mulligatawny   Toasted Sesame Crackers

Baked Ham — Spiced Cherry Sauce

White Bread

Green Cole Slaw   Pineapple — Pimiento Ring — Fruit Garni

Macaroni Soufflé

Orange Torte   Prize Chocolate Cake

Coffee   Tea   Milk

Suggested wine: Rosé

ADVANCE PREPARATION SCHEDULE

Deep Freeze	Previous Day	Early Morning
Bread (see Index)	*Olives*	*Relishes*
Chocolate Cake	*Crabmeat*	*Ham*
	Mulligatawny	*Sauces*
	Pineapple Ring	*Salad*
	Orange Torte	*Boil macaroni*
		Frost cake

RELISH TRAY

A simple relish tray comprised of cauliflower buds, green pepper rings, carrot sticks, celery sticks, celery hearts, and garlic olives.

GARLIC OLIVES

3 8½ ounce cans ripe olives   Olive oil
8 cloves garlic, sliced

Place olives in self-sealing quart jar and fill with olive oil. Add garlic and seal tightly. Place in refrigerator. Let stand at least 24 hours; may be kept 2 to 3 weeks as flavor improves over longer period. Makes 3 cups.

CRABMEAT DIP

1 6-ounce can crabmeat
½ cup chili sauce
½ cup mayonnaise
1 small clove garlic, minced
1 teaspoon dry mustard
1 tablespoon prepared horseradish
1 tablespoon Worcestershire
⅛ teaspoon Tabasco
⅛ teaspoon salt
2 hard-cooked eggs, chopped fine

Flake and bone crabmeat. Combine all ingredients; blend well. Refrigerate several hours before serving. Serve with Chippers. Makes approximately 2 cups.

TUREEN OF MULLIGATAWNY

2 fryers, 2 to 3 pounds each
¼ cup seasoned flour (see Index)
¼ cup butter
½ green pepper, diced
1 medium-sized onion, finely chopped
2 garlic cloves, minced
2 quarts water
1 tablespoon salt
1 #2 can garbanzos (chick peas)
3 tablespoons ground coriander
3 tablespoons poppy seeds
4 teaspoons powdered turmeric
½ cup flaky or grated coconut (packaged)
Dash of cayenne
2 tablespoons butter
4 whole cloves

Wash chickens and dry. Place seasoned flour in paper bag, shake chicken pieces in flour until well coated. Heat butter in a large kettle (4-quart will do). Add chicken pieces to butter and brown evenly; add green pepper, onion, garlic, and cook slowly for 5 minutes. Add water and salt; simmer about 1 hour or until chicken is tender. Remove chicken from stock; cool and cut meat from bones in large chunky pieces.

Whirl garbanzos with their liquid in blender or press through sieve and add to stock, with ground coriander, poppy seeds, turmeric, coconut, and cayenne. Heat 2 tablespoons butter in skillet, add cloves for 1 minute, remove and add flour to butter. Cook until butter is lightly browned. Stir in 2 cups of the soup stock and when smooth return to soup and blend well. Check seasonings, add salt if necessary, and simmer 15 minutes. Add chicken pieces. Serve in bowls; pass a mound of hot rice garnished with lemon slices. Dip cut edge of lemon in paprika and make a thick coating for color.

BAKED HAM — SPICED CHERRY SAUCE

We suggest a cooked, read-to-serve canned ham for this busy day. Heat according to directions and serve with Spiced Cherry Sauce.

SPICED CHERRY SAUCE

1 #2 can sour red pitted cherries   2 tablespoons cornstarch
¾ cup sugar   ¼ teaspoon cinnamon
            ½ lemon, thinly sliced

Place undrained cherries and sugar in a saucepan. Dissolve cornstarch in ½ cup of cherry juice. Combine with cherry-sugar mixture in saucepan. Add cinnamon and cook, stirring constantly, until thick and translucent. Add lemon and simmer an additional 15 minutes. Serve hot with Baked Ham.

Suggestion: This sauce is equally delicious on a roast of pork, or lamb.

GREEN COLE SLAW

2 cups crisp shredded cabbage   3 tablespoons sugar
½ cup chopped parsley   3 tablespoons vinegar
⅓ cup green onions, sliced thin 2 tablespoons salad oil
            1 teaspoon salt

Chill cabbage, parsley, and green onions; combine. Mix sugar, vinegar, oil and salt; stir to dissolve sugar. Pour over vegetables. Toss lightly.

PINEAPPLE-PIMIENTO RING — FRUIT GARNI

2 packages lemon-flavored gelatin   ½ pound pimiento cream cheese,
2 cups boiling water   softened
1 #2½ can crushed pineapple,   1 cup mayonnaise
   with juice   1 cup heavy cream, whipped

Place gelatin in large bowl of electric mixer. Add boiling water and dissolve. Cool and set in refrigerator. When of jelly-like consistency remove and beat until frothy and thick, about 10 minutes. Blend cheese and mayonnaise, combine with pineapple and juice; add to gelatin. Pour into 6-cup oiled mold. When firm, unmold on platter, garnish with watercress, pears, and pineapple slices. Tint the pears with red coloring to a blushing rosiness. If desired, use a bowl of Strawberry Rose Dressing (see Index) in the center of the mold.

Garnish:

1 #2½ can pineapple slices   1 #2 can pears
Watercress sprigs

MACARONI SOUFFLE

1 cup macaroni, uncooked   1 teaspoon Worcestershire
  (approximately 4 ounces)   ½ teaspoon salt
1 cup grated aged Cheddar cheese   Freshly ground pepper
1 cup butter   Paprika
1 cup milk   ¼ teaspoon dry mustard
3 eggs, separated   1 cup bread crumbs

Cook macaroni according to package directions. Drain; mix with cheese. Combine butter, milk and egg yolks. Bring to boil; pour over bread crumbs. Let stand 5 minutes to absorb liquid. Add to macaroni and cheese. Stir well. Beat egg whites until stiff; fold into macaroni. Bake in a preheated 350° oven 30 to 40 minutes.

ORANGE TORTE

¾ cup butter   1 teaspoon baking soda
1 cup sugar   1 cup dairy sour cream
2 eggs   1 cup walnuts, finely chopped
2½ cups cake flour   1 8-ounce package pitted dates,
1 teaspoon baking powder   finely cut (optional)
Grated rind of 1 orange

Cream butter and sugar well; add eggs one at a time, beating well after each addition. Sift flour and baking powder; blend in grated rind and add to egg mixture. Combine soda and sour cream, beating well for about 3 minutes. Add dates and nuts; mix well. Pour into greased tube pan. Bake in 375° oven for 1 hour. Remove from oven and immediately pour Orange Topping over cake; let cool in pan at room temperature for several hours or overnight.

Orange Topping:

> 1 cup powdered sugar, combined with 1 cup orange juice

PRIZE CHOCOLATE CAKE

⅓ cup butter	2½ teaspoons baking powder
1 cup sugar	½ teaspoon salt
2 egg yolks	1 cup milk
2½ (1 ounce) squares unsweet- ened chocolate, melted	1 teaspoon vanilla
	⅔ cup chopped walnuts
1½ cups all-purpose flour, sifted	2 egg whites *or* ¼ cup
½ cup sugar	

Cream butter; add 1 cup sugar gradually. Add unbeaten egg yolks and cream until fluffy. Blend melted chocolate to creamed butter mixture. Sift flour, baking powder and salt. Add to chocolate mixture alternately with milk. Add vanilla; blend in nuts. Beat egg whites until stiff and gradually beat in remaining ½ cup sugar. Fold carefully into batter. Pour into two well-greased and floured round 8-inch cake pans. Bake 30 to 35 minutes in a preheated 350° oven. Cool in pans. Frost with Whipped Cream Frosting.

Whipped Cream Frosting:

½ teaspoon unflavored gelatin	⅛ teaspoon salt
2 tablespoons cold water	2 tablespoons confectioners'
1 cup heavy cream	sugar
½ teaspoon lemon juice	

Soften gelatin in cold water. Scald 2 tablespoons of cream. Pour over gelatin, stirring until dissolved. Refrigerate until of jelly-like consistency. Beat with egg beater until smooth. Whip remaining cream; add salt, sugar, lemon juice; fold into gelatin mixture. Sufficient to cover and fill two 8-inch layers.

Bachelors and Benedicts Dinner

(SERVES APPROXIMATELY 8)

Paprika Roll   Papoose Frankfurters
Round Crackers   Edam Sauce
Beef Tenderloin à la Boeuf
Broiled Tomatoes
Baked Noodles Florentine
Rye Rolls
Old-Fashioned Compote   Corn Relish
California Cheesecake
Espresso

Suggested wine: red Bordeaux

ADVANCE PREPARATION SCHEDULE

Deep Freeze	Previous Day	Early Morning
Paprika Roll	*Compote*	*Prepare frankfurters*
		Noodle casserole
		Sauce for beef
		Cheesecake

PAPRIKA ROLL

1 8-ounce and 1 3-ounce package
  cream cheese
1 8-ounce wedge sharp Cheddar
  cheese, finely grated
1 small garlic clove, minced

1 teaspoon fresh onion juice
¼ teaspoon Worcestershire
½ cup finely chopped pimiento-
  stuffed olives (optional)
Paprika

Cream cheese should be at room temperature and then mashed until of a smooth consistency. Add grated Cheddar cheese, garlic, and remaining ingredients, except paprika; blend until thoroughly mixed. Sprinkle a large piece of wax paper with paprika, to make a solid red coating on the cheese roll. Roll cheese mixture back and forth on paprika to form a long roll or 2 small ones. Coat the cheese well, including the two ends, so that it looks like a "rind." The roll should be about 2 inches in diameter to fit on a cracker when sliced. Roll onto fresh wax paper and store in refrigerator until firm; it can be frozen. Serve on cheeseboard; slice and place on round crackers. The flavor improves at room temperature.

PAPOOSE FRANKFURTERS

1 8-ounce package buttermilk refrigerator biscuits	2 4¼-ounce jars cocktail sausages

Open biscuits as instructed. Pat each biscuit flat and square; cut into 5½-inch strips. Wrap each frankfurter spirally with a strip. Press ends of dough so that it holds. Place on ungreased 10-inch square cake pan. Bake in a preheated 475° oven 15 minutes or until browned. Serve hot on toothpicks with sauce. May be wrapped early in the day and refrigerated until ready to serve. Makes 18.

EDAM SAUCE

½ pound processed Edam cheese	1 teaspoon Dijon-type mustard
¼ cup dry white wine	½ teaspoon Worcestershire

Melt cheese in double boiler, stir in wine, mustard, Worcestershire, and blend well. Serve in chafing dish, as a dip for the frankfurters.

BEEF TENDERLOIN A LA BOEUF

4 to 6 pounds tenderloin	½ teaspoon pepper
1½ teaspoons salt	3 tablespoons butter, softened

Season meat on both sides with salt and pepper; spread with softened butter. Broil about 2 inches from source of heat for 10 minutes on each side. Remove from broiler to roasting pan. Cover with sauce and bake uncovered in a preheated 350° oven for 10 minutes. Total cooking time varies with thickness of meat and desired degree of doneness. Should be served rare and presented whole with sauce atop.

Garnish with broiled tomato halves or watercress. If served sliced, pour sauce atop after slicing.

Sauce:

¼ cup butter
1 clove garlic, minced
½ pound mushrooms
1½ cups sliced onions
¼ pound hamburger
2 tablespoons chili sauce
1 tablespoon seasoned steak
  sauce
⅛ teaspoon marjoram
⅛ teaspoon thyme
4 drops Tabasco sauce
2 teaspoons Worcestershire
½ cup dry red wine
½ cup condensed beef bouillon
1 teaspoon salt
¼ teaspoon pepper
½ teaspoon flour

In 12-inch skillet, melt butter; sauté garlic, mushrooms, and onions for 5 minutes or until onions are limp. Add hamburger, breaking with fork, stirring constantly until brown. Add remaining ingredients, stir well, and simmer slowly until ready for tenderloin. (Can be made in advance but should be kept hot.)

BROILED TOMATOES

4 medium tomatoes
½ teaspoon salt
4 tablespoons dried bread crumbs
Freshly ground black pepper
1 tablespoon melted butter

Cut tomatoes in half; do not peel. Combine salt, butter, and breadcrumbs. Spread each cut side of the 8 halves of tomatoes with mixture. Dust with pepper. Place on broiler rack and broil under medium heat or about 5 minutes until crumbs are browned. Serve around beef. They may be baked in a preheated 350° oven for 25 minutes.

BAKED NOODLES FLORENTINE

2 8-ounce packages broad noodles
1 medium onion, chopped fine
1 tablespoon butter
2 cups dairy sour cream
¼ cup butter, melted
1 10-ounce package frozen
  spinach, cooked and drained
3 eggs, lightly beaten
½ teaspoon salt

Cook noodles in boiling salted water (1 teaspoon salt to 1 quart of water) for 7 minutes or until tender; blanch with cold water and drain. Sauté onion in 1 tablespoon butter.

In a large bowl, combine sour cream and melted butter; add

noodles, spinach, eggs, onion, and salt. Mixture should be quite loose; if necessary, add additional sour cream. Pour into well-greased 2-quart casserole; bake in a preheated 375° oven 45 minutes, or until lightly browned.

OLD-FASHIONED COMPOTE

½ pound large pitted prunes ¼ pound figs
½ pound dried apricots 1½ cups hot water
¼ pound dried peaches 2 tablespoons honey
¼ cup white wine

Place prunes, apricots, peaches, and figs in saucepan filled with hot water; cover tightly and let stand 1 hour. Blend in honey and wine; re-cover and chill overnight. To serve, place over low heat, only until hot.

CORN RELISH

16 large ears fresh corn on the cob ¾ cup water
4 cups (1 small head) finely chopped cabbage 1¼ cups cider vinegar
1 cup diced celery 1 teaspoon celery seed
2 cups diced green pepper 4 teaspoons dry mustard
1½ cups chopped onion 1 teaspoon turmeric
¾ cup sugar ¼ teaspoon cayenne pepper
¼ cup fresh lemon juice ½ teaspoon garlic powder
 5 teaspoons salt
 ¾ cup chopped pimiento

Cook corn on cob in boiling water to cover 2 to 3 minutes, using 1 teaspoon salt to 1 quart water. Cool corn, cut from cob; mix with cabbage, celery, green pepper, and onion. Combine sugar, lemon juice, water, vinegar, celery seed, mustard, turmeric, pepper, garlic powder, and salt in a 5-quart kettle. Bring to boiling point. Add vegetables and cook 25 minutes, stirring frequently. Stir in pimiento and heat. Pack in hot, sterilized jars; seal at once. Keep four or five weeks before using. Makes about 3 pints.

CALIFORNIA CHEESECAKE

Crust:

1 6-ounce box zwieback 1 teaspoon cinnamon
1 cup sugar ¼ pound butter

Grind zwieback; mix with sugar, cinnamon, and butter. Line bottom and sides of 12-inch spring form with mixture, ready for baking.

Filling:

1¼ cups sugar	1 lemon, juice and rind
2 8-ounce packages cream cheese	1 teaspoon vanilla
	¼ cup flour
8 eggs, separated	Pinch salt
1 quart dairy sour cream	

Cream sugar and cream cheese; add beaten egg yolks. Then add lemon juice and rind, vanilla, flour, salt, and sour cream; fold in beaten egg whites. Fold mixture into lined spring form and bake 5 minutes in a preheated 375° oven; lower heat to 275° for 1 hour. Leave in open oven to cool; then refrigerate. To serve, cover with Strawberry Glaze.

Strawberry Glaze:

1 quart strawberries	¼ cup water
⅓ cup sugar	1 tablespoon cornstarch
1 teaspoon butter	

Crush enough berries to make ½ cup. Boil berries, sugar, water, and cornstarch for 2 minutes; add butter. Strain and cool. Arrange whole berries on cake. Pour glaze over cheesecake.

Spinster Dinner

(SERVES 6)

Escargots in Mushrooms

Ginger Baked Chicken   Curried Rice

Eggplant Soufflé

California Salad   Green Goddess Dressing

Toast Melba

Apples à la Nellie Virginia

Chocolate Cinnamon Bars

Coffee   Milk

ADVANCE PREPARATION SCHEDULE

Deep Freeze	Previous Day	Early Morning
Cinnamon bars	*Salad Dressing*	*Apples Virginia*
		Chicken
		Rice
		Assemble salad ingredients

ESCARGOTS IN MUSHROOMS

1 7½-ounce can snails (24)   1 pound fresh mushrooms
2 tablespoons butter

Prepare snails according to directions on can. Do not use shells. Remove stems from mushrooms. Heat 2 tablespoons butter in saucepan, add mushroom caps, and sauté 5 minutes. Place on baking sheet; set 1 snail in each cap. Cover with Butter Sauce and bake in a preheated 425° oven 7 minutes, or until thoroughly heated.

Reserve mushroom stems for sauce or seasoning in another recipe. Serve in living room from chafing dish, or for first course dining serve in individual portions with sprig of parsley garnish.

Butter Sauce:

½ cup butter   ¼ cup chopped parsley
1 clove garlic, minced   1 teaspoon salt
⅛ teaspoon nutmeg

Melt butter for escargots in saucepan in which mushrooms were sautéed. Blend in garlic, parsley, salt, and nutmeg. Heat, do not boil.

GINGER BAKED CHICKEN

¼ pound butter   ½ teaspoon paprika
3 2-pound frying chickens   1 teaspoon dry ginger
2 small onions, sliced   Salt and pepper to taste
1 cup sherry   1 cup chicken bouillon
½ cup tomato juice   Cucumber slices
Pimiento strips

Melt butter in heavy skillet; place chickens in skillet and brown until golden. Remove and place in baking dish. Add onions to remaining butter in skillet, sauté until soft; add sherry, tomato juice, paprika, ginger, salt, pepper, and bouillon. Heat and stir mixture 1 minute, blending thoroughly. Pour over chicken in baking dish. Place in a preheated 350° oven and bake uncovered for 1 hour and 15 minutes, or until tender. Turn chicken carefully every half hour.

Serve on platter with Curried Rice mounded in center; garnish with slices of scored cucumber and pimiento strips. Score cucumber by drawing lines length of cucumber with tines of fork.

CURRIED RICE

2 quarts boiling salted water	3 tablespoons butter
1 cup well-rinsed long-grain rice	1 tablespoon curry powder
1 tablespoon minced parsley	

Drop long-grain rice into rapidly boiling water a little at a time so that water does not cease to boil. Cook exactly 10 minutes. Drain; dry in top of double boiler over hot water. Melt butter in skillet; add curry powder and parsley. Combine this mixture with rice; blend well.

EGGPLANT SOUFFLE

2 eggplants	4 egg yolks, beaten
2 tablespoons butter	4 egg whites, beaten stiff
2 tablespoons flour	1 tablespoon chopped parsley
1 cup milk	1 cup grated Parmesan cheese

Peel eggplant and cut into squares. Drop into boiling salted water (½ teaspoon salt to 1 cup water). Cook until tender; drain and mash with fork. Melt butter in saucepan, add flour and milk gradually; cook until thick. Pour a small amount of sauce slowly into beaten egg yolks, blend, and gradually return this mixture to white sauce; add eggplant and parsley. When cool, fold in beaten egg whites. Pour into buttered 2-quart casserole, alternating layers with grated cheese, ending with cheese on top. Place casserole in pan of hot water. Bake in a preheated 325° oven 50 minutes to 1 hour. Serve immediately.

CALIFORNIA SALAD

3 heads Bibb lettuce
2 tomatoes, in sixths
1 16-ounce can hearts of palm, cut in 2-inch slices
1 4-ounce can artichoke hearts
Paprika

Make a bed of ½ head Bibb lettuce for each serving. Arrange tomatoes and hearts of palm with artichoke heart in center. Cover with 4 tablespoons Green Goddess Dressing and sprinkle with paprika.

GREEN GODDESS DRESSING

1 clove garlic, minced
½ teaspoon salt
½ teaspoon dry mustard
1 teaspoon Worcestershire
2 tablespoons anchovy paste
3 tablespoons tarragon wine vinegar
3 tablespoons minced chives *or* scallions
⅓ cup minced parsley
1 cup mayonnaise
½ cup dairy sour cream
⅛ teaspoon black pepper

Thoroughly blend all ingredients with rotary beater. This dressing will keep for several days.

APPLES A LA NELLIE VIRGINIA

6 medium-size juice oranges
6 large firm cooking *or* baking apples
Lemon juice
Granulated sugar

Grate rind of 3 oranges, being careful to grate lightly to avoid any of the white membrane; squeeze oranges and reserve juice. Peel apples, beginning with stem end, and peel ⅔ to ¾ of the way down; moisten peeled apple with lemon juice to prevent discoloration. Remove core, but only halfway; if apple is completely cored, it may collapse. Roll apples in sugar and place them in flat saucepan in single layer; sprinkle with grated orange peel. Add additional sugar to orange juice to taste; pour over apples. Cover pan and simmer over very low heat; do not permit them to boil; baste every 5 minutes with the orange juice. Cook until tender, being careful that they are not overcooked. When apples are tender, remove from pan and put each in individual dessert dish. Cook orange juice until reduced by about one-third, then pour over apples. Serve hot or cold with Cointreau Whipped Cream.

Topping:

1 cup heavy cream, whipped	2 tablespoons confectioners'
1 tablespoon Cointreau *or*	sugar
Grand Marnier	

Blend whipped cream with confectioners' sugar and add liqueur.

CHOCOLATE CINNAMON BARS

2 cups all-purpose flour	1 whole egg
1 teaspoon baking powder	1 egg yolk
1⅓ cups sugar	1 egg white, slightly beaten
4 teaspoons cinnamon	1 6-ounce package (1 cup)
½ cup (¼ pound) butter *or*	semi-sweet chocolate pieces
margarine, softened	½ cup chopped pecans *or* walnuts

Sift together flour, baking powder, 1 cup sugar, and 3 teaspoons cinnamon; add butter, whole egg and egg yolk. Blend well with wooden spoon or on low speed of electric mixer. Turn into lightly greased 11″ x 7″ x ¾″ jelly roll pan; spread evenly with spatula. Beat egg white slightly; brush egg white over mixture. Combine remaining ⅓ cup sugar, 1 teaspoon cinnamon, chocolate pieces, and nuts. Sprinkle over top. Bake in a preheated 350° oven 25 minutes; cool and cut into bars.

Pre-Nuptial Dinner

(SERVES 8)

This exciting dinner may become even more dramatic if each course is served separately in the Continental manner. At least two waitresses are needed; three would be better.

Individual Cheese Soufflés
Mushroom Bouillon au Chablis — Parsley Pancake Strips
Chateaubriand Foie Gras
Cucumbers with Capers
Wild and White Rice Mold
Brioches
Pimiento Hearts of Palm — French Dressing
Cantaloupe Alaska
Butter Wafers
Coffee   Tea

Suggested wine: Musigny or other red Burgundy

ADVANCE PREPARATION SCHEDULE

Deep Freeze	Previous Day	Early Morning
Ice cream balls	*Bouillon*	*Cucumbers*
Cookies	*French Dressing*	*Rice Mold*

INDIVIDUAL CHEESE SOUFFLES
(Double the recipe for 8)

1½ cups dairy sour cream	2 tablespoons chopped chives
1 cup sifted flour	½ cup grated non-processed
1¼ teaspoons salt	Gruyère cheese
¼ teaspoon freshly ground black pepper	5 eggs, separated

Combine sour cream, flour, salt, and pepper; mix until smooth. Stir in chives and cheese. Beat egg whites until stiff, but not dry. Using same beater in a separate bowl, beat yolks until thick and lemon-colored. Gradually add yolks to cream mixture, stirring constantly; carefully fold in egg whites. Pour into 4 individual 1½-cup oven-proof dishes, ungreased. Place in shallow pan of hot water and bake until set in a preheated 350° oven 30 to 40 minutes. Serve immediately.

MUSHROOM BOUILLON AU CHABLIS

2 ounces dried mushrooms
1 quart water
1 teaspoon salt
2 tablespoons chicken fat *or* butter
1 stalk celery
½ teaspoon salt

2 bouillon cubes
1 carrot
1 leek
1 beef or lamb shank (approximately 1 pound)
1 clove garlic
6 cups water

¼ cup Chablis

Wash mushrooms thoroughly and soak overnight in water. Next day cook in water in which they were soaked, add salt and simmer 2 hours; strain, reserving stock. Place butter in 3-quart kettle, heat and add celery, carrot, leek, bone, and garlic; sauté until lightly browned. Add water, salt, and bouillon cubes; cover, and simmer 2 hours. Strain, and add mushroom stock to soup stock. Heat; add wine and serve with Parsley Pancake Strips.

PARSLEY PANCAKE STRIPS

2 tablespoons flour
1 egg

½ cup milk
½ teaspoon chopped parsley

1 teaspoon butter

Combine flour, egg, milk and parsley; beat well. Heat butter in 6-inch skillet, add 1 tablespoon batter to make thin pancake, tilting pan to cover bottom. Brown lightly on both sides. Cut into fine julienne strips, about 2 inches long, and add to each serving of consommé as it is poured.

CHATEAUBRIAND FOIE GRAS

3 pounds heart of beef tenderloin, trimmed
8 ounces foie gras with truffles *or* liver pâté

1 teaspoon salt
4 tablespoons butter
1 tablespoon concentrated beef stock
8 slices toast

Make a slit the length of tenderloin, forming a pocket; fill with pâté and lace together with pins and strings. Sprinkle with salt and brush with 2 tablespoons butter. Place in a preheated oven and broil 6 to 7 minutes. Brush again with 2 tablespoons butter combined with beef stock. Place under moderate broiler and cook for about 12 minutes for rare, longer for better done. Dip toast in pan drippings, slice Chateaubriand and arrange on toast.

CUCUMBERS WITH CAPERS

4 medium-size cucumbers
Water to cover
½ teaspoon salt
2 tablespoons butter

2 tablespoons flour
1½ cups chicken stock, *or*
1½ cups hot water and
2 chicken bouillon cubes
1 tablespoon capers

Peel cucumbers; cut in half lengthwise and remove seeds; dice. Place in saucepan with salt and just enough water to cover. Heat butter in saucepan, add flour, blend, and add stock, stirring until thickened. Add capers, drain cucumbers, and simmer additional 10 minutes.

WILD AND WHITE RICE MOLD

To boil rice:

1 cup white long-grain rice
1 teaspoon salt

2½ cups water

Wash rice thoroughly; place in saucepan with water and salt. Bring to boil, cover, and lower heat. Simmer 25 minutes until water is absorbed.

1 pound mushrooms
6 tablespoons butter
3 tablespoons grated onion
½ teaspoon salt
3 cups cooked rice

1 13-ounce can cooked wild rice
¼ cup bouillon *or* water
¼ teaspoon garlic powder
Watercress (optional)
Preserved kumquats

Wash mushrooms and separate caps of mushrooms from stems. Chop stems coarsely. Melt 2 tablespoons butter in saucepan, add mushroom stems and onion, and sauté for 5 minutes. Combine with white rice, blend well; add wild rice, salt, garlic powder, and remaining 4 tablespoons of butter and bouillon. Pour into well-greased 6-cup mold, place in pan of hot water and bake in a preheated 350° oven for 40 minutes. To serve, turn out on heated platter, sautéed mushroom caps in center of ring; garnish with bed of watercress and clusters of kumquats.

BRIOCHES

½ cup milk	¼ cup lukewarm water
½ cup (¼ pound) butter	1 egg, separated
⅓ cup sugar	3 whole eggs, beaten
1 teaspoon salt	3¼ cups sifted all-purpose flour
1 package dry yeast	1 teaspoon sugar

Scald milk, cool to lukewarm; cream butter, adding sugar gradually; add salt. Soften yeast in water; blend with milk and creamed mixture. Add egg yolk, whole eggs, and flour; beat with wooden spoon for 2 minutes. Cover; let rise in warm place, 80° to 85°, until doubled in bulk, about 2 hours. Punch down, then beat thoroughly. Cover tightly with foil and refrigerate overnight. To bake, stir dough down and turn into floured bowl. Cut off ¼ of dough, and reserve. Divide remaining dough into 16 pieces and form into balls. Place in well-greased 2¾-inch muffin pans. With moistened finger make a depression in each ball. Cut small piece of dough into 16 pieces and form into balls. Place a small ball in each depression; cover and let rise in warm place until doubled in bulk, about 1 hour. Beat remaining egg white with teaspoon of sugar, brush over brioches. Place on lowest rack in a preheated 400° oven and bake until brown, 15 to 20 minutes.

PIMIENTO HEARTS OF PALM

Salad:

1 can hearts of palm	6 cups torn escarole
2 tablespoons chopped pimiento	

Form a bed of escarole. Cut hearts of palm in 2-inch pieces; place on escarole. Sprinkle with pimiento and serve with dressing.

FRENCH DRESSING

1 cup salad oil
¼ cup cider vinegar
2 tablespoons red wine vinegar
2 tablespoons tarragon vinegar
1 tablespoon plus 1 teaspoon
   sugar

¼ teaspoon paprika
½ teaspoon dry mustard
⅛ teaspoon cayenne pepper
¼ teaspoon black pepper
Pinch thyme
2 whole garlic cloves

Blend or shake well all ingredients except garlic. Add whole garlic cloves and allow cloves to remain in dressing for at least 2 days. Makes 1½ cups.

CANTALOUPE ALASKA

4 cantaloupes
4 tablespoons Crème de Menthe
4 egg whites
¼ teaspoon salt

½ cup sugar
2 drops mint extract
3 pints firm vanilla ice cream
Flaked coconut

Cut cantaloupes in half crosswise. Cut a small slice from bottom if necessary, to make them stand upright. Remove seeds and pour 1½ teaspoons Crème de Menthe in each half. Beat egg whites with salt until stiff, adding mint extract. Place scoops of ice cream into halves, and cover ice cream and cut surface of melon completely with meringue. Sprinkle with coconut and bake in a preheated 450° oven for 2 minutes, or until golden brown. Serve at once.

BUTTER WAFERS

¾ cup soft butter *or* margarine
½ cup sugar
1 egg
1 teaspoon vanilla
¼ teaspoon salt

1¾ cups sifted all-purpose flour
1 7-ounce package chocolate
   mint candy wafers *or*
   rum wafers

Cream together butter, sugar, egg, vanilla, and salt. Stir in flour. Chill about 1 hour. Shape in 1-inch balls. Place 2 inches apart on ungreased cooky sheet. Flatten each by pressing a wafer in center. Bake in a preheated 400° oven 8 to 10 minutes. Remove immediately from pan. Makes 4 dozen.

These cookies store well in a covered container.

Formal Wedding Breakfast

(SERVES 6)

Apricot Bowle   Cheese Crisps

Fillets of Sole Marguery   Watercress Sandwiches

Breast of Chicken in French Marinade

Wild Rice Portugaise

White Asparagus on Curly Endive — Herb Dressing

Chiffon Roll à la Crème

Beverage

Suggested wine: Chablis

ADVANCE PREPARATION SCHEDULE

Previous Day	**Early Morning**
Chiffon Roll	*Marinate chicken*
Cheese Crisps	*Fillets of Sole*
Dressing	*Watercress Sandwiches*
Soak wild rice	*Sauce for Chiffon Roll*
	Bake Cheese Crisps

APRICOT BOWLE

Fresh apricots — a minimum of one per guest	Brandy — to cover apricots
	Champagne

Soak required number of apricots overnight in brandy to cover. To serve, drain and prick apricots with a fork to release flavor. Place one in each large goblet for individual service. Fill with iced champagne. Refill as needed. For variation, use small fresh cling peaches the same way. Drained brandied whole peaches or apricots are delectable as a substitute, but there is no need to prick these for flavor.

CHEESE CRISPS

2 ounces cream cheese, softened
2 ounces aged Cheddar cheese
  (finely grated)
½ cup (¼ pound) butter,
  softened

1 cup all-purpose flour
Egg white
Paprika
2 tablespoons of caraway *or*
  other seeds

Combine cream cheese and Cheddar cheese; blend thoroughly. Add butter and flour; mix well. Shape into a ball, wrap in wax paper, and chill in refrigerator several hours. Roll out very thin and cut into various shapes as for cookies. Brush tops with egg white and dust with paprika; sprinkle with caraway or other seeds of your choice. Bake in a preheated 375° oven 10 to 12 minutes.

FILLETS OF SOLE MARGUERY

6 small fillets of sole *or* flounder
¾ cup white table wine
1½ tablespoons lemon juice
6 tablespoons butter *or*
  margarine
½ teaspoon salt
⅛ teaspoon pepper
Dash paprika

½ lemon, sliced
1½ tablespoons flour
½ cup cream
2 egg yolks, slightly beaten
¾ teaspoon sugar
2 teaspoons minced parsley
12 small oysters
12 small shrimps, cooked

Garnish

Arrange fillets in buttered baking dish, pour over wine, lemon juice, and 4 tablespoons melted butter; season with salt, pepper, paprika and top with lemon slices. Bake in a preheated 400° oven 20 minutes, or until fish flakes easily. Transfer, with broad spatula, to hot serving platter and keep warm. Reserve liquid in pan.

For sauce, melt remaining butter in top of double boiler; over direct heat, blend in flour and add liquid from baking pan. Stir constantly over low heat until thickened and smooth. Add cream to beaten yolks, stir in a small amount of hot sauce, then return to double boiler. Place pan over hot water and cook 1 minute. Blend in sugar.

For garnish, heat butter in skillet, add oysters, and sauté until oysters curl at edges, about 2 or 3 minutes.

To assemble, pour sauce over fish on platter, sprinkle with parsley, and garnish with oysters and heated shrimp.

WATERCRESS SANDWICHES

1 loaf thin-sliced white bread
1 3-ounce package cream cheese,
   softened
1 cup slivered almonds, toasted

2 tablespoons finely chopped
   watercress
¼ teaspoon salt
Sprigs of watercress

Trim crusts from bread and flatten with a rolling pin so as to shape nicely. Beat cheese with rotary or electric beater until fluffy. Add almonds, watercress, and salt; spread a generous teaspoonful on each slice. Roll as for a jelly roll, placing seam side down on flat pan, and refrigerate until serving time. Tuck a sprig of watercress in end of each sandwich. Wrap in wax paper and refrigerate. Makes 24 sandwiches.

BAKED CHICKEN IN FRENCH MARINADE

½ cup (¼ pound) butter
1 clove garlic, minced (optional)
2 tablespoons chopped parsley
2 tablespoons brown sugar
1 cup sauterne

1 teaspoon seasoned salt
3 2-pound broiling chickens
1½ teaspoons salt
½ teaspoon ground black pepper
1 teaspoon paprika

2 teaspoons flour

Melt butter and add garlic, parsley, brown sugar, sauterne, and seasoned salt, mixing thoroughly. Season quartered chickens on both sides with salt, pepper, and paprika. Marinate with butter mixture and let stand for 2 hours. Place skin side down in 10″ x 14″ baking dish. Bake uncovered, in marinade, in preheated 350° oven for 1 hour, basting frequently. Turn chicken, sprinkle with flour and baste frequently until brown. Serve with Wild Rice Portugaise. Fluffy White Rice (see Index) may be substituted.

WILD RICE PORTUGAISE

1 cup wild rice
1 cup grated American cheese
1 cup chopped fresh or
   canned mushrooms
1 cup chopped ripe olives

½ cup chopped onion
1 cup hot water
½ cup salad oil
1 cup canned tomatoes
½ teaspoon garlic salt

Soak rice overnight, drain, wash again and drain. Add to remaining ingredients. Place in greased 2-quart casserole, cover and bake for 1 hour in a preheated 350° oven.

WHITE ASPARAGUS ON CURLY ENDIVE

1 quart curly endive
1 #2 can asparagus stalks (white)

1 green pepper
Paprika

Place asparagus in stacks of 3 on a bed of endive. Slip spears through rings of green pepper and dust with paprika.

HERB DRESSING

1 cup mayonnaise
1 teaspoon prepared mustard
⅛ teaspoon Tabasco sauce
1 teaspoon chili powder

2 teaspoons onion juice
4 tablespoons vinegar
½ teaspoon ground marjoram
½ teaspoon ground thyme

1 teaspoon salt

Blend ingredients together. Place in a small jar, cover, and shake.

CHIFFON ROLL A LA CREME

6 eggs
⅛ teaspoon salt
¾ teaspoon cream of tartar

¾ cup granulated sifted sugar
1 teaspoon vanilla
¾ cup cake flour, sifted

¾ cup confectioners' sugar

Grease a 15" x 10" jelly roll pan; line bottom with wax paper and grease again. Separate eggs, dropping whites into bowl of electric mixer. Beat yolks about 1 minute. Add salt to egg whites and beat with electric beater until foamy; add cream of tartar and beat until stiff but not dry. Fold yolks into beaten whites carefully; fold in sugar, vanilla, and then flour, just until blended. Do not over-mix. Pour into prepared pan and spread evenly from center to sides. Bake in a preheated 400° oven from 13 to 15 minutes, or until light brown. Lightly dust clean dish towel with confectioners' sugar. Loosen cake from sides of pan with spatula and invert it into sugared towel. Lift off pan and peel off paper gently. Trim crusts from cake with sharp knife and roll up cake gently from narrow end, rolling towel with it. Cool about 10 minutes. Unroll, remove towel, spread with Cream Cheese Filling.

Cream Cheese Filling:

3 8-ounce packages cream cheese   1 teaspoon vanilla
2 egg yolks   Grated rind of lemon
¼ cup sugar   ⅛ teaspoon salt

Soften cheese and mash; Add yolks, sugar, vanilla, and rind. Beat well, preferably in electric mixer or blender. Fill jelly roll with ⅔ of cheese mixture, reserving ⅓ for sauce.

Sauce:

⅓ cheese filling   1 cup dairy sour cream
1 tablespoon sugar

Combine filling, sour cream, and sugar; serve over roll.

Formal Wedding Dinner

(SERVES 6)

Chicken Liver Pâté in Aspic   Champagne
Salted Nuts   Decorated Mints
Jellied Wine Consommé
Fillet of Sole Poulette
Breasts of Chicken in Pineapple Shells
Wild Rice Amandine   Carrots en Cognac
Bridal Salad — Pink French Dressing
Cheddar Disks
Ice Cream Bridal Molds   Coconut Cake Blanc
Coffee

Suggested wine: Chablis or white Burgundy

Only the very brave would undertake the entire organization of this important day. We hope you can have professional help for serving and for your table decor. The menu, gauged for six, is a suggestion for this happy day or for any important occasion. The recipes may be increased to serve more.

ADVANCE PREPARATION SCHEDULE

Deep Freeze	Previous Day	Early Morning
Cake	*Chicken Liver Pâté*	*Fillet of sole*
	Jellied Consommé	*Chicken*
	French Dressing	*Rice*
		Cheddar Disks
		Frost cake

Please Note: If this menu is used intact, it would necessitate two ovens. If you have only one oven, the fish may be baked in advance and completed later with the sauce. The other baked foods could be completed while the fish is being served.

CHICKEN LIVER PATE IN ASPIC

Aspic for Pâté:

2 envelopes (2 tablespoons) unflavored gelatin	2 cups hot water
	2 chicken bouillon cubes
¼ cup cold water	1 tablespoon dry sherry

Soak gelatin in cold water; dissolve in hot water. Add bouillon cubes, stir until dissolved; add sherry. Place small molds or plastic holders for egg storage in a tray of ice water. Pour ¼ inch of this aspic liquid in each mold. Drop 1-inch balls of pâté into each mold. Pour in additional liquid to cover pâté. Refrigerate until jelled. Serve on toast rounds. Makes 2 dozen tiny aspic molds.

Pâté:

1 pound chicken livers	½ teaspoon ground cloves
Flour	¼ teaspoon lemon juice
⅛ pound unsalted butter	½ teaspoon dry mustard
½ teaspoon salt	1 teaspoon anchovy paste
Dash cayenne pepper	1 tablespoon grated onion
½ pound sweet butter, softened	2 tablespoons cognac
½ teaspoon sweet basil	1 tablespoon Benedictine
2 tablespoons chopped truffles (optional)	

Coat livers with flour; sauté 10 minutes in butter. Add salt, cayenne pepper, softened butter, sweet basil, cloves, lemon juice, dry mustard, anchovy paste, grated onion, cognac, Benedictine, and truffles. Place in container of electric blender or food mill and blend to a paste. Pack into a 1½-cup mold and refrigerate at least 24 hours. Form into 1-inch balls.

Note: These may be stored in an earthenware crock and kept for other menus.

JELLIED WINE CONSOMME

4 cups rich beef consommé *or* 3 10½-ounce cans, undiluted	½ teaspoon salt
	⅛ teaspoon pepper
2 tablespoons unflavored gelatin	½ teaspoon lemon juice
½ cup water	Finely chopped sweet onion and
1 teaspoon sugar	parsley
1 cup dry red wine	

Soften gelatin in water. Bring consommé to a boil; stir in gelatin, add sugar, and dissolve. Add red wine, salt, pepper, and lemon juice; cool and refrigerate for about 3 hours or until set. Break the jellied consommé lightly with a fork and serve in cups, garnished with chopped sweet onion and parsley.

FILLET OF SOLE POULETTE

2 pounds fillet of sole	1 bay leaf
1 cup white wine	Thyme
1 cup water	1 teaspoon salt

Place sole in saucepan. Add wine, water, bay leaf, thyme and salt; bring to a boil, reduce heat, and simmer 8 to 10 minutes. Remove fish from liquid, draining carefully and place in a buttered baking dish. Reserve fish stock. Cover with Poulette Sauce and bake in a preheated 350° oven 15 minutes.

Poulette Sauce:

2 tablespoons butter	1 tablespoon lemon juice
1 tablespoon flour	1 tablespoon minced parsley
2 cups strained fish stock	1 cup tiny shrimp, cooked, *or*
2 egg yolks	1 4-ounce jar cooked shrimp

Melt butter in saucepan. Add flour; stir until smooth; add fish stock.

Cook slowly until creamy. Combine egg yolks, lemon juice, and parsley; add slowly to cream sauce. Stir in shrimp and pour over cooked sole. Bake in a preheated 350° oven another 15 minutes.

BREASTS OF CHICKEN IN PINEAPPLE SHELLS

1 slice white bread	Pinch cayenne pepper
¼ cup half and half cream	½ teaspoon monosodium
¼ pound veal, ground	glutamate
¼ pound lean pork, ground	6 1-pound chicken breasts,
¼ pound lean beef, ground	deboned
1 medium onion, minced	2 tablespoons melted butter
8 water chestnuts, coarsely	1 teaspoon salt
chopped	3 small fresh pineapples, halved
1 tablespoon soy sauce	2 tablespoons honey
¼ teaspoon powdered ginger	2 teaspoons sesame seeds

Soak bread in cream. Combine with meats. Add onion, chestnuts, soy sauce, ginger, cayenne and monosodium glutamate. Mix well. Divide stuffing among the boned chicken breasts. Roll up and fasten with toothpicks. Place in greased shallow roasting pan. Brush with butter and salt. Bake in a preheated 350° oven 35 minutes, or until tender.

Split pineapples lengthwise, through leaves, leaving crown. Remove and discard cores. Remove pineapple flesh from skin, cut into chunks, and return to shells. Cut each cooked breast of chicken into 4 slices, to within ¼ inch of the bottom. Reshape each fanlike on top of a pineapple half. Spread honey over each chicken breast and sprinkle with sesame seeds. Put into a preheated 400° oven to toast seeds.

WILD RICE AMANDINE

2 cups wild rice	4½ cups chicken broth
½ cup olive oil	½ teaspoon salt
2 tablespoons chopped onion	⅛ teaspoon pepper
2 tablespoons chopped chives	½ cup almonds, blanched and
3 tablespoons chopped green	shredded
peppers (optional)	

Wash wild rice in cold water several times and drain. Heat olive oil in saucepan; stir in onion, chives, and green pepper. Add rice, heat, stirring constantly until rice begins to turn yellow. Stir in chicken broth, salt, pepper, and almonds. Pour into well-buttered 6-cup casserole, cover and bake 1¼ hours in a preheated 350° oven, or until rice is tender.

CARROTS EN COGNAC

8 large carrots	1 teaspoon sugar
⅓ cup butter	¼ teaspoon thyme
1 teaspoon salt	⅓ cup cognac or other brandy

Wash carrots and pare. Cut into ¼-inch strips and arrange in a buttered 1-quart casserole. Melt butter in saucepan; add sugar, salt, thyme, and brandy. Pour over carrot strips. Bake 1 to 1¼ hours in a preheated 350° oven.

BRIDAL SALAD

6 cups limestone lettuce, shredded	1 can hearts of palm (1-inch
1 6-ounce can artichokes	pieces)
	Pimiento

Arrange individual portions on bed of lettuce; dot with pimiento. Serve with Pink French Dressing.

PINK FRENCH DRESSING

1 cup lemon juice	1 tablespoon salt
1 cup catsup	¾ cup sugar
2 cups salad oil	Garlic, optional for another
1 medium onion, grated, or	occasion
2 teaspoons onion juice	

Combine all ingredients in blender and beat well.

CHEDDAR DISKS

½ cup (¼ pound) butter	1 cup all-purpose flour
1 cup (½ pound) grated	½ teaspoon salt
aged Cheddar cheese	Dash cayenne
1 tablespoon caraway seeds (optional)	

Cream butter; add cheese, flour, salt, and cayenne. Knead until smooth; chill 1 hour or more. Form dough into long roll 1 inch in diameter. Wrap in wax paper and chill. Slice as for icebox cookies. Sprinkle with caraway seeds and bake in a preheated 350° oven until pale gold. Makes about 2 dozen.

Caution: Overbaking spoils cheese flavor.

COCONUT CAKE BLANC

3 cups sifted cake flour	4 egg yolks, well beaten
2 teaspoons baking powder	1 cup milk
¼ teaspoon salt	1 teaspoon vanilla
1 cup (½ pound) butter	1 cup shredded coconut, packed
1 pound confectioners' sugar	lightly
4 egg whites, well beaten	

Sift flour once, then measure. Add baking powder and salt. Sift 3 times. Cream butter thoroughly and add sugar gradually. Continue creaming until light and fluffy; add egg yolks and beat well. Add flour mixture alternately with milk, beating after each addition. Stir in vanilla and coconut. Fold in egg whites carefully. Bake in two 9-inch or three 8-inch pans in a preheated 375° oven 25 to 30 minutes. Remove and cool on cake racks. Frost with Butter Cream Frosting.

Butter Cream Frosting:

⅓ cup butter *or* margarine, softened	3 cups confectioners' sugar
	3 tablespoons cream
1 teaspoon vanilla	

Cream butter until light and fluffy; add 1 cup sugar; beat until well blended. Add cream, vanilla, and remaining sugar, beating until thick and smooth and of spreading consistency.

Sufficient for a three-layer cake. For a smaller cake, use the following:

¼ cup butter *or* margarine, softened	2 cups confectioners' sugar
	2 tablespoons cream
½ teaspoon vanilla	

Same method as for larger amount.

Post-Wedding Brunch

(SERVES 6)

Hot Consommé *or* Bull Whip

Chicken Livers Stroganoff

Rice Rosé

Chippers

Marinated Baby Cucumbers

Strawberry French Toast   Schnecken

Suggested wine: Montrachet or a red Bordeaux

ADVANCE PREPARATION SCHEDULE

Deep Freeze	Previous Day	Early Morning
Schnecken	*Consommé*	*Prepare French Toast*
	Cucumbers	*to sauté*

HOT CONSOMME

2 pounds lean beef	1 teaspoon salt
1 veal bone	3 peppercorns
1 pound chicken wings	2 sprigs parsley
2 quarts cold water	1 bay leaf
⅓ cup diced carrots	1 parsnip
⅓ cup diced celery	1 tablespoon sherry per serving
⅓ cup diced onion	(optional)
1 10-ounce can tomato soup	

Place beef, veal bone, and chicken wings in kettle; cover with cold
water and bring to a boil; add remaining ingredients except sherry.
Cover and simmer very slowly for 2 hours; strain, cool and refrig-

erate. When cold, remove solidified fat. To serve, reheat and add seasoning to taste, and sherry to individual servings.
The soup stores for several days, or freezes well.

BULL WHIP

4 ounces canned beef bouillon   1 jigger vodka

Mix in blender with crushed ice. Serve with wedge of fresh lime.
1 serving.

CHICKEN LIVERS STROGANOFF

½ pound chicken livers	½ cup hot water
2 tablespoons dehydrated onion flakes	1 chicken bouillon cube
	1 teaspoon seasoned salt
2 tablespoons water	⅓ teaspoon tarragon
¼ cup butter	1 tablespoon sherry
½ pound sliced mushrooms	1 cup dairy sour cream
1 teaspoon flour	1 teaspoon chopped parsley

Wash livers and cut in two; combine onion flakes and 2 tablespoons water. Heat butter in large skillet; add livers and mushrooms; sauté for 5 minutes, turning frequently. Remove livers and mushrooms; drop onion flakes into sauce; cook 3 minutes, but do not brown. Blend flour, water, and bouillon cube until smooth. Blend in seasoned salt and tarragon; add to onions and cook another 3 minutes. Return mushrooms and livers to seasonings in skillet; add sherry and sour cream, reheat slowly but thoroughly. Do not boil, as cream may curdle. Pour onto platter and serve with mounds of Rice Rosé. Sprinkle with parsley.

RICE ROSE

1 8-ounce package long grain rice	1 teaspoon salt
2 quarts water	4 tablespoons butter
2 teaspoons paprika	¼ cup blanched slivered almonds

Cook rice according to package directions. Blend in butter and paprika until thoroughly mixed. Combine with almonds. To reheat, place in top of double boiler over hot water. Mix to prevent sticking. To serve, toss with butter.

MARINATED BABY CUCUMBERS

1 quart new cucumbers, cut in
  ¼-inch slices
¼ cup white vinegar
¼ cup water
4 teaspoons sugar

1 teaspoon celery seed
¼ teaspoon dried dill weed
1 medium onion, sliced thin
¼ cup commercial Italian style
  salad dressing

If new pickle cucumbers are not obtainable, the full-grown variety
will do, although the small ones have a special freshness. Place
cucumbers in a bowl; combine vinegar, water, sugar, celery seed,
dill weed, onion, and dressing; pour over cucumber slices. Refrigerate for several hours or overnight. These cucumbers can be stored
in the refrigerator for a week.

STRAWBERRY FRENCH TOAST

1 5½-ounce can
  evaporated milk
3 tablespoons water
1 egg, slightly beaten
1 teaspoon vanilla
1 tablespoon sugar
¼ teaspoon salt

¼ teaspoon cinnamon
6 slices bread
1 cup crushed cornflakes
¼ cup butter
1 10-ounce package frozen
  strawberries, thawed
1 cup dairy sour cream

Combine milk, water, egg, vanilla, sugar, salt, and cinnamon.
Blend well. Dip bread in mixture and then in cornflakes. Heat
butter in skillet, add bread slices; sauté slowly until brown on both
sides, being careful that bread does not burn. Serve topped with
strawberries and sour cream.

SCHNECKEN

Dough:

1 1-ounce cake yeast, *or* 1 package
  dry yeast
1 cup lukewarm milk
1 cup cold milk
1 cup (½ pound) butter

2 eggs
1 cup sugar
4 to 5 cups all-purpose flour,
  sifted
1 teaspoon salt

Dissolve yeast in lukewarm milk; if using dry yeast, dissolve in
warm milk; set aside 5 minutes. Melt butter and add cold milk;
add eggs and mix well. Sift together sugar, flour, and salt; add
butter mixture. Stir well, add yeast sponge and beat well. Cover and

allow to rise until double in bulk, in warm (85°) protected spot, for 2½ hours.

Glaze:

> 1 cup brown sugar ⅓ cup water
> 72 pecan halves

While dough is rising, combine brown sugar and water (glaze ingredients) in saucepan and boil 1 minute. Place 1 tablespoon of mixture in well-buttered 1½-inch muffin tins and half a pecan in bottom of each tin, flat side up. Set aside.

Filling:

> ½ cup sugar   ½ cup pecans, coarsely chopped
> 1 teaspoon cinnamon   ½ cup raisins
> ¼ cup butter, cut in small pieces

Remove dough to floured board and add sufficient flour to make dough firm enough to handle. Prepare ¼ recipe at a time. Roll out on floured board, about ¼ inch thick in large rectangle. Sprinkle with filling ingredients; roll up as for a jelly roll, with seam side down, and cut into 1-inch slices. Place each slice, cut side down, in prepared pans. Bake in a preheated 375° oven about 20 minutes; remove from pans while hot. Makes about six dozen small 1½-inch schnecken.

Honeymooners' Return

(SERVES 8)

Suggested aperitif: Positano or dry sherry

Salmon Cream Puffs

Beef Bourguignonne   Egg Barley — Mushroom Caps

Orange Prunier

Chocolate Soufflé — Sauce Maxim

Coffee   Milk

Suggested wine: a Château Burgundy

ADVANCE PREPARATION SCHEDULE

Previous Day	Early Morning
Orange mold	*Beef*
Cream puffs for stuffing	*Sauce Maxim (without whipped cream)*

SALMON CREAM PUFFS

½ cup water	⅛ teaspoon salt
¼ cup (⅛ pound) butter, cut in pieces	½ cup all-purpose flour, sifted
	2 eggs

Combine water, salt, and butter in saucepan and bring to a boil. When butter is melted, pour in the flour all at once. Stir vigorously with a wooden spoon over low heat until the mixture forms a ball in the pan. Continue cooking and stirring for about 4 minutes. Remove from heat; beat in the eggs one at a time until smooth. Drop batter from teaspoon onto ungreased cooky sheet in tiny balls, ½ inch in diameter. Leave 2-inch space between mounds. Bake in a preheated 400° oven until golden and dry, about 20 minutes. When cool, store in a tin box or in foil. To serve, slice off top, fill and replace at a jaunty angle. Makes 18 small puffs.

Filling:

¼ pound smoked salmon, finely chopped	½ cup heavy cream, whipped
	⅛ teaspoon dill weed

Blend well.

BEEF BOURGUIGNONNE

5 pounds beef chuck, cut into large cubes	2 leeks, coarsely chopped
Flour	3 cups coarsely chopped onions
7 tablespoons butter	4 tablespoons chopped parsley
4 tablespoons olive oil	1 bay leaf
Salt and pepper	· 1 teaspoon thyme
¼ cup cognac, warmed	3½ cups Burgundy
½ pound bacon, diced	Water to cover meat
2 cloves garlic, minced	36 small whole onions, dry *or* canned
2 carrots, coarsely chopped	½ teaspoon sugar

Roll beef cubes in flour; heat 4 tablespoons each of butter and olive oil in skillet, add beef, and brown evenly on all sides over high heat. Sprinkle meat with salt and pepper. Pour cognac over all and ignite. When flame dies, place meat in casserole. To skillet, add bacon, garlic, carrots, leeks, chopped onions, and 2 tablespoons chopped parsley. Cook, stirring, until bacon is crisp and vegetables are lightly browned. Transfer to casserole with meat and add bay leaf, thyme, Burgundy, and enough water just to cover meat. Cover and place in preheated 350° oven; bake 2 hours. Remove from oven. Blend 1 tablespoon each of butter and flour with a little casserole gravy and stir into casserole. Return to oven and continue cooking about 2 hours longer or until meat is fork tender. Brown whole onions in 2 tablespoons butter combined with sugar; add enough water to glaze onions and to keep them from burning. Cover and cook until onions are almost tender. To serve, add onions to casserole and garnish with parsley sprigs.

Note: This recipe serves 12. We suggest giving the bride the balance to start the freezer supply.

EGG BARLEY

1 8-ounce package egg barley   Salt and pepper

Cook according to package instructions. Serve hot, bordered with Mushroom Caps.

MUSHROOM CAPS

1 pound fresh mushroom caps   2 tablespoons olive oil
2 tablespoons butter   Juice ½ lemon

Sauté mushrooms in butter and oil until lightly browned on one side; sprinkle with lemon juice and turn to brown other side.

ORANGE PRUNE MOLD

1 pound large prunes   ⅛ teaspoon salt
2 3-ounce packages lemon-   ¾ cup boiling water
  flavored gelatin   2¼ cups orange juice, strained
        Orange sections, etc.

Wash prunes and soak in cold water 30 minutes. Bring to a boil and cook about 30 minutes; cool, remove pits, being careful to preserve shape of prunes. Dissolve gelatin in boiling salted water, add orange juice. Place layer of prunes in bottom of oiled 6-cup mold. Add gelatin to cover and congeal in refrigerator; repeat until prunes and gelatin have been utilized. To serve, place mold on large platter, border with and alternate orange sections, mandarin oranges, grapefruit, and avocado wedges, in attractive pattern.

Variation:

Intersperse fruit border with rounds of stiffly beaten whipped cream to be used in other menus as a fruit dessert.

CHOCOLATE SOUFFLE

3 tablespoons butter	3 1-ounce squares unsweetened chocolate, melted
¼ cup sifted all-purpose flour	4 egg yolks, beaten
¾ cup plus 1 tablespoon sugar	1 teaspoon vanilla
1½ cups milk	
6 egg whites	

Melt 2 tablespoons butter in upper part of double boiler. Combine flour and ¾ cup sugar; add to melted butter and mix until smooth. Add milk and chocolate; cook, stirring, over hot water until thick. Add egg yolks and cook 2 minutes more; add vanilla. Remove from heat; cool slightly. Beat egg whites until stiff and fold into cooled mixture. Grease 8-inch (1½-quart) soufflé dish with 1 tablespoon butter and sprinkle with 1 tablespoon sugar. Pour soufflé mixture into dish; set it in another container of hot water. Bake in preheated 350° oven for 40 minutes. Cool and remove from dish by inverting on serving platter. Serve with Sauce Maxim.

SAUCE MAXIM

9 egg yolks	½ cup Grand Marnier
1½ cups sugar	2 cups heavy cream, whipped

Beat yolks and sugar in top of double boiler over hot (not boiling) water for about 20 minutes until mixture is firm and makes a ribbon when dropped from beater. Remove pan from hot water and place in pan of ice water. Continue beating until cool. Mix in Grand

Marnier. Chill thoroughly. To serve, gently fold in whipped cream; spoon around soufflé, or serve from separate bowl.

Caution: If using a glass double boiler, let cool before placing in ice water.

Variation:

For a delectable dessert, serve Sauce Maxim over whole, hulled strawberries, or pour into bowl and border with cooked or canned pears. Delicious!

Bride's First Luncheon

(SERVES 6)

Strawberries in Port
Eggs Benedict   Shoestring Potatoes
Hollandaise Sans Souci
Kumquat Compote   Applesauce Cake
Coffee

For her first guest menu, one of our favorite campus brides chose recipes that would be well accommodated in serving pieces received as gifts. Especially nice to use gifts from guests invited for this occasion.

ADVANCE PREPARATION SCHEDULE

Deep Freeze	Previous Day	Early Morning
Applesauce Cake	*Kumquats*	*Hollandaise*
		Wash and hull berries
		Split muffins and hollow for toasting
		Defrost cake

STRAWBERRIES IN PORT

1 quart strawberries   Port to cover

Strawberries and port have a definite affinity, but care should be taken that they do not marinate too long as the berries will become soft. Simply wash berries and hull; place in bowl and add enough port to cover. Refrigerate 1 hour and serve. One quart of berries serves six. Serve in a deep glass bowl.

EGGS BENEDICT

6 English muffins	12 thin slices boiled ham
Butter, softened	12 eggs
12 slices black olive *or* truffle	Paprika

Tear muffins in half, removing some of the soft dough in center to make room for the egg. Toast lightly and spread with butter. Place a slice of ham on each muffin, tucking it into the hollow. Break an egg on each, place on cooky sheet, and bake in preheated 350° oven for 6 minutes or until whites are set. Place on individual plates or on a platter. Cover each egg with Hollandaise and sprinkle with paprika; top with olive or truffle slice.

With this recipe, the worry of the broken poached egg is eliminated. We suggest packaged or canned shoestring potatoes; to serve, heat quickly in a preheated 375° oven. Serve 2 eggs for each guest.

Shoestring Potatoes:

1 4-ounce can serves 4.

HOLLANDAISE SANS SOUCI

A wonderful never-fail Hollandaise. The version in our *Thoughts for Buffets* remains a favorite, but we offer this adaptation for variety.

¼ cup (⅛ pound) butter	Dash cayenne
1 cup dairy sour cream	½ teaspoon powdered mushroom
4 tablespoons lemon juice	(optional)
¼ teaspoon salt	

Melt butter in saucepan; stir in sour cream and blend well, add lemon juice, salt, cayenne, and powdered mushroom. Heat, but do not allow to boil. The mushroom powder, though not necessary, adds a delightful flavor.

Serve extra sauce in a sauce bowl.

KUMQUAT COMPOTE

1 16-ounce can kumquats   ¼ cup walnut meats, chopped (optional)

Pour kumquats and syrup into saucepan; heat to boiling point and serve hot; sprinkle with walnuts.

APPLESAUCE CAKE

1 1-pound box graham crackers
¾ cup sugar
1½ teaspoons cinnamon
½ cup butter, melted
4 eggs, separated

3 tablespoons lemon juice
1 14½-ounce can evaporated milk
1 8-ounce can applesauce
1 teaspoon vanilla
1 cup heavy cream, whipped

Crush crackers. Mix with cinnamon and 1 tablespoon of the sugar; add melted butter and blend. Grease 9-inch spring form thoroughly and line bottom and sides with cracker mixture, pressing firmly. Beat yolks until thick; add remaining sugar, lemon juice, milk, applesauce and vanilla. Beat egg whites until very stiff, fold carefully into applesauce mixture. Pour into lined spring form. Bake in a preheated 350° oven one hour. Cool, and top with whipped cream.

Baby Shower Luncheon

(SERVES 6)

Pineapple "Cradle" Appetizer
"Baby" Frogs' Legs   "Play Pen" Potato Balls
"Bib" Lettuce — "Baby Blue" Cheese Salad Dressing
Marron Bassinet Mold
Coffee

Suggested wine: Chablis

ADVANCE PREPARATION SCHEDULE

Deep Freeze	Previous Day	Early Morning
Marron Mold	*Dressing*	*Prepare pineapple*
		Crisp lettuce
		Prepare potatoes
		Prepare frogs' legs

PINEAPPLE "CRADLE" APPETIZER

1 large pineapple	6 pipe cleaners
2 tablespoons chopped candied ginger	6 small blossoms

Cut chilled pineapple in sixths, leaving leafy top attached. Remove hard core from each section and loosen fruit from peel as close as possible. Cut into bite-size pieces, in length and across. Sprinkle with ginger. Attach pipe cleaners as for a handle and tuck flowers into leaf side of "cradle," spearing with toothpick if necessary.

"BABY" FROGS' LEGS

12 pairs frogs' legs	½ teaspoon sugar
Juice of 1 lemon	3 tablespoons fresh or dried
⅓ cup flour	tarragon
¼ pound butter or margarine	3 tablespoons chopped fresh
2 garlic cloves, crushed	chives
2 tablespoons lemon juice	3 tablespoons chopped parsley
½ teaspoon salt	1 tablespoon cognac, warmed
¼ teaspoon pepper	½ cup dry white wine

Wash frogs' legs. Place in bowl, add juice of 1 lemon, cover with cold water. Let soak in refrigerator for 2 hours. Drain and dry thoroughly. Dredge with flour. Heat shortening in skillet until foamy. Add garlic and 2 tablespoons lemon juice. Cook for 1 minute; add frogs' legs, shaking pan and turning them frequently until golden brown on both sides. Add salt, pepper, sugar, tarragon, chives, and parsley. Cook for 1 minute. Flame warm brandy and add; add white wine and cook for 1 minute. Serve immediately.

"PLAY PEN" POTATO BALLS

6 potatoes   ¼ cup shortening
1 teaspoon salt

Pare potatoes and form balls with French cutter, allowing approximately 5 balls per person. Let stand in cold, salted water until needed. Heat shortening in skillet and place balls in pan: cover closely. Cook slowly, shaking pan over heat to brown evenly. Cook about 5 minutes or until tender. Sprinkle with salt. Drained canned potato balls may be prepared in the same manner.

"BIB" LETTUCE
"Baby Blue" Cheese Dressing

3 heads Bibb lettuce

Wash lettuce and halve each head, permitting it to remain in clusters. Refrigerate until ready to serve. Arrange on individual salad plates and serve with Cheese Dressing.

Blue Cheese Dressing:

⅓ cup blue cheese
1 cup dairy sour cream
¼ teaspoon garlic salt
¼ teaspoon paprika
¼ teaspoon celery salt

⅛ teaspoon freshly ground black pepper
3 tablespoons lemon juice
¼ cup chopped *or* sliced ripe olives

Mash cheese until creamy. Stir in other ingredients; blend well. Makes about 1½ cups.

MARRON BASSINET MOLD

1 cup chopped marrons
¼ cup rum
⅔ cup sugar

⅓ cup water
5 egg yolks, beaten very light
1½ cups heavy cream, beaten stiff

Rock salt and ice

Pour rum over chopped marrons; let stand several hours or overnight. Boil sugar and water for 10 minutes; then pour in a fine stream, beating constantly, over egg yolks. Cook in double boiler, beating all the while until mixture thickens. Chill thoroughly. Drain marrons. Sprinkle ¼ cup of marrons into a 6-cup melon mold; fold egg mixture and whipped cream together and then fold in the ¾ cup of marrons. Pour into mold. Cover and pack 3 to 4 hours in rock salt and ice. If rock salt is not available, dessert can be placed in freezer for several hours or overnight. The difference is mainly in the texture; either is good.

Ornament with tiny pink and blue satin bows on toothpicks, staggered attractively. Insert one end of toothpick through knot, other end into mold. Elevate enough to clear the food. Bows may be purchased already tied. Decorate and place in freezer until ready to serve.

Grandma Visits Luncheon

(SERVES 6)

Minted Melon Balls

Tuna Fish Mold   Herbed Crackers

Asparagus Roquefort Salad   Applesauce Bread

Biscuit Tortoni

Coffee

ADVANCE PREPARATION SCHEDULE

Deep Freeze	Previous Day	Early Morning
Bread	Tuna Mold	Melon balls
	Biscuit Tortoni	Dressing for salad

MINTED MELON BALLS

2 cantaloupes   Juice of 1 orange

Juice of 1 lemon   ¼ cup sugar

Fresh mint

Cut cantaloupe into balls with melon ball cutter; place in bowl. Combine lemon juice, orange juice, and sugar and pour over melon balls. Chill. Serve in stemmed glasses and garnish with fresh mint.

TUNA FISH MOLD

2 envelopes (2 tablespoons)   ¾ cup milk
unflavored gelatin   ⅓ cup lemon juice
¼ cup cold water   1 tablespoon butter or
2 eggs, separated   margarine
1 teaspoon salt   2 cups flaked tuna fish
1 teaspoon dry mustard   1 cup mayonnaise
¼ teaspoon paprika   2 hard-cooked eggs, quartered
2 tablespoons sugar   Watercress

Soften gelatin in cold water. Beat egg yolks and mix with salt, mustard, paprika, and sugar. Add milk, then lemon juice slowly, stirring constantly. Place in a double boiler and cook over hot water until mixture thickens, stirring constantly. Add butter and softened gelatin; stir until gelatin is dissolved. Cool; chill in refrigerator until mixture starts to thicken. Fold in tuna, mayonnaise, and stiffly beaten egg whites. Pour into oiled 5-cup fish or ring mold and chill until firm. Unmold and garnish with quartered eggs and watercress; add a dusting of paprika.

ASPARAGUS ROQUEFORT SALAD

2 pounds fresh asparagus, cooked and chilled
1 head Romaine lettuce

¼ cup Roquefort cheese (optional garnish)

Roquefort Dressing:

¼ cup Roquefort cheese, crumbled
1 8-ounce can tomato sauce
2 tablespoons chili sauce *or* catsup

4 teaspoons lemon juice
1 teaspoon onion, grated
½ teaspoon paprika
Dash of Tabasco
½ teaspoon salt (optional)

Mash cheese with fork; add tomato sauce, chili sauce, lemon juice, grated onion, paprika, Tabasco, and salt. Beat with rotary beater until smooth. Arrange asparagus spears on lettuce; top with Roquefort Dressing; garnish with additional Roquefort cheese.

A simple dressing could be served the children.

APPLESAUCE BREAD

⅓ cup shortening
1 cup sugar
1 egg
2 cups sifted all-purpose flour
1 teaspoon baking powder
½ teaspoon soda

½ teaspoon salt
¼ teaspoon nutmeg
⅓ cup orange juice
1 tablespoon grated orange rind
¾ cup raisins
½ cup chopped nuts

1 cup applesauce

Cream shortening and sugar until light and fluffy; add egg and beat well. Combine sifted flour, baking powder, soda, salt, and nutmeg; add alternately with orange juice, beating until smooth after each addition. Stir in raisins, nuts, and applesauce. Turn mixture into 3 greased 1-pound (#2 size) empty cans. Bake in a preheated 350° oven 45 minutes. Makes 3 small loaves.

BISCUIT TORTONI

2 cups heavy cream, whipped	1 cup macaroon crumbs
⅓ cup confectioners' sugar	(crushed macaroon cookies)
1 teaspoon vanilla	1 cup chopped blanched,
2 egg whites, beaten stiff	toasted almonds
16 whole almonds	

Blend whipped cream and confectioners' sugar and vanilla. Fold in beaten egg whites, macaroon crumbs, and chopped almonds. Line an 8½" x 4½" x 2½" loaf pan with wax paper; extend paper above sides of pan to facilitate lifting dessert. Pour mixture into pan; garnish top with remaining almonds and freeze rapidly. When firm, lift out of pan and slice. Return to pan and place in freezer until ready to serve.

Silver Anniversary Dinner

(SERVES 8)

Caviar Mousse — Lemon Garni   Relish Bowl
Zuppa Rapallo
Beef Wellington
Pea Soufflé Amandine   Vineyard Carrots
Meringue Belle
Coffee

Suggested wine: pink Sparkling Burgundy

ADVANCE PREPARATION SCHEDULE

Previous Day

Caviar Mousse
Zuppa Rapallo (without sherry)

Early Morning

Roast the beef;
wrap in pastry

CAVIAR MOUSSE — LEMON GARNI

1 tablespoon unflavored gelatin	2 cups dairy sour cream
2 tablespoons cold water	⅛ teaspoon dry mustard
½ cup boiling water	4½ ounces black caviar
1 tablespoon lemon juice	Paprika
1 teaspoon Worcestershire	Lettuce
2 tablespoons mayonnaise	Lemon wedges

Soak gelatin in cold water; dissolve in boiling water. Add lemon juice and Worcestershire. Combine mayonnaise with sour cream and mustard; pour into first mixture and blend well. Fold in caviar. Mix and pour into greased 4-ounce individual molds. Dip edges of lemon slices in paprika to form thick coating. Serve in lettuce cups; garnish with paprika lemon wedges.

ZUPPA RAPALLO

1½ quarts broth, chicken *or* beef	1 lemon peel, grated
¼ cup cornstarch	1 #2 can tomatoes
2 6-ounce cans tomato paste	1 hard-cooked egg, chopped
Salt and pepper to taste	1 cup chopped cooked sweetbreads
½ teaspoon Worcestershire	¼ cup sherry (optional)
Dash Tabasco	

Make a paste of ½ cup broth and cornstarch; add to remaining broth and simmer, stirring, to medium thickness; add tomato paste, salt, pepper, Worcestershire, and Tabasco. Simmer 20 minutes; strain. Add lemon peel, tomatoes, egg, and sweetbreads; heat thoroughly; stir in sherry and serve at once. Freeze leftover.

BEEF WELLINGTON

1 7-pound fillet of beef	1 bay leaf
4 tablespoons butter	Pinch of rosemary
Salt and pepper	¼ cup water
1 stalk celery	½ cup pâté de foie gras
1 onion, sliced	Pie Pastry, rolled ⅛ inch thick
1 carrot, sliced	1 egg yolk, beaten slightly
2 tomatoes, diced	(optional)
2 sprigs parsley	

Trim fillet and spread with butter; sprinkle with salt and pepper.

Put in a flat pan with celery, onion, carrot, tomatoes, parsley, bay leaf, rosemary, and water; roast in a preheated 400° oven for about 25 minutes. Remove and cool. Reserve drippings and vegetables in pan for sauce. When fillet is cold, spread it with pâté de foie gras and wrap it in Pie Pastry. Trim the edges of the pastry, moisten them with a little cold water, and press firmly together; bake the rolled fillet on a baking sheet in a preheated 450° oven for about 15 minutes or until the crust is delicately browned. Watch carefully that crust does not become too brown, as beef will be overdone. For a shiny crust, brush the surface with beaten egg yolk before baking. Garnish with parsley and stacks of Vineyard Carrots. Serve very hot with Sauce Wellington.

Domestic pâté de foie gras serves well for this purpose, or see Index.

There could be leftovers for lunch as this is a very generous recipe.

Pie Pastry Crust:

½ cup butter, softened	3⅓ cups sifted all-purpose flour
8 teaspoons granulated sugar	1½ teaspoons salt
⅔ cup shortening, softened	⅓ to ⅔ cup cold water

Combine butter and sugar in a large bowl, and beat with fork until smooth; then blend well with shortening. Combine flour and salt; blend with butter mixture. Gradually stir in water until mixture cleans the side of bowl. Knead on lightly floured surface until just well mixed. For Beef Wellington, the pastry should be rolled ⅛ inch thick. Remaining dough, if any, can be frozen and used for pie or tarts, if desired, at a later time.

Sauce Wellington:

1 cup beef *or* veal stock	1 large truffle, chopped, *or* a few chopped ripe olives
¼ cup pâté de foie gras	

Add beef or veal stock, pâté de foie gras, and truffle to the roasting pan after removing beef; simmer the sauce for 15 minutes and serve separately.

VINEYARD CARROTS

2 pounds young carrots, cut in julienne strips	½ teaspoon ground ginger
	1 teaspoon fine granulated sugar
1 cup peach juice	2 tablespoons butter

Cook carrots in peach juice until tender; add ginger, sugar and butter. Continue cooking for 3 or 4 minutes, tossing gently. Drain and serve very hot.

PEA SOUFFLE AMANDINE

2 10-ounce packages frozen peas, cooked	¼ cup toasted almonds, ground
	½ cup cream
¼ cup milk	2 drops almond extract
½ teaspoon salt	3 egg yolks, well beaten
2 tablespoons flour	3 egg whites, beaten stiff

Cook peas according to package directions and drain. Press cooked peas through a sieve with milk, or purée in electric blender, making about 2 cups of purée; add salt and flour. Heat almonds and cream to boiling point and combine with purée. Add extract and egg yolks. Fold in stiffly beaten egg whites; pour into a greased 6-cup soufflé dish. Bake in a preheated 350° oven about 25 minutes. Serve immediately.

MERINGUE BELLE

Large Meringue Shell	1 quart coffee ice cream
Pink "Kisses"	3 packages frozen raspberries
1 quart raspberry ice	(defrosted)
1 quart vanilla ice cream	1 pint heavy cream, whipped
Pink flowers	

Meringue Shell:

8 egg whites	2 cups sugar
1 teaspoon baking powder	2 teaspoons vinegar
¼ teaspoon salt	2 teaspoons vanilla

Beat egg whites until frothy, add baking powder, salt, and beat until stiff. Add sugar, beating continually (at high speed if using electric mixer), 1 tablespoon at a time, until stiff and glossy. Add vinegar and vanilla slowly, continuing to beat. Cover baking sheets with wax paper and outline a circle 9″ in diameter. Cover circle with meringue ¼ inch thick, then add a rim 1½ inches high, and about 2 inches wide, forming a shell. Tint remaining meringue with a few drops of red food coloring until delicate pink. Make individual meringues (kisses) for decoration. Use a pastry tube, or drop off meringue from tablespoon in mounds 1 inch in diameter. Swirl mixture to a peak. Place large shell ring and "kisses" in a preheated 250° oven. Bake 30 to 40 minutes or until crisp. Remove from oven and from paper. Cool on racks.

To assemble, place meringue shell on serving platter. Fill with alternate scoops of coffee ice cream, vanilla ice cream, and raspberry ice. Hold a 4-ounce glass in center as shell is filled so that it is sunk into ice cream balls with rim at level of top. Arrange pink flowers in glass. Scatter several "kisses" over ice cream. Border base with whipped cream and remaining kisses. A sprinkling of silver candies would be in keeping.

Serve with raspberries. (Have the ice cream formed into balls and frozen.)

The shell may be baked 2 or 3 days in advance. The meringue shell with ice cream may be frozen for about 4 or 5 days.

Preferably, make the shell in advance, assemble it to serve; or assemble it in the morning and freeze until serving time.

Special Events

THE TORCH of the Olympic games has been the insignia of sports from Greece to the present era. It represents the zestful activities, companionship, hearty competition, and conviviality which follow those events. May the following menus climax the day's enthusiasms and good fellowship and welcome the conquering heroes' return.

WEEKEND GUESTS

Friday Evening — Jet Age Supper

(GREETING NON-SCHEDULED ARRIVALS)

(SERVES 8)

Cocktails

Sardine Pâté   Crabmeat Bouchées   Seviche
Stuffed Celery
Cold Beef Fillet Marinara   Spaghetti Missouri
Assorted Sliced Breads
Hollywood Cheesecake
Coffee

Suggested wine: any light red wine

ADVANCE PREPARATION SCHEDULE

Previous Day	Early Morning
Crabmeat Bouchées	*Sardine Pâté*
Seviche	*Marinate beef*
Cheesecake	

SARDINE PATE

2 sweet onions	Salt
2 3¾-ounce cans sardines	Mayonnaise
4 hard-cooked eggs	Lemon juice to taste
Freshly ground pepper	Cognac, about 1 teaspoon

Slice onions paper-thin into bowl. Add sardines, eggs, pepper, salt, and enough mayonnaise to make of a spreading consistency. Squeeze in a little lemon juice; add a bit of cognac. Refrigerate for about 1 hour; taste again and adjust seasonings. Serve with Melba toast or assorted crackers. Makes about 2 cups.

CRABMEAT BOUCHEES

2½ tablespoons butter	½ teaspoon dried tarragon
3 tablespoons flour	2 teaspoons chopped parsley
½ cup chicken stock *or* broth	1 teaspoon mushroom powder
½ cup heavy cream	¼ teaspoon rosemary
2 cups crabmeat, fresh, frozen, *or* canned	½ teaspoon salt

Melt butter in a saucepan; stir in flour and gradually add chicken stock, stirring constantly. Cook for a few minutes, stirring, and slowly add heavy cream, blending it into the mixture thoroughly. Remove the sauce from the heat and add crabmeat, tarragon, parsley, mushroom powder, rosemary, and salt. Spread the mixture on a platter to cool, form it into small balls, and brown lightly in hot, deep fat. Serve hot with wooden picks to accompany cocktails. Makes about 50 bouchées. Freeze extras to have on hand.

SEVICHE

1 pound of fish, fresh sole *or* flounder
Juice of 12 limes, if not available use 5 California lemons
2 tomatoes, ripe, chopped
¼ onion, chopped
1 green chili pepper, chopped

1 teaspoon oregano
Few strips red pimiento
2 tablespoons chopped parsley
1¼ teaspoons salt
¾ teaspoon white pepper
¼ teaspoon dry mustard
12 small green olives

1 avocado, sliced

Dice raw fish; place in earthenware crock; pour lime (or lemon) juice over, mix rest of ingredients; add and marinate for approximately 2 to 3 hours in refrigerator. Garnish with avocado and pimiento.

STUFFED CELERY

2 bunches celery
Cream Cheese Filling
Blue Cheese Filling

Toast rounds
Paprika
Parsley, chopped

One bunch of celery to be filled with Cream Cheese Filling, one with Blue Cheese Filling.

Keep bunches separate. Wash in iced, salted water; cut off leaves just above stalks. Separate stalks, dry well. Fill stalks of first bunch with Cream Cheese Filling starting with inside heart stalks. As each one is filled, replace it as closely as possible to its natural position in bunch. When all stalks are filled and in place, tie them together, wrap in wax paper and refrigerate at least 1 hour.

Repeat with second bunch filled with Blue Cheese Filling. To serve, cut in ¼-inch rounds and serve on toast rounds; dust cream cheese with paprika and blue cheese with chopped parsley.

Cream Cheese Filling:

1 3-ounce package cream cheese
3 drops Tabasco
¼ teaspoon monosodium glutamate
¼ teaspoon seasoned salt

Mix and blend very well.

Blue Cheese Filling:

¼ pound blue cheese
Pinch cayenne pepper
3 tablespoons butter, softened

Mix and blend very well.

COLD BEEF FILLET MARINARA

1 fillet of beef, about	¾ cup soy sauce
3 to 4 pounds	1 tablespoon Worcestershire
¼ cup olive oil	2 2-ounce cans liver pâté

Marinate beef in olive oil, soy sauce, and Worcestershire for several hours, turning several times. Broil 10 minutes each side (longer if desired). Chill. Spread liver pâté over beef, as if icing cake.

Aspic Garnish (optional):

| 1 package unflavored gelatin | ¼ cup Madeira *or* port |
| 1 can consommé | |

Heat gelatin, wine, and consommé; pour into shallow pan and chill. Cut in strips or cubes and decorate top of pâté-coated beef with this aspic.

SPAGHETTI MISSOURI

1 1-pound package spaghetti	2 pounds ground beef
½ cup cold water	3 10½-ounce cans tomato soup
½ cup butter	1 cup grated Parmesan cheese
1 green pepper, chopped	Salt, red pepper, paprika
2 medium onions, chopped	2 tablespoons Worcestershire
1 pound fresh mushrooms, sliced	Oregano
	Basil

Cook spaghetti 2 minutes less than package directions; blanch in cold water. Melt butter in large skillet; sauté pepper with onions until just glazed. Add mushrooms and sauté a few minutes longer. Pour into well-buttered baking casserole. Place meat in saucepan; add tomato soup, Parmesan cheese, salt, red pepper, paprika, Worcestershire, a pinch of oregano, and basil. Simmer sauce for 2 hours. Mix thoroughly in casserole with mushroom mixture and cooked spaghetti; bake 1 hour in preheated 350° oven.

HOLLYWOOD CHEESECAKE
(Must be prepared at least one day in advance)

1¼ cups graham cracker *or* zwie-	¼ cup granulated sugar
back crumbs, crushed fine	¼ cup melted butter *or* margarine
¼ teaspoon cinnamon (optional)	1 teaspoon unsalted shortening

Remove all ingredients for this cake from refrigerator an hour before preparation. Sift cracker crumbs and cinnamon. Combine with sugar and butter; mix with fork until well blended and moist. Grease 10-inch spring form (without tube) with 1 teaspoon unsalted shortening. Cover sides of pan with about 1 cup of crumb mix, to within 1 inch of top. Pour rest of mix into bottom of pan and with large spoon press down until smooth and compact. Keep in refrigerator or cool place while preparing filling.

First part of Filling:

1 pound cream cheese	3 eggs or 2 large eggs
(2 8-ounce packages)	(½ cup)
½ cup granulated sugar	¾ teaspoon vanilla

Combine cream cheese, sugar, eggs, and vanilla; beat until smooth, about 2 or 3 minutes. Pour into crumb-lined pan, spread uniformly. Bake in preheated 375° oven 20 minutes. Remove from oven, place on cake rack, and let stand at room temperature for about 15 minutes. Raise oven temperature to 475° while preparing second part of filling.

Second part of Filling:

1 pint dairy sour cream	¼ cup granulated sugar
1 teaspoon vanilla	

Mix sour cream, sugar, and vanilla only until well blended. Spoon over cooled, baked first part of filling, starting from side to center. Bake at 475° for about 10 minutes. Remove from oven and let stand at room temperature on cake rack for 5 or 6 hours or until absolutely cold. When filling is cold, loosen sides with spatula, release clamp, and remove rim carefully. Do not cut cake until following day. Cover pan with wax paper and store in coldest part of refrigerator. This cake may then be kept for 3 or 4 days. When ready to serve, cut in wedges and with spatula release carefully from bottom of pan. Should be about 1¼ inches high.

Saturday Morning — Sideboard Morning Coffee

(SERVES 8)

Pitchers of Juices — Orange — Pineapple — Tomato
Kedgeree
Apple Butterhorns   Date Nut Bread
Whipped Cream Cheese

ADVANCE PREPARATION SCHEDULE

Deep Freeze   **Early Morning**

Butterhorns   *Ice juices*
Date Bread   *Whipped Cheese*

KEDGEREE

1 pound dried codfish	4 hard-cooked eggs
4 cups hot cooked fluffy rice (1⅓ cups raw)	2 teaspoons salt
½ cup (¼ pound) butter *or* margarine	⅛ teaspoon pepper, coarsely ground

Soak codfish for 12 hours in water to cover. Drain. Cover with water, bring to a boil, simmer until tender. Drain and flake coarsely. Heat butter in serving skillet, add fish, eggs and rice; toss lightly. Season with salt and pepper. Place over warmer; toss occasionally so rice remains fluffy.

Note: This well-traveled recipe has endured many changes in its contacts. In India as "Kitcheri" it was comprised of rice and lentils. Appropriated in Scotland, it was named "Kedgeree." Our recipe with codfish has a New England accent.

APPLE BUTTERHORNS

1 cake yeast	1 teaspoon lemon rind, grated
½ cup lukewarm milk	1 teaspoon salt
1 cup shortening	2 cups sifted all-purpose flour
¼ cup sugar	¼ cup (⅛ pound) butter, melted
1 egg, beaten	1 cup finely chopped apples
½ cup chopped dates	

Dissolve yeast in warm milk. Melt shortening, add sugar, and cool to lukewarm. Mix in egg, lemon rind, salt, yeast. Beat in flour, and refrigerate overnight. Roll three 9-inch circles. Spread with melted butter, chopped apples, and dates. Cut each circle into 8 pie-shaped wedges; moisten edges with warm water and roll each wedge toward point, making horns. Cover. Let rise in warm place 2½ hours, or until doubled in bulk. Bake in a preheated 375° oven 12 to 15 minutes. Frost while warm with Confectioners' Icing.

Confectioners' Icing:
Blend confectioners' sugar and water.

DATE NUT BREAD

1 cup chopped dates	2 eggs
¾ cup chopped nuts	½ teaspoon vanilla
¼ teaspoon soda	½ cup granulated sugar
¾ teaspoon salt	1¾ cups all-purpose flour
¼ cup butter, melted	¼ cup brown sugar, firmly packed
¾ cup boiling water	1½ teaspoons baking powder

Combine dates, nuts, soda, and salt in a mixing bowl; add butter and water; allow to stand for 15 minutes, stirring to blend; combine eggs, vanilla, and granulated sugar. Sift flour, brown sugar, and baking powder together and add to egg mixture; blend in dates and nuts, but do not mix any more than necessary. Grease an 8″ x 4″ x 3″ loaf pan, line with wax paper, and grease again; fill with batter. Bake in a preheated 350° oven 50 to 60 minutes. When done, toothpick inserted in center will come out clean. Cool before removing. Loosen sides with spatula and turn out on rack. To slice perfectly, allow loaf to stand several hours.

This bread remains moist for several days (if it lasts that long) and freezes well. May also be used for sandwiches, sliced thin, with cream cheese.

WHIPPED CREAM CHEESE

1 8-ounce package cream cheese,   ½ cup dairy sour cream
softened

Place cheese and sour cream in blender or mixing bowl. Whirl
quickly until light and smooth. Pile lightly in decorative bowl.

Saturday Luncheon

(SERVES 8)

Skillet Tuna

Cucumber Relish Mold — Anchovy Beets

Parmesan Bread

Plum Dumplings

Coffee   Tea

ADVANCE PREPARATION SCHEDULE

Previous Day	Early Morning
Cucumber Mold	*Tuna (without sherry)*
	Prepare bread
	Prepare dumplings
	Anchovy Beets

SKILLET TUNA

2 tablespoons butter
¼ pound fresh mushrooms
1 tablespoon minced onion
1 10-ounce can cream of
  mushroom soup
½ cup milk
2 7-ounce cans tuna fish
1 6½-ounce can water
  chestnuts, sliced

1 10-ounce package frozen peas,
  cooked
2 tablespoons sliced pimiento
1 tablespoon chopped chives
¼ teaspoon black pepper
½ teaspoon salt
1 teaspoon Worcestershire
3 tablespoons sherry

Melt butter in 10-inch skillet; sauté mushrooms and onions; stir milk into soup gradually and add; heat thoroughly. Drain tuna, break into chunks; add chestnuts, peas, pimiento, chives, pepper, salt, and Worcestershire. Just before serving stir in the sherry and reheat. Serve over rice or toast points.

CUCUMBER RELISH MOLD

2 tablespoons unflavored gelatin
1½ cups cold water
2 tablespoons instant minced onion
2 teaspoons salt
2 teaspoons sugar
2 cups grated cucumber
2 cups dairy sour cream
4 tablespoons prepared horseradish
4 tablespoons vinegar
3 hard-cooked eggs

Soften gelatin in cold water in medium saucepan; stir in onion, salt, and sugar. Heat just to boiling; remove from heat, stir to dissolve gelatin completely. Cool. Stir in grated cucumber, sour cream, horseradish, and vinegar. Pour into a greased 6-cup mold and chill in refrigerator for at least 4 hours. Unmold on a bed of torn greens of your choice; garnish with Anchovy Beets and quartered hard-cooked eggs.

ANCHOVY BEETS

1 #1 can whole baby beets   1 2-ounce can rolled anchovies

Drain beets; scoop out centers of each beet with a small melon ball cutter or knife. Drain anchovies; place one in hollow of each beet.

PARMESAN BREAD

2 cups warm water (105° to 115°)
2 packages active dry yeast
2 tablespoons sugar
2 teaspoons salt
2 tablespoons butter or margarine, softened
½ cup plus 1 tablespoon grated Parmesan cheese
1½ tablespoons dried oregano leaves
4¼ cups sifted all-purpose flour

If possible, check temperature of warm water with a thermometer. Sprinkle yeast over water in large bowl of electric mixer. Let stand for a few minutes; then stir to dissolve yeast. Add sugar, salt, butter,

½ cup cheese, oregano, and 3 cups flour. Beat at low speed until blended; at medium speed 2 minutes, until smooth. Scrape bowl and beaters; using a wooden spoon, gradually beat in remainder of flour. Cover the bowl with wax paper and a towel. Let rise in a warm place (85°) free from drafts for 45 minutes, or until quite light, bubbly, and more than double in bulk. Grease a 1½- or 2-quart casserole lightly; set aside; stir down batter. Beat vigorously ½ minute, or about 25 strokes. Turn into casserole and sprinkle evenly with 1 tablespoon grated cheese. Bake in a preheated 375° oven, 55 minutes, or until nicely browned. Turn out onto wire rack to cool, or serve slightly warm, in wedges. Makes 1 round loaf.

PLUM DUMPLINGS

10 fresh plums *or* 1 #2½ can plums, drained
10 cubes sugar (dots) for fresh plums
2 cups all-purpose flour
3 tablespoons butter
2 cups riced, cooked potatoes, chilled
1 teaspoon salt
2 eggs
¼ cup melted butter
¾ cup bread crumbs

Drain canned plums, or slit fresh plums and remove pits. Insert a cube of sugar in fresh plums. Combine flour and butter with knives or pastry blender until the consistency of cornmeal. Add potatoes and salt and stir in eggs. Knead dough well, until smooth. Roll out on floured board to ¼-inch thickness. Cut in 2½-inch squares. Place a plum on each square, moisten edges, and pinch opposite corners together to enclose plum. Drop gently into large kettle of boiling water and cook 10 minutes in a continuous boil. Separate dumplings if they stick together while boiling. Heat melted butter in skillet, add bread crumbs, blend, and brown lightly; add dumplings. Coat well; serve with sugar.

Variation:

Use cooked dried apricots.

Saturday Dinner

(SERVES 8)

Salmon Caviar Rolls   Chopped Liver Roll
Cocktail Rye
Turkey La Prise — Mushroom Rice Dressing
Mandarin Orange Compote in Orange Shells
Ratatouille   Bowknot Rolls
Angel Torte   Coffee

Suggested wine: Sauterne

ADVANCE PREPARATION SCHEDULE

Deep Freeze	Previous Day	Early Morning
Rolls	*Liver Roll*	*Salmon Rolls*
	Orange Compote Shells	*Dressing*
	Compote dressing	*Arrange vegetables*
	Angel Torte, unfrosted	*Bowknot Rolls (see Index)*

SALMON CAVIAR ROLLS

12 thin slices smoked salmon   4 tablespoons chopped ripe olives
1 2-ounce can domestic caviar   Lemon slice — sprig watercress

Cut sliced salmon into about 3-inch lengths. Mix caviar with ripe olives. Heap a teaspoon in center of each slice. Roll and chill. Garnish with lemon slices and a sprig of watercress tucked in one end.

CHOPPED LIVER ROLL

1 pound calves' liver, sliced   1 tablespoon mayonnaise
2 tablespoons chicken fat *or* butter   ¼ teaspoon black pepper
2 small onions   1 teaspoon salt
2 hard-cooked eggs   Stuffed green olives, sliced
4 tablespoons chicken fat *or* butter   Sprigs parsley
1 loaf sliced cocktail rye bread

Gently sauté liver in 2 tablespoons shortening, about 5 minutes on each side; cool. Grind liver, add onions, eggs; grind again. Add 4 tablespoons fat, mayonnaise, salt, and pepper; blend thoroughly. Shape into a long roll approximately 1½ inches in diameter (as for icebox cookies) but slightly oval to conform to loaf of cocktail rye bread. Wrap in foil and refrigerate. To serve, remove foil and place on platter with whole sliced loaf of bread alongside. Top liver with round of stuffed green olive rings; garnish abundantly with parsley. Each guest slices his own portion to be placed on a piece of the bread.

TURKEY LA PRISE

1 tablespoon salt	1 teaspoon seasoning salt
½ teaspoon ground pepper	1 15- to 18-pound turkey
2 teaspoons paprika	¼ to ½ cup shortening

Combine salt, pepper, paprika, and seasoning salt; rub into turkey inside and out. Fill cavity loosely with Mushroom Rice Dressing; skewer and lace opening. Place in roasting pan, coat well with shortening and place in a preheated 350° oven; baste every 20 minutes with additional shortening; roast 2½ hours or until tender. When thigh is soft to the touch, turkey is done. Remove and allow to stand ½ hour before carving. Place on large platter, garnish with Mandarin Orange Compote in Orange Shells on crisp sprigs of parsley. Place before the host for his carving pleasure. Be certain the tools are sharp.

MUSHROOM RICE DRESSING

Liver and gizzard of turkey	¾ pound mushrooms, sliced
6 tablespoons shortening	1½ teaspoons pepper
2 onions, chopped	4½ cups cooked brown rice

Grind liver and gizzard; melt shortening, add onions, and sauté slowly for 10 minutes, stirring frequently. Add mushrooms, sauté for 10 minutes and remove from pan. Set aside. Place ground liver and gizzard in saucepan; sauté for 5 minutes. Combine with onions, mushrooms, salt, pepper, and rice. Stuff turkey lightly, and lace with pins and string.

Turkey Gravy:

½ cup cold water	2 tablespoons butter, melted
2 tablespoons flour	1 teaspoon gravy browner

Deglaze roasting pan with cold water, loosening all the flavorful drippings. Make a paste of flour, butter, and gravy browner, adding pan drippings if needed. Return to pan; heat and stir until smooth and slightly thickened. Makes about 2 cups.

MANDARIN ORANGE COMPOTE IN SHELLS

1 large *or* 2 small fresh pineapples	1 pint dairy sour cream
4 11-ounce cans *or* 4 packages frozen mandarin oranges, drained	½ cup flaked coconut
1 8-ounce package marshmallow miniatures	Parsley sprigs

Peel and core pineapple; cut into bite-sized pieces. Combine with mandarin oranges. Refrigerate. Combine marshmallows with sour cream and refrigerate overnight. Next day, beat thoroughly. To serve, combine with pineapple and oranges, add coconut, toss lightly and serve in Orange Shells. Border turkey and add crisp parsley for contrast.

ORANGE SHELLS

Cut 4 oranges in sharp angles through center so that halves separate in saw-tooth edge points. Remove pulp carefully. Shells will be serving receptacles for compote.

Use orange sections for breakfast following morning.

RATATOUILLE (VEGETABLE CASSEROLE)

¼ cup olive oil	5 small zucchini, sliced ¼ inch thick
1 clove garlic, minced	
3 onions, sliced thin	5 small tomatoes, sliced thin
4 green peppers, sliced thin	1 teaspoon salt
1 eggplant, sliced ¼ inch thick	⅛ teaspoon coarsely ground pepper
1 teaspoon olive oil	

Heat ¼ cup olive oil in 2-quart saucepan; add garlic and sauté for

3 minutes. Remove from heat and place vegetables in pan in layers; sprinkle each layer with salt and pepper; add 1 teaspoon olive oil on top. Simmer, covered, over low heat for 30 to 35 minutes, gently moving contents from time to time. Cook uncovered for final 10 minutes to reduce sauce. Serve hot or cold.

ANGEL TORTE

4 egg whites	1 cup sugar
¼ teaspoon salt	1 teaspoon vanilla
¼ teaspoon cream of tartar	1 teaspoon vinegar
	½ cup chopped pecans

Remove egg whites from refrigerator 1 hour before using and place in large bowl of electric mixer. Beat until foamy, add salt and cream of tartar. Add sugar slowly, while beating at medium speed; add vanilla and vinegar and beat until stiff. Fold in pecans. Place aluminum foil on cooky sheet, grease and mark two 9-inch circles. Turn meringue within circles, place in a preheated 275° oven and bake 45 minutes. Loosen meringues from foil. Set one meringue on flat plate, spread with half of filling, cover with second meringue and second half of filling. Refrigerate overnight. To serve, frost with whipped cream and garnish with chocolate curls.

Filling:

½ pound sweet baking chocolate	1½ cups heavy cream, whipped
⅛ teaspoon salt	½ cup heavy cream, whipped, for
¾ cup strong brewed coffee	decoration (optional)
2 tablespoons cognac	

Place chocolate, salt, and coffee in saucepan; heat, stirring, until chocolate melts; add cognac and stir until smooth. Cool, fold in 1½ cups whipped cream. Spread on layers. Refrigerate. Decorate with chocolate curls, made by shaving chocolate from a bar with a vegetable peeler. Use ½ cup heavy cream, whipped, for decor.

Late Tête-à-Tête

(SERVES 8)

Orange Apricot Ring

Fresh Fruit Garni   Strawberry Rose Dressing

Cheese Platter   Apples

Herb crackers   Sesame crackers

French bread

Zwieback Cookies   Butterhorns   Coffee Brownies

Sanka or Brandy

Suggested wine: red Burgundy or a California Pinot Noir

ADVANCE PREPARATION SCHEDULE

Previous Day	Early Morning
Orange Apricot Ring	*Dressing*
Zwieback Cookies	*Fruit*
Butterhorns	
Coffee Brownies	

ORANGE APRICOT RING

1 #2½ can apricots, drained
3¾ cups liquid, comprised of:
   Juice from apricots,
   1 6-ounce can frozen orange
     juice, defrosted
   Sufficient water

2 tablespoons unflavored gelatin
2 tablespoons cognac
1 8-ounce package cream cheese,
   softened
2 tablespoons cream

Refrigerate drained apricots. Combine liquids; pour ½ cup in small saucepan and add gelatin. Place over heat and stir until dissolved; blend into remainder of liquid. Pour half into oiled 6-cup mold; refrigerate until of jelly-like consistency. Place apricots rounded side down in mold; if there are extras, make a second row. Place in refrigerator to set. Add cognac to second half of liquid, reserving 2 tablespoons, then place in refrigerator until of jelly-like consistency. Mix cream cheese and cream with 2 tablespoons of uncongealed reserved liquid; then blend well. When mold with apricots is set, spread a layer of the cheese mixture, then cover with second half of gelatin mixture. Set in refrigerator until firm, about 2 hours.

STRAWBERRY ROSE DRESSING

1 3-ounce package cream cheese
⅓ cup orange juice, fresh *or* frozen
1 tablespoon lemon *or* lime juice
1 tablespoon honey
Dash salt
1 cup strawberries, fresh *or* frozen

Mash cream cheese with a fork until softened. Gradually add orange juice, lemon or lime juice, honey, and salt. With rotary beater or blender, beat in sieved pulp of strawberries. Makes 1½ cups.

FRESH FRUIT GARNI

1 honeydew melon
¼ watermelon
1 Cranshaw melon *and/or*
1 cantaloupe
1 quart strawberries
1 pint blueberries

Place honeydew balls in center of apricot ring. Arrange short spokes of watermelon, Cranshaw and/or cantaloupe, sliced with serrated knife, around the mold; intersperse with unhulled strawberries and dot with blueberries.

CHEESE PLATTER

Serve cheese at room temperature to best savor its texture and flavor. For variety, arrange alternate wedges of Port de Salut and Danish Tilsit around red Dutch Edam. Serve with unsalted crackers and French bread. For eye appeal, place paper doilies on serving tray and cover with transparent wax paper cut to conform to tray. Without the paper, the doilies would only have nuisance value.

ZWIEBACK COOKIES

6 egg whites
¾ cup sugar
1 cup all-purpose flour
1 teaspoon baking powder
½ cup plus 1 tablespoon
butter, melted

½ teaspoon vanilla
¼ cup chopped, blanched
almonds *or* toasted filberts
Powdered *or* Vanilla Sugar

Beat egg whites very stiff and add sugar. Sift flour and baking powder; add alternately with melted butter; then stir in vanilla and nuts. Bake in buttered, floured loaf pan 35 to 40 minutes in a preheated 350° oven or until light golden brown. When cool, remove from pan and allow to stand overnight. Cut in thin slices and roll each in powdered sugar or Vanilla Sugar. Spread pieces on cooky sheets and bake in 300° oven until golden brown.

Vanilla Sugar:

2 vanilla beans   1 pound granulated sugar

Place in a covered jar and let stand for one week. The flavor of the beans lasts for six months and the sugar may be replenished during that time. The flavor of vanilla sugar is exceptional and may be used wherever sugar and vanilla are indicated. 1 tablespoon sugar contains the equivalent of ¼ teaspoon vanilla. Adjust ingredients of recipe accordingly.

BUTTERHORNS

1 cake compressed yeast
1 tablespoon sugar
¼ cup warm water
1 cup (½ pound) butter
3 cups sifted all-purpose flour
1 teaspoon salt

¾ cup lukewarm half and half
cream
3 egg yolks, well beaten
¾ cup thick preserves (approximately), strawberry, cherry,
or your choice

Combine yeast and sugar in a small bowl, add water and stir until dissolved. In a large bowl combine butter, flour, and salt; blend with 2 knives or pastry cutter until dough resembles coarse cornmeal. Add yeast mixture, then cream, and mix very well. Beat in egg yolks. Cover and allow to stand free from drafts for ½ hour. Place in refrigerator overnight.

Divide dough in 4 portions. Roll each portion into a circle and cut into 8 wedges. Place 1 teaspoon preserves on wide end of each wedge; roll from wide end to point and shape into crescent. Place on buttered cooky sheet, cover and stand in warm place, free from drafts; let rise about an hour. Preheat oven to 400°; bake rolls for about 25 minutes.

Variation:

Make half of dough into crescents. Use other half for:

MERINGUE COFFEE CAKE

3 egg whites 1 teaspoon vanilla
¾ cup sugar ½ cup chopped pecans

Beat egg whites until stiff but not dry; add sugar and vanilla, beat until very stiff. Roll out second half of dough into large circle, spread with meringue, and sprinkle with chopped nuts. Roll (tuck in sides of dough before rolling) and shape into a large crescent. Place on greased cooky sheet. Cut through dough at 1½-inch intervals ⅔ to opposite side of crescent. Turn each portion on its side at outside edge to make a large swirl. Cover. Let rise 1 hour in warm place until double in bulk. Bake in a preheated 375° oven 25 to 30 minutes. Cool; sprinkle with powdered sugar.

Note: This dough cannot be kept under refrigeration as it becomes too flaky and tender. Bake it at once, and freeze the excess.

COFFEE BROWNIES

4 1-ounce squares chocolate 4 eggs
1 cup (½ pound) butter 2 cups sugar
1 tablespoon instant coffee 1 cup all-purpose flour
1 cup chopped nuts

Melt chocolate with butter and cool; add instant coffee. Beat eggs with sugar and flour; add nuts. Combine all ingredients. Pour into greased 13″ × 9″ × 2″ baking pan. Bake 25 to 30 minutes in a preheated 350° oven in 8″ square pan.

Sunday Supper — For the Road

(SERVES 8)

Bloody Marys   Orange Blossoms

Fruit Cup

Turkey Asperge   Escarole Bowl — Curry French Dressing

Harvest Moon Cake   Coffee

ADVANCE PREPARATION SCHEDULE

Deep Freeze   **Early Morning**

Cake   *Frost cake*
                Curry French Dressing
                Wash greens
                Cook asparagus

FRUIT CUP

No doubt there will be fruit and apricot ring left from the "Late Tête-à-Tête" evening menu. We suggest this fruit and the orange sections removed from the orange shells of the previous dinner be used for individual fruit cups combined with any berries in season.

TURKEY ASPERGE

5 tablespoons flour	1½ cups turkey *or* chicken broth
1 teaspoon salt	½ cup grated American cheese
¼ teaspoon onion salt	1½ cups cooked asparagus spears
¼ cup melted butter	8 slices turkey
2½ cups milk *or* light cream	2 tablespoons toasted,
1⅓ cups instant rice	slivered almonds

Stir flour, ½ teaspoon of salt, and onion salt into butter; add milk. Cook over low heat, stirring constantly until thickened. Pour rice into 2-quart shallow baking dish. Add remaining ½ teaspoon salt to broth; pour over rice, with ¼ cup cheese. Top with asparagus; next, layer the turkey and cover with sauce. Sprinkle with remaining ¼ cup cheese. Bake in a preheated 375° oven, for about 20 minutes. Top with almonds.

This, of course, may be made with leftover turkey from Saturday's dinner.

ESCAROLE BOWL

2 quarts escarole

Tear greens; place in bowl and toss with Curry French Dressing.

CURRY FRENCH DRESSING

½ teaspoon curry powder	1 teaspoon salt
½ cup salad oil	2 teaspoons sugar
5 tablespoons malt vinegar	½ teaspoon paprika
½ teaspoon grated onion	

Let stand at least ½ hour. Mix well. Makes ¾ cup.

HARVEST MOON CAKE

2 cups sifted cake flour	¾ cup brown sugar, firmly packed
2 teaspoons baking powder	2 egg yolks, unbeaten
¼ teaspoon salt	⅔ cup milk
⅓ cup butter	1 teaspoon vanilla

Sift flour once, measure, add baking powder and salt; sift together 3 times. Cream butter thoroughly, add sugar gradually, and cream together until light and fluffy. Add egg yolks; beat well. Alternate flour with milk, a small amount at a time, beating after each addition until smooth. Add vanilla, and bake in greased 8″ x 8″ x 2″ pan in a preheated 350° oven 45 minutes, or until done when tested. Spread with Harvest Moon Frosting.

Harvest Moon Frosting:

2 egg whites, unbeaten	Dash salt
1 cup brown sugar, firmly packed	¼ cup water
1 teaspoon vanilla	

Put egg whites, sugar, salt, and water in top of double boiler. Beat with rotary egg beater until thoroughly mixed. Place over rapidly boiling water, beating constantly while cooking for 7 minutes, or until frosting stands in peaks. If electric beater is used, 2 minutes is sufficient time. Remove from heat; add vanilla and beat until thick enough to spread. After covering cake with frosting, draw tip of silver knife in parallel lines across top, to form pattern.

SPORTS EVENTS

Brunch Before the "Double Header"

(SERVES 6)

Gimlets

Melon Platter

Lobster Omelet

Cornbread   Strawberry Preserves

Zucchini Salad

Chocolate Yeast Cake

Coffee

Suggested wine: Rosé

ADVANCE PREPARATION SCHEDULE

Deep Freeze	Previous Day	Early Morning
Chocolate Yeast Cake, unfilled	*Chocolate Yeast Cake, unfilled* (or *deep freeze*)	*Prepare melon*
Cornbread		*Lobster filling*
	Strawberry Preserves (*see Index*)	*Cornbread* (or *deep freeze*)
		Zucchini
		Fill cake

MELON PLATTER

1 small honeydew melon	1 cantaloupe
⅛ watermelon	1 pint blueberries

Cut honeydew and watermelon with French cutter into 4-inch slices. Stak 3 slices of each and place alternately around Melon Basket in center of platter.

Melon Basket:

With a sharp paring knife, make a diagonal 1½-inch gash through center of cantaloupe. Next cut in opposite direction to form a triangle. Repeat completely around center of melon. Force halves apart. Discard seeds and remove melon with ball cutter, leaving shell to form basket. Refill with melon balls, and garnish with blueberries.

LOBSTER OMELET

Filling:

3 4-ounce frozen rock lobster	1 cup milk
tails, *or*	½ pound fresh mushrooms, sliced
1 7-ounce can lobster	2 tablespoons butter
¼ cup (⅛ pound) butter	¼ teaspoon salt
2 tablespoons flour	Paprika

Drop lobster tails into boiling, salted water (½ teaspoon salt to each cup of water). When water comes to a boil again, simmer tails just 2 minutes. Drain immediately and drench with cold water. Cut away thin membrane from underside of tails, remove meat from shells. Dice lobster meat. Melt butter in saucepan; stir in flour and cook 1 minute. Add milk; cook and stir until slightly thickened. Sauté mushrooms in 2 tablespoons butter for 5 minutes; add salt, paprika, and diced lobster meat. Heat thoroughly. Pour over omelet.

Omelet:

5 eggs, separated	½ teaspoon salt
5 tablespoons milk	2 tablespoons butter

Beat egg yolks with milk and salt until creamy. Beat egg whites until very stiff; fold into yolks. Melt butter in a 12-inch skillet or omelet pan. Pour in egg mixture. Bake in a preheated 400° oven

8 minutes, or until browned on top. When omelet is done, pour hot lobster filling over top. Fold omelet in half over filling and gently slide out of pan onto heated platter.

CORNBREAD

1 cup white cornmeal	2 eggs
3 tablespoons flour	½ cup (¼ pound) butter *or*
4 teaspoons baking powder	margarine
½ cup milk	⅓ teaspoon salt

Sift cornmeal, flour, baking powder, and salt together; add milk and unbeaten eggs. Melt butter and add when cooled. Pour into 8″ x 8″ x 2″ greased pan; bake in a preheated 425° oven 25 minutes. Serve hot. May be reheated if baked earlier.

ZUCCHINI SALAD

6 fresh zucchini, sliced thin

Marinate sliced zucchini in Vinaigrette Dressing, chill and serve on individual salad plates.

Vinaigrette Dressing:

½ cup wine vinegar	1 tablespoon finely chopped
1 cup salad oil	parsley
1 teaspoon salt	2 tablespoons sweet pickle relish
½ teaspoon Worcestershire	1 tablespoon finely chopped chives
½ teaspoon dry mustard	*or* 1 teaspoon grated onion
⅛ teaspoon freshly ground pepper	

Mix ingredients thoroughly. Add to sliced zucchini and toss lightly.

CHOCOLATE YEAST CAKE

¾ cup milk
¼ cup warm water
1 ¼-ounce package active dry yeast
1 tablespoon sugar
3 cups sifted all-purpose flour
¾ cup soft butter *or* margarine
2 cups sugar
⅔ cup cocoa

½ cup hot water
3 eggs, beaten
1 teaspoon baking soda
½ teaspoon salt
¼ teaspoon nutmeg
¼ teaspoon cinnamon
½ teaspoon vanilla
1 cup chopped pecans

Scald milk; cool to lukewarm. Place warm water (110° to 115°) in large mixing bowl. Add yeast and stir until dissolved; then lukewarm milk, 1 tablespoon sugar and 2 cups flour; beat until smooth. Cover with clean towel and let rise in a warm place about 45 minutes, or until mixture is light and spongy. Cream butter with 2 cups sugar and set aside. Combine cocoa and hot water, stirring until smooth. Cool to lukewarm and blend with the sugar and yeast mixtures. Beat in eggs and the remaining 1 cup flour, baking soda, salt, nutmeg, cinnamon, and vanilla. Beat by hand 10 minutes, or electric mixer set at low speed, 6 minutes. When smooth, stir in pecans. Turn into well-greased 10-inch tube pan. Let rise in a warm place about 2 hours, or until doubled in bulk. Bake in a preheated 350° oven 45 minutes or until done. When slightly cool, turn out on wire rack, and let stand until cold.

Filling:

2 cups cold half and half cream, *or* 1 cup milk and 1 cup heavy cream

1 3¼-ounce package instant vanilla pudding
1 tablespoon instant coffee
Confectioners' sugar

About half an hour before serving, pour cold half and half cream into deep mixing bowl; add instant pudding and coffee; mix well with rotary beater about 1 minute; let stand. Split cake carefully into 3 layers on serving plate and fill with pudding. Sift confectioners' sugar over top and sides. (Serves 10 to 12.)

Note: Store leftover cake in refrigerator; however, a whipped cream filling is more attractive when served immediately.

Winter Sports Brunch

(SERVES 8)

Hot Rum Bowl   Dubonnet
Sliced Smoked Sturgeon   Thin Pumpernickel
Crown Cheese Soufflé   Spiced Orange Wedges
Old Wives' Coffee Cake
Coffee

ADVANCE PREPARATION SCHEDULE

Deep Freeze	Previous Day	Early Morning
Coffee Cake	*Orange Wedges*	*Prepare soufflé container*

SLICED SMOKED STURGEON

1 pound smoked sturgeon,   1 lemon, sliced
   sliced thin   1 tablespoon chopped parsley
                  Paprika

Cut sliced sturgeon into squares of about 1½ inches. Place in over-lapping rows on serving plate. Garnish with lemon slices; sprinkle lightly with parsley and paprika.

CROWN CHEESE SOUFFLE

½ cup (¼ pound) butter *or*   ½ cup heavy cream
   margarine   2 cups grated natural Swiss
1 cup all-purpose flour   cheese
2½ teaspoons salt   ½ cup snipped fresh chives
¼ teaspoon pepper   8 eggs, separated
⅛ teaspoon nutmeg   9 slices white bread (about)
2 cups milk   6 lean bacon slices

Melt butter in large saucepan; stir in flour, salt, pepper, and nutmeg. Add milk and cream, blending slowly and thoroughly. While cooking, stir constantly, until smooth and thickened. Reserve 2 tablespoons of the grated cheese. Blend in remainder of cheese; add chives and stir egg yolks into mixture, one at a time. Cool slightly. Butter a china soufflé or casserole dish which measures 10 cups to brim. Line bottom of dish with about 3 bread slices cut to fit. Cut 6 more bread slices in half lengthwise; place them upright and side by side, in a circle around inner edge of dish. Lace a strip of bacon, in figure-eight fashion, around each 2 slices. Fold a 35-inch length of aluminum foil, 12 inches wide, in half lengthwise; wrap around outside of dish, so that a collar 3 inches high stands above rim; fasten with cellophane tape. Beat egg whites stiff; carefully fold into cooled cheese mixture, and pour into soufflé dish. Sprinkle with reserved grated cheese. Bake in a preheated 350° oven 1 hour and 40 minutes, or until golden. Carefully remove foil collar and serve at once.

SLICED ORANGE WEDGES

4 oranges, unpeeled	2 cups sugar
1¼ cups water	½ cup vinegar
½ teaspoon soda	12 whole cloves
3 pieces stick cinnamon	

Cover oranges with water; add soda, and bring to a boil, reduce heat and simmer 20 minutes, or until easily pierced with a fork. Drain; cut in eighths. Combine in saucepan: sugar, water, vinegar; cloves and cinnamon. Simmer over low heat until sugar is dissolved, then boil rapidly 5 minutes. Add orange wedges and simmer about 20 minutes. Cool, cover, and refrigerate.

OLD WIVES' COFFEE CAKE

1 cake compressed yeast	¼ cup mashed potatoes
2 tablespoons lukewarm water (for dry yeast, use *warm* water)	¾ cup potato liquid (from boiled potato)
1 cup (½ pound) butter, melted	1 teaspoon vanilla
½ cup sugar	4 cups all-purpose flour
2 eggs, well beaten	1 teaspoon salt

Dissolve yeast in lukewarm water. Cream butter and sugar until very smooth. Use no less than a 2-quart bowl. Add yeast, combined eggs, potato, and potato liquid, half of each at a time, beating well with a wooden spoon after each addition. Add vanilla. Sift flour and salt together, beat in 1 cup at a time, and when all is added, beat for 2 minutes. The batter will be quite moist. Brush with oil or melted butter; cover and place in refrigerator overnight. In the morning, remove ½ of dough and place on well-floured board. Roll with floured rolling pin to a rectangle 18 by 14 inches. Spread with ½ Filling ingredients (see below): first spread with butter, then with nuts, raisins, cinnamon and sugar. Roll from the longer side into a roll, seam side down. Seal ends and place in a circle in 4 cup ring or 9″ baking pan. Cover and let stand in warm (85°) temperature, away from drafts for 2 hours and 15 minutes. Repeat with second half of dough, to make 2 rings. Bake in preheated oven 350°, 45 to 55 minutes. Remove to racks and spread with confectioners' frosting.

Cake Filling:

¼ cup melted butter	½ cup white *or* dark raisins
½ cup nuts, coarsely chopped pecans *or* walnuts	1½ teaspoons ground cinnamon
	¼ cup sugar

If raisins are dry, soak in boiling water for 15 minutes. Drain. Mix well.

Confectioners' Frosting:

1 cup sifted confectioners' sugar	½ teaspoon vanilla *or*
2 tablespoons warm milk	lemon juice
½ teaspoon grated lemon rind (optional)	

Drizzle over cake while still warm. One large cake may be baked instead of two. Rolled dough will be thicker.

Old Wives' Coffee Cake recognizes the merit of old-fashioned cooking and use of the herbs and concoctions of our early days, as witness the use of the potatoes and liquid in this recipe. Our young wives may happily hark back to our many inheritances of the kitchen. Incidentally, our hostess who contributed this claims it to be "a great cake."

Luncheon — Set Sail

(SERVES 8 TO 10)

Beet Borsch en Gelée

Shrimp Louis — Pineapple Garni   Spinach Ring

Port du Salut and Flatbread

Fruit Blitz Torte

ADVANCE PREPARATION SCHEDULE

Previous Day	Early Morning
Dressing	*Filling for cake*
Bake cake	
Beet Borsch	
Shrimp	
Spinach mold	
Flatbread	

BEET BORSCH EN GELEE

2 #2½ cans sliced *or* whole beets   2 tablespoons sugar
2 cans water   Juice of 3 lemons
1 teaspoon salt   2 envelopes (2 tablespoons)
1 whole onion   unflavored gelatin
2 eggs, beaten   ½ cup dairy sour cream
3 ounces caviar (black or red) *or* chopped chives

Pour beets and liquid of 1 can of beets, plus liquid from second can of beets, into kettle (reserving ½ cup); add water, salt, and onion; simmer 20 minutes. Combine eggs, sugar, lemon juice, and gelatin. Let stand a minimum of 5 minutes. Strain beet liquid into egg mixture, stirring constantly. Beat well with electric mixer or rotary beater. Chill. Garnish with sour cream, 1 tablespoon for each serving, topped with caviar or chopped chives. Though imported caviar is very special, our domestic variety serves the purpose. Remember to drain domestic caviar well.

SHRIMP LOUIS

3 pounds shrimp, cooked   1 #2½ can sliced pineapple
2 heads Bibb lettuce

Make a border of Bibb lettuce; place pineapple rings on lettuce around spinach mold, and then place shrimps on top of pineapple. Serve with Louis Dressing.

Louis Dressing:

1½ cups chili sauce	1 cup mayonnaise
¼ cup chopped celery	1 teaspoon lemon juice
¼ cup chopped sour pickles	½ teaspoon Worcestershire
½ cup finely chopped hard-boiled eggs	2 tablespoons chopped parsley

Blend ingredients well. Makes 3½ cups.

SPINACH RING

1 3-ounce package lemon-flavored gelatin	1 cup hot water
½ teaspoon salt	1 cup cold water
⅛ teaspoon pepper	1 cup small-curd cottage cheese
2 teaspoons lemon juice	1 cup mayonnaise
1 teaspoon cider vinegar	¾ cup chopped celery
	1½ cups finely chopped spinach

Blend together gelatin, salt, pepper, lemon juice, vinegar, and dissolve in hot water. Add cold water; cool, and refrigerate until of syrup-like consistency. Beat in cottage cheese and mayonnaise; fold in celery and spinach. Pour into a greased 6-cup mold and refrigerate for several hours until firm. Unmold on a bed of greens, as indicated in recipe for Shrimp Louis.

Serve with a platter of Port du Salut Cheese and Flatbread.

PORT DU SALUT

Cheese and green salad are very compatible, and Brie, Camembert, or Swiss Gruyère are always favorites. Add this combination in other menus for deserved approval.

FLATBREAD

2 cups sifted all-purpose flour	½ teaspoon salt
½ cup yellow cornmeal	¼ cup butter
⅔ cup warm water	

Sift flour again with cornmeal and salt. Combine butter with pastry blender until crumbly; stir in warm water, chill 1 hour. Remove from refrigerator and form into marble-sized balls. Roll each into paper-thin 4-inch rounds. Place on ungreased cooky sheet and bake in a preheated 375° oven 5 minutes, or until lightly browned. Cool. Makes 90 wafers.

Stored in tightly covered containers, they will keep for some time.

FRUIT BLITZ TORTE

½ cup butter *or* margarine
½ cup sugar
4 egg yolks
1 teaspoon vanilla
1 cup all-purpose flour
1 teaspoon baking powder
3 tablespoons milk
4 egg whites

¾ cup sugar
½ cup chopped almonds *or* pecans
1 cup heavy cream, beaten stiff
2 cups sliced peaches *or* strawberries, sugared and drained (drained frozen fruit may be used)

Cream butter; beat in ½ cup sugar, egg yolks, and vanilla gradually. Sift flour and baking powder together; add alternately with milk. Spread mixture in two 9-inch loose-bottom cake pans. Whip egg whites until stiff but not dry; add ¾ cup sugar gradually. Spread ½ of meringue over batter in each pan. Sprinkle with chopped nuts and bake in a preheated 350° oven 35 minutes. Cool on a rack. About ½ hour before serving, add fruit to stiffly beaten cream and spread thickly between layers of cake. Refrigerate until ready to serve.

Variation:

Omit fruit filling and replace with scoops of assorted flavors of ice cream. Frost Torte with whipped cream, garnish with berries.

19th Hole Luncheon

(SERVES 12)

Chilled Tomato Cream Soup   Melba Toast
Della Robbia Fruit Salad Platter   Poppy-Seed Dressing
Sandwich Loaf au Gratin
Vienna Slices
Coffee

Suggested wine: Rosé

ADVANCE PREPARATION SCHEDULE

Deep Freeze	Previous Day	Early Morning
Vienna Slices	*Tomato Cream Soup*	*Prepare fruit*
	Poppy-Seed Dressing	*Prepare sandwich*

CHILLED TOMATO CREAM SOUP

6 ripe tomatoes, sliced thin
6 small green onions, bulbs and tops, chopped fine
1 clove garlic, minced
¼ teaspoon dried basil
½ teaspoon salt
⅛ teaspoon ground pepper
2 tablespoons tomato paste
3 tablespoons flour
2 10½-ounce cans chicken broth
3 ounces dry sherry

Combine tomatoes, onions, garlic, basil, salt, and pepper. Cook gently for 10 minutes or until tomatoes are tender. Combine tomato paste and flour; blend well. While stirring constantly, add broth and sherry until mixture comes to a boil. Cool and refrigerate for at least 3 hours. Serve small portions, topped with sour cream mixture; or combine with the broth. Very rich; serve in Pots de Crème or demitasse cups for interest.

This recipe divides well to serve a lesser number.

Topping:

1 cup dairy sour cream
1 teaspoon curry powder
1 teaspoon finely grated lemon peel

Combine sour cream with curry powder and grated lemon peel.

DELLA ROBBIA FRUIT SALAD PLATTER

2 quarts strawberries   2 pounds grapes
2 melons, honeydew, watermelon, *or* cantaloupe

Place strawberries in center of chilled serving platter. Arrange rows of sliced melons in season; ring platter with small bunches of grapes. Serve with Poppy-Seed Dressing. A French cutter for slicing melons is effective.

POPPY-SEED DRESSING

¾ cup sugar
1 teaspoon salt
1 teaspoon dry mustard
⅓ cup white vinegar
¼ teaspoon celery salt

½ cup salad oil
1½ tablespoons poppy seeds
1 drop green food coloring
  (optional)

Combine sugar, salt, mustard, vinegar, and celery salt in blender or electric mixer. While beating, slowly add salad oil until thoroughly blended. Add poppy seeds and coloring. The dressing keeps well; it will separate; shake well before using. Makes 1½ cups. Add coloring for eye appeal.

SANDWICH LOAF AU GRATIN

1 loaf crusty French bread, cut
  into 16 1-inch slices, sliced
  within ¼ inch of bottom crust

8 slices Cheddar cheese
8 slices Swiss cheese
¼ cup butter, melted

Place Cheddar and Swiss cheese alternately in sliced loaf of French bread. Press loaf lightly together. Brush with melted butter; place in a preheated 400° oven for 15 minutes until toasted, and cheese is melted. Permit guests to break off individual slices at the table.
    An unusually delicious sandwich.

VIENNA SLICES

2 cups all-purpose flour	2 tablespoons milk
1 teaspoon baking powder	1 teaspoon lemon extract
¼ teaspoon salt	½ cup apricot *or* raspberry jam
½ cup sugar	4 egg whites, beaten partially
⅔ cup butter	½ cup sugar
4 egg yolks, slightly beaten	1 cup pecans, ground

Sift flour, baking powder, salt, and ½ cup sugar. Cut butter in as for pie crust. Combine egg yolks, milk, and lemon extract. Add to dry ingredients and mix well. Press dough in bottom and up sides, about ½ inch thick, in a 9″ x 12″ x 2″ pan. Spread jam on top. Gradually beat other ½ cup sugar into egg whites until stiff. Fold in nuts and pile lightly on top of jam. Bake in a preheated 350° oven 30 minutes. Cool and cut into diamond shapes. The yield will vary, according to the size of the pieces. Cut them to the number of your requirement.

Skiing on Sunday Brunch

(SERVES 8)

Bavarian Bouillon   Vegetable Thin Crackers

Ham à la Crème   Fried Parsley

Swiss Asparagus   Citrus Caesar Salad

Spiced Glazed Walnuts

Ski Cake — Avalanche Frosting

Mountain Mocha

ADVANCE PREPARATION SCHEDULE

Deep Freeze	Previous Day	Early Morning
Danish Pastry	*Salad dressing*	*Prepare asparagus*
	Walnuts	*Crisp salad greens*
	Bouillon	

BAVARIAN BOUILLON

1 quart water
8 beef bouillon cubes
Salt and pepper
1 tablespoon grated onion

½ teaspoon celery seed
2 teaspoons grated Parmesan
cheese

Heat water to boiling, add bouillon cubes, reduce heat, and simmer 3 minutes. Add salt and pepper to taste, onion, and celery seed. Sprinkle each serving with ½ teaspoon cheese.

HAM A LA CREME

2 tablespoons butter, unsalted
8 ¼-inch slices baked ham
1 cup dry white wine
1 pound fresh mushrooms,
chopped
2 tablespoons butter

½ cup boiling water
¼ teaspoon salt
1 teaspoon lemon juice
4 teaspoons flour
1½ cups half and half cream
2 tablespoons cream

Heat 1 tablespoon butter in each of 2 skillets; add ham slices and sauté lightly on each side. Add wine and cook slowly until wine is reduced about half. Remove ham to warm platter. Sauté chopped mushrooms for 5 minutes in another pan, in 2 tablespoons butter. Add boiling water, salt, lemon juice, and stir in flour to make a light roux. Blend mixture to reduced liquid in which ham was sautéed; add cream. Heat and pour over ham. Garnish with Fried Parsley.

FRIED PARSLEY

2 dozen sprigs parsley leaves

Wash parsley and dry thoroughly. Remove stems, using only leafy sprigs. Drop sprigs into hot (390°F.) deep fat and fry a few seconds, or until crisp. Drain on absorbent paper, sprinkle with salt, and serve at once.

SWISS ASPARAGUS

1 pound fresh asparagus
¼ cup butter
⅓ cup chopped onions
1½ teaspoons salt

2 teaspoons instant non-fat
dry milk
1 teaspoon shredded Swiss cheese
3 tablespoons lemon juice
Dash paprika

Trim asparagus, remove tough ends of stalks, and wash. Place in saucepan of hot water, sufficient to cover, and simmer for 5 minutes. Remove and drain. Heat butter in a skillet, add onions, and sauté until golden. Add asparagus, cover, and steam over low heat 10 minutes. Turn onions and asparagus into shallow baking dish. Combine salt, dry milk, cheese, and spread over asparagus; sprinkle with lemon juice. Bake in a preheated 350° oven 15 minutes. Dust with paprika and brown carefully under broiler. Serve at once.

CITRUS CAESAR SALAD

1 clove garlic, split	3 tablespoons lemon juice
2 cups salad oil	1 11-ounce can mandarin oranges,
½ teaspoon Worcestershire	drained
¼ teaspoon dry mustard	1 6-ounce jar artichoke hearts,
¼ teaspoon paprika	quartered
1 teaspoon sugar	2 avocados, peeled and sliced
½ teaspoon salt	2 quarts salad greens

1½ cups croutons

Combine garlic, salad oil, Worcestershire, mustard, paprika, sugar, and salt in a pint jar. Shake well, refrigerate overnight. In the morning discard garlic. Arrange greens in a larger bowl, placing orange and artichoke sections and avocados attractively. Moisten evenly with oil mixture, add lemon juice and croutons, and mix gently.

If avocados are cut in advance, moisten with lemon juice or juice of mandarin oranges to prevent discoloration. If cut at the last moment they have a lovely fresh look.

SPICED GLAZED WALNUTS

2 cups sugar	2 1-inch pieces cinnamon stick
1 cup hot water	4 whole cloves
Dash cream of tartar	3 whole allspice

1 pound shelled, halved walnuts

Dissolve sugar in water. Add cream of tartar and spices. Bring to a boil and cook, without stirring, for 15 minutes or until syrup begins to turn pale amber. Immediately set pan into a pan of cold water to stop the cooking and then place over hot water to keep syrup soft while it is being used. Drop walnut halves, one at a time, into the hot syrup, then place on wax paper to dry and harden. Peel off paper and place in a tightly sealed metal box.

SKI CAKE

½ cup (¼ pound) butter, softened
1 cup sugar
2 cups sifted cake flour
1 tablespoon baking powder

1 cup milk
1 teaspoon vanilla
⅔ cup coarsely shaved unsweetened chocolate
2 egg whites

Cream butter; gradually blend in ½ cup sugar until mixture is light and fluffy. Sift flour and baking powder together; then sift into butter alternately with milk. Blend in vanilla and shaved chocolate. Beat egg whites until soft peaks form; gradually add remaining ½ cup sugar, beating until thick and glossy. Gently fold into chocolate batter. Pour into two 9-inch greased pans and bake 30 minutes in 350° oven. Turn out on racks to cool; when cool, frost with Avalanche Frosting.

AVALANCHE FROSTING

½ cup butter, softened
1½ cups confectioners' sugar

2 egg yolks
1 8-ounce package chocolate bits

Mix butter until creamy; blend in sugar until mixture is soft and fluffy. Beat egg yolks until very light and thick; mix into butter and sugar. Melt chocolate bits in a saucepan over hot water. Place one of the cakes on a large platter and spread about ⅓ of the frosting (butter mixture) on top of it; repeat same procedure for second layer. Spread remaining frosting over the rest of the cake. Pour the melted chocolate chips over the entire cake.

MOUNTAIN MOCHA

6 cups strong hot brewed coffee
3 ½-ounce squares sweet chocolate, shaved

1 cup heavy cream, whipped

Pour piping hot coffee into mugs. Add ½ square of shaved chocolate to each. (Use a vegetable peeler.) Stir well. Serve a mound of whipped cream on each.

Well worth the skiing.

Post-Polo Dinner

(SERVES 6)

Shrimps Rémoulade Mississippi

Relishes   Cheese Squares

Steak Luigi

Asparagus Polonaise   Baked Potatoes Amandine

Strawberry Roll

Café Diable

ADVANCE PREPARATION SCHEDULE

Previous Day

Boil shrimp
Cake for roll
Refrigerate Cheese Squares dough

Early Morning

Cheese Squares
Polonaise

SHRIMP REMOULADE MISSISSIPPI

2 pounds shrimp, cooked and   Shredded lettuce
   cleaned   Capers

Rémoulade Sauce:

1 tablespoon minced garlic
1 teaspoon prepared English
   mustard
1 teaspoon paprika
¼ teaspoon salt
¼ teaspoon pepper
⅛ teaspoon cayenne

2 teaspoons prepared horseradish
4 anchovies, mashed
1 tablespoon minced green
   onion
¼ cup wine vinegar
½ cup salad or olive oil
½ cup sherry

Combine garlic, mustard, and paprika in a large bowl, and mix thoroughly; add oil and vinegar, alternately, until well blended. Add remaining sauce ingredients and again, blend well. Place shrimp in this sauce, cover bowl, and marinate about 3 hours. Drain shrimp and serve on shredded lettuce. Garnish with capers.

CHEESE SQUARES

½ cup Cheddar cheese spread   2 cups all-purpose flour
½ cup butter *or* margarine   ½ teaspoon salt
⅛ teaspoon cayenne

Soften the cheese spread at room temperature; blend with butter. Sift flour with salt and cayenne; cream with butter and cheese. The mixture will be crumbly. Place in wax paper, pack tightly, and chill several hours. Roll to ½-inch thickness, folding crumbs over and over until the cheese mixture is firm. Cut into 1-inch squares and place on a baking sheet, leaving space between the squares. Bake in a preheated 375° oven 20 minutes.

STEAK LUIGI

1 3- to 3½-pound sirloin   Salt and pepper to taste

Italian Sauce:

1 cup salad oil
½ teaspoon garlic salt
½ teaspoon onion salt
15 peppercorns
½ teaspoon crushed red pepper

½ teaspoon salt
¼ teaspoon freshly ground
  pepper
3 green peppers, cut in 2-inch
  squares

Combine sauce ingredients and boil rapidly for 5 minutes. Season steak with salt and pepper. Heat 1 tablespoon oil in skillet, add steak, and brown quickly and evenly for about 1 minute. Turn. Baste with Italian Sauce constantly, while steak pan-fries. Cook until of desired doneness. To serve, pour Sauce over steak and serve immediately.

Note: Cook about 10 minutes for a medium (1½ inches thick) steak.

ASPARAGUS POLONAISE

2 10-ounce packages frozen   2 tablespoons butter, melted
  asparagus   1 teaspoon lemon juice

Cook asparagus according to package directions. When tender, drain and place on warm serving platter; brush with mixture of melted butter and lemon juice. To serve, spoon Polonaise Sauce over asparagus.

Polonaise Sauce:

2 tablespoons butter, melted	⅛ teaspoon salt
1 cup dry bread crumbs	⅛ teaspoon pepper
1 hard-cooked egg, chopped fine	

Melt butter in saucepan, add bread crumbs, and sauté until lightly browned. Remove skillet from heat; mix in egg, salt, and pepper.

BAKED POTATOES AMANDINE

4 potatoes in skins	2 tablespoons milk
2 tablespoons butter	1 teaspoon salt
1 egg, well beaten	1 tablespoon butter
¼ cup slivered almonds	

Scrub potatoes, drop in boiling water and cook until tender, about 20 minutes. Peel and mash while still warm; combine with butter, egg, milk, and salt. Shape into fingers about 3 by 1 inches. Melt remaining 1 tablespoon butter, add almonds, and brown slightly; coat each potato finger by pressing almonds on surface and place on buttered baking sheet. Heat in preheated 375° oven for 15 minutes while steak is baking. Both should be ready to be served at the same time. The prepared potatoes will freeze nicely. Defrost and sauté when serving the leftovers.

STRAWBERRY ROLL

4 eggs, separated	¾ cup all-purpose flour, sifted
¾ cup granulated sugar	¼ teaspoon salt
1 teaspoon vanilla	1 teaspoon baking powder
Confectioners' sugar	

Beat egg whites until stiff; add ½ cup of the granulated sugar. Beat egg yolks until thick and lemon colored; add balance ¼ cup of granulated sugar and vanilla. Fold egg whites into the beaten egg yolks. Sift flour with salt and baking powder, and fold into egg mixture.

Line 8″ x 10″ pan with wax paper, letting it extend over edge of pan. Do not grease. Pour batter into pan and spread evenly, using a spatula. Bake 12 minutes in a preheated 375° oven. Sprinkle confectioners' sugar on a tea towel. When cake is done turn immediately onto the towel. Peel off wax paper carefully so as not to tear cake. Trim crusts. Cover with wax paper and roll lightly in towel. Cool.

To prepare, open roll; fill with Strawberry Filling; reroll in wax paper, with open seam on bottom. Place in refrigerator to chill for no longer than 1 hour, as it would become soggy. To serve, remove wax paper, and sprinkle lightly with confectioners' sugar.

Strawberry Filling:

1 cup heavy cream, whipped	½ teaspoon vanilla
¼ cup granulated sugar	1 pint sliced strawberries

Blend cream, sugar, and vanilla and spread on cake.

CAFE DIABLE

½ cup brandy	Thin outer peel of 1 lemon
9 lumps sugar	4 whole cloves
Thin outer peel of 1 orange	Stick of cinnamon
4 cups hot brewed black coffee	

Heat all ingredients, except coffee, in chafing dish or café diable pan until sugar is dissolved, stirring occasionally. Heat bowl of a ladle over a match; fill with a small amount of mixture. Add 1 sugar lump to ladle and ignite. Lower ladle into chafing dish to light brandy. While brandy is flaming, pour hot coffee into chafing dish. When flame dies, ladle coffee into demitasse cups. For additional flavor drop a 1-inch stick of cinnamon into each cup.

Fireside Chat Supper

(SERVES 4)

Welsh Rarebit

Pimiento Olives   Toast Points

Limestone Salad Moulé

Apple Schnitten

Coffee

ADVANCE PREPARATION SCHEDULE

Early Morning

Moulé dressing
Crust for Apple Schnitten

WELSH RAREBIT

1 tablespoon butter	1 teaspoon dry mustard
1 pound sharp Cheddar cheese, diced	2 teaspoons Worcestershire
	Dash cayenne
¾ cup stale beer *or* ale	4 slices toast
1 egg, slightly beaten	⅛ teaspoon paprika

Have the boiling water in chafing dish low enough not to touch upper container. Melt butter in upper section, add cheese, and stir until melted. Add beer very slowly, blending well. Cheese will thicken again. Combine egg, mustard, Worcestershire, cayenne, and add a small amount of the cheese mixture while stirring. Slowly return the egg mixture to the cheese, blending thoroughly. Stir until heated and serve over buttered toast points, two to a serving. Sprinkle with paprika. Prepare additional Rarebit as needed. Have ingredients in readiness.

Note: The Rarebit may be prepared in a double boiler.

LIMESTONE SALAD MOULE

2 heads limestone lettuce

Moulé Dressing:

1 3-ounce package cream cheese	¼ cup dairy sour cream
½ teaspoon grated onion	1 tablespoon chili sauce
¼ teaspoon garlic salt	½ of 7½-ounce can undrained minced clams
¼ teaspoon salt	
2 tablespoons white dinner wine (Rhine, sauterne, Chablis, etc.)	2 tablespoons finely chopped green onions

Wash and crisp lettuce. Cut into bite-size pieces and toss with Moulé Dressing.

APPLE SCHNITTEN

½ cup (¼ pound) butter	½ lemon, grated rind
¼ cup sugar	½ teaspoon almond extract
1 cup all-purpose flour	Confectioners' sugar
⅓ cup finely ground almonds	2 cups applesauce (approximately)

Cream butter; add sugar and remaining ingredients, except applesauce. Mix well. Pat on buttered cooky sheet into a 12″ x 9″ rectangle. Bake in a preheated 400° oven 10 minutes, until light golden brown. While warm cut into 12 even pieces. Dot 6 pieces heavily with confectioners' sugar and score with a heated 2-tined fork heated over flame. Cool. Just before serving, put together with thick sweetened applesauce, topped with sugared strip.

Broomstacking Supper

(SERVES 10)

Fish Chowder

Relishes   Crusty Bread or Crisp Crackers

Salad Ravigote

Butter Cream Coffee Kuchen or Tea Ring Scandinavia

Grape Platter

Assorted Cheeses

Coffee

ADVANCE PREPARATION SCHEDULE

Previous Day	Early Morning
Coffee Kuchen	*Chowder*
Tea Ring	*Crisp greens*

FISH CHOWDER

1½ pounds flounder *or* halibut, skinned and boned	2 medium onions, chopped
	Salt
8 potatoes, sliced thin	Pepper
1 #2½ can tomatoes	1½ cups (¾ pound) butter
1 quart half and half cream	

Cut fish in about 1-inch squares and place in saucepan. Combine with potatoes, tomatoes, and onions; add water to cover, salt, and pepper; bring to a rolling boil, then cook on medium heat, stirring frequently to prevent fish adhering to pan. Cook about 6 hours, or until all ingredients are very soft. Remove from heat, add butter; when melted, add cream. To serve, reheat.

Note: This chowder can be prepared in an iron kettle over barbecue coals. Cook about 3 hours.

SALAD RAVIGOTE

5 stalks celery, in ½-inch slices	4 large heads Bibb lettuce
1 head leaf lettuce	2 heads Boston lettuce
3 tomatoes, peeled and sliced	

Wash all lettuce; drain and crisp in refrigerator. Line large salad bowl with leaf lettuce. Separate leaves of Bibb lettuce, and tear Boston lettuce into bite-sized pieces. Place in lined bowl, add celery slices, and mix gently. Arrange tomato slices over lettuce and celery. Chill. To serve, cover with Sauce Ravigote. Toss lightly.

Sauce Ravigote:

2 hard-cooked eggs, coarsely chopped	1 tablespoon prepared mustard
	1 tablespoon chopped parsley
2 tablespoons lemon juice	¼ teaspoon dried tarragon
⅓ cup wine vinegar	½ teaspoon salt
⅔ cup olive oil	¼ teaspoon freshly ground
½ onion, chopped fine	pepper

Mix egg with lemon juice and vinegar. Add oil very slowly, blending well. Add remaining ingredients, and again blend well. Mix well before serving.

BUTTER CREAM COFFEE KUCHEN

Kuchen Dough:

1 ⅔-ounce package compressed yeast	½ cup sugar
	½ teaspoon salt
2 tablespoons sugar	4 egg yolks, well beaten
1 cup scalded milk	1 teaspoon vanilla
⅔ cup butter, softened	5 cups all-purpose flour

Combine yeast with 2 tablespoons sugar. Pour milk over butter, add ½ cup sugar, and salt; blend in eggs and vanilla. Cool, and when lukewarm combine with yeast mixture. Mix well, add flour gradually, beating until dough becomes too stiff to mix. Turn out on floured board and knead very gently for 2 or 3 minutes or until smooth. Place in well-greased bowl, brush top with melted shortening, cover, and allow to rise in warm place free from drafts for about 1½ to 2 hours. Dough should double in bulk. Turn out on floured board. Divide dough in half, making one cake at a time, reserving the other half. Roll one part of dough into a 10″ x 15″ rectangle.

Spread with Butter Cream Filling, reserving ⅓ cup of filling. Sprinkle with ½ cup finely chopped nuts. Cut lengthwise into 3 strips. Twist each slightly, then braid. (Place a knife at start of braid to hold it together.) Spread reserved ⅓ cup of Butter Cream Filling in bottom of 10-inch bread pan. Place braided dough in pan on Butter Cream, brush with slightly beaten egg yolk, and sprinkle with 2 tablespoons broken nuts. Cover pan with towel and allow to rise in warm place until double in size, about 1½ to 2 hours. Bake in a preheated 350° oven about 45 minutes until lightly browned.

Note: Do not serve this cake warm. It is unusual, in that it is better as the cake absorbs the Butter Cream Filling.

Repeat procedure with other half of reserved dough, or prepare Tea Ring Scandinavia.

Butter Cream Filling:

½ cup (¼ pound) butter, softened	1 cup sifted confectioners' sugar
	2 teaspoons vanilla
½ cup pecans, chopped fine	

Beat butter with rotary beater until light and fluffy, add sugar gradually; blend in vanilla.

Topping:

1 egg yolk, slightly beaten	2 tablespoons pecans, broken

TEA RING SCANDINAVIA

1 egg, slightly beaten	½ cup light brown sugar,
1 tablespoon cream	finely packed
1 cup nuts, coarsely chopped	1 cup raisins
(walnuts *or* hazelnuts)	¼ cup butter, melted

Combine all ingredients except butter and blend well.

Roll the reserved half of dough into an oblong ½ inch thick. Brush with melted butter. Combine remaining ingredients and blend well. Spread evenly over rolled dough. Roll as for a jelly roll. Bring ends together, forming a ring. Lift into well-greased 9-inch spring form, seam end down. With a sharp knife cut halfway through ring about 1½ inches apart on outside edge. Turn each division upward to show filling. Brush with melted butter and allow to rise until double in size, about 1½ to 2 hours. Bake in a preheated 400° oven about 15 minutes; reduce heat to 350° and bake additional 15 minutes. Remove at once. Cool on cake rack. Frost with Confectioners' Sugar Icing (see Index).

GRAPE PLATTER

Arrange a low bowl with a variety of grapes. Pile them high in contrasting colors. Intersperse clusters of kumquats with leaves. Place a bowl of nuts and large raisins on table.

ASSORTED CHEESES — CRACKERS

Suggested Cheeses: Muenster, Stilton, Gorgonzola.

To the Hounds Brunch

(SERVES 8 TO 10)

Glazed Apples   Blueberry Peaches
Deviled Turkey
Macedoine of Vegetables
Whole-Wheat Toast   Cottage Cheese Swirls
Rice Cream Vienna

Suggested wine: May Wine

ADVANCE PREPARATION SCHEDULE

Deep Freeze	**Previous Day**	**Early Morning**
Cheese Swirls	*Cook turkey*	*Apples*
(reheat to serve)	*Salad dressing*	*Blueberry Peaches*
	Rice Cream	*Assemble Deviled Turkey*

GLAZED APPLES

10 red cooking apples	2 cups water
1½ cups sugar	¼ cup currant jelly
¼ cup sugar	

Wash and core apples; starting at stem, peel ⅓ way down. Arrange apples in shallow pan, stem side up. Boil 1½ cups sugar and water together for 10 minutes; add apple peel for color, but remove before using syrup. Bake apples in a preheated 350° oven, basting frequently with syrup, for about 45 minutes or until apples are tender when pierced with fork. Remove from oven, place teaspoon of jelly in each, and sprinkle with 1 teaspoon sugar each. Place apples in broiler, at low heat, basting often until brown. Serve warm with cream or chilled.

Variation:

Instead of currant jelly, use mincemeat, orange marmalade, raisins and nuts, or a cooked prune. Apples are also delicious served with Orange Sauce.

Orange Sauce:

Drain juice from apples; add 1½ cups orange juice, 1 teaspoon grated orange rind; boil 10 minutes and pour over apples.

BLUEBERRY PEACHES

½ pint dairy sour cream	2 tablespoons sugar
½ pint blueberries	6 tablespoons cinnamon
8 large peaches, sliced, *or* 2 10-ounce packages frozen peaches	

Combine sour cream and blueberries; spoon over sliced peaches. Serve with generous sprinkling of combined sugar and cinnamon. This may be served individually or in a large partitioned bowl with peaches in 1 section, blueberries in second, and sugar and cinnamon in third.

Variation:

Use peeled and sliced oranges instead of peaches. This is an excellent fruit dessert, as well.

DEVILED TURKEY

1 cup ripe olives, pitted	1 teaspoon Worcestershire
2 tablespoons onion, chopped	Dash Tabasco
¼ cup butter	1 cup celery, sliced thin
6 tablespoons flour	3 cups diced, cooked turkey
1 teaspoon dry mustard	1 2-ounce jar pimiento, chopped
2 teaspoons salt	⅔ cup dry bread crumbs,
3 cups milk	buttered

Cut olives into large pieces. Sauté onion in butter slowly, 3 to 4 minutes. Blend in flour, mustard, and salt. Add milk, Worcestershire, and Tabasco; cook, stirring, until thickened. Add celery, turkey, pimiento, and olives; heat thoroughly. Pour into 1 large or 2 small shallow baking dishes, or individual baking shells, and top with crumbs. Bake in a preheated 350° oven for about 20 minutes; if using large casserole increase time about 10 to 15 minutes.

Buttered Crumbs:

For each ½ cup bread crumbs, add 1 tablespoon melted butter or margarine.

MACEDOINE OF VEGETABLES

1 9-ounce package frozen artichoke hearts

1 envelope garlic salad dressing mix

1 4-ounce can button mushrooms, drained

1 8-ounce can French style green beans, drained

2 cooked carrots, cut into strips

1 red onion, sliced thin

Lettuce

Anchovy fillets

Pimiento

Cook artichoke hearts according to directions; drain and cool. Combine salad dressing mix according to package directions. Place artichoke hearts, mushrooms, beans, carrots, and onion in mixing bowl and cover with dressing. Refrigerate and let marinate 2 hours or more. Serve on lettuce leaves and garnish with anchovies and pimiento.

COTTAGE CHEESE SWIRLS

Dough:

2 cups all-purpose flour

1 egg, well beaten

2 tablespoons vegetable oil

1 teaspoon salt

1 teaspoon baking powder

½ cup water, room temperature

Place flour in a large bowl, making a well in center of flour. Pour egg, oil, salt, and baking powder in well; blend with flour. Stir vigorously, while adding water. Dough will be medium soft. Keep stirring (a wooden spoon is best) until smooth; knead lightly. Cover and allow to stand while preparing Filling.

Filling:

2 cups dry cottage cheese

2 cups creamed cottage cheese

4 eggs, well beaten

1 teaspoon salt

2 tablespoons butter, melted

Flour

½ cup dairy sour cream

Blend cottage cheeses, eggs, and salt until smooth. Divide dough into two parts. Roll out half of dough to ⅛-inch thickness; brush with 1 tablespoon melted butter. Spread half of cottage cheese mixture evenly over dough, covering to the very edges. Roll from length into a long roll as for jelly roll. Prepare other half the same way. Slice into rounds 1 inch thick. Flatten these rounds slightly by dipping both open ends lightly into flour, to keep cottage cheese covered. Shake off surplus flour. Bake in a well-buttered pan in a preheated 375° oven until thoroughly well baked and medium brown, about ¾ hour. Spread lightly with sour cream. Serve hot. Makes approximately 12.

RICE CREAM VIENNA

¾ cup rice	1 package unflavored gelatin
4 cups milk	2 tablespoons water
¾ cup sugar	2 cups heavy cream, whipped
1 cup raspberry syrup	

Cook rice in milk 25 minutes until soft; add sugar and cool. Combine gelatin and water; stir over heat until dissolved; cool. Add gelatin and whipped cream to rice. Rinse melon mold in cold water. Pour in mixture. Grease inner rim of mold cover and seal. Leave in refrigerator at least 2 hours. Before serving, dip mold for a few seconds in hot water to release it. Turn out on platter and cover with bottled raspberry syrup or frozen raspberries, defrosted.

Football Warm-Up Lunch or Supper

(SERVES 8)

A WARM-UP BEFORE THE GAME OR A HEARTY RETURN

Baked Onion Soup Tally-Ho   All-American Bread Sticks
Tartare Steak San Marco   Dilled Brussels Sprouts
Gourmet Mushrooms   Pickled Watermelon Rind
Apricot Mold   Almond Bars
Coffee
Beer

ADVANCE PREPARATION SCHEDULE

Previous Day	Early Morning
Brussels Sprouts	*Onion Soup*
Gourmet Mushrooms (see Index)	*Apricot Mold*
Pickled Watermelon Rind (see Index)	*Almond Bars*

BAKED ONION SOUP TALLY-HO

8 ¾-inch slices French bread
1 cup grated Parmesan cheese
2 tablespoons butter
2 tablespoons flour
1 cup water

4 10½-ounce cans condensed onion soup (made with beef stock)
2 10½-ounce cans condensed beef consommé, gelatin added
2 #2 cans tomatoes

2 10½-ounce cans water

Toast bread: remove centers with cooky cutter or rim of juice glass. Place each slice of bread in a 16-ounce ovenproof casserole or marmite. Sprinkle 1 tablespoon of the cheese in center of each slice. To prepare soup, place butter in 4-quart saucepan, and brown lightly; add flour, blend until golden brown. Add 1 cup water slowly; cook until thickened. Add onion soup, consommé, tomatoes, and water; bring to a boil; lower heat, and simmer 5 minutes. Ladle mixture over French bread in casseroles, dividing it proportionately. Reserve approximately 1 cup of the soup. Place individual soups in a preheated 275° oven for about 45 minutes. As soup bakes, replenish reduced liquid with reserve amount of soup. Remove from oven and serve immediately while bubbling hot; sprinkle additional tablespoon of cheese over each serving. In smaller bowls this could serve 12. As suggested for this menu it is very filling.

ALL-AMERICAN BREAD STICKS

Melted butter
⅔ cup sifted all-purpose flour
1⅓ cups cornmeal
1 tablespoon sugar

4 teaspoons baking powder
1 teaspoon salt
1 egg
1 cup milk

3 tablespoons melted butter

Set oven at 425°. Grease corn-stick pans liberally with melted butter. Place in oven to heat while preparing batter. Combine flour, cornmeal, sugar, baking powder, and salt in bowl. Beat egg in small bowl; add milk and melted butter. Add liquid ingredients to dry ingredients. Blend until dry ingredients are just moist. Do not overbeat. Fill hot corn-stick pan, re-butter hot pan, fill with batter, and bake. Repeat until all batter is used. Makes 14 to 21 sticks.

May be baked in well-greased 8″ x 8″ x 2″ pan and cut in squares.

TARTARE STEAK SAN MARCO

The following is the basic recipe for each pound of meat; three pounds will serve eight generously for this menu.

1 pound freshly ground lean chuck *or* round of beef	¼ teaspoon dry mustard
1 egg yolk	1 small ice cube
1 teaspoon salt	4 strips anchovy fillets, cut in half lengthwise
1 teaspoon Worcestershire	4 pimiento-stuffed olives, sliced
1 teaspoon cognac	Sprigs of parsley; baby dill pickles; plum tomatoes, for garnish
1 tablespoon grated onion	
½ teaspoon coarsely ground pepper	Thin-sliced caraway rye and pumpernickel
1 teaspoon capers	

Be certain meat is very fresh and freshly ground. Place in shallow bowl; distribute over the meat, as evenly as possible, egg yolk, salt, Worcestershire, cognac, onion, ground pepper, capers, mustard, and ice cube. Blend ingredients thoroughly, using 2 forks; handle as lightly as possible. Return to refrigerator quickly until ready to serve; then shape to approximate the form of a football. Crisscross anchovy fillets through center to simulate lacings of a football. Use sliced olive rings as grommets. Ring the loaf with sprigs of parsley; interspersed with baby dill pickles and plum tomatoes. Surround entire platter with thinly sliced caraway rye and pumpernickel.

DILLED BRUSSELS SPROUTS

1 10-ounce package frozen
brussels sprouts *or*
1 quart fresh brussels sprouts,
cooked
⅓ cup wine vinegar

½ teaspoon sugar
1 teaspoon seasoning salt
⅓ cup water
1 teaspoon dill seed
3 tablespoons olive or salad oil

Cook frozen brussels sprouts 2 minutes less than package directions, drain. Heat vinegar and sugar and pour over sprouts. When cool add seasoning salt, water, dill seed, and oil; toss lightly but thoroughly. Chill a minimum of 12 hours. Serve on toothpicks.

APRICOT MOLD

2 3-ounce packages apricot
flavored gelatin
2 cups hot water

1 #2½ can apricots
½ pint dairy sour cream
1 pint vanilla ice cream

Dissolve gelatin in hot water; let cool in refrigerator. Drain apricots. Purée apricots through sieve or food mill and add to gelatin. Whip sour cream and ice cream together, add to mixture. Place in 6-cup melon mold. Refrigerate until set.

ALMOND BARS

½ pound butter
½ cup powdered sugar
1 cup sifted all-purpose flour

1 teaspoon orange extract
1 cup almonds, finely ground

Cream butter and sugar thoroughly; add remaining ingredients and mix thoroughly in mixer. Spread batter thinly on a 12" x 15" cooky sheet; bake 12 to 15 minutes or until slightly brown in a briefly preheated 375° oven. Remove from oven and sprinkle with powdered sugar. When it has cooled slightly, cut in squares and remove carefully from pan.

Bowling Award Dinner

(SERVES 8)

Artichoke Melange Appetizer   Melba Toast
Crabmeat Tetrazzini   Hard Rolls   Braised Peas
Finnish Cucumbers
Pumpkin Chiffon Torte   Coffee

Suggested wine: Rhine

ADVANCE PREPARATION SCHEDULE

Deep Freeze	Previous Day	Early Morning
Hard Rolls	*Hard-cook eggs*	*Cucumber*
	Pumpkin Torte	*Appetizer*
		Prepare Tetrazzini for baking

ARTICHOKE MELANGE APPETIZER

4 hard-cooked eggs, chopped
1 cup canned artichoke hearts, water pack
2 cups red caviar
6 sweet pickles, chopped

10 ripe olives, chopped
Mayonnaise, thinned with cream
2 tablespoons coarsely chopped pimiento

In a glass bowl arrange layers of each of the first 3 ingredients; spread a thin coating of mayonnaise over each layer. Top with pickles and olives and border with pimiento. Serve with Melba Toast.

CRABMEAT TETRAZZINI

3 tablespoons butter
1 medium onion, chopped fine
1 large green pepper, chopped fine
3 10½-ounce cans tomato soup
1 pound fresh mushrooms, cut in thick slices, *or* 2 7½-ounce jars mushrooms
2 7½-ounce cans of crabmeat, flaked

1 1-pound package thin spaghetti
½ teaspoon onion salt
½ teaspoon celery salt
½ teaspoon salt
⅛ teaspoon black pepper
¼ teaspoon paprika
1 pound sharp Cheddar cheese

Cook spaghetti 2 minutes less than package directions and drain. Heat butter in large saucepan. Add onion, green pepper, and fresh mushrooms; sauté until soft. Add tomato soup, mushrooms (if canned), crabmeat, cooked spaghetti, and seasonings. Dice ¾ of the cheese and add, cooking gently until almost melted. Pour into buttered baking dish; top with remainder of cheese. Bake in a preheated 400° oven until cheese is brown; about 30 to 45 minutes.

BRAISED PEAS

1 tablespoon butter	½ teaspoon salt
½ teaspoon beef extract	¼ teaspoon pepper
1 tablespoon water	¼ teaspoon thyme *or* mint
1 teaspoon sugar	2 10-ounce packages frozen peas

Combine butter, meat extract, water, sugar, salt, pepper, and thyme in saucepan. Break up block of peas with fork. Cover and simmer until tender, about 10 to 15 minutes.

FINNISH CUCUMBERS

6 small cucumbers   Salt

Peel the cucumbers, cut them into very thin slices, using a potato slicer if possible. Place on a flat dish and sprinkle with salt. Set aside for at least 1 hour, then drain off all the liquid. Rinse them well in iced water, drain again, and dry. Mix cucumbers with the following dressing.

Finnish Dressing:

2 tablespoons finely chopped fresh dill	Freshly ground black pepper
	¼ teaspoon dry mustard
1 cup dairy half and half sour cream	1 fresh tomato, peeled and mashed
1 clove garlic, minced	¼ cup salad oil
1 teaspoon sugar	2 tablespoons tarragon vinegar
Salt	Paprika

Add the chopped dill to the sour cream with the garlic, sugar, salt, and pepper to taste. Then add the dry mustard and fresh tomato pulp. Last, mix in the oil and vinegar very slowly. Allow the cucumbers to marinate in the Finnish Dressing for at least 1 hour. Serve very cold in lettuce cups. Dust with paprika.

PUMPKIN CHIFFON TORTE

18 double ladyfingers, separated
2 tablespoons unflavored gelatin
½ cup cold water
1½ cups brown sugar
½ teaspoon salt
1 teaspoon nutmeg
¼ teaspoon dry ginger
1 cup half and half cream

5 egg yolks, slightly beaten
1 1-pound, 13-ounce can pumpkin
½ cup sugar
5 egg whites, beaten stiff
1 cup heavy cream, whipped
¼ cup salted pecans, chopped, toasted

Place ladyfingers around sides and on bottom of a 10-inch greased spring form. Soften gelatin in water. Combine brown sugar, salt, spices, and cream in a heavy pan. Cook to boiling point, stirring constantly; add gelatin and dissolve. Pour small amount of mixture slowly over egg yolks. Return to pan; cook over low heat for 3 minutes, stirring constantly. Add pumpkin and mix thoroughly. Chill until partially thickened. Beat remaining sugar into stiffly beaten egg whites gradually. Fold into pumpkin mixture. Pour into prepared spring form. Chill overnight or for at least 12 hours. Top with whipped cream and pecans.

Fisherman's Boast Dinner

(SERVES 8)

Antipasto International — Lemon French Dressing
Red Snapper en Papier   Assorted Cocktail Crackers
Squash Casserole   Oven French Fries
Almond Rolls
Old-Fashioned Lemon Chiffon Pie
Coffee

ADVANCE PREPARATION SCHEDULE

Deep Freeze	Previous Day	Early Morning
Almond Roll	*Lemon Dressing*	*Chill antipasto ingredients*
	Pie shell	*Squash for baking*
		Crisp potatoes
		Wrap Red Snapper
		Lemon pie

ANTIPASTO INTERNATIONAL

1 head Boston lettuce
1 7-ounce can tuna, drained and flaked
1 1-pound, 4-ounce can green beans, marinated
1 3¾-ounce can sardines in oil, drained

1 avocado, peeled and diced
12 cherry tomatoes
2 4-ounce cans artichokes, halved
1 2-ounce can anchovy fillets
½ cup salad olives, pimiento-stuffed

1 cup Lemon French Dressing

Arrange a border of lettuce leaves. Center platter with mound of tuna. Outline with green beans. Space sardines around platter with 3 or 4 in each mound. Fill in between with avocado, cherry tomatoes, hearts of artichokes, and crisscross anchovy fillets over tomatoes. Toss olives over all and marinate with Lemon French Dressing. If arranged in advance, be certain to dip avocado in lemon juice to prevent discoloration, or marinate in the Lemon French Dressing.

Note: This salad is a combination of French Niçoise, Italian Antipasto, and American license, and is a many-sided recipe for the inventive cook. A piquant antipasto in this menu, but adding crisp greens as a salad and an entrée it becomes a complete meal. Add an additional vegetable or two (beets, potatoes, or green beans) and it becomes a savory luncheon dish. To make it really substantial, add 3 cooked, diagonally sliced frankfurters, and the men cheer.

LEMON FRENCH DRESSING

⅓ cup lemon juice
⅔ cup salad oil
3 tablespoons sugar
¼ teaspoon dry mustard (optional)

1 teaspoon salt
1 teaspoon paprika
Dash pepper

Combine lemon juice, oil, sugar, salt, paprika, pepper, and mustard;

beat until thoroughly blended. Chill. Makes 1 cup (approximately).

RED SNAPPER EN PAPIER

4 fillets of red snapper
¼ cup olive oil
¼ cup lemon juice
1 teaspoon salt

1 small garlic clove, slivered
(optional)
2 teaspoons oregano
Parsley

Slices of lime

Cut 6 small slits in each fillet. Combine oil, lemon juice, oregano and salt, and dip each piece of fish in this liquid; coat well. Tuck a sliver of garlic and a dash of oregano in each slit. Wrap the four fillets in one layer in brown paper, making 1 package, and bake 35 minutes in a preheated 325° oven. To serve, remove from package, place on heated platter. Garnish with parsley and lime slices. (Serves 4. To serve 8, make 2 packages, doubling all ingredients.)

SQUASH CASSEROLE

2 10-ounce packages frozen
squash, defrosted, or
2 pounds fresh squash (2 cups
mashed)
1 egg, beaten

1 3-ounce package cream cheese,
softened
½ teaspoon salt
⅛ teaspoon pepper
½ teaspoon Worcestershire

If using frozen squash, defrost in saucepan for 10 minutes, according to package directions.

To boil fresh squash, scrub well; do not peel. Remove slice from blossom stem end, and cut in cubes or slices. Place in 1 inch of water, using ½ teaspoon salt per cup of water, and boil 15 to 20 minutes, or until tender. Drain and mash (fresh or frozen). Beat egg into cheese and add to squash. Stir in salt, pepper, and Worcestershire. Place in 1½-quart buttered casserole; bake ½ hour in a preheated 350° oven.

OVEN FRENCH FRIES

6 medium potatoes
2 tablespoons salad oil

2 tablespoons water

Peel potatoes and slice in ½-inch strips, as for French-fried potatoes. Wash and drain. Place in shallow baking dish. Combine oil and water and pour over potatoes. Toss, so that each strip is moistened. Preheat oven to 475° and bake 30 minutes, turning strips once or twice. For additional crispness, place under broiler for a minute or two to brown them further. Sprinkle with salt.

French Fries are an enticing tidbit, and we suggest an increase in the number of potatoes if your family is "potato minded."

ALMOND ROLLS

See Index for Parker House Rolls.

Roll dough and cut in 1-inch circles, shape as directed. Place a split blanched almond on each; brush with slightly beaten egg yolk. Let rise and bake according to recipe directions.

OLD-FASHIONED LEMON CHIFFON PIE

Pie Crust:

1½ cups sifted all-purpose flour	5 tablespoons vegetable
¼ teaspoon baking powder	shortening
½ teaspoon salt	4 tablespoons cold milk *or*
5 tablespoons butter	water

Sift flour, baking powder and salt together 3 times. Cut cold shortening into dry ingredients with a pastry blender or knife until it resembles coarse meal. Gradually add cold milk. Turn onto floured board; knead a few seconds to hold mixture together. Wrap in wax paper and refrigerate ½ hour. Place on floured board again. Roll into desired size. Dough should be in large enough circle to fit loosely into 9-inch pie pan and hang over the edge about 1 inch.

Turn edge of crust under rim and flute with fingers or pie cutter. Prick dough well with fork. Bake about 25 minutes in a preheated 400° oven. Makes one 9-inch shell or 8 small shells.

Lemon Filling:

¼ cup cornstarch	¼ cup hot water
¾ cup granulated sugar	2 tablespoons butter
⅛ teaspoon salt	2 medium-size lemons,
2 egg yolks, beaten	grated rind and juice, *or*
¼ cup cold water	⅓ cup juice

Combine cornstarch, sugar, and salt. Combine eggs with cold water and add to cornstarch mixture. Stir hot water in slowly. Simmer mixture over heat until thick, stirring constantly. Add butter, rind, and juice of lemon. Bring to a boil and continue cooking 3 more minutes. Cover, let stand while preparing Chiffon Meringue.

Chiffon Meringue:

2 egg whites ¼ cup granulated sugar

Place egg whites in bowl of electric mixer; beat until it clings to bowl. Add sugar gradually and beat until very stiff. Fold in hot lemon mixture; pour into baked pie shell. Cover with Meringue Topping.

Meringue Topping:

½ cup egg whites (about 4) ½ teaspoon vanilla
6 tablespoons granulated sugar

Beat egg whites until stiff but not dry. Add sugar gradually and continue to beat until thoroughly blended and stiff. Blend in vanilla. Pile onto cooled Lemon Filling. Be sure to enclose custard by spreading meringue over rim. Bake on top rack of preheated 450° oven 7 or 8 minutes, until golden brown. Remove; place on rack to cool. To serve, cut with a wet knife.

TV Football Tray Supper

(SERVES 10 TO 12)

Vegetable Bowl — Lively Dip
Clam Sauce Spaghetti
Bagel Puffs
Cucumber Mold
Candy Apple Deep-Dish Pie

ADVANCE PREPARATION SCHEDULE

Previous Day	Early Morning
Dip	*Cabbage bowl*
Cucumber Mold	*Vegetables*
	Clam Sauce
	Bagel
	Apple Pie

VEGETABLE BOWL

1 large head cabbage, hollowed out in center to hold small glass bowl for dip; spread outside leaves, flower-like

Raw vegetables: carrot curls, cauliflowerets, green pepper strips, radishes, cucumber wheels, broccoli, etc.

Place cabbage "bowl" in center of large round platter or tray. Fill small bowl with dip. Place in center of cabbage. Surround with mounds of each vegetable to make a pleasing color arrangement.

LIVELY DIP

1 cup mayonnaise
½ cup chili sauce, drained
1 clove garlic
½ teaspoon dry mustard
⅛ teaspoon cayenne pepper
¼ teaspoon lime juice
1 tablespoon prepared horseradish

Combine ingredients and blend well. Place in refrigerator overnight before serving. This dip is an excellent salad dressing as well.

BAGEL PUFFS

½ cup vegetable shortening
1½ cups cold water
½ teaspoon sugar
½ tablespoon salt (1½ teaspoons)
4 eggs
1½ cups matzo meal

Combine first four ingredients in a saucepan; heat until mixture comes to a boil, add matzo meal all at once. Remove from heat, cool slightly, add 1 egg at a time, beating after each addition.

Grease cooky sheet and drop batter from tablespoon onto sheet in a 2-inch mound. Dip finger into cold water and pierce center of dough through to make a hole as for a doughnut. Bake 45 to 60 minutes in a preheated 400° oven. Makes 14 to 16.

CLAM SAUCE SPAGHETTI

⅔ cup butter
⅓ cup olive oil
3 cloves garlic, minced
4 8-ounce cans minced clams
Salt and freshly ground pepper to taste
2 teaspoons basil (optional)

1 cup chopped parsley
2 12-ounce bottles clam juice
2 1-pound packages thin spaghetti
⅓ cup grated Parmesan cheese (optional)
2 cans whole clams (for garnish)

Melt butter and oil in saucepan; add minced garlic and simmer 5 minutes. Add minced clams, salt and pepper, basil; simmer 10 minutes. Add ¾ cup parsley and clam juice; let cook for another 20 minutes. Boil spaghetti in large pan of water according to package directions; drain. Just before serving, heat whole clams. Mix spaghetti well with first clam mixture; garnish with whole clams and the remainder of parsley. Sprinkle with Parmesan cheese. Sauce can be made well in advance and reheated just before serving.

CUCUMBER MOLD

4 cucumbers, cut in small pieces (with seedy part removed)
½ teaspoon salt
2 3-ounce packages lime-flavored gelatin

2 cups hot water
2 cups dairy sour cream
¼ cup sugar
Paprika

Salt cucumbers, cover with wax paper, and weight down with heavy can overnight. Drain and chop fine. Dissolve gelatin in hot water; cool and let thicken slightly; whip until frothy and fold in remaining ingredients. Pour into a well-oiled 5-cup melon mold and refrigerate until firm.

To serve, turn out on large platter; garnish with curly endive, orange and grapefruit sections. Dust the mold with paprika for color contrast.

CANDY APPLE DEEP-DISH PIE

4 pounds tart cooking apples
Butter
Brown sugar

½ cup raisins
½ cup chopped pecans
¼ cup lemon juice

Pare and slice apples; place a layer in a greased 3-quart casserole or baking dish. Dot with butter and sugar and sprinkle with raisins and nuts. Continue in this way, sprinkling lemon juice over each layer of apples, until all of the apples are used. Put Streusel Topping over casserole and bake in a preheated 350° oven for ¾ to 1 hour, until apples are tender. Serve with a warm hard sauce, whipped cream, or ice cream.

Streusel Topping:

> ½ cup (¼ pound) butter   1 cup all-purpose flour
> 2 cups light brown sugar

Mix butter, flour, and sugar until crumbly. Spread evenly over top of apple casserole.

VARIED ACTIVITIES

The Deciding Vote Brunch

(SERVES 5)

Parsley Soup

Soufflé Omelet   Curry Ham Sauce   Shrimp Sauce

Cheese Straws [see Index]   Baking Powder Biscuits [see Index]

Strawberry Rhubarb Forms

Karidopita

(Greek Honey Cake)

Coffee   Tea

Suggested wine: Riesling

ADVANCE PREPARATION SCHEDULE

Previous Day	Early Morning
Strawberry mold	*Sauces*
Cake	*Soup*

PARSLEY SOUP

2 10½-ounce cans frozen   ½ cup lemon juice
  potato soup   Salt
2½ cups milk   Pepper
1 large bunch parsley   5 radish roses (for garnish)

Cook potato soup according to directions, bring to boiling point, add milk, and bring to a boil again. Remove from heat and cool. Wash parsley, drain, and remove stems. Place half of stemmed parsley in blender, turn on low speed once or twice. Add ½ of lemon juice and whirl again until finely minced. Add second half of parsley and repeat procedure with lemon juice. Be certain parsley is as fine as possible. Add about 2 cups of potato soup mixture. Whirl at low speed until finely puréed; remove and repeat with balance of soup. Remove from blender and combine all of soup and minced parsley. Season to taste with salt and pepper. Chill until icy cold. Serve in parfait glasses, spear radish roses with toothpicks, and place one on rim of each glass for a perky garnish. Makes approximately 1 quart.

SOUFFLE OMELET

5 eggs, separated   ¾ teaspoon salt
5 tablespoons water   Dash pepper
½ teaspoon baking powder   2 tablespoons butter

Beat egg whites with rotary beater until stiff but not dry. In another bowl, beat yolks until thick and lemon colored. Add water, baking powder, salt, and pepper to yolks and mix well. Fold yolk mixture into whites until well blended. Heat butter in a 9-inch skillet or omelet pan. Reduce to low heat, pour batter into pan, cover, and cook slowly for 12 minutes until light brown at the bottom. Place on lower rack of preheated 275° oven, uncovered, and bake 10 minutes until slightly brown. Serve with sauces.

Notes:

(a) Beat the whites first, and the unnecessary washing is eliminated, as the beater can then be used for the yolks.

(b) For successful preparation, do not make an omelet for a larger quantity than 6 eggs. If more is needed make two omelets.

(c) Use a rotary hand beater for best results.

CURRY HAM SAUCE

1½ tablespoons butter	¼ teaspoon curry powder
1½ tablespoons flour	½ cup diced ham
1 cup milk	1 teaspoon Worcestershire
¼ teaspoon salt	½ cup dairy sour cream

Melt butter in saucepan; add flour; cook until smooth and bubbling. Add milk gradually, stirring until smooth. Add salt, curry powder, diced ham, and Worcestershire. Blend in sour cream. Reheat slowly before serving; do not boil. Makes approximately 2 cups.

SHRIMP SAUCE

2 tablespoons flour	12 shrimps (about ½ pound),
¼ cup (⅛ pound) butter	cooked and chopped
1 cup half and half cream	2 tablespoons sherry
¼ teaspoon salt	1 teaspoon chopped parsley
⅛ teaspoon coarsely ground pepper	

Heat butter, add flour, cook until bubbly. Add cream, simmer slowly, stirring until thickened; then add salt and pepper. Blend in shrimp and heat through; add sherry. To serve, sprinkle with parsley. Makes approximately 2 cups.

STRAWBERRY RHUBARB MOLD

1 10-ounce package frozen, sweetened rhubarb	1 3-ounce package lemon gelatin
1 10-ounce package frozen strawberries, drained	4 drops red coloring
	Bibb lettuce

Cook rhubarb according to package directions, or until shredded. Drain. Combine rhubarb and strawberry juices. If necessary, add sufficient water to make 1¾ cups liquid. Heat 1 cup liquid, add gelatin and dissolve; add remaining ¾ cup, cool and place in refrigerator until jelly-like. Add drained rhubarb and strawberries and blend well. Pour into five 4-ounce moistened or greased molds. To serve, unmold on individual salad plates on beds of Bibb lettuce.

KARIDOPITA
(Greek Honey Cake)

¾ cup butter	¼ teaspoon salt
¾ cup sugar	½ teaspoon cinnamon
3 eggs	¼ cup milk
1 cup all-purpose flour, sifted	½ teaspoon grated orange rind
1½ teaspoons baking powder	1 cup walnuts

Cream butter and sugar thoroughly. Add eggs, one at a time, beating well after each. Sift together flour, baking powder, salt, and cinnamon; add to batter. Stir in milk and orange rind. Beat well, then blend in nuts. Pour into a greased and floured 8″ x 8″ x 2″ pan. Bake in a preheated 350° oven 30 minutes, or until done when tested. Remove from oven and cut into diamond shapes in pan while still hot. Pour on cold Syrup; refrigerate and let soak until ready to serve. Makes about 3 dozen pieces.

Syrup:

½ cup sugar	¾ cup water
1 cup honey	¾ teaspoon lemon juice

Mix sugar, honey and water in saucepan, simmer 5 minutes. Skim and add lemon juice, boil another 2 minutes. Cool.

Traditionally Greek desserts are very sweet and this recipe is no exception. The cake is quite moist and rich and is very good without the Syrup. It may be served separately.

Welcome Home Dinner

(SERVES 8)

Clam Fondue   French Bread

Sirloin Tip Roast

or

Roast Beef Tenderloin

Cranberry Chutney

Peas Paisan   Individual Potato Puddings

Marinated Artichoke Salad

Soufflé au Grand Marnier   Demitasse

Suggested wines: Chablis (with the Fondue)

Claret or red Burgundy (with Roast Beef)

ADVANCE PREPARATION SCHEDULE

Previous Day

Cranberry Chutney
Artichoke Salad

Early Morning

Assemble Fondue
Brown meat
Grand Marnier sauce

CLAM FONDUE

3 tablespoons butter	4 tablespoons catsup
1 small onion, diced	1 tablespoon Worcestershire
½ green pepper, diced	¼ teaspoon cayenne pepper
¼ pound processed Cheddar cheese	2 7½-ounce cans minced clams, drained

2 tablespoons sherry

Melt butter in top of double boiler; add onion, green pepper, and sauté until soft but not browned. Add processed cheese, catsup, Worcestershire, and cayenne pepper; place over hot water and cook until cheese melts. To serve, add clams and sherry; blend well and heat thoroughly. Give each guest a fork on which to spear broken bits of the French bread. Serve the Fondue in a chafing dish or casserole with warmer, and let the dipping begin. Makes about 3 cups.

SIRLOIN TIP ROAST
or
ROAST BEEF TENDERLOIN

4½ pounds sirloin tip, *or*
  beef tenderloin
Seasoned flour
  2 tablespoons shortening
  2 large Bermuda onions, ¼-inch
  slices

1 can tomatoes
¼ pound mushrooms, sliced and
  sautéed (optional)

Dredge roast thoroughly in seasoned flour; reserve remaining flour. Melt shortening in roasting pan, add onions, and sauté lightly over direct heat. Move onions to the side and brown the meat until crusty. Remove meat to flat rack and place over sliced onions; insert meat thermometer, pour tomatoes over roast, and bake in a preheated 325° oven, uncovered, until thermometer reaches 140°, or about 1¼ hours for rare (tenderloin 45 to 60 minutes). Add a little water to tomato-onion mixture if it becomes dry. For gravy, make a paste of about 1 tablespoon of reserved seasoned flour and 2 tablespoons water. Combine with 1 cup of pan drippings and heat; add mushrooms. Slice meat and arrange on large platter; serve gravy separately. Garnish with round ¼-inch slices of grapefruit, unpeeled and seeded. Mound each with Cranberry Chutney.

Seasoned Flour:

¼ cup flour, ½ teaspoon salt, ¼ teaspoon paprika, and any additional seasonings such as monosodium glutamate, garlic salt, seasoned salt, etc.

Note: The alternate tenderloin is suggested for your preference as the recipe serves for either cut.

CRANBERRY CHUTNEY

2 cups water
2 cups sugar
1 pound fresh cranberries
¼ cup vinegar
½ teaspoon salt

1 cup seeded raisins
2 tablespoons brown sugar,
  firmly packed
¼ teaspoon powdered ginger

Bring water and sugar to boil; add remaining ingredients. Simmer until berries are all popped, about 10 minutes. Cool and refrigerate.

PEAS PAISAN

3 tablespoons butter
1 cup scallions *or* green
   onions, sliced
2 10-ounce packages frozen peas
1 teaspoon sugar
1½ teaspoons salt

¼ teaspoon savory
¼ teaspoon marjoram
2 tablespoons minced parsley
1 cup water
¼ teaspoon freshly ground
   pepper

Melt butter in saucepan, add scallions, and sauté about 5 minutes or until tender but not brown. Add frozen peas, sugar, salt, herbs, water, and pepper. Cover and cook over low heat 10 minutes or until peas are tender. To serve, drain and heap on platter, border with Potato Puddings.

INDIVIDUAL POTATO PUDDINGS

6 medium baking potatoes
1 medium onion, grated
3 eggs
½ teaspoon salt

⅛ teaspoon baking powder
⅛ teaspoon white pepper
¾ cup flour (about)
¼ cup shortening, melted

Peel and grate potatoes on fine or medium grater. Allow to stand a few minutes, then squeeze out excess moisture until dry as possible. Combine with onion and add eggs, salt, baking powder, pepper. Stir in sufficient flour to make a batter just stiff enough to drop from a spoon. Add shortening. Grease twelve 3-inch muffin tins and dust lightly with flour. Fill tins with batter and bake in a preheated 350° oven for 45 minutes or until brown. Makes 12 puddings.

Note: The amount of liquid in potatoes will vary, hence the amount of flour used must vary as well.

MARINATED ARTICHOKE SALAD

3 carrots, sliced julienne
¾ cup water
3 tablespoons olive oil
3 tablespoons lemon juice
1 small bay leaf (optional)
2 teaspoons salt

¼ teaspoon garlic salt
2 9-ounce packages frozen
   artichokes
2 heads romaine lettuce
1 teaspoon oregano
Salad greens

Place carrots, water, oil, lemon juice, bay leaf, salt, and garlic salt in a saucepan. Boil gently for 5 minutes. Add frozen artichoke hearts and continue boiling until tender, about 5 to 10 minutes. Do not remove from liquid. Refrigerate until chilled thoroughly. To serve, drain and arrange on bed of luxurious greens. Dust with oregano.

SOUFFLE AU GRAND MARNIER

3 tablespoons butter	½ cup sugar
2 tablespoons flour	3-inch piece of vanilla bean
1 cup milk	4 egg yolks, slightly beaten
¼ teaspoon salt	5 egg whites, beaten stiff

Melt butter in saucepan; add flour and blend well. Gradually add milk, stirring constantly; mix in salt, sugar, and vanilla bean. When sauce is thick and smooth, remove from heat. Remove vanilla bean and cool. Add egg yolks and beat well; fold in egg whites. Butter an 8-inch soufflé dish, sprinkle with sugar, and pour in batter. Set dish in a pan of hot, not boiling water; bake in a preheated 400° oven 15 minutes; reduce heat to 375° and bake 20 to 25 minutes longer. Sprinkle with powdered sugar and serve with Grand Marnier Sauce on the side.

Grand Marnier Sauce:

1 cup milk	½ cup granulated sugar
1-inch piece of vanilla bean	¾ cup heavy cream
4 egg yolks, well beaten	⅓ teaspoon salt
3 tablespoons Grand Marnier	

Scald milk with vanilla bean in top of double boiler; remove vanilla bean. Beat egg yolks while adding sugar gradually. Stir in heavy cream and add the scalded milk slowly, continually beating until blended. Place over hot water and cook, stirring constantly until the mixture coats the spoon. Remove from the fire, cool; then beat in Grand Marnier.

Round Number Birthday Dinner

(SERVES 8)

Asparagus Appetizer   Pickled Shrimp
Cocktail Rye Toast
Breast of Chicken Gourmet
Poppy-Seeded Noodles   Lima Beans Bonne Femme
Lighted Cream Puff Ring
Coffee   Liqueur

Suggested wine: red Burgundy

ADVANCE PREPARATION SCHEDULE

Previous Day	Early Morning
Shrimp	*Toast*
	Sauté chicken
	Cream Puff Ring (without filling)
	Marinate asparagus

ASPARAGUS APPETIZER

1 quart water
1 teaspoon salt
24 asparagus stalks *or*
   2 #2 cans white asparagus,
   drained

Vinaigrette Dressing (see **Index**)
   or Garlic Cheese Dressing
   (*Thoughts for Buffets*)
4 heads Bibb lettuce

Place water and salt in bottom of double boiler. Remove tough ends of asparagus and peel stalks partway up from ends. Tie in a bunch; bring water and salt to a boil and stand the bunch in water. Reverse top of double boiler to cover asparagus. Steam about 12 minutes or until tender. Remove, drain, and cool. Marinate with Vinaigrette Dressing. Or to serve, make a bed of lettuce; place 3 asparagus spears on each and ribbon with Garlic Cheese Dressing; garnish with Pickled Shrimp.

PICKLED SHRIMP

To boil shrimp:

2½ pounds fresh shrimp	½ cup celery tops
3½ teaspoons salt	½ cup mixed pickling spice

Combine shrimp, salt, celery tops, and pickling spice; cover with boiling water and boil 5 minutes. Drain and cool with cold water. Shell and devein shrimp.

To pickle shrimp:

2 cups sliced onion   7 *or* 8 bay leaves

Place shrimp in bowl with onion and bay leaves in alternate layers. Cover with Marinade and let stand in refrigerator a minimum of 24 hours. Remove from Marinade and serve well chilled.

Marinade:

1¼ cups salad oil	2½ teaspoons celery seed
¾ cup white vinegar	1½ teaspoons salt
2½ tablespoons capers and juice	Dash Tabasco

Mix ingredients and blend well.

COCKTAIL RYE TOAST

Cut cocktail rye in ⅛-inch slices; spread with softened butter. Place in a preheated 325° oven and bake about 20 minutes, until edges curl and bread is browned. Toast will curl attractively if crusts are removed before baking. Serve hot or cold.

BREAST OF CHICKEN GOURMET

8 chicken breasts, split   ¼ cup butter
½ cup dry white wine

Remove skin from chicken breasts; melt butter in skillet. Add breasts and sauté until just delicately brown, turning occasionally. Sprinkle wine over chicken; cover and steam until tender, 20 to 25 minutes. Cover with Gourmet Sauce, and reheat; do not allow to boil. This recipe lends itself to the use of dark meat equally well.

Gourmet Sauce:

2 tablespoons butter
½ medium-size onion, chopped
　fine (*or* 1 tablespoon minced
　dehydrated onion)

½ teaspoon gravy browner
½ cup dry white table wine
2 cups dairy sour cream
Salt and pepper to taste
Green pepper rings

Melt butter in saucepan; add onion and gravy browner; simmer, stirring, for 5 minutes. Blend in wine and sour cream; heat, but do not boil. Remove from heat. When chicken is tender, pour this sauce over it; add salt and pepper to taste. Place on platter circling mound of Poppy-Seeded Noodles; garnish with raw green pepper ring.

POPPY-SEEDED NOODLES

1 quart water
½ teaspoon salt
1 8-ounce package medium-
　size noodles

3 tablespoons butter
1 tablespoon poppy seeds

Bring water and salt to a boil; add noodles and cook about 10 minutes, or according to package directions. Drain. Melt butter in saucepan, blend in poppy seeds; add noodles and stir over low heat until poppy seeds are well distributed and noodles heated.

Variation:

Caraway seeds may be substituted for poppy seeds; or, for a crunchy taste, add ⅓ cup chopped, blanched, and browned almonds.

LIMA BEANS BONNE FEMME

12 small white onions, peeled
½ cup diced lean ham
2 tablespoons butter
1 teaspoon flour
3 cups baby limas *or*
　2 packages frozen

4 lettuce leaves, shredded
1 cup water
1 teaspoon salt
1 tablespoon chopped parsley
3 tablespoons butter

Sauté ham and onions for 5 minutes in 2 tablespoons butter. Stir in flour; add limas, lettuce, water, salt, and parsley. Bring to boil; cover tightly and cook about 15 to 20 minutes until beans are tender. Keep hot, and stir in remaining butter just before serving.

CREAM PUFF BIRTHDAY RING

Cream Puff Paste:

½ cup water	⅛ teaspoon salt
¼ cup (⅛ pound) butter	½ cup all-purpose flour
	2 eggs

Bring water, butter, and salt to boiling point; add flour all at once and stir over heat until mixture leaves sides of pan and forms a ball. Remove from heat and continue beating about 2 minutes to cool mixture slightly. Add eggs, 1 at a time, beating thoroughly after each addition, until mixture has a satin-like sheen. Grease cooky sheet and mark circle about 10 to 12 inches in diameter. Mark a second circle in center about 6 to 8 inches. Fill ring formed by these 2 circles with Cream Puff Paste, using pastry tube, or drop from tablespoon. Bake in a preheated 450° oven 5 minutes; reduce heat to 300° and bake about 20 minutes longer. Cool, split in half, fill with Chocolate Rum Filling and top with Topping Garnish.

Chocolate Rum Filling:

1 egg, beaten	¼ cup cold water
1 egg yolk	¼ pound sweet cooking chocolate
3 tablespoons flour	
3 tablespoons sugar	¼ cup water
¾ cup scalded milk	1 egg white, beaten stiff
1 tablespoon unflavored gelatin	2 tablespoons rum
	1 cup heavy cream, whipped

Combine beaten egg, egg yolk, flour, and sugar in saucepan; add scalded milk. Bring to a boil; stir and cook until smooth. Soften gelatin in water for 5 minutes and stir into egg mixture. Combine chocolate and ¼ cup water in saucepan and heat until melted; add to mixture. Beat until thoroughly blended. Place over pan of ice cubes until cool and thickened. Fold in beaten egg white and rum. Carefully split cream puff circle in half horizontally. Fill with Chocolate Rum Filling. Cover filling with whipped cream and finally Topping Garnish.

Topping Garnish:

¼ cup white corn syrup	¼ cup blanched, slivered almonds
1 tablespoon confectioners' sugar	

Brush top layer of cream puff lightly with corn syrup; garnish with almonds and sprinkle lightly with confectioners' sugar. Carefully place over filling and whipped cream. This is a rich dessert, requiring only small portions. To serve, place large candle, 3 inches in diameter and about 10 inches tall, in center of Cream Puff Ring and bring the lighted candle dessert to the table to the accompaniment of Happy Birthday cheers.

Voting Age Birthday Dinner

(SERVES 8)

Curried Cucumber Soup   Crackers
Lobster Chambord
Duchess Potatoes Amandine
Hearts of Palm — Spiced Seed Dressing
Raspberried Peaches
Ballot Cake
Coffee

Suggested wine: Rhine or Moselle

ADVANCE PREPARATION SCHEDULE

Deep Freeze	Previous Day	Early Morning
Cake	*Soup*	*Potatoes*
	Rice	
	Peaches	
	Dressing	
	Lobster	

CURRIED CUCUMBER SOUP

4 cups diced, unpared cucumbers
1 cup finely diced, peeled, raw potatoes
⅔ cup sliced leeks *or* green onions
¼ cup chopped parsley
2 14½-ounce cans chicken broth (about 3½ cups)

½ cup water
1½ teaspoons dry mustard
½ teaspoon curry powder
¼ teaspoon white pepper
1½ teaspoons salt
⅔ cup heavy cream, chilled
¾ cup diced, unpared apple

Mix cucumbers, potatoes, leeks, parsley, chicken broth, water, mustard, curry powder, pepper, and salt together in a saucepan. Cover and bring to a boil; cook gently until potatoes are tender, about 10 minutes. Force through a sieve or food mill and cool slightly; then chill. To serve, blend cream carefully into chilled mixture. Fold in apple; garnish each serving with tiny sprigs of parsley.

Note: This is especially attractive served in Pots de Crème cups.

LOBSTER CHAMBORD

4 large live lobsters	Salt and pepper
1 tablespoon salad oil	Dash paprika
1 tablespoon butter	2 cups light cream
½ cup Pernod	1 cup fish broth or consommé
2 tablespoons brandy, warmed	1 tablespoon butter
2 tablespoons flour	

Note: To cut live lobsters, wash and insert knife where tail and body connect. Split lengthwise. Turn on back and cut spinal cord, using a sharp scissors or knife. Crack claws. This may be done at your market. Remove dark vein and spongy tissue. Reserve tomalley (greenish liver) and coral (roe). Both are delicious.

Cut lobsters into medium pieces and sauté them in combined oil and butter for 5 minutes, or until the pieces turn red on all sides, but do not overcook. Pour off fat. Add the Pernod and stir with the brown bits that cling to the pan. Add 2 tablespoons warmed brandy; flame the brandy and let it burn out. Simmer the sauce until reduced to ⅓ its original volume; add salt, pepper, and a dash of paprika. Stir in cream and broth; cover pan and bring liquid to a boil. Add mashed tomalley and roe. Reduce heat and simmer 15 minutes. Transfer to serving dish and keep hot. Make a paste of butter and flour and add to the sauce, gradually. Simmer, stirring until smooth and thick. Strain through a fine sieve over the heated lobster and serve at once.

DUCHESS POTATOES AMANDINE

4 potatoes, in skins	2 tablespoons milk
2 tablespoons butter	1 teaspoon salt
1 egg, well beaten	1 tablespoon butter
¼ cup slivered almonds	

Scrub potatoes, drop in boiling water and cook until tender, about 20 minutes. Peel and mash while still warm; combine with butter, egg, milk, and salt. Shape into fingers about 3″ x 1″. Melt remaining 1 tablespoon butter, add almonds, and brown slightly; coat each potato finger by pressing almonds on surface and place on buttered baking sheet. Heat in a preheated 375° oven for 15 minutes.

HEARTS OF PALM

1 #2 can hearts of palm   1 1½-ounce can pimiento
3 heads Boston lettuce

Place 3 stalks of palm on bed of lettuce. Cut pimiento in strips and place 2 crosswise over hearts of palm. Serve with Spiced Seed Dressing.

SPICED SEED DRESSING

1½ teaspoons celery seed   1 tablespoon onion, grated
1½ teaspoons mustard seed   ½ teaspoon salt
¾ cup salad oil   1 egg yolk
2 tablespoons vinegar   Pinch of sugar

Combine all ingredients and blend well. Makes approximately 1 cup.

RASPBERRIED PEACHES

8 whole fresh peaches   2 10½-ounce packages frozen
2 cups water   raspberries, defrosted
1½ cups sugar

Skin peaches by plunging them first into boiling water, then immediately into cold water. Slip off the skins, leaving the peaches whole and perfect. Combine water and sugar in a saucepan; boil 5 minutes to make a syrup. Place peaches in syrup and cook 2 minutes, turning so that all the surface of the peach is coated. Remove carefully; cool, and refrigerate. Purée raspberries through a sieve, food mill, or blender, and pour over the refrigerated peaches. Let stand several hours or overnight, basting occasionally. Serve from bowl, or in individual compotes.

Note: Fresh raspberries may be used in season. Wash carefully. Remove peaches from syrup; pour boiling hot syrup over the raspberries. Cool and pour over refrigerated peaches and proceed as above. The home-type canned peaches may be used, but the flavor is surpassed by the fresh. A refreshing dessert either way. An elaboration, for a special occasion; place the peaches on meringue shells and spoon the raspberry sauce over them.

BALLOT CAKE
(Lemon Cake)

1 13½-ounce package deluxe yellow cake mix	4 eggs
1 4-ounce package instant lemon pudding	1 cup ice water
	⅔ cup salad oil

Place all ingredients in electric mixer and beat 10 minutes on medium speed. Pour into a buttered and floured angel food pan; bake in a preheated 350° oven 50 minutes.

Note: The use of mixes and preparations was stressed in *Thoughts for Buffets* and therefore we have used a minimum in this book.

Friday Night Supper

(SERVES 10)

Hearts of Artichokes Marinés

Trout Platter   Lemon Sauce

Radish Roses   Sliced Cucumbers

Old-Fashioned Noodle Pudding   Individual Egg Twists

Claret Fruit Compote

Pecan Torte

Coffee   Tea

ADVANCE PREPARATION SCHEDULE

Deep Freeze   **Previous Day**   **Early Morning**
Torte   *Noodle Pudding*   *Artichokes*
    Salt trout   *Cook trout*
    Compote
    Lemon Sauce
    (*without whipped cream*)

HEARTS OF ARTICHOKES MARINES

3 10-ounce packages frozen   ⅛ teaspoon tarragon (optional)
   artichoke hearts   2 heads iceberg lettuce
6 tablespoons lemon juice   1 green pepper, chopped
½ cup olive oil   2 hard-cooked eggs, chopped
½ teaspoon salt   1 tablespoon capers
⅛ teaspoon freshly ground pepper   1 2-ounce can rolled anchovies

Cook artichoke hearts; drain and chill. Marinate for 1 hour in combined lemon juice, oil, and seasonings in refrigerator. To serve, arrange antichoke hearts in lettuce cups; sprinkle with green pepper and hard-cooked eggs. Top each with capers and anchovies. Serve icy cold as appetizer or salad.

TROUT PLATTER

10 1-inch slices of white trout   ½ cup chopped celery, with leaves
1½ teaspoons salt   1 tablespoon lemon juice *or*
Water to cover   vinegar
2 onions, sliced

Wash fish and rub with salt. Let stand overnight. In the morning, rinse fish and place in large saucepan, in one layer; cover with water. Add onions, celery, and lemon juice; bring to a boil, reduce heat and simmer about 10 minutes or until fish flakes easily. Remove carefully to serving platter. Refrigerate until cold.

To serve, pour Lemon Sauce around fish, and garnish with parsley and carrot flowers.

LEMON SAUCE

4 eggs, slightly beaten	2 tablespoons flour
1 cup lemon juice	¼ cup water for paste
⅞ cup water	¼ cup butter
¾ cup sugar	1 cup heavy cream, whipped
1 teaspoon salt	¼ cup slivered almonds
1 tablespoon dry mustard	(optional)

Combine eggs, lemon juice, water, and sugar in top of double boiler. Make a paste of salt, mustard, flour, and water and blend with egg mixture. Place over boiling water and cook, stirring until thick. Add butter, heat until well blended. Remove, cool and fold in whipped cream just before serving. Add slivered almonds with whipped cream. Makes 3 cups.

OLD-FASHIONED NOODLE PUDDING

1 pound broad noodles, cooked (*al dente*)	6 eggs, well beaten
	¾ cup sugar
1 pound small-curd cottage cheese	1 quart milk
1½ teaspoons salt	

Note: This pudding must be started in advance to insure sufficient refrigeration. Bake it the previous day or early morning if used for dinner.

Combine noodles, cottage cheese, eggs, sugar, milk and salt and pour into well-greased 14″ x 10″ baking pan. Place in a preheated 350° oven and bake 1 hour, or until tested by inserting knife. If knife is clean when removed, pudding is done. Cool and refrigerate in baking pan about 8 hours or more. Cut in 3-inch squares, without removing from pan, and reheat in a preheated 350° oven for about 25 minutes before serving. Remove portions to large platter and garnish with parsley. Serve very hot.

INDIVIDUAL EGG TWISTS

This recipe makes 1 large and 18 individual twists. Freeze the large bread, or the unbaked dough, and use with another menu.

1 cake compressed, *or*	1 tablespoon sugar
1 package dry yeast	¼ cup shortening
¼ cup lukewarm water	2 eggs, beaten
2 cups hot water	6 cups all-purpose flour
1 tablespoon salt	1 egg yolk, slightly beaten
¼ cup poppy seeds	

Dissolve compressed yeast in lukewarm water (dry yeast in warm water). Combine salt, sugar, and shortening in mixing bowl and blend in hot water. Cool, and when lukewarm add dissolved yeast and beaten eggs. Add flour gradually; mix until too stiff to stir with a spoon. Place on a floured board and knead until smooth and elastic, about 10 minutes. Place in a greased bowl, cover and set in a warm place to rise until double in bulk, about 2 hours. Cut off ⅔ of dough for large loaf (twist). Divide in 4 parts, use 3 for large braid; roll each 1½ inches thick. Hold beginning ends of the 3 strips of dough together by weighting with a knife, then braid the 3 pieces, forming a loaf. Divide fourth strip in three, make a small braid; place over large loaf as ornamental top. Place on well-greased pan; cover, let rise again until doubled in bulk. Brush with beaten egg yolk and sprinkle with poppy seeds. Bake in a preheated 400° oven 15 minutes; reduce heat to 350° and bake 30 to 45 minutes more, or until brown. Instead of 1 large loaf, 2 or 3 smaller loaves may be made.

Individual Loaves: Use remaining ⅓ of recipe for individual loaves. Cut into 18 small pieces and cut each piece into 3 strips. Braid these strips to make small twists (rolls). Place on well-greased pan; let rise until doubled in bulk. Brush with beaten egg and sprinkle with poppy seeds. Bake in a preheated 350° oven about 20 to 25 minutes until brown.

CLARET FRUIT COMPOTE

½ pound dried apricots	3 cups claret
½ pound dried peaches	1½ cups sugar
½ pound dried apples	1 1-pound package frozen *or*
½ pound dried prunes	1 #2 can sour cherries
½ pound dried pears	

Wash dried fruit and soak in cold water 2 hours. Pour claret in saucepan; add sugar and dissolve. Simmer slowly until consistency of heavy syrup. Drain soaked dried fruit and cherries; add fruit to syrup, cover and simmer 1½ hours, or until fruit is tender. Serve warm or cold as individual compotes.

Note: For a smaller quantity use 1 pound dried mixed fruits with ¾ cup sugar, 1½ cups claret, and 1 cup sour cherries.

PECAN TORTE

2 tablespoons flour	1 cup sugar
½ teaspoon salt	1 tablespoon orange juice, *or* rum
½ teaspoon baking powder	½ cup pecans, grated
4 egg yolks	4 egg whites, beaten stiff

Sift flour, salt, and baking powder together. Beat egg yolks until thick and lemon colored; add to flour mixture. Beat in sugar, orange juice, and pecans; blend well. Fold egg whites into batter and pour into two 8-inch greased layer cake pans. Bake in a preheated 350° oven 25 minutes. No longer than 3 hours before serving, spread Filling between layers and frost with Chocolate Cream.

Filling:

½ cup heavy cream, whipped   1½ teaspoons grated orange rind

Combine whipped cream and orange rind.

Chocolate Cream:

1 6-ounce package chocolate chips	½ cup dairy sour cream
	Dash salt
Whole pecans	

Melt chocolate chips over hot water. Stir in sour cream and salt. Spread on cake and garnish with whole pecans.

Friends and Family Dinner

(SERVES 6 TO 8)

Marinated Shrimp on the Rocks   Saltines

Bohemian Veal

Sesame Sprouts   Potato Dumplings

Cranberry Mold   Lemon Fluff Pie

Coffee   Milk

Suggested wine: red or white Bordeaux

ADVANCE PREPARATION SCHEDULE

Previous Day	Early Morning
Marinate shrimp	*Clean sprouts*
Cranberry Mold	*Prepare dumplings*
Lemon pie	*Prepare veal*

MARINATED SHRIMP ON THE ROCKS

3 medium yellow onions, sliced thin
1 cup vegetable oil
¾ cup cider vinegar
¼ cup capers and juice
½ teaspoon salt
⅛ teaspoon freshly ground pepper
¼ cup sugar

Juice of 1 lemon
1 teaspoon Worcestershire
1 bay leaf
½ teaspoon garlic powder
¼ teaspoon dry mustard
½ teaspoon parsley flakes
3 pounds shrimp, cooked, cleaned, and deveined

Black olives

Combine all ingredients except shrimp and olives. Blend very well. Immerse shrimp in this marinade and allow to stand a minimum of 2 hours. Toss shrimp every half hour. To serve, fill large bowl with chopped ice; drain shrimp and arrange with olives on ice. Have colored toothpicks available. Use number of shrimp needed, refrigerate remainder (shrimp will store for several days) or reduce recipe. Makes about 60 shrimp.

BOHEMIAN VEAL

3 pounds veal steak	¼ teaspoon Worcestershire
Flour	¼ teaspoon dried rosemary
3 tablespoons cooking oil	2 tablespoons catsup
½ teaspoon salt	1 cup sauterne *or*
⅛ teaspoon pepper	other white table wine
½ teaspoon garlic salt	1 cup dairy sour cream
½ teaspoon paprika	Watercress
½ teaspoon dry mustard	1 tomato

Cut veal into serving size pieces. Dredge with flour and brown on both sides in heated oil. Combine salt, pepper, garlic salt, paprika, mustard, Worcestershire, rosemary, catsup, and wine, stirring until blended. Pour over browned veal; cover and simmer until tender, about 50 minutes. Remove to platter; keep hot. Add sour cream to drippings left in pan and heat but do not boil. Pour over meat. Garnish with watercress, and a quartered tomato.

SESAME SPROUTS

3 pounds brussels sprouts *or*	¼ cup butter, melted
2 10-ounce packages frozen	¼ cup sesame seeds

Wash fresh brussels sprouts, removing the discolored outside leaves, and leave whole. Boil 12 minutes in sufficient water to cover. For frozen, cook according to package directions. Melt butter; add sesame seeds, and heat until very light brown. To serve, pour over sprouts.

POTATO DUMPLINGS

½ cup grated raw potatoes	2 eggs, slightly beaten
2 tablespoons shortening	¾ cup flour
1 tablespoon chopped onion	Melted butter *or* margarine
6 medium potatoes, cooked and riced (about 2 pounds)	½ tablespoon caraway seeds (optional)
1 tablespoon salt	

Drain grated raw potato in strainer, stirring occasionally. Heat shortening in skillet; add onion and cook slowly until yellowed. Add grated potato and cook until a paste is formed. Let cool; add riced potatoes, salt, eggs, and flour, stirring until smooth. Form into balls the size of walnuts. Drop into boiling, salted water. Cook for about 3 minutes after dumplings rise to top of water, or until cooked through to center. Remove from water, drain and serve with melted butter or margarine. Optional: sprinkle with seeds.

Note: Omit caraway seeds with this menu, since seeds are used in the brussels sprouts recipe.

CRANBERRY MOLD

1 orange, unpeeled
1 16-ounce can whole
  cranberries
1 7-ounce can crushed pineapple
1¾ cups liquid

1 package cherry-flavored gelatin
¼ cup coarsely chopped walnuts

Garnish:

Greens and orange slices

Grind orange and combine with cranberries and pineapple. Drain and measure juice, adding sufficient water to make 1¾ cups liquid. Bring 1 cup of this liquid to a boil; add gelatin and dissolve. Add remaining ¾ cup of liquid. Mix well and refrigerate until of jelly-like consistency; remove from refrigerator; add strained fruits and nuts. Pour into oiled 4-cup mold; refrigerate until firm. Unmold on greens and garnish with unpeeled orange slices.

LEMON FLUFF PIE

Chocolate Crumb Crust:

1¼ cups finely crushed chocolate
  wafers
1 tablespoon sugar

¼ cup melted butter
Pinch of salt

Mix together wafers, sugar, melted butter, and salt; press firmly into 9-inch pie pan to form pie shell.

Filling:

4 egg yolks, beaten slightly
¼ teaspoon salt
2 teaspoons grated lemon peel
½ cup lemon juice
1 cup sugar

1 tablespoon unflavored gelatin
¼ cup cold water
4 egg whites
1 cup heavy cream
2 tablespoons sugar

Cook egg yolks, salt, lemon peel, lemon juice, and ½ cup sugar in double boiler over hot water until thick; about 5 minutes. Remove from heat. Soak gelatin in cold water for 5 minutes, then add to egg yolk mixture. Stir until dissolved; cool. Beat egg whites until stiff; gradually add ½ cup remaining sugar and beat 1 minute longer; fold into cooked mixture with ½ cup cream, whipped. Pile lightly in prepared Chocolate Crumb Crust. Whip the remaining ½ cup cream; sweeten with 2 tablespoons sugar and swirl around edge of pie.

Our Man of the Year Dinner

(SERVES 8)

Chicken Shrimp Soup   Cheese Wafers
Olives   Green Onions
Red Wine Tenderloin in Aspic
Horseradish Sauce   Caraway Rye Bread
Caesar Salad
Iced Poppy-Seed Cake
Cognac   Coffee

Suggested wine: red Burgundy or Bordeaux

ADVANCE PREPARATION SCHEDULE

Deep Freeze	Previous Day	Early Morning
Cheese wafers	*Tenderloin*	*Soup*
Cake		*Horseradish Sauce*
		Assemble salad
		ingredients (without eggs)
		Custard Filling
		Assemble cake
		Chocolate Icing

CHICKEN SHRIMP SOUP

Great Gumbo! This soup was served to a group of our hostesses who unanimously voted approval.

6 tablespoons butter	3½ cups water
8 chicken wings	8 sprigs parsley
¼ cup flour	1 tablespoon salt
2 large onions, chopped	¼ teaspoon pepper
2 cloves garlic, minced	1 teaspoon seasoning salt
6 celery stalks, cut in ¼-inch dice	1 teaspoon oregano
	1 tablespoon sugar
1 pound small shrimp, cooked, deveined	½ teaspoon celery seed
	1 bay leaf
1 6½-ounce can crabmeat	¾ teaspoon crushed red pepper in ½-inch pieces
1 #2½ can tomatoes	

8 okra, fresh *or* frozen, cut

Heat butter in 2-quart saucepan. Remove tips of chicken wings and cut in half at the joint; dredge with flour, place in butter, brown evenly. Add onions and garlic; sauté for 10 minutes, or until lightly browned; blend in celery. Now add shrimp, crabmeat, tomatoes, water, and parsley; the salt, pepper, seasoning salt, oregano, sugar, celery seed, bay leaf, and red pepper. Simmer for 1 hour; add okra and cook 10 minutes. Serve in bowls with a scoop of Fluffy Rice (see Index). (Serves 12.)

Note: Freeze leftovers and serve for luncheon another day with salad, rolls, and dessert.

CHEESE WAFERS

¼ cup butter	½ cup sharp Cheddar cheese
¼ teaspoon Tabasco	spread

⅔ cup all-purpose flour

Cream butter and Tabasco; blend cheese spread and flour. Combine mixtures. Form into a 2-inch roll. Place in refrigerator and chill several hours until firm. Cut into thin slices, about ¼ inch, and place on greased cooky sheet. Bake in a preheated 400° oven 12 to 15 minutes. May be frozen for future use. Good as accompaniment for clear soup or salads.

RED WINE TENDERLOIN IN ASPIC

1 6- to 7-pound beef tenderloin   Seasoned salt
¼ cup butter, softened   ½ cup dry red wine
Salt   3 cups Red Wine Aspic

Garnish:

Pimiento-stuffed olives, sliced   2 hard-cooked eggs
2 tablespoons capers   Leaf lettuce

Place tenderloin on rack in roasting pan. Tuck narrow end under (or remove it to use for another recipe) to make roast uniformly thick. Spread butter over meat, season with salts. Insert meat thermometer and place in a preheated 425° oven for 30 minutes. Reduce heat to 300° and baste meat with wine. Continue to cook 20 more minutes per pound for rare, or until meat thermometer registers 140°. Baste meat every 15 minutes with wine and pan drippings. If drippings in pan dry out too quickly add about 2 tablespoons of butter and ¼ cup water. Cool thoroughly. Mold in Red Wine Aspic.

Red Wine Aspic:

3 cups liquid comprised of   2 tablespoons unflavored gelatin
1 10-ounce can beef broth
½ cup dry red wine
natural pan juices from
tenderloin, drained

Measure liquid. If insufficient, add water to make 3 cups. Soak gelatin in ½ cup of cold liquid. Heat remainder, add soaked gelatin and dissolve.

Note: To use as garnish in other recipes, chill until set and chop coarsely. For Red Wine Tenderloin proceed as follows: Oil two 9″ x 5″ x 3″ bread pans. Pour in each about ½ inch of liquid, and place slices of olives in pattern for decoration. Place in refrigerator until set. Cut tenderloin in 2 pieces, and place each half in a bread pan over congealed gelatin. Pour remaining gelatin around each. If any remains, pour into small mold for garnish. Place pans in refrigerator to jell until very firm.

Unmold on lettuce-lined platter, placing both halves of beef together to form one piece. Remove aspic from small mold, chop coarsely and place it around beef. Chop whites and yolks of eggs separately and place them in ribbonlike rows with capers at either end of platter. Add a few pimiento olives for contrast.

HORSERADISH SAUCE

½ cup prepared horseradish   2 tablespoons sugar
1 cup mayonnaise   ½ teaspoon salt
1 cup heavy cream, whipped

Blend horseradish, mayonnaise, sugar, and salt together. Fold in whipped cream. Chill.

CAESAR SALAD

2 coddled eggs   6 anchovy fillets, shredded
1 garlic, clove, minced   ¾ cup olive oil
¼ teaspoon pepper   3 tablespoons cider vinegar
⅛ teaspoon salt   8 cups romaine lettuce, torn
½ teaspoon prepared English   ¾ cup Parmesan cheese
   mustard   1½ cups Croutons

To coddle eggs, bring water to a boil; remove from heat. Place raw eggs (with shells) in water; cover and let stand for 2 minutes. Mix garlic, pepper, salt, mustard, anchovy fillets, olive oil, and vinegar; let set for 2 hours. Open coddled eggs and toss with lettuce. Add anchovy mixture and toss lightly; sprinkle with Parmesan cheese and Croutons (see Index).

ICED POPPY-SEED CAKE

¾ cup poppy seeds   2 cups sifted cake flour
¾ cup milk   2 teaspoons baking powder
¾ cup butter   ½ teaspoon salt
1½ cups sugar   4 egg whites, beaten stiff
1 teaspoon vanilla   Chocolate Icing

Blend poppy seeds and milk; allow to stand 2 hours. Cream butter with sugar and vanilla until light and fluffy. Sift dry ingredients together and add to creamed mixture alternately with poppy seeds and milk. Fold in egg whites carefully and pour into 2 greased 8-inch layer cake pans; bake in a preheated 350° oven 25 to 30 minutes, or until cake tests done. (Test by piercing with toothpick; if toothpick comes out clean, cake is done.) Cool and fill with

Custard Filling. Ice with Chocolate Icing or dust with confectioners' sugar.

Custard Filling:

½ cup sugar	4 egg yolks, beaten
1 tablespoon cornstarch	¼ teaspoon salt
1 cup milk, scalded	1 teaspoon vanilla
	½ cup chopped nuts

Mix sugar with cornstarch in saucepan. Add scalded milk and cook until slightly thickened, stirring constantly. Stir small amount of hot mixture into beaten egg yolks; then return to rest of filling and cook, stirring until smooth and of custard consistency. Add salt, vanilla, and chopped nuts. Cool.

Chocolate Icing:

2 1-ounce squares unsweetened chocolate	3 tablespoons butter, softened
	2 cups confectioners' sugar, sifted
3 tablespoons hot milk	1 teaspoon vanilla

Combine chocolate with hot milk and stir until melted. Add butter, blend in sugar until smooth; then add vanilla and beat thoroughly. If icing appears dull, add a few more drops of hot milk. Spread on cake and allow to set several hours before cutting.

Variation:

Use prepared chocolate pudding for top, sides, and layers. Sprinkle with chopped nuts.

Travelogue Dinner

(SERVES 10)

Artichokes with Tarragon Mayonnaise

Manicotti or Cannelloni   Tomato Sauce

Circle Salad

Vanilla Nut Cookies   Tipsy Oranges

Coffee   Tea

Previous Day	Early Morning
Noodle dough	*Fillings*
Tomato sauce	*Crêpes*
Cook artichokes	*Crisp vegetables*
Mayonnaise	

ARTICHOKES WITH TARRAGON MAYONNAISE

4 large artichokes, 2½ to 3 pounds	2 tablespoons lemon juice
¼ cup salad *or* olive oil	1 clove garlic
	1 teaspoon salt
⅛ teaspoon pepper	

Trim stalks from base of artichokes; remove any discolored leaves. Wash artichokes well in cold water; drain. Tie each with twine, to hold leaves in place. Fill 8-quart saucepan with 6 quarts water; add oil, lemon juice, garlic, salt, and pepper; bring to boil. Plunge artichokes into boiling liquid. Reduce heat; simmer gently 30 minutes, or until base tests tender. Drain artichokes well. Let cool; refrigerate, covered, at least 4 hours or until ready to serve.

Tarragon Mayonnaise:

4 egg yolks	1 teaspoon dry mustard
6 tablespoons tarragon vinegar	2 cups salad oil
2 teaspoons salt	2 teaspoons dried tarragon leaves

Prepare one half mayonnaise at a time to prevent curdling. In electric blender, combine 2 egg yolks, 2 tablespoons vinegar, 1 teaspoon salt, and ½ teaspoon mustard with ¼ cup oil. Cover; blend 15 seconds at high speed. Then very slowly drizzle in ¾ cup oil while blending; blend about 1 minute in all. Turn mayonnaise into bowl. Repeat blending as above, using same amounts of ingredients. Place wax paper directly on surface of mayonnaise; refrigerate several hours, or until ready to serve. Beat in remaining 2 tablespoons vinegar. Remove twine from artichokes. Open each like a flower; remove choke, and discard. With scissors, snip off spike ends of leaves. Fill center of each artichoke with about ½ cup Tarragon Mayonnaise. Arrange on large serving platter. Garnish with bouquet of parsley and carrot flowers. Guests peel off leaves and dip them into mayonnaise.

MANICOTTI

Pancakes:

6 eggs	½ teaspoon salt
1 cup milk	1½ cups flour

Beat eggs lightly, add milk, salt, flour, and beat until smooth. Grease a 7-inch skillet lightly, heat and pour ¼ of batter, spreading to cover bottom of pan. Cook until lightly browned (on one side only) and cooked through; do not turn over. Place on wax paper browned side up, until batter is used.

Spread a tablespoon of filling on each pancake, fold in thirds, overlapping, and arrange side by side in 1 layer in shallow greased baking pan. Cover with 3 cups of Tomato Sauce. Bake 30 minutes in a preheated 350° oven.

Cheese Filling:

1½ cups ricotta *or* cottage cheese	2 eggs
½ cup grated Romano cheese	⅛ teaspon pepper
¼ cup chopped parsley	1½ teaspoons salt

Combine ricotta and Romano cheese, parsley, eggs, pepper, and salt. Mix well.

Meat Filling:

2 tablespoons oil, salad *or* olive	1½ cups diced Swiss *or* Mozzarella cheese
2 onions, chopped	1 cup soft bread crumbs
1 clove garlic, minced	1 egg, slightly beaten
½ pounds mushrooms, chopped coarsely	1½ teaspoons salt
1½ pounds ground beef	½ teaspoon oregano
	¼ teaspoon coarsely ground pepper

Heat oil in skillet, add onions and garlic; brown lightly. Stir in mushrooms, cook 3 minutes; add beef, then cheese, crumbs, egg, and seasonings. Blend well with wooden spoon; fill pancakes (Manicotti).

TOMATO SAUCE

3 tablespoons shortening	1 #2 can Italian tomatoes
½ cup chopped onions	½ cup tomato paste
1 clove garlic, minced	¼ teaspoon oregano
⅓ cup mushrooms, sliced, fresh *or*	¼ teaspoon salt
canned	⅛ teaspoon freshly ground pepper

Heat shortening, add onions and garlic, sauté until onions are transparent; add mushrooms, cook 1 minute. Add tomatoes, tomato paste, and seasonings; simmer 15 minutes.

CANNELLONI

Noodle Dough:

2 eggs	1 teaspoon salt
2 tablespoons skim milk	1½ cups sifted all-purpose flour

Beat eggs until frothy. Add milk, salt and flour; mix with a fork until dough holds together. Knead on heavily floured board until dough loses stickiness and becomes smooth. Cover and let stand 30 minutes. Divide in half. Roll each piece of dough as thin as possible (1/16 inch approximately) on a lightly floured board. Let stand uncovered 10 to 15 minutes. Cut into twelve 4-inch squares. Cook in 4 quarts boiling salted water, uncovered, for 10 minutes. Remove, drain on paper towel.

Crêpe Batter:

3 eggs, beaten	2 tablespoons butter, melted
1 cup milk	¾ cup unsifted all-purpose flour
½ teaspoon salt	Salad oil

Beat the eggs, milk, salt, and butter together. Stir the unsifted flour into egg mixture until well blended. Heat 1 teaspoon oil in a 7-inch skillet; pour in 3 to 4 tablespoons batter, tilting skillet quickly to coat bottom, using just enough batter to make a very thin pancake. Cook on medium-high heat until lightly browned, turn over and brown reverse side lightly. Slide out onto a platter; stack the pancakes carefully. Makes 18 wrappers.

Cannelloni Filling:

2 pair calves' brains, cooked	Pinch nutmeg
1 cup cooked spinach *or* chard	2 tablespoons olive oil
½ pound sausage meat	½ cup cracker crumbs
1 tablespoon chopped parsley	½ cup grated Parmesan cheese
1 teaspoon oregano	3 eggs, lightly beaten
½ tablespoon chopped onion	½ teaspoon salt
1 clove garlic, minced	¼ teaspoon pepper

To cook brains: Soak brains in salted water (½ teaspoon salt to 1 cup water) for ½ hour. Drain. Bring fresh salted water to rolling boil, add brains, cover, reduce heat and simmer 15 minutes. Drain and place in ice water to harden. Remove membranes with a very sharp knife; brains are very tender.

Squeeze spinach completely dry, combine with brains, and put through food chopper twice; blend with sausage meat, parsley, oregano, onion, garlic, and nutmeg. Mix well; add olive oil, Parmesan, cracker crumbs, eggs, salt, and pepper. Blend well.

Cannelloni Sauce:

4 tablespoons butter	½ teaspoon salt
½ onion, grated	⅛ teaspoon oregano
½ cup flour	Pinch nutmeg
2 cups chicken broth	2 egg yolks, beaten
2 cups hot milk	½ cup grated Parmesan cheese
¼ cup butter	

Heat butter in saucepan, add onion, and cook until transparent. Do not brown. Blend in flour until bubbly, add broth and milk and stir until thickened. Add salt, oregano, and nutmeg. Stir a small amount of hot liquid into eggs and return to saucepan. Heat.

When all the pancakes are completed, fill each, using 1 heaping tablespoon of filling. Fold into package shape or into a roll with open ends. Place seam sides down, in greased, shallow serving-baking dish, side by side. Cover with sauce, sprinkle with a layer of grated Parmesan, and dot with butter. Place in a preheated 350° oven and heat until sauce bubbles, 30 to 35 minutes. Serve from casserole piping hot.

CIRCLE SALAD

2 heads Chinese cabbage	2 Italian onions (sweet red)
2 bunches watercress	¾ cup Herbed French Dressing

Wash greens thoroughly; remove stems from watercress. Cut cabbage in ¼-inch slices. Do not separate stalks. Cut onions in ¼-inch rings. Drain and crisp in refrigerator. To serve, arrange cabbage slices and watercress alternately in a large bowl; circle top with onion rings. Cover with Herbed French Dressing (see Index) and toss lightly.

TIPSY ORANGES

10 navel oranges	⅓ cup sugar
⅓ cup whiskey	¼ cup butter
2 cups orange juice	⅓ cup sugar
¼ cup brandy (optional)	

Peel 2 oranges very carefully, removing only thin outer peel (zest). Sliver peeling and marinate 30 minutes in whiskey. Combine with orange juice and ⅓ cup sugar; simmer 15 minutes until it becomes glazed and bubbly. Reserve.

Peel 8 oranges carefully, leaving each whole. Remove all white parts so that pulp is completely uncovered. Arrange in ovenproof dish. Cream butter and second ⅓ cup sugar; top each orange with proportionate amount of mixture. Broil 6 inches from heat for 10 minutes, basting often until topping carmelizes. Watch to prevent burning. To serve, add reserved syrup and place over direct medium heat for 10 minutes, basting twice. Warm brandy, set aflame, and pour over oranges. Delicious hot or cold.

VANILLA NUT COOKIES

2 tablespoons and 2 teaspoons butter	1½ teaspoons vanilla
	½ cup sifted cake flour
2 cups brown sugar, firmly packed	1 teaspoon baking powder
	½ teaspoon salt
2 eggs, well beaten	1½ cups chopped pecans

Cream butter and sugar; add eggs, vanilla, and beat well. Combine flour, baking powder, and salt; blend into butter mixture. Stir in pecans. Line a cooky sheet with unglazed paper. Drop ½ teaspoon of batter, a minimum of 2 inches apart. Bake in a preheated 375° oven for 6 minutes.

Special Note: This is a very thin batter and spreads considerably.

Cheers for Fifty Years Dinner

(SERVES 6 TO 8)

Sunflower Shrimp

Mushroom Duxelles   Pumpernickel Rounds

Chicken Vin Blanc   Parslied Potato Balls

Sesame Green Beans   Soft Rolls

Celebration Salad

Chocolate Ambrosia   Coffee

Suggested wine: red Burgundy or Pinot Blanc

ADVANCE PREPARATION SCHEDULE

Previous Day	**Early Morning**
Dressings	*Cook artichokes*
Chocolate Ambrosia	*Mushrooms for heating*
	Assemble chicken

SUNFLOWER SHRIMP

2 artichokes
1 clove garlic (optional)
1 1½-ounce jar tiny Danish
Shrimp

1 cup Spiced French Dressing
Catsup
Parsley
Radishes

Cut off stems of artichokes and any brown tips of leaves; wash thoroughly and let stand in salted water about 30 minutes. Drain. Place in boiling salted water to cover; add garlic and simmer 25 to 45 minutes or until bottom leaves pull away easily from stalk. Turn upside down to drain; refrigerate. Drain shrimp, marinate in Spiced French Dressing (see Index), and place in refrigerator for a minimum of 1 hour. To serve, use a round 14-inch platter; separate artichoke leaves from stalk and place them flat and petal-wise, as close together as possible, covering surface of platter completely. Place a shrimp on base of each petal, to be eaten with edible portion of the artichoke leaf. Add color by dotting each shrimp with a small dab of catsup. Garnish platter with a bouquet of parsley and radishes in the center, or with a bowl of olives and radishes. Remove choke (spiny substance) from the heart. Next day cut heart in fourths; combine and marinate with leftover cucumber and tomatoes.

Note: This serves as an excellent side salad as well.

MUSHROOM DUXELLES

1 pound large, fresh mushrooms	2 tablespoons butter
2 tablespoons butter	2 tablespoons flour
½ cup minced cooked chicken	1¼ cups hot water
1 tablespoon lemon juice	2 chicken bouillon cubes
½ teaspoon salt	½ cup heavy cream
⅛ teaspoon pepper	Paprika
1 tablespoon coarsely chopped green pepper	

Wash mushroom and remove stems. Melt butter in saucepan; add mushroom caps, sauté 8 minutes, and remove from heat. Grind mushroom stems, add to same pan in which mushroom caps were sautéed, and cook 10 minutes.

Combine ground stems, chicken, lemon juice, salt, pepper, and green pepper. Fill mushroom caps and set in chafing dish or heated servers. Heat 2 tablespoons butter in saucepan; blend in flour and cook until smooth. Add hot water, bouillon cubes, and cream; heat thoroughly and pour over filled caps. Sprinkle with paprika. Serve with toast points.

Variation:

Substitute crabmeat for chicken, in other menus.

CHICKEN VIN BLANC

8 chicken breasts	4 teaspoons potato flour
Salt	2 teaspoons tomato paste
Pepper	2 cups chicken stock *or* broth
6 tablespoons butter	½ cup white wine *or* sherry
4 tablespoons brandy	8 thin slices Gruyère cheese

Season chicken with salt and pepper. Melt butter in skillet, add chicken, and sauté until brown and tender, about 30 minutes. Remove chicken to an oven-to-table serving dish. Warm brandy in ladle; flame, pour over chicken, and allow flame to burn out. Stir flour and tomato paste into browned butter in skillet; add chicken stock and wine. Stir over heat until mixture comes to a boil. If too thick, add more wine or stock. Top each chicken breast with a slice of Gruyère cheese; pour sauce over, and brown quickly under preheated broiler.

PARSLIED POTATO BALLS

3 pounds potatoes	½ cup finely chopped parsley
¼ cup butter	¾ teaspoon salt

Peel potatoes; make 1 quart of potato balls, using French cutter. Boil in salted water 10 to 15 minutes, or until just tender. Drain thoroughly. Heat butter in skillet, blend in parsley and salt; add potato balls and toss lightly until completely coated. Heat thoroughly and serve at once.

SESAME GREEN BEANS

1 teaspoon sesame seeds	2 tablespoons pimiento
¼ cup butter	2 pounds green beans, cooked *or*
Juice of 1 lemon	2 10½-ounce packages frozen

Brown seeds in butter lightly. Add lemon juice and pimiento. Pour over cooked green beans. To serve, mound in center of serving platter and surround with Parslied Potato Balls.

CELEBRATION SALAD

½ clove garlic, minced	2 tablespoons tarragon vinegar
¼ teaspoon salt	8 to 10 chopped anchovies
¼ cup mayonnaise	2 teaspoons minced parsley
¼ cup dairy sour cream	Dash pepper
Boston and Bibb lettuce (very crisp)	

Mash garlic and salt. Blend with remaining ingredients, except greens. Toss lightly with greens in salad bowl. Serve immediately.

CHOCOLATE AMBROSIA

1½ dozen lady fingers, split	1 tablespoon Cointreau (or
6 tablespoons sweet sherry	Orange Curaçao)
12 ounces sweet cooking	6 egg yolks, well beaten
chocolate	6 egg whites, beaten stiff
1 tablespoon sugar	¼ cup almonds, slivered
1 tablespoon water	1 cup heavy cream, whipped

½ teaspoon vanilla

Line sides and bottom of a medium sized (9-inch) spring form pan with split lady fingers, placing rounded sides against the sides and bottom of the cake pan. Moisten bottom layer only slightly with 2 tablespoons of the sherry. Melt chocolate in top of double boiler, adding sugar, water, Cointreau, and well beaten egg yolks. Cool; fold in stiffly beaten egg whites. Pour half of chocolate into prepared spring form; sprinkle with slivered almonds, add a layer of split lady fingers, flat side down. Moisten with another 2 tablespoons sherry, and pour in remaining chocolate filling. Again, sprinkle with slivered almonds, cover with split lady fingers, flat side down, and moisten with balance of sherry. Refrigerate for at least 12 hours. (Serves 10 to 12.)

Decorate with whipped cream combined with vanilla, forced through pastry tube to a large "50" and serve it with gaily lighted gold candles.

Moving Day Dinner for New Neighbors

(SERVES 6)

Sherry Cheese Blend — Melba Toast Rounds

Vienna Herring Salad

Tongue Monterey   Farfel and Mushrooms

Baked Fruited Lima Beans

German Cole Slaw

Apple Slices   Camptown Brownies

Coffee

Suggested wine: Beaujolais

ADVANCE PREPARATION SCHEDULE

Deep Freeze	Previous Day	Early Morning
Brownies	*Tongue*	*Cheese dip*
	Apple Slices dough	*Herring salad*
		Prepare farfel and mushrooms for baking
		Lima beans
		Apple slices
		Cole slaw

SHERRY CHEESE BLEND

1 8-ounce wedge blue cheese
1 8-ounce package cream cheese
2 5-ounce packages chive cream cheese
4 tablespoons olive juice
4 tablespoons sherry
1 teaspoon Tabasco
½ cup grated onion
½ cup stuffed olives, chopped
Paprika

Have ingredients at room temperature before mixing. Blend all together, except paprika, until well mixed and creamy. Pour into serving bowl, top with paprika and serve with melba toast rounds. This recipe is too generous for six, but it may be used another day as dressing with Tomato Aspic. (See Index for Aspic.) Makes 3 cups.

VIENNA HERRING SALAD

1 12-ounce jar herring in wine
2 slices rye bread
¼ cup oil
¼ cup dry white wine
2 tablespoons vinegar *or* lemon juice
1 tablespoon sugar
1 small onion, sliced
1 apple, unpeeled and sliced
3 hard-cooked eggs
1 tablespoon parsley
Paprika
1 loaf cocktail rye bread

Drain herring; remove all spices, reserving onions. Soak 2 slices rye bread in combined oil, wine, vinegar, and sugar. Place herring, onions reserved from herring, and fresh onion, apple and 2 eggs in chopping bowl; chop until thoroughly mixed and smooth. Mash soaked rye bread, add mixture to herring combination; blend well and refrigerate. To serve, place mixture in bowl and sprinkle with yolk of remaining egg; garnish with parsley and sprinkle with paprika. Serve with cocktail rye bread.

TONGUE MONTEREY

1 pound prunes	½ cup brown sugar, firmly packed
1 fresh tongue	1 sliced lemon and juice
1 10-ounce can tomato soup	1 beef bouillon cube
1 onion, sliced	

Wash and soak prunes overnight. Wash tongue and place in kettle with water to cover; do not season. Simmer tongue slowly until done, about 3 to 3½ hours; it is cooked when fork-tender. Peel, place in casserole; add prunes, tomato soup, brown sugar, lemon and juice, bouillon, and onion. Bake 30 to 45 minutes in a preheated 350° oven.

Note: To improve flavor, prepare previous day. Reheat before serving.

FARFEL AND MUSHROOMS

1 onion	1½ quarts water
½ pound fresh mushrooms	1 chicken bouillon cube
¼ cup butter	½ teaspoon salt
1 8-ounce box farfel	

Grind onion and mushrooms together; melt butter in skillet and add mushroom mixture. Cook 10 minutes. Combine water, bouillon cube, and salt in saucepan; add farfel and boil 15 minutes. Drain, do not rinse. Combine the two mixtures; pour into 1½-quart buttered casserole. Set casserole in pan of boiling water, and bake in a preheated 350° oven 30 minutes.

BAKED FRUITED LIMA BEANS

1 #2 can lima beans	6 slices crisp, cooked bacon
1 #2½ can pears,	(optional)
with juice	¼ cup brown sugar, firmly
¼ cup butter	packed
½ cup chili sauce	

Heat beans in own liquid, then drain, reserving liquid. Use half of beans to cover bottom of well-greased baking dish. Drain pears, reserve juice, and place drained pears, round side up, on the beans. Melt butter in bean liquid; add ¼ cup of this same to baking dish, reserving remainder for basting. Fill space around pears with balance of beans. Mix brown sugar and chili sauce with ¼ cup of the pear juice. Pour over fruit and bean mixture, and bake about 30 minutes in a preheated 350° oven. Keep basting with bean and butter liquid. Five minutes before serving, arrange cooked bacon on top of beans, between pears. If made in advance, reheat in oven.

Note: A suggested delicious buffet accompaniment for ham or turkey.

GERMAN COLE SLAW

1 medium-sized head white cabbage	¼ cup vinegar
	2 egg yolks, beaten
2 quarts boiling water	1 teaspoon salt
2 onions, grated	¼ teaspoon pepper
1 green pepper, finely chopped	3 tablespoons olive oil
1 cup dairy sour cream	

Wash cabbage; cut very fine; place in bowl and blanch with hot water. Drain, and squeeze out all water. Combine with onion, green pepper, and vinegar. Beat eggs, salt, and pepper together; add oil very gradually, beating steadily in blender or electric mixer. Pour over cabbage, toss thoroughly; add sour cream; stir until evenly blended. Refrigerate until serving time.

APPLE SLICES

4 cups cake flour, sifted	½ cup dairy sour cream
1 cup and 6 tablespoons sugar	1 tablespoon fine bread crumbs
½ teaspoon salt	3 pounds greening apples,
1 cup butter	sliced and peeled
4 eggs, separated	½ teaspoon cinnamon

Mix together flour, 4 tablespoons sugar, and salt. Cut in butter with pastry blender; beat egg yolks and mix with sour cream; add to dry mixture, stirring well. Form into ball, wrap in wax paper, and place in refrigerator a minimum of 5 hours (overnight is fine). Cut chilled dough into 4 parts. Grease a 14" x 16" sheet pan well. Roll dough to fit pan, so that it is easier to handle, using 2 parts for bottom and 2 parts for top. Use hands freely to patch dough if necessary. Sprinkle bottom crust with bread crumbs. Spread with apples. Add cinnamon to 1 cup sugar and sprinkle over apples.

Cover with remaining pastry; seal edges. Brush top with slightly beaten egg whites and sprinkle over this remaining 2 tablespoons sugar. Bake in a preheated 375° oven 40 to 50 minutes until browned and crisp looking. While still warm, brush on frosting. Cool before cutting into squares. Makes about 12 slices.

White Frosting:

¾ cup confectioners' sugar 2 tablespoons hot cream *or* milk
¼ teaspoon vanilla

Mix sugar with hot cream or milk; add vanilla. Drizzle over hot cake as it comes out of oven, tilting pan so that frosting runs.

CAMPTOWN BROWNIES

2 1-ounce squares unsweetened chocolate
½ cup butter
½ cup semi-sweet chocolate pieces
2 eggs
1 cup sugar
1 teaspoon vanilla
½ cup sifted all-purpose flour
1 cup miniature marshmallows
½ cup broken nutmeats

Place chocolate squares, butter, and chocolate pieces in top of double boiler; melt over hot water. Beat eggs with rotary beater until very thick and lemon colored; blend well with chocolate mixture; add sugar, vanilla, flour, marshmallows, nutmeats and mix. Pour into greased and floured 9″ x 9″ pan. Bake in a preheated 350° oven 30 minutes. Cool 10 to 15 minutes; cut and remove from pan. Makes 16 brownies.

For a Cold Winter Night

(SERVES 6 TO 8)

Deviled Pâté Glacé
Pot Roast à la Françoise
Basque Potatoes   Mushroom Spinach Bake
Chinese Celery Salad   Hard Rolls   Spiced Cherry Conserve
Lemon Meringue Pie
Coffee

ADVANCE PREPARATION SCHEDULE

Previous Day	Early Morning
Cherry Conserve	*Spinach*
Pâté	*Lemon Pie*
Pot Roast	

DEVILED PATE GLACE

1 envelope unflavored gelatin
¼ cup cold water
1 10½-ounce can beef consommé
1 8-ounce package cream cheese

1 4½-ounce can deviled ham
1 teaspoon prepared horseradish
1 teaspoon Worcestershire
½ teaspoon celery seed

⅛ teaspoon oregano

Garni:

1 head Boston lettuce   1 jar whole pickled beets

Soak gelatin in cold water for 5 minutes. Heat consommé to boiling, add moistened gelatin and mix until dissolved. Oil a 2-cup mold, pour in sufficient consommé to cover bottom (about ½ cup). Place in refrigerator to congeal. Blend cream cheese, ham, horseradish, Worcestershire, celery seed and oregano together until very smooth. Mix with remaining gelatin consommé. Pour cheese mixture over congealed consommé in mold and return to refrigerator to congeal. To serve, unmold on bed of Boston lettuce, garnish with whole pickled beets and serve with icebox rye bread.

POT ROAST A LA FRANCOISE

2 tablespoons shortening
5- to 6-pound brisket of beef
1 teaspoon salt
½ teaspoon freshly ground pepper

½ teaspoon paprika
2 onions, ½-inch slices
2 bay leaves (optional)
2 tablespoons Worcestershire

¾ cup sherry

Heat shortening in large heavy-bottomed pan or Dutch oven. Dust meat with salt, pepper, and paprika. Place in heated shortening with onions and brown evenly. Add bay leaves and Worcestershire. Reduce heat, add sherry, and simmer slowly. The cooking should be done "short," with very little liquid. Add more sherry if needed, to prevent meat from sticking to bottom of pan. Simmer 3 to 4 hours until fork-tender. Allow meat to cool in its own juices. Skim fat from gravy; thicken, if desired, by adding 2 tablespoons flour for each cup of gravy. Make a paste of flour and 2 tablespoons gravy and stir into pan while heating. Slice meat and place on hot platter. Serve gravy separately.

Note: Prepare the brisket a day in advance, as flavor improves and congealed fat is removed more easily. Delicious served cold as well as hot.

BASQUE POTATOES

6 medium-size potatoes	¼ cup grated carrots
Salted water	2 cups beef broth *or* 2 bouillon
2 tablespoons butter	cubes, dissolved in 2 cups of
½ cup onion, chopped	water
1 clove garlic, mashed	¾ teaspoon salt
¼ cup chopped celery	2 tablespoons snipped parsley

Peel and cut the potatoes into 1-inch cubes; cover with salted water and let stand while preparing the sauce. Heat butter in saucepan, add onion, garlic, celery, and carrots; sauté until tender, about 15 minutes. Add the drained potatoes, cook a few minutes, stirring gently so as not to break them. Add the broth (or 2 bouillon cubes dissolved in 2 cups of water) and salt. Bring to a boil, lower heat, cover and cook slowly until the potatoes are done. Sprinkle with parsley. This is attractive served in a tureen and ladled out.

MUSHROOM SPINACH BAKE

1 pound fresh mushrooms	Salt
2 tablespoons butter	2 teaspoons dehydrated minced
3 pounds spinach, cooked and	onion
chopped, *or* 2 packages frozen	2 tablespoons butter *or* margarine,
spinach, cooked and chopped	melted
Garlic salt	

Wash and dry mushrooms; slice off stems. Sauté both caps and stems in butter for several minutes with round side down first, until brown. Drain spinach; combine with salt, onion, and butter. Line a flat baking pie dish, about 10″ x 1½″, with spinach mixture and arrange sautéed mushrooms and stems on top. Sprinkle mushrooms with garlic salt and cover with Sauce.

Sauce:

1 cup canned evaporated milk	1 cup American *or* Cheddar cheese, freshly grated

Heat milk and cheese to simmering point and cook gently for 2 or 3 minutes. Let sauce stand about 5 minutes; spoon carefully over mushrooms. Bake about 20 minutes in a preheated 350° oven; then broil for several minutes until top is brown.

Note: May be used as a main luncheon or supper dish, or as an accompaniment.

CHINESE CELERY SALAD

1 bunch Chinese celery	2 large green peppers, sliced
French Dressing	

Wash celery, place in refrigerator to crisp. Slice in ½-inch rounds, place on salad plates, garnished with green pepper rings, and marinate with French Dressing (see Index). Chill thoroughly.

SPICED CHERRY CONSERVE

1 #2 can pitted tart cherries	1 tablespoon lemon juice
½ cup brown sugar	2 whole cloves
1 3-inch stick cinnamon *or* ¼ teaspoon cinnamon	¼ teaspoon nutmeg
	¼ teaspoon salt
¼ cup coarsely broken nutmeats	

Pour cherries and syrup into saucepan; add sugar, cinnamon, lemon juice, cloves, nutmeg, and salt. Simmer 5 minutes. Remove stick cinnamon and cloves; drain cherries, returning juice to pan. Simmer until reduced to ½ cup; add cherries and nutmeats and cook 5 minutes longer. Cool and refrigerate. Serve as a relish. Makes 2 cups.

LEMON MERINGUE PIE

1 9-inch baked pie shell (see Index)	2 cups water
	2 lemons, juice and grated rind
⅔ cup sugar	4 egg yolks, well beaten
3 tablespoons flour	2 tablespoons butter

Mix sugar and flour; add water, lemon juice and rind, and beaten egg yolks, stirring slowly to avoid lumps. Cook in double boiler until thick, stirring constantly. Add butter to hot lemon mixture and whip hard until smooth. Cool. Fill pie shell 15 minutes before serving.

Meringue:

4 egg whites	½ teaspoon cream of tartar
¼ cup confectioners' sugar	¼ teaspoon baking powder
2 tablespoons grated lemon rind	

Beat egg whites until soft peaks form; add confectioners' sugar, cream of tartar, and baking powder; continue beating until stiff and glossy. Place over pie; top with grated lemon rind. Brown under flame quickly before serving.

Alumni Get-Together Supper

(SERVES 12)

Mushroom Rolls   Liver Mousse Pâté

Green Goddess Dip   Cauliflower Buds

Chippers   Pumpernickel

Dilled Brussels Sprouts

Cioppino Fisherman's Wharf

Pimiento French Bread

Date Cake

Coffee   Beer

ADVANCE PREPARATION SCHEDULE

Deep Freeze	Previous Day	Early Morning
Date cake	*Mushroom Rolls*	*Crisp cauliflower*
French Bread	*Liver pâté*	*Cioppino*
	Brussels sprouts	
	Dip	

For the finger foods and get-together nibbles use the convenience of the lazy suzan or sectional dish, interspersed with crackers and pumpernickel. Add radishes, and/or olives and greens for garnish.

MUSHROOM ROLLS

Dough:

1 cup sifted flour	½ cup butter, softened
½ teaspoon salt	3 tablespoons dairy sour cream

Combine all ingredients with a wooden spoon, blending well. Form into a ball; wrap in wax paper; chill overnight.

Filling:

4 tablespoons butter	½ teaspoon freshly ground
2 small onions, chopped	pepper
1½ pounds fresh mushrooms, chopped	2 hard-cooked egg yolks, chopped
1½ teaspoons salt	

Melt 2 tablespoons butter in skillet; add onions and sauté 10 minutes. Remove onions, melt additional 2 tablespoons of butter, and sauté mushrooms for 10 minutes. Add all remaining ingredients, including sautéed onions; mix well. Divide chilled dough into 3 pieces and prepare one at a time; roll out very thin. Spread ⅓ of mushroom mixture on each and roll up as for jelly roll. Bake in a preheated 400° oven 15 minutes on buttered cooky sheet. Cut into 1-inch slices and serve hot.

LIVER MOUSSE PATE

1 cup fresh liver sausage *or* braunschweiger	½ teaspoon steak sauce
⅓ cup sour cream *or*	¼ teaspoon basil
¼ cup heavy cream	1 tablespoon butter, melted
1 tablespoon cognac *or* brandy	1 tablespoon chopped pistachio
⅛ teaspoon coarsely ground fresh pepper	nuts
	Watercress
	Icebox rye bread

Combine liver sausage, sour cream, cognac, pepper, sauce, and basil in blender. Whirl until very smooth and well puréed. (Pâté may be puréed through food mill or sieve.) Pour into buttered crock or mold, pour melted butter over top to seal, and chill in refrigerator at least 4 hours to blend flavors. (Flavor improves if this stands a few days.) To serve, turn out on small platter; garnish with watercress, sprinkle with nuts, and border with icebox rye bread. Makes 1 generous cup.

GREEN GODDESS DIP

1 clove garlic, minced	1 tablespoon tarragon vinegar
1 2-ounce can anchovy fillets, chopped fine	½ cup dairy sour cream
	1 cup mayonnaise
3 tablespoons finely chopped chives	⅓ cup finely chopped parsley
	Salt and pepper to taste

Combine ingredients in order given; blend thoroughly, pour into serving bowl and chill. Remove from refrigerator ½ hour before serving. Can be made several days in advance. Makes 2 cups.

An excellent salad dressing, as well.

CAULIFLOWER BUDS

1 head fresh white cauliflower

Wash cauliflower; break into buds and crisp in salted water in refrigerator. To serve, drain and pile into bowl or sectional dish. Serve with Lemon Blue Cheese Dressing (see Index).

PICKLED MUSHROOMS

1 pound small fresh mushrooms	¼ cup salad oil or olive oil
½ teaspoon salt	½ cup wine vinegar
1 pint boiling water	2 tablespoons grated onion
1 clove garlic, minced	

Scrub mushrooms; do not remove stems. Add salt to boiling water, then mushrooms; cook 10 minutes. Drain well. Combine oil, vinegar, onion, and garlic; add mushrooms and marinate in refrigerator at least 12 hours. Serve on picks.

May be served as salad on lettuce; use chopped parsley for garnish.

DILLED BRUSSELS SPROUTS

1 10-ounce package frozen brussels sprouts *or* 1 quart fresh brussels sprouts, cooked	1 teaspoon seasoned salt
	⅓ cup water
	1 teaspoon dill seed
¼ cup wine vinegar	3 tablespoons olive oil
1 teaspoon sugar	

Cook frozen brussels sprouts according to package directions; drain. Heat vinegar and pour over sprouts. When cool, add remaining ingredients and toss lightly but thoroughly. Chill a minimum of 12 hours. Serve on toothpicks.

These are zesty.

CIOPPINO FISHERMAN'S WHARF

½ cup olive *or* salad oil	2 teaspoons salt
2 garlic cloves, minced	¼ teaspoon pepper
1¼ cups chopped onion	¾ cup water
¾ cup chopped green onion	1½ pounds halibut steak *or* flounder
¾ cup chopped green pepper	
1 11½-ounce jar whole clams	½ pound raw shrimp, shelled and deveined
1 #2½ can tomatoes	
1 6-ounce can tomato paste	3 6½-ounce cans king crabmeat, drained, *or* 2 10-ounce packages frozen crabmeat, defrosted
1¾ cups Burgundy	
⅓ cup chopped parsley	
2 teaspoons oregano	
½ teaspoon basil	

Pour oil into 6-quart kettle and heat; add garlic, onion, green pepper and sauté 10 minutes; stir occasionally. Drain clams; reserve ¼ cup liquid. Add clam liquid, undrained tomatoes, tomato paste, Burgundy, parsley, oregano, basil, salt, pepper, and water to sautéed vegetables, mixing well. Bring to a boil; reduce heat and simmer uncovered, and stirring, for 10 minutes. Cut halibut in 1-inch pieces; discard skin and bones. Remove cartilage from crabmeat. Add halibut, shrimp, crabmeat, and clams to tomato mixture. Simmer, covered, 15 minutes. Simmer uncovered 15 minutes. Serve very hot.

A delicious American adaptation of an Italian version of French bouillabaisse.

PIMIENTO FRENCH BREAD

1 package active dry yeast	1¾ to 2 cups all-purpose flour
¾ cup warm water	½ cup chopped, pimiento-stuffed
2 tablespoons shortening,	olives
softened	⅓ cup walnuts
1 teaspoon sugar	1 egg white
1 teaspoon salt	2 tablespoons water

Dissolve yeast in warm water; stir in shortening, sugar, salt, then add 1 cup flour and beat well. Blend in olives and nuts, and sufficient remaining flour to make a soft dough, firm enough to handle. Turn onto a lightly floured board and knead gently about 5 minutes or until smooth. Shape dough into a round. Place in greased bowl, turning so that entire surface is greased. Cover with cloth and let rise in a warm place until doubled in bulk, 1½ to 2 hours. Punch down and let rise again until doubled, about 45 minutes. Punch down once more, cover, and allow dough to rest 15 minutes. Shape into long loaf; taper ends. Place on lightly greased cooky sheet. Make deep slashes 2 inches apart on top. Let rise uncovered 1 hour. Preheat oven to 375°. Half an hour before baking, place pan of water on top shelf of oven to remain during baking. Brush bread with cold water. Bake 20 minutes.

Mix egg white and 2 tablespoons water; brush loaf with mixture and return to oven. Bake 25 minutes longer. Recipe may be doubled for 2 loaves.

DATE CAKE

1 cup boiling water	1 cup sugar
1 cup chopped dates	½ teaspoon allspice
1 teaspoon baking soda	1 tablespoon melted butter
1 cup all-purpose flour	1 egg, beaten
½ cup chopped nuts	

Combine boiling water, chopped dates, and baking soda in saucepan; bring to a boil, remove from heat. Mix flour, sugar, and spice together. Add butter to egg and beat into flour mixture. Combine with date mixture; add nuts, and blend well. Pour into shallow greased 9-inch pan and bake in a preheated 250° oven 1 hour. Remove and cool on rack.

Happy Landings Dinner

(SERVES 6)

Salt Water Skillet Windsor
Kobe Flaming Collops
Salzburg Potatoes   Carottes Croquante
Granada Cream Cake
Coffee

Suggested wine: Rosé

ADVANCE PREPARATION SCHEDULE

Deep Freeze	Previous Day	Early Morning
Cake	*Marinate beef*	*Arrange Skillet Windsor*
		Carrots
		Frost cake

SALT WATER SKILLET WINDSOR

1 tablespoon grated onion	½ teaspoon salt
1 cup chopped celery	1 teaspoon Worcestershire
1 4½-ounce can shrimp	1 cup mayonnaise
1 6½-ounce can crabmeat	¼ cup butter, melted
1 cup bread crumbs	

Combine all ingredients in a bowl, except butter and crumbs, and
mix well. Spoon into 6 individual shells or chafing dish. Blend butter
with bread crumbs and spread over the top. Bake in a preheated
350° oven 30 minutes. Serve with assorted crackers.

KOBE FLAMING BEEF COLLOPS

1 cup dry red wine	2 teaspoons salt
2 tablespoons vinegar	Dash black pepper
½ cup oil	3 pounds beef, cut in 2-inch cubes
2 onions, sliced thin	6 small tomatoes
1 clove garlic, crushed	Whole mushroom caps
½ teaspoon marjoram	2 green peppers, cut in 1-inch
½ teaspoon rosemary	squares
Dash cayenne pepper	1 lemon, sliced in 6ths
Brandy	

Blend wine, vinegar, oil, onions, garlic, marjoram, rosemary, cayenne pepper, salt, and black pepper together in a spouted pint bowl. Pour over beef at room temperature, marinate for at least 4 hours. Drain beef and save marinade. Spear a tomato on each of 6 skewers, alternately adding beef, mushroom caps, and green pepper. Top with section of lemon. Broil under moderate heat for 10 minutes, turning frequently and basting with marinade.

Note: For sheer drama moisten a fluff of cotton with brandy and tip each skewer to present a flaming torch of collops.

SALZBURG POTATOES

1 tablespoon butter, melted	1 teaspoon paprika
1 small onion, chopped fine	½ teaspoon salt
3 medium raw potatoes, peeled and sliced thin	2 tablespoons flour
	1 cup dairy sour cream

Heat butter in 9-inch skillet; add onion and sauté until brown. Add potatoes; blend in paprika and salt. Cover with water to level of potatoes and simmer slowly until soft, about 15 minutes. Combine flour with liquid from potatoes, mix well, return to skillet and cook 5 minutes. Add sour cream slowly and heat thoroughly.

CAROTTES CROQUANTE

12 medium carrots, cooked	½ clove garlic
¼ cup olive *or* salad oil	1 tablespoon chopped green onion tops *or* chives
1 teaspoon salt	
1 teaspoon paprika	1 tablespoon finely chopped green pepper
½ teaspoon dry mustard	
¼ teaspoon basil	1 tablespoon pickle relish
⅛ teaspoon ground black pepper	1 tablespoon fresh lemon juice
1½ tablespoons cider vinegar	

Cut carrots into julienne strips. Cook in 1 inch of boiling water with 2 teaspoons salt until crisp-tender, about 10 minutes. Drain well. Combine remaining ingredients; pour over carrots. Cover and refrigerate for at least 1 hour. Serve as a cold vegetable.

GRANADA CREAM CAKE

8 eggs, separated	1 tablespoon grated orange rind
1 teaspoon cream of tartar	¼ cup orange juice
¼ teaspoon salt	1 cup plus 2 tablespoons cake
1⅓ cups sugar	flour, sifted

1 egg yolk, reserved for frosting

Place egg whites in large bowl of electric mixer at room temperature for at least 2 hours. Sprinkle cream of tartar and salt over egg whites and beat until stiff but not dry; gradually beat in ⅔ cup sugar. Beat 7 egg yolks until thick and lemon-colored; add remaining sugar gradually, beating constantly; add orange rind and juice, continuing to beat thoroughly; fold into egg white mixture. Add flour by sifting a small amount at a time over egg white mixture, folding carefully until ingredients are well blended. Pour batter into an ungreased 10-inch tube pan. Bake in a preheated 325° oven about 1¼ hours or until cake springs back when dented with the finger. Invert pan to cool a minimum of 1 hour before removing. Turn out on wire cooling rack. Cut into 3 layers; spread two larger layers with Orange-Cream Filling; top with the smallest and frost both top and sides with Orange Frosting.

Orange-Cream Filling:

¾ cup sugar	1 tablespoon orange rind, grated
3 tablespoons flour	1 egg, slightly beaten
¼ cup orange juice	1 cup heavy cream

Mix sugar and flour in a saucepan; add orange juice, rind, and egg; mix well. Cook, stirring, until thickened. Cool and fold in whipped cream.

Orange Frosting:

⅓ cup butter	¼ cup orange juice
1 egg yolk, reserved from cake	3 tablespoons light cream
3½ cups confectioners' sugar, sifted	½ cup pistachio nutmeats, sliced (optional)

Cream the butter. Mix slightly beaten egg yolk, orange juice, and cream; add alternately with sugar to creamed butter; mix well. Spread frosting on top and sides of cake, making gentle swirls and peaks. Sprinkle with pistachio nuts.

Cum Laude Dinner

(SERVES 6 TO 8)

Crabmeat Soufflé

Consommé Julienne   Cheese Straws

Chicken à la Champagne

Chinese Pea Pods   Potato Puffs

Green Salad Varié   Sesame-Curry Dressing

Chocolate Mousse

Coffee

Suggested wine: white Burgundy or Champagne

ADVANCE PREPARATION SCHEDULE

Previous Day	Early Morning
Consommé	*Sauté chicken*
Chocolate Mousse	*Prepare puffs*
	Dressing

CRABMEAT SOUFFLE

1 tablespoon butter	2 cups fresh crabmeat, *or* 2
2 tablespoons finely chopped	10½-ounce packages frozen,
green pepper	defrosted
1 teaspoon finely chopped onion	½ teaspoon salt
2 cups Cream Sauce	⅛ teaspoon pepper
4 egg yolks	⅛ teaspoon dry mustard

5 egg whites, beaten stiff

Melt butter in saucepan; add green pepper and onion. Sauté until tender, then combine with Cream Sauce (see Index). In a large bowl beat egg yolks until thick and lemon colored. Add Cream Sauce; blend well and carefully stir in crabmeat, salt, pepper, and dry mustard. Fold egg whites into crabmeat mixture. Pour this soufflé batter into a straight-sided 2-quart buttered soufflé dish or casserole; place in a shallow pan of hot water and bake in a pre-heated 350° oven 40 minutes, or until the soufflé rises and is well browned. Serve at once.

CONSOMME JULIENNE

1 tablespoon butter *or* margarine	1 teaspoon salt
1 cup carrot strips, julienne sliced	Dash pepper
½ cup finely shredded cabbage	1 teaspoon sugar
¼ cup leek, julienne sliced	5 chicken bouillon cubes
¼ cup celery, julienne sliced	1 quart boiling water
1 onion, sliced thin	2 tablespoons chopped parsley

Melt butter in a medium saucepan and add vegetables, seasonings, and sugar. Cover, and cook over low heat for about 5 minutes, or until vegetables are tender. Dissolve bouillon cubes in boiling water; add cooked vegetables and simmer 5 minutes. Serve garnished with parsley, accompanied by toasted crackers or cheese straws.

CHICKEN A LA CHAMPAGNE

3 2-pound frying chickens	1 cup champagne
2 teaspoons salt	1 cup chicken bouillon *or*
¼ cup flour	consommé
2 tablespoons butter	2 tablespoons butter
1 tablespoon salad oil	1 cup sliced fresh mushrooms
2 tablespoons Curaçao	½ cup heavy cream

Garni:

2 oranges, unpeeled, cut in   6 clusters grapes
12 wedges

Disjoint chickens. Sprinkle with salt and dust with flour. Heat 2 tablespoons butter and oil in skillet; add floured chicken and sauté 10 minutes on each side. Remove from skillet to a casserole and place uncovered in a preheated 350° oven for 20 minutes to continue browning. Remove from oven and pour the Curaçao and champagne over chicken. Cover with bouillon and place over low heat; simmer until tender, approximately 20 minutes.

Heat 2 tablespoons butter in another skillet, add mushrooms and sauté 5 minutes. Stir in cream and pour over chicken. Serve from chafing dish, adding orange wedges and green seedless grapes to each portion as it's served.

CHINESE PEA PODS

2 pounds Chinese pea pods
1 4-ounce can water chestnuts, sliced
1 cup boiling water

1 chicken bouillon cube
2 tablespoons soy sauce
1 tablespoon cornstarch
¼ cup pea pod liquid
1 tablespoon chopped parsley

Wash pea pods and remove tips and strings; if large, cut in half. Place in saucepan with water chestnuts and boiling water. Add bouillon cube and stir until dissolved. Cover and simmer 10 minutes. Combine soy sauce, cornstarch, and liquid from peas, blend well and return to peas. Simmer until blended and liquid is clear. Adjust seasoning. Mound in center of platter; sprinkle with chopped parsley and arrange a border of Potato Puffs.

POTATO PUFFS

2½ cups mashed potatoes
2 eggs, well beaten
1 teaspoon salt

½ teaspoon baking powder
½ teaspoon dried minced onion
½ teaspoon celery salt
Vegetable shortening

Combine potatoes, eggs, salt, baking powder, onion, and celery salt; blend well. Heat shortening in large kettle to 390°; drop heaping tablespoons into hot fat. Deep fry until golden brown; remove and drain on paper towels. Place in 300° oven to keep hot, while balance is frying. Dust with paprika.

Note: To test fat for proper heat, a thermometer is the most reliable. However, to test for temperature of 375° to 400° a cube of bread dropped in the fat will brown in 40 seconds.

GREEN SALAD VARIE

2 quarts greens, romaine, Boston, and curly endive

1 cup mayonnaise
½ onion, chopped (with juice)
Juice of ½ lemon
¼ teaspoon dry mustard
1½ tablespoons prepared mustard

¼ teaspoon curry powder
½ teaspoon salt
⅛ teaspoon coarsely ground pepper
2 tablespoons sesame seeds, toasted

Combine mayonnaise, onion, lemon juice, dry and prepared mustards, curry, salt, and pepper. To serve, toss with salad greens and sprinkle with sesame seeds.

Note: To toast sesame seeds, place in pan on lower rack of broiler and toast 2 minutes, or until light brown; shake the pan and watch carefully to avoid scorching.

CHOCOLATE MOUSSE

1 pound German sweet cooking chocolate	2 tablespoons Grand Marnier
10 eggs, separated	½ cup strong brewed coffee
	1 cup heavy cream, whipped

Melt chocolate in double boiler; cool. Separate eggs; beat yolks until thick and lemon colored. Add Grand Marnier and coffee. Combine with chocolate and blend until smooth. Beat egg whites until very stiff. Fold carefully into chocolate mixture and pour into 8-cup greased mold. Refrigerate 24 hours. Unmold and garnish with whipped cream and chocolate curls. (Serves 10.)

A heritage recipe laden with the goodness of Grandmother's cooking. It recalls her axiomatic comment "that when deliciously conceived, what extravagance goes in must be good on the turning out."

Bon Voyage Dinner

(SERVES 8)

Atlantic Cucumber Boats — Sauce Verte   Piroschki Russe
Caneton aux Herbes de Provence
Noodles Warsaw   Belgian Beet Compote
Hard Rolls
Kahlua Sundae   Yankee Meltaways
Demitasse

ADVANCE PREPARATION SCHEDULE

Deep Freeze	Previous Day	Early Morning
Meltaways	*Beet Compote*	*Shrimp*
Piroschki	*Coffee ice cream*	*Cucumber Boats*
	Marshmallow sauce	*Prepare ducks in foil*
	Sauce Verte	*Prepare noodles to bake*

CUCUMBER BOATS

4 cucumbers of similar size
3 green peppers
1 cup chopped, firm tomatoes
½ teaspoon salt
⅛ teaspoon freshly ground pepper
2 green onions, chopped fine

1 cup finely cut celery
1 tablespoon minced parsley
½ cup French Dressing (about)
(see Index)
1 pound shrimps, cleaned and
deveined

Peel cucumbers; slice in half lengthwise. Remove seeds, leaving one half slightly hollowed, and chill. Cut each green pepper in 3 triangles as for sail of boat. Spear a toothpick through vertical side of triangle and then stick one into each cucumber sailboat. Fill hollow with Macedoine Salad.

Macedoine Salad:

Toss together chopped tomatoes, salt, pepper, green onions, celery, and parsley; marinate lightly with French Dressing; fill cucumber boats and top with a row of 3 or 4 shrimp. Serve with Sauce Verte.

Variation:

Seafood fillings in these boats are excellent to use for other menus.

SAUCE VERTE

1 tablespoon chives
1 tablespoon tarragon
2 tablespoons parsley
1 teaspoon dill weed
1 teaspoon chervil

1 4-ounce jar strained baby
spinach
1 cup mayonnaise
1 drop green food coloring
(optional)

Combine chives, tarragon, parsley, dill weed, and chervil and chop fine; blend with spinach and mayonnaise and add food coloring if desired. Chill thoroughly and allow to stand several hours so flavors may "marry."

PIROSCHKI

1 package dry yeast	3 eggs, separated
½ cup warm water	2 tablespoons sugar
3 cups all-purpose flour	¼ cup (⅛ pound) butter, melted
½ cup milk	1 teaspoon salt

Soften yeast in warm water, add 2 cups flour and milk, beat well; cover and let stand in warm spot about 1 hour. Beat egg whites until stiff. Beat yolks with sugar until lemony and smooth. Add butter and salt to egg yolks; fold in egg whites. Add to yeast dough and blend. Add remaining flour, turn out on floured board. Knead well (more flour might be needed) until dough is smooth and elastic. Place in greased bowl; cover, let rise again until doubled in bulk, about 1 hour. Pinch off balls of about a rounded tablespoon and roll ¼ inch thick. Place 1 teaspoon Meat Filling on each; fold over and place seam down. Shape into rounds. Let rise again, about 20 minutes, until dough is light. Bake in a preheated 425° oven 15 minutes. To glaze before baking, brush with mixture of 1 egg yolk and 1 tablespoon water.

Meat Filling:

4 tablespoons butter	½ cup hot water
½ pound lean beef, ground twice	½ teaspoon salt
1 large onion, grated	1 teaspoon Worcestershire
1 beef bouillon cube	¼ cup cracker crumbs

Heat butter in skillet, add meat, sauté until pink has disappeared. Add onion and brown lightly. Dissolve bouillon cube in water and add to meat and onion mixture; add salt, Worcestershire, and cracker crumbs. Blend well, adjust seasonings, and cool.

CANETON AUX HERBES DE PROVENCE

2 ducklings, quartered	½ teaspoon rosemary
½ teaspoon salt	½ teaspoon sage (optional)
½ cup butter	1 teaspoon chopped parsley
2 tablespoons flour	1 teaspoon prepared white
Duck liver	mustard
2 shallots *or* green onions	2 cups dry white wine
1 teaspoon thyme	2 tablespoons browned flour
½ teaspoon chervil	(see note following recipe)

Wash and dry quarters of duckling; sprinkle with salt. Heat butter in skillet and brown the ducklings well. The original French recipe from Noves says "stiffen the duck" and that is exactly what should be done.

The ducks are baked in papillotes or foil packages with a sauce which is prepared as follows:

Pour off all but 2 tablespoons of butter from skillet in which ducklings were "stiffened." Add flour and stir well, scraping all the delicious bits in the pan to blend with the sauce and continue stirring until the flour browns. Grind the duck liver and combine with shallots, herbs, parsley, mustard, and wine; add to the pan in which the duck was "stiffened." Cook, stirring constantly, for 5 minutes. Place ducks in the papillotes. Cut aluminum foil into 8 pieces large enough to enclose quarters of duckling. To form papillotes, turn up the four sides of foil, to form container. Place a spoonful of the sauce in each; place quarter of duck on sauce, and cover with another tablespoon of same mixture. Fold the long edges together and turn up the ends package-wise, so juices are sealed in completely.

Preheat oven to 450°. Place papillotes with duck in oven; reduce heat to 325°; bake for 35 minutes.

Serve each guest a papillote so that he may enjoy the full luscious aroma as it is opened. Additional sauce may be prepared to serve separately if desired.

Note: Browned flour was another ingredient which, in our interpretation of the recipe, is browned in the butter when making the roux. The French preparation, however, browns the flour first in a 400° oven, until it turns a golden brown. A quick procedure — one which, being original, may pique your curiosity sufficiently to try it.

NOODLES WARSAW

1 cup buckwheat groats
1 egg, beaten
2 cups boiling water
2 teaspoons salt
2 tablespoons butter
2 onions, chopped
8-ounces broad noodles, broken, cooked and drained

⅛ teaspoon freshly ground pepper
1 teaspoon Worcestershire
1 beef bouillon cube
½ cup boiling water
1 tablespoon butter

Place groats in saucepan, stir in egg until well blended. Add water and 1 teaspoon salt; cover and cook over low heat for 12 minutes. Melt butter in skillet; add onion and sauté for 10 minutes while stirring. Combine groats, onions, noodles, pepper, Worcestershire, and remaining salt. Dissolve bouillon cube in boiling water and add. Place in buttered 2-quart casserole and bake in a preheated 350° oven about 30 minutes. If noodles become too dry for your taste, add soup stock made with 1 bouillon cube and ¾ cup boiling water and 1 tablespoon butter.

This dish, because of the dry texture, is a good accompaniment to any roast that has its own sauce or gravy.

BELGIAN BEET COMPOTE

½ pound unsweetened prunes   4 tablespoons sugar
3 cups undrained julienne   2 tablespoons vinegar
   beets   2 teaspoon concentrated
½ teaspoon salt   orange juice

Combine all ingredients in a saucepan. Cover and simmer very slowly 25 minutes or until prunes are tender. A truly fine accompaniment to roast meat or poultry.

KAHLUA SUNDAE

For each portion:

1 large scoop of Coffee Ice Cream   Serving of Marshmallow Sauce
   1 tablespoon of Kahlua, poured over Coffee Ice Cream
              and Marshmallow Sauce

Coffee Ice Cream:

4 eggs   9 marshmallows, diced
1½ cups sugar, sifted   ½ cup instant coffee
1 cup light cream   1 teaspoon vanilla
1½ tablespoons flour   1 quart heavy cream, whipped

Beat eggs and add sugar gradually. Add cream and then flour. Beat into marshmallows. Pour into top of double boiler and cook over water until thick. Add coffee while mixture is still hot; cool. Fold vanilla into whipped cream. Pour into ice cube trays; place in freezer for several hours, or overnight, until firmly frozen. Serve with Marshmallow Sauce.

Marshmallow Sauce:

2 pounds marshmallows	Pinch of salt
1 teaspoon vanilla	¼ cup cream

Place marshmallows in double boiler, add salt and cream. Cook, stirring, until marshmallows are melted. Cool slightly, add vanilla. Serve hot or cold.

MELTAWAYS

1 cup (½ pound) butter *or* margarine	¼ teaspoon salt
½ cup powdered sugar	¼ cup finely chopped walnuts
1 teaspoon vanilla	Currant jelly
2¼ cups cake flour	Confectioners' sugar

Cream butter, sugar, and vanilla. Sift flour and salt together and add, mixing very thoroughly; combine with chopped nuts. Drop by teaspoon on ungreased cooky sheet; make a hollow in center of each cooky. (The top of the handle of a wooden spoon does very well.) Drop ⅛ teaspoon jelly in center of each cooky. Bake about 8 minutes in a preheated 400° oven. While still warm sprinkle with confectioners' sugar. Makes approximately 50.

Meltaways freeze well.

The Boss Comes to Dinner

(SMALL DINNER PARTY)

(SERVES 6)

Salade Niçoise   Toast Melba

Baked Steak Citron   Delmonico Potatoes

Artichoke Hearts Polonaise   Parker House Rolls

Bowl of Lingonberries

Cheesecake Eugénie

Coffee

Suggested wine: red Burgundy

ADVANCE PREPARATION SCHEDULE

Previous Day	Early Morning
Cheesecake	*Prepare artichokes*
	Prepare salad ingredients
	for assembling later
	Sauce for potatoes

SALADE NICOISE

2 7½-ounce cans white tuna fish, drained
1 quart salad greens
15 small ripe pitted olives
6 hard-cooked eggs, cut in wedges

4 tomatoes, peeled and quartered
8 or 10 anchovy fillets (#2 small can)
½ cup basic French Dressing (see Index) plus 2 tablespoons wine vinegar

Toss tuna fish, greens, and olives in a large bowl. Surround with egg wedges, tomatoes, and place crossed strips of anchovies over all. Just before serving combine dressing with the wine vinegar; pour over salad and toss gently. Serve as a first course appetizer salad.

BAKED STEAK CITRON

½ cup chili sauce
1 3-inch sirloin steak (for 6)
4 tablespoons butter
½ teaspoon salt

⅛ teaspoon paprika
2 onions, sliced
1 lemon, sliced
2 tomatoes, sliced thick

½ pound fresh mushrooms

Spread chili sauce on steak; dot with 2 tablespoons butter; season with salt and paprika. Cover with overlapping alternate slice of onion, lemon, and tomatoes. Bake 45 minutes in a preheated 450° oven for rare. Place 2 tablespoons butter in skillet, add mushrooms, and simmer for 8 minutes. Top steak with mushrooms. Present on a wooden plank, if possible, and carve, for the enjoyment of your guests, at the table.

Note: If you find a similarity to the "Baked Steak" in *Thoughts for Buffet,* please note the slight addition of flavorful ingredients, creating a subtle variation.

DELMONICO POTATOES

¼ cup butter *or* margarine
1 cup slightly crushed cornflakes
3 tablespoons flour
½ teaspoon salt
Dash pepper

1½ cups milk
1 8-ounce package processed sharp or mild cheese, sliced thin *or* shredded
1 1-pound package frozen French fries

Melt butter in a saucepan. Blend 1 tablespoon with cornflakes; set aside. Stir flour, salt, and pepper into remaining butter in saucepan. Add milk. Cook over low heat, stirring until mixture is smooth and thick. Spread half the frozen French fries over bottom of 1½-quart baking dish. Pour half the sauce over potatoes; cover with half the cheese. Repeat. Sprinkle cornflakes over top. Bake in a preheated 375° oven about 25 minutes or until heated through.

ARTICHOKE HEARTS POLONAISE

2 tablespoons olive oil
1 small clove garlic, crushed
½ pound large mushrooms, sliced thick
1 10-ounce package frozen artichoke hearts

2 teaspoons flour
¼ cup chopped parsley
2 tablespoons dry white wine
¼ teaspoon salt
⅛ teaspoon freshly ground pepper

Pour olive oil into a large skillet and heat; sauté garlic and add mushrooms. Cook until juice is absorbed and mushrooms are slightly brown, about 10 minutes. In a separate saucepan cook artichoke hearts according to package directions; add to mushrooms. Sprinkle flour over all, tossing through mixture. Add parsley, wine, salt, and pepper. Bring to boiling point. Serve immediately. Browned bread crumbs may be used instead of flour.

LINGONBERRIES

Available in many markets. One 14-ounce jar is sufficient.

CHEESECAKE EUGENIE

2 8-ounce packages cream cheese	1 teaspoon vanilla
1 cup sugar	1 teaspoon lemon juice
2 cups dairy sour cream	5 egg whites, beaten stiff
5 egg yolks, beaten	¼ cup chopped glazed fruit

Cream softened cheese with sugar. Blend with sour cream; add egg yolks and vanilla and mix well. Fold in egg whites. Pour into a 10-inch spring form pan and bake in a preheated 300° oven 1 hour. Turn off the heat and leave cake in oven for another ½ hour. Remove and cool. Refrigerate overnight. Top with glazed fruit. The cake is large and is an imposing dessert. A next-day treat as well.

Between Planes Dinner

(SERVES 6 TO 8)

Blue Cheese Tartar Balls   Surprise Appetizers

Chicken Palourde

Accordion Potatoes   Broiled Spinach

Raspberry Ring

Chocolate Bombe

Spritz Cookies

Coffee

Suggested wine: white or red Chianti

ADVANCE PREPARATION SCHEDULE

Deep Freeze	Previous Day	Early Morning
Bombe	*Raspberry Ring*	*Lobster shells*
Cookies		*Prepare potatoes for frying*
		Chicken
		Prepare zucchini
		Potatoes for baking

BLUE CHEESE TARTAR BALLS

1 pound lean sirloin steak, ground
1 small onion, grated
½ teaspoon salt
¼ teaspoon pepper

1 3-ounce package cream cheese, softened
¼ pound blue cheese, softened
1 egg, lightly beaten
¼ cup chopped parsley

Grind meat and combine with onion, salt, and pepper. Be certain meat is very fresh. Cream the cheeses together until smooth and form into balls the size of a marble. Enclose balls in covering of ground meat, then dip in beaten egg. Roll in parsley and spear each ball on toothpick or cocktail skewer. To serve, pile into a pyramid, on platter. Border with cocktail rye slices.

SURPRISE APPETIZERS

1 cake compressed yeast, or
    1 ounce dry yeast
⅓ cup lukewarm water
¾ pound boiled potatoes, puréed
6 tablespoons butter, melted
¼ cup warm milk
½ teaspoon salt

2¾ cups flour
5 egg yolks, beaten
1 cup ham, baked or boiled
¼ cup finely chopped parsley
2 tablespoons half and half cream

Dissolve compressed yeast in lukewarm water, or dry yeast in warm water. Combine puréed (or well mashed) potatoes, butter, milk, and salt. Add half of flour, beating well; stir in yeast and egg yolks. Beat in remaining flour. Let stand ¾ hour, to rest the dough.

Chop ham and parsley very fine. Add enough cream to hold ham and parsley together. Roll dough on floured board to ¼-inch thickness. Cut dough in 2-inch rounds. Fill one round with a level tablespoon of ham mixture and cover with second round. Seal edges together; use tines of fork. Drop in deep fat (360°) and fry until brown. A puffy surprise.

CHICKEN PALOURDE

1 cup all-purpose flour
2 teaspoons salt
¼ teaspoon pepper
3 2-pound broilers, cut into small pieces

¼ cup salad oil or butter
Paprika
1 cup half and half cream
1 7½-ounce can minced clams, with juice

Combine flour, salt, and pepper in a paper bag; add chicken pieces and shake until well coated. Heat salad oil in deep skillet; add chicken, sprinkled generously with paprika, and sauté until golden brown. Turn often over high heat. Remove all but 3 tablespoons fat. Add cream; lower heat, cover, and cook gently 5 to 10 minutes, or until tender. Add clams with juice and cook 5 more minutes. Arrange chicken on platter, cover with sauce, and border with Accordion Potatoes.

ACCORDION POTATOES

10 medium-size potatoes	2 teaspoons salt
½ cup melted butter	⅛ teaspoon pepper
1 teaspoon paprika	

Scrub potatoes well and peel. Slash them thinly, about three-quarters way through from top to bottom, leaving bottom whole. Dry well and roll potatoes in melted butter, place in roasting pan, and bake in a preheated 375° oven 2½ hours. Sprinkle with salt and pepper; baste frequently. After about 2 hours of roasting, sprinkle potatoes with paprika. Continue roasting about 30 minutes more, or until done.

Note: If potatoes are peeled in advance, soak in ice water until ready to prepare for baking. These may also be roasted with the meat; allow more baking time if lower oven temperature is required. Though the flavor is similar to other roasted potatoes, the slashes give a different look. Serve around chicken platter.

Variation:

Sprinkle with ½ cup grated Cheddar cheese after about 2 hours roasting time (for another menu).

BROILED SPINACH

2 10-ounce packages chopped frozen spinach	2 tablespoons butter, melted
2 teaspoons butter	¾ cup (6 ounces) canned mushrooms, stems and pieces, drained
1 teaspoon salt	
⅛ teaspoon pepper	2 slices processed Cheddar cheese
½ teaspoon nutmeg	

Heat 2 teaspoons butter in skillet, add frozen spinach, cover and cook until defrosted and heated. Break up spinach as it defrosts. Blend in salt, pepper, and nutmeg. In another skillet heat 2 tablespoons butter and sauté mushrooms lightly. Add cheese and cook until cheese is melted. Combine with spinach and pour into shallow buttered casserole. Cover with Topping.

Topping:

3/4 cup dairy sour cream
2 tablespoons prepared horseradish
1 teaspoon prepared mustard
1/2 teaspoon salt
Paprika

Combine sour cream with horseradish, mustard and salt; spread over entire surface of hot spinach, sprinkle with paprika. Place under broiler about 2 inches from heat until evenly browned.

RASPBERRY RING

2 10-ounce packages frozen raspberries, defrosted
2 3-ounce packages raspberry-flavored gelatin
3½ cups liquid (berry juice and water)
1 cup dairy sour cream
2 ripe bananas, sliced

Drain raspberries. Add sufficient water to juice to make 3½ cups liquid. Heat 2 cups liquid to boiling point, add gelatin, and dissolve. Add remaining liquid and place in refrigerator until of jellylike consistency. Fold in drained raspberries; pour half into well-oiled 6-cup mold. Place mold in refrigerator until firm. Keep remaining half of gelatin mixture in cool place, but do not refrigerate. Remove firm gelatin mold from refrigerator. Cover with sour cream, then with layer of sliced bananas. Cover with remaining gelatin and return to refrigerator until firm and ready to serve.

Serve on platter garnished with watercress, bananas halved and rolled in chopped nuts, and whole canned apricots.

CHOCOLATE BOMBE

1 pint vanilla ice cream
2 1-ounce squares unsweetened chocolate, melted
½ cup water
½ cup sugar
1/8 teaspoon salt
2 egg yolks, slightly beaten
1 teaspoon vanilla
2 tablespoons rum
2 cups heavy cream, whipped
½ cup chopped marrons

Line a 1½-quart melon or other mold with ice cream and freeze firm, about 1 hour. Melt chocolate in water over low heat, stirring until blended. Add sugar, salt, and simmer 3 minutes, stirring constantly. Pour slowly over egg yolks, blending well. Cool; add vanilla and rum. Fold whipped cream into chocolate mixture, then fold in marrons. Spoon into center of mold and freeze overnight. Unmold to serve; garnish with whipped cream and chocolate curls.

SPRITZ COOKIES

1 cup (½ pound) butter, softened	⅔ cup sugar
	2 egg yolks
2¼ cups all-purpose flour	

Cream butter until very light. Add sugar gradually, and cream with butter until light and fluffy. Add egg yolks, mix thoroughly, and add flour. Place dough in pastry tube (or cooky press) and force through various openings to shape an assortment, directly onto a lightly buttered baking sheet. Bake in a preheated 350° oven about 10 minutes or until edges are lightly browned. These cookies are very dainty.

Note: Cooky sheet liners of parchment-like paper are available in most stores. They come in various sizes, eliminate buttering the pan and prevent the cookies from becoming too brown on underside.

Citation Celebration Dinner

(SERVES 8)

Caviar Roulade

Mushroom Consommé   Open-Face Cucumber Sandwiches

Breast of Turkey — Oyster or Italian Dressing

Prunes and Carrots

Broccoli Mold Amandine   Toasted French Bread

Double Chocolate Torte or Soufflé Stephanie

Coffee

Suggested wine: white Bordeaux or Burgundy

ADVANCE PREPARATION SCHEDULE

Deep Freeze	Previous Day	Early Morning
Cake	*Cake for Roulade*	*Sauce for Roulade*
	Consommé	*Broccoli Mold*
		Prunes and Carrots
		Dressing
		Frost cake

CAVIAR ROULADE

4 tablespoons butter   2 cups milk
½ cup flour   4 eggs, separated
¼ teaspoon salt

Preheat oven to 325° with rack on lowest bracket of oven. Grease a 10″ x 15″ jelly roll pan; line with greased wax paper and sprinkle with flour. Melt butter, blend in flour with wire whisk; add milk and cook, stirring until mixture boils. Simmer, stirring, 1 minute. Stir in slightly beaten egg yolks, very slowly. Beat egg whites until stiff and fold in, add salt. Spread batter in prepared pan and bake on lowest rack about 10 minutes. Remove cake; place on a wet towel and roll tightly. Before serving unroll and add filling.

Filling:

1 3-ounce package cream cheese   6 ounces imported *or* domestic
1 cup dairy sour cream   black caviar
1 teaspoon onion juice

While roll is baking, mix the cream cheese and 3 tablespoons sour cream with half the caviar; spread lightly on turned-out cake. Roll the cake like a jelly roll. Serve with a sauce made by blending the remaining sour cream, onion juice, and caviar. To serve, slice cake thinly, jelly-roll fashion, and top each slice with a spoonful of the sour cream and caviar sauce. This makes very generous servings.

Note: Though domestic caviar tends to produce a gray color, it has fine flavor. Red caviar may be substituted.

OPEN-FACE CUCUMBER SANDWICHES

6 slices bread   2 tablespoons mayonnaise
1 slim cucumber   Paprika

Cut bread with 1½-inch cooky cutter, 2 rounds per slice. Slice cucumber in ¼-inch slices. Spread bread rounds with mayonnaise. Place cucumber slice on each and dust with paprika for color. Sandwiches have a nicer appearance if cucumber slices conform to bread rounds. In selecting cucumber, the best are firm and slender, not too large.

MUSHROOM CONSOMME

2 tablespoon butter	1 tablespoon flour
¼ pound fresh mushrooms, chopped	6 cups chicken stock
	½ cup heavy cream, whipped
1 tablespoon chopped onion	Nutmeg

Heat butter in saucepan, add mushrooms, onion, and sauté about 5 minutes. Add flour, stirring until well blended. Add chicken stock; salt if necessary. Serve in cups and garnish with a dollop of whipped cream and a dash of nutmeg.

A good time-saver is undiluted commercial chicken soup. If you are a purist, see Index for Chicken Soup.

BREAST OF TURKEY
(Oyster or Italian Dressing)

2 teaspoons salt	2 full breasts of turkey,
½ teaspoon pepper	(about 12-pound turkeys), *or*
1 teaspoon paprika	upper half of 12-pound turkey
1 teaspoon seasoned salt	¼ cup shortening

Combine salt, pepper, paprika, and seasoned salt; rub into breasts, inside and out. Fill cavity loosely with dressing; place in roasting pan in a preheated 350° oven, baste with melted shortening every 20 minutes, for about 2 hours, or until tender. When joint of wing moves easily, turkey is done. Remove and allow to stand ½ hour before slicing.

Variation:

If using breasts only, fill breasts and roll to enclose filling, and fasten with skewers. Proceed as above. Bake until fork-tender, about 30 minutes to the pound. Either the filleted breasts or the upper half of the turkeys are available in most markets.

OYSTER DRESSING

2 cups boiling water	½ cup chopped celery leaves
1 package onion soup mix	1 cup (½ pound) butter *or*
2½ quarts bread cubes	margarine
½ cup chopped parsley	1 pint small oysters, drained

Pour boiling water over soup mix; let stand. Cut slices of bread into cubes. Toast in oven until dry. Sauté parsley and celery leaves in butter for 5 minutes. Add oysters and pour over bread cubes. Toss. Pour over onion soup mixture. Stir, and stuff turkey cavities. Surplus dressing may be baked separately in a well-greased casserole.

ITALIAN DRESSING

4 matzos, crumbled in 1-inch pieces	½ cup almonds
	½ pound sausage, mild Italian
½ cup (¼ pound) butter	2 eggs, slightly beaten
2 medium onions, chopped	½ teaspoon salt
1¼ cups chopped celery tops	⅛ teaspoon pepper
Pinch sugar	Dash tarragon
2 cloves garlic	Dash marjoram
½ pound mushrooms	Dash thyme
¼ to ½ cup orange juice	

Place matzos in bowl; cover with warm water; drain immediately. Brown in saucepan in 2 tablespoons melted butter. Remove from heat and set aside. Brown onion, celery tops, sugar, and garlic in 2 additional tablespoons butter until celery turns a deep green. In another skillet, heat 4 tablespoons butter and sauté mushrooms and almonds for 5 minutes. Brown sausage under broiler. Drain fat and cut into small slices. Combine matzos, celery mixture, mushrooms, almonds, and sausage; add eggs, season with salt, pepper, tarragon, marjoram, and thyme. Moisten with orange juice. Fill turkey cavity lightly and lace opening with skewers and thread. Makes enough to stuff a 10-pound turkey.

Note: Matzos, an oversized cracker, are available in packages.

PRUNES AND CARROTS

½ pound jumbo prunes
1 14-ounce jar baby carrots
1 tablespoon cornstarch
¼ cup carrot liquid

1 tablespoon brown sugar
½ cup orange juice
½ teaspoon salt
1 tablespoon butter

Wash prunes; place in pan with enough water to cover; simmer slowly for 15 minutes, tightly covered. Drain carrots, reserving ¼ cup liquid. Mix carrot liquid with cornstarch, stirring until smooth. Add brown sugar, orange juice, and salt. Melt butter in saucepan, add cornstarch mixture; cook, stirring until blended and thickened. Add carrots and prunes. Stir gently; heat. Flavor improves if prepared in advance and reheated just before serving. Serve with broccoli mold.

BROCCOLI MOLD AMANDINE

4 packages frozen chopped broccoli *or* 3 pounds fresh broccoli
¼ pound Cheddar *or* American cheese

Milk
3 eggs, slightly beaten
¼ pound almonds, blanched
¼ cup (⅛ pound) butter, melted
Salt and pepper to taste

Cook broccoli rapidly in boiling salted water; drain. Put through ricer or chop fine. Place cheese in saucepan, stir slowly until melted, add milk to thin. Add cheese, eggs, almonds, butter, salt and pepper to broccoli; mix thoroughly. Put mixture in a well-buttered 6-cup mold. Place mold in a pan half filled with water and bake in a preheated 375° oven for 45 minutes. Turn out on platter and garnish with prunes and carrots.

Note: Cook frozen broccoli according to package directions. Drain.

DOUBLE CHOCOLATE TORTE

½ cup sifted cake flour
½ teaspoon double-acting baking powder
¼ teaspoon salt
4 eggs, unbeaten (at room temperature)

¾ cup sugar
1 teaspoon vanilla
3 1-ounce squares unsweetened chocolate
2 tablespoons sugar
¼ teaspoon soda

3 tablespoons cold water

Sift flour once and measure. Combine baking powder, salt, and eggs in bowl. Beat with rotary egg beater, adding ¾ cup sugar gradually until mixture becomes thick and light-colored. Gradually fold in flour and vanilla. Melt chocolate over hot water. Remove from heat and cool. Then add 2 tablespoons sugar, soda, and cold water; blend. Quickly beat into batter until chocolate mixture is completely blended. Line a 15″ x 10″ pan with wax paper. Pour in batter and bake in a 375° oven 18 to 20 minutes. Turn cake out onto cloth; quickly remove wax paper and cut off crisp edges of cake. Cool on cake rack. Cut cake in 4 equal parts and split each quarter through the middle, making 8 thin layers. Put together with Chocolate Frosting, using about ¼ cup between layers. Cover top and sides of torte with remaining frosting. Chill several hours. (Makes 12 servings.)

Chocolate Frosting:

4½ 1-ounce squares unsweetened chocolate	3 cups sifted confectioners' sugar
	⅓ cup milk
½ cup butter	2 egg whites, unbeaten
1 teaspoon vanilla	

Melt chocolate and butter together. Add sugar, milk, egg whites, and vanilla. Mix well. Place in bowl of ice water and beat with rotary egg beater until of spreading consistency. Makes about 3 cups of frosting.

SOUFFLE STEPHANIE

¼ pound finely minced glacé fruit, soaked in	½ teaspoon salt
	4 eggs, separated
½ cup brandy	½ cup sugar
4 tablespoons butter	½ cup crushed nut brittle
4 tablespoons flour	1 tablespoon sugar
1 cup scalded milk	1 teaspoon vanilla

Combine glacé fruit and brandy and soak several hours. Heat butter in saucepan. Add flour and blend until smooth and bubbly. Stir in milk and salt; cool. Beat yolks until thick and lemon colored; Add ½ cup sugar and vanilla. Combine with yolk mixture. Add nut brittle and fold in stiffly beaten whites. Drain glazed fruits. Grease a 2-quart casserole or soufflé dish and sprinkle with

1 tablespoon sugar. Pour half of soufflé mixture into prepared dish; add glacéd fruits in a layer; cover with remaining soufflé. Place in pan of boiling water and bake in a preheated 375° oven 1 hour. Serve at once.

Teacher Comes to Dinner

(SERVES 4)

Tomato Frappé

Escalopes de Veau

Dilled Green Beans   Basque Potatoes

Caramel Fruit Compote

Marble Cake

Suggested wine: red Burgundy or Bordeaux

ADVANCE PREPARATION SCHEDULE

Deep Freeze	Previous Day	Early Morning
Compote	*Frappé*	*Escalopes de Veau*
	Marble Cake	
	Basque Potatoes	
	(*see Index*)	

TOMATO FRAPPE

4 tomatoes	2 teaspoons mayonnaise
¼ cup chopped chow-chow	½ cup chopped celery
1 teaspoon anchovy paste	

Peel uniform size tomatoes and scoop out. Mix pulp with chow-chow, mayonnaise, celery, and anchovy paste. Fill the tomatoes; wrap each in cheesecloth or plastic wrap; refrigerate until cold.

ESCALOPES DE VEAU

8 slices veal steak, very, very thin
¼ pound cooked ham, 4 slices
¼ pound Swiss cheese, 4 slices
¼ cup flour
1 egg, beaten

¼ cup bread crumbs
2 tablespoons butter
Parsley
Lemon wedges
Paprika

Flatten slices of veal to about 4" x 5" size, using edge of saucer or meat hammer. Place slice of ham and 1 slice of Swiss cheese on top of veal, and cover with another slice of veal. Fasten together with toothpicks. Salt both sides, roll in flour, dip in egg, then in bread crumbs. Heat butter in skillet and sauté veal slowly until nicely browned on both sides. If made in advance, set aside. To serve, place in a preheated 350° oven for 20 minutes. Remove. Pour browned butter on top, sprinkle with chopped parsley, garnish with lemon wedges coated with paprika. Place on platter in a preheated 350° oven 20 minutes before serving.

DILLED GREEN BEANS

1 package frozen green beans
2 tablespoons butter, melted

½ teaspoon dried dill weed
Salt

Cook beans according to package directions until just tender and drain. Add melted butter and dill; salt to taste; toss lightly and serve.

CARAMEL FRUIT COMPOTE

2 #2½ cans Elberta peaches
1 #2 can pitted Bing cherries
1 11-ounce package dried apricots
Juice of ½ large orange

Juice of ½ lemon
¼ teaspoon grated orange rind
¼ teaspoon grated lemon rind
1 cup brown sugar, firmly packed

Drain peaches and cherries; reserve juice, separately. Mix peaches, apricots, cherries, orange juice, lemon juice, orange rind, lemon rind, and brown sugar; add the peach juice; omit the cherry juice. Bake in a preheated 325° oven 1½ hours.

This recipe serves 12. It is excellent to have on hand. We suggest using amount required, and freezing remainder.

MARBLE CAKE

Chocolate Custard:

1 egg	3 tablespoons Dutch cocoa
½ cup sugar	½ cup boiling water

Beat egg with sugar in a saucepan; add cocoa and boiling water. Bring to a boil and cook until thick, stirring constantly. Set aside to cool while preparing white cake.

Cake Batter:

¾ cup butter	1 teaspoon baking soda
1 cup sugar	2 teaspoons baking powder
2 eggs	¼ teaspoon salt
2 cups cake flour	¾ cup milk
1 teaspoon vanilla	

Cream butter, add sugar, then 1 egg at a time. Beat well after each addition. Sift flour, baking soda, baking powder, and salt together; add alternately with milk. Begin and end with flour. Add vanilla last.

Pour Chocolate Custard on top of batter in bowl, being careful to blend with spatula only once. Pour into buttered 7" x 11" pan, leaving large areas of dark and light to achieve marbleized effect. Bake in a preheated 350° oven 35 to 40 minutes. Frost top with chocolate icing or dust with powdered sugar. Delicious plain if desired.

The Soirée Dinner

(SERVES 6 TO 8)

Crisp Vegetable Carrousel — Sauce Iberis

Chicken Bretagne

Spinach Soufflé

Crusty Noodle Ring

Hot Pickled Pineapple   French Bread

Crêpes Suzette

Irish Coffee

CRISP VEGETABLE CARROUSEL

Arrange a lazy susan or large platter with an assortment of crisp vegetables. All types of raw vegetables are excellent with Sauce Iberis (a dunking sauce): cherry tomatoes, cauliflower, radishes, cucumber sticks, etc. Form spokes of peeled cucumber sticks making sections around bowl of sauce. Place cherry tomatoes, cauliflowerets, radishes, and celery fans in between. Dust cucumbers with paprika for eye appeal. Shrimps are a fitting inclusion.

To make decorative vegetables, see Index.

SAUCE IBERIS

1 cup mayonnaise	1 tablespoon chopped parsley
½ teaspoon dry mustard	3 tablespoons chopped pimiento
¼ teaspoon garlic salt	olives
1 tablespoon anchovy paste	3 tablespoons chopped gherkins
½ teaspoon Tabasco	*or* sweet pickle relish
2 tablespoons tarragon vinegar	1 teaspoon chopped onion

3 hard-cooked eggs, chopped fine

Combine mayonnaise, mustard, garlic salt, anchovy paste, Tabasco, tarragon vinegar, parsley, olives, gherkins, onion, and eggs. Blend well. Serve in bowl in center of platter or lazy susan (carrousel) surrounded by vegetables for dipping. Makes 2 cups. A dunking sauce for shrimp, raw cauliflower, etc.

CHICKEN BRETAGNE

2 2¾- to 3-pound frying chickens
1½ teaspoons salt
⅛ teaspoon pepper
½ cup (¼ pound) unsalted butter
15 small white onions

½ pound small white mushrooms, quartered
½ cup dry white wine
1 teaspoon wine vinegar
3 large tomatoes, peeled, seeded, and coarsely chopped
¼ cup heavy cream

Garnish:

2 tablespoons chopped parsley   Quartered tomatoes

Cut chicken in quarters; season quarters, necks, and giblets with salt and pepper. Heat butter until foaming; brown chickens and giblets until golden. Cover pan and cook about 18 minutes. Blanch onions in boiling water and drain. Combine with chickens; add mushrooms. Simmer for 5 minutes; drain off all but 1 tablespoon of remaining browned butter in pan. Stir in white wine, vinegar, and tomatoes. Cook uncovered over medium heat for 5 minutes. Remove chicken, mushrooms, and onions to deep serving dish and keep warm.

Add cream to the sauce; simmer slowly until sauce thickens; adjust seasonings. Pour sauce through sieve for smoothness; heat and pour over chicken. Sprinkle with parsley and garnish with quartered tomatoes. Serve very hot.

SPINACH SOUFFLE

6 tablespoons butter
7 tablespoons flour
1½ cups milk
1½ teaspoons salt
¾ cup egg whites (about 6 egg whites)

1 tablespoon flour
1½ cups chopped, firmly packed raw spinach
4 egg yolks
1 tablespoon instant minced onion

¼ teaspoon black pepper

Place a shallow baking pan on oven rack. Set a 2-quart ungreased casserole in pan. Pour boiling water around casserole to depth of at least 1 inch. Preheat oven to 325°. While oven and casserole are preheating, melt butter in a saucepan. Add 7 tablespoons flour; blend well. Add milk all at once and cook, stirring constantly, until mixture thickens.

Add salt to egg whites and beat until stiff and glossy, but not dry. Blend 1 tablespoon flour into the spinach. Beat egg yolks; add onion, pepper, and spinach, then blend into white sauce. Fold spinach mixture into egg whites, a quarter of it at a time. Remove hot casserole from oven. Spoon in soufflé.

Using a spatula, make a groove around soufflé about 1 inch deep and 1 inch from edge of casserole. Return casserole to pan of hot water in oven and bake for 60 to 70 minutes or until a knife inserted halfway between center and outside edge comes out clean. Serve at once.

CRUSTY NOODLE RING

¼ cup (⅛ pound) butter ½ cup dark brown sugar
1 cup pecan halves

Melt butter in bottom of 6-cup ring mold, add brown sugar, pressing into bottom of mold. Place unbroken pecans firmly into brown sugar to form a pattern.

Noodles:

½ pound broad noodles ½ teaspoon cinnamon
2 eggs, slightly beaten ⅓ cup sugar
¼ cup (⅛ pound) butter, melted ½ teaspoon salt
Watercress

Boil noodles; drain well and combine with eggs, butter, cinnamon, sugar, and salt. Spread in prepared mold over sugar-pecan mixture and bake in a preheated 350° oven for 1 hour. Unmold on platter, center with bowl of Hot Pickled Pineapple and garnish with watercress.

HOT PICKLED PINEAPPLE

1 #2 can crushed pineapple, 3 tablespoons brown sugar
drained 2 tablespoons cider vinegar
1 tablespoon butter

Toss all ingredients together in a pie pan. Place in a preheated 350° oven and bake 30 minutes, stirring occasionally. Serve warm.

CREPES SUZETTE

Suzette butter:

½ cup unsalted butter
¼ cup granulated sugar
Grated rind of 1 orange

Grated rind of 1 lemon
½ cup orange juice
3 tablespoons orange liqueur

Cream the butter; add sugar, orange rind, and lemon rind. Add orange juice and liqueur slowly and blend well. Set aside in refrigerator until firm.

Crêpes:

1½ cups sifted all-purpose flour
¼ cup confectioners' sugar
⅛ teaspoon salt
¾ cup milk
¾ cup cold water

¼ cup butter, melted
2 tablespoons Curaçao
3 egg yolks
Butter *or* oil for greasing
    skillet

Combine flour, sugar, salt, milk, and water in electric blender or mixer and beat. Add butter, Curaçao, egg yolks, and beat again until smooth. Scrape down flour from sides of bowl.

A 6-inch skillet makes about 12 crêpes. A 5-inch skillet makes about 18 crêpes. Grease a skillet and heat. Pour in 2 to 3 tablespoons batter and tilt skillet quickly to cover surface. Cook about 1 minute on each side or until brown. Stack and set aside until final preparation.

To assemble:

2 tablespoons granulated sugar
Suzette butter
2 tablespoons cognac

2 tablespoons Curaçao
2 tablespoons kirsch
18 crêpes

Heat chafing dish, add sugar, and permit it to melt partially. Add ¼ cup of Suzette butter and cognac. Heat to bubbling. Place as many crêpes in pan as possible to heat through. Fold each in fourths and set to side of pan, until all are heated. Arrange them in center of pan, pour on the Curaçao and kirsch, avert your face and light the liqueur. Spoon the sauce over the crêpes as they are served, 2 or 3 to each guest.

IRISH COFFEE

There is an excellent recipe for Irish Coffee in our *Thoughts for Buffets*.

Kitchen Party Luncheon

(SERVES 6)

Scallops New Orleans   Brown Rice
Viennese Kaiserschmarrn
(Kaiser's Nonsense)
Fried Cheese   Fruit Coffee Ring
Spiced Candied Cherries
Coffee   Tea

ADVANCE PREPARATION SCHEDULE

Deep Freeze	Previous Day	Early Morning
Coffee Ring	*Spiced Candied Cherries*	*Scallops*
		Coat cheese for frying

SCALLOPS NEW ORLEANS

1½ pounds fresh scallops   3 cups cooked Brown Rice
3 fresh fish fillets, cut in pieces
(sole *or* flounder)

Marinade:

½ cup white wine   1 teaspoon chopped parsley
3 tablespoons lemon juice   ½ teaspoon chopped tarragon
2 drops aromatic bitters   1 medium onion, chopped
(optional)

Combine all Marinade ingredients in a large bowl and blend well. Add fish and scallops; marinate several hours, or overnight.

Sauce:

1 green pepper, diced	Pepper to taste
1 pimiento, diced	½ cup chili sauce
½ pound fresh mushrooms, sliced	½ cup tomato sauce
6 green onions and tops, sliced	½ cup water
2 teaspoons capers	1 bay leaf
½ small cauliflower, cut in pieces	1 clove garlic, minced
½ teaspoon salt	Chopped parsley

Combine sauce ingredients in large saucepan; simmer over low heat for 30 minutes.

Drain fish and scallops and add to Sauce; simmer for 15 minutes; remove bay leaf. Serve hot on a bed of cooked Brown Rice (see Index).

VIENNESE KAISERSCHMARRN
(Translation — "Kaiser's Nonsense")

2 eggs, beaten	2 tablespoons sugar
½ cup milk	2 tablespoons raisins
⅛ teaspoon salt	1 cup all-purpose flour
2 tablespoons butter	

Combine eggs, milk, and salt; add sugar, raisins; beat well. Add flour. Batter should be light. Melt butter in skillet; add batter; lift the batter with a fork around the edge of pan so uncooked batter runs underneath. Slice with knife while still cooking in pan. Remove when slightly browned and soft. Pancake will be in chunks. Serve with sugar and cinnamon.

Note: A good breakfast dish with fruit compote. Legend has it that this recipe relates to a happy moment in the otherwise rigid routine in the life of the Emperor Franz Joseph. He enjoyed this simple dish each morning, without fail, to the amusement of those about him, who in turn named it "Kaiser's Nonsense."

SPICED CANDIED CHERRIES

2 cups cider vinegar	1 cup water
2 cups sugar	1 stick cinnamon
1 pound candied cherries	

Combine vinegar, sugar, water, cinnamon, in saucepan; bring to a boil. Simmer 10 minutes. Add cherries; bring to a boil again. Remove from heat, cool and refrigerate. Serve as a relish.

FRUIT COFFEE RING

1½ teaspoons (1 envelope) dry yeast
1 teaspoon sugar
⅓ cup warm water
⅓ cup scalded milk
⅓ cup butter *or* margarine
3 tablespoons sugar
½ teaspoon salt
2⅓ cups sifted all-purpose flour

1 egg, beaten
Salad oil
4 tablespoons butter
½ cup blackberry filling
½ cup apricot filling
1 teaspoon grated orange rind (optional)
1 teaspoon orange juice
1 egg yolk

1 tablespoon cold water

In small bowl, sprinkle yeast and sugar into warm water; stir until dissolved. In large bowl, combine scalded milk, butter, sugar, and salt; cool until lukewarm. Add half of flour, beating well with spoon until smooth and elastic. Stir in yeast and egg; beat well. Add remainder of flour, a little at a time, beating well to make a soft dough. Turn onto lightly floured surface, cover, let rest 10 minutes. Knead dough until light and smooth; turn into large greased bowl; brush surface lightly with salad oil. Cover with damp cloth; let rise in warm place (85°F.), free from draft, about 2 hours, or until doubled in bulk.

Divide dough in three pieces. Roll, dot with small quantity of butter on two pieces, top with third piece, and roll butter into dough. Repeat until all butter is used. Divide dough into 3 pieces. With stockinette-covered rolling pin, roll each piece of dough into 20″ x 5″ strip. Spread one strip with filling (combine apricot preserve and orange rind). Spread second strip with blackberry filling. Place third strip on top. Roll up from 20-inch side as for jelly roll. Pinch together at ends to seal completely. Place on a large greased cooky sheet; form into a ring and fasten two ends together. Beat egg yolk with water and brush ring with mixture; cover with damp cloth and let rise in warm place until doubled in bulk, or about 1 hour. Bake in a preheated 375° oven for about 30 minutes, or until light brown. When cool, ice with Confectioners' Frosting.

Confectioners' Frosting:

> 1 cup confectioners' sugar   2 tablespoons warm milk
> ½ teaspoon vanilla *or* lemon juice

Mix together, drizzle over cake.

Variation:

Use any of your favorite fillings.

Make raspberry filling by combining ⅓ cup red raspberry preserve with 2 teaspoons lemon rind.

FRIED CHEESE

> 6 3-inch squares mild hard cheese   2 eggs, slightly beaten
> (¼ inch thick)   1 cup fine bread crumbs
> 2 tablespoons butter *or* oil

Dip the cheese squares in the eggs so that they are well coated; dredge with crumbs thoroughly. Heat butter and sauté squares until lightly browned. Turn once to brown second side. Serve at once.

Note: They may be coated with egg and crumbs and refrigerated until ready to serve.

Young Executives Dinner

(SERVES 6 TO 8)

Soup Perc

Crown Roast of Pork

Spiced Apples   Minted Pears

Glazed Onions

Combination Salad — Stockyard Dressing

Frosted Bowknots   Chocolate Chip Whipped Cream Pie

Coffee

ADVANCE PREPARATION SCHEDULE

Deep Freeze	Previous Day	Early Morning
Bowknots	*Pears*	*Soup*
		Frost Bowknots
		Pie
		Roast for baking
		Walnut Dressing
		Onions for baking

SOUP PERC

1 quart extra-strength chicken broth
1 head lettuce, leaves separated

1 cucumber, peeled, seeded, and cubed
Salt and pepper

Place broth, lettuce, and cucumber in 2-quart kettle. Simmer for 10 minutes. Cool slightly. Pour into blender and whirl thoroughly. Season to taste, as the flavor should be subtle. Reheat to serve.

CROWN ROAST OF PORK

5-pound crown roast of pork
1 teaspoon salt
½ teaspoon pepper

Spiced crab apples, drained
Minted pears
Parsley sprigs

"French" the chops of roast: cut meat from ends of rib bones, and cut through backbone for easier carving. Wipe roast with damp paper towels. Place in shallow roasting pan and sprinkle with salt and pepper. Wrap each rib bone with aluminum foil to prevent overbrowning. Insert a meat thermometer into thick part of the meat, without touching any bone. Fill center of roast with crushed foil to keep crown shape during preparation. Roast meat in a preheated 325° oven, uncovered, for 2½ hours. Remove the foil from the center of roast. Fill center with Walnut Dressing. Cover the dressing loosely with square of foil. Continue roasting pork until internal temperature is 185° on thermometer. Remove foil from each of the rib bones. Place the roast on a serving board or platter. Garnish with crab apples, minted pears, and parsley sprigs. Makes 6 to 8 servings (two ribs for each serving).

WALNUT DRESSING

2 cups thinly sliced apples	⅛ cup lemon juice
¾ cup orange sections	⅛ cup sugar
¾ cup chopped walnuts	¾ tablespoon grated orange rind
¼ cup dry white wine	

Combine apples, orange sections, walnuts, lemon juice, sugar, orange rind, and wine in a bowl. Cover. Refrigerate at least 1 hour. Fill crown roast with this cold dressing.

GLAZED ONIONS

⅓ cup butter	Dash cayenne
1 teaspoon beef extract	Pinch nutmeg
1 tablespoon brown sugar	Pinch ground cloves
1 teaspoon salt	3 dozen very small white onions

Melt butter in casserole on top of stove; add beef extract, sugar, salt, cayenne, nutmeg, and cloves. When blended, add onions and stir until well coated. Cover and bake in a preheated 350° oven about 1 hour, shaking casserole lightly three or four times to prevent onions from sticking.

Variation with another menu:

Add 1 cup whole blanched almonds. They are delicious in this recipe but were omitted here because of the nuts in the roast dressing.

MINTED PEARS

1 8-ounce glass mint jelly	½ teaspoon mint flavoring
½ cup vinegar	2 or 3 drops green vegetable
¼ cup light corn syrup	coloring
1 #2½ can pear halves, drained	

Combine jelly, vinegar, and syrup in a skillet and simmer 15 minutes until jelly is dissolved. Add pears, mint flavoring, and coloring and simmer 15 more minutes. Do not overcook. Serve drained, hot or cold.

Variation:

Do not drain pears. Add to syrup ½ teaspoon mint flavoring and

2 to 3 drops green coloring, or enough to color pears. Refrigerate several hours. Serve cold.

COMBINATION SALAD

6 cups Boston lettuce, torn
2 tomatoes, peeled and cut in 6ths
1 cup raw fresh mushrooms, scrubbed and sliced thin
1 cucumber, thinly sliced

Arrange in salad bowl, moisten with Stockyard Dressing; toss lightly but thoroughly to cover all ingredients.

STOCKYARD DRESSING

1 cup dairy sour cream
¼ cup half and half cream
2 tablespoons mayonnaise
½ teaspoon curry powder
½ teaspoon Worcestershire
½ teaspoon steak sauce
½ teaspoon prepared horseradish
½ teaspoon dry mustard
1 small clove garlic, minced
2 dashes Tabasco
Dash salt and pepper

Combine sour and sweet creams, mayonnaise, curry powder, Worcestershire, steak sauce, horseradish, mustard, garlic, Tabasco, salt and pepper, and mix well. Keep refrigerated. Makes 1¼ cups.

Note: Delicious and tangy; would be good with broiled chicken.

FROSTED BOWKNOTS

1 package active dry yeast
¼ cup warm water
1 cup milk, scalded
½ cup shortening
⅓ cup sugar
1 teaspoon salt
3½ to 4 cups sifted all-purpose flour
1 egg

Soften yeast in water in a large mixing bowl. Combine milk, shortening, sugar, and salt; cool to lukewarm. Add 1 cup of the flour and beat well. Beat in softened yeast and egg and then beat in remaining flour gradually to form a soft dough and continue until very smooth. Cover with a towel and let rise in warm place 1½ to 2 hours until doubled in bulk. Turn out on floured board and roll to an 18″ x 10″ rectangle, ½ inch thick. Cut strips 10 inches long and ¾ inch wide and roll lightly with fingers; tie loosely in a knot, tucking ends underneath. Arrange on greased baking sheets. Cover and let rise again until almost double, about 45 minutes. Bake in a preheated 375° oven 12 minutes or until light brown. Spread with Orange Frosting. Makes 20 rolls.

Orange Frosting:

> 1 teaspoon orange peel, grated   2 tablespoons orange juice
> 1 cup confectioners' sugar, sifted

Blend orange peel, orange juice, and sugar well. Brush icing on with pastry brush.

Variation:

These are very good as a plain dinner roll; omit the orange frosting.

CHOCOLATE CHIP WHIPPED CREAM PIE

> 3 tablespoons sugar
> 1 tablespoon flour
> 1 cup (15) graham crackers, crushed fine
> ½ cup butter
>
> ½ cup milk
> 15 marshmallows
> 1 pint heavy cream, whipped
> 2 4-ounce bars sweet cooking chocolate, grated

Combine sugar, flour, and graham crackers; mix well; add butter. Press into 9-inch pie shell to make crust. Place in a preheated 350° oven for 10 minutes. Cool before filling. Pour milk and marshmallows in double boiler and stir until melted. Cool; fold in whipped cream. Add grated chocolate to cooled mixture. Turn into baked pie shell to chill for several hours.

Optional garnish:

Shave chocolate curls from solid bar of sweet cooking chocolate with vegetable peeler. Arrange a border around edge of filling.

For the Visiting Dignitary

(FORMAL DINNER)

(SERVES 6)

Pierogi   Glazed Shrimp   Artichoke Hearts Caviar

Avgholemono Soup

Rock Cornish Hens Wildnut   Herb Green Beans

Avocado Green Salad — Horseradish Dressing

Date Rum Cake

Coffee

Suggested wine: Montrachet or other white Burgundy

ADVANCE PREPARATION SCHEDULE

Deep Freeze	**Previous Day**	**Early Morning**
Cake	*Shrimp*	*Artichoke hearts*
Pierogi	*Soup*	*Frost cake*
		Wild rice
		Salad dressing

PIEROGI

Unstretched Strudel Dough:

2½ cups sifted all-purpose flour	1 egg
½ teaspoon salt	⅔ cup ice water
1 teaspoon baking powder	4 tablespoons salad oil

Sift flour, salt, and baking powder into a bowl. Make a well in the center and drop the egg, water, and oil into it. Work into the flour and knead until smooth and elastic. Place a warm bowl over dough and let rest for 30 minutes. Roll out in a rectangle as thin as possible and spread with one of the fillings. Roll up like a jelly roll, brush with oil or melted butter. Bake in a preheated 350° oven for 30 to 35 minutes. Cut into 1-inch slices while hot. Makes 36.

Cabbage Filling:

6 cups finely shredded cabbage	1½ teaspoons salt
½ cup minced onions	½ teaspoon pepper
⅓ cup butter *or* chicken fat	2 teaspoons sugar

Cook cabbage and onions in butter or fat over low heat for 25 minutes, stirring occasionally. Add salt, pepper, and sugar. Cool. Roll up in Strudel Dough.

Liver Filling:

½ cup chicken fat	1 cup diced onions
1½ pounds calf's liver, cubed	1½ teaspoons salt
¼ teaspoon pepper	

Heat chicken fat in saucepan, add liver and onions, and sauté until liver loses its redness. Pour liver, onions, and fat remaining in the pan into a chopping bowl or meat grinder. Chop or grind thoroughly; add salt and pepper. Spread on oiled Strudel Dough and roll up. Divide into 4 small strudels.

GLAZED SHRIMP

1 envelope (1 tablespoon) unflavored gelatin	1 teaspoon Worcestershire
2 tablespoons cold water	1 drop Tabasco
½ cup catsup	1 pound shrimp, cooked and cleaned
½ cup chili sauce	Small cabbage

Soften gelatin in cold water and dissolve over hot water. Combine with all remaining ingredients except shrimp. Place in refrigerator until of jelly-like consistency. Place shrimps on toothpicks and dip into thickened sauce. Let drip; then stick into cabbage. (Cut a slice from stem end so cabbage stands evenly.) Place in refrigerator to set. Can be prepared hours in advance. Makes about 20.

ARTICHOKE HEARTS CAVIAR

1 #303 (15-ounce) can artichoke hearts	1 3-ounce package cream cheese
1 2-ounce jar caviar, red *or* black	1 tablespoon cream

Drain artichoke hearts. Soften cheese; blend with cream and mash until smooth. Spread leaves of artichoke hearts from center slightly. Place 1 teaspoon cheese in center of each and top with generous ½ teaspoon caviar. Refrigerate until serving time. Makes 14–16.

AVGHOLEMONO SOUP

2 quarts chicken broth, strained	3 eggs
¼ cup rice	¼ cup lemon juice
	Salt

Heat broth to boiling, add rice and cook 20 minutes. Beat eggs with a rotary beater until frothy; add lemon juice, blending well and, while continuing to beat, slowly add 2 cups of the hot broth. To serve, combine egg-lemon-soup mixture and salt to taste; bring to a simmer and cook 3 minutes. Do not allow to boil or soup will curdle. See Index for Chicken Soup, or use canned broth.

History has repeated itself with this Byzantine heirloom, which has remained a favorite since the sixth century.

ROCK CORNISH HENS WILDNUT ·

6 Cornish hens	½ cup butter, melted
1 tablespoon salt	3 slices bacon (optional)

Wash and prepare the hens for roasting. Sprinkle cavities lightly with salt. Stuff and truss them; brush with melted butter and lay ½ slice bacon over each bird. Roast uncovered in a preheated 375° oven 1 to 1½ hours or until tender, basting every 20 minutes with melted butter added to pan drippings. The secret of a flavorful Cornish hen is continuous basting with butter. Add more if the ½ cup is exhausted before poultry is tender.

Wild Rice and Almond Stuffing:

1 cup wild rice	½ teaspoon salt
½ cup chopped onion	½ cup almonds, toasted °
½ cup sliced, fresh mushrooms	and slivered
3 tablespoons butter	½ teaspoon thyme

° To toast almonds, heat 2 tablespoons butter in skillet, add almonds and heat unti lightly browned. Watch closely, as they burn easily.

Wash and cook wild rice according to package directions, or see

Index. Sauté onion and mushrooms in butter for 5 minutes. Mix with rice, add salt, almonds, and thyme. Makes about 3½ cups (enough for 6 hens).

Arrange Cornish hens on platter; garnish with ½-inch slices of 2 or 3 unpeeled navel oranges. Tuck sprigs of parsley between slices and in wings of hens.

Note: Do not stuff hens until just before roasting.

HERB GREEN BEANS

1½ pounds green beans	¼ cup minced celery
¼ cup butter	¼ cup snipped parsley
¾ cup minced onions	¼ teaspoon dried rosemary
1 small clove garlic, crushed	¼ teaspoon dried basil

Cook beans in boiling salted water until tender. Drain. Melt butter in saucepan, add onions, garlic, and celery; sauté 5 minutes. Add parsley, rosemary, basil and salt. Simmer, covered, for 10 minutes. Toss well with beans. Serve piping hot.

AVOCADO GREEN SALAD

1 head curly endive   2 avocados
2 scallions, chopped

Trim and wash endive thoroughly. Cube avocados and arrange on a bed of endive. Sprinkle with scallions and serve with Horseradish Dressing.

HORSERADISH DRESSING

1½ tablespoons prepared horseradish	1 tablespoon sugar
1 cup dairy sour cream	¼ teaspoon paprika
1 tablespoon tarragon vinegar	1 tablespoon snipped chives
1 tablespoon snipped fresh dill *or* 1 teaspoon dried dill	¾ teaspoon salt

Combine horseradish, sour cream, and vinegar. Mix until smooth. Stir in dill, sugar, paprika, chives, and salt. Refrigerate, covered, at least 15 minutes. Makes 1 cup.

DATE RUM CAKE

¾ cup butter	1 teaspoon baking soda
1½ cups dark brown sugar, firmly packed	1 cup boiling water
	2 eggs, well beaten
1 pound dates, chopped	1½ cups cake flour, sifted
1 pound walnuts, chopped	¾ teaspoon salt

1 tablespoon rum

Cream butter and brown sugar until well blended; add dates and nuts that have been put through the grinder. Add soda to boiling water and pour over creamed mixture. Stir until cool. Add eggs. Gradually stir in flour and salt, beating until smooth. Then add rum and stir until well blended. Turn batter into a greased 13″ x 9″ pan and bake in a preheated 300° oven 1 hour and 15 minutes. Cool in the pan on a wire rack for 10 minutes. Frost with Rum Butter Icing or serve with whipped cream.

Rum Butter Icing:

2 cups confectioners' sugar	2 tablespoons cream
¼ cup butter, softened	1 teaspoon rum

Dash mace

Blend sugar and butter together; add cream, rum, mace, and beat until smooth.

Come See Our Movies Dinner

(SERVES 6)

Jellied Pickled Fish

Chinese Beef and Vegetables   Pilaf

Garlic Bread

Grecian Pears   Anise Cookies

Coffee   Milk

ADVANCE PREPARATION SCHEDULE

Deep Freeze	Previous Day	Early Morning
Anise cookies	*Pickled Fish*	*Chinese Beef*
	Pears	

JELLIED PICKLED FISH

4 onions, sliced	¾ cup white vinegar
6 slices pike	2 tablespoons sugar
1½ teaspoons salt	2 teaspoons pickling spice
¼ teaspoon pepper	2 bay leaves
2 cups water	Parsley
4 slices lemon	

Combine 2 sliced onions, pike, salt, pepper, and water in a sauce-pan. Bring to a boil and cook over low heat 25 minutes. Carefully remove the fish and place in a bowl or jar, alternating the layers with the remaining 2 sliced onions. Mix the vinegar, sugar, pickling spice, and bay leaves with the fish stock. Bring to a boil and pour over the fish; cover and let pickle in the refrigerator for 2 days before serving. Will keep about two weeks. The liquid in this recipe will be jelled. Chop it coarsely to use as garnish over individually served fish slices. Ornament further with sprigs of parsley and lemon slices.

CHINESE BEEF AND VEGETABLES

2 tablespoons Oyster Sauce	1 cup celery, sliced in 2-inch lengths
¼ teaspoon salt	
1 teaspoon fresh ginger, chopped	12 water chestnuts, sliced
½ teaspoon sherry	½ pound fresh bean sprouts, *or* 1 16-ounce can sprouts, *or* ½ pound snow peas
1½ pounds beef tenderloin, *or* flank steak, sliced thin and cut in 1½-inch strips	
	1 tablespoon cornstarch
4 tablespoons oil	½ cup soup stock or water
1½ cups onions, sliced lengthwise	1 teaspoon soy sauce

Combine Oyster Sauce, salt, and ginger. Coat beef with mix-ture. Place 2 tablespoons of oil in saucepan; sauté beef until lightly browned, about 5 minutes. Remove from pan. Heat re-maining 2 tablespoons oil, add onions, celery, and sauté lightly

3 to 4 minutes; add chestnuts, drained, bean sprouts, and sautéed beef. Make a paste of cornstarch and soup stock; add soy sauce and sherry; blend with beef mixture. Cook until thickened and clear, about 5 minutes. Serve with Pilaf.

Oyster Sauce:

1 pint oysters   3 tablespoons soy sauce

Drain oysters; reserve liquid. Grind oysters and add to oyster liquid. Place in pot, bring to boil; reduce heat, simmer ½ hour, strain, and add soy sauce. Stores well — use as a sauce or a dip.

PILAF

2 onions, chopped	3 cups beef broth
3 tablespoons butter, softened	3 tablespoons catsup
2 cups raw rice	½ teaspoon salt
⅛ teaspoon pepper	

Sauté onions in butter; add rice and sauté until brown. Add broth, catsup, salt, and pepper; simmer, covered, for 40 minutes. If more liquid is needed after 30 minutes, add enough water to cover and cook last 10 minutes. Do not stir. Let stand 10 minutes. To serve, turn out carefully and toss lightly.

GARLIC BREAD

2 loaves French bread	2 tablespoons grated Parmesan
½ cup butter, melted	cheese (optional)
1 clove garlic, minced	

Cut bread in 1-inch slices within ¼ inch of bottom crust. Combine butter, garlic, and cheese; spread each cut slice with mixture. Press bread back to loaf shape; wrap each loaf in aluminum foil. Bake in a preheated 375° oven 15 minutes, or until heated. Serve in foil, shaping it basket-like as it is opened.

GRECIAN PEARS

6 fresh Comice *or* Anjou pears
3 cups sugar
2 cups water
4 drops red food coloring
   (optional)

1 4-inch stick cinnamon
3 or 4 whole cloves
Dairy sour cream
Mace

Peel pears and core from blossom end, leaving stems on. Combine sugar, water, and food coloring in large saucepan. Simmer over low heat, stirring until sugar is dissolved. Add pears to this syrup and boil gently about 15 minutes, or until tender. Turn often to color evenly. Remove from heat and place pears with syrup in bowl. Add cinnamon stick and cloves. Refrigerate several hours. To serve, place chilled pears in individual compotes. Press gently to flatten bottoms, in order to stand them upright. Garnish with a mint leaf tucked in a stem end. Add syrup. Spoon sour cream around pears. Sprinkle with mace. Makes 6 portions.

Note: As with most Greek desserts, the pears are quite sweet and the syrup thick. Reduce sugar to 1 cup for the calorie-conscious and serve as a compote as well.

ANISE COOKIES

3 eggs
1 cup sugar
1 tablespoon anise seeds

1½ cups all-purpose flour
½ teaspoon baking powder

Beat eggs and sugar 30 minutes by hand, or 20 minutes with electric mixer. Sift flour with baking powder; add anise seed. Combine with egg mixture and beat 5 minutes. Drop from teaspoon on well-greased and floured cooky sheets, 1 inch apart. Let stand overnight, or 10 hours, at room temperature before baking. Bake in a preheated 350° oven 10 to 15 minutes.

Festival Dinner

(SERVES 4)

Chilled Potato Soup Gourmet
Coq au Vin   Green Rice Puddings
Beet and Egg Salad — Herb Croutons
Mardi Gras Cake   Coffee

Suggested wine: a red Burgundy

ADVANCE PREPARATION SCHEDULE

Deep Freeze	**Previous Day**	**Early Morning**
Cake	*Soup*	*Coq au Vin*
		Prepare puddings
		Crisp greens

POTATO SOUP GOURMET

1 10½-ounce can frozen cream of potato soup, slightly thawed
1 cup water
½ cup dairy sour cream
¼ cup sliced radishes
2 tablespoons chopped green onions

Heat soup and water in a saucepan until soup is thawed; stir occasionally. Remove from heat and cool. With a rotary beater, beat in a small amount of sour cream at a time until mixture is smooth. Stir in radishes and green onions. Chill thoroughly, 2 to 3 hours.

COQ AU VIN

2 medium onions, chopped
½ pound fresh mushroms, halved
1 cup (½ pound) butter
1½ teaspoons salt
½ teaspoon pepper
2 2½-pound chickens, disjointed
½ teaspoon paprika
½ teaspoon monosodium glutamate
1 cup Burgundy
4 slices bacon (optional)
1 tablespoon flour
Watercress

Using 12-inch frying pan, brown onions and mushrooms in butter

with ½ teaspoon salt and ¼ teaspoon pepper. Remove from pan.
Season chicken with remaining salt and pepper, paprika, monosodium glutamate, and brown thoroughly in remaining butter. Add
wine. Cut bacon into 2-inch lengths and fry in separate skillet to
soft, not crisp, stage. Drain. Return onions and mushrooms to
chicken, together with drained bacon. Simmer, covered, over low
heat for 45 minutes, or until tender, adding a little hot water if
necessary. Remove chicken and keep warm. There should be a cup
of liquid remaining; if not, add hot water to make that amount.
Make a paste of 1 tablespoon flour with chicken liquid; add to the
sauce and simmer 10 minutes. To serve, place chicken on platter
encircled by Green Rice Puddings and watercress sprigs. Serve
sauce separately.

GREEN RICE PUDDINGS

2 cups rice, cooked	1 small onion, grated
½ cup grated Cheddar cheese	2 eggs, well beaten
1 cup chopped parsley	½ cup milk
1 teaspoon Worcestershire	

Combine cooked rice, cheese, parsley, onion, eggs, milk, and
Worcestershire and blend well. Pour into eight 3-inch well-greased
muffin tins and bake in a preheated 350° oven 30 to 45 minutes, or
until browned.

BEET AND EGG SALAD — HERB CROUTONS

1 quart salad greens	3 hard-cooked eggs, sliced
(Boston lettuce, Bibb, curly	½ cup canned julienne beets,
endive)	drained
1 cup French dressing	Herb croutons

Wash greens; drain and place in refrigerator to crisp. To serve, toss
with French dressing; arrange egg slices and beets over greens, and
scatter Croutons over all.

HERB CROUTONS

4 slices bread (1 cup cubes)	¼ teaspoon thyme
1 tablespoon butter	¼ teaspoon marjoram

Toast bread, trim off crusts, and cut into ½-inch cubes. Melt butter;

add thyme and marjoram. Toss and turn the bread cubes with the herb butter over moderate heat. Cool and add to greens just before serving.

MARDI GRAS CAKE

⅔ cup butterscotch morsels
¼ cup water
2¼ cups sifted all-purpose flour
1 teaspoon salt
1 teaspoon soda
½ teaspoon baking powder

½ cup shortening
1 cup sugar
¼ cup brown sugar, firmly packed
3 eggs, unbeaten
1 cup buttermilk or sour milk

Melt butterscotch morsels in water in saucepan. Cool. Sift together flour, salt, soda, and baking powder. Cream shortening with white and brown sugars. Add eggs, one at a time, beating well after each addition. Add butterscotch mixture and mix well. Add dry ingredients alternately with buttermilk, beginning and ending with dry ingredients. Turn batter into 2 greased and floured 9-inch layer pans. Bake in a preheated 375° oven for 30 minutes or until done. Cool. Put layers together with Butterscotch Filling. Makes 8 to 12 slices.

Butterscotch Filling:

½ cup sugar
1 tablespoon cornstarch
½ cup evaporated milk
⅓ cup water

⅓ cup butterscotch morsels
1 egg yolk, beaten
2 tablespoons butter, softened
1 cup chopped coconut

1 cup chopped pecans or walnuts

Combine sugar and cornstarch. Blend in milk, water, morsels, and egg yolk. Cook and stir until thickened. Remove from heat; stir in butter, coconut, and nuts. Cool. Spread between cake layers and on top to within ½ inch of the edge. If the entire recipe is used for filling, dust top with confectioners' sugar.

Hong Kong Dinner

(SERVES 6)

Water Chestnut Ramaki

Chinese Spareribs *or* Spareribs Aloha

Chicken Sub Gum Soup

Crab Foo Yong   Rice   Foo Yong Sauce

Cauliflower Vinaigrette

Pineapple Crème de Menthe

Tea

Suggested wine: Champagne (for contrast)

ADVANCE PREPARATION SCHEDULE

Previous Day	Early Morning
Marinate pineapple	*Sauce for spareribs*
Vinaigrette dressing	*Foo Yong Sauce*
(without oil)	*Cook Cauliflower*

WATER CHESTNUT RAMAKI

1 7-ounce can water chestnuts   ⅓ cup catsup
7 bacon strips, cut in half   ½ cup granulated sugar

Wrap water chestnuts in bacon strips, skewering firmly with tooth-pick. If larger than bite size, cut water chestnuts in halves or thirds. Use half strip of bacon for each piece of chestnut; fatty bacon is best. Place in baking pan, fairly close together and place pan in a preheated 300° to 325° oven. Drain off fat as it collects, until bacon appears as dry as possible, but not burned; about one hour. Combine catsup and sugar. Pour this sauce over wrapped water chestnuts; sauce need not cover completely. Return pan to 300° oven for another hour. Chestnuts should now be ready, coated in thick, gooey sauce that clings and does not drip. Be sure to place chestnuts with toothpicks sticking upward so that they are not sticky to handle. If the picks look burned, replace with fresh ones just before serving. Replace in oven briefly, and serve hot.

CHINESE SPARERIBS

2 racks spareribs, cut in half
½ cup soy sauce
½ cup honey
3 tablespoons vinegar
½ cup sherry

1½ cups chicken broth *or*
  2 chicken bouillon cubes dissolved in 1½ cups hot water
1 tablespoon sugar
1 clove garlic, minced

1 teaspoon powdered ginger

Score ribs between bones, but do not separate them; place in a shallow pan. Combine soy sauce, honey, vinegar, sherry, broth, sugar, garlic, and ginger and pour over meat. Allow to stand 2 hours, turning every half hour. Drain; reserve liquid. Place ribs on a rack in shallow pan and roast in a preheated 325° oven about 2 hours. Pour off fat as it accumulates and baste frequently with marinade. To serve, separate into portions of 1 or 2 ribs.

SPARERIBS ALOHA

3 pounds lean country *or*
  baby spareribs

1 teaspoon salt
⅛ teaspoon pepper

Have butcher split ribs into serving pieces — 2 ribs to a portion. Season with salt and pepper and bake in a preheated 350° oven 1¼ hours. Drain fat. Bake another hour at 325°, basting every 10 minutes with Aloha Sauce.

Sauce:

½ cup diced onions
¼ cup diced green pepper
2 8-ounce cans tomato
  sauce

1 tablespoon Worcestershire
⅓ cup white vinegar
1 #2 can pineapple tidbits
  and syrup

Combine onions, green pepper, tomato sauce, Worcestershire, vinegar, pineapple, and syrup, blending well.

Spareribs Aloha is suggested instead for those who enjoy a moist rib.

CHICKEN SUB GUM SOUP

1 teaspoon salad oil
½ cup mushrooms, sliced
½ cup celery, thinly sliced
6 cups chicken broth
1 teaspoon salt

1 cup cooked chicken, diced
4 water chestnuts, coarsely
   diced
½ cup bean sprouts
1 egg, beaten

Heat oil in saucepan; add mushrooms and celery; cook for 1 minute. Stir in chicken broth, salt, chicken, chestnuts, and sprouts; simmer 10 minutes. To serve, drizzle egg into soup slowly, mixing steadily.

CRAB FOO YONG

2 6-ounce packages frozen
   crabmeat, thawed, or 2 6-ounce
   cans crabmeat
½ cup finely chopped celery
¼ cup finely chopped green
   pepper
¼ cup thinly sliced green onions
1 1-pound 3-ounce can bean
   sprouts, drained
1 4-ounce can mushrooms, stems
   and pieces

6 eggs, slightly beaten
½ teaspoon salt
½ teaspoon monosodium
   glutamate
⅛ teaspoon pepper
Dash Tabasco (optional)
1 tablespoon cornstarch
2 tablespoons soy sauce
3 tablespoons salad oil

Flake crabmeat, removing all bones; combine with celery, green pepper, green onions, bean sprouts, and mushrooms; mix lightly. Blend eggs with salt, monosodium glutamate, pepper, and Tabasco; add cornstarch combined with soy sauce. Pour mixture over crabmeat, mixing carefully. Use a scant ½ cup for each pancake. Heat 1 tablespoon salad oil in 10-inch skillet, and pour 4 cakes into pan; cook on medium heat until delicately browned. Turn only once, and brown reverse side. Repeat cooking procedure 3 times. Place cakes on heated platter and keep warm until all are prepared. Pour Foo Yong Sauce over pancakes and serve at once with fluffy Steamed Rice.

STEAMED RICE

2 cups long grain rice   3 cups water

Wash under running water until water is clean. Combine in a saucepan with the water; cover tightly and bring to a boil over high heat. Reduce heat to lowest point and cook 20 minutes; do not uncover. Makes 6 cups.

FOO YONG SAUCE

1 tablespoon cornstarch   1 chicken bouillon cube
½ teaspoon sugar   1 tablespoon soy sauce
1 cup water

Blend cornstarch, sugar, bouillon cube, soy sauce, and water. Stir constantly while cooking, until mixture thickens and is clear. Serve piping hot over Crab Foo Yong.

CAULIFLOWER VINAIGRETTE

1 head cauliflower
Boiling, salted water
2 tablespoons finely chopped
   stuffed green olives

1 tablespoon capers
6 anchovies, chopped
Lettuce

Separate cauliflower into flowerets; cook in boiling salted water (½ teaspoon salt to 1 cup water) for 5 minutes. Drain in strainer and immediately run cold water over cooked flowerets. Place in bowl and add olives, capers, and anchovies. Toss lightly with Vinaigrette Dressing; allow to cool; refrigerate 1 to 2 hours. To serve, arrange in lettuce-lined bowl.

Vinaigrette Dressing:

1 teaspoon chopped onion
1 teaspoon chopped chives
1 teaspoon chopped parsley
   ¾ cup olive oil

1 teaspoon salt
¼ teaspoon ground pepper
2 tablespoons wine vinegar

Combine onion, chives, parsley, salt, and pepper with wine vinegar. Let stand at least ½ hour. Add olive oil and blend thoroughly.

PINEAPPLE CREME DE MENTHE

1 fresh pineapple, prepared
Sweetened lime juice to cover
½ cup confectioners' sugar

1 quart pineapple sherbet
6 ounces green Crème de Menthe
6 green maraschino cherries

Peel and core fresh pineapple. Cut in horizontal, round slices ½ inch thick. Marinate in lime juice, sweetened with confectioners' sugar. Refrigerate overnight. When ready to serve, remove from marinade and place each slice in deep, individual dessert bowls. To simplify eating, cut each slice in wedges. Serve with a scoop of pineapple sherbet, topped with 1 ounce Crème de Menthe and a green maraschino cherry.

Campaign Rally Dinner

(SERVES 8)

Brisket of Beef with Limas
Winter Fruit Compote
Tomato Platter — Texas French Dressing
Sliced Caraway Rye
Lemon Angel Torte
Beer   Coffee

Suggested wine: Beaujolais

ADVANCE PREPARATION SCHEDULE

Deep Freeze	Previous Day	Early Morning
Cake	*Brisket*	*Assemble cake fruit*
	Dressing	*Assemble meat*
	Angel Torte	

BRISKET OF BEEF WITH LIMAS

8 pounds brisket of beef, lean   ⅓ cup brown sugar
1 pound white large lima beans   Juice of ½ lemon
1 tablespoon prepared mustard   1 teaspoon salt
¾ cup chili sauce   3 cups cold water (approx.)

Note that *lean* brisket is designated. Place meat in roaster without rack and surround with raw lima beans. Combine mustard, chili sauce, sugar, lemon juice, salt, and spread over meat and beans.

Pour water over beans. Cover roaster and place in a preheated 350° oven, allowing 30 minutes roasting time for each pound. Baste frequently; add water to pan when necessary. When almost tender and beans are a reddish brown, remove brisket and let stand at room temperature. Remove fat from meat and when cold slice medium thick (about ¼ inch). Slices should not be too thin. Place over beans.

To serve, reheat in 350° oven for about 30 minutes, basting 2 or 3 times. Serve from oven casserole or arranged on platter.

Increase the size of this recipe according to your needs. Do not hesitate to make a larger amount than necessary, as cold brisket is especially delicious.

WINTER FRUIT COMPOTE

1 #2 can pineapple, drained
1 #2 can pears, drained
1 #2 can peaches, drained
¼ cup sherry
1 1-pound, 4-ounce can applesauce
⅛ teaspoon nutmeg
½ teaspoon cinnamon
¼ cup butter

Grease a 1½ quart casserole very well. Drain fruit and arrange alternately in casserole. Combine sherry, applesauce, nutmeg, cinnamon, and pour over fruit. Dot with butter. Bake in a preheated 350° oven 40 minutes. Serve hot or warm.

TOMATO PLATTER

2 large cucumbers, unpeeled
4 large tomatoes, sliced thick
2 tablespoons chopped parsley
2 sweet Italian onions, sliced thin

Score cucumbers in length with a fork before slicing and arrange as a border on platter. Place sliced tomatoes within border. Sprinkle with chopped parsley and spread onion rings over all. Marinate with Texas French Dressing (about ½ cup). Serve ice cold.

TEXAS FRENCH DRESSING

¼ cup sugar
1 teaspoon prepared mustard
1 teaspoon paprika
1½ teaspoons salt

1 10½-ounce can tomato soup
¼ cup white vinegar
½ cup salad oil
1 teaspoon Worcestershire

¼ pound blue cheese, crumbled

Combine sugar, mustard, paprika, salt, undiluted tomato soup, vinegar, oil, Worcestershire, and blue cheese in blender or in bowl of electric mixer. Beat at high speed in electric mixer 2 minutes, but only a whirl in blender. Makes 1 pint.

Note: This is a heavy type of dressing; stores well in refrigerator.

LEMON ANGEL TORTE

1 envelope (1 tablespoon) unflavored gelatin
½ cup cold water
6 egg yolks, slightly beaten
¾ cup sugar

¾ cup lemon juice
1½ teaspoons grated lemon rind
6 egg whites
¾ cup white corn syrup
1 10-inch angel food cake

1 cup heavy cream, whipped

Soften gelatin in water. Combine egg yolks, sugar, lemon juice, and rind in double boiler and cook over hot, but not boiling water, while stirring, until mixture coats a spoon. Remove from heat and add gelatin; stir until dissolved. Cool slightly. Beat egg whites until stiff, gradually add syrup while beating constantly. Fold into yolk custard, then fold in whipped cream. Tear cake into small pieces. Butter a 10-inch spring form, cover bottom with layer of torn cake and pour custard over it. Alternate layers of cake and custard until all is used. Place in refrigerator and chill until firm. To serve, remove rim of pan and frost with Fruit Frosting.

Fruit Frosting:

¼ teaspoon almond extract
¼ cup chopped candied fruit

1 cup heavy cream, whipped
10 candied cherries, halved

Fold almond extract and candied fruit into whipped cream. Frost cake and decorate with candied cherries.

For the Clergy Dinner

(SERVES 8)

Filled Fish Mold

Braised Leg of Veal

Butter Pecan Sprouts   Gnocchi Parmigiana

Egg Twist Bread

Orange Sherbet Mold

Chocolate Icebox Cake

Coffee

ADVANCE PREPARATION SCHEDULE

Deep Freeze	Previous Day	Early Morning
Bread	*Fish*	*Veal*
	Orange Sherbet	*Gnocchi*
	Chocolate Icebox Cake	
	Wrap veal	

FILLED FISH MOLD

1½ 1-pound jars gefilte fish (small fish balls, or large pieces)

1 #2 can julienne beets, chopped

2 3-ounce packages lemon-flavored gelatin

2 tablespoons prepared horseradish

If using large pieces of gefilte fish, cut through width into ¼-inch slices. Drain fish and beets. Measure liquids, adding sufficient water to make 3½ cups. Bring to a boil; add gelatin; dissolve. Cool; place in refrigerator until of jelly-like consistency. Remove, fold in beets and horseradish, and pour into well-oiled 6-cup mold. Arrange fish balls, or fish slices, in the partially congealed gelatin to form a regular pattern; return to refrigerator for several hours to set. Turn out on a lettuce-lined platter; center with bowl of white prepared horseradish. Garnish with sliced cucumbers and radishes. Serve with assorted crackers.

Note: Homemade gefilte fish is, of course, delicious in this recipe.

As the strength of prepared horseradish varies, adjust amount to your taste.

BRAISED LEG OF VEAL

1 6-pound leg of veal	2 tablespoons shortening
1 clove garlic, split	3 onions, sliced
½ cup thin French dressing	3 celery stalks, sliced
1 teaspoon salt	1 10-ounce can chicken broth
⅛ teaspoon pepper	4 small carrots
1 teaspoon oregano	½ pound small fresh mushrooms
Pinch rosemary	½ cup dry white wine

Remove outer skin, wash and dry veal, and rub with clove of garlic. Saturate a large piece of cheesecloth until very moist in French dressing. Wrap around veal, so as to enclose meat completely. Refrigerate overnight; meat may be refrigerated as long as 24 hours for added flavor.

Remove veal from refrigerator and let stand at room temperature 1 hour. Season with salt, pepper, oregano, and rosemary. Heat shortening in iron skillet or Dutch oven. Add onions and celery and sauté lightly. Add veal with onions and celery, pour bouillon over this; cover, reduce heat, and simmer slowly until tender, about 4 hours. Use more water if necessary. Add carrots and cook about 10 minutes; now add mushrooms and wine and simmer 8 to 10 minutes longer. Remove to hot platter, arrange carrots and mushrooms around meat and garnish with sprigs of celery.

Cold veal, sliced, is especially good for leftover suppers or sandwiches.

BUTTER PECAN SPROUTS

3 pounds fresh Brussels sprouts or 2 10-ounce packages frozen

Wash and remove discolored leaves of fresh sprouts and leave whole. Cook 12 minutes in sufficient water to cover. Cook frozen sprouts according to package directions. Drain and cover with Butter Pecan Sauce.

Butter Pecan Sauce:

¼ cup butter *or* shortening   ¼ cup coarsely chopped pecans

Brown butter until golden, add pecans, and heat through.

GNOCCHI PARMIGIANA

3 cups milk
½ cup (¼ pound) butter
1 teaspoon salt

¾ cup Cream of Wheat *or* Farina
2 cups grated Parmesan cheese
1 egg, lightly beaten

Combine 2 cups of milk, butter, and salt in saucepan and bring to a boil. Add Cream of Wheat to balance of milk and add to heated mixture. Cook, stirring, until thickened. Remove from heat and add 1 cup grated cheese, egg, and blend well. Pour into 8" x 10" pan, cool and place in refrigerator to chill very thoroughly. Cut into 1-inch rounds or squares and layer in overlapping rows in shallow baking dish. Melt remaining butter, pour over Gnocchi, and sprinkle with remainder of cheese. Bake in a preheated 425° oven until lightly browned, about 25 minutes. Remove from casserole and arrange on platter with Butter Pecan Sprouts.

EGG TWIST BREAD

(Cholla)

7½ cups unsifted all-purpose flour
⅔ cups sugar
1 package dry yeast
1 heaping tablespoon salt

2 cups warm water
⅛ cup melted vegetable shortening
3 eggs

2 cups sifted all-purpose flour

Sift 7½ cups flour into a very large bowl. Make a hollow in center of flour, put sugar in hollow, and sprinkle yeast on the sugar. Pour salt around the flour. Pour 1 cup of warm water (not hot) on the yeast and sugar, cover, let stand in a warm place to ferment for about 15 to 30 minutes. Melt shortening, let cool until just warm. Beat the eggs, reserve about ⅛ cup of egg. Add remainder of eggs, the warm shortening, and 1 cup of warm water to the flour mixture. Mix very well in bowl, then place on floured board; add 1 cup of flour while kneading dough. Knead well for about 10 minutes until soft and pliable. Sprinkle 2 tablespoons flour in bowl and return the dough to bowl. Let rise until doubled in bulk. Remove dough and return to floured board. Knead again, about 10 minutes, until soft and pliable. Cut into three parts, making 3 loaves. Take one part, cut into three. Knead each piece to the count of twenty. Then knead and roll each piece to the length of the bread pans.

Then braid the three pieces and place in a buttered and floured bread pan. Do the same with the other two parts. Let rise until doubled; brush with the reserved ⅛ cup of egg, and bake in a preheated 350° oven for about 50 minutes.

Note: To braid dough; place knife over the tips of the three pieces of dough, which will hold the dough in place while it is being braided.

ORANGE SHERBET MOLD

2 3-ounce packages orange gelatin
2 cups boiling water
⅓ cup lemon juice

1 pint orange sherbet
1 can drained mandarin oranges
1 7-ounce can crushed pineapple, with juice

Dissolve gelatin in water; cool and add lemon juice. Place in refrigerator until of jelly-like consistency. Beat in sherbet and fold in orange segments and pineapple. Place in twelve 4-ounce greased molds, or in 1 greased 6-cup mold. Turn out on platter lined with leaf lettuce and decorate with clusters of grapes.

CHOCOLATE ICEBOX CAKE

18 lady fingers, split
8 ounces sweet cooking chocolate
3 tablespoons water
4 egg yolks, beaten

2 tablespoons confectioners' sugar
½ cup chopped nuts (optional)
4 egg whites, stiffly beaten

1 cup heavy cream, whipped

Melt chocolate in double boiler, add water, and blend; remove from heat and add egg yolks, one at a time, beating vigorously until smooth and blended. Add confectioners' sugar, chopped nuts, and blend; fold in cream first, then egg whites. Line a 2-quart soufflé dish, or spring form, with lady fingers; pour in mixture. Chill a minimum of 12 hours in refrigerator. To serve, remove spring form rim, or serve from soufflé dish.

Election Alert Supper

(CELEBRATION FOR HAPPY RETURNS)

(SERVES 8)

Seafood Marsala

Cocktail Relishes Cucumber Daisies

Fresh Pepper Salad Old Glory Mold

Toffee Squares

Coffee Sanka

ADVANCE PREPARATION SCHEDULE

Deep Freeze	Previous Day	Early Morning
Toffee Squares	*Pepper salad*	*Seafood*
	Mold	*Cocktail Relishes*

SEAFOOD MARSALA

1 8-ounce package spaghetti, cooked
1 quart raw oysters, drained
1 quart raw scallops, drained
2 cups shrimp, cooked
2 cups fresh crabmeat

1 pound Steamed Mushrooms, drained and sliced
1¼ quarts Cream Sauce Marsala
¼ cup bread crumbs
¼ cup grated American cheese
2 tablespoons butter

Prepare Steamed Mushrooms:

1 pound mushrooms
¼ cup water

2 tablespoons butter
¼ teaspoon salt

Combine mushrooms, water, butter, and salt in top of double boiler; cover tightly and steam over hot water for 20 minutes.

Reserve liquid from oysters, scallops, and Steamed Mushrooms for Cream Sauce Marsala. Combine all seafoods. Grease a 3-quart casserole and cover bottom with ⅓ of the spaghetti. Add a layer of ½ the seafood, then ½ the mushrooms; repeat layers, ending with last third of spaghetti. Pour Cream Sauce Marsala over contents of casserole. Spread bread crumbs and cheese over top and dot with butter. Place in a preheated 350° oven for 45 minutes. Serve piping hot in casserole on doily-lined platter.

Cream Sauce Marsala:

⅓ cup butter
½ cup flour
1 quart milk, heated (reserved liquid from oysters, scallops, and mushrooms, plus sufficient milk to make 1 quart)

½ teaspoon salt
⅛ teaspoon white pepper
1 teaspoon Worcestershire
⅛ teaspoon thyme
⅛ teaspoon oregano
¼ cup Marsala

Melt butter in saucepan; add flour and heat until bubbly and smooth. Do not brown. Stir in milk liquid slowly; blend in salt, pepper, Worcestershire, thyme, oregano, and Marsala. Cook until heated and smooth. Makes about 1½ quarts.

COCKTAIL RELISHES

Cocktail onions
Pickled beets
Green pimiento olives
Cheese cubes

Pitted black olives
Sausage cubes
Pickle slices
Ham cubes

Using 3 different relishes from the above list, arrange them on picks in taste and color selection, such as pickle slice, sausage cube, and cheese cube, or pickled beet, olive, and ham cube, etc. Multicolored picks add to the festive look. Have a sufficient number in reserve to replenish the centerpiece as needed.

Note: The centerpiece may be embellished with a base of gala leaves and green and yellow Cucumber Daisies.

CUCUMBER DAISIES

Score long thin cucumbers with tines of fork. Cut off ends and scoop out seeds with an apple corer. Fill hollow with softened pimiento cheese. Chill, and when cold, slice in ¼-inch widths.

FRESH PEPPER SALAD

8 green or red peppers
1½ teaspoons salt
¼ teaspoon pepper
¼ cup water

½ teaspoon garlic powder
1 bay leaf
1 cup cider vinegar

Cut the peppers in half, discarding the seeds and fibers. Pierce each pepper with a fork and hold it over a flame or heat until the skin browns and blisters. Rub the skin off, then slice the peppers. Combine the salt, pepper, garlic powder, bay leaf, vinegar, and water in a saucepan. Bring to a boil and pour over the peppers. Chill for a few hours. Remove the bay leaf. This salad will keep two days.

OLD GLORY MOLD

1 9-ounce can crushed pineapple
1 8½-ounce can blueberries
1 13-ounce jar maraschino cherries
1 3-ounce package cherry gelatin
1 3-ounce package lime gelatin
1 3-ounce package lemon gelatin
1 cup condensed milk, chilled

Drain pineapple, blueberries, and cherries, separately; reserve juices and place each fruit in separate bowls. Add enough water to each juice to make 1¾ cups liquid of each. Heat separately. Dissolve cherry gelatin in hot cherry liquid. Dissolve lime gelatin in hot pineapple liquid. Dissolve lemon gelatin in hot blueberry liquid. Cool each, and set in refrigerator to chill until of jelly-like consistency. Beat milk with rotary or electric beater until stiff. Mix ⅓ of milk with each gelatin mixture, beating until well blended. Place the 3 bowls in refrigerator until mixture is partially congealed. Fold cherries into cherry flavor, pineapple into lime flavor, and blueberries into lemon flavor. Lightly grease an 8-cup mold and add a cup of each flavor alternately, until all is used. Place in refrigerator again for several hours, until set. Unmold on large cake plate (white, preferably, for Old Glory effect).

TOFFEE SQUARES

1 cup (½ pound) butter
½ cup brown sugar, firmly packed
½ cup white sugar
1 egg yolk
2 cups all-purpose flour
1 teaspoon cinnamon
1 teaspoon vanilla
1 cup chopped pecans or walnuts
1 egg white, slightly beaten

Cream butter with both brown and white sugars, and blend in the egg yolk; use an electric mixer for efficient blending. Add flour, cinnamon, vanilla, and ½ cup of nuts. Mix well. Butter an 18″ x 12″

cooky sheet and press dough evenly over entire surface. The dough will be quite thin. Brush with egg whites and sprinkle remaining nuts evenly over dough. Place in a preheated 325° oven and bake on lower rack for 20 minutes. Change to upper rack and bake 10 to 15 minutes, or until nicely browned. Cut in squares while warm. Makes 50 2-inch squares.

Derby Dinner

(SERVES 8)

Persimmon Tulips

Prime Ribs of Roast Beef — Clubhouse Sauce

Memphis Eggplant   Southern Corn Custard

Artichoke Salad — Anchovy Dressing   Jockey Biscuits

Walnut Meringue

and/or

Pineapple Chiffon Pie

Coffee

This authentic menu of a noted Southern hostess is worthy of repetition.

ADVANCE PREPARATION SCHEDULE

Deep Freeze	Previous Day	Early Morning
Jockey Biscuits	*Dressing*	*Eggplant*
	Pie shell	*Prepare corn*
		Bake pie

PERSIMMON TULIPS

6 persimmons (medium size)   2 heads Bibb lettuce
¾ cup basic French Dressing

Wash persimmons. Score peeling, dividing each in 6 sections. Release sections, cutting them ¼ inch thick to within ½ inch of base; they will resemble petals of tulip. To serve, place on bed of lettuce on individual salad plates, and cover each with 2 tablespoons basic French Dressing (see Index).

A simple, beautiful first course, and balm to the calorie-conscious guest, as well.

PRIME RIBS OF ROAST BEEF

1 standing rib roast of beef (use a 5-rib roast to serve 6). The first 4 ribs are the choice selection of beef. Tender care is suggested for wrapping and storing. More detailed information is in "Kitchen Comfort." A rib roast should be no less than 3 ribs; the leftover roast is a favorite, served cold. There are two schools of thought on the preparation of the stalwart rib roast: the energetic hot oven, fast method as opposed to the lower-temperature slow method. The first produces a rugged glaze while with the second procedure there is less shrinkage, but very little crust.

Salt
Freshly ground pepper
1 teaspoon seasoned salt
½ cup Burgundy, for basting (optional)
2 tablespoons butter

The seasoning for both methods is the same, though it may be varied to your taste. This one we find excellent. Wipe the roast with a damp cloth. Use a pepper grinder to dust roast and rub the salt and pepper into the meat, very thoroughly. Sprinkle with seasoned salt; insert meat thermometer at thickest part of roast, being careful not to touch any bone, and place rib side down in roaster on roasting rack; do not cover.

Place butter in bottom of pan and roast in a preheated 450° oven, basting with Burgundy and pan juices every 10 minutes. Continue roasting until required temperature is indicated on thermometer, or use time schedule.

Fast Method Time Schedule:

Figure 12 minutes per pound for rare
Figure 18 minutes per pound for medium
Figure 23 minutes per pound for well done

Let stand 15 minutes before carving.

Slow Method Time Schedule:

22 minutes per pound for rare
25 minutes per pound for medium
30 minutes per pound for well done

Prepare and season as in Fast Method. Insert thermometer and place in a preheated 325° oven. Do not add water and do not cover. It is not necessary to baste, though the Burgundy adds a fine flavor. Let stand 15 minutes before carving.

Meat Thermometer Reading:

140° F. for rare
160° F. for medium
170° F. for well done

CLUBHOUSE SAUCE

1 small clove garlic, minced (optional)
1 teaspoon salt
½ pound fresh mushrooms, sliced
1 medium onion, sliced
¼ cup butter
1 teaspoon flour
2 tablespoons chili sauce
¼ teaspoon thyme
⅛ teaspoon Tabasco
1 teaspoon Worcestershire
½ cup dry red wine
1 teaspoon beef extract

Sauté garlic, salt, mushrooms, and onion in butter for 5 minutes. Blend in flour until smooth. Add chili sauce, thyme, Tabasco, Worcestershire, wine, and beef extract and simmer 10 minutes. Pour over roast or serve separately. Makes about 1 cup.

MEMPHIS EGGPLANT

3 medium-size eggplants
3 cups water
1½ teaspoons salt
4 tablespoons butter, melted
1 large onion, minced
1 cup celery, cut in ½-inch slices
1½ pounds boiled shrimp, deveined, halved
⅓ teaspoon salt
⅛ teaspoon paprika
¼ cup cracker crumbs
Butter for topping

Peel eggplants and cut in large pieces. Pour water and salt into saucepan, add eggplant, and simmer 10 minutes or until tender. Drain well and mash thoroughly. Heat 2 tablespoons butter in skillet, add onion and celery, sauté until lightly browned. Combine with mashed eggplant, add remaining 2 tablespoons butter, shrimp, ⅓ teaspoon salt, and paprika. Turn into buttered 2-quart serving casserole. Sprinkle with cracker crumbs and dot with additional butter. Bake in a preheated 350° oven 30 to 40 minutes until browned and well heated. Serve from casserole.

SOUTHERN CORN CUSTARD

2 #2 cans creamed corn
1 14½-ounce can evaporated milk
4 whole eggs, lightly beaten

¼ cup butter
2 tablespoons flour
Dash paprika and dash salt

Force corn through sieve or food mill; add milk, eggs, butter, flour, paprika, salt, and mix well. Pour into a greased 2-quart casserole, place in pan of hot water, and bake in a preheated 350° oven 45 minutes or until firm. (Test by piercing with toothpick which will be dry when removed from custard.)

This is a delicious substitute for potatoes or rice and will give a party air to a simple dinner, as well.

ARTICHOKE SALAD

1 head iceberg lettuce, torn
coarsely
5 heads Bibb lettuce, separate
leaves

1 cup coarsely chopped parsley
1 6-ounce can artichoke hearts,
halved
12 cherry tomatoes

Combine lettuce and parsley and place on individual serving plates. Arrange artichokes and cherry tomatoes on lettuce. Serve dressing separately.

ANCHOVY DRESSING

1 cup mayonnaise
1 2-ounce can flat anchovies,
drained

1 small clove garlic, minced
¼ cup lemon juice

Combine mayonnaise, flat anchovies, garlic, and lemon juice; blend very well.

JOCKEY BISCUITS

2 cups all-purpose flour	⅓ cup shortening
2½ teaspoons baking powder	2 tablespoons chopped chives
1 teaspoon salt	2 tablespoons chopped pimiento

1 cup milk

Sift flour, baking powder, and salt into mixing bowl. Blend shortening, chives, and pimiento with pastry blender or 2 knives until it resembles coarse meal; stir in milk gently, but thoroughly. Drop by tablespoons about 1 inch apart on greased baking sheet. Bake in a preheated 425° oven 12 to 15 minutes, or until golden brown. Serve piping hot. Makes 18 biscuits, about 2 inches in diameter.

WALNUT MERINGUE

3 egg whites, beaten	1 teaspoon vinegar
1 cup sugar	1 cup finely chopped unsalted
10 single soda crackers, unsalted, crushed	walnuts
	1 teaspoon vanilla
1 teaspoon baking powder	1 cup heavy cream, whipped

1 pint strawberries

The egg whites should be moist and not too stiff. While continuing to beat, gradually add sugar, crackers, baking powder, vinegar, nuts and vanilla. Grease 9-inch pie pan, pour in meringue, and bake 30 to 35 minutes in a preheated 350° oven. Cool. To serve, top with whipped cream and large, bright strawberries.

PINEAPPLE CHIFFON PIE

3 tablespoons cornstarch	2 cups crushed pineapple,
2 cups canned pineapple juice	drained
1 cup sugar	4 egg whites, beaten stiff
⅛ teaspoon salt	Baked 9-inch pie shell

Mix the cornstarch with ¼ cup pineapple juice to make a smooth paste. Place remainder of juice in a saucepan; blend in cornstarch paste, ½ cup of sugar, and salt. Cook over low heat, stirring constantly, until thickened; then mix in the pineapple and cool. Beat the egg whites until stiff but not dry; beat in the remaining sugar. Fold into the pineapple mixture, and pour into pie shell. Chill.

Use half the following pie crust recipe — making just a shell, or prepare the full recipe and freeze half for another day.

Crust:

2 cups sifted flour	6 tablespoons ice water
¾ teaspoon salt	¾ cup shortening

Cut flour, salt, shortening to size of peas; blend in water; form a ball. Roll out dough to ¼-inch thickness; cover a 9-inch pie pan loosely; it should extend 1 inch beyond edge. Fold back to form a standing rim and flute with thumb and finger to make a rope edge. Bake in a preheated 450° oven 10 to 12 minutes or until lightly browned.

To utilize yolks, see Index.

For tomorrow's planning — a delicious remake of today's roast beef.

DICED SOUTHERN BEEF

2 pounds roast beef *or* pot roast	2 large sweet potatoes, peeled and sliced
¼ pound butter	
2 large onions, thinly sliced	2 sweet pimiento peppers, halved
2 large green peppers, sliced and seeded	½ teaspoon salt
1 8-ounce can of tomato sauce	⅛ teaspoon freshly ground pepper

Cut beef, onions, and peppers in ½-inch squares. Melt butter in shallow ovenware serving skillet. Add onions and green peppers; sauté until onions are soft and lightly browned. Add beef, sweet potatoes, and tomato sauce, salt and pepper, and bake in a preheated 325° oven 1 hour.

"Ten and Tin" Anniversary Dinner

(SERVES 8)

Demi Cheese Puffs   Petit Beef Balls
Poulet et Langouste Marengo   Braised Endive
Pineapple Noodle Pudding
Iceberg Salad — Watercress Dressing
Bananas Flambées   Date Meringues
Coffee

Suggested wine: Champagne

ADVANCE PREPARATION SCHEDULE

Previous Day

Cook lobster and cut
Dressing (without watercress)
Date Meringues

Early Morning

Sauce for Poulet
  (without lobster and tomatoes)
Prepare beef for balls
Sauté chicken
Assemble Noodle Pudding
Crisp lettuce

DEMI CHEESE PUFFS

2 egg whites, lightly beaten   ¼ pound Swiss cheese, grated
¼ cup fine dry bread crumbs

Mix egg whites and cheese and shape into marble-sized balls. Roll in crumbs. Fry in hot oil, heated to 375°. Balls puff up and become light. Accompany with cocktail picks and serve very hot. Makes 24.

Variations:

After you have tried these delicacies as they are, you may wish to improvise a little. Make deviled puffs by adding onion juice, a little mustard, and a dash of Tabasco. Switch to another cheese: Cheddar and Herkimer are both good. Such seasoners as salad herbs, chili powder, or curry may be added to the cheese or to the crumb coating.

PETIT BEEF BALLS

1½ pounds sirloin of beef, ground
2 tablespoons black caviar
¼ teaspoon onion juice
½ teaspoon anchovy paste
1 teaspoon mushroom sauce, bottled

2 tablespoons chili sauce
Salt and pepper to taste
2 tablespoons cream
1 egg
3 to 4 slices bacon, chopped raw
Pumpernickel bread

Combine all ingredients except bacon; mix well and shape into 1-inch balls. Place each ball on thin round of pumpernickel bread; sprinkle top with chopped bacon and broil until brown. The beef balls should be kept small, the bread rounds cut thin. Makes 50 to 60.

POULET ET LANGOUSTE MARENGO
(Chicken and Lobster Marengo)

4 chicken breasts, skinned and split
Salt and pepper
¼ cup butter
2 tablespoons dry sherry
½ pound sliced fresh mushrooms
2 tablespoons flour
1½ cups chicken stock
1 bay leaf, crushed

1 tablespoon tomato paste
2 tablespoons chopped chives
½ teaspoon salt
⅛ teaspoon pepper
2 10-ounce packages frozen lobster tails
3 ripe tomatoes, cored and quartered

Sprinkle chicken breasts with salt and pepper. Heat butter in large skillet until it begins to foam. Add chicken breasts and brown to a golden glow. Spoon sherry over chicken and remove chicken from skillet. Place in a shallow baking dish, cover with foil, and bake in a preheated 300° oven 25 to 30 minutes, or until tender.

Add mushrooms to skillet and sauté until tender, about 8 minutes. (If skillet is dry, add 1 tablespoon butter.) Blend in flour; add chicken stock and simmer, stirring constantly until thickened. Season with bay leaf, tomato paste, chives, salt and pepper. Simmer slowly for 15 minutes. Cook frozen lobster tails according to package directions (or see Index). Remove lobster meat from shells and cut into bite-sized pieces. Add lobster meat and tomatoes to sauce; simmer very slowly, 5 to 8 minutes more, until lobster and tomatoes are just heated through. Serve chicken breasts on a large platter, topped with sauce. Arrange Braised Endive, spoke-like, around platter.

Note: This sauce can be made in advance; add lobster and tomatoes just before heating to serve.

BRAISED ENDIVE

8 endive heads, halved	¼ cup water
2 tablespoons butter	Salt
1 teaspoon beef extract	Pepper

Place endive in saucepan, dot with butter, and add beef extract which has been blended with water. Cover tightly and simmer 20 minutes, turning to glaze endive. If liquid is absorbed, add a little water to prevent sticking. Salt and pepper to taste. Serve around "Poulet."

Note: This is very good with roasts as well.

PINEAPPLE NOODLE PUDDING

1 12-ounce package egg noodles, cooked	6 tablespoons sugar
6 eggs, well beaten	½ cup cream
½ cup white seedless raisins	1 cup creamed cottage cheese
1 7-ounce can crushed pineapple, well drained	6 small graham crackers, crushed
	¼ cup butter

Mix noodles, eggs, raisins, pineapple, sugar, cream, and cottage cheese; place in a buttered casserole. Sprinkle with crushed graham crackers; dot with butter. Bake in a preheated 350° oven for about 1 hour.

ICEBERG SALAD — WATERCRESS DRESSING

1 cup salad oil	1 teaspoon salt
⅓ cup tarragon vinegar	1 teaspoon prepared mustard
⅓ cup catsup	1 teaspoon Worcestershire
⅓ cup sugar	⅓ cup chopped watercress

Beat all ingredients together, adding watercress last. Serve this dressing over wedges of iceberg lettuce.

BANANAS FLAMBEES

½ cup (¼ pound) butter ¼ cup Banana Cordial
½ cup light rum 8 bananas, not too ripe
2 tablespoons sugar Confectioners' sugar
2 tablespoons cognac

Melt butter; add rum, sugar, and cordial in a chafing dish. Add bananas and simmer, covered, for 5 minutes. Remove cover and cook until lightly browned. Warm cognac; ignite and pour over bananas. Sprinkle with confectioners' sugar; serve from chafing dish and serve hot.

Note: Serve with rum-flavored whipped cream — if you have a special taste for rum.

DATE MERINGUES

4 egg yolks ¼ teaspoon baking powder
¾ cup sugar ½ teaspoon salt
½ cup (¼ pound) butter, softened 1 cup fresh dates, cut small
2 1-ounce squares unsweetened 4 egg whites
 chocolate, melted 1 tablespoon lemon juice
1 teaspoon vanilla ½ cup sugar
½ cup all-purpose flour, sifted ½ teaspoon salt

Beat egg yolks until light. Gradually add sugar, beating until creamy. Blend in butter, chocolate, and vanilla. Sift together flour, baking powder, and salt. Fold into chocolate mixture. Turn into a greased 9-inch square pan and bake in a preheated 375° oven 20 minutes.

Beat egg whites until soft peaks are formed. Gradually beat in lemon juice, sugar, and salt. Beat to stiff peaks; fold in dates. Remove baked mixture from oven; immediately cover with meringue, spreading evenly over top of hot fudge layer and return to oven. Reduce heat to 350° and bake about 20 minutes longer or until meringue is golden brown and set. Cool before cutting into 1½-inch squares. Makes about 24.

Note: With another menu, add ½ teaspoon rum extract when adding lemon juice.

Petits Luncheons

So MUCH is shared in a small group, which makes every day important in itself. Discriminating selections for a small menu lend significance to the mosaic of these patterns of living.

Petit Summer Luncheon

(SERVES 6)

Lemon Beet Cup   Crab Honeydew — Persian Dressing

Corn Sticks   Jam

Blueberry Cake

Iced Coffee   Orange Iced Tea

ADVANCE PREPARATION SCHEDULE

Deep Freeze	Previous Day	Early Morning
Corn Sticks	*Soup*	*Melon*
	Blueberry Cake crust	*Salad dressing*
		Blueberry cake
		Orange Iced Tea

LEMON BEET CUP

2 #303 (1-pound) jars whole
   baby beets
2 jars beet liquid
½ teaspoon salt

2 eggs, well beaten
3 tablespoons sugar
3 tablespoons lemon juice
¾ cup dairy sour cream

Drain beet juice into saucepan; add water and salt. Cut beets in half and add to liquid; simmer 15 minutes. Pour small amount of hot liquid slowly into eggs, while stirring well. Add sugar and return to liquid; then add lemon juice and blend well. Refrigerate. Serve ice cold with a tablespoon of sour cream on each cupful.

CRAB HONEYDEW

2 6½-ounce cans crabmeat
3 small honeydew melons (or
   Persian)

1 cup sliced celery
2 tablespoons minced onion
¼ cup slivered almonds

Remove cartilage from crabmeat carefully and reserve the large chunks for topping. Cut melons in half; remove seeds. Scoop out center and form melon balls with cutter, or cut into bite-sized chunks. Scallop edges of melon shells with knife or scissors. Combine melon pieces with crabmeat (except the reserved chunks), celery, onion and almonds.

Persian Dressing:

½ cup heavy cream, whipped
½ cup mayonnaise

¼ teaspoon curry powder
¼ teaspoon salt

Combine whipped cream, mayonnaise, curry and salt and blend well. Fold half of Persian Dressing into crab-melon mixture. Pile into melon shells. Garnish with reserved crab chunks. Place remaining dressing in serving bowl to serve separately.

CORN STICKS

1 cup yellow cornmeal
1 cup sifted all-purpose flour
4 teaspoons baking powder
1 teaspoon salt
¼ cup sugar
2 eggs

1 cup milk
3 tablespoons butter or margarine,
   melted
1 8¾-ounce can cream style corn
   (approximately 1 cup)

Sift cornmeal, flour, baking powder, salt and sugar into a small bowl. Beat eggs lightly in large bowl; stir in milk, butter and corn. Add cornmeal mixture, stirring until well blended. Pour into greased corn stick or muffin pans, filling almost full. Bake 20 minutes in a preheated 425° oven, or until corn sticks are golden and the surface is firm to the touch. Let cool 3 minutes in pans. Turn out, and serve at once. Makes 18.

Note: Corn sticks may be removed from pans and cooled completely on wire racks, then refrigerated for two or three days. To serve, reheat for 15 minutes in 325° oven.

BLUEBERRY CAKE

½ cup (¼ pound) butter 1 egg, beaten
1 cup sugar   2 cups all-purpose flour
½ teaspoon baking powder

Combine butter, sugar, egg, flour, and baking powder; press into bottom and sides of buttered pan, 7″ x 11″. Place in refrigerator overnight. The next day sprinkle a little flour over crust and add filling.

Filling:

2 pints blueberries   1 tablespoon flour
¾ cup sugar   ½ cup brown sugar
2 tablespoons butter

Wash blueberries and turn into pastry-lined pan; mix sugar and flour and cover berries. Sprinkle with brown sugar and dot with butter.

Topping:

1 egg, well beaten   ½ cup half and half cream
1 teaspoon vanilla

Combine egg, cream, and vanilla and spread over top of filling. Bake in a preheated 450° oven 10 minutes; reduce heat to 350° and bake for 50 minutes.

Variation:

Substitute Italian plums or peaches.

ORANGE ICED TEA

1 quart strong tea	1 lemon, juice and rind
2 oranges, juice and rind	½ cup granulated sugar

Prepare 1 quart strong tea and steep for 5 minutes. Cut rinds of oranges and lemon into large strips and place in 2 quart bowls. Pour hot tea over them; add sugar. Let stand 15 to 20 minutes. Remove rinds and add juice of oranges and lemon. Chill in refrigerator, and serve over ice.

ICED COFFEE

To enjoy the full flavor of coffee in iced coffee, pour hot freshly prepared double-strength coffee into ice-filled glasses. Have additional ice cubes ready, if necessary. The cubes may be made of frozen coffee.

Note: For safety against breakage, be certain to pour hot coffee directly into ice-filled glasses.

Petit Luncheon

(SERVES 6)

Crêpes Colette
Cucumber Salad
Strawberry Ice
Surprise Squares
Coffee   Tea

ADVANCE PREPARATION SCHEDULE

Previous Day

Pancakes
Cucumber Salad
Strawberry Ice
Surprise Squares

CREPES COLETTE

Pancakes:

2 eggs	¼ teaspoon salt
1 tablespoon butter, melted	⅓ cup unsifted all-purpose flour
¼ teaspoon sugar	⅔ cup milk

Beat eggs with rotary beater until creamy; beat in butter, sugar, salt, flour, and milk until smooth. Lightly grease and heat a 6-inch skillet and pour in 2 tablespoons batter; quickly tilt skillet so batter covers bottom completely; cook until golden. Use a broad spatula and turn to brown other side; remove and stack on wax paper. Repeat with rest of batter, making 12 pancakes; add more butter as needed. Wrap lightly in wax paper and store in refrigerator. May be made early same day.

Filling:

1 10½-ounce can condensed cream soup, undiluted (chicken, celery, *or* mushroom)	2 cups cooked, diced, chicken
	½ cup sliced ripe olives
	1 teaspoon Worcestershire
¼ cup milk	2 tablespoons chopped parsley
1 cup Swiss cheese, grated	12 Crêpes Colette
Sprinkle of paprika	

Combine soup, milk, and ½ cup of cheese; heat until cheese melts. Mix with chicken, olives, Worcestershire, and parsley. Place ¼ cup mixture on each pancake; roll and secure seam with a wooden pick. Place in greased shallow baking pan. Sprinkle with remaining ½ cup cheese and paprika. Bake in a preheated 375° oven 25 minutes, or until cheese melts.

CUCUMBER SALAD

1 3-ounce package lemon-flavored gelatin	1 cup finely chopped, drained cucumber
1 cup hot water	1 teaspoon minced onion
1 cup small-curd cottage cheese	¼ cup chopped nuts
	⅛ teaspoon white pepper
½ cup mayonnaise	½ teaspoon salt
1 tablespoon chopped pimiento	

Dissolve gelatin in hot water; cool, add cottage cheese, and beat well with rotary beater. Add mayonnaise, cucumber, onion, nuts, pimiento, salt, and pepper; blend well, and pour into 6 individual well-greased molds. Refrigerate until firm. To serve, unmold on lettuce cups and decorate with more pimiento.

STRAWBERRY ICE

1 pint water	2 quarts strawberries
3 cups sugar	Juice of 1 lemon

Boil water and sugar until thick, about 20 minutes. Mash berries and press through a sieve, add lemon juice. When syrup is cold, add berries and place in deep freezer for several hours until firm. Serve in sherbet glasses garnished with mint leaves and a whole strawberry.

This is a refreshing icy dessert, and as many find an icy dessert refreshing, this one has been included.

SURPRISE SQUARES

1 cup flour, sifted	¼ cup brown sugar, firmly packed
⅛ teaspoon salt	1 egg, separated
⅛ teaspoon soda	1½ teaspoons water
½ teaspoon baking powder	½ teaspoon vanilla
½ cup butter *or* margarine	½ package chocolate bits
¼ cup granulated sugar	½ cup brown sugar, firmly packed

Sift together flour, salt, soda, and baking powder. Cream shortening, granulated sugar, and ¼ cup brown sugar until smooth. Add egg yolk, water, vanilla, and mix well; stir in flour mixture thoroughly. Press firmly into well-greased 8″ x 8″ x 2″ pan. Top with rows of chocolate bits. Beat egg white until stiff, and gradually beat in ½ cup brown sugar; spread lightly over chocolate bits and dough to cover entire pan. Bake 25 minutes in a preheated 375° oven. Remove and cut into 1½-inch squares. Makes about 48 squares.

Petit Luncheon

(SERVES 8)

Salmon Delmonico   Rice Ring

Bibb Lettuce — Roquefort Goddess Dressing

Brown-and-Serve Rolls

Strawberry Parfait Pie

Coffee

ADVANCE PREPARATION SCHEDULE

Previous Day

Roquefort dressing
Pie

Early Morning

Brown-and-Serve Rolls (see Index)
Salmon
Rice Ring for baking

SALMON DELMONICO

¼ cup (⅛ pound) butter
¼ cup flour
2 cups milk
1 egg yolk, slightly beaten
1 tablespoon lemon juice
⅛ teaspoon coarsely ground pepper

1 teaspoon salt
1 tablespoon butter
½ pound fresh mushrooms, sliced (optional)
1 1-pound can salmon, coarsely flaked

Melt ¼ cup butter; add flour and cook, stirring, until blended. Add milk, egg yolk, lemon juice, pepper, salt, and stir over low heat until slightly thickened. Heat 1 tablespoon butter in another skillet, add mushrooms, sauté 5 minutes. Combine with salmon and add to sauce, blending carefully. Heat. Serve with Rice Ring.

RICE RING

1¼ cups butter, melted
⅓ cup finely diced green pepper
4 cups boiled rice (1⅓ cups raw)

½ teaspoon salt
⅛ teaspoon pepper
⅓ cup minced parsley

Heat butter, add green pepper, sauté lightly. Combine with rice, salt, pepper, reserving 1 tablespoon parsley, and add balance to rice mixture. Blend well and press into greased 6-cup mold. Bake in a preheated 400° oven 10 minutes. Unmold ring on large platter and fill with Salmon Delmonico. Surround with pickled peach halves, hollow side up and centered with currant jelly. Sprinkle reserved parsley over salmon.

Variation:

Tuna fish can be substituted for salmon.

BIBB LETTUCE — ROQUEFORT GODDESS DRESSING

1 cup mayonnaise	1 clove garlic, crushed, *or*
½ cup dairy sour cream	1 teaspoon garlic salt
¼ cup minced parsley	½ teaspoon minced green onion
¼ cup wine vinegar	3 ounces Roquefort cheese,
1 tablespoon lemon juice	crumbled
1½ tablespoons anchovy paste	4 heads Bibb lettuce

Combine all ingredients except lettuce and mix well. Makes 2 cups. Wash, drain, and dry lettuce; separate leaves and arrange on salad plates. Serve with desired amount of dressing. This dressing and avocado are good teammates.

STRAWBERRY PARFAIT PIE

1 meringue shell, or Graham	½ cup cold water
Cracker Crust (see Index)	1 pint vanilla ice cream
1 3-ounce package strawberry-	1 cup sliced, fresh *or* frozen
flavored gelatin	strawberries
1 cup hot water	

Prepare shell. Dissolve gelatin in hot water. Add cold water; stir. Cut ice cream in 6 pieces. Add to gelatin mixture. Stir until ice cream melts. Chill mixture in refrigerator until it begins to thicken and mound when spooned (20 to 30 minutes). Gently fold in strawberries. Pour into cooled pastry shell. Chill until firm, about 20 to 25 minutes. Trim with sliced berries.

Petit Brunch

(SERVES 6)

Broiled Grapefruit Ceres
Eggs en Soufflé
Canadian Bacon — Orange Sauce
Corn Spoon Bread
Bundt Kuchen or Gugelhupf   Coffee

Suggested wine: Moselle or a white California

ADVANCE PREPARATION SCHEDULE

Deep Freeze	Early Morning
Bundt Kuchen	*Prepare grapefruit*
	Orange Sauce
	Bake Spoon Bread

BROILED GRAPEFRUIT CERES

6 grapefruit halves	6 tablespoons sherry
6 tablespoons sugar	Pomegranate seeds (optional)

If grapefruit are very juicy, do not separate sections. Remove core and sprinkle each half with 1 tablespoon sugar. Place under pre-heated broiler for about 10 minutes or until browned. Remove, and pour 1 tablespoon of sherry over each. Sprinkle with pomegranate seeds. Serve at once.

Of myths, pomegranates, and cooks — Proserpine was to be returned to her home from the infernal regions, if she agreed to abstain from food during her sojourn there. When Pluto's cook revealed that she had eaten six pomegranate seeds, he was turned into an owl by Ceres, Proserpine's mother. However, Minerva took pity upon him and became his mentor. That the goddess of Wisdom protected the cook is a source of pride to the long line of cooks who have followed.

EGGS EN SOUFFLE

6 Eggs Mollets	3 tablespoons flour
3 tablespoons butter	2 cups milk
¼ cup diced onion	¼ teaspoon salt
¼ cup diced carrots	¼ teaspoon freshly ground pepper
¼ cup diced celery	¼ teaspoon oregano
¼ cup chopped leek *or* green onions (white only)	3 egg yolks, beaten
	3 egg whites, beaten stiff

Shell Eggs Mollets and reserve in warm water until needed.

Heat 1 tablespoon of the butter in saucepan; add onion, carrots, celery, leek, and cook until soft; do not brown. Add remaining butter, stir in flour until smooth, then stir in milk. Add salt, pepper, oregano; reduce heat, cover and simmer slowly for 20 minutes. Strain sauce into bowl, cool and stir in yolks. Fold in beaten whites. Grease a 1½-quart soufflé dish or casserole, and pour in ⅓ of soufflé mixture; place Eggs Mollets in sauce, in one layer; add remaining mixture. Bake in a preheated 325° oven 20 to 25 minutes, until brown and high. Serve at once.

Eggs Mollets:

Remove eggs from refrigerator a minimum of 20 minutes before cooking. Place in fast-boiling water; time them from the moment the water reboils. Cook 6 minutes and plunge into cold water. White will be set and yolk still creamy. Shell at once; reheat, or keep warm submerged in hot water until needed.

CANADIAN BACON — ORANGE SAUCE

Allow 2 to 3 slices bacon per serving. Place in large, heavy skillet over low heat. Allow 5 minutes cooking time, but turn slices frequently. Lean part will be reddish brown. Serve with Orange Sauce.

ORANGE SAUCE

¼ cup prepared horseradish	½ cup orange juice
1 tablespoon prepared mustard	¼ cup orange rind
2 tablespoons lemon juice	2 ounces currant jelly
1 tablespoon lemon rind	1 tablespoon white vinegar

Heat all ingredients together in a saucepan until the jelly melts. Serve piping hot with Canadian Bacon. Makes about 1½ cups sauce.

Note: Prepared horseradish varies in strength, so the quantity should be adjusted to taste. This is delicious for baked ham as well.

CORN SPOON BREAD

1 10-ounce package frozen cut corn, cooked	2 tablespoons butter
	2 teaspoons salt
3 cups milk	3 egg yolks, slightly beaten
1 cup yellow cornmeal	1 teaspoon baking powder
3 egg whites, stiffly beaten	

Cook corn according to package directions. Do not overcook. Mix and set aside 1 cup of milk with cornmeal. Heat remaining 2 cups milk and add. Cook slowly, stirring constantly for 15 minutes, until thickened. Remove from heat, add butter and salt. Mix well, and allow to cool for 5 minutes. Add egg yolks and baking powder; drain cooked corn, cool and add to egg mixture. Fold in stiffly beaten egg whites until no flecks of white are visible. Pour into greased 2-quart casserole, and bake in a preheated 325° oven for 40 to 50 minutes, until golden.

BUNDT KUCHEN

½ cup (¼ pound) butter	¼ cup citron, cut in strips
2 cups sugar	¼ cup coarsely chopped candied cherries
3 cups all-purpose flour	
4 teaspoons baking powder	¼ cup slivered blanched almonds
1 cup milk	6 egg whites, beaten stiff
6 egg yolks, beaten	1 teaspoon vanilla
½ lemon rind, grated	Confectioners' sugar

Cream butter and sugar. Sift flour and baking powder together; combine with milk. Then add to creamed butter, alternately with beaten egg yolks. Blend in lemon rind, citron, cherries, almonds; fold in stiffly beaten egg whites; stir in vanilla. Pour into greased 9-inch tube pan and bake in a preheated 350° oven 1 hour and 10 minutes. Turn out on rack; coat thickly with confectioners' sugar.

GUGELHUPF

½ cup warm water
1 package dry yeast
3 cups unsifted all-purpose flour
½ cup slivered blanched almonds
½ cup butter or margarine, melted and cooled

¼ teaspoon salt
½ cup sugar
½ cup milk, scalded and cooled
3 eggs, slightly beaten
¾ cup seedless raisins
3 tablespoons grated lemon rind

Measure water into large mixing bowl; sprinkle yeast over it and stir until dissolved. Blend in ½ cup of flour; cover and let stand in warm place, free from drafts, about ½ hour, until light and bubbly.

Grease a 9-inch fluted tube pan (Turk's head) heavily and press almonds into sides of pan. Combine butter, salt, and sugar; add to cooled milk. Beat alternately with remaining flour into yeast sponge and then beat in eggs, 1 at a time. Mixture should be very smooth, softer than dough but heavier than batter. Add raisins and lemon rind; mix well. Cover; let rise again in warm place for about 1 hour until within ¾ inch of rim. Place in a preheated 400° oven, reduce at once to 375°, and after 5 minutes to 350°; bake 45 minutes in all. If top browns too quickly, cover lightly with a sheet of brown paper.

Petit Luncheon

(SERVES 4)

Deviled Turkey Steak — Sauce Diablo
Green Beans Marinara   French Bread
Peach Crisp
Coffee

ADVANCE PREPARATION SCHEDULE

Deep Freeze	Previous Day	Early Morning
Turkey	*Marinate mushrooms*	*Green Beans*
		Streusel for Peach Crisp

DEVILED TURKEY STEAK

4 thick slices white
meat of turkey
(about 6 ounces each)

½ cup bread crumbs
¼ cup butter to moisten
(about)

Dip slices of turkey into Sauce Diablo, then in bread crumbs; coat well. Place under preheated broiler until nicely browned. Transfer to shallow baking pan. Moisten with melted butter and bake in a preheated 250° oven 15 minutes. Serve with additional Sauce Diablo.

SAUCE DIABLO

1 tablespoon dry mustard
1 tablespoon salt
2 tablespoons Worcestershire
1 cup salad oil
2 tablespoons sugar
2 tablespoons vinegar
½ bay leaf
1 clove
4 peppercorns

1 tablespoon butter
1 tablespoon flour
½ cup hot water
1 beef bouillon cube
2 tablespoons currant jelly
¼ cup orange juice
1 teaspoon lemon juice
1 tablespoon grated orange rind
Red food coloring

Mix mustard, salt, Worcestershire, oil, sugar, vinegar, bay leaf, clove, and peppercorns in saucepan; let simmer until light brown; stir frequently to prevent sticking. Make a paste of butter, flour, water, and bouillon cube. Add to first mixture and simmer for 20 minutes; add currant jelly, orange juice, lemon juice, orange rind, and mix well. Skim the top; strain through cheesecloth. To make sauce glisten, add a few drops of red vegetable coloring. Makes 2 cups.

GREEN BEANS MARINARA

1 #2 can French-cut string
beans, drained
½ pound marinated mushrooms,
drained (see Index)

1 sweet Italian onion, sliced thin
½ cup prepared Italian dressing
1 2-ounce jar pimiento, chopped
Sprinkle of freshly ground pepper

Combine beans, mushrooms, and onions; cover with dressing. Toss lightly; garnish with pimiento and pepper. Serve very cold.

PEACH CRISP

½ cup sugar   6 fresh peaches, peeled and sliced,
½ cup butter   *or* 1 #2½ can sliced peaches,
½ cup flour   drained
½ teaspoon cinnamon (optional)

Combine sugar, butter, and flour in a medium-size bowl. Cut into crumbly consistency with knives or pastry blender. Layer sliced peaches in 10″ x 2″ x 6″ greased baking dish. Spread crumbled mixture over peaches. Bake 25 to 30 minutes in a preheated 375° oven. Serve warm or cold.

Petit Luncheon

(SERVES 6 TO 8)

Lobster San Rafael
Toasted Sesame or Fancy Cheese Crackers
Soufflé Pancakes or Dollar Pancakes
Green Grape Bowl
Coffee

ADVANCE PREPARATION SCHEDULE

Previous Day   **Early Morning**

Cook lobster   *Lobster casserole*
                        Grapes
                        Pancake batter

LOBSTER SAN RAFAEL

6 lobster tails (2 10-   ½ medium onion, sliced
  ounce packages frozen)   ½ cup button mushrooms
Salt   ¼ cup dry white wine
6 whole peppercorns   1 10½-ounce can Manhattan
1 bay leaf   style clam chowder
2 tablespoons butter   ⅓ cup dried bread crumbs
    2 tablespoons butter

Boil lobster tails for 7 minutes, using 1 quart water to 1 teaspoon salt, peppercorns, and bay leaf. Remove from shell when cool. Cut in bite-size pieces; heat butter in saucepan, add onions, and sauté lightly; add mushrooms and blend in wine and chowder. Combine with lobster meat. Pour into individual ramekins or shells. Sprinkle with bread crumbs, dot with butter, and bake in a preheated 300° oven 20 to 25 minutes. May be baked in a 1½-quart casserole — allow 30 minutes for heating.

Variation:

Substitute Parmesan cheese for bread crumbs.

SOUFFLE PANCAKES

6 tablespoons buttermilk pancake mix	6 egg yolks
½ teaspoon salt	6 tablespoons dairy sour cream
	6 egg whites, beaten stiff

Butter to grease griddle

Place the dry pancake mix and salt in a mixing bowl. Beat yolks until thick and lemon colored; combine with sour cream and mix just enough to blend. Carefully fold in beaten whites. The egg whites should be stiff but not too dry. Drop batter from a tablespoon onto a lightly greased, hot griddle. (The griddle is hot enough when water dropped on it will sputter.) When bubbles begin to appear on top of the pancake, turn, and brown on the other side. Serve with Green Grape Bowl.

DOLLAR PANCAKES
(low calorie)

1 cup creamed cottage cheese, small curd	¼ teaspoon salt
3 eggs	¼ teaspoon baking powder
3 tablespoons flour	¼ teaspoon vanilla
	Butter to grease skillet

Combine cottage cheese, eggs, flour, salt, baking powder, and vanilla, and mix well in blender or with rotary beater; the batter will be very thin. Drop on lightly greased skillet from tablespoon to form silver-dollar-sized pancakes. Brown lightly on both sides. Serve as desired with syrup, or jelly.

An electric skillet at the table is in accord with a lazy summer day. The batter is thin; the pancakes very tender. Use a hot skillet, and be certain the pancakes are nicely browned before turning.

GREEN GRAPE BOWL

2 pounds seedless green grapes   2 cups dairy sour cream
1 cup brown sugar

Remove grapes from stems and mix with sour cream. Serve in bowl with an accompanying bowl of brown sugar.

Petit Luncheon

(SERVES 4)

Chef's Salad Bowl — Canadian Dressing
French Toast Americana   Blackberry Jam
Coffee   Tea

ADVANCE PREPARATION SCHEDULE

Previous Day	**Early Morning**
Dressing	*Assemble salad ingredients*
French Toast	

CHEF'S SALAD BOWL

1 medium-size head Boston lettuce, torn in bits
1 cup chicken, julienne strips
½ cup celery, cut in ½-inch slices
8 cherry tomatoes, *or* 2 medium, quartered

2 hard-cooked eggs, quartered
1 4-ounce can artichoke hearts
2 large slices Swiss cheese, julienne
Thousand Island Dressing (optional)

Toss lettuce, chicken, and celery together in large salad bowl. Circle tomatoes, eggs, and artichoke hearts around edge of bowl. Cut cheese in 1-inch strips, spread in center, and dust with paprika.

Serve the colorful salad at the table. Pour Canadian Dressing over all; toss lightly and well.

CANADIAN DRESSING

⅔ cup prepared bottled French   ¼ cup juice of pickled fruit *or*
  dressing, heavy type   sweet pickles
              2 tablespoons bourbon

Combine dressing, juice of pickled fruit, and bourbon and blend well.

FRENCH TOAST AMERICANA

1 loaf unsliced bread,   4 eggs, beaten
  preferably egg bread   1 teaspoon vanilla
1 quart milk   Pinch of salt
              1 tablespoon butter

Cut loaf of bread into 6 slices. Combine milk, eggs, vanilla, and salt. Place bread in mixture and soak overnight. To serve next day, heat butter in skillet and sear slices quickly on both sides. Place on cooky sheet and bake in a preheated 325°–350° oven 20 to 25 minutes. Serve with Blackberry Jam, maple syrup, powdered sugar, or honey.

BLACKBERRY JAM

4 cups blackberries   3 cups sugar

Wash berries, place in saucepan, combine with sugar. Mash a few berries, stir and cook over low heat until sugar is dissolved. Bring to a rolling boil, stirring frequently from bottom of pan, using caution that the mixture does not stick. Boil until a small amount dropped on a plate does not spread. Pour into hot sterilized jars at once and seal immediately.

Petit Luncheon

(SERVES 6)

Shrimp in Eggplant Shells
Pickled Beets
Graham Gems
Layered Coconut Custard   Pecan Balls
Coffee   Tea

ADVANCE PREPARATION SCHEDULE

Deep Freeze	Previous Day	Early Morning
Pecan Balls	*Pickled Beets*	*Prepare eggplant for baking*
		Custard
		Graham Gems

SHRIMP IN EGGPLANT SHELLS

1 large eggplant	½ teaspoon salt
2 tablespoons butter	⅛ teaspoon white pepper
2 small green peppers, finely sliced	Cayenne pepper
	¼ teaspoon seasoning salt
2 small onions, finely sliced	1½ pounds shrimp, cooked
6 stalks celery, finely sliced	2 teaspoons butter
1¼ cups finely crushed, unsalted butter crackers	Parsley

Wash eggplant, cut off top, scoop out pulp ¼ inch from shell. Cover shell with salt water and set aside until needed. Soak pulp in salt water 30 minutes; drain. Cover with fresh salt water and cook until tender, about 5 minutes. (For salt water use ½ teaspoon for each cup of water.) Heat butter in saucepan; add green peppers, onions, and celery, sauté until tender. Combine the eggplant pulp with green peppers, onion and celery mixture, add 1 cup cracker crumbs. Season with salt, white pepper, cayenne, and seasoning salt; adjust to taste. Add shrimp.

Drain and dry eggplant shells. Pour mixture into shells, top with remaining ¼ cup cracker crumbs, and dot with 2 teaspoons butter. Place in shallow pan, add a small amount of water to pan, and bake 30 to 40 minutes in a preheated 350° oven. Place on serving platter surrounded by heavy clusters of parsley. This entrée should be highly seasoned to assure the flavor of its Southern origin.

PICKLED BEETS

8 medium-size fresh beets *or*	2 bay leaves
1 16-ounce can beets	½ teaspoon pickling spice
½ cup water	½ teaspon salt
⅓ cup lemon juice	1 teaspoon prepared horseradish
2 tablespoons sugar	Lettuce
2 hard-cooked eggs	

If using fresh beets, scrub and cook until tender; peel, slice, and place in bowl. Combine water, lemon juice, sugar, bay leaves, pickling spice, salt, in a saucepan and bring to a boil; stir in horseradish. Pour over beets; refrigerate until needed. May be made several days in advance. Serve in lettuce cups and sprinkle with sieved hard-cooked eggs.

Variation:

Prepare green beans instead of beets. Makes 2 cups.

GRAHAM GEMS

1 cup fine graham cracker crumbs	1 tablespoon butter, melted
¾ cup milk	½ cup sifted all-purpose flour
1 egg	1½ teaspoons baking powder
	¼ teaspoon salt

Soak crumbs in milk. Beat in egg and melted butter. Sift flour, baking powder, and salt together; blend into crumbs lightly. Spoon batter into 6 large muffin tins, greased on the bottom. Bake in a preheated 400° oven 25 minutes.

LAYERED COCONUT CUSTARD

2 cups finely grated coconut	¼ cup sugar
2 cups milk	¼ teaspoon salt
4 eggs	1 teaspoon vanilla

Combine coconut and milk in electric blender and whirl 10 seconds at high speed. Pour mixture into a sieve over a small bowl and press out as much liquid as possible. Reserve the coconut liquid and half the coconut. Beat eggs until foamy; add sugar, salt, and beat until thick and lemon colored. Add coconut liquid, reserved coconut, and vanilla. Beat well and pour into a 1½-quart buttered casserole. Set in shallow pan of hot water and bake in a preheated 300° oven 1 hour and 15 minutes. Cool. To serve, place on doily on platter, or spoon into custard dishes.

PECAN BALLS

1 cup (½ pound) butter
¼ cup sugar
2 teaspoons vanilla
2 cups finely ground pecans
2 cups all-purpose flour
Confectioners' sugar

Cream butter until soft; add sugar, vanilla, and pecans. Sift in flour. Roll into small balls, ½ inch in diameter, and place on greased cooky sheet. Bake in a preheated 300° oven 45 minutes. Remove and roll in confectioners' sugar while still warm. Makes about 4 dozen.

Petit Luncheon

(SERVES 6 TO 8)

Chicken Livers and Apples
Shasta Salad — Shasta French Dressing   Buttermilk Horns
White Cloud Angel Food Cake
Coffee   Tea

ADVANCE PREPARATION SCHEDULE

Previous Day
Shasta French Dressing
Angel Food Cake

Early Morning
Arrange Buttermilk Horns
Frost cake
Marinate salad

CHICKEN LIVERS AND APPLES

6 tart apples	1½ tablespoons cornstarch
4 tablespoons butter	2 tablespoons apple juice
¼ cup brown sugar	¾ cup apple juice
1½ pounds chicken livers	1 tablespoon lemon juice
Salt	2 tablespoons currant jelly
Pepper	1 8-ounce package medium
1 to 2 tablespoons undiluted	noodles, cooked
canned bouillon or ½	
bouillon cube	

Peel and core apples; cut into sixths or eighths, depending on size. Melt 2 tablespoons butter in large skillet. Add apples and sprinkle with brown sugar. Cook over low heat about 10 minutes or until apples are soft, not mushy, turning occasionally. Remove from pan. In same pan, melt remaining 2 tablespoons butter. Add livers and sauté 5 minutes. Season with salt, pepper, and bouillon. Cook 3 minutes longer over medium heat. Combine cornstarch with 2 tablespoons apple juice to form smooth paste. Add ¾ cup of apple juice, lemon juice, and currant jelly. Add sauce to livers, stirring until it thickens.

Serve the livers on top of green or white egg noodles; border with the apples.

Variation:

Orange juice may be used in place of apple juice.

SHASTA SALAD

1 head romaine lettuce	2 tablespoons minced green onions
½ pound fresh mushrooms	2 pimientos, minced
2 hard-cooked eggs, cut into eighths	½ 8-ounce can bamboo shoots, drained

Reserve 8 whole lettuce leaves to line a salad bowl or individual salad plates. Tear remaining lettuce into bite-size pieces. Wash mushrooms in a small stream of running cold water; wipe dry with absorbent paper toweling. Cut in quarters from rounded side through stem. Place in a deep mixing bowl; add eggs, green onion, pimiento, lettuce, and bamboo shoots cut into 2-inch lengths; and toss gently. Pour into lettuce-lined salad bowl or individual salad plates. To serve, marinate with Shasta French Dressing.

SHASTA FRENCH DRESSING

1 cup olive oil	¼ teaspoon salt
1 cup red wine vinegar	¼ teaspoon chopped fresh mint
¼ teaspoon freshly ground	(optional)
pepper	¼ teaspoon oregano
1 clove garlic	

Combine all ingredients in a bottle. Refrigerate. To serve, shake vigorously.

BUTTERMILK HORNS

1 package prepared, ready-to-bake, vacuum-packed buttermilk biscuits (8 biscuits)	¼ cup (⅛ pound) butter, melted
	¼ cup sesame seeds

Remove biscuits and separate. Pull each lengthwise; twist and curve ends crescent-shaped. Dip in butter, then in sesame seeds, and place on cooky sheet. Bake as directed on package.

WHITE CLOUD ANGEL FOOD CAKE

1¼ cups sifted cake flour	¼ teaspoon salt
½ cup sifted sugar	1¼ teaspoons cream of tartar
1½ cups egg whites	1 teaspoon almond extract
1⅓ cups sugar	

Measure sifted flour, add ½ cup sugar, and sift together four times. Combine egg whites, salt, cream of tartar, and flavoring in large bowl. Beat with rotary beater or electric mixer until moist, soft peaks form; add remaining sugar, a fourth at a time, beating well with each addition. Sift flour and sugar mixture carefully into egg whites in four additions. Fold in with large spoon after each addition. Bring spoon through batter with large gentle strokes. Do not beat. Pour into 10-inch ungreased tube pan. Bake in a preheated 350° oven 35 or 40 minutes, or until cake springs back when pressed with finger. Turn cake upside down in pan, elevated on prongs of pan or on cake rack. If there are no prongs, the tube of the pan may be set upside down over the neck of a soft drink bottle, as cake cools best when air circulates around it. Cool thoroughly, as it will fall if at all warm. Cut with serrated knife with sawing motion for light fluffy slices.

Seven-Minute White Frosting:

⅔ cup sugar	¼ cup water
⅔ cup white corn syrup	2 egg whites
½ teaspoon vanilla	Salt

Combine ingredients and beat 2 minutes with rotary beater or electric beater. Pour into top of double boiler. Place over boiling water and beat at high speed continually with electric beater until mixture is thick and glossy, about 5 to 7 minutes.

Petit Luncheon

(SERVES 6)

Salmon Salad Gelée   Sour Cream Cucumbers
Rosemary Rolls
Broccoli Tips — Mustard Mayonnaise
Strawberries Delmonico
Ginger Cookies
Coffee

Suggested wine: Rhine

ADVANCE PREPARATION SCHEDULE

Deep Freeze	**Previous Day**	**Early Morning**
Cookies	Salmon salad	Purée raspberries
	Mustard Mayonnaise	Wash strawberries, hull
	(see Index)	Broccoli
	Cucumber dressing	Cucumbers
		Rosemary Rolls (see Index)

SALMON SALAD GELEE

1 10½-ounce can tomato soup, undiluted
1 3-ounce package cream cheese
2 tablespoons unflavored gelatin
¼ cup water
1 1-pound can salmon, flaked
1 cup diced celery
1 green pepper, diced
1 cup mayonnaise
1 tablespoon Worcestershire
1 medium onion, grated
2 tablespoons sweet pickle relish
½ teaspoon salt

Heat soup until steaming; add cream cheese, and dissolve; blend thoroughly. Soften gelatin in water; add to soup and cheese mixture; stir well. Combine with salmon, celery, green pepper, mayonnaise, Worcestershire, onion, relish, and salt. Pour into 6-cup oiled fish mold and place in refrigerator for a minimum of 2 hours. Unmold on greens; place bowl with Sour Cream Cucumbers in curve of fish; border with Broccoli Tips.

SOUR CREAM CUCUMBERS

1½ tablespoons vinegar
¾ teaspoon salt
1 tablespoon sugar (scant)
1 cup dairy sour cream
Dash pepper
2 tablespoons chopped chives
2 tablespoons chopped fresh dill
   or 1 tablespoon dill seed
1 teaspoon celery seed
¼ teaspoon mustard
2′ firm, fresh cucumbers

Mix vinegar, salt, sugar, and sour cream; add pepper, chives, dill, celery seed, and mustard. Score cucumbers in length with tines of fork and slice paper thin. Add to dressing; chill. Flavor is improved if cucumbers stand 2 to 3 hours in dressing.

BROCCOLI TIPS

2½ pounds broccoli   1 teaspoon salt

Soak broccoli in cold water 15 minutes; drain well, remove large leaves and tough ends of stalk. Cut in 2-inch lengths, making gashes in ends of larger stalks. Place in a large saucepan with water 1 inch deep. Cover closely and steam about 10 minutes. Do not permit it to become too soft. Remove, drain, and sprinkle with salt. Chill. Place around fish mold; serve Mustard Mayonnaise in separate serving dish.

STRAWBERRIES DELMONICO

1 10-ounce package frozen   3 pints strawberries
raspberries

Defrost raspberries and purée in blender or through sieve. Wash strawberries and hull. Place in glass bowl. To serve, pour raspberry purée over berries.
Delightful embellished with a scoop of vanilla ice cream.

GINGER COOKIES

¾ cup shortening   3 teaspoons baking soda
1 cup sugar   ¼ teaspoon salt
⅓ cup dark molasses   1 teaspoon ginger
1 egg   1 teaspoon cinnamon
2 cups flour   1 teaspoon ground cloves

Combine shortening, sugar, molasses, egg, flour, baking soda, salt, ginger, cinnamon, and cloves; mix well. Make small marble-size balls, place on a greased cooky sheet; flatten with bottom of a glass and sprinkle with sugar. Bake in a preheated 350° oven 15 minutes. Makes 50 to 55 cookies.

Petit Luncheon

(SERVES 6)

Artichokes Ris de Veau   Toasted Hard Rolls
Celery and Olives
Strawberry Bavarian Pie
Coffee   Tea

ADVANCE PREPARATION SCHEDULE

Deep Freeze	Previous Day	Early Morning
Pie crust	*Prepare pie*	*Boil artichokes*
	Cook sweetbreads	*Glaze pie*

ARTICHOKES RIS DE VEAU
(with Sweetbreads)

6 artichokes   Salted water
1 tablespoon vinegar

Clean artichokes with vegetable brush; cut off stems evenly so they will stand. Slice off about ¾-inch from top of artichoke. Place in boiling salted water, add vinegar, and cook about 20 to 45 minutes or until a leaf pulls away easily. Remove and drain upside down. Press down on artichoke to separate leaves and remove choke. This thorny substance inside at base may be pulled out with the fingers, and the residue carefully scraped away so as not to waste any of the delicate and delicious heart. Set aside in warm place. To serve, spread leaves sufficiently to form cup large enough to hold serving of Diced Sweetbreads.

Diced Sweetbreads:

3 pair sweetbreads	1½ cups **Bechamel Sauce**
2 tablespoons butter	2 tablespoons sherry
1 cup fresh sliced mushrooms	2 tablespoons chopped truffles (optional)

Prepare sweetbreads (see Index), and dice in ½-inch pieces. Melt butter in saucepan, add mushrooms, sauté for 5 minutes, then add sweetbreads. Blend in Bechamel Sauce, sherry, truffles, and heat to piping hot. Pour into prepared artichokes.

Bechamel Sauce:

2 tablespoons butter	2 cups half and half cream, heated
2 tablespoons flour	
½ teaspoon salt	2 tablespoons sherry
⅛ teaspoon pepper	

Heat butter in saucepan, blend in flour, and add cream, stirring until smooth. Add salt and pepper; blend in sherry. Makes 2 cups sauce.

STRAWBERRY BAVARIAN PIE

1 teaspoon unflavored gelatin	3 egg yolks, beaten slightly
2 tablespoons cold water	2 tablespoons butter
2 cups milk	1 teaspoon vanilla
½ cup granulated sugar	1 8-inch pie shell, baked
¼ cup flour	(see Index)
½ teaspoon salt	

Soften gelatin in cold water. Scald milk in double boiler. Mix ½ cup sugar in medium bowl, add flour and salt; slowly stir in milk. Return to double boiler top; cook over direct heat, stirring until mixture thickens and coats spoon. Then cook over boiling water 10 minutes. Slowly stir this mixture into egg yolks. Return to double boiler and cook until thickened, about 5 minutes; remove from heat. Add butter and softened gelatin, stirring until dissolved. Cool and add vanilla. Pour into baked pie shell and refrigerate until firm. Top with Strawberry Glaze when pie is set.

Strawberry Glaze:

¼ cup granulated sugar 4 teaspoons cornstarch
1 10-ounce package frozen sliced strawberries, defrosted

Mix sugar with cornstarch in a saucepan. Drain juice from berries, reserving berries, and slowly stir juice into cornstarch until smooth. Simmer, stirring occasionally, until clear and thickened. Cool, then stir in berries.

Variation:

Substitute other frozen berries or fruits of your choice.

Petit Brunch

(SERVES 6)

Omelets Lorraine
Broiled Tomatoes
Waffled Crackers
Nectar Parfait Spice Cookies
Coffee

ADVANCE PREPARATION SCHEDULE

Deep Freeze	Previous Day
Cookies	*Waffle Crackers*
	Parfait

OMELETS LORRAINE

12 eggs	6 tablespoons grated Parmesan
3 tablespoons water	cheese
½ teaspoon salt	4 strips bacon, cooked and
¼ teaspoon Tabasco	crumbled
6 tablespoons butter	

Break eggs into large mixing bowl. Combine water, salt, and Tabasco; add to eggs. Beat with a rotary beater only until well blended (do not beat until frothy). Heat pan; it is hot enough when drop of water sputters. For each omelet, melt 1 tablespoon butter in heated pan. Add 1 tablespoon bacon. Add ⅙ of the egg mixture, or about ⅓ cup. Stir about 7 times, heat slightly, then sprinkle with 1 tablespoon cheese. Cook until set but moist on top. Tip pan and roll omelet out onto hot dish so that it overlaps, browned side up.

BROILED TOMATOES

3 medium tomatoes	1½ teaspoons Worcestershire
¾ teaspoon prepared mustard	½ teaspon basil
1 tablespoon grated onion	3 tablespoons bread crumbs
¼ teaspoon salt	1 tablespoon butter

Heat oven to 375°. Wash tomatoes. Cut out stem ends and cut in half, crosswise. Arrange cut side up on cooky sheet or foil, on broiler pan. Combine mustard, onion, salt, Worcestershire, and basil; spread over tomato. Cover with crumbs and dot with butter. Broil without turning, 15 minutes, or until nicely browned.

Variation:

These may be baked uncovered in a preheated 350° oven for 30 minutes.

WAFFLED CRACKERS

1 cup all-purpose flour	2 egg yolks, beaten
1½ teaspoons baking powder	¾ cup milk
¼ teaspoon salt	2 tablespoons oil, shortening,
1½ teaspoons sugar	*or* butter, melted
2 egg whites, beaten stiff	

Sift flour, baking powder, salt, and sugar together into mixing bowl. Combine egg yolks and milk and add to flour mixture; stir in oil. Mix until smooth; fold in egg whites. Drop by tiny spoonfuls onto preheated waffle iron and bake. Serve warm, or reheat in a preheated 350° oven.

NECTAR PARFAIT

1 cup pitted cooked prunes	Slivered unblanched almonds
1 cup apricot whole fruit nectar	1 pint vanilla ice cream
1 3-ounce package lemon-flavored gelatin	

Cut prunes into small pieces. Drain thoroughly. Heat nectar to boiling and dissolve gelatin in it. Add ice cream by big spoonfuls, stirring until it melts. Chill in refrigerator until very thick and almost set. Swirl in prunes. Pour into tall parfait glasses. Top with a circle of almonds. Chill until firm, about 30 minutes.

SPICE COOKIES

2 cups sugar	2 teaspoons salt
½ cup shortening	2 teaspoons cinnamon
4 cups all-purpose flour	2 teaspoons ginger
2 eggs	2 teaspoons nutmeg
½ cup molasses	2 teaspoons allspice
1 teaspoon baking soda	

Combine all ingredients in mixing bowl, blending well with fingers. Form into balls about ¾ inch in diameter. Roll each ball in granulated sugar. (For convenience, push dough to one side and pour sugar in bottom of a bowl.) Place about 2½ inches apart on ungreased cooky sheet; bake 10 minutes in a preheated 375° oven. Makes 10 dozen cookies.

Note: This cooky dough may be refrigerated; use as needed.

Petit Luncheon

(SERVES 4 OR 5)

Chicken Nouillettes   Caraway Sticks
Salad Victor — Mustard Dressing
Fruit Pancake
Coffee

ADVANCE PREPARATION SCHEDULE

Previous Day

Celery
Mustard Dressing

Early Morning

Chicken Nouillettes
Defrost fruit
Freeze skillet

CHICKEN NOUILLETTES

1 tablespoon butter	1 teaspoon salt
1/3 cup chopped onion	3 tablespoons sherry
2 cups fine noodles	1 cup dairy sour cream
2¾ cups chicken broth	2½ cups diced, cooked chicken
½ teaspoon grated lemon peel	¼ cup slivered almonds,
½ teaspoon monosodium	toasted
glutamate	3 tablespoons minced parsley

Heat butter in saucepan and add onion; sauté until tender, but not brown. Add noodles, broth, lemon peel, monosodium glutamate, and salt; bring to a boil. Cover; cook over low heat 25 minutes, or until noodles are tender. Stir in sherry, sour cream, and chicken; heat. To serve, pour on a heated platter, top with nuts and parsley; garnish with a sprig or two of crisp parsley.

SALAD VICTOR

1 bunch Pascal celery	Leaf lettuce
2 cups water	2 firm tomatoes
2 chicken bouillon cubes	2 hard-cooked eggs, sliced
	Paprika

Clean celery and separate stalks. Cut into 12 to 16 4-inch lengths, allowing 3 or 4 for each serving. Heat water; add bouillion cubes and dissolve. Tie celery in bundles to keep firm and drop into boiling bouillon; cook slowly about 20 minutes, or until tender. Remove from water; drain, untie, and place in refrigerator to chill.

To serve, cover salad plates with lettuce and center each with a thick slice of tomato; place celery across tomato and garnish each salad with half an egg, sliced. Dust egg and celery with paprika, and serve with Mustard Dressing.

MUSTARD DRESSING

⅔ cup salad oil	1 tablespoon vinegar
⅔ cup evaporated milk	1 teaspoon salt
(or 1 6-ounce can)	1 teaspoon Worcestershire
¼ cup prepared mustard	Dash Tabasco

Pour oil, then milk into a 1-pint jar; add mustard, vinegar, salt, Worcestershire, and Tabasco. Cover tightly and shake well until thoroughly blended. Refrigerate; shake well again before serving.

Note: Dressing becomes thick as it stands, and is excellent with cold meats or poultry. Makes 1⅔ cups.

FRUIT PANCAKE

2 tablespoons butter	½ teaspoon salt
3 eggs	½ cup flour
½ cup milk	

Coat a 10-inch frying pan thickly with butter. Place in freezer 45 minutes to an hour. Beat eggs with electric beater (or rotary beater) until very light. Add salt and flour; blend well; add milk, beating continually. Remove pan from freezer; pour in egg batter. Place in preheated 475° oven and bake 10 minutes; reduce heat to 425°. Bake 10 minutes more and reduce heat to 350°; bake a final 10 to 15 minutes or until done. Pancake should puff up at the sides, crisp and brown. For larger frying pans, double the recipe. This one serves 4. Serve with Fruit Filling.

Fruit Filling:

1 tablespoon confectioners' sugar	2 10-ounce packages frozen straw-
Juice of 1 lemon	berries, *or* peaches, drained

Place pancake on hot platter and sprinkle with sugar and lemon juice. Spread with strawberries or peaches, fold over; top with additional confectioners' sugar.

Petit Luncheon

(SERVES 6 TO 8)

Crabmeat Creole — Fluffy Rice
Relish Tray   Half and Half Rolls
Pudding Cérise
Sesame Praline Cookies
Coffee   Tea

ADVANCE PREPARATION SCHEDULE

Deep Freeze	**Previous Day**	**Early Morning**
Rolls	*Cookies*	*Crabmeat Creole*
		Pudding
		Rice

CRABMEAT CREOLE

½ cup (¼ pound) butter
1 large green pepper, sliced thin
2 medium-size onions, sliced thin
2 thin slices of ham, cut julienne
2 #2 cans tomatoes
½ pound fresh mushrooms, sliced
1 clove garlic, minced

¾ cup dry white wine
2 pounds fresh crabmeat
2 cups chicken consommé
1 teaspoon salt
⅛ teaspoon pepper
⅛ teaspoon paprika
Dash cayenne pepper

Fluffy Rice (see Index)

Heat butter in saucepan; add green pepper, onions and ham. Sauté gently until onions and pepper are tender. Add tomatoes, mushrooms, garlic, wine, crabmeat, and consommé; simmer 10 minutes. Season with salt, pepper, paprika, and cayenne; adjust to taste. Place scoop of rice in each bowl. Serve creole from tureen with Louisiana elegance.

RELISH TRAY

½-inch slices celery cabbage　　Carrot curls
Almond-stuffed green olives　　Italian onion rings

HALF AND HALF ROLLS

1 cake compressed yeast
2 tablespoons granulated sugar
⅓ cup lukewarm water
¼ cup boiling water
2 tablespoons shortening,
　softened

1½ teaspoons salt
¼ teaspoon baking soda
1 cup half and half sour cream
3½ cups (about) all-purpose flour,
　sifted with ½ teaspoon baking
　powder

Crumble yeast and sugar together in a small bowl; add lukewarm water. Pour boiling water over softened shortening. Add salt, baking soda, and sour cream, very gradually. Cool. When lukewarm, add the dissolved yeast, then the sifted flour and baking powder slowly, beating thoroughly with wooden spoon. When too heavy to mix with spoon, turn out onto a floured canvas cloth and knead gently several minutes, adding a little more flour if necessary. Place in a well-greased bowl; rub top of dough with melted shortening. Cover with a towel and let stand in warm spot, free from drafts, until double in bulk. Turn out onto floured canvas and knead a few seconds. Cut into 24 uniform pieces and shape each into rounds, dipping fingers into flour or melted shortening to prevent sticking. Arrange about ¼ inch apart in a round 10-inch pan. Brush top with melted shortening and let stand again until doubled in bulk, about 1 hour, depending on temperature of room. Bake in a preheated 400° oven about 30 minutes, or until golden brown.

These rolls are more delicious if not served too hot, because of their unusual moisture. They may be baked in advance and reheated for about 10 minutes in a 400° oven just before serving. Also, this dough may be shaped into loaves and baked about 50 to 60 minutes at 400°. Freezes well.

PUDDING CERISE

1 cup all-purpose flour
1 cup sugar
½ teaspoon baking
　powder
1 egg, beaten

2 tablespoons butter, melted
1 cup canned sweet cherries,
　drained
1 cup chopped nuts — walnuts
　or pecans

Mix flour and sugar, then sift. Add baking powder, egg, butter, cherries, and nuts. Spoon into well-greased 4- or 5-ounce baking dishes. Bake 45 minutes in a preheated 500° oven.

Variation:

Serve with Sauce Maxim (see Index).

SESAME PRALINE COOKIES

¾ cup butter, melted	1 egg, beaten
1½ cups dark brown sugar, firmly packed	½ cup sesame seeds
	1 cup sifted all-purpose flour
1 teaspoon vanilla	¼ teaspoon salt

Mix together butter, sugar, and vanilla; beat until well blended. Stir in egg and sesame seeds. Add flour and salt; mix thoroughly. Drop by ½ teaspoonful onto well-greased cooky sheets. Bake only 6 or 8 cookies at a time in a preheated 350° oven for 4 to 5 minutes, or until lightly browned. Cool for 1 to 2 minutes before removing from sheet. Reheat if difficult to remove. Cookies will be thin and crisp. Store in a tightly covered container to keep crisp. Makes about 100 small cookies.

Petit Luncheon

(SERVES 8)

Soufflé Choice

Layer Cheese *or* Layer Sole

or

Cottage Cheese *or* Layer Crabmeat

Cinnamon Puffs

Tomatoes Kobb

Fruit Cup au Kirsch   Golden Refrigerator Cookies

Coffee   Tea

ADVANCE PREPARATION SCHEDULE

Deep Freeze	Previous Day	Early Morning
Cookies	*Layer soufflés for baking*	*Tomatoes Fruit Cup Cinnamon Puffs*

LAYER CHEESE SOUFFLE

8 slices white bread
6 eggs, well beaten
2 cups milk
1 tablespoon butter
½ teaspoon onion flakes

¾ teaspoon salt
¼ teaspoon pepper
¾ cup grated strong Cheddar cheese

Trim crusts of white bread and cut bread into small cubes. Combine eggs, milk, butter, and seasonings; beat well. Alternate layers of cheese and bread cubes in ungreased 2-quart casserole. Cover with liquid mixture and place in refrigerator overnight. Bake in a preheated 350° oven 1 hour.

LAYER SOLE SOUFFLE

8 slices white bread, crusts removed
4 eggs, well beaten
2¾ cups milk, scant
½ cup mayonnaise
2 tablespoons chopped parsley

½ cup chopped celery
1 pound sole *or* halibut, cooked
1 10½-ounce can cream of mushroom soup
8 square slices American cheese
¼ cup grated American cheese

Butter a 9-inch baking dish; line sides and bottom with bread. Dice remaining bread in cubes. Combine eggs, milk, mayonnaise, parsley, and celery; blend well. Slice sole or halibut in 1½-inch squares; add, and moisten thoroughly. Alternate layers of sole mixture, bread cubes, and cheese slices. Pour undiluted mushroom soup over all and top with grated cheese. Bake in a preheated 350° oven 1 hour.

COTTAGE CHEESE SOUFFLE

8 slices stale bread
Butter
Garlic salt
6 eggs, separated
½ cup dry white wine
1 cup chicken bouillon

1 teaspoon salt
2 teaspoons Worcestershire
2 teaspoons grated onion
2 pounds small-curd cottage cheese
Grated Parmesan cheese
Paprika

Butter bread, dust with garlic salt and cut each slice into thirds. Line a 2-quart casserole with bread slices. Combine egg yolks, wine, bouillon, salt, Worcestershire, onion, and cottage cheese. Beat egg whites stiffly, fold into mixture. Pour into bread-lined casserole; sprinkle with cheese and paprika. Bake in a preheated 325° oven 30 to 40 minutes, or until set and golden brown. Serve immediately.

LAYER CRABMEAT SOUFFLE

3 7-ounce packages frozen crab-meat (thawed) or 3 cans crab-meat
8 slices white bread (crust removed)
8 square slices American cheese
4 eggs, well beaten

2½ cups milk
½ cup mayonnaise
½ cup chopped celery
¼ cup chopped parsley
1 10½-ounce can cream of mushroom soup (undiluted)
¼ cup grated American cheese

Separate crabmeat and remove cartilage. Butter a 2-quart baking dish generously; line with squares of bread and slices of cheese. Combine crabmeat, eggs, milk, mayonnaise, celery, and parsley; pour over bread and cheese. Refrigerate overnight. Place in a preheated 375° oven for 15 minutes. Remove and cover with mushroom soup. Sprinkle with grated cheese. Return to 350° oven and bake 1 hour and 15 minutes more. Serve while hot.

Note: May be refrigerated and reheated.

CINNAMON PUFFS

⅓ cup shortening
½ cup sugar
1 egg
½ teaspoon salt

½ cup dairy sour cream
1½ cups sifted all-purpose flour
1½ teaspoons baking powder

Preheat oven to 375°. Lightly grease 16 (2-inch size) muffin-pan cups. With wooden spoon, or portable electric mixer at medium speed, cream shortening, sugar, and egg in medium bowl. Mixture should be light and well blended. Stir in sour cream. Sift flour with baking powder and salt directly onto creamed mixture. Mix until smooth. Fill muffin-pan cups ⅔ full; bake 20 minutes. Remove from pans and dip into Cinnamon Puff Topping.

Cinnamon Puff Topping:

> ½ cup sugar   1 teaspoon cinnamon
> ⅓ cup butter *or* margarine, melted

Combine sugar with cinnamon, mixing well. Dip tops of hot muffins into butter, then into sugar mixture. Serve warm. Makes 16.

TOMATOES KOBB

4 large beefsteak tomatoes
½ teaspoon salt
¼ teaspoon freshly ground pepper
¼ teaspoon grated onion
4 tablespoons mayonnaise
1 teaspoon curry powder
1 teaspoon chopped parsley

Peel and quarter tomatoes; seed and chop coarsely. Season with salt, pepper, and grated onion. Place in refrigerator for 5 or 6 hours before serving; chill thoroughly. Combine mayonnaise and curry powder. Serve tomatoes in bowls with a large tablespoon of curried mayonnaise on each. Sprinkle with chopped parsley.

FRUIT CUP AU KIRSCH

1 cup mandarin orange sections, drained
½ cup preserved kumquats, drained and sliced
1 cup fresh *or* frozen raspberries, drained
1 cup seedless green grapes
½ cup Kirsch
1 cup white wine
1 cup juices of drained fruits

Combine oranges, kumquats, raspberries, grapes, Kirsch, wine, and juices of fruits; refrigerate 2 hours, so flavors will "marry." Serve in sherbet cups.

Variation:

Substitute or add other fruits, depending on amount needed. Fruit juice may be used instead of white wine. The Kirsch is a delightful "must."

GOLDEN REFRIGERATOR COOKIES

¾ cup all-purpose flour, sifted
½ teaspoon soda
½ teaspoon salt
½ cup granulated sugar
½ cup brown sugar, firmly packed

½ cup butter *or* margarine, softened
1 egg
½ teaspoon vanilla
1½ cups quick-cooking rolled oats

¼ cup chopped walnuts, *or* currants, *or* chocolate bits

Sift flour once (on wax paper); measure, add soda, salt, and sift into a bowl. Add granulated and brown sugars, butter, egg, and vanilla. Beat until smooth, about 2 minutes; stir in oats and nuts. Shape into 3 rolls, about 1½ inches in diameter; wrap in wax paper and chill thoroughly. Slice ¼ inch thick and place on ungreased cooky sheet. Bake in a preheated 350° oven 10 to 12 minutes, or until lightly browned.

Note: The dough can be made in advance, shaped into rolls, and kept in the refrigerator, to slice and bake as needed.

Petit Luncheon

(SERVES 6)

Cantaloupe and Shrimp
Barbecued French Loaf
Coffee Meringues Glacées
Coffee

ADVANCE PREPARATION SCHEDULE

Deep Freeze	Previous Day	Early Morning
Meringues	*Boil shrimp*	*Arrange loaf*
		Assemble shrimp sauce

CANTALOUPE AND SHRIMP

3 large cantaloupes	Watercress
3 cups hot cooked rice	1 #2½ can sliced pineapple
(see Index)	6 shrimp, cooked and cleaned

Cantaloupes are delicious containers for a hot shrimp luncheon dish. Halve cantaloupes, remove seeds, cut ¼-inch slice from bottom to level melon. Add interest by notching the cut edges for a saw-toothed effect. Place on individual plates and fill each with ½ cup rice; cover with Shrimp Sauce and a dash of paprika. Garnish with a bouquet of watercress, as a fringe for a pineapple slice, topped with a reserved shrimp.

Shrimp Sauce:

1 10-ounce can frozen	⅛ teaspoon nutmeg
cream of shrimp soup	2 tablespoons sherry
1 cup dairy sour cream	1½ pounds cooked, cleaned shrimp

Reserve 6 shrimp for garnish (see ingredients under Cantaloupe and Shrimp). Combine shrimp soup, sour cream, nutmeg, and sherry in top of double boiler. Heat until blended; then stir in 1 pound cooked shrimp and heat through again.

BARBECUED FRENCH LOAF

1 loaf French bread	2 tablespoons poppy seed
⅓ cup butter *or*	¼ cup prepared mustard
margarine	½ pound Swiss cheese, sliced and
1 medium onion, minced	cut in 2½-inch squares

Make diagonal cuts in loaf of bread about 1 inch apart three-fourths of the way through (do not cut to bottom of loaf). Cream butter; blend in onion, poppy seed, and mustard. Spread one side of each slice with creamed mixture and insert a slice of cheese in each cut. Spread remainder of mixture over top. Bake in a preheated 375° oven for 20 minutes or until loaf is light golden brown and cheese is melted. Serve at once.

COFFEE MERINGUES GLACEES

6 egg whites	3 tablespoons instant coffee
½ teaspoon cream of tartar	¼ teaspoon salt
1½ cups sugar	1½ cups cornflakes, crushed

Lemon Sherbet

Beat egg whites until frothy; add cream of tartar and salt. Gradually add sugar, while beating until stiff and glossy. Fold in remaining ingredients. Swirl 3-inch circles on a greased cooky sheet. Hollow out centers slightly to form nests. Bake in a preheated 275° oven 1 hour and 15 minutes. Fill with fresh Lemon Sherbet (see Index) or your favorite ice cream. Can be served with sauce if desired. Makes approximately 18.

Note: Meringues freeze very well. Have them on hand as they are very versatile for many fillings.

Petit Brunch

(SERVES 4 TO 6)

Cranberry Cocktail

Brown Rice and Shrimp   Cheese Canapés

Puffball Henrici — Hot Strawberries

or

Apple Pancake Torte

Coffee

ADVANCE PREPARATION SCHEDULE

Previous Day	Early Morning
Cook shrimp	*Boil rice*
Canapé roll	

CRANBERRY COCKTAIL

2 pints bottled cranberry juice
2 tablespoons lemon juice
1 cup orange juice

2 8¾-ounce cans crushed
  pineapple, undrained
2 cups finely cracked ice

In electric blender combine cranberry juice, lemon juice, orange juice, pineapple, and ice. Blend at high speed, covered, for 30 seconds. Chill in pitcher; serve in stemmed cocktail or parfait glasses.

BROWN RICE AND SHRIMP

2 cups brown rice
4 cups beef broth
1½ teaspoons salt
2 tablespoons minced ginger
  root or 1 teaspoon dry ginger
3 tablespoons oil or butter
1 cup chopped almonds

1 pound fresh shrimp, cooked
  and deveined
Julienne strips of meat: ham,
  chicken, pork, etc.
½ cup minced green onion
  (optional)

Wash rice. Pour broth into saucepan; add salt and ginger. Bring to a boil; add rice slowly so as not to disturb boiling point. Cover tightly and reduce heat to a very slow simmer. Cook 45 minutes, remove from heat, and let stand 10 minutes longer, covered. Heat butter in saucepan, add shrimp, and sauté very slowly for 5 minutes. Toss with hot rice; adjust seasoning. Turn into hot casserole or chafing dish and garnish with strips of meat, onions, and almonds.

Note: This is a dry rice. Add more broth, if needed, before placing in casserole.

CHEESE CANAPES

1 8-ounce package Cheddar
  cheese
1 8-ounce package American
  cheese
1 8-ounce package cream cheese
1 tablespoon prepared horseradish

1 teaspoon Worcestershire
1 clove garlic, chopped fine
Salt and pepper
½ cup finely cut almonds,
  buttered and browned
2 teaspoons paprika

Put cheeses through food mill; add horseradish, Worcestershire, garlic, salt and pepper. Shape into a 2-inch roll. Combine almonds and paprika; press cheese roll into mixture until well coated. Roll in wax paper and chill for several hours. Slice and serve on round crackers. Stores well in refrigerator for several days.

PUFFBALL HENRICI — HOT STRAWBERRIES

½ cup flour	½ cup milk
⅛ teaspoon salt	2 eggs
½ teaspoon sugar	2 tablespoons salad oil
¼ teaspoon baking powder	2 packages frozen strawberries

Combine flour, salt, baking powder and sugar. Pour in milk and beat until smooth. Add unbeaten eggs and mix well. Pour oil into an 8-inch skillet. Heat until a drop of water sputters in pan. Tip skillet to coat all sides and bottom thoroughly. Pour off excess and pour in batter. When crisp and brown on the bottom, turn pancake over. It is a large pancake, easier to handle with 2 pancake turners, or invert the pancake into another hot greased skillet. As soon as the pancake is turned, push it down in the center; the outer edges will then rise above the sides of the skillet when baked. Place immediately in hot oven. Bake 15 minutes.

Heat the strawberries to boiling. Remove pancake from oven and slip it out of the skillet onto a paper towel. Lift half the hot berries out of juice with a slotted spoon and place in pancake. Roll up jelly-roll fashion, place on platter, and sprinkle with powdered sugar. Serve with balance of berries. Serves 2 or 3.

Note: This recipe is for 1 skillet and serves 2 large or 4 small portions. The following recipe is for 2 skillets.

APPLE PANCAKE TORTE

1 cup sifted flour	½ teaspoon vanilla
¼ cup sugar	4 tablespoons butter
⅛ teaspoon salt	2 large red Delicious apples,
2 eggs, separated	pared, cored and sliced thin
¾ cup milk	½ cup sugar
1 teaspoon cinnamon	

Sift flour, sugar, and salt into mixing bowl. Combine egg yolks, milk, and vanilla; blend well and add to dry ingredients, stirring until smooth. Beat egg whites until stiff and fold into batter. Melt 1 tablespoon butter in an 8-inch rounded ovenware skillet; tip skillet so that sides are buttered. Pour in half the batter and cook over low heat, spreading batter up the sides of the pan to form a bowl-shaped pancake. When batter is just slightly brown, arrange half the apple slices over the pancake, overlapping slices to completely cover the batter. Sprinkle with half the combined sugar and cinnamon and dot with 1 tablespoon butter. Place under preheated broiler until sugar is melted and bubbly, about 10 minutes, or place in a preheated 400° oven and bake 15 minutes. Loosen edge of pancake with spatula and slide onto heated serving plate. Repeat with second half of batter and with other ingredients, or use 2 skillets.

Note: One pancake serves 3 amply for dessert, or 2 for a luncheon portion.

Interlude for Two

COOKING for two is fun, but a true problem in mathematics. In using a recipe, how does one subtract to prepare little enough, and how much does one add to balance the necessary ingredients? In a larger recipe, what does one do with the remainder?

The freezing compartment is a boon. Leftovers become delicious concoctions. Many items may be refrigerated for several days. Serve them with a stimulating evening cocktail for two, or to share with the unexpected guest.

And now for your eating pleasure, a few menus tailored for the twosome.

Interlude for Two Dinner

Steak Diane

Wild Rice   Burgundy Beets

Lettuce Avocado Salad

Dutch Peaches and Cream Pie

Coffee   Tea   Milk

Suggested wine: red Bordeaux

ADVANCE PREPARATION SCHEDULE

Early Morning

Beets
Crisp lettuce
Dressing
Pie

STEAK DIANE

2 tablespoons butter
6 ¼-inch slices fillet of beef
½ teaspoon salt
⅓ teaspoon pepper
2 teaspoons cognac (about)
1 tablespoon butter

½ cup fresh mushroom caps, sliced
½ cup strong beef stock *or* canned
  undiluted beef consommé
1 teaspoon frozen chives
1 teaspoon minced parsley

Heat butter in a large skillet and brown beef quickly on both sides. Season with salt and pepper; place on heated plates. Warm cognac in a metal ladle, set aflame, and pour over beef. Add mushrooms to skillet and sauté quickly for about 3 minutes, then add beef stock, chives, parsley, and butter. Pour over beef, and serve with Wild Rice.

WILD RICE

Prepare 1 cup rice according to package directions, or see Index.

BURGUNDY BEETS

¼ cup sugar
¼ cup dry red wine
½ teaspoon salt
Dash pepper
1 teaspoon cornstarch

2 tablespoons lemon juice
  or vinegar
1 #303 can beets
1 tablespoon butter *or*
  margarine

Combine sugar, wine, salt, and pepper in saucepan. Make a paste of cornstarch and lemon juice; blend with sugar mixture. Cook, stirring constantly, until thickened. Add beets and butter; heat through.

LETTUCE AVOCADO SALAD

1 pint assorted lettuce (romaine, Bibb, iceberg)	1 small avocado
	2 teaspoons chopped pimiento

Line salad plates with romaine lettuce. Form cups of Bibb lettuce on romaine; add a layer of shredded iceberg lettuce. Use French cutter for avocado and arrange slices; sprinkle with pimiento. Serve with Watercress Dressing (see Index).

DUTCH PEACHES AND CREAM PIE

6 ripe peaches, stoned and halved	¼ cup flour
	½ teaspoon cinnamon
1 9-inch unbaked Pie Shell (see Index)	1 cup dairy sour cream
	2 tablespoons sugar
½ cup sugar	½ teaspoon cinnamon

Place peach halves, cut side up, in pie shell, overlapping as little as possible. Combine ½ cup sugar, flour, and ½ teaspoon cinnamon; mix well and sprinkle over peaches. Pour sour cream evenly over all and then sprinkle with remaining combined sugar and cinnamon. Bake 10 minutes in a preheated 450° oven, then turn heat down to 350° and bake ½ hour longer. Serve warm.

Note: Cut recipe in half for 3 to 4 individual pies, depending on size of pans.

Interlude for Two Dinner

Watercress Soup

Lobster Diavolo   Spaghettini

Peaches Romanoff   Gâteaux Vites

Coffee

Suggested wine: Orvieto or white Chianti

ADVANCE PREPARATION SCHEDULE

Early morning

Soup
Cook spaghettini
Peaches Romanoff

WATERCRESS SOUP

2 tablespoons butter	2 cups hot milk
1 medium-size onion, minced	½ teaspoon salt
2 bunches watercress, chopped	Dash pepper
1 tablespoon flour	1 egg yolk
3 cups hot chicken bouillon	½ cup heavy cream

Heat butter in pan; add onion and sauté over low heat until golden. Add watercress, cover pan, and cook 5 minutes. Blend in flour, bouillon, milk and simmer 15 minutes. Rub through fine sieve or whirl 1 minute in blender. Add salt, pepper, and reheat. Combine egg yolk and cream; stir in ¼ cup of the hot soup slowly. Return to soup, stirring well. Serve in cups with a sprig of watercress as garnish. Delicious served cold as well.

Note: To prepare watercress, tie in bunches and wash thoroughly under running water. Drain, shake dry, and snip the leaves fine, using scissors.

LOBSTER DIAVOLO

2 1-pound lobsters, live	½ garlic clove, minced
3 tablespoons olive oil	1 pinch ground cloves
1 small onion, finely chopped	1 pinch mace
1 #2 can tomatoes	¼ teaspoon salt
2 sprigs parsley, chopped	⅛ teaspoon pepper
½ teaspoon thyme	2 tablespoons cognac

Split the lobsters; heat oil in saucepan, add onion, and sauté lightly; place lobsters in oil and cook over high heat until they have changed color. Reduce heat and continue cooking 10 minutes. Add tomatoes, parsley, thyme, garlic, cloves, mace, salt, and pepper. Cover; cook for 15 minutes or until the lobsters are tender. Heat cognac, ignite it, and pour flaming over the lobsters. A perfect chafing dish maneuver.

SPAGHETTINI

4 ounces (half an 8-ounce package) spaghettini

Boil according to package directions; drain and blanch. Keep heated in colander placed over boiling water. Serve in separate bowl as an accompaniment to lobster.

GATEAUX VITES

1 egg white, beaten stiff	¼ teaspoon salt
1 cup brown sugar	½ teaspoon vanilla
1 cup pecan chips	

Blend egg white, brown sugar, salt, vanilla, and pecan chips well. Spread in well-buttered cooky pan, about 9 inches square. Bake in a preheated 350° oven 18 to 20 minutes. Cut while hot.

PEACHES ROMANOFF

2 egg yolks, beaten until frothy	1 pound fresh peaches (about 3) or 1 8-ounce can sliced peaches, drained
⅓ cup sugar	
½ cup orange juice	1 tablespoon lemon juice
⅓ cup heavy cream, whipped	Maraschino cherries

Place egg yolks in top of double boiler; add sugar and orange juice and continue beating well until light and lemon colored. Cook over water which is just simmering (not boiling), stirring constantly until thick and smooth. Cool and place in refrigerator to chill. Fold in whipped cream.

Fresh peaches should be prepared as close to serving time as possible. Peel and slice quite thick, and brush with lemon juice to keep from turning dark. Fold into custard and heap into compotes. Garnish with cherries, or fresh berries in season, if you prefer. Low glass compotes are effective. Makes 2 generous servings.

Interlude for Two Dinner

Squabs Choucroute   Parsley Potatoes
Nesselrode Pie
Coffee   Tea   Milk

Suggested wine: Pinot Chardonnay

SQUABS CHOUCROUTE

2 squabs	1 carrot, diced
2 tablespoons seasoned flour	2 tablespoons chopped celery
2 tablespoons butter	1 chicken bouillon cube
2 tablespoons chopped onion	1 cup boiling water

Split squabs in half and dredge with seasoned flour. Melt butter in saucepan and sauté squabs slowly until lightly browned. Place them in a casserole. To remaining butter mixture in saucepan, add onion, carrot, and celery; sauté, stirring for about 5 minutes. Dissolve bouillon cube in water, blend ½ cup with onion mixture, and pour over squabs. Baste with remaining ½ cup bouillon. Cover casserole and place in a preheated 350° oven; roast about 1 hour or until tender. Do not allow squabs to become dry. Baste occasionally and if liquid is not sufficient add additional water and bouillon cube. To serve, place on platter, border with Sweet Sauerkraut.

Sweet Sauerkraut:

1 tablespoon shortening	Dash pepper
⅓ cup chopped onions	1 tablespoon cooking sherry
2 tablespoons sugar	1 #303 can tomatoes
½ bay leaf	1 #2 can sauerkraut, drained

Heat shortening in saucepan, add onion and sauté for 5 minutes. Add sugar, bay leaf, and pepper. Cover and simmer 5 minutes. Stir in sherry, tomatoes, and sauerkraut; place in greased baking pan. Bake ½ hour in a preheated 350° oven.

PARSLEY POTATOES

1 pound new potatoes, small	1 tablespoon snipped parsley
3 tablespoon butter, melted	Paprika (optional)

Scrub potatoes well and pare off a narrow strip through center (for appearance). Boil in salted water, ½ teaspoon per cup, for about 35 minutes. Drain; shake in pan over heat to dry. Place on serving plate, pour butter over potatoes; sprinkle with parsley and paprika.

Note: If using old (mature) potatoes, pare first, then prepare as for new potatoes.

NESSELRODE PIE

3 eggs, separated
⅓ cup sugar
2 tablespoons unflavored gelatin
¼ cup water
⅓ cup rum
½ teaspoon vanilla

1 cup whipping cream, beaten stiff
1 baked 9-inch pie shell, *or* Crumb Crust (see Index)
¼ cup coarsely chopped candied fruit

1 square (1-oz.) unsweetened chocolate

Beat egg yolks until thick, then beat in sugar gradually. Dissolve gelatin in the water combined with 2 tablespoons of the rum. Place over boiling water and heat carefully until clear and slightly simmering. Add slowly to egg and sugar mixture; gradually beat in remaining rum with an electric or rotary beater. Beat egg whites until stiff and fold into yolk mixture; add vanilla, then fold in cream and candied fruit. Pour into prepared pie shell; shave chocolate with vegetable slicer, spread thickly over top and place in refrigerator. Chill thoroughly before serving.

Interlude for Two Dinner

Chicken Breasts Artichauts
Coconut Sweet Potatoes   Butterhorns
Senf Gurken
Baked Alaska Shortcakes
Coffee   Tea   Milk

ADVANCE PREPARATION SCHEDULE

Deep Freeze	Early Morning
Baked Alaskas	*Potatoes for baking*
	Butterhorns (see Index)

CHICKEN BREASTS ARTICHAUTS

1 package frozen artichoke hearts	¼ teaspoon freshly ground pepper
	½ teaspoon poultry seasoning
4 chicken breasts, cleaned	4 strips uncooked bacon
2 teaspoons oregano	½ cup chicken consommé
1 teaspoon salt	½ cup Vermouth
Parsley	

Defrost artichokes sufficiently to separate them and place in bottom of roasting pan. Sprinkle chicken breasts with oregano, salt, pepper, and seasoning and place on artichokes. Spread a strip of bacon on each breast; combine consommé and Vermouth and pour over all. Bake in a preheated 325° oven for 1 hour and 15 minutes, or until tender. Arrange on platter, border with Coconut Sweet Potatoes, and garnish with parsley.

COCONUT SWEET POTATOES

4 large sweet potatoes, cooked and peeled	¾ cup light molasses
	½ teaspoon salt
¼ cup butter	¼ teaspoon pepper
¾ cup orange juice	¼ cup flaked coconut

Slice sweet potatoes diagonally, about ⅜ inch thick. Arrange overlapping slices in greased 8″ x 8″ baking dish; dot with butter. Mix orange juice, molasses, salt, and pepper. Drizzle about half this sauce over potatoes. Bake in a preheated 350° oven 15 minutes. Remove from oven, baste with remaining sauce, and sprinkle with flaked coconut. Return to oven and bake 15 minutes longer.

BAKED ALASKA SHORTCAKES

3 large egg whites	½ cup sugar
¼ teaspoon cream of tartar	1 pint ice cream, any flavor
4 prepared shortcake shells	

Beat egg whites with cream of tartar until they hold a soft peak, then beat in sugar gradually. Continue beating until meringue is stiff and glossy. Place the shortcake shells on a baking sheet. In the center place a scoop of ice cream. Completely cover ice cream with a thick coating of the meringue. Place in a preheated 500° oven for 3 to 5 minutes, or until meringue is delicately brown. Serve at once. The two extra shortcakes are good to keep in the freezer for another time.

Variation:

Make fruit baskets. Fill shells with well-drained fruit salad. Spoon a rim of whipped cream around the edge, and finish with an orange peel "handle."

SENF GURKEN

Senf Gurken are zesty pickled yellowed cucumbers, deliciously prepared with mustard, and are available in most markets. They are packed in 12-ounce jars and are served cold as a relish.

Interlude for Two Dinner

Clam Bisque
Pocket Lamb Chops   Pineapple Relish
Zucchini au Gratin   Potato Pancakes for Two
Dessert Fruitcake
Coffee   Milk

Suggested wine: Margaux

ADVANCE PREPARATION SCHEDULE

Early Morning

Stuff chops
Assemble pancake ingredients
Assemble zucchini for baking
Pineapple Relish (see Index)

CLAM BISQUE

1 10½-ounce can cream of celery soup
¾ cup water

2 tablespoons white wine
1 10½-ounce can clam juice
1 teaspoon chopped parsley
Paprika

Combine all ingredients in saucepan; simmer 5 minutes. Serve with garnish of chopped parsley and dust with paprika.

POCKET LAMB CHOPS

2 2-inch rib *or* loin lamb chops
2 large *or* 4 small fresh mushrooms
⅛ teaspoon salt

⅛ teaspoon seasoned salt
2 tablespoons chili sauce
1 teaspoon butter
Water

Make a slit in thick side of each chop and insert the mushrooms; skewer the slit together with a toothpick or metal skewer. Place chops in pan and broil 5 minutes on each side. Remove from broiler, sprinkle with salt and seasoned salt, cover with chili sauce; dot with butter; add sufficient water to just cover bottom. Place in oven, reducing heat to 350°, and bake about 20 minutes, basting often, until browned and tender. Serve with sauce from pan.

ZUCCHINI AU GRATIN

3 medium zucchini, cut into ½-inch rounds
2 teaspoons oil
1 small onion, cut fine
¼ teaspoon coarse pepper
Dash garlic powder

½ teaspoon seasoned salt
1 tablespoon grated Parmesan cheese
2 tablespoons tomato sauce *or* paste
Sliced Swiss cheese

Scrub zucchini; do not peel. Cut into ¼-inch rounds. Heat oil in skillet, add zucchini and onion; sauté 5 minutes. Add pepper, garlic powder, seasoned salt, and Parmesan; combine well. Place in greased 1-quart casserole and brush with tomato sauce or paste; cover with slices of Swiss cheese. Bake in a preheated 350° oven until cheese melts. Serve hot immediately.

POTATO PANCAKES FOR TWO

2 large, raw grated potatoes	½ teaspoon baking powder
1 egg, beaten	1 tablespoon milk
1 teaspoon grated onion	¼ teaspoon salt
1 tablespoon flour	Dash pepper

¼ cup shortening

Drain potatoes thoroughly and combine with all ingredients except shortening; mix well. Heat shortening and drop batter from tablespoon. Fry until browned on both sides. Stack on paper towels and keep warm until served. Makes 12 small pancakes.

DESSERT FRUITCAKE

1 #303 can fruit cocktail, drained	1 teaspoon soda Pinch salt
1 cup sugar	¼ cup brown sugar
1 cup cake flour	½ cup angel flake coconut
1 egg	⅛ cup butter, softened

Pour fruit cocktail into strainer; allow to stand to drain fruit thoroughly. Place into large bowl of electric mixer, add remaining ingredients, and beat 3 minutes at medium speed. Turn batter into well-greased 8-inch square cake pan. Bake in a preheated 350° oven 25 minutes; add topping and bake 20 minutes more.

Topping:

¼ cup light brown sugar   ½ cup chopped walnuts

Mix together and sprinkle over top of cake. Add whipped cream garnish if desired.

Interlude for Two Dinner

Sukiyaki Rice

Strawberry Almond Tree Teahouse Kipfel

Hot Sake Tea

ADVANCE PREPARATION SCHEDULE

Deep Freeze

Kipfel

Early Morning

Prepare vegetables

Clean berries

SUKIYAKI

2 tablespoons salad oil

1½ pounds tenderloin *or* sirloin, sliced ¼ inch thick, about 2 inches across

1 cup "cellophane" (translucent noodles)

1 white onion, sliced thin

3 green onions, sliced thin

½ 8-ounce can sliced bamboo shoots, drained

1 8-ounce can water chestnuts

1 cup sliced celery

½ pound spinach, washed

¼ pound mushrooms, sliced

½ green pepper, cut in strips

¼ cup soy sauce

¼ cup sherry

¼ cup beef broth, consommé, *or* bouillon

1 tablespoon sugar

½ teaspoon monosodium glutamate

The appearance of the vegetables before preparation, as well as after, is a source of pride; arrange the tenderloin and crisply fresh vegetables attractively on platter in individual sections. If possible, cook the Sukiyaki at the table, with the guests as audience as well as participants. An electric skillet is convenient.

Heat electric skillet to medium, add oil (or heat oil in skillet on stove); add meat and sauté lightly. Push the meat to one side and place vegetables in pan, each separately, in mounds. Do not mix them. Combine soy sauce, sherry, broth, sugar, monosodium glutamate and pour over contents. Cover and cook 5 minutes; uncover and cook an additional 5 minutes, tossing vegetables lightly, until heated and bubbly. Serve from skillet with Fluffy Rice (see Index). (Serves 4; divide in half for 2.)

STRAWBERRY ALMOND TREE

1 pint fresh strawberries	½ teaspoon Benedictine
1 tablespoon Kirsch	½ cup heavy cream, whipped
1 tablespoon confectioners' sugar	½ cup slivered almonds

Wash berries; do not hull. Sprinkle with Kirsch and sugar, then chill. Add Benedictine to whipped cream and place in a bowl. Serve from Strawberry Almond Tree. Dip the berries first in the whipped cream and then in the almonds.

Directions for Strawberry Almond Tree:

Fill a long-stemmed compote or large goblet with strawberries, and place it in a 6-inch or 7-inch bowl. Fill the bowl around the base of the compote with whipped cream. Place this on a 9-inch or 10-inch serving plate and spread the almonds on the plate around the bowl. This arrangement is attractive with other dipped fruits or dipped appetizers.

TEAHOUSE KIPFEL

1 cake compressed yeast	2 egg yolks
2¼ cups sifted flour	½ cup dairy sour cream
½ cup (¼ pound) butter *or* margarine	½ cup confectioners' sugar

Crumble yeast into flour in large mixing bowl. Cut in butter with pastry blender until mixture resembles coarse meal. Blend in egg yolks and sour cream thoroughly. Press into ball on lightly floured board and knead until smooth, about 7 minutes. Dough will be sticky; do not hesitate to dust with additional flour. Divide into 3 parts, wrap each in wax paper, and chill for 2 hours. Prepare filling before removing from refrigerator. Set aside. Sprinkle board with confectioners' sugar, roll each piece of dough into an 8-inch circle; cut each circle into 8 pie-shaped wedges. Place a full tea-spoonful of filling onto each wide end and roll up to point. The dough is very tender and as it is rolled the filling spreads to the outside. This is characteristic; however, if the ends of the dough are cupped the filling will not spread onto the pan or burn. Place on greased baking sheets, curling ends slightly to form crescents. Bake in a preheated 375° oven for 20 minutes or until golden brown. Dust with confectioners' sugar. Makes 2 dozen.

Filling:

1 cup walnuts, finely chopped	1 teaspoon vanilla
½ cup sugar	Pinch of salt
	2 egg whites

Combine walnuts, sugar, and vanilla. Add salt to egg whites, beat until stiff and fold into walnut mixture.

Interlude for Two Dinner

Herbed Edam   Toasted Sesame Crackers
Deviled Drumsticks   Wheat Pilaf
White Asparagus Polonaise
Rum Cream Cake
Coffee   Tea   Milk

Suggested wine: Médoc

ADVANCE PREPARATION SCHEDULE

Previous Day	Early Morning
Herbed Edam	*Prepare drumsticks for baking*
Cooky crust	*Rum Cream Cake*

HERBED EDAM

1 Edam cheese	⅛ teaspoon freshly ground pepper
1 tablespoon Worcestershire	½ teaspoon chervil
	Tabasco to taste

Hollow the cheese and crumble the removed portion. Mix cheese with the Worcestershire, pepper, chervil, and Tabasco, blending thoroughly. Refill the Edam shell. Let ripen several hours, preferably overnight. Serve with toasted sesame crackers.

DEVILED DRUMSTICKS

½ cup flour ¼ cup (⅛ pound) butter
6 chicken drumsticks, *or* 4 leg
and thigh portions

Put flour in a paper bag, add drumsticks, and shake until well coated. Heat butter in a skillet and brown chicken evenly. Place in a preheated shallow baking dish. Cover with Deviled Sauce. Bake in a preheated 300° oven about 40 minutes or until tender. Remove to platter, serve piping hot around a mound of Wheat Pilaf. Serve extra sauce separately.

Deviled Sauce:

1 cup brown sugar
1 tablespoon cornstarch
¼ teaspoon ginger
¼ teaspoon dry mustard
¼ teaspoon oregano
⅛ teaspoon coarse black pepper
2 cloves garlic, crushed with 1
teaspoon salt

2 tablespoons minced onion
4 whole cloves
1 cup dry red wine
1 tablespoon tarragon *or*
white vinegar
1 cup prepared fresh purple
plums *or* 1 #2 can plums,
pitted and drained

Combine sugar, cornstarch, ginger, mustard, oregano, pepper, salt and garlic, onion, cloves, wine, vinegar, and plums in heavy saucepan. Simmer for 20 minutes and pour over drumsticks.

Note: To prepare fresh plums: cut in halves, remove seeds, and cut each plum half crosswise 3 times.

WHEAT PILAF

1 cup water
1 tablespoon butter
¾ cup packaged seasoned wheat pilaf
1 envelope seasoning included
in package

Combine water, butter, and seasoning and bring to a rolling boil; stir in pilaf, cover, and let stand for 10 minutes. Stir lightly with a fork before serving.

WHITE ASPARAGUS POLONAISE

1 6¾-ounce can white asparagus, heated and drained

Cover with Polonaise Butter.

Polonaise Butter:

2 tablespoons butter	½ teaspoon parsley, chopped
1 tablespoon bread crumbs	(optional)
⅛ teaspoon lemon juice	

Melt butter and blend in bread crumbs, lemon juice, and parsley. Stir over low heat until golden. Serve hot over heated asparagus.

RUM CREAM CAKE

6 egg yolks	1 pint heavy cream,
1 cup sugar, less 1 tablespoon	whipped
1 tablespoon unflavored	½ cup Jamaica rum
gelatin	Grated chocolate *or*
½ cup cold water	pistachio nuts, chopped

Beat egg yolks until light; add sugar and beat again. Soak gelatin in cold water 5 minutes; place over low heat and let come to a boil, while stirring. Pour over sugar and egg mixture and stir briskly. Fold whipped cream into egg mixture; add rum slowly. Cool, but do not permit filling to become firm. Pour into Cooky Crust pie shell. When set, sprinkle with grated chocolate or chopped pistachio nuts. (Serves 6. Leftovers may be used the following day.)

Cooky Crust:

¼ pound stick (minus 1 inch)	1 cup all-purpose flour
butter	3 tablespoons ice water

Cut off 1 inch of butter from ¼ pound stick. Mix remaining butter with flour, using only a fork. Work ice water into mixture; knead lightly; roll out and place loosely in a buttered 9-inch pie plate. Prick well with a fork, flute the rim, and bake in a preheated 350° oven until golden brown.

Interlude for Two Dinner

Lemon Blue Cheese   Pumpernickel Slices   Crackers
Shrimp Curry   Fruited Brown Rice
Green Salad
Pecan Pie
Coffee   Tea   Milk

Suggested wine: white Burgundy

ADVANCE PREPARATION SCHEDULE

Previous Day	Early Morning
Prepare cheese	*Rice*
Boil shrimp	*Pecan Pie*

LEMON BLUE CHEESE

1 4-ounce package blue cheese	¼ teaspoon pepper
½ teaspoon garlic salt	Juice of 1 lemon
½ teaspoon salt	1 pint dairy sour cream
½ teaspoon paprika	Ripe olives, sliced *or* chopped
½ teaspoon celery salt	(optional)

Cream blue cheese in small bowl of electric mixer or with rotary beater. Add remaining ingredients. Chopped or sliced ripe olives may be added for texture. Serve with crackers or pumpernickel slices.

Note: Stores well. Keep in refrigerator as a dip ready for unexpected guests.

SHRIMP CURRY

4 scallions *or* green onions, cut fine	16 shrimp, cooked
1 tablespoon butter	1 pint dairy sour cream *or* half and half
1 10-ounce can frozen cream of shrimp soup, defrosted	sour cream
	1 tablespoon curry powder

Melt butter in saucepan, sauté scallions until tender; add cream of shrimp soup and shrimp. Blend in sour cream and curry powder and bring to a boil. Serve with Fruited Brown Rice.

To cook shrimp:

¾ pound raw shrimp	1 bay leaf
4 cups water	2 celery stalks with leaves
1 small onion	2 teaspoons salt
1 clove garlic	Dash cayenne
1 tablespoon lemon juice	

Wash shrimp and drain. Combine water and remaining ingredients and bring to a boil. Add shrimp. Bring to boil again, reduce heat and simmer 8 to 10 minutes. Allow them to cool in the liquid. Remove shells and devein.

Note: Although the black intestinal vein is edible, it is suggested that it be removed, as the clean pink shrimp is more appetizing. Cleaned and deveined frozen shrimp are available; less cooking time is needed.

Variation:

Fill a 2-cup greased mold or 4 individual molds with hot cooked white rice, firmly packed. Set aside in a warm place. To serve, unmold on platter, center or border with Shrimp Curry. The rice will unmold easily. A dusting of paprika or chopped parsley gives color contrast.

FRUITED BROWN RICE

2 cups brown rice, cooked	2 tablespoons seedless white
¼ cup orange marmalade	raisins
¼ teaspoon salt	

Grease 4 4-ounce muffin pan cups. Combine rice, marmalade, raisins, and salt; blend well. Fill greased pans with rice mixture, firmly packed. Place in shallow pan, in 1 inch of hot water. Bake in a preheated 350° oven 35 minutes or until thoroughly heated. Unmold and place around Shrimp Curry. The fruit of the rice recipe substitutes for the usual curry accompaniments, though they may be added if you wish.

GREEN SALAD

Oil and Vinegar Dressing (see Index)

Use greens of your choice.

PECAN PIE

1 cup sugar	3 egg yolks, well beaten
14 square soda crackers, crumbled	1 teaspoon vanilla
1 cup coarsely chopped pecans	3 egg whites, beaten stiff

Combine sugar, crackers, pecans, egg yolks, and vanilla. Blend well
and fold in egg whites. Butter a 9-inch pie plate and pour mixture
into middle of pan. Do not try to spread it. Bake 25 minutes in a
preheated 350° oven.

Variation:

Cover with 1 pint strawberries, hulled and sweetened. Border with
whipped cream.

Interlude for Two
Celebration Dinner

Lobster Salad Asta
Steak in a Paper Bag
Noodles Polonaise   Italian Zucchini
Zabaglione   Sponge Cake
Coffee   Tea   Milk

Suggested wine: Beaujolais (Fleurie)

ADVANCE PREPARATION SCHEDULE

Deep Freeze	Previous Day	Early Morning
Cake	*Cook lobster*	*Potatoes*
		Prepare steak for baking
		Crisp greens
		Zabaglione

LOBSTER SALAD ASTA

1 whole fresh lobster *or*   1 cup cantaloupe balls
1 8-ounce package frozen   Boston lettuce
           Curly endive

Cut fresh lobster into bite-size pieces, or separate frozen lobster from bones and fiber. Combine with melon balls and toss with Asta Dressing; garnish with chopped parsley. Serve on a bed of Boston lettuce and curly endive.

Asta Dressing:

2 tablespoons mayonnaise   2 teaspoons catsup
2 tablespoons dairy sour cream   ½ teaspoon brandy
⅛ teaspoon paprika   ½ teaspoon white wine
⅛ teaspoon freshly ground pepper   ½ teaspoon prepared horseradish
¼ teaspoon salt   Parsley, chopped

Combine all ingredients and chill thoroughly. Excellent with other seafoods.

STEAK IN A PAPER BAG

1 2½-inch-thick sirloin strip *or*   2 teaspoons freshly ground
   boneless rib of eye steak   pepper
1 tablespoon salad oil   1 clove garlic, split
1 teaspoon salt   ½ to 1 cup coarse bread crumbs

Brush steak with oil; rub well with salt, pepper, and garlic. Press bread crumbs onto steak to form thick coating. Place in brown paper bag; close with skewer or string. For rare steak, roast 35 minutes in a preheated 375° oven.

NOODLES POLONAISE

4 ounces noodles, cooked

Keep noodles heated in sieve or colander over hot water. To serve, turn onto platter or bowl and spread with Polonaise Sauce. Serve very hot.

Polonaise Sauce:

2 tablespoons butter   2 tablespoons dried bread crumbs

Heat butter in small skillet; add bread crumbs and sauté slowly until golden brown.

ITALIAN ZUCCHINI

1 tablespoon butter
3 small zucchini squash, thin-sliced with skin
½ onion, diced
½ green pepper, diced

1 teaspoon salt
Dash freshly ground pepper
2 fresh tomatoes, peeled and diced

Heat butter in skillet; add zucchini, onion, and green pepper; sauté for 5 minutes. Add salt, pepper, and tomatoes; simmer for 15 minutes.

ZABAGLIONE

3 egg yolks
3 teaspoons sugar

3 tablespoons light corn syrup
3 tablespoons red wine

Combine egg yolks, sugar, corn syrup, and red wine in top (preferably with a rounded bottom) of double boiler. Place over slowly boiling water. Cook, beating constantly but gently with a rotary beater, until mixture is light and holds its shape, about 3 minutes. Serve warm or chilled.

Variation:

Orange juice, rum, or other wine may be used in place of red wine.

SPONGE CAKE

1½ cups sifted cake flour
½ cup sugar
¼ teaspoon salt
1 teaspoon cream of tartar

5 eggs, separated
¾ cup light corn syrup
½ teaspoon vanilla extract
½ teaspoon lemon extract

Combine flour, ¼ cup of the sugar, and salt; sift together twice. Add cream of tartar to egg whites; beat until soft mounds are formed. Gradually beat in remaining ¼ cup sugar. Add corn syrup slowly to egg white mixture; continue beating until firm peaks are formed. Beat egg yolks until thick and lemon colored; add vanilla and lemon extracts. Fold egg yolks into egg white mixture. Sift in the dry ingredients, ¼ cup at a time; fold in gently.

Pour batter into ungreased 15½" x 10½" x 1" jelly roll pan. Cut through batter with spatula to remove air bubbles. Bake in a preheated 325° oven for 30 to 35 minutes, or until cake springs back when touched lightly with finger. Invert pan; let cake hang in pan about 20 minutes, or until just slightly warm. Elevate by setting corners on upside down custard cups. Remove cake from pan and cut as desired.

Note: Use ½ and freeze remainder. Keeps very well. Cake may also be baked in an ungreased 10-inch spring form in 325° oven for about 50 minutes, or in a 13" x 9" x 2" oblong pan for about 45 minutes, or in two 9" x 2" round layer pans at 325° for about 35 minutes.

The World
Around Us

THE CHALLENGE of cooking is met by learning and doing.

Cooking, like other talents, is inherent in some, cultivated in others. Happily we may combine enjoyment and the art of cooking.

Symphony Luncheon

(SERVES 6)

Crisp Salad — Herb French Dressing

Brie Cheese   Salted Nuts

Sweetbreads Grand Vefour   Hot Frosted Asparagus

Icebox Rolls

Strawberries Jamaica   Pecan Sandwich Cookies

Coffee

Suggested wine: Muscadet or other light white wine

ADVANCE PREPARATION SCHEDULE

Deep Freeze	Previous Day	Early Morning
Rolls in freezer	*Cook sweetbreads*	*Prepare rolls for baking*
	Rolls	*(if not in deep freeze)*
	Cookies	*Prepare asparagus*
	French Dressing	*Strawberries (see*
		recipe)

CRISP SALAD

1 stalk celeriac, sliced thin	1 3-ounce jar button mushrooms,
4 tomatoes, sliced in thirds	drained
2 green peppers, 6 slices	1 tablespoon chopped green
each	onions

Make a bed of the celeriac and place alternate slices of tomatoes and green peppers on it; center with mushrooms, sprinkle with onion. Serve with Herb French Dressing.

Note: Brie Cheese and crisp salad is a Continental favorite which Americans share.

Herb French Dressing:

3 green onions, chopped	½ teaspoon basil
1 stalk celery, chopped	1⅓ cups oil
⅓ cup chopped parsley	⅔ cup tarragon vinegar
1 teaspoon salt	Pinch rosemary
½ teaspoon pepper	Pinch marjoram

Reserve 1 tablespoon of chopped green of onion for garnish. Combine all ingredients; shake well and chill.

SWEETBREADS GRAND VEFOUR

3 pair medium-size sweetbreads	1 tablespoon peanut oil
5 tablespoons flour	¾ cup bread crumbs
1 egg	½ cup (¼ pound) butter

To cook sweetbreads: see Index.

Blanch and drain sweetbreads; divide each in 2; cover with damp cloth and place under a weight for 1 hour to flatten them. Roll sweetbreads in flour, dip in egg mixture beaten with oil, then in bread crumbs. Heat butter in frying pan; cook sweetbreads over

low flame for 10 minutes, until evenly browned. Serve with Grand
Vefour Sauce.

Worthy of its originator.

Grand Vefour Sauce:

1 tablespoon butter	½ medium onion, chopped fine
1 cup milk, slightly salted	1 tablespoon cream
2 tablespoons flour	1 teaspoon salt
2 tablespoons butter	⅛ teaspoon pepper
⅔ pound mushrooms, chopped fine	½ teaspoon Worcestershire

Heat 1 tablespoon butter in saucepan; bring milk to a boil, add
flour and milk to butter, stirring briskly until mixture boils again.
Melt 2 tablespoons butter in saucepan; sauté mushrooms and onion
until onions are softened. Cook over medium heat until liquid is
evaporated. Add this mixture to the sauce and stir thoroughly. Remove from heat; blend in cream, salt, pepper, and Worcestershire.
Reheat and serve over sweetbreads.

HOT FROSTED ASPARAGUS

2 large bunches asparagus   1 egg white
1 cup mayonnaise

Cook asparagus and drain. Beat egg white until fluffy; fold in
mayonnaise. Frost (spread) hot well-drained asparagus by covering
completely with egg white mixture and place under preheated
broiler until tinted a light brown.

ICEBOX ROLLS

½ cup sugar	2 cakes compressed yeast *or*
1 tablespoon salt	2 packages dry yeast
2 tablespoons butter *or* margarine	¼ cup warm water
	1 teaspoon sugar
2 cups boiling water	2 eggs, beaten
8 cups all-purpose flour, sifted before measuring	

Dissolve sugar, salt, and shortening in boiling water; cool to lukewarm. Stir dry yeast into warm water with sugar.

Note: Use lukewarm water for compressed yeast, warm water
for dry yeast. Add first mixture to yeast mixture, then add beaten

eggs and 2 cups flour. Beat well. Add remaining flour, mix well, cover and place in refrigerator for at least 2 hours, or until needed. Shape into rolls 3 hours before baking. Cover and set in a warm place until double in bulk (about 2 hours). Bake in a preheated 425° oven for 15 minutes.

To shape rolls: Always roll dough on lightly floured surface.

For your random choice.

Cloverleaf Rolls: Make 3 small balls for each roll and place in greased muffin tins. Cups should be about ½ full.

Bowknots: Roll dough to 18″ x 10″ rectangle. Cut strips 10 inches long, ¾ inch wide. Roll strips tightly with fingers, being careful not to stretch length of strips. Tie as for a knot.

Parker House: Roll dough about ¼ inch thick and cut with 2½-inch cutter. Make a crease just off center with dull side of silver knife. Fold larger side over small side and overlap; seal edges.

Round Buns: Roll and shape to any desired size. Brush tops with melted butter or slightly beaten egg yolk for smooth brown finish. Place on greased baking sheet. Makes about 4 dozen.

STRAWBERRIES JAMAICA

1 quart strawberries	1½ ounces rum
1 cup orange juice	1 tablespoon chopped fresh mint

Wash strawberries and drain. Combine orange juice and rum; pour over berries and sprinkle with mint. Cover and let stand in refrigerator for 1 to 2 hours (no more), shaking the bowl occasionally to distribute the rum. Do not mix with a spoon, to avoid bruising berries. Serve with a garnish of mint.

PECAN SANDWICH COOKIES

1½ cups (¾ pound) butter	3 cups sifted all-purpose flour
¾ cup sugar	1½ cups finely ground pecans
1 teaspoon vanilla	

Cream butter and sugar; add flour, nuts and vanilla. Mix together and knead until pliable. Roll out ¼ inch thick and cut with a small round cooky cutter. Bake in a preheated 350° oven until light brown, about 20 minutes.

Filling:

⅓ cup water	⅞ cup unsalted butter, softened
1 cup sugar	½ cup ground pecans
3 egg whites, stiffly beaten	Pecan halves

Cook water and sugar until it forms a thread when dropped from a spoon. Pour sugar syrup very slowly into beaten egg whites beating constantly. When partially stiff, beat in butter, small portions at a time. Spread between 2 cookies and on the edges. Roll edges in ground pecans; top each with a dab of filling and half a pecan.

Luncheon for Neighbors

(SERVES 6)

Rocky Tomato Juice

Asparagus Egg Curry   Spiced Purple Plum Mold

Crusty Rolls   Lime Marmalade

Macaroon Sherry Bavarian

Coffee

Suggested wine: Pouilly Fuissé or a white Burgundy

ADVANCE PREPARATION SCHEDULE

Previous Day	**Early Morning**
Plum Mold	*Curry sauce*
Tomato cubes	
Macaroon Bavarian	
(without garnish)	
Hard-cook eggs	

ROCKY TOMATO JUICE

1 1-quart jar tomato juice	1 teaspoon celery salt
1 tablespoon lemon juice	⅛ teaspoon basil
Dash Tabasco (optional)	

Combine tomato juice with seasonings. Pour 2 cups into freezer tray. To serve, place 3 frozen cubes in each 6- to 8-ounce glass, fill with unfrozen juice poured over cubes. Add a dash of Tabasco.

ASPARAGUS EGG CURRY

⅓ cup minced scallions *or* onion
¼ cup (⅛ pound) butter
3 tablespoons flour
1 tablespoon curry powder
2½ cups milk
1 teaspoon salt

¼ teaspoon coarse pepper
8 hard-cooked eggs
4 10-ounce packages frozen asparagus spears *or*
3 pounds fresh

Sauté scallions in butter until golden. Remove from heat and blend flour and curry powder to make a smooth paste. Add to onion, reheat, and gradually add milk, stirring until thickened. Season with salt and pepper; add more if needed. Peel and slice hard-cooked eggs and add to the sauce. Cook frozen asparagus spears according to package directions, or use 3 pounds fresh asparagus (see Index) when in season. Drain well and arrange on a deep platter. Serve curried eggs over asparagus.

SPICED PURPLE PLUM MOLD

1 #2½ can Italian blue plums
1¾ cups plum juice plus water
1 3-ounce package cherry-flavored gelatin
¼ teaspoon cinnamon

⅛ teaspoon ground cloves
⅛ teaspoon nutmeg
1 #2 can Queen Anne cherries, drained (optional)

Drain plum juice and add sufficient water to make 1¾ cups liquid. Heat 1 cup to boiling point, add gelatin, and dissolve; then add remaining liquid. Refrigerate until of jelly-like consistency. Pit plums and purée in food mill or through sieve. Add puréed plums and seasonings and pour into 6 individual molds. May be served as salad or as meat accompaniment. Serve on greens garnished with cherries.

Note: Very tangy; use interesting molds.

MACAROON SHERRY BAVARIAN

20 to 24 almond macaroons
1 cup sherry (cream sherry
    preferred)
2 tablespoons unflavored gelatin
1 cup cold water

2 cups hot milk
5 eggs, separated
1 cup sugar
1 4-ounce bottle maraschino
    cherries, halved

Soak macaroons in sherry. Add gelatin to cold water and soak for
5 minutes; add hot milk and stir until dissolved. Combine egg yolks
with sugar and beat until light. Mix with gelatin mixture; place
in top of double boiler and cook slowly until thick and smooth,
stirring constantly. Overcooking will tend to curdle mixture. Cool
before folding in stiffly beaten egg whites. Line a 1-quart oiled
mold with macaroons, interspersing cherries to form an attractive
pattern. Pour in mixture and chill until firm. Unmold on platter;
garnish with a border of whipped cream and cherries.

Summer Artists' Luncheon

(SERVES 4)

Summer Fruit Soup   Sesame Crackers
Southern Crab Cakes — Lobster Sauce   Sally Lunn
French Endive Salad — Anchovy Dressing
Macaroons Porcupine   Beverage

Suggested wine: Vouvray or a white Burgundy

ADVANCE PREPARATION SCHEDULE

Previous Day

Crab Cakes
Anchovy Dressing

Early Morning

Fruit soup
Crisp vegetables

SUMMER FRUIT SOUP

2 cantaloupes	1 tablespoon cornstarch
2 oranges	1 teaspoon grated orange rind
3 cups fresh red raspberries	¾ cup orange juice
5 tablespoons sugar	¼ cup fresh lemon juice

Cut cantaloupes in halves; remove seeds. Cut out balls using melon ball cutter, first making an even row around upper edge of melon halves to "scallop" the shell. Pare and section oranges; arrange sections and cantaloupe balls in cantaloupe shells and chill. Purée raspberries in blender and strain or press through a sieve to remove seeds; add sugar. Blend small amount of purée with cornstarch. Add remaining purée; cook and stir until mixture comes to a boil and is thickened. Add orange rind, orange juice, and lemon juice; chill. To serve, pour raspberry sauce over fruit in cantaloupe shells. Garnish with fresh mint sprigs if desired. Makes 4 servings.

SOUTHERN CRAB CAKES

3 cups cooked crabmeat	1 tablespoon mayonnaise
1½ teaspoons salt	2 teaspoons snipped parsley
⅛ teaspoon pepper	Flour
1 teaspoon dry mustard	1 egg, slightly beaten
2 teaspoons Worcestershire sauce	2 tablespoons water
	Dried bread crumbs
1 egg yolk	Butter or shortening

Mix together crabmeat, salt, mustard, pepper, Worcestershire, egg yolk, mayonnaise, and parsley. Press mixture firmly into 8 small cakes. Refrigerate. Just before serving, dip cakes in flour, then in egg combined with water, then into crumbs. Melt butter in skillet. Sauté cakes quickly over high heat until golden brown.

LOBSTER SAUCE

1 6½-ounce can lobster meat	1 egg yolk, beaten
4 tablespoons butter	1 tablespoon milk
2 tablespoons flour	½ teaspoon salt
1 cup chicken broth	⅛ teaspoon paprika
1 cup half and half cream	2 tablespoons sherry

Drain lobster and cut in medium-size pieces. Melt 2 tablespoons butter in skillet, add lobster; set aside to keep warm. Place 2 table-spoons butter in a 2-quart saucepan; heat, add flour, and cook until smooth. Stir in chicken broth; add cream. Cook until mixture is thickened. Remove from heat. Blend egg yolk with milk and stir slowly into sauce. Add salt, paprika, sherry, and the heated lobster. Serve hot over Crab Cakes.

SALLY LUNN

¼ cup warm water	1 teaspoon salt
1 package dry yeast	1 egg
¾ cup lukewarm milk	¼ cup (⅛ pound) butter
1½ tablespoons sugar	2¾ cups flour

Pour water into mixing bowl of electric beater or large mixing bowl. Add yeast and stir until dissolved. Add milk, sugar, salt, whole egg, butter, and flour. Beat 2 minutes with electric beater. Dough will spiral to top of beaters; do not be concerned, as it re-moves easily. (If beaten by hand, use a wooden spoon for 5 min-utes. Beating is the secret of Sally Lunn.) Cover and let rise in warm spot, free from drafts, for about 1¼ to 1½ hours. Sponge should be very light to the touch. Beat down with a spoon; pour into greased 9-inch tube pan. Let rise again for 1¼ to 1½ hours. Dough should rise to within an inch of the top. Bake in a pre-heated 350° oven 45 to 50 minutes, or until lightly browned. Serve hot with butter and preserves. May be baked in 4-inch muffin tins. Allow to remain in oven 30 minutes.

FRENCH ENDIVE SALAD

4 stalks French endive   2 heads Bibb lettuce
2 tablespoons chopped pimiento

Cut each endive in 3 sections and place on bed of Bibb lettuce. Sprinkle with pimiento; serve Anchovy Dressing separately.

ANCHOVY DRESSING

1 small garlic clove, minced
1 small onion, minced
¼ teaspoon each of dried basil, thyme, and oregano
1 small can flat anchovy fillets and anchovy oil

1 teaspoon Worcestershire sauce
1 tablespoon catsup
⅓ cup wine vinegar
⅔ cup imported olive oil
Black pepper to taste

In the bottom of a wooden bowl, place garlic and onion. Add herbs, anchovies and their oil. Mash to a pulp with a wooden spoon or potato masher, or mix in a mortar with pestle. Add seasonings and olive oil. Beat with a fork to mix. The dressing should be thick, and needs to be mixed well before each portion is ladled out. Store in refrigerator. Makes 1 cup.

MACAROONS PORCUPINE

2½ dozen macaroons
6 eggs, separated
1 cup sugar
1½ teaspoons flour

Pinch salt
8 ounces sherry
6 tablespoons sugar
20 blanched almonds

Line buttered serving casserole with macaroons. Beat egg yolks thoroughly until lemon colored and thick; place in top of double boiler. Add 1 cup sugar, flour, and salt to sherry; mix until smooth. Place over hot water and cook, stirring, until thick. Beat egg whites until very stiff and fold in 6 tablespoons sugar. Blend with custard and pour over macaroons. Arrange almonds, point upright, in regular design over surface of pudding. Place under broiler until slightly browned. Delicious hot; and an equally good cold leftover. (Makes 10 servings.)

Fashion Show Luncheon

(SERVES 8)

Salmon Ring Mold

Egg and Tomato Garni   Thousand Island Dressing

Ham and Chutney Canapés   Persimmon Caviar

Pâté Chicken Almond

Melba Toast   Sesame Crackers

Quick Coffee Cake   Cherry Kuchen

Coffee

Suggested wine: Rosé

ADVANCE PREPARATION SCHEDULE

Deep Freeze	Previous Day	Early Morning
Coffee Cake	*Salmon Mold*	*Cherry Kuchen*
	Dressing	*Canapés*
	Ham and Chutney	*Clean persimmons*
	Chicken Pâté	
	Lorenzo Dressing	

SALMON RING MOLD

1 10½-ounce can tomato soup	1 cup diced celery
1 3-ounce package cream cheese, softened	1 cup mayonnaise
2 envelopes (2 tablespoons) unflavored gelatin	1 green pepper, diced
	1 onion, grated
½ cup cold water	1 tablespoon Worcestershire
1 1-pound can salmon	½ teaspoon salt
	⅛ teaspoon pepper

Garni:

Leaf lettuce	3 tomatoes, quartered
4 hard-cooked eggs, sliced *or* quartered	Lemon slices
	Paprika

Heat soup in double boiler; add cream cheese and stir until dissolved. Soften gelatin in water, add soup mixture, and stir until dissolved. Combine with all other ingredients, including salt and pepper. Pour into an oiled 6-cup ring mold; refrigerate for at least 3 hours, or until firm. Unmold on a flat lettuce-lined platter. Garnish with sliced or quartered hard-cooked eggs, tomato wedges, and lemon slices. Dust eggs with paprika. Serve with bowl of Thousand Island Dressing in center of mold.

THOUSAND ISLAND DRESSING

1 cup mayonnaise
¼ cup chili sauce
¼ cup dairy sour cream
2 tablespoons catsup
2 tablespoons lemon juice
1 hard-cooked egg, grated *or* minced
2 tablespoons finely minced pimiento
2 tablespoons finely minced green pepper
2 tablespoons finely minced celery
2 tablespoons finely minced green onion
2 tablespoons finely minced cucumber
1 tablespoon chopped parsley
1 teaspoon salt
¾ teaspoon sugar
½ teaspoon paprika
¼ teaspoon freshly ground pepper

Mix ingredients thoroughly and let stand several hours before using. Stir or shake before serving.

HAM AND CHUTNEY CANAPES

1 cup ground ham (corned beef may be substituted)
½ cup chutney
½ teaspoon prepared horseradish
1 teaspoon olive oil
20 rounds of white bread
6 strips of bacon, cut in squares

Grind ham and chutney together; add horseradish and enough oil to moisten and bind. Pile high on rounds of white bread (toasted on one side). Top with a little square of bacon, and broil. Makes 20 canapés.

PATE OF CHICKEN ALMOND

2 cups minced cooked chicken
¼ cup butter
3 tablespoons sherry
¼ cup minced onion *or* 1 small clove garlic, minced
1 teaspoon lemon juice
Dash Tabasco
¼ cup slivered, toasted almonds

Blend chicken with butter; add remaining ingredients except for almonds. Mix well; place pâté in small bowl and let stand to blend flavors. Unmold to serve and sprinkle with almonds. Makes approximately 2 cups.

PERSIMMON CAVIAR

4 persimmons, halved   1 2-ounce can caviar
Sprigs watercress

Open persimmons in center; scoop out a small amount, enough to insert a spoonful of caviar. Add a sprig of watercress. Garnish platter with ring of watercress and serve with Lorenzo Dressing.

Lorenzo Dressing:

⅔ cup olive oil   ¼ teaspoon Worcestershire
⅓ cup white vinegar   Dash paprika
1 teaspoon salt   ½ cup chili sauce
¼ cup chopped watercress

Combine all ingredients, mix well. To keep watercress crisp, wash carefully, shake dry, and refrigerate until just before preparing or serving. Especially helpful when used as a garnish.

QUICK COFFEE CAKE

½ pint dairy sour cream   ¼ pound pecans, chopped
2 cups all-purpose flour   1 cup white raisins
½ cup (¼ pound) butter   Powdered sugar
1 10-ounce jar sweet
orange marmalade

Cream together sour cream, flour, and butter; refrigerate for ½ hour. Cut dough into 4 equal parts. Roll out in oblong pieces and fill with layers of marmalade, nuts, and raisins. Fold each oblong in half and place on greased baking sheet. Bake in a preheated 350° to 375° oven 40 minutes, or until golden brown. Cut into 2-inch strips while hot. Sprinkle with powdered sugar.

CHERRY KUCHEN

Dough:

½ cup (¼ pound) butter,   1 cup all-purpose flour, unsifted
softened   1 egg yolk
¼ teaspoon sugar

Cut butter into flour with 2 knives or pastry blender, until consistency of coarse cornmeal. Add egg yolks and sugar; blend until dough forms a soft ball. Press with fingertips into a 7" x 11" baking pan. Cover with custard.

Custard:

3 eggs	1 teaspoon vanilla
1 cup sugar	1 #2 can cherries, drained
Confectioners' sugar	

Beat eggs, sugar, and vanilla together; gently blend in cherries. Pour into dough-lined pan. Bake in a preheated 325° oven 1 hour, or until custard is set and firm. Sprinkle with confectioners' sugar. To serve, cut in squares.

The Hostess Cooks Dinner

(SERVES 6)

Salmon Trout Chaudfroid

Sesame Rye Crackers

Cucumber Sandwiches

Potted Squab   Cauliflower Salad

Cinnamon Rolls

Chocolate Soufflé — Mint Marshmallow Sauce

Coffee   Tea

ADVANCE PREPARATION SCHEDULE

Deep Freeze	Previous Day	Early Morning
Rolls	Boil trout	Squab for roasting
		Cauliflower Salad
		Chaudfroid sauce
		Glaze trout
		Mint Sauce
		Cucumber Sandwiches
		(see Index)

SALMON TROUT CHAUDFROID

2 quarts water, *or* enough to cover fish
2 medium onions
2 carrots
1 stalk dill
½ cup vinegar
6 whole peppercorns

1 teaspoon thyme
2 tablespoons salt
1 6-pound salmon trout, whole, wrapped in cheesecloth
Radishes *or* carrots (for decoration)
Watercress

Court Bouillon for fish:

Combine water, onions, carrots, dill, vinegar, and seasonings in a large saucepan; boil for 10 minutes.

Place the whole trout on a sheet of foil as large as the fish and then wrap in cheesecloth; leave ends long enough for handles. Lower into the court bouillon. Simmer very gently for about 45 minutes. Remove the trout, using ends of cheesecloth to raise it, and unwrap; slip it off with foil, lay upright on a rack to cool. Place rack over a pan (to catch Chaudfroid Sauce drippings). Prepare Chaudfroid Sauce; pour over fish. It may be necessary to coat fish 3 or 4 times so that it is well covered. (Use sauce which drips into pan if needed.) If sauce sets before it is used, stir over hot water until of correct texture. This amount will cover one large fish. To trim, reserve a small amount of sauce for last coating; when coating has set to your satisfaction, decorate fish with petals of radishes or carrots, and watercress leaves. Pour over reserved sauce to hold in place. (Spear with toothpicks until set.) Remove fish with foil to platter; garnish with watercress sprigs and cucumber sandwiches.

This recipe is larger than needed for the menu. Use leftovers for luncheon next day. A fine substitution for the whole trout is the Seafood Mold Chaudfroid (see Index), which may be made with the Chaudfroid Sauce recipe.

Chaudfroid Sauce:

¼ cup (⅛ pound) butter
¼ cup flour
2 cups warm milk
1 teaspoon salt

2 drops yellow coloring
¾ cup cold water
3 envelopes (3 tablespoons) unflavored gelatin
¼ cup mayonnaise

Melt butter in saucepan; blend in flour; cook until bubbly. Stir in milk slowly to avoid lumps, then add salt and coloring. Soak gelatin in cold water until softened and add to sauce. Combine with mayonnaise very slowly. Let stand in cool place until consistency of heavy cream.

POTTED SQUAB

6 squabs
1 teaspoon salt
¼ teaspoon black pepper
½ cup (¼ pound) melted butter or margarine
2 medium onions, quartered

1 cup white wine
¼ cup tomato paste
1½ cups green peas, fresh or frozen
1 #2 can small potatoes, drained

Clean squabs; wipe with damp cloth. Sprinkle with salt and pepper. Pour butter into casserole; arrange birds; add onions and wine. Bake uncovered in a preheated 425° oven 15 minutes. Cover, reduce heat to 350°, bake 45 minutes longer. Baste frequently. Add tomato paste, peas, and potatoes for last 10 minutes of baking. Arrange on platter with vegetables. Garnish each squab with a crisp sprig of parsley (optional).

CAULIFLOWER SALAD

1 small head cauliflower
½ teaspoon sugar
½ teaspoon salt
⅛ teaspoon pepper
2 teaspoons grated lemon peel
2 tablespoons lemon juice
2 tablespoons minced onion
¼ cup olive oil

1 clove garlic
1 small head lettuce
½ green pepper, cut in strips
½ cup sliced green olives
½ pimiento, cut in strips
4 hard-cooked eggs, quartered
Freshly ground black pepper
2 or 3 tablespoons olive oil

Cook cauliflower in boiling salted water until just tender-crisp. Do not overcook. Drain, cool, and separate into flowerets. Combine sugar, salt, pepper, lemon peel, lemon juice, onion, and the ¼ cup olive oil, blending well. Pour this marinade over cauliflower; let set for 30 minutes or longer. Drain; reserve the marinade, adding 2 or 3 tablespoons olive oil and garlic. Tear lettuce into bowl; add marinated cauliflower, green pepper, green olives, pimiento, and eggs. Remove garlic clove and pour marinade over salad. Toss lightly. Add freshly ground pepper. Serve in lettuce cups for individual salads, or let the host take over the salad bowl.

CINNAMON ROLLS

1 cup (½ pound) butter *or* margarine, melted	¼ cup warm water
	1 tablespoon sugar
1 cup dairy sour cream	4 cups all-purpose flour
2 eggs, well beaten	¾ cup sugar
1 package dry yeast	½ teaspoon salt

Combine butter, sour cream, and eggs. Dissolve yeast in warm water and add 1 tablespoon sugar. Sift flour, ¾ cup sugar, and salt together; add to butter mixture. Then add yeast and stir briskly until batter comes away from sides. Place in refrigerator for at least 6 hours. Divide in 4 parts (¼ makes 12 rolls). Roll each part in 8-inch circles; cut each circle into 12 wedges, roll each by starting at wide end. Brush with melted butter, sprinkle with Topping. Place on greased baking sheet, brush with beaten egg yolk. Let rise at room temperature, covered and away from drafts, 1½ to 2 hours, or until double in bulk. Bake in a preheated 400° oven about 15 minutes. Repeat with each of the four portions.

Topping:

½ teaspoon cinnamon	½ cup chopped nuts *and/or*
½ cup sugar	½ cup raisins
1 egg yolk, beaten	

Combine all ingredients; blend well.

CHOCOLATE SOUFFLE

4 1-ounce squares unsweetened chocolate	4 eggs, separated
	1 cup sugar
1¾ cups evaporated milk	1 teaspoon vanilla

Add chocolate to milk in top of double boiler. When melted, beat until smooth and cool. Beat yolks until lemon colored; gradually add sugar, beaten chocolate milk mixture, and vanilla. Beat whites until stiff but not dry; fold into chocolate and egg yolk mixture. Turn into greased casserole, place in pan of hot water, and bake in a preheated 350° oven 50 to 60 minutes. Serve at once with Mint Marshmallow Sauce.

The soufflé may be popped into the oven just as dinner is served and should be fluffed and piping hot on schedule. If this proves too much of a problem for the hostess-cook, a Bavarian dessert or mousse, which may be prepared the day before, is suggested. Make selection from Index.

Mint Marshmallow Sauce:

1 cup prepared marshmallow sauce	½ teaspoon mint flavoring
¼ cup half and half cream, *or* milk	4 drops green food coloring

Thin marshmallow sauce with cream; blend with mint flavoring and green food coloring.

Canasta Luncheon

(SERVES 8)

Decanter of May Wine
Baked Shrimp Casserole   Deviled Breadsticks
Tossed Green Salad — French Dressing Varié
Apple Kuchen

ADVANCE PREPARATION SCHEDULE

Deep Freeze	Previous Day	Early Morning
Kuchen	*Dressing*	*Shrimp casserole*
	Breadsticks	*Cook egg*
		Crisp greens

BAKED SHRIMP CASSEROLE

2 tablespoons butter	½ cup dry sherry
½ pound mushrooms, sliced	1 tablespoon Worcestershire
1 medium onion, minced	½ teaspoon paprika
2 fresh tomatoes, sliced	1 teaspoon salt
2 tablespoons flour	¼ teaspoon pepper
½ cup cream	1 tablespoon chopped parsley
1 8½-ounce can tomatoes	3 cups fluffy cooked rice

3 pounds shrimp, cooked and cleaned

Melt butter in a 12-inch frying pan; sauté mushrooms and onion. Add tomatoes and simmer for 10 minutes. Remove from heat, cool; blend in flour and cream. Add remaining ingredients and transfer to a 2-quart casserole. Bake in a preheated 350° oven 20 to 30 minutes.

DEVILED BREADSTICKS

¼ cup (⅛ pound) butter   ¾ teaspoon salt
2 small cloves garlic, crushed   1 4-ounce box extra-thin
3 tablespoons Worcestershire   Italian breadsticks

Melt butter in a saucepan; add garlic, Worcestershire, and salt. Place breadsticks in a single layer in an oblong baking pan and pour butter mixture over all, turning so that they are well coated. Bake in a preheated 250° oven 1 hour, turning occasionally, until sticks are crisp and dry. Drain on paper toweling. Makes 36 to 48 breadsticks.

TOSSED GREEN SALAD

2 cups Chinese cabbage, cut   3 hard-cooked eggs, sliced
  in ½-inch slices   ½ teaspoon dill seed
1 cup julienne-sliced beets   2 cups torn chicory

Place in a salad bowl, cover with dressing, and toss lightly.

FRENCH DRESSING VARIE

1 cup salad oil   ½ cup sugar
¼ cup tarragon vinegar   1 teaspoon salt
½ cup chili sauce   ¼ teaspoon paprika
½ cup lemon juice   1 egg
        1 teaspoon grated onion

Combine all ingredients and beat until smooth with an electric beater.

APPLE KUCHEN

1 cup all-purpose flour	1 tablespoon bread crumbs
½ teaspoon baking powder	5 cups sliced fruit
½ cup sugar	(apples, plums, peaches)
½ cup (¼ pound) butter	⅔ cup sugar
1 egg, beaten	1 teaspoon cinnamon
2 tablespoons milk	1 egg yolk

¼ cup dairy sour cream

Combine flour, baking powder, and ½ cup sugar. Cut in butter with pastry blender. Add beaten egg and milk and mix well. Spread in an 8-inch square pan, sprinkle with bread crumbs; cover with sliced fruit and sprinkle fruit with sugar and cinnamon. Beat egg yolk with sour cream and pour over fruit. Bake in a preheated 400° oven 35 to 40 minutes.

Sewing Club Brunch

(SERVES 4)

Senegalese Soup Cup   Rye Melba Rounds
Cocktail Sausage Eggs   Fruit Tea Bread
Lingonberries
Half-Pound Cake
Coffee

ADVANCE PREPARATION SCHEDULE

Deep Freeze	Previous Day	Early Morning
Half-Pound Cake	*Soup (without cream or chicken)*	*Sausages*

SENEGALESE SOUP CUP

¼ cup butter
2 onions, diced
1 large apple, cored, peeled, and chopped
1 tablespoon curry powder
2 tablespoons flour

1 teaspoon salt
1 quart chicken broth
1 cup half and half cream
1 cup coarsely chopped cooked chicken
¼ cup chopped parsley
Paprika

Melt butter in saucepan; add onions and apple, and sauté until soft but not brown. Add curry and cook slowly for 5 minutes. Blend flour and salt with enough chicken broth to make a paste and stir into onion mixture; add remaining broth and bring to a boil. Remove from heat and press through a fine sieve or whirl in blender. Cool and chill in refrigerator. To serve, add very cold cream and chicken. Blend carefully. Garnish with parsley and dust with paprika. Serve in small handled cups.

COCKTAIL SAUSAGE EGGS

¼ cup butter, melted (about)
½ cup sliced raw mushrooms
4 eggs
Seasoned salt
1 4-ounce jar cocktail sausages

1 teaspoon marjoram
¾ cup beer
½ cup catsup
2 tablespoons sherry
Few dashes Tabasco
1 tablespoon minced chives

Put 1 teaspoon melted butter in each of 4 custard cups. Add a few mushroom slices to each. Break 1 egg carefully into each cup, taking care to keep the yolk whole. Sprinkle with seasoned salt to taste. Spoon 1 teaspoon melted butter on each egg. Bake in a pre-heated 350° oven 15 minutes.

Meanwhile, sprinkle sausages with marjoram and simmer gently in the beer for 10 minutes. Combine catsup, sherry, and Tabasco in a small saucepan and heat just to boiling point. To serve, place a few sausages on top of each cooked egg; sprinkle with chives and serve hot sauce separately.

FRUIT TEA BREAD

⅓ cup shortening
⅔ cup sugar
2 eggs
⅓ cup chopped candied orange rind
¼ cup chopped citron
½ cup ground, uncooked, dried apricots

1¾ cups sifted all-purpose flour
1 teaspoon baking powder
½ teaspon baking soda
½ teaspoon salt
1 cup ripe mashed bananas
1 teaspoon vanilla
Whipped cream cheese

Cream shortening and sugar until light and fluffy. Add eggs and beat thoroughly. Stir in orange rind, citron, and apricots. Sift flour, baking powder, baking soda, and salt together. Combine bananas and vanilla; add to egg mixture alternately with dry ingredients, in thirds, mixing until smooth after each addition. Turn into greased loaf pan about 8½" x 4½" x 3". Set aside to rest for 20 minutes. Bake in a preheated 350° oven for 1 hour and 10 minutes. Serve with Whipped Cream Cheese.

Whipped Cream Cheese is available at most markets, or whip 1 3-ounce package of softened cream cheese with 1 tablespoon dairy sour cream.

LINGONBERRIES

Lingonberries are deliciously refreshing and are obtainable in 16-ounce jars. Serve them from a bowl or in individual compotes.

HALF-POUND CAKE

1 cup (½ pound) butter, softened
2 cups sugar
4 eggs, separated

3 cups all-purpose flour
1 tablespoon baking powder
1 cup milk
Grated rind of 1 lemon

Cream butter and sugar, add egg yolks, then flour, which has been sifted 3 times with baking powder. Add milk gradually, then lemon peel. Beat egg whites until stiff, and add. Bake in a greased angel food cake pan or fancy iron mold 1½ hours in a preheated 325° oven. Remove the cake from the oven and let it stand for 10 minutes, then invert it on a rack. If an angel food pan is used.

invert it over the neck of a soft drink bottle. Sprinkle top with confectioners' sugar before serving.

Note: This is an all-purpose cake; cut it into 4 sections, wrap and freeze separately — to be served with a cup of afternoon coffee, or toasted when it is slightly stale.

Luncheon for Art's Sake

(SERVES 6)

Jellied Consommé Madrilène
Braised Sweetbreads Piquant
Oriental Garden Celery
Dutch Poppy-Seed Loaf — Whipped Butter
Tinted Cloud Blintzes   Sunkissed Strawberry Preserves

or

Blintz Soufflé — Blueberry Sauce
Coffee

Suggested wine: Rosé

ADVANCE PREPARATION SCHEDULE

Deep Freeze	Previous Day	Early Morning
Poppy-Seed Loaf	*Consommé*	*Assemble blintzes*
	Curry mayonnaise	
	Sweetbreads	
	Preserves	

JELLIED CONSOMME MADRILENE

½ cup cold water
2 envelopes (2 tablespoons) unflavored gelatin
1 cup chicken broth *or* 2 chicken bouillon cubes, 1 cup water

3 cups tomato juice
½ cup chopped green pepper
1 teaspoon sugar
2 teaspoons lemon juice
1 teaspoon Angostura bitters
Lemon slices

Pour water into a small bowl. Sprinkle gelatin evenly over water. Let stand about 5 minutes to soften. Blend together in saucepan the broth (or bouillon cubes dissolved in water), tomato juice, green pepper, and sugar. Cover and simmer 6 to 8 minutes until green pepper is tender. Strain. Add the lemon juice, bitters, and softened gelatin to the hot broth. Stir until gelatin is completely dissolved. Pour into a bowl and cool. Cover and refrigerate until firm, about 5 hours. Just before serving, break mixture lightly with fork. Garnish each serving with lemon slices and a teaspoon of Curry Mayonnaise.

Curry Mayonnaise:

1 cup mayonnaise	½ clove garlic, minced
1 teaspoon curry	(optional)
1 teaspoon lemon juice	Dash salt

Combine and mix well.

BRAISED SWEETBREADS PIQUANT

6 pair sweetbreads	¼ cup chopped onion
2 cups water	1 teaspoon salt
1 tablespoon lemon juice	⅓ cup melted butter
2 stalks celery	½ cup bread crumbs
1 sprig parsley	½ cup chili sauce

Wash sweetbreads and drain. Bring water to a boil and add sweetbreads, lemon juice, celery, parsley, onion, and salt. Simmer, covered, 20 minutes. Remove, drain, and while holding under cold water, slip off membranes and cut out dark veins and tissues. Split thick sweetbreads in half lengthwise. Dip cooked sweetbreads in butter, then coat thoroughly with crumbs. Place on baking pan and spread each piece with chili sauce. Place in a preheated 350° oven for 15 minutes. If not golden brown, place under broiler for 1 or 2 minutes.

Suggestion: To serve as appetizer, cut into 1½-inch pieces (will serve 12). To serve as main luncheon dish, mound Oriental Garden Celery around sweetbreads.

ORIENTAL GARDEN CELERY

2 large bunches celery
¼ cup butter, margarine, *or* oil
3 tablespoons soy sauce

1 teaspoon sugar
Grating of fresh ginger root
or dash ground ginger

Select tender inner stalks from celery. Wash thoroughly and dry on absorbent paper. Cut each stalk into diagonal slices ¼ inch thick. Heat butter, add celery, and sauté quickly over high heat 3 to 5 minutes, or until almost tender, stirring constantly. Add soy sauce, sugar, and ginger; heat thoroughly.

DUTCH POPPY-SEED LOAF

2 tablespoons shortening
¾ cup sugar
2 eggs
3 cups sifted all-purpose flour

3½ teaspoons baking powder
1 teaspoon salt
⅓ cup poppy seeds
1 teaspoon grated lemon grind

1⅓ cups milk

Beat shortening, sugar, and eggs with electric mixer until light and fluffy. Sift dry ingredients; combine with poppy seeds and lemon rind. Add to egg mixture, alternating with milk. Beat until smooth after each addition. Turn into a greased and floured 9″ x 5″ x 3″ pan and bake in a preheated 350° oven 1 hour and 15 minutes. Serve warm with cream cheese and jam. To reheat, wrap in foil and place in a preheated 350° oven for 20 minutes.

TINTED CLOUD BLINTZES

Batter:

2 eggs
2 tablespoons shortening, melted
½ cup milk

⅓ cup flour
½ cup water
⅛ teaspoon salt

Beat eggs until lemon colored; add shortening. Stir in milk alternately with flour, then blend in water (adding salt) and mix until smooth. Batter is very thin. Grease a 7-inch skillet and heat; pour in 3 tablespoons batter, tilting pan quickly to spread. Bake until lightly browned on both sides. Stack until ready to fill.

Filling:

2 egg yolks, beaten
1½ cups dry cottage cheese, sieved

6 tablespoons dairy sour cream
2 tablespoons sugar
1 tablespoon butter, melted

Combine yolks and cottage cheese; add sour cream, sugar, and butter. Mix until smooth and creamy.

Meringue:

3 egg whites	Dash salt
¼ teaspoon cream of tartar	⅓ cup sugar

Beat whites till frothy; add cream of tartar and salt. Then add sugar, gradually, and beat until shiny and stiff. To assemble, spread 1 tablespoon filling on each pancake; roll and place seam side down on greased cooky sheet. Repeat until all are filled. Place in a preheated 400° oven for about 10 minutes and spread each blintz with 1 tablespoon defrosted frozen strawberries, or Strawberry Preserves. Cover with meringue and return to oven for about 8 minutes until browned. Makes 18.

Variation:

For a special event, warm ¼ cup Curaçao slightly and pour over meringue; ignite and serve.

SUNKISSED STRAWBERRY PRESERVES

2 quarts strawberries   2 cups sugar
3½ cups sugar

Wash strawberries in cold water. Place in colander. Pour boiling water over berries, then hull. Place in saucepan, add 2 cups of sugar, boil slowly 10 minutes. Move berries by shaking pan but do not stir them; skim, add 3½ cups sugar. Simmer approximately 30 minutes, or until liquid thickens when dropped from spoon. Keep skimming. Pour on large platter; place in sun to absorb rays. Next day, pour into hot 4-ounce jars; seal with paraffin.

BLINTZ SOUFFLE

18 blintzes (see Index)	1 teaspoon salt
¼ cup (⅛ pound) butter, softened	2 tablespoons orange juice
	1 cup dairy sour cream
2 tablespoons sugar	1 teaspoon vanilla
3 egg yolks, beaten	3 egg whites, beaten stiff
Cinnamon and sugar	

Place blintzes in single layer in shallow greased baking pan.

Cream butter and sugar; combine with egg yolks, salt, and orange juice. Blend in sour cream and vanilla; fold in egg whites and pour over blintzes. Bake in a preheated 350° oven 1 hour. Serve immediately, with Blueberry Sauce, additional sour cream, or cinnamon and sugar.

Blueberry Sauce:

    2 10-ounce packages frozen,   1½ cups sugar
      unsweetened blueberries,
      defrosted

Combine blueberries with sugar; beat with rotary beater until sugar is dissolved.

Book Review Luncheon

(SERVES 4)

Crabmeat Tomato Roses — Thousand Island Dressing Civette
Mushrooms on Toast Points   Giant Popovers
Strawberry Bavarian Cream
Coffee

ADVANCE PREPARATION SCHEDULE

Previous Day

Thousand Island Dressing
Bavarian Cream

Early Morning

Tomatoes

CRABMEAT TOMATO ROSES

    4 large ripe tomatoes   1 ounce caviar
    2 6-ounce packages frozen crab-   ½ cup French Dressing
      meat, thawed and drained   (see Index)
                1 hard-cooked egg, chopped fine

Cut thin slice off top of each tomato. Remove pulp and seeds. Sprinkle inside of tomato shells with salt and turn upside down to drain. Flake crabmeat and combine with caviar; marinate with French Dressing. To serve, open tomato shells slightly by slitting them in 6 sections, ⅓ down from stem. Fill with mixture and sprinkle with chopped egg. Serve with Thousand Island Dressing Civette. The amount of dressing in these calorie-conscious days is a personal decision. We suggest that it be served separately.

THOUSAND ISLAND DRESSING CIVETTE

1⅓ cups mayonnaise	3 tablespoons catsup
¼ cup minced green pepper	1 tablespoon minced chives
¼ cup chili sauce	1 tablespoon tarragon vinegar
1 teaspoon paprika	

Blend mayonnaise thoroughly with green pepper, chili sauce, catsup, chives, vinegar, and paprika. Makes about 2 cups.

MUSHROOMS ON TOAST POINTS

1 pound large mushrooms	2 tablespoons butter
¼ teaspoon salt	⅔ cup half and half cream
⅛ teaspoon coarsely ground pepper	Toast points

Scrub mushrooms; remove stems (use stems minced for sandwiches in sauce); place cap side up in flat, well-greased baking dish. Add salt and pepper; dot with butter, pour cream over them, and bake in a preheated 400° oven 10 to 12 minutes. Serve on toast points.

GIANT POPOVERS

¼ teaspoon salt	2 eggs plus 1 egg white
1 cup all-purpose flour	1 cup milk

Preheat oven to 450° while making batter. Sift salt and flour into bowl. Beat eggs and add milk, then stir gradually into flour to make smooth batter. Beat with eggbeater until full of bubbles. Lightly grease six 4-inch individual ovenware custard dishes and preheat. Fill hot dishes half full and bake at 450° for 30 minutes; lower the oven to 350° and continue baking 10 minutes more. Serve piping hot with butter and jelly or preserves.

STRAWBERRY BAVARIAN CREAM

2 envelopes (2 tablespoons) unflavored gelatin	¼ teaspoon salt
¼ cup cold water	1½ teaspoons vanilla
2½ cups milk	8 almond macaroons
¾ cup sugar	1 cup heavy cream
	Fresh or frozen strawberries

Soak gelatin in water 5 minutes; scald milk, add sugar, salt, and blend in gelatin until dissolved. Cool; place in refrigerator until of jelly-like consistency and add vanilla. Beat with electric or rotary beater until thick and fluffy. Crumble macaroons and add. Whip cream until stiff and fold into mixture. Pour into greased 6-cup ring mold and refrigerate until firm. Unmold on serving platter; place strawberries in center and garnish outer edge with additional berries and mint leaves.

Cookies could be added. See the Index to help you decide.

Garden Walk Tea

(SERVES 12)

Cheese Chutney Canapés   Watercress Sandwiches

Limed Lobster

Chicken Salad Supreme   Frozen Salad — Raspberry Dressing

Small Hard Rolls

Spice Cupcakes   Danish Pastry Peterson

Coffee   Tea

ADVANCE PREPARATION SCHEDULE

Deep Freeze	Previous Day	Early Morning
Cupcakes	*Tomato Dressing*	*Watercress Sandwiches*
Frozen Salad	*Cook chicken*	*Chicken Salad*
Danish Pastry		*Chutney Canapés for broiling*
		Raspberry Dressing
		Limed Lobster

CHEESE CHUTNEY CANAPES

5 slices fresh bread
3 tablespoons chutney
1 3-ounce package cream cheese, softened

½ cup grated Herkimer cheese
1 egg white, beaten very stiff
⅛ teaspoon baking powder

Cut 3 small rounds from each slice of bread; toast rounds on one side. Place dab of chutney in center of each round, on untoasted side. Mix together cream cheese, Herkimer cheese, egg white, and baking powder; make a border around chutney with this mixture by spreading from tip of knife. Heat and brown under broiler just before serving.

WATERCRESS SANDWICHES

½ cup finely chopped watercress
1 3-ounce package cream cheese, softened
½ cup chopped pecans
½ teaspoon prepared horseradish

⅛ teaspoon salt
10 slices fresh bread
2 tablespoons mayonnaise
Paprika
Watercress leaves

Combine watercress, cheese, pecans, horseradish, and salt; blend well. Cut 3 small rounds from each slice of bread, or cut bread in strips for variety; toast on one side, spread other side with mayonnaise. Mound cheese spread on mayonnaise; dust with paprika and garnish with a watercress leaf.

LIMED LOBSTER

½ cup chopped celery
¼ cup chopped scallions (*or* green onions)
1 7-ounce can lobster
1 clove garlic (optional)
1 teaspoon salt
½ teaspoon sugar

½ teaspoon curry
¼ teaspoon each: black pepper, oregano, coriander
2 tablespoons olive oil
1½ tablespoons lime juice (*or* lemon juice)

Combine celery, scallions, and lobster. Salt lightly. Mash garlic to liquid and add salt, sugar, curry, pepper, oregano and coriander. Blend oil and lime juice. Let lobster marinate in sauce in refrigerator for several hours. Serve as dip on toast rounds or crackers.

Note: Crab may be substituted for lobster.

CHICKEN SALAD SUPREME

4 cups cubed cooked chicken
4 tablespoons chopped green
    olives
1½ cups chopped celery
1 cup toasted, chopped almonds
¼ cup chopped mixed sweet
    pickles

4 hard-cooked eggs, sliced
1½ cups mayonnaise
Leaf lettuce
Tomato wedges
¼ cup chopped ripe olives
Watercress

Combine chicken, olives, celery, almonds, pickles, eggs, and mayonnaise; toss lightly and chill. Serve on leaf lettuce, garnished with tomato wedges, ripe olives, and watercress. Tomato French Dressing may be sprinkled over or served separately. This recipe may be divided exactly in half to serve 6.

Tomato French Dressing:

1 tablespoon sugar
1 teaspoon salt
1 teaspoon dry mustard
1 teaspoon paprika
1 10½-ounce can condensed
    tomato soup

1 cup vinegar
1 tablespoon Worcestershire
1 cup salad oil
1 clove garlic, crushed
1 small onion, crushed

Combine ingredients in bottle or jar; cover and shake thoroughly. Makes 1 quart. Keeps very well — an "old reliable" standby.

FROZEN SALAD

2 3-ounce packages cream cheese,
    softened
1 cup mayonnaise
1 cup sugar
Dash salt and paprika
1 #2½ can sliced pineapple

1 4-ounce bottle maraschino
    cherries, cut fine
1 green pepper, chopped
1 cup chopped walnuts
1 cup heavy cream, whipped
Curly endive

Blend cheese with mayonnaise, sugar, salt and paprika. Cut half the pineapple into small pieces and fold into mayonnaise mixture; add cherries, green pepper, and walnuts. Fold in whipped cream. Pour into 6-cup lightly greased melon mold and place in freezer. To serve, unmold on platter on bed of curly endive. Cut remaining pineapple slices in half; use as garnish.

RASPBERRY DRESSING

½ cup frozen raspberries, thawed	3½ tablespoons white vinegar
¼ cup sugar	½ teaspoon dry mustard
	¼ teaspoon salt
¾ cup salad oil	

Sieve raspberries; add sugar and 1½ tablespoons vinegar. Let stand 1 hour. Mix together mustard, salt, remaining vinegar; blend well. Gradually add salad oil, beating until smooth and slightly thickened. Add raspberry mixture in thirds, beating after each addition. Makes about 1½ cups.

SPICE CUPCAKES

½ cup (¼ pound) butter, softened	1¾ cups sifted all-purpose flour
1 cup sugar	1 teaspoon soda
1 egg, beaten	½ teaspoon salt
1 cup apple butter	1½ teaspoons baking powder
1 teaspoon vanilla	2 tablespoons lemon juice
	⅔ cup evaporated milk

Cream butter in large mixing bowl; add sugar gradually and cream until mixture is light and fluffy. Add egg and mix well. Blend in apple butter and vanilla. Sift flour with soda, salt and baking powder. Stir lemon juice into evaporated milk. Add milk mixture alternately with dry ingredients to the egg mixture, beginning and ending with dry ingredients; mix only enough to blend. Spoon mixture into muffin pans which have been lined with paper baking cups. Bake in a preheated 350° oven 20 to 25 minutes. Remove from oven and cool on rack. Frost with Almond Butter Frosting. Makes 24 cupcakes.

Almond Butter Frosting:

¼ cup butter	2 tablespoons evaporated milk
2 cups confectioners' sugar, sifted	½ cup toasted, chopped almonds

Melt butter; heat slowly until bubbly. Remove from heat and stir in about a third of the sugar. Add evaporated milk and remaining sugar; beat until smooth and thoroughly blended. Stir in almonds. If too thick for easy spreading, add a few more drops evaporated milk.

DANISH PASTRY PETERSON
(Danska Wienerbrød)

1½ cakes compressed yeast	¼ cup sugar
1¼ cups lukewarm milk	3½ cups all-purpose flour
1 egg	1½ cups (¾ pound) butter

1 egg, slightly beaten (for glaze)

Dissolve yeast in milk; add 1 egg and sugar. Add about 1 cup flour gradually and beat with wooden spoon until smooth and glossy. Add remaining flour and knead until easy to handle. Roll out on well-floured board to a 14″ x 14″ square. Spread center third of dough with ⅓ of the butter. Fold over in 3 parts and roll out again. Do this 3 times. Let stand in a cool place about ½ hour, then roll and prepare in the desired shape as follows:

Envelopes: Roll dough out thin and cut in 4″ x 4″ squares. Spread with 1 tablespoon Filling. Fold corners in toward center and press down edges.

Combs: Roll dough out thin and cut in strips 5 inches wide. Cut triangles 3 inches wide at base. Place Filling in middle and fold both sides of length over to center. Turn onto pearl-sugar (fine grained) and chopped almonds. Cut in pieces 4 inches long and gash one folded side of each 5 times.

Crescents: Roll dough out thin and cut in strips 5 inches wide. Cut triangles 3 inches wide at base. Place Filling on base and roll up. Place pastries on buttered baking sheet and chill in refrigerator several hours or overnight to rise.

Remove from refrigerator, brush filled envelopes or crescents with slightly beaten egg. Bake in a preheated 450° oven until golden yellow. When cold, spread envelopes and crescents with icing made of 1 cup of confectioners' sugar mixed with 2 tablespoons water or sherry.

Almond Paste Filling:

¼ pound almonds, blanched	½ cup sugar

1 egg

Grind blanched almonds and mix with sugar. Add egg gradually and work until smooth.

Vanilla Cream Filling:

½ cup milk	1 egg yolk
1 tablespoon flour	1 tablespoon sugar
½ teaspoon vanilla	

Mix all ingredients except vanilla in double boiler. Cook over boiling water, stirring constantly, until thick. Cool, stirring occasionally, and add vanilla.

Note: Apple sauce or various fruit fillings may be used for variety.

Bridge Luncheon

(SERVES 4)

Beet Consommé   Deviled Crab in Toast Cups
Orange-Olive Salad — Tart French Dressing
Vienna Spice Torte
Coffee   Tea

ADVANCE PREPARATION SCHEDULE

Previous Day	Early Morning
Beet Consommé	*Toast cups*
French Dressing	*Slice oranges*

BEET CONSOMME

4 fresh beets	1 tablespoon strained lemon juice
2 cups water	1 2-ounce jar imported black
4 cups chicken broth	*or* domestic red caviar
2 envelopes (2 tablespoons)	Dairy sour cream
unflavored gelatin	Freshly ground nutmeg
¼ cup sherry	(optional)

Peel and dice beets; cook in 2 cups of salted water 20 to 30 minutes. Drain, reserving 1 cup of beet liquid, and heat with broth. Soak gelatin in sherry; dissolve in hot beet mixture. Cool. Add lemon juice and refrigerate until it starts to set. Place about 1 teaspoon caviar in the bottom of each of 4 bouillon cups. Carefully add partially set beet consommé. Chill until firm. Serve with a teaspoon of sour cream (or yogurt for the calorie-conscious). Sprinkle lightly with nutmeg.

DEVILED CRAB

1½ tablespoons butter	½ teaspoon dry mustard
1½ tablespoons flour	1 teaspoon Worcestershire
¾ cup half and half cream	¼ teaspoon salt
1 cup crabmeat, fresh *or* canned	½ cup chopped celery (optional)

4 teaspoons cognac

Make Toast Cups.

Melt butter in saucepan; add flour; stir until creamy. Blend in cream, stirring constantly for 5 minutes, until cooked. Add crabmeat, mustard, Worcestershire, salt, and celery; combine and add cognac. Pour into Toast Cups. To heat, place in a preheated 350° oven 15 to 20 minutes until thoroughly heated.

BUTTERED TOAST CUPS

4 slices thin-sliced bread   ¼ cup melted butter

Remove crusts from bread. Dip in melted butter and press each slice into a 3-inch muffin pan to form a cup. Place in a preheated 375° oven about 12 to 15 minutes, until lightly browned. Leave in muffin pan.

ORANGE-OLIVE SALAD

2 large oranges	1 tablespoon chopped parsley
⅓ cup sliced ripe olives	⅓ cup Tart French Dressing
¼ teaspoon grated onion	4 lettuce cups

Pare oranges and cut 8 slices crosswise about ⅛ inch thick. Arrange in lettuce cups. Combine olives, onion, parsley and French Dressing and spread lightly over oranges.

TART FRENCH DRESSING

½ teaspoon salt	⅔ cup salad oil
1 teaspoon sugar	¼ teaspoon Tabasco
½ teaspoon dry mustard	⅓ cup vinegar
½ teaspoon paprika	⅓ cup lemon juice

Mix dry ingredients thoroughly; add oil and Tabasco and stir until well blended. Add vinegar and beat or shake well. Beat or shake again just before serving. Makes 1 cup.

VIENNA SPICE TORTE

⅓ cup slivered almonds	¼ teaspoon salt
1 tablespoon butter	½ teaspoon ground nutmeg
1 tablespoon sugar	¼ teaspoon ground ginger
½ teaspoon cinnamon	⅛ teaspoon ground cloves
¼ cup all-purpose flour	2 tablespoons butter
2 tablespoons non-fat dry milk	1 teaspoon grated lemon rind
1½ teaspoons baking powder	½ cup sugar
½ teaspoon cinnamon	2 egg whites, unbeaten

⅓ cup water

Prepare filling.

Sour Cream Filling:

½ cup sugar	2 egg yolks, unbeaten
1 teaspoon cornstarch	1 teaspoon grated lemon rind
1 cup dairy sour cream	½ teaspoon almond extract

Combine sugar and cornstarch in saucepan; stir in sour cream and egg yolks; mix well. Cook over medium heat, stirring constantly until thickened. Add lemon rind and almond extract. Cool at least 15 minutes.

Line an 8-inch cake pan with foil. Place almonds and butter in pan and toast in a preheated 400° oven 10 minutes, until golden. Stir frequently to prevent burning. Combine sugar with cinnamon and sprinkle over almonds.

Sift together flour, dry milk, baking powder, cinnamon, salt, nutmeg, ginger, cloves. Combine butter, lemon rind, and sugar; cream well; add egg whites and beat very well. Add dry ingredients alternately with water, beginning and ending with dry ingredients and blending well. Pour over filling. Bake in a preheated 350° oven

40 to 45 minutes; cool and turn out on serving plate; remove foil while still warm. Serve warm.

Noon Committee Meeting Luncheon

(SERVES 8)

Blueberry Mold — Summer Fruit Platter
Nora's Honey Dressing
Crusty Deviled Ham Sandwiches
Cream Cheese Tarts　　Chocolate Peek-a-Boos
Iced Tea　　Hot Coffee

ADVANCE PREPARATION SCHEDULE

Deep Freeze	Previous Day	Early Morning
Tarts	*Blueberry Mold*	*Ham Sandwiches*
	Dressing	

BLUEBERRY MOLD — SUMMER FRUIT PLATTER

2 pints fresh blueberries	1 pint dairy sour cream
½ cup orange juice	Grated rind of 1 lemon
½ cup sugar	½ teaspoon nutmeg
2 boxes lemon-flavored gelatin	½ teaspoon cinnamon
1 cup boiling water	½ teaspoon monosodium
1 cup blackberry brandy	glutamate

Garnish:

1 quart strawberries	1 medium-size honeydew
¼ large watermelon	8 small bunches grapes

Combine 1 pint fresh blueberries, orange juice, and sugar; bring to a boil; cool. Dissolve gelatin in boiling water; cool; mix all the ingredients together including remaining pint of uncooked blueberries. Pour into well-oiled 6-cup mold. To serve, unmold on large platter. Fill center with strawberries; surround with alternating wedges of watermelon and honeydew in spoke fashion; arrange bunches of grapes artistically. Serve with Nora's Dressing.

NORA'S HONEY DRESSING

1 teaspoon salt	1 teaspoon dry mustard
1 teaspoon celery seed	1 teaspoon paprika
½ cup sugar	¼ cup vinegar
½ cup honey	1 cup oil

Combine salt, celery seed, sugar, honey, mustard, and paprika in electric mixer (or use rotary beater). Add 1 tablespoon of the vinegar and ¼ cup of the oil; beat ½ minute. Continue beating about 5 minutes, while adding remaining vinegar and oil, alternately.

A good dressing for fruit salads.

CRUSTY DEVILED HAM SANDWICHES

1½ dozen small crisp rolls *or* 1½ dozen Brown-and-Serve rolls	1 egg, beaten
	3 tablespoons dairy sour cream
¾ pound cooked ham, baked *or* boiled	½ teaspoon seasoned salt
	½ teaspoon oregano
2 tablespoons sweet pickle relish	¼ teaspoon dill weed
½ teaspoon Worcestershire	

Cut rolls in half and remove center, leaving only crusts. Chop ham thoroughly, or put through meat grinder using fine cutter. Combine with relish, egg, sour cream, salt, oregano, dill weed and Worcestershire. Place a rounded tablespoon of mixture in half of the split rolls and cover with other half. Preheat oven to 350°; place prepared rolls on greased baking sheet and bake 15 minutes. Serve at once. If brown-and-serve rolls are used, place in a preheated 400° oven for 15 minutes. To insure a crusty roll, place a pan of hot water on oven rack below the other pan during baking time.

CREAM CHEESE TARTS

Filling:

1 8-ounce package cream cheese, softened	1 egg, beaten
	¼ cup sugar
1 teaspoon vanilla	

Cream together.

Crust:

1¼ cups graham cracker crumbs	6 tablespoons butter *or* margarine, melted

Combine and mix very well. Place 1½-inch cupcake papers inside of 1½-inch muffin pans and line each with 1 level tablespoon crust mixture; press firmly; add 1 heaping tablespoon or little more of cheese filling. Bake in a preheated 375° oven about 10 minutes, or until crack begins to appear on surface of cheese. Remove from oven; cool for 10 minutes. Add 3 cherries from can of prepared cherry pie crust filling on top of each tart. Return to oven for 4 or 5 minutes to set.

May be frozen for no more than one week. Makes 2 dozen small tarts.

CHOCOLATE PEEK-A-BOOS

1 cup all-purpose flour	4 eggs
¼ teaspoon salt	1½ teaspoons vanilla
¼ cup sugar	1 6-ounce package semi-sweet
1 cup milk	chocolate bits
¼ cup (⅛ pound) butter	Confectioners' sugar

Sift flour, salt, and sugar together; heat milk and butter to boiling point. Add dry ingredients all at once to hot liquid, stirring constantly. Cook until mixture leaves sides of pan in smooth, compact ball; stir vigorously. Remove from heat. Add eggs, one at a time, and beat; add vanilla. Drop dough by ½ teaspoonfuls onto ungreased baking sheets. Place 2 chocolate bits on each cooky. Cover bits with a teaspoon of dough. Bake in a preheated 375° oven about 17 minutes. Sprinkle with confectioners' sugar. Cool.

Blockbuster Luncheon

(SERVES 8)

Mushroom Crêpes
Hawaiian Salad Bowl
Coffee Raisin Pilau
Flaky Butter Cookies
Coffee   Tea   Milk

ADVANCE PREPARATION SCHEDULE

Deep Freeze	Early Morning
Cookies	*Assemble crêpes*
	Pilau

MUSHROOM CREPES

Crêpes:

4 eggs	1½ cups all-purpose flour
¼ teaspoon salt	2 tablespoons butter, melted
2 cups milk	

Beat eggs well; add combined salt and flour, then butter. Add milk gradually while beating to a smooth batter. Make 1 crêpe at a time. Grease a 7-inch skillet lightly and pour in 3 tablespoons of batter, tilting the pan from side to side so batter covers bottom. Sauté lightly on both sides and remove to paper towel. Fill with 1 tablespoon of Mushroom Filling; roll and place alongside each other in baking dish. Cover with Sherry Sauce and bake for 15 minutes in a preheated 350° oven until thoroughly heated.

Mushroom Filling:

2 tablespoons butter	½ teaspoon salt
1½ cups coarsely chopped	⅛ teaspoon tarragon leaves
fresh mushrooms	½ teaspoon seasoned salt
3 tablespoons bread crumbs	

Heat butter in saucepan; add mushrooms and sauté 5 minutes. Add salt, tarragon leaves, seasoned salt, and bread crumbs.

Sherry Sauce:

2 tablespoons butter	1 teaspoon lemon juice
2 tablespoons flour	1 cup half and half cream
1 teaspoon instant minced onion	1 cup chicken consommé
	½ teaspoon salt
1 teaspoon Worcestershire	½ cup sherry

Melt butter, add flour and onion; cook until smooth and bubbly. Gradually add Worcestershire, lemon juice, cream, consommé, salt, and sherry; cook slowly until thick.

HAWAIIAN SALAD BOWL

1 10½-ounce package miniature marshmallows	2 11-ounce cans mandarin oranges, drained
1 pint dairy sour cream	1 4-ounce package flaked coconut
1 large fresh pineapple, cubed	Head lettuce

Combine marshmallows and sour cream; let stand a few hours with pineapple, oranges, and coconut; chill thoroughly. Serve in lettuce cups.

Note: Canned pineapple may be substituted, but is sweeter.

COFFEE RAISIN PILAU

1 8-ounce package precooked rice	⅛ teaspoon salt
2 cups regular strength brewed coffee	⅛ teaspoon nutmeg
	½ cup brown sugar, firmly packed
½ cup golden seedless raisins	
½ cup chopped walnuts	1 cup heavy cream, whipped

Prepare precooked rice, using coffee instead of water. Stir in raisins, walnuts, salt, nutmeg, and brown sugar. Blend well and cool. Fold in whipped cream. Serve chilled in sherbet glasses. Top with spoonful of reserved whipped cream.

FLAKY BUTTER COOKIES

1 cup (½ pound) butter, softened	1 egg
1 3-ounce package cream cheese, softened	2¼ cups sifted all-purpose flour
	⅛ teaspoon salt
1 cup sugar	½ teaspoon vanilla

Cream butter, cheese, and sugar. Add egg, then flour, salt, and vanilla. Add more flour if necessary (¼ cup). Divide dough into rolls, wrap in wax paper and place in freezer or refrigerator until ready to bake. Dough will keep indefinitely in freezer. Slice cookies paper thin while cold, with a sharp knife, and bake on a cooky sheet in a preheated 375° oven until edges are brown, about 6 to 8 minutes. Remove from cooky sheet while warm. Cookies will be very crisp as soon as they have cooled.

Lazy Summer Day Luncheon

(SERVES 6)

Scorpion and Matai
(Blender Drinks)
Crab Louis or Seafood Mold Chaudfroid
Oranges in Bloom with Cheese Platter
Meringue Coffee Cake
Coffee   Tea

SCORPION
(1 serving)

1½ ounces lemon juice	2 ounces light rum
2 ounces fresh orange juice	1 ounce brandy
1 ounce orgeat syrup	

Mix in blender with shaved ice. Serve in 14-ounce or 16-ounce glass filled with cubed ice.

MATAI
(1 serving)

Juice of 1 fresh lime *or*	½ teaspoon Simple Syrup
1 tablespoon bottled lime juice	Dash orgeat syrup
1 ounce light rum	Dash orange curaçao
1 ounce Jamaica rum	Stick fresh pineapple

Fill a 14-ounce or 16-ounce glass with shaved ice. Pour all ingredients over ice and stir. Add pineapple stick as swizzle.

Simple Syrup:

1 cup sugar   1 cup water

Combine in saucepan and boil 5 minutes. Make ¾ cup.

Note: Simple Syrup has been added for convenience. It is indispensable for non-alcoholic drinks as well. Sugar does not dissolve easily and the syrup makes a perfect blend. Use it to taste.

CRAB LOUIS

1½ pounds crabmeat, fresh or frozen	Tomato slices
Lettuce	Artichoke hearts, canned or frozen
	1 hard-cooked egg, chopped fine

Pick over crabmeat, leaving the meat in as large pieces as possible. Arrange a bed of shredded lettuce on 6 individual salad plates and place a mound of crabmeat on each. Encircle the crabmeat with halved tomato slices and wedges of artichoke hearts; sprinkle generously with egg. Chill thoroughly. Serve with Sauce Louis.

Sauce Louis:

1 cup mayonnaise	2 tablespoons grated onion
⅓ cup heavy cream, whipped	2 tablespoons chopped parsley
½ cup chili sauce	1 tablespoon lemon juice
	Few grains cayenne

Combine all ingredients and blend well.

Note: Delicious with many other seafoods.

SEAFOOD MOLD CHAUDFROID

2 envelopes (2 tablespoons) unflavored gelatin	2 cups diced celery, ½-inch pieces
½ cup cold water	½ cup sliced pimiento olives
2½ cups mayonnaise	¼ cup 1-inch green pepper strips
4 6½-ounce cans crabmeat, or 1½ pounds fresh crabmeat	1 2-ounce jar pimiento, chopped
	1 teaspoon salt
	¼ teaspoon paprika

Garnish:

Watercress   Pickled onions
Quartered hard-cooked eggs   Tomatoes

Soak gelatin in cold water; dissolve over heat while stirring. Add
to mayonnaise very slowly. Combine carefully with remaining ingredients and blend well. Pour into well-oiled 6-cup fish mold. If
smaller mold is used, pour balance into individual molds and use
as garnish. Place in refrigerator several hours or overnight. Unmold on lettuce-lined platter. Center with Sauce Louis and garnish
with watercress, hard-cooked eggs, a sprinkling of pickled onions,
and tomatoes.

Variation:

Substitute shrimp, lobster, or tuna for crabmeat. The mold may be
glazed with Chaudfroid Sauce as for Salmon Trout Chaudfroid (see
Index).

ORANGES IN BLOOM WITH CHEESE PLATTER

Score through the peel of each orange, dividing it into 6 sections.
Do not cut the pulp. Peel down each sixth carefully; do not remove
it, but fold each point in under orange with peeling outside, so
that it forms a base of folded petals. Remove as much white membrane as possible from pulp, separate sections, and spread open
as a flower. Sprinkle with pomegranate seeds or currants, depending
on the season. Tangerines may be arranged in this fashion. Serve
around a wheel of Brie or Bel Paese cheese, or use a variety of
cheeses. A bouquet of kumquats may be made for garnish. Peel
them in 5 sections.

MERINGUE COFFEE CAKE

2 cakes compressed yeast   4 egg yolks, well beaten
1 teaspoon sugar   1 cup milk, scalded and cooled
⅓ cup lukewarm water   4 egg whites, beaten stiff
4 cups sifted all-purpose flour   1 cup sugar
⅓ teaspoon salt   ½ teaspoon vanilla
1 cup (½ pound) butter   ½ cup ground nuts
3 tablespoons sugar   ½ cup sugar
              2 teaspoons cinnamon

Dissolve yeast with 1 teaspoon sugar in water. Sift flour and salt into large bowl and cut in butter with a pastry blender or knives, as for pie crust. Add remaining sugar; mix well. Combine egg yolks and milk; add to flour mixture; blend in yeast mixture; cover. Refrigerate overnight.

Next day, roll out to ¼-inch thickness. Add sugar and vanilla to beaten whites and beat again until stiff and glossy. Spread ½ the meringue over dough. Combine cinnamon, sugar, and nuts; sprinkle half over meringue. Roll up dough as for jelly roll. Place in well-buttered tube pan or ring mold; spread with remaining meringue and sugar mixture. Let rise in warm spot for 1 hour. Bake in a preheated 350° oven 1 hour. Let cool in pan before removing.

This is another favorite recipe we introduced in *Thoughts for Buffets* as "Continental Coffee Cake," and for your convenience have included it here with slight variations.

Two Tables of Bridge Luncheon

(SERVES 8)

Shrimp Creole   Green Rice Ring
Fruit Garni
Parker House Rolls
Coffee Cream Soufflé
Coffee   Tea

ADVANCE PREPARATION SCHEDULE

Previous Day	Early Morning
Coffee soufflé	*Shrimps*
	Creole sauce
	Fruit

SHRIMP CREOLE

1 quart water	3 peppercorns
1 tablespoon caraway seeds	2 teaspoons salt
1 slice lemon	2 pounds raw shrimp

Combine water in saucepan with seeds, lemon, peppercorns, and salt; boil for 5 minutes; add shrimp, bring to a boil, and cook 5 minutes. Let shrimps cool in water in which they were cooked; reserve ¾ cup liquid. Drain, clean, devein, and refrigerate.

Creole Sauce:

½ cup (¼ pound) butter	1 teaspoon salt
3 medium onions, chopped fine	⅛ teaspoon pepper
1 stalk celery with leaves, diced	2 teaspoons sugar
2 medium green peppers with seeds, diced	⅛ teaspoon ginger
	Pinch ground cloves
2 teaspoons minced parsley	Pinch cinnamon
1 6-ounce can tomato purée	1 tablespoon cornstarch
1 cup canned tomatoes	3 tablespoons cold water
¾ cup shrimp liquid	½ pound fresh mushrooms
1 tablespoon butter	

Heat butter in saucepan; add onion and sauté until soft and transparent, about 5 minutes. Add celery, green peppers, and parsley; simmer slowly 15 minutes. Blend in tomato purée, tomatoes, shrimp liquid, salt, pepper, sugar, ginger, cloves, and cinnamon; cover and simmer slowly 1 hour. Make a paste of cornstarch and water; add to sauce and cook until clear and slightly thickened. Place mushrooms in top of double boiler, add butter, and steam 10 minutes. Combine mushrooms with their butter liquid, and shrimps with sauce. Heat. To serve, pour into center of Green Rice Ring.

GREEN RICE RING

3 cups rice, cooked	2 tablespoons Parmesan cheese
3 eggs, separated	1 small onion, grated
¾ cup minced parsley	Salt, pepper, paprika to taste
2 tablespoons Worcestershire	

Place rice in a bowl; add beaten egg yolks, parsley, cheese, onion, salt, pepper, paprika, Worcestershire; mix well. Beat egg whites until stiff and fold in carefully. Pour into well-oiled 6-cup ring mold;

place in pan of hot water and bake in a preheated 350° oven 45 minutes. Unmold on hot platter.

FRUIT GARNI

2 large grapefruit	1 #2½ can sliced pineapple,
2 avocados	drained
¼ cup lemon juice	Watercress

Peel grapefruit and separate into segments. Peel avocados, cut in ½-inch slices with French cutter, and dip in lemon juice to prevent discoloration. Place pineapple rings around rice ring; alternate grapefruit sections and avocado slices, in a mound, on each pineapple slice. Garnish with watercress. Thin slices of unpeeled red apple may be added to grapefruit and avocado for color.

To make grapefruit segments:

Peel grapefruit through pulp so that all of peeling is completely removed and grapefruit clear of white pulp. Slip a knife into each side of membrane adjoining segment, thus releasing it. Pry it loose carefully. Peel it over a bowl so as to catch all juices.

COFFEE CREAM SOUFFLE

2 envelopes (2 tablespoons) unflavored gelatin	2 egg yolks
	2 tablespoons brandy
⅓ cup cold double-strength brewed coffee	2 cups heavy cream, whipped
	2 egg whites
2½ cups hot double-strength brewed coffee	⅛ teaspoon salt
	¼ cup grated, unsweetened chocolate
1 cup sugar	
1½ cups creamed cottage cheese	

Soften gelatin in cold coffee; dissolve in hot coffee. Add ⅔ cup sugar. Stir until dissolved; cool, and refrigerate until of jelly-like consistency.

Purée cottage cheese through a sieve. Add egg yolks and brandy; beat 3 minutes in electric mixer or with rotary beater; add gelatin mixture and beat well; fold in cream. Beat egg whites until they form soft peaks; add remaining ⅓ cup sugar and salt. Gradually, while continuing to beat, fold egg whites into cheese mixture very carefully, until mixture mounds when removed with a spoon.

Secure a double strip of aluminum foil firmly around a 1-quart soufflé dish or casserole, extending 2 inches above top rim of dish. Spoon gelatin mixture into prepared soufflé dish. Chill until firm. Remove strip. Garnish top with a border of grated chocolate.

The Board Meets
Winter Brunch

(SERVES 6)

Vegetable Chowder   Cheese Puffs
Eggs Leo   Rye Rolls
Strawberry Preserves
Apple Pancakes
Coffee

Suggested wine: Manzanilla, or any good pale dry sherry

ADVANCE PREPARATION SCHEDULE

Previous Day	**Early Morning**
Preserves	*Chowder*
	Arrange pancake ingredients

VEGETABLE CHOWDER

4 tablespoons butter	1½ cups green beans, cut in
1 cup sliced onions	1-inch pieces
1 green pepper, diced	1½ cups diced carrots
2 teaspoons salt	1 cup diced potatoes
¼ teaspoon pepper	3 cups water
1 14½-ounce can evaporated milk	

Melt butter; add onions, green pepper, salt, and pepper. Sauté until lightly browned. Add green beans, carrots, potatoes, and water; cook until vegetables are tender, about 15 minutes. Add milk; heat and serve. Serve with Cheese Puffs (see Index).

EGGS LEO

12 slices bacon	6 eggs
2 onions, sliced fine	Salt
6 slices tomato	Ground black pepper
Dashes Worcestershire	

Sauté bacon in pan until almost done; then put aside, removing all but 3 tablespoons bacon fat. Sauté onions in bacon fat until brown. Place tomato slices on top of onions; add bacon. Break eggs carefully over bacon, add salt; cover and let cook until eggs are firm. Before serving, sprinkle with pepper and Worcestershire.

STRAWBERRY PRESERVES

4 cups firm strawberries   3 cups sugar
⅓ cup lemon juice (optional)

Wash and hull strawberries; place them in alternate layers with sugar in preserving kettle. Let stand overnight. Place on heat and bring very slowly to boiling point, stirring as little as possible until sugar dissolves. Boil rapidly for 25 minutes; add lemon juice and boil 5 more minutes. Watch closely that it does not burn. Pour at once into hot sterilized jars and seal. Make no more than 4 cups of berries at a time. The preserves should be of medium consistency. Berries vary in liquid content and therefore may need more or less cooking according to the variety.

APPLE PANCAKES

3 eggs	2 tart apples
½ cup milk	3 tablespoons butter
½ cup all-purpose flour	1 tablespoon sugar
1 teaspoon sugar	1 teaspoon cinnamon
Dash salt	3 tablespoons lemon juice

Beat eggs slightly and add milk. Combine flour, 1 teaspoon sugar, and salt; add to milk, stirring until smooth. Peel and slice apples. Heat 2 tablespoons butter in a 10-inch ovenware skillet; place apples in butter and sauté until heated. Tilt skillet so that pan is completely coated. Pour batter over apples and place in a preheated 500° oven. Combine sugar and cinnamon. When pancake is set but not browned, sprinkle with sugar and cinnamon mixture; dot with 1 tablespoon butter. Return to oven until brown. Before serving, sprinkle with lemon juice. Roll up and cut into 6 portions.

These are small portions of a delicious pancake. To double the recipe, use a second skillet.

Dinner and on to
the Theater

(SERVES 6)

Frogs' Legs Madeira — Parslied Toast Points
Olives   Salted Nuts
Beef Tenderloin Macedoine
Almond Cabbage   Parker House Rolls
Ambassador Salad
Eggs à la Neige
Nut Tarts
Orange Cinnamon Coffee

Suggested wines: dry Madeira (with the Frogs' Legs)
red Burgundy (with the Beef)

ADVANCE PREPARATION SCHEDULE

Deep Freeze	Previous Day	Early Morning
Parker House Rolls (*see Index*)	*Eggs à la Neige*	*Toast Points* *Frogs' Legs* *Crisp greens* *Cabbage* *Ambassador Salad Dressing* *Nut Tarts* (*see Index*)

FROGS' LEGS MADEIRA

12 pairs frogs' legs (about 2 pounds), fresh *or* frozen
2 tablespoons lemon juice
¼ cup half and half cream
1 teaspoon salt
¼ cup flour
½ cup (¼ pound) butter
1 clove garlic, minced (optional)
¼ cup Madeira
1 cup dairy sour cream

If frozen frogs' legs are used, follow package directions; if fresh, cut away bones above ankles and soak in cold water for 2 hours. For either, sprinkle with lemon juice. Combine cream and salt, dip in the frogs' legs, and coat with flour. Heat butter in saucepan and add garlic. Add frogs' legs and brown quickly in hot butter; add Madeira and simmer 5 minutes. Combine with sour cream and heat, but do not boil. Serve at once on Parslied Toast Points.

PARSLIED TOAST POINTS

6 slices bread, halved   2 tablespoons butter
¼ cup chopped parsley

Cut bread in triangles; using a minimum of butter, brown the points quickly to a crisp consistency; dip in chopped parsley. Keep warm until served with Frogs' Legs Madeira. Garnish with parsley sprigs.

BEEF TENDERLOIN MACEDOINE

1 4-pound whole beef tenderloin
3 tablespoons shortening
1 pound mushrooms, sliced
1 large Bermuda onion, diced
1 large green pepper, diced
1 teaspoon salt
¼ teaspoon pepper
½ teaspoon seasoned salt
1 clove garlic (optional)
½ cup catsup
Watercress

Sear meat rapidly under broiler on both sides; place on bottom broiler pan. Melt shortening in saucepan; add mushrooms, onions, green pepper, and sauté for 5 minutes. Season meat and vegetables with salt, pepper, seasoned salt, and garlic. Place mushroom mixture around meat in broiler pan. Liberally cover vegetables with catsup. Roast, uncovered, in a preheated 325° oven 30 to 40 minutes until desired doneness of meat is reached. Garnish platter with watercress and border with Almond Cabbage squares. Serve sauce separately.

More vegetables may be required for larger tenderloin. There should be enough to surround meat completely; do not use rack, as meat and vegetable flavors should blend.

ALMOND CABBAGE

5 cups finely shredded cabbage	⅓ cup potato flour
2 teaspoons salt	½ cup seedless white raisins
⅓ cup butter *or* chicken fat	1 cup sliced blanched almonds
½ cup boiling water	2 tablespoons sugar
1½ cups cubed white bread	4 eggs

Place the cabbage and salt in the butter; cook over low heat for 30 minutes, stirring frequently. Cool. Pour the water over the bread; squeeze dry and mash. Add potato flour, raisins, almonds, and sugar. Separate the eggs and add the yolks and cabbage. Mix until smooth. Beat the egg whites until stiff but not dry and fold into the mixture. Turn into a greased 2-quart shallow baking pan. Bake in a preheated 350° oven 25 to 35 minutes, or until set. To serve, cut into squares.

AMBASSADOR SALAD

1 clove garlic	Juice of 2 lemons
½ cup olive oil	1 cup croutons
4 to 5 heads Bibb lettuce	1 egg, coddled
Salt and freshly ground pepper, to taste	½ cup grated Parmesan, Romano, *or* blue cheese
1 2-ounce can anchovies	

Split garlic, add to oil; let stand several hours. Tear Bibb lettuce in bits and heap in large salad bowl. Season with salt and pepper. Remove garlic and blend ¼ cup of this oil with lemon juice. Moisten croutons in remaining oil. To coddle egg, place in boiling water; turn off heat and allow to stand 1 minute. Remove and break egg over salad; add cheese and toss gently with large fork and spoon until well blended. Have anchovies and croutons in small bowls accompanying salad. To serve, toss croutons into salad and place anchovy on top of each individual salad, as it is portioned.

Croutons:

1 loaf day-old French bread

Prepare croutons in oven, using no butter. Cut day-old French bread in ½-inch slices; remove crusts. Cut into ½-inch cubes. Arrange on cooky sheet; bake in a preheated 350° oven until delicately brown. Shake frequently to brown evenly.

EGGS A LA NEIGE

Meringues:

4 cups milk	¾ cup sugar
6 egg whites	¼ teaspoon salt

Make meringues the day before or early in the day. Scald milk in large skillet. Beat egg whites until frothy; gradually add sugar and salt, while beating stiff. Onto hot milk, drop 3 large mounds of meringue, 1 inch apart; cook 5 minutes, turning once with slotted spoon; drain on paper towel. Reserve 1½ cups milk for custard sauce. Repeat; cool, then refrigerate meringues.

Custard Sauce:

1½ cups heavy cream	6 egg yolks
¾ teaspoon vanilla	½ cup sugar
1½ cups milk used for meringues	Pinch salt
	1½ tablespoons flour

In double boiler, scald cream with vanilla and milk. Beat egg yolks until light; then beat in sugar, salt, flour, and a little of cream-milk mixture. Stir this into rest of cream-milk mixture; cook over hot (not boiling) water; continue stirring until sauce coats metal spoon.

To serve:

2 pints fresh strawberries	1 1-ounce square unsweetened chocolate

Let custard sauce and meringues cool in refrigerator until 20 minutes before serving. Then hull and wash strawberries. Slice them into a deep serving dish. Heap the chilled meringues over strawberries; then pour on the custard sauce. Lastly, with vegetable parer, shave the chocolate over all.

ORANGE CINNAMON COFFEE

6 tablespoons coffee	6 3-inch slices candied orange
6 cups water	peel
3 teaspoons cinnamon	

After measuring coffee into coffee maker, add water, cinnamon, and orange peel and brew as usual.

6 p.m. Before the Opera Dinner

(SERVES 4)

Shrimp Marseilles   Sesame Crackers
Veal Parmesan Napoli   Green Noodles Alfredo
Glazed Carrots   Mushrooms Gourmet
French Lace Horns — Caramel Sauce
Coffee

Suggested wine: Valpolicella or other Italian red wine

ADVANCE PREPARATION SCHEDULE

Deep Freeze	Previous Day	Early Morning
French Horns	*Boil shrimps*	*Marinate shrimps*
	Marseilles dressing	*Carrots*
		Sauce

SHRIMP MARSEILLES

¼ cup salad oil	⅛ teaspoon pepper
2 tablespoons wine vinegar	⅛ teaspoon garlic powder
1 tablespoon grated onion	⅛ teaspoon dry mustard
¼ teaspoon salt	2 avocados
1 pound shrimp, cooked and deveined	

Prepare dressing: beat together the oil, vinegar, onion, salt, pepper, garlic powder, and mustard. Cut avocados in half lengthwise and remove pits. Scoop out pulp and chop coarsely; reserve shells. Chop shrimp coarsely and combine with avocado. Pour dressing over and mix lightly but thoroughly. Chill for 1 hour. To serve, fill avocado shells and place on paper doilies or green leaves.

VEAL PARMESAN NAPOLI

4 large rib veal chops	Flour to dredge
1 teaspoon lime juice	½ cup Parmesan cheese, grated
½ teaspoon salt	1 egg, beaten
⅛ teaspoon freshly ground pepper	2 tablespoons vegetable
2 tablespoons butter	shortening

¾ cup dry white wine

Brush chops with lime juice; sprinkle with salt and pepper. Dip first in hot butter, second in flour, third in cheese. Refrigerate ½ hour until coating is set. Then proceed to dip again, first in beaten egg, second in flour, and third in cheese. Refrigerate 2 hours. Heat shortening in skillet; add chops and sauté quickly until brown on both sides. Add wine; cover and simmer slowly, 30 to 40 minutes or until tender. Serve with Green Noodles Alfredo or around a mound of macaroni or spaghetti.

GREEN NOODLES ALFREDO

1 ½-pound package green noodles	1 cup grated Parmesan cheese
½ cup (¼ pound) butter or margarine	½ cup half and half cream

Cook noodles according to package directions. Drain, but do not rinse. Place on heated platter. Keep warm. Melt butter or margarine in saucepan, stir in cheese and cream; simmer, stirring constantly until cheese is melted and smooth. Pour piping hot over drained noodles and toss gently. Serve with extra Parmesan.

Note: A picture emerges of Alfredo the Elder, in Rome, tossing his pasta with grace and flourish, the famous gold spoon shining with action. Then, with a final flourish, honoring the lady of his choice at the table by presenting her with the platter and its last portion, to be eaten with the celebrated gold spoon.

GLAZED CARROTS

1½ pounds carrots	1 tablespoon cornstarch
½ teaspoon salt	¼ cup carrot liquid
1 tablespoon butter, melted	½ cup orange juice

Scrape carrots well, and cut into slices with French cutter. Place in saucepan; add sufficient salted water to cover (½ teaspoon salt per cup of water). Cover pan and cook 15 to 20 minutes. Drain, reserving ¼ cup of liquid. Mix cornstarch with carrot liquid, add orange juice and salt. Melt butter in saucepan; add orange juice mixture and cook, stirring until blended and thickened. Add carrots and reheat. The flavor improves when allowed to stand before serving.

MUSHROOMS GOURMET

1 pound fresh mushrooms	⅛ teaspoon thyme
½ cup water	⅛ teaspoon tarragon
3 tablespoons dairy sour cream	½ teaspoon ginger
3 tablespoons mayonnaise	¼ teaspoon salt

Scrub mushrooms and slice thinly through stems and caps. Bring water to a boil, add mushrooms, cover and steam slowly for 3 minutes. Drain. Combine sour cream, mayonnaise, herbs, and salt; toss with mushrooms. Refrigerate. Serve very cold on a generous bed of fresh crisp lettuce.

FRENCH LACE HORNS

1 cup sifted all-purpose flour	¼ cup butter
1 cup finely chopped nuts	¼ cup vegetable shortening
½ cup light corn syrup	⅔ cup brown sugar, firmly packed

Combine flour and nuts. Melt butter and shortening in a saucepan; add syrup and sugar and bring to boiling point. Remove from heat and blend in combined flour and nuts gradually. Drop rounded teaspoonfuls on greased cooky sheet, 3 inches apart. Bake in a preheated 325° oven 8 to 10 minutes. Cool 1 minute. Remove carefully with a large spatula and roll at once to form a cone. To serve, fill with ice cream. May be filled and frozen. Serve with Hot or Cold Caramel Sauce. Makes about 4 dozen.

Note: Allow to cool without rolling and they then become dainty French Lace Cookies.

COLD CARAMEL SAUCE

⅓ cup butter   1 egg, well beaten
1 cup dark brown sugar   ¼ cup heavy cream, whipped
½ teaspoon vanilla

Cream butter and sugar well; blend with egg. Fold in whipped cream and vanilla.

HOT CARAMEL SAUCE

½ cup granulated sugar,   ¾ cup cream
caramelized   1 tablespoon butter
½ cup granulated sugar   1 teaspoon vanilla

To caramelize sugar, place in heavy skillet over low heat; stir constantly until melted and brown. Place granulated sugar and cream in double boiler and heat to boiling point. Add caramelized sugar and stir until well blended. Remove from heat, add butter and vanilla and beat thoroughly. May be reheated over hot water. Store in jar in refrigerator.

One-Man Show Cocktail Party

(SERVES 15 TO 20)

Oysters Polonaise   Sole en Escabèche
Shrimp Fromage   Stuffed Eggs à la Russe
Tri-Cheese Ball   Chicken Pâté
Coconut Crabmeat Appetizers
Quick Pickles   Olives   Spiced Mushrooms
Chocolate Pretzels   Date Squares
Coffee
Almondettes
(candy)

Suggested wine: Rhine or Moselle

ADVANCE PREPARATION SCHEDULE

Deep Freeze	Previous Day	Early Morning
Date Squares	*Sole en Escabèche*	*Coat Tri-Cheese Ball*
Chocolate Pretzels	*Tri-Cheese Ball*	*with nuts*
	(without nuts)	*Prepare crabmeat*
	Chicken Pâté	*Oyster topping*
	Shrimp Fromage	
	Spiced Mushrooms	

OYSTERS POLONAISE

4 dozen oysters	1 teaspoon Worcestershire
1 clove garlic, cut	1 cup fine bread crumbs
¼ cup dry sherry	¼ cup minced chives
Rock salt	¼ cup minced parsley
3 teaspoons butter	¼ teaspoon dried tarragon
3 teaspoons Roquefort *or* blue cheese	

Remove oysters from their shells and rub the deep shell lightly with cut clove of garlic; sprinkle a few drops of dry sherry in each shell. Return oysters to the shells. Cover a baking sheet with rock salt and place it in a hot oven until salt is heated. Melt butter, Roquefort cheese, and Worcestershire in a saucepan. Add bread crumbs, chives, parsley, and crushed dried tarragon; blend well. Spread a small amount of mixture over each oyster, covering each evenly. Arrange the filled oyster shells on the hot salt and place in a preheated 500° oven. Cook until the tops are delicately browned.

SOLE EN ESCABECHE

2 tablespoons butter	1 clove garlic, minced
½ cup olive *or* salad oil	¾ cup orange juice
½ cup flour (about)	Juice of 2 limes
8 fillets of sole, fresh *or* frozen	Dash Tabasco
1½ teaspoons salt	2 unpeeled oranges, sliced
½ teaspoon white pepper	1 lime, sliced thin
2 onions, sliced in thin rings	Grated orange peel (optional)
1 green pepper, sliced in thin rings	

Heat butter and 2 tablespoons of olive oil in a skillet. Flour fish lightly, place in heated butter and oil; sauté until just golden brown and tender. Season with salt and pepper. Cut slices in approximately 1½-inch squares. Place in flat dish or pan. Combine onion, pepper rings, and garlic with remaining oil and add to oil in saucepan; sauté about 2 minutes. Combine with orange and lime juice, Tabasco; salt and pepper to taste. Pour mixture over hot fish. Cool, refrigerate 24 hours. To serve, garnish with orange and lime slices and sprinkle with grated orange peel.

SHRIMP FROMAGE

1½ pounds raw shrimp	½ cup catsup
1 8-ounce package cream cheese	1 tablespoon prepared
1 medium onion, grated	horseradish

Dash Tabasco

Cook shrimp (see Index). Clean and cut in ½-inch pieces. Add remaining ingredients and chill well. Serve as spread with assorted crackers.

STUFFED EGGS A LA RUSSE

12 hard-cooked eggs, cooled and shelled	⅛ teaspoon Worcestershire
⅓ cup mayonnaise	¼ teaspoon salt
2 tablespoons butter *or* margarine, melted	Dash pepper
	1 8-ounce jar red caviar
	1 small bunch watercress

Halve eggs crosswise. Carefully remove yolks and set aside. Cut zigzag scalloped edges on whites for decoration. Cut a thin slice from bottom of each, to make a firm base so egg halves will stand upright. Refrigerate, covered, until ready to fill. Press yolks through sieve into a medium bowl. With wooden spoon beat yolks with mayonnaise, butter, Worcestershire, salt, and pepper until smooth. Fill each egg half with about 1 teaspoon drained caviar. Put egg yolk mixture through a pastry tube with a No. 6 decorating tip; pipe onto caviar, swirling high. Or mound egg yolk mixture on caviar with a teaspoon. Garnish top of each with a few caviar globules. Arrange on serving platter, cover with plastic wrap or foil; refrigerate until ready to serve, for 3 to 4 hours. Border Chicken Pâté mold with stuffed eggs and abundant watercress sprigs.

TRI-CHEESE BALL

4 ounces blue cheese	1 tablespoon grated onion
1 6-ounce packages sharp Cheddar cheese	½ teaspoon Worcestershire
3 ounces cream cheese	½ cup finely chopped nutmeats preferably walnuts or pecans
1 tablespoon minced parsley	¼ cup finely chopped nutmeats

Allow cheeses to stand at room temperature to soften. Combine with parsley, onion, Worcestershire and the ½ cup nutmeats; blend well. Place mixture on wax paper and shape into a ball. Refrigerate for 1 to 2 hours and then roll ball in the ¼ cup nutmeats. Refrigerate until 1 hour before serving time. Use as a spread on crackers.

CHICKEN PATE

1 cup light liver sausage	1½ cups Chicken Aspic
2 cups finely ground cooked chicken	⅞-ounce jar truffles *or* black olives, sliced
1 cup heavy cream, whipped	

Combine liver sausage and chicken; fold in cream. Reserve one truffle; slice and cut into stars. Slice remaining truffles and fold into chicken mixture.

Prepare Chicken Aspic. Pour ½ cup cooled Chicken Aspic into a 6-cup greased mold. Place in refrigerator just until jellied. Watch closely as the small amount sets quickly. Arrange truffle stars attractively as garnish in the jellied aspic layer. Return to refrigerator until set. Combine chicken mixture with remaining cup of aspic, blend well and pour over congealed layer in mold. Refrigerate until firm. To serve, unmold on large platter. Border with Eggs à la Russe and thin-sliced cocktail rye bread. Intersperse with sprigs of green garnish and Radish Roses (see Index).

Chicken Aspic:

1 tablespoon unflavored gelatin	2 cups strong chicken bouillon
	1 tablespoon sherry

Sprinkle gelatin over bouillon and let stand for 5 minutes. Heat slowly and stir until gelatin is dissolved; add sherry and cool.

Note: For a quick bouillon, combine one 10½-ounce can chicken broth and ¼ cup water.

COCONUT CRABMEAT APPETIZERS

4 tablespoons butter
¾ cup minced onion
½ cup finely grated coconut, or prepared grated coconut
2 6½-ounce cans crabmeat, drained

1¼ teaspoons salt
2 teaspoons curry powder
1 clove garlic, minced
1 egg
2 tablespoons cold water
½ cup dry bread crumbs
½ cup vegetable oil

Melt butter and sauté onion lightly until brown. Combine onion, coconut, crabmeat, salt, curry powder, garlic, egg, and water in blender and blend until very smooth. (Or beat ingredients together with rotary beater until smooth.) Form into ¾-inch balls and roll in dry bread crumbs. Heat oil in a skillet; brown the balls on all sides. Drain and pierce with cocktail picks. Serve in heated container. Makes 24 balls.

QUICK PICKLES

2 cucumbers
1 teaspoon mustard seed
1 teaspoon celery seed

1 medium onion, sliced
¼ cup water
¼ cup sugar
¾ cup vinegar

Cut cucumbers into long slices (as for dill pickles). Place in a quart jar. Add mustard seed, celery seed, and sliced onion. Bring water to a boil; add sugar and vinegar and pour into jar. Let stand 4 to 6 hours before serving. Serve cold.

SPICED MUSHROOMS

1 pound small white button mushrooms (about 40)
Lemon juice
¾ cup olive oil
1 clove garlic, minced

Salt, cayenne, and black pepper
Red pepper
Coriander seed
Mustard seed
Finely shredded lemon rind
2 tablespoons brandy

Wash mushrooms in lemon juice and water. Cut the ends of the stems, even with the caps. This holds the caps in firm buttons. Do not peel. Dry well on a cloth and place in a pint jar. Heat 2 tablespoons of oil in a shallow pan, add garlic, and cook for 1 minute.

Add remaining oil and the rest of the ingredients, except the mushrooms. Cook very slowly, covered, for 15 to 20 minutes. Remove from heat, pour over mushrooms, and allow to cool. Cover tightly. Mushrooms keep for several days and the flavor will improve.

CHOCOLATE PRETZELS

½ cup (¼ pound) butter *or* margarine
⅔ cup sugar
1 egg, beaten
2 squares unsweetened chocolate, melted

1 teaspoon vanilla extract
1½ cups sifted all-purpose flour
1 teaspoon cinnamon
⅛ teaspoon salt
½ cup chocolate bits, melted (optional)

¼ cup chopped nuts (optional)

Cream butter and sugar; beat in egg. Add chocolate, vanilla, and blend well. Combine with flour and cinnamon, blend thoroughly. The batter will be soft. Chill dough thoroughly until very firm, to facilitate shaping. Remove half and form cookies of this first half; leave remainder chilled in refrigerator until ready to use. Cut off 1 teaspoon of chilled dough for each cooky; roll between palms to thickness of pencil. Form into pretzel shape. Bake on ungreased cooky sheet in a preheated 350° oven 10 to 12 minutes. While hot, dip pretzels in melted chocolate bits, then in nuts. Cool on cake rack. Makes about 40 pretzels.

Variation:

May be made in circles.

DATE SQUARES

1 cup water
1 cup sugar
1 cup chopped dates
1½ cups all-purpose flour

½ teaspoon salt
1½ cups oatmeal
1 cup shortening, melted
½ cup chopped nutmeats

1 cup brown sugar

Place water, sugar, and chopped dates in a saucepan and boil until thick and smooth. Cool until lukewarm. Mix flour, salt, oatmeal, shortening, nutmeats, and brown sugar together for crumb crust. Grease brown paper well and line an 8-inch square pan. Place ¾ of crumb crust in pan and pat down well. Add date mixture and cover with remainder of crumb crust. Bake 45 minutes in a pre-heated 350° oven. Cut into squares while still warm, but not hot.

Note: Men especially seem to enjoy these and they are grand to mail for gifts.

ALMONDETTES
(Candies)

1 cup granulated sugar	1 teaspoon white vinegar
1 cup dark corn syrup	1 teaspoon vanilla
¼ cup (⅛ pound) butter	Whole almonds, unblanched
3 1-ounce squares unsweetened chocolate, melted	

Place sugar, syrup, and butter in a saucepan; bring to a boil and add chocolate and vinegar. Boil until it reaches hard-ball stage (forms a hard ball when dropped into cold water). Add vanilla. Pour into buttered pan to ½ inch in depth and let stand ½ hour. Cut in 1-inch squares and roll each around an almond. Roll each in wax paper, twisting ends to secure it.

Topical Review Dinner

(SERVES 6)

Crabmeat Choux   Artichokes Brûlés

Steak au Poivre

Celery Chablis   Mushroom Pilaf

Barbary Salad   Swedish Limpa Bread

Trilby Mousse   Butter Rosettes

Coffee

ADVANCE PREPARATION SCHEDULE

Deep Freeze	Previous Day	Early Morning
Choux	*Mousse*	*Mushroom pilaf*
Limpa Bread	*Rosettes*	*Crab filling*
		Crisp vegetables

CRABMEAT CHOUX

1 6-ounce can crabmeat *or*   ½ cup mayonnaise
  1 package frozen crabmeat   ½ cup chili sauce
1 small clove garlic, mashed   1 tablespoon prepared
2 hard-cooked eggs, sieved   horseradish
⅛ teaspoon Tabasco   ¼ teaspoon dry mustard
              Choux Puffs (see Index)

Drain and flake crabmeat. Mix with balance of ingredients and chill before serving. A delicious spread or dip.

To serve, slit Choux Puffs ⅓ way down, fill with spread, and replace top.

ARTICHOKES BRULES

1 6-ounce can artichoke bottoms   8 thin slices bread
  (8 to 12)   Mayonnaise

Place artichoke bottoms on 3-inch rounds of bread; cover all with mayonnaise. Bake in a preheated 450° oven until brown, about 5 minutes.

STEAK AU POIVRE

6 teaspoons freshly ground   6 teaspoons butter, softened
  black pepper   ¼ cup cognac, warmed, per
6 12-ounce minute steaks, *or*   skillet
  club steaks   Watercress
Salt for skillet   Sliced lemon
              Tomatoes, broiled

Press the pepper into the steaks on both sides with the heel of the hand (1 teaspoon for each steak). Sprinkle sufficient salt on the skillet to just cover bottom. Use 2 skillets if necessary. Turn the heat high and when the salt begins to brown, add the steaks. Cook 1 minute on each side reduce heat and cook to desired doneness (about 2 more minutes for rare). Remove steaks; place a teaspoon of butter on each. Rinse each hot skillet with ¼ cup cognac and pour over steaks. Ignite cognac and pour it blazing over steaks, if you wish.

Serve with watercress, lemon slices dipped in paprika, and broiled tomatoes.

CELERY CHABLIS

5 tablespoon butter *or* margarine
4 cups celery, sliced ½-inch diagonally
1 teaspoon salt
½ teaspoon white pepper

2 tablespoons finely chopped green onions
⅔ cup slivered, blanched almonds
1 tablespoon coarsely chopped green onion tops

3 tablespoons dry white wine

Heat 3 tablespoons butter in skillet; add celery, salt, pepper and onions. Sauté gently until celery is barely tender. Brown almonds lightly in remaining butter; add to celery with onion tops and wine. Cook 2 or 3 minutes longer to blend flavors. Serve very hot.

MUSHROOM PILAF

½ cup butter
1½ cups raw rice
1 10½-ounce can condensed onion soup

1 10½-ounce can condensed beef consommé
½ pound fresh mushrooms, sliced

1½ cups shredded Cheddar cheese (optional)

Melt butter in 2-quart casserole; stir in rice to coat grains with butter. Add soup, consommé, and mushrooms; mix well. Cover and bake in a preheated 325° oven about 55 minutes, or until rice is tender and liquid is absorbed. Stir occasionally during baking. Remove cover, top contents with cheese, and return to oven for an additional 5 minutes.

BARBARY SALAD

4 heads Bibb lettuce
½ cup diced celery
12 slices cucumber
2 hard-boiled eggs, quartered

1 large tomato, cut in 6ths
2 tablespoons grated Parmesan cheese
4 slices crisp bacon, crumbled

Arrange lettuce to conform to contour of a deep glass bowl. Layer the celery over it, then the cucumbers (more if desired).

Border with eggs and tomatoes. Sprinkle with cheese, then with bacon. It looks beautiful. Just toss it with flourish and Chutney French Dressing.

Chutney French Dressing:

To 1 cup of basic French Dressing, add 2 tablespoons finely chopped chutney.

SWEDISH LIMPA BREAD

2 packages active dry yeast
1½ cups warm water
¼ cup molasses
⅓ cup sugar
1 tablespoon salt
2 tablespoons shortening, softened
Finely grated rind of 1 *or* 2 oranges (about)
4 cups (about) sifted rye and wheat flour (Bohemian style)
Cornmeal

In mixing bowl dissolve yeast in warm water; add molasses, sugar, salt, shortening, and orange rind. Mix in flour with spoon until smooth, adding enough flour to handle easily. Turn onto floured board, knead until smooth. Let rise in warm place until doubled in bulk. Shape into 2 round loaves, slightly flattened, on opposite corners of greased baking sheet; sprinkle with cornmeal, cover with damp cloth; let rise about 1 hour. Bake in a preheated 375° oven 30 to 35 minutes, or until brown. May be baked in loaf pans.

TRILBY MOUSSE

1 pint heavy cream, whipped
¾ cup sugar
¼ cup (2 ounces) miniature marshmallows, *or* pieces

Fold whipped cream, sugar and marshmallows together carefully. Pour into 2 ice cube trays. Refrigerate several hours or overnight, until frozen. Remove by spoonfuls into serving dishes, top each with slivered almonds and center with maraschino cherry or colorful berry. (Serves 8 to 10.) Leftovers may be stored in the deep freeze.

Topping:

1 teaspoon butter
⅓ cup slivered almonds
8 to 10 maraschino cherries *or* berries

Heat butter and brown almonds lightly.

BUTTER ROSETTES

⅝ pound butter, softened	3 cups sifted all-purpose flour
¾ cup sugar	¾ teaspoon baking powder
3 eggs, separated	1 teaspoon vanilla
Candied cherries	

Cream butter with sugar; add egg yolks, 1 at a time, blending well. Sift flour with baking powder and gradually blend into egg mixture; add vanilla. Form into a ball. Wrap in wax paper and refrigerate at least 2 to 3 hours or longer. Save egg whites for decorating.

Remove dough from refrigerator; let stand long enough to become pliable enough for use in cooky press. Use small star insert, rolling out long strands. Break off enough to form a star. Cookies are small and dainty. Brush with beaten egg white and decorate with ⅛ of candied cherry. Bake on ungreased cooky sheet in a preheated 375° oven for 20 to 25 minutes, until golden brown.

Note: These have a festive party look and are appropriate for any occasion.

Before the Benefit Cocktail Supper

(SERVES 16 TO 18)

Hot Olive Tarts

Crabmeat Brochette

Chicken Liver Pâté in Aspic — Cocktail Rye Bread

Spiced Shrimp

Savory Steak Slices or Tenderloin Slices

Indonesian Chicken Curry

Molded Beet Borscht — Zucchini Garnish

Swedish Tea Cakes   Starlight Crisps   Fudge Squares

Coffee

Service for a group is always a matter of judgment. We offer quantity menus and leave it to you to adjust the amounts to your needs. Perhaps more curry, fish, or the other finger foods may be increased in using these recipes.

ADVANCE PREPARATION SCHEDULE

Deep Freeze	Previous Day	Early Morning
Olive Tarts	*Chicken Liver Pâté*	*Crabmeat*
Tea Cakes	*Molded Borscht*	*Curry*
Fudge Squares	*Marinate steak*	*Fluffy or Fruited*
Starlight Crisps	*Spiced shrimp*	*Rice (see Index)*

HOT OLIVE TARTS

¼ cup butter, softened
1 8-ounce package cream cheese
1 cup all-purpose flour
½ teaspoon salt
36 pimiento-stuffed olives

Blend butter, cream cheese, flour, and salt thoroughly; chill overnight. Roll very thin and cut in 1½-inch squares. Place a pimiento-stuffed olive in center and bring up corners to completely cover. Bake in a preheated 400° oven until brown, 15 minutes. These may be stored in freezer in a plastic bag before baking. If baked frozen, increase heat to 425° and bake slightly longer. Makes 36 tarts.

CRABMEAT BROCHETTE

1 pound fresh crabmeat
1 teaspoon salt
1 teaspoon dry mustard
16 slices bacon, halved
1 teaspoon chopped ripe olives
3 tablespoons sherry
1 cup dried bread crumbs

Remove all bony substance from crabmeat, flake, and blend with salt, mustard, olives, sherry, and bread crumbs. Shape into balls the size of walnuts. Roll a strip of bacon around each ball and fasten with toothpick to prevent from falling apart. Broil until well browned all around, about 15 to 20 minutes. Makes 32 balls.

CHICKEN LIVER PATE IN ASPIC

1 pound chicken livers, yellow
    if possible
½ small onion
2 whole eggs
2 eggs, separated

1 pint heavy cream
2 tablespoons finely chopped
    parsley
Dash salt
Dash pepper

Put chicken livers and onion through grinder, then press through a sieve. Add the 2 whole eggs and 2 egg yolks, cream, parsley, salt, and pepper. Beat remaining 2 egg whites until stiff, and add to mixture. Grease a 9-inch loaf pan with butter; fill with mixture and place in pan of boiling water. Bake in a preheated 350° oven 1 hour. Cool and remove from pan.

Aspic:

1 envelope (1 tablespoon)
    unflavored gelatin
1½ cups canned chicken
    consommé *or* broth

Juice of 1 lemon
Stuffed olives
Slices pimiento
Sprigs parsley

Icebox rye bread

Dissolve gelatin in hot consommé and add lemon juice. Pour approximately ½ inch of liquid into pan and place sliced olives and pimiento in pattern to decorate. When set, replace liver loaf in pan and pour remaining aspic on top. Allow it to run down sides. Refrigerate until set and unmold on parsley-garnished platter. Serve on thin slices of icebox rye bread.

SPICED SHRIMP

2 pounds shrimp, uncooked
1 onion, sliced
1 cup salad oil
1 cup vinegar
½ of 3¼-ounce jar capers and
    juice

1 tablespoon pickling spices
½ teaspoon sharp prepared
    mustard
2 teaspoons Worcestershire
Juice of 1 lemon
½ teaspoon garlic powder

Cook shrimp 5 minutes; shell, clean, and devein. Mix onion, salad oil, vinegar, capers and juice, pickling spices, mustard, Worcestershire, lemon juice, and garlic powder together; pour over shrimp. Store in covered jar in refrigerator for 3 days before serving. Makes approximately 40.

SAVORY STEAK SLICES

2 pounds prime flank steak   ⅔ cup dry white wine
⅔ cup soy sauce   ¼ cup salad oil
                Cocktail rye bread

Flank steak should be cut about 2 inches thick, or be halved
lengthwise. Trim excess fat from meat. Combine soy sauce and
wine; cover meat and marinate in mixture 24 hours in refrigerator.
Remove and drain; brush meat with oil and place 6 inches under
preheated broiler. Broil 1 minute on each side; turn and broil 5
minutes longer, until medium rare. Baste with pan juices. Serve
warm. Place on cutting board, slice in thin diagonal slices, and
serve on cocktail rye slices. Accompany with mustard, pickles, and
relish.

TENDERLOIN SLICES

1 small fillet of beef, about   ½ teaspoon freshly ground
  4 pounds   pepper
¼ cup (⅛ pound) butter   ½ teaspoon rosemary
1 teaspoon salt   ½ cup dry red wine
              About 50 small Parker House Rolls

Rub fillet thoroughly with butter, salt, pepper, and rosemary. Insert meat thermometer in thickest part. Place fillet in a preheated
450° oven and roast 30 to 40 minutes or until thermometer registers
120° for very rare, or 135° for medium. Baste frequently with wine.
Place on serving board; cut in ¼-inch slices and then halve each
slice. Place on opened roll. Makes about 50 small sandwiches.
Freeze leftovers.

INDONESIAN CHICKEN CURRY

2 cups finely grated coconut   ¾ cup all-purpose flour
3 cups milk   1 teaspoon salt
½ cup butter *or* margarine   ¼ teaspoon pepper
¾ cup sliced onions   4 cups chicken stock
1 clove garlic, minced   4 cups cooked chicken, cut
2 tablespoons curry powder   in large pieces
½ teaspoon dry ginger

Place coconut and milk in electric blender, cover, and blend at high speed for 40 seconds. Only half the coconut and the milk can be blended at one time because of the quantity. Pour mixture into a sieve placed over a small bowl and press out as much liquid as possible. Reserve both coconut liquid and coconut.

Heat butter in a large skillet, add onions and garlic, and brown until onions are golden; remove from heat. Add curry, ginger, flour, salt, pepper, and stir to blend. Return to heat. Add chicken stock and coconut liquid gradually. Cook, stirring constantly, until slightly thickened. Add chicken and simmer 10 to 15 minutes, or until mixture is thoroughly heated and flavors blended. Sprinkle half the reserved coconut over the curry and serve over hot Fluffy or Fruited Rice in chafing dish. Serve remaining coconut as a condiment.

Curry Side Dishes:

3 hard-cooked egg yolks	1 cup chopped raisins
3 hard-cooked egg whites	1 cup grated coconut
1 cup chopped peanuts	(canned or fresh)

1 cup chutney

Separate egg yolks from whites; press each through sieve (whites first). Place each of these accompaniments in separate dishes, convenient to the Chicken Curry, that each guest may serve himself.

MOLDED BEET BORSCHT

2 envelopes (2 tablespoons) unflavored gelatin	6 tablespoons sugar
½ cup cold water	⅔ cup red wine vinegar
2 16-ounce cans diced *or* shoestring beets	2 tablespoons instant minced onion
	2 cups dairy sour cream

Dill weed *or* chervil

Soften gelatin in water; drain liquid from beets; combine with sugar and vinegar. Heat to simmering. Dissolve gelatin in hot liquid; chill in refrigerator until syrupy. Stir in beets and onions. Pour into 6-cup ring mold. Chill until firm. Unmold on platter and center with bowl of sour cream, sprinkled with dill weed or chervil.

ZUCCHINI GARNISH

12 zucchini   Freshly ground pepper

Scrub and slice zucchini thin. Circle Beet Mold and sprinkle with freshly ground pepper.

SWEDISH TEA CAKES

1 cup (½ pound) butter	1 teaspoon vanilla
½ cup sugar	2 cups sifted cake flour
1 egg, well beaten	½ teaspoon salt

Cream butter and sugar until light and fluffy; add egg and vanilla; blend. Add flour and salt; mix well. Place about 1 teaspoon batter in 1½-inch greased muffin pans, about 1 inch deep. Press batter up sides and over bottom leaving center hollow. Place about 1 teaspoon Filling in each hollow. Bake in a preheated 350° oven 25 to 30 minutes. Makes 36 cakes.

Filling:

2 eggs, well beaten	¼ teaspoon salt
½ cup sugar	½ pound almonds, finely ground

Combine eggs, sugar, salt, and almonds; blend well. Fill center hollows of cakes and bake as directed.

FUDGE SQUARES

1 cup butter	2 cups sugar
6 1-ounce squares unsweetened chocolate	1 cup all-purpose flour, sifted
	2 teaspoons vanilla
6 eggs, beaten until light and foamy	1½ cups broken walnuts *or* pecans

Melt butter with chocolate in saucepan. To eggs, add sugar and beat until thickened; add flour and vanilla. Beat well and add the chocolate-butter mixture; beat until it bubbles. Add nutmeats. Pour mixture into 11″ x 17″ x 1½″ pan. Bake in a preheated 350° oven about 25 minutes. When done, it will buckle and appear to break. Remove from oven; let cool about 2 or 3 minutes, then cut into

1-inch squares, or larger if you prefer. Makes about 12 dozen 1-inch squares.

Note: These are more glamorous when covered with a chocolate frosting.

STARLIGHT CRISPS

1 cake compressed yeast	½ cup butter *or* margarine
¼ cup lukewarm water	½ cup shortening
3½ cups sifted all-purpose flour	2 eggs, beaten
1½ teaspoons salt	½ cup dairy sour cream
3 teaspoons vanilla	

Soften yeast in lukewarm water. (For dry yeast use warm water.) Sift together flour and salt; cut in butter and shortening. Blend in beaten eggs, sour cream, vanilla, and softened yeast. Mix thoroughly. Cover and chill for 2 hours. Roll out ½ of chilled dough on pastry board; sprinkle with ¾ cup Vanilla Sugar Spread; fold over and put aside. Take remaining ½ chilled mixture, sprinkle with remaining sugar spread; fold over and place both mixtures together, giving 4 layers of dough. Cut into 4″ x 1″ strips. Twist each strip 3 times. Place on ungreased baking sheets. Bake in a preheated 375° oven 15 to 20 minutes until golden brown.

Vanilla Sugar Spread:

1½ cups sugar   2 teaspoons vanilla

Combine sugar and vanilla and use as spread.

Opening Night
Sandwich Supper

(BEFORE THE CURTAIN)

(SERVES 6)

Liver Pâté   Pitted Black Olives   Toast Rounds
Jonathan Ham Sandwich
Chef's Special Sandwich
Williamsburg Club Sandwich
Alsatian Slaw
Blueberry Torte
Coffee

Suggested wine: Rosé

ADVANCE PREPARATION SCHEDULE

Previous Day	Early Morning
Liver pâté	*Chicken salad*
Chicken	*Blueberry Torte*
Slaw	*Chef's Sandwich sauce*
	Assemble sandwich ingredients

LIVER PATE

1 pound livers, chicken, duck,   Pepper
   or turkey   Pinch each: allspice, basil,
6 tablespoons butter   thyme, marjoram
1 tablespoon curry   ½ cup dry Vermouth
Salt   3 tablespoons dairy sour cream

Sauté livers slowly in butter 15 minutes, mashing with fork; add curry, salt, pepper, and herbs; remove from stove; blend in Vermouth and force through sieve or food mill, or a quick spin in the blender. Add cream and blend well. Place in covered container and store in refrigerator for a minimum of 3 days before serving. Makes about 2 cups.

JONATHAN HAM SANDWICH

12 slices white sandwich bread	12 slices baked ham
Mayonnaise to spread	6 small Jonathan apples,
Mustard to spread	unpeeled, sliced thin
12 slices Swiss cheese	

Spread bread lightly with mayonnaise, then with mustard. Cover each slice with 1 slice ham, 4 apple slices, and 1 slice of cheese. Arrange sandwiches on baking sheet. Broil until cheese melts, and is slightly brown. Serve hot, 2 slices per serving.

CHEF'S SANDWICH

3 tablespoons butter	2 tablespoons butter
3 tablespoons flour	¼ pound small fresh mushrooms
1 cup milk	3 slices toast, halved
½ cup cream	12 slices cooked turkey or
¼ cup sherry	chicken
¼ teaspoon salt	⅓ cup Parmesan cheese, grated
⅛ teaspoon ground pepper	(approx.)

Melt 3 tablespoons butter; add flour and stir until golden. Heat combined milk and cream and add to butter and flour, stirring vigorously until thickened; blend in sherry, salt, and pepper. Melt 2 tablespoons butter, add mushrooms, and sauté for 5 minutes; add to sauce. Grease a 10-inch heat-proof platter and arrange toast halves on it. Place 3 slices of chicken or turkey on each half slice of toast; pour sauce over all, and sprinkle well with cheese. Place under broiler and heat until bubbly and brown.

WILLIAMSBURG CLUB SANDWICH

1 large avocado	1½ cups Colony Chicken Salad
½ cup French Dressing	6 thick slices tomato
6 slices toast	2 tablespoons chopped parsley
Olives, pickles, parsley sprigs	

Peel and slice avocado, marinate in French Dressing (see Index) for ½ hour; place toast slices singly on flat surface and on each spread ¼ cup Chicken Salad; drain avocado slices and place on salad. Cover each sandwich with 1 thick slice of tomato and sprinkle with chopped parsley. Place on serving platter; garnish with olives, pickles, and sprigs of parsley.

Colony Chicken Salad:

1 cup diced cooked chicken	¼ cup mayonnaise
½ cup diced celery	¼ teaspoon salt
¼ teaspoon seasoned salt	

Combine all ingredients and toss lightly. Chill.

This simple chicken salad has been included as the sandwich filling to complement the other ingredients. It is a very good and basic recipe, to which you can add your choice of supplements. For a more elaborate and delicious recipe prepare Chicken Salad Supreme (see Index).

ALSATIAN SLAW

1 head of cabbage, boiling water to cover	1 green pepper, diced
¾ cup sugar	1 large onion, diced
1 cup red wine vinegar	Salt
	1 cup oil, olive *or* salad

Shred cabbage, and pour boiling water over it. Let stand. Combine sugar and vinegar in a saucepan and bring to a boil. Strain cabbage, add green pepper, onion, hot vinegar mixture, salt, and oil. Chill, and let stand overnight.

BLUEBERRY TORTE

1 cup all-purpose flour	1 tablespoon cream
⅓ cup sugar	1 quart blueberries
1 teaspoon baking powder	1 cup sugar
½ cup (¼ pound) butter	1 tablespoon flour
1 egg	½ lemon, juice

Sift flour, sugar, and baking powder together. Cream butter and add to dry ingredients; mix well. Beat egg with cream and add to flour and butter mixture. Pastry will be thin and crumbly in texture. Spread thinly on bottom and partway up sides of 9-inch spring form pan. Wash and drain berries; dry thoroughly. Mix sugar and flour, add the berries, and toss lightly to coat them well. Sprinkle with lemon juice. Place in pastry lined pan and bake in a preheated 375° oven 45 to 60 minutes, depending on moistness of berries. For those who are blueberry minded, add an extra pint.

Opening Night
Chafing Dish Supper

(AFTER-THEATER CRITIQUE)

(SERVES 8 TO 10)

Crab Mousse Ring — Fruit Garni

Chicken Curry   Fluffy Rice   Curry Accompaniments

Oriental Pork   Crisp Chinese Noodles

Tomato Beef

Relish Salad Bowl — Tart French Dressing

Brandied Pears Chantilly

Almond Squares   Coconut Crescents   Chocolate Crumbles

Espresso

Suggested wine: white Burgundy

ADVANCE PREPARATION SCHEDULE

Deep Freeze	Previous Day	Early Morning
Almond Squares	*Crab ring*	*Curry*
Chocolate Crumbles	*Pears*	*Oriental Pork*
Coconut Crescents	*French Dressing*	*Frost grapes*
	Marinate salad	*Tomato Beef*

CRAB MOUSSE RING

1½ cups fresh crab *or*
  2 6-ounce cans
3 tablespoons lemon juice
2 tablespoons white wine
  vinegar
2 teaspoons prepared
  horseradish
½ teaspoon salt
½ teaspoon black pepper
1 envelope (1 tablespoon)
  unflavored gelatin

¼ cup cold water
½ cup hot water
1 cup mayonnaise
½ cup dairy sour cream
2 eggs, hard-cooked
Tomato wedges
Pink grapefruit
Avocado
Frosted Grapes

Mix crabmeat with lemon juice, vinegar, horseradish, salt, and pepper. Soften gelatin in cold water for 5 minutes, then dissolve in hot water. Blend mayonnaise and sour cream with gelatin. Add crabmeat and arrange sliced eggs in bottom of a 5-cup oiled ring or fish mold. Pour in crab mixture, and place in refrigerator. Chill until firm. Unmold on serving platter, and garnish with tomato wedges, pink grapefruit, sliced avocado, and clusters of Frosted Grapes, placing in alternate rows, to circle mold. Serve Thousand Island or Louis Dressing separately.

Frosted Grapes:

To frost grapes, wash and dry thoroughly, dip in slightly beaten egg whites, then in sugar. Coat evenly; place on platter to dry. Especially attractive when placed on Galax or other shiny leaves.

CHICKEN CURRY

2 apples, peeled	1½ tablespoons curry powder
1 large onion	3 cups chicken broth
3 stalks celery	3 tablespoons cornstarch
2 tablespoons salad oil	1 teaspoon lemon juice
¼ teaspoon garlic powder	3 cups diced, cooked chicken
1½ teaspoons dry ginger	*or* turkey
1 teaspoon salt	

Chop apples, onion, and celery coarsely. Heat oil, add apple mixture, and sauté until tender. Add garlic powder, ginger, salt, and curry. Make a paste of 3 tablespoons of the broth and cornstarch; blend into mixture with remaining broth. Simmer, stirring constantly, until thickened. Blend in lemon juice and chicken. Heat thoroughly, stirring frequently, as the curry has a tendency to stick. Serve with Fluffy Rice and Curry Side Dishes (see Index).

FLUFFY RICE

2 cups long-grain rice   3 cups hot water   1 teaspoon salt

Wash rice thoroughly in cold water. Drain well and combine with the hot water. Add salt. Place in saucepan. Cover tightly and bring to a quick boil. Reduce heat, simmer slowly for about 25 to 45 minutes, depending on type, or until rice is dry and the water has been absorbed. Do not remove cover or stir while cooking. When rice is done, turn off heat and allow to stand 20 minutes. Prepare sufficient rice to be served with any or all the casserole recipes.

ORIENTAL PORK

1½ cups quick-cooking rice
2 tablespoons oil *or* fat
1 pound boneless fresh pork, cut into ¾-inch cubes
Salt and pepper
2 cups drained fruit liquid plus water
3 tablespoons cornstarch
1 tablespoon soy sauce
3 tablespoons prepared mustard
2 tablespoons vinegar

¼ cup molasses
½ teaspoon dry ginger
1 3½-ounce can pineapple chunks, drained
1 11-ounce can mandarin oranges, drained
1 large green pepper, diced
1 3-ounce can chow mein noodles (optional)
1 11-ounce can water chestnuts, sliced (optional)

Prepare rice according to package directions; for added flavor dissolve 2 chicken bouillon cubes in boiling water before adding rice. Spread in 3-quart shallow casserole. Heat oil in large skillet, add pork, and sauté until evenly browned; sprinkle with salt and pepper. Measure juice from drained canned fruits; add sufficient water to total 2 cups liquid. Make a paste of cornstarch and fruit liquid; mix until well blended and combine with soy sauce, mustard, vinegar, molasses, and ginger. Pour over pork. Cook and stir until thickened and clear. Cover and simmer slowly for 15 minutes, stirring occasionally. Add pineapple, oranges, green pepper, and simmer for 5 minutes more. Pour mixture over rice in casserole. Bake in a preheated 350° oven for 30 minutes. Sprinkle chow mein noodles and water chestnuts over top during last 5 minutes of baking.

This versatile dish has many uses and may be refrigerated (before adding to rice) for baking later. It lends itself to leftover cooking, and may be prepared for chafing dish service. Chicken may be a substitute for the pork.

TOMATO BEEF

3 tablespoons cornstarch	¼ cup soy sauce
½ teaspoon salt	2 medium green peppers,
Dash pepper	¼-inch strips, sliced
3 pounds beef tenderloin,	1 beef bouillon cube
¼-inch slices of leftover beef	¾ cup hot water
3 tablespoons salad oil	¼ cup red wine

3 tomatoes, cut in wedges

Combine cornstarch, salt, pepper, and dredge meat in mixture. Heat oil and sauté meat quickly on each side, about 1 minute; sprinkle with soy sauce. Add green peppers; sauté 2 more minutes. Dissolve bouillon cube in hot water and blend with beef; stir in and add wine and tomatoes. Set aside until ready to serve. Then bring to a quick boil, sufficient to heat, and serve at once. Do not allow tomatoes to become mushy. May be served from casserole or on platter with tomatoes and peppers over meat.

RELISH SALAD BOWL

1 7-ounce can ripe olives, pitted	2 quarts crisp salad greens
1 8-ounce can artichoke hearts, drained	10 tomato slices
	10 mild onion slices
1 8-ounce can button mushrooms, drained	1 large cucumber, sliced
	2 tablespoons sesame seeds, toasted
¼ cup Tart French Dressing	

Tart French Dressing (additional)

Cut olives into large wedges, place in bowl. Cut artichokes in half; combine with drained mushrooms and add to olives. Pour Tart French Dressing (see Index) over all. Toss gently and chill.

To serve, fill salad bowl with an assortment of crisp greens outlined with petal-like leaves; romaine, limestone lettuce, chicory, watercress, etc. Arrange marinated vegetable slices on greens; drizzle any remaining marinade over all. Sprinkle with sesame seeds. Serve with Tart French Dressing.

BRANDIED PEARS CHANTILLY

10 fresh pears *or* 2 #2½ cans
    pear halves
3 cups water
1½ cups sugar
Dash nutmeg

¼ teaspoon dry ginger
⅛ teaspoon ground cloves
½ cup brandy
½ cup Cointreau
1 cup heavy cream, whipped

Peel, core, and halve fresh pears. Combine water, sugar, nutmeg, ginger and cloves; bring to a boil. Simmer raw pears gently in this syrup about 15 minutes or until tender. If using canned pears, simmer gently in syrup 5 minutes. Remove from heat, add brandy and Cointreau; pour over pears. Cool; refrigerate and baste occasionally. Serve in tall stemmed individual compotes; garnish with whipped cream.

ALMOND SQUARES

1 cup (½ pound) butter
1 cup sugar
¾ cup sifted all-purpose flour

1 cup ground almonds
¼ teaspoon salt
6 egg yolks

16 almonds, blanched

Cream the butter; add sugar gradually, beating until light and fluffy. Combine flour, almonds, and salt. Add ⅙ at a time to the butter mixture, alternating with egg yolks, mixing well after each addition. Turn into a buttered 8-inch square pan. Mark 16 squares with a dull-edged knife, and place an almond in the center of each square. Bake in a preheated 350° oven 35 minutes or until browned. Cut through marked squares while still warm.

COCONUT CRESCENTS

1 cup (½ pound) butter
½ cup confectioners' sugar
1¼ cups all-purpose flour

¼ teaspoon vanilla
1 cup chopped pecans
1 cup grated coconut

Cream butter and sugar together, mix in flour. Add vanilla, pecans and coconut and blend well. Roll dough with hands into pencil-like rope; cut into 1½-inch lengths and shape into crescents.
Place on a cooky sheet, leaving space between each crescent for spreading. Bake in a preheated 350° oven until light brown, about 12 minutes.

CHOCOLATE CRUMBLES

1 8-ounce package semi-sweet bits
1 15-ounce can sweetened condensed milk

24 graham crackers, rolled very fine
1 teaspoon vanilla

Mix ingredients well; press into well-buttered 8″ x 8″ pan. Bake in a preheated 375° oven 15 to 18 minutes. Cut in 2-inch squares with wet knife while still warm. Makes 16 squares.

To roll graham crackers:

Drop a few at a time into paper bag (close bag so crumbs won't spill out) and crush with rolling pin. A still faster method is a quick whirl in the blender.

Downbeat Jazz Festival

(SERVES 8)

Shrimp Crab Mold — Sharp Salad Dressing
Toast Curls
Steak Verzany
Braised Celery Fans   Broiled Potatoes
Cloverleaf Rolls
Spicy Cantaloupe
Vanilla Torte
Coffee   Espresso   Tea

Suggested wine: Sylvaner

ADVANCE PREPARATION SCHEDULE

Deep Freeze	Previous Day	Early Morning
Rolls (see Index)	*Mold*	*Steak sauce*
	Dressing	*Assemble Torte*
	Toasted rye bread	
	Bake Torte	
	Spicy Cantaloupe	

SHRIMP CRAB MOLD

1½ teaspoons (½ envelope)
  unflavored gelatin
¾ cup cold water
2 3-ounce packages cream
  cheese
1 10½-ounce can tomato soup

1 cup mayonnaise
1 pound shrimp, cleaned
  and deveined
1 6-ounce can crabmeat,
  deveined
1 cup chopped celery
½ cup ground nuts

Soak gelatin in cold water. Cream the cheese until fluffy. Heat
soup, add gelatin, stir until dissolved. Add mayonnaise, shrimp,
crabmeat, celery, nuts, and blend. Pour into well-oiled 8-cup fish
mold and refrigerate until firm. Unmold on bed of shredded lettuce.
Garnish with pimiento, stuffed olives, and lemon wedges and serve
with Thousand Island Dressing (see Index). Caviar may be added
to Dressing, or another choice is Sharp Salad Dressing.

SHARP SALAD DRESSING

¾ cup mayonnaise
2 tablespoons bottled
  barbecue sauce

2 tablespoons chili sauce
2 tablespoons prepared
  horseradish

Combine mayonnaise, barbecue sauce, chili sauce, and horseradish;
mix well and refrigerate.

TOAST CURLS

Cut paper-thin slices from unsliced cocktail rye bread, remove
crusts, and bake. Toast rye slices in a preheated 350° oven until
brown and crisp, about 10 minutes. Butter and serve hot.

STEAK VERZANY

½ cup (¼ pound) beef marrow,
  diced
¼ cup (⅛ pound) butter
½ cup chopped shallots or onions
¼ teaspoon thyme
¼ teaspoon garlic, minced
1 cup champagne (smallest size
  bottle)

1 teaspoon steak sauce
1 tablespoon chopped parsley
4- to 4½-pound sirloin, or
  porterhouse steak
1 teaspoon salt
½ teaspoon pepper

Poach the beef marrow in salted water to cover for 10 minutes. Drain. Melt the butter; add onions and cook over low heat for 5 minutes. Add thyme, garlic, champagne, and steak sauce. Cover and cook over low heat until reduced to half. Add parsley and marrow. Broil steak to desired degree of doneness, add salt and pepper, pour sauce over. Serve at once.

Note: Sauce is delicious with broiled liver, but marrow should be omitted.

BRAISED CELERY FANS

3 bunches celery 1 teaspoon concentrated
2 tablespoons butter beef extract
Paprika, parsley

Trim discolored edges at bottoms of celery bunches. Cut off base of each bunch, including heart in a 3-inch piece. Upper portion may be used for other purposes (relish or cooking). Clean and wash. Place in ice water about an hour. Drain and cut in ¼-inch slices through heart. Melt butter; blend in beef extract and sauté celery slices until soft and lightly brown. Serve 2 or 3 slices (fans) for each portion. Use as a border on steak platter. Dust with paprika and garnish with parsley.

BROILED POTATOES

6 potatoes, medium size, cut in   6 teaspoons salt
  ¼-inch slices, white or sweet   ⅛ teaspoon freshly ground
1 onion, chopped, *or*   pepper
  1 tablespoon instant   2 tablespoons butter
  minced onion

Wash and slice potatoes (with or without skins); arrange on flat baking pan or large cooky sheet. Sprinkle with onion, salt, pepper, and place dab of butter on each slice. Broil at 400° (preheated) on lower broiler rack away from heat. Potatoes will be done in about 15 minutes, tender and slightly brown. Broil a few minutes longer for more crispness and a browner look. Serve layered on flat dish.

SPICY CANTALOUPE

1 large cantaloupe	¼ cup brown sugar, firmly packed
⅔ cup canned fruit juice	¼ cup wine vinegar
(pineapple, grapefruit, etc.)	1 ½-inch stick cinnamon
3 whole cloves	¼ teaspoon dry ginger

Peel cantaloupe; cut into cubes. Place in large flat dish. Combine remaining ingredients in a saucepan, bring to a boil, reduce heat, and simmer 10 minutes. Pour over cantaloupe, cool; place in refrigerator overnight. Serve cold as relish. Makes 1 pint.

VANILLA TORTE

Sunshine Cake:

7 eggs, separated	¼ cup orange juice
¼ cup sugar	1¼ cups sifted cake flour
½ teaspoon cream of tartar	

Have eggs at room temperature. Beat yolks well, about 2 to 3 minutes in electric mixer. Add sugar gradually, beating continually; add orange juice and beat until light and fluffy. Sift flour again and fold in slowly. Whip egg whites, adding cream of tartar when they start to foam. Beat until stiff, but not dry. Fold yellow batter into beaten egg whites, very gently; bake in 10-inch spring form in a preheated 325° oven 1 hour. Invert pan and allow to cool before removing from pan. Loosen around edges to release.

Vanilla Torte Filling:

3 egg yolks	1 cup milk
2 tablespoons all-purpose flour	1 teaspoon vanilla
1 tablespoon sugar	

Combine egg yolks, flour, milk, vanilla, and sugar; cook in double boiler until thick. Let cool.

Vanilla Meringue:

3 egg whites	¼ cup sugar
½ teaspoon cream of tartar	½ teaspoon vanilla

Beat egg whites until foamy, add cream of tartar, and beat until mounds form; add sugar and beat until stiff. Frost entire cake with meringue, forming graceful swirls. Bake in a preheated 375° oven about 15 minutes, or until lightly browned. Meringue will be accented by the deeper brown of the crests of the swirls.

Variations:

May be sliced in half, filled with custard and frosted, or filled with whipped cream and frosted with cream and topped with shaved chocolate, or chopped candied cherries.

For a cooling summer dessert, serve with a scoop of your favorite ice cream and chocolate or strawberry sauce.

For "weightwatchers," serve plain, or with a shake of confectioners' sugar.

Summer Stock Buffet Party

(SERVES APPROXIMATELY 10)

Mushroom Canapés   Chicken-Almond Appetizers
Shrimp Cocktail Mold   Pinwheels
Chicken Loire
Curried Lamb   Meat Balls Fritzi
Claret Strawberry Bowl
Lemon Icebox Cake   Finger Fruit and Relish Tray
Chocolate Layer Cake
Coffee

Suggested wine: Rosé

ADVANCE PREPARATION SCHEDULE

Deep Freeze	Previous Day	Early Morning
Meat balls	*Refrigerate pinwheels*	*Mushroom Canapés*
Cake	*Shrimp Mold*	*Marinate chicken*
	Curried Lamb	*Prepare appetizers*
	Icebox Cake	*Prepare fruit*
		Frost cake

MUSHROOM CANAPES

4 tablespoons butter	2 tablespoons chopped parsley
½ pound mushrooms, coarsely chopped	½ cup dairy sour cream
	12 slices bread, thin-sliced
1 teaspoon grated onion	Paprika

Heat butter in saucepan; add mushrooms and onion; sauté until lightly browned. Combine with parsley and sour cream. Cut each slice of bread into two 1½-inch rounds. Pile mixture on bread; dust with paprika. Brown in a preheated 350° oven 15 minutes. May be made in advance and browned when ready to serve. Makes 2 dozen.

CHICKEN-ALMOND APPETIZERS

1 tablespoon butter	1 teaspoon capers (optional)
1 tablespoon flour	2 tablespoons toasted and chopped almonds
½ cup warm milk	
1 tablespoon sauterne	4 slices bread, toasted and cut in fourths
½ teaspoon salt	
1 cup cooked, finely chopped chicken	¼ pound Cheddar cheese, sliced

Melt butter in skillet; add flour, stirring until smooth. Stir milk in slowly. When thickened, add wine, salt, chicken, capers, and almonds. Spread on toasted bread squares and top with a small slice of Cheddar cheese. Bake or broil until bubbly and heated through thoroughly. Makes 16 canapés.

PINWHEELS

1 loaf white bread, unsliced	2 tablespoons pickle relish
8 ounces prepared pimiento cheese spread	2 tablespoons liquid from stuffed olives

Small-size stuffed olives

Cut the loaf of bread into 4 thin slices, cut lengthwise; trim the crusts. Blend pimiento cheese spread with pickle relish and olive liquid; spread each slice of bread with cheese mixture. Arrange a row of olives, placed lengthwise, across the narrow end of each slice; roll, beginning at this end, as in making jelly roll. Wrap each roll in wax paper and place in refrigerator until ready to serve. Cut each roll into 7 or 8 pinwheels.

SHRIMP COCKTAIL MOLD

½ cup finely cut celery
4 tablespoons chopped green pepper
4 hard-cooked eggs
2 pounds shrimp, cooked and ground

4 ounces cream cheese
6 tablespoons chili sauce
1 tablespoon Worcestershire
2 teaspoons prepared horseradish
2 teaspoons onion juice
Cherry tomatoes

Grind celery, green pepper, and eggs; add remaining ingredients and mix well. Place mixture in greased 6-cup mold, and chill. Garnish with cherry tomatoes and Dilled Brussels Sprouts (see Index).

CURRIED LAMB

4 cups cold cooked Lamb
6 tablespoons butter
1 medium-size onion, diced
1 clove garlic, minced
1 apple, diced

4 stalks celery, diced
4 tablespoons flour
2 teaspoons salt
4 teaspoons curry powder
4 cups lamb stock *or* tomato purée

Trim fat from lamb. Place butter in saucepan; sauté onion, garlic, apple, and celery until soft and yellowed. Stir in flour, salt, and curry powder; cook for 1 minute. Add lamb stock or tomato purée and stir until sauce boils. Add lamb and simmer 10 minutes. Serve with Boiled Rice and Curry Side Dishes (optional, see Index).

CHICKEN LOIRE

½ cup tarragon vinegar
½ cup lemon juice
2 frying chickens, cut into small serving pieces
2 eggs, slightly beaten
1 tablespoon water
2 cups crushed cornflakes

½ cup butter
2 tablespoons butter
½ cup chopped onion
½ pound fresh mushrooms, sliced
1 10½-ounce can cream of mushroom soup
1½ cups light cream

Combine vinegar and lemon juice; add chicken pieces, cover, and marinate in refrigerator for 2 hours. Remove chicken from marinade. Blend eggs with water; dip chicken in mixture, then roll in crushed cornflake crumbs. Melt ½ cup butter in heavy skillet; brown chicken evenly. Melt 2 tablespoons butter in a small skillet; add onion and mushrooms and sauté until golden. Pour 2 tablespoons of marinade in bottom of large shallow casserole. Add browned chicken, mushrooms, and onion. Combine soup and cream; pour over chicken. Bake in a preheated 350° oven 45 minutes to 1 hour, or until chicken is tender; 15 to 20 minutes before chicken is ready to be removed from oven, sprinkle with remaining cornflakes.

MEAT BALLS FRITZI

1 8-ounce can tomato sauce	1 large grated potato
1 cup of water	1 large grated onion
1 10-ounce glass of tomato preserves	2 eggs
	1 tablespoon French Dressing mix
2 pounds ground round steak	1 teaspoon salt

In 4-quart saucepan, cook tomato sauce, water, and preserves for 5 minutes. Mix remaining ingredients lightly but thoroughly. Shape into balls the size of a walnut, drop into sauce and simmer, covered, for 1 hour. These can be prepared in advance and freeze well.

Variation:

Grape jelly may be substituted for the tomato preserves and chili sauce for the tomato sauce.

FINGER FRUIT AND RELISH TRAY

On a tray or platter, about 10″ x 14″, arrange 24 wax paper baking cups, muffin size. Fill the cups, arranging them with interest, with any or all of the following, or with others of your own selection.

Bunches of grapes	Carrot sticks
Pineapple wedges on toothpicks	Celery fans
	Plums
Small apples	Pickles
Orange wedges	Cubes of cheeses
Strawberries	Radish roses

CLARET STRAWBERRY BOWL

2 quarts strawberries ¼ cup sugar (optional)
1 cup claret

Wash and hull berries, leaving whole. Sprinkle with sugar. Pour claret over berries and chill in refrigerator 1 hour before serving. Served in a large glass bowl the strawberries are an attractive appointment.

LEMON ICEBOX CAKE

1½ cups (¾ pound) unsalted butter	Juice and rind of 1½ lemons
3 cups powdered sugar	2¼ cups chopped nuts
6 eggs, separated	2½ dozen ladyfingers, split in half

1 cup heavy cream, whipped

Cream butter and sugar; add egg yolks, one at a time, beating well. Add lemon juice, rind, and nuts. Beat egg whites until stiff and fold into mixture.

Line sides and bottom of a 9-inch spring form with ladyfingers. Pour in ½ of mixture; add a layer of ladyfingers, and then remaining mixture; top with layer of ladyfingers. Chill until set. Before serving, frost with whipped cream. Border with a sprinkling of yellow decorating sugar (optional).

Whipped Cream Frosting:

We suggest the use of Whipped Cream Frosting as an alternate, as the gelatin holds it better for storage.

1 teaspoon unflavored gelatin   1 cup heavy cream, chilled
4 teaspoons cold water   ¼ cup confectioners' sugar
¼ teaspoon vanilla

Combine gelatin and cold water; dissolve over hot water. Beat heavy cream; pour slightly cooled gelatin into cream; add sugar and vanilla, continuing to beat until stiff; use care not to overbeat. Chill in refrigerator for 15 minutes before frosting cake. Cake may then be refrigerated in advance of serving.

CHOCOLATE LAYER CAKE

3 eggs, well beaten	3 teaspoons baking powder
1½ cups heavy cream, whipped	1½ cups sugar
2¼ cups cake flour	½ teaspoon salt
1½ teaspoons vanilla	

Fold beaten eggs lightly into whipped cream. Sift flour, baking powder, sugar, and salt together twice; then sift slowly into cream mixture, folding in gently. Add vanilla. Pour into 2 greased and floured 9-inch cake tins. Bake 25 to 30 minutes in a preheated 350° oven. Frost and layer with Chocolate Frosting.

Chocolate Frosting:

2 1-ounce squares chocolate	⅓ teaspoon salt
2 cups sifted confectioners' sugar	1 egg, beaten well
⅓ cup shortening, softened	

Melt chocolate over hot water; blend with remaining ingredients and beat until smooth and fluffy.

Variation:

A very good cake with berries and heavy cream, whipped.

Dinner Club Meets

(SERVES 8)

Escargots Bourguignonne

Pickled Mushrooms   Green Goddess Dip

Whole Wheat Thins

Crown Roast of Lamb — Celery Root Dressing

Casserole Peas   Scotch Scones

Cheesecake Regency

Coffee or Mexican Coffee

Suggested wine: Rhine or claret

ADVANCE PREPARATION SCHEDULE

Deep Freeze	Previous Day	Early Morning
Scones	Rolls	Prepare escargots
	Mushrooms (see Index)	Dressing
	Cake	Crown roast
	Green Goddess Dip	Hollandaise
	(see Index)	Peas
		Cheesecake

ESCARGOTS BOURGUIGNONNE

2 cups dry white wine   1 tablespoon chopped shallot
1 clove garlic, minced   *or* green onion
2 dozen canned snails and shells

Boil together wine, garlic, and shallot until the wine is reduced to ¾ cup. Strain through a fine sieve. Have snails and their shells assembled. Pour 1 scant teaspoon of the reduced wine in the bottom of each shell, replace the snails in their shell, and seal with parsley butter.

Parsley Butter:

1 cup butter   ½ teaspoon lemon juice
½ cup chopped parsley

Cream butter with lemon juice, and blend in parsley. Place the prepared snails on a baking sheet and heat in a preheated 400° oven about 10 minutes.

CROWN ROAST OF LAMB

1 16-rib crown roast of lamb   Freshly ground pepper
1 clove garlic, minced (optional)   1 teaspoon rosemary
Salt   Dressing for center

Have roast tied together in crown fashion, two 8-rib sections of two loins, with bones cut evenly across the top. If surplus for serving is desired, increase to two 10-rib sections, allowing 2 ribs per serving. Wipe with a damp cloth and cover each bone with aluminum foil to prevent charring. Rub with minced garlic, salt, freshly ground pepper, and rosemary. Place on rack in roasting pan and sear in a preheated 450° oven 10 minutes. Reduce heat to 350° and continue to roast, allowing 15 minutes per pound for the over-all roasting. Remove and fill center with Celery Root Dressing. Place under broiler until lightly browned, then remove foil from bones and replace with paper frills or preserved kumquats.

CELERY ROOT DRESSING

1 pound potatoes, cooked	½ cup Hollandaise Sauce
1 pound celery root, fresh	½ teaspoon salt
or canned, cooked	⅛ teaspoon freshly ground pepper

Combine potatoes with celery root and purée or mash thoroughly. Heat over boiling water; blend in Hollandaise, salt, and pepper. Fill center of crown and place under broiler until lightly browned.

Garnish:

1 #2½ can peach halves, heated   3 teaspoons mint jelly
                       Parsley

Serve on platter garnished with drained peach halves, hollow side up, on parsley sprigs; fill each with 1 teaspoon mint jelly.

I Hollandaise Sauce:

¼ cup butter, softened	Dash nutmeg
2 egg yolks	¼ teaspoon salt
2 teaspoons lemon juice	¼ cup boiling water

Cream butter until soft and smooth. Beat in egg yolks, one at a time, then lemon juice and seasoning. Put in refrigerator in bowl that can be set over hot water. Just before serving set over hot, *not* boiling water, stirring constantly while heating. When hot add the ½ cup boiling water very gradually. Makes about ⅔ cup.

II Quick Blender Hollandaise:

½ cup butter	2 tablespoons fresh lemon juice
4 egg yolks	¼ teaspoon salt
Pinch cayenne	

Melt butter until bubbling; *do not* brown. Place egg yolks, lemon juice, salt, and cayenne in blender. Cover container, and whirl motor quickly on and off. Remove cover; turn motor on high and immediately add hot butter, pouring steadily. Turn off motor as last drop of butter is poured. Makes about 1 cup.

Note: If either Hollandaise sauce is used for topping other foods, serve immediately, while hot.

CASSEROLE PEAS

2 tablespoons butter
½ pound fresh mushrooms, sliced
2 packages frozen peas
1 10½-ounce can mushroom soup, undiluted

1 can bean sprouts, drained
1 4-ounce can water chestnuts, sliced
Toasted slivered almonds *or* French-fried onion rings (optional)

Heat butter in saucepan, add mushrooms, sauté for 5 minutes. Combine with peas, soup, bean sprouts, and water chestnuts. Place in lightly buttered casserole and bake in a preheated 350° oven 20 to 25 minutes. Toasted slivered almonds or broken up French-fried onion rings may be sprinkled over top before baking.

This recipe from *Thoughts for Buffets* has been so popular that we present it again (with slight variations).

SCOTCH SCONES
(From Edinburgh, Scotland)

2 cups all-purpose flour
2 teaspoons baking powder
½ teaspoon salt
2 teaspoons sugar
4 teaspoons butter

1 orange rind, grated
1 lemon rind, grated
½ cup raisins, finely chopped
2 eggs, minus ⅓ of 1 white
⅓ cup light cream

Sugar (for topping)

Sift flour once; measure, add baking powder, salt, and sugar; sift again. Cut in butter with pastry blender or knives; add fruit rind and raisins. Reserve about ⅓ of egg white for glaze. Beat remaining eggs well and add cream. Add all at once to flour mixture and stir until all flour is dampened; stir vigorously until mixture forms a soft dough and follows spoon around bowl. Turn out on floured board and knead about 30 seconds. Roll ½ inch thick and cut in triangles. Place on ungreased baking sheet, brush top lightly with slightly beaten egg white. Sprinkle with sugar. Bake in a preheated 450° oven 12 to 15 minutes, or until browned.

CHEESECAKE REGENCY

Graham Cracker Crumb Crust:

1½ cups packaged graham cracker crumbs

¼ cup sugar
½ cup butter *or* margarine, melted

Combine crumbs and sugar in small bowl; blend in butter. Press firmly over bottom and about 2½ inches up sides of a heavily buttered 9-inch spring-form pan; chill.

Filling:

3 8-ounce packages cream cheese	⅛ teaspoon salt
1½ cups sugar	4 eggs
	1 teaspoon vanilla

Let cream cheese soften in large bowl. Blend in sugar, add salt, and beat until fluffy. Add eggs, 1 at a time, beating well after each addition. Beat in vanilla, then pour into Crumb Crust. Bake in a preheated 350° oven 50 minutes, or until firm in center. Remove cake from oven; let stand 15 minutes. Reset oven to very hot, 450°.

Topping:

2 cups dairy sour cream	1 teaspoon vanilla
	¼ cup sugar

Combine sour cream, sugar, and vanilla in small bowl; spread over top of cake. Return to 450° oven to bake 10 minutes, or just until topping is set. Cool cake on wire rack, then chill completely.

To remove cake from spring form, loosen around edge with knife; release spring and remove sides of pan; leave cake on metal base for easy handling and serving. For a party touch, top with a rosette of sliced fresh strawberries. Makes one 9-inch cake for generous serving of 12 to 16 wedges.

Variation:

Add ½ teaspoon almond extract to cake.

MEXICAN COFFEE

2 cups strong freshly brewed coffee	1 cup milk
	½ cup heavy cream, whipped
1½ cups chocolate syrup	Grated rind of 1 orange

Combine coffee, syrup, and milk. Heat. Top with spoonful of whipped cream and a sprinkling of orange rind.

Served in the living room, this Mexican specialty, in a lovely pot, provides a gracious finale to complete the dinner. The whipped cream and orange are attractive in small bowls placed on the tray.

Poker Club Dinner

(SERVES 6)

Pecan Mushrooms
Cabbage Provençale   Beer
Celery Cheese Salad   Rye Rolls
Linzer Torte
Coffee

ADVANCE PREPARATION SCHEDULE

Deep Freeze

Linzer Torte

Early Morning

Pecan Mushrooms for broiling
Stuff celery
Cabbage Provençale

PECAN MUSHROOMS

1 pound large fresh mushrooms
1 tablespoon olive oil
1 small onion
¼ cup chopped pecans
3 tablespoons butter
1 teaspoon basil

3 tablespoons bread crumbs
Dash Tabasco
1 teaspoon Worcestershire
½ teaspoon salt
3 tablespoons Parmesan
    cheese

Remove stems of mushrooms; brush caps with olive oil. Chop stems, onion, and pecans coarsely; sauté in butter 5 minutes. Add basil, bread crumbs, Tabasco, Worcestershire, and salt. Place caps in pan and broil 2½ minutes on each side. Fill caps with bread crumb mixture. Sprinkle with Parmesan cheese and place under broiler for 5 minutes more, or until heated.

STUFFED CABBAGE PROVENCALE

3 pounds lean ground beef,
    round *or* chuck
1½ cups cooked white rice, firm

1 large onion, grated
2 teaspoons salt
Fresh-ground pepper
1 large head cabbage

Combine beef, rice, onion, salt, and pepper; blend thoroughly.

Cover and refrigerate while preparing other ingredients. Place whole head of cabbage in boiling water just long enough to allow the leaves to become flexible. Drain well and set aside on large platter.

Gingersnap Sauce Provençale:

1 #2½ can Italian tomatoes	1 tablespoon sugar
1 8-ounce can tomato sauce	1 tablespoon minced parsley
1 cup water	1 small onion, grated
3 tablespoons lemon juice	8 gingersnaps

Combine tomatoes, tomato sauce, water, lemon juice, sugar, parsley, and onion; simmer for ¾ of an hour. While this is cooking, prepare stuffed cabbage. Remove meat mixture from refrigerator. Scoop a proportionate amount of this mixture into each cabbage leaf, folding the leaves package-wise around the meat, and secure them further with toothpicks. Place the cabbage rolls, a few at a time, in a heavy skillet, with enough butter to cover bottom of skillet. Carefully turn the cabbage rolls as they sauté over a medium to hot flame until lightly browned and glazed. Remove and carefully place them in the cooked tomato mixture. Gently cook both sauce and cabbage rolls together for another 40 minutes. Now remove cabbage rolls again. Add the gingersnaps to the tomato sauce. Simmer slowly for 5 minutes, breaking down the bulk of the whole small tomatoes, and any remaining lumps from the gingersnaps. Place cabbage rolls in a casserole or chafing dish and pour sauce over them. Reheat in chafing dish, or if serving in casserole place in a preheated 350° oven for 20 minutes until steaming.

An old-fashioned recipe, prosaic in content but a savory offering for guests as well as family.

CELERY CHEESE SALAD

1 3-ounce package blue cheese	1 large bunch celery
1 4-ounce jar prepared blue	Caraway seeds
cheese spread	Romaine *or* curly endive

Mash blue cheese; blend thoroughly with cheese spread. Wash and separate celery into stalks. Dry thoroughly. Fill hollows of celery with cheese mixture, level with knife, sprinkle with caraway seeds, and press to adhere; refrigerate. Just before serving, arrange romaine

or endive on chilled salad plates. Slice celery stalks crosswise into
bite-size pieces. Place 6 or 8 pieces on bed of greens; dust lightly
with paprika.

LINZER TORTE

1½ cups sifted all-purpose flour	½ cup firmly packed brown sugar
¼ cup sugar	½ cup (¼ pound) butter
½ teaspoon double-acting baking powder	1 egg, beaten
½ teaspoon salt	⅓ cup blanched almonds, ground
½ teaspoon cinnamon	1 tablespoon flour

Sift together flour, sugar, baking powder, salt, and cinnamon. Cut
in brown sugar and butter. Add egg and almonds. Blend with
pastry blender. Reserve a generous ½ cup of dough for topping;
blend this with 1 tablespoon flour and chill.

Press remaining dough evenly into bottom and sides of an
8-inch pie pan. Do not cover rim. Fill with Cream Filling and top
with Raspberry Sauce. Roll out chilled ½ cup of dough on floured
pastry cloth or board; cut in ½-inch strips with pastry wheel. Slip
long spatula under strips and transfer to top of torte, arranging
strips over filling, crisscross fashion. With another strip, circle the
pie, covering the ends of the lattice strips. Do not cover rim of
pie pan. Bake in a preheated 375° oven 45 minutes.

Cream Filling:

1 egg	¼ teaspoon salt
⅓ cup sugar	1½ cups milk, scalded in
¼ cup sifted flour	top of double boiler
1 teaspoon vanilla	

Beat egg until fluffy, about 2 minutes. Add sugar gradually; beat
until thick and lemon colored. Blend in flour and salt. Gradually
add scalded milk. Cook over boiling water, stirring constantly, until
thick. Cover and continue cooking for 4 to 5 minutes, stirring occasionally. Add vanilla. Cool.

Raspberry Sauce:

1 10-ounce package thawed, frozen raspberries, undrained	2 tablespoons sugar
	2 tablespoons cornstarch
1 tablespoon lemon juice	

Combine undrained raspberries, sugar and cornstarch in sauce-pan. Add lemon juice. Bring to boil and cook for 5 to 10 minutes, until mixture begins to thicken. Cool.

If raspberries are absorbed in baking, raspberry jam may be added to topping of sauce when torte is removed from oven.

Curling We Must Go
Stag Supper

(SERVES 8)

Lentil Soup
Poor Boy Sandwich
Head Lettuce — Spice French Dressing
Wheel of Brie Cheese — Water Crackers
Rice Custard International
Coffee

Suggested wine: red Burgundy

ADVANCE PREPARATION SCHEDULE

Previous Day	Early Morning
Soup (without frankfurters)	*Rice Custard*
Dressing	*Assemble sandwich ingredients*

LENTIL SOUP

2 cups lentils	3 carrots
2½ quarts water	1 tablespoon salt
2 onions, diced	¼ teaspoon pepper
2 tablespoons fat	1 bay leaf
or butter	8 frankfurters, sliced thin

Wash and drain lentils; combine with water; bring to a boil and cook over medium heat 1 hour. Heat fat in skillet; add onions and brown. Add to lentils with carrots, salt, pepper, and bay leaf. Simmer, covered, over low heat 2 hours. Discard bay leaf and rub mixture through food mill or sieve. Return to saucepan. Add frankfurters and cook over low heat 10 minutes. Croutons are a tasteful garnish.

POOR BOY SANDWICH

1 pound ground beef
⅓ cup grated Parmesan cheese
¼ cup grated onion
1 6-ounce can tomato paste
1 teaspoon salt
¼ cup chopped black olives
½ teaspon oregano
Pepper
1 long French bread, halved lengthwise
3 tomatoes, sliced
1 4-ounce package sliced cheese, mozzarella, cheddar, etc.

Combine ground beef, grated cheese, onion, tomato paste, salt, olives, oregano, pepper; arrange mixture on halves of French bread. Bake 15 minutes in a preheated 350° oven; arrange slices of tomato and cheese on top of meat mixture and broil about 10 minutes at least 6 inches from heat. Serve with a garnish of assorted pickles on leaf lettuce.

HEAD LETTUCE — SPICE FRENCH DRESSING

1½ cups olive oil
½ cup wine vinegar
1 tablespoon tarragon vinegar
1 teaspoon garlic salt
1 teaspoon dry mustard
1 teaspoon sugar
½ teaspoon coarsely ground pepper
1 teaspoon paprika
1 tablespoon Worcestershire
2 green peppers, sliced
2 heads Iceberg lettuce

Combine all ingredients; blend well. Serve with platter of thick slices from solid heads of lettuce. Top each slice with ring of pepper.

RICE CUSTARD INTERNATIONAL

5 eggs
1 cup granulated sugar
½ teaspoon vanilla
½ teaspoon salt
1 quart milk
1 cup cooked rice
⅓ cup raisins (optional)
Cinnamon

Break eggs in mixing bowl; add sugar, salt, vanilla, and milk. Blend well with wire whisk, but do not overbeat. Sprinkle cooked rice on bottom of greased baking pan and pour mixture over it. Place in a pan of boiling water and bake in a preheated 300° oven 1 hour, until set. Raisins may be added if desired. Sprinkle top lightly with cinnamon. Serve in low compotes, hot or cold.

Duplicate Bridge Party Continental Dinner

(SERVES 8)

Pea Soup St. Germain — Croutons
Chicken Paprika Vienna
Spaetzle   Bohnen Suess und Sauer
Brandy Pear Compote
Sacher Torte
Coffee

Suggested wine: Rhine

ADVANCE PREPARATION SCHEDULE

Deep Freeze	**Previous Day**	**Early Morning**
Sacher Torte (unfrosted)	*Pea Soup* *Pear Compote*	*Spaetzle dough* *Prepare beans* *Frost Torte* *Chicken*

PEA SOUP ST. GERMAIN

4 tablespoons butter	2 teaspoons salt
3 10-ounce packages frozen peas	½ teaspoon sugar
½ cup lettuce, shredded, firmly packed	½ cup water
½ cup green part of leeks *or* green onion tops, chopped	1 quart chicken consommé
	Pinch chervil (optional)

Melt butter in saucepan; add peas, lettuce, leek tops, salt, sugar, and water. Cover and simmer until peas are thoroughly cooked. Purée vegetables through a fine sieve or food mill; add to the consommé. Heat and serve. Garnish with small croutons and pinch of chervil.

CROUTONS

3 slices bread, cut in ¼-inch cubes	2 tablespoons melted butter
	¼ teaspoon garlic salt (optional)

Toss bread in melted butter until lightly browned and crisp. Dust with garlic salt before toasting.

CHICKEN PAPRIKA VIENNA

4 medium-size onions, sliced	2 teaspoons salt
6 tablespoons cooking oil	¼ cup flour
4 teaspoons paprika	3 cups hot water
2 roasting chickens, cut in eighths	6 tablespoons dairy sour cream (optional)
¼ cup tomato paste	Parsley
1 green pepper, sliced	

Sauté onions in oil; add paprika, cut-up chicken, tomato paste, green pepper, and salt. Simmer for 10 minutes. Stir in flour and simmer additional 5 minutes; add hot water and cook slowly, covered, until tender, stirring occasionally. Reserve a cup of gravy for Spaetzle (check with Spaetzle recipe). Sour cream may be added to remaining gravy. Arrange chicken on platter, bordered with Spaetzle and gravy. Garnish with parsley.

SPAETZLE

4 eggs, well beaten 2 teaspoons salt
½ cup water 2 cups all-purpose flour
1 egg, beaten, for gravy

Mix eggs, water, 1 teaspoon salt, and flour; beat well. Batter should be stiff and smooth. Boil 6 cups water with second teaspoon salt in 8-quart pot; drop dough into water from a wet teaspoon, making small dumplings. Boil 5 minutes. Drain, rinse with hot water, drain again. Put 1 cup of the reserved chicken gravy in heavy pan; heat Spaetzle in it. Stir beaten egg into ¼ cup of this heated gravy and return to chicken to simmer for 2 or 3 minutes more.

Note: The Spaetzle are simple to prepare and delicious with many other recipes. Rinse them in hot water; drain as directed, and use them in soups and with gravies.

BOHNEN SUESS UND SAUER

2 pounds green beans ⅔ cup cold water
2 teaspoons salt ¼ cup cider vinegar *or*
¼ cup butter *or* margarine lemon juice
2 tablespoons all-purpose flour 2 tablespoons granulated sugar

Cut green beans into 1-inch or 2-inch pieces, or French cut. (See glossary). Cook in salted water, covered, until tender. Drain, leaving about 2 tablespoons liquid in pan. Melt butter, blend in flour, and brown slightly. Stir in cold water and cook, stirring, until smooth. Combine sauce with beans and continue stirring, until heated. Add vinegar and sugar; simmer a few minutes longer.

BRANDY PEAR COMPOTE

4 large firm fresh pears *or* ½ cup strawberry preserves
1 #2½ can pears ¼ cup peach *or* apricot brandy

Peel, core, and cut pears into sixths. Place in saucepan with preserves; cover and simmer slowly for 20 minutes. Add ½ cup water and brandy; cook 10 minutes or until pears are tender. If canned pears are used, simmer only 8 minutes. Refrigerate.

SACHER TORTE

10 egg yolks, beaten	12 ounces semi-sweet chocolate
1 cup sugar	morsels
2 cups ground walnuts	2 tablespoons strong brewed
2 tablespoons bread	coffee
crumbs	10 egg whites, beaten stiff
1 teaspoon finely ground	½ cup tart jelly, currant *or*
coffee	raspberry (more if necessary)

Beat egg yolks with sugar until lemon colored. Stir walnuts into egg yolks; add bread crumbs and ground coffee. Melt chocolate in hot, strong brewed coffee, cool; add to yolk mixture. Fold in stiffly beaten egg whites. Pour into 9-inch greased spring form; bake 1 hour in a preheated 350° oven. Cool on cake rack. Cover top and sides with a thin layer of tart jelly, then with Chocolate Frosting.

Chocolate Frosting:

4 1-ounce squares	1 cup sugar
unsweetened chocolate	2 egg yolks, beaten
½ cup strong brewed	¼ cup (⅛ pound) unsalted
coffee	butter, softened

Combine chocolate and coffee in saucepan. Heat until dissolved and add sugar. Cook until smooth and thickened, stirring frequently. Remove from heat; beat in egg yolks and butter. Cool and spread on cake. This is a large cake and will freeze well for another occasion.

Family Fare

A FESTIVE menu is in order with the family around the dining table. Activities are recounted, plans discussed, opinions exchanged. Family Fare gives recognition to these important "guests" and the thoughtful "hostess mother" provides the background with her own warmth.

Family Fare Brunch

(SERVES 8)

Swiss Omelet

Tomato Indienne

Cinnamon Toast Toffees

Fruit Caprice — Foamy Sauce

Coffee   Tea   Milk

Suggested wine: dry Riesling

ADVANCE PREPARATION SCHEDULE

Previous Day	Early Morning
Fruit Caprice	*Start toffees*
	Tomato Indienne
	(see Index)

SWISS OMELET

8 egg yolks	2 teaspoons baking powder
½ cup milk	¼ cup (⅛ pound) butter
⅓ cup mashed sardines	8 egg whites
⅛ teaspoon garlic powder	½ teaspoon salt
¼ teaspoon cloves	2 cups shredded Swiss cheese

Combine egg yolks with milk, sardines, garlic powder, and cloves; beat lightly. Mix in baking powder. In each of two 9-inch skillets or round layer cake pans, melt half the butter. Beat egg whites with salt until stiff but not dry. Fold in egg yolk mixture. Pour half the batter into each skillet. Cook over low heat 5 minutes or until bottom is nicely browned. Bake in a preheated 325° oven 10 minutes, or until done. Sprinkle 1 cup of cheese over top of each, fold in half, and turn out onto warm plate. Serve immediately. Make additional omelets as required.

CINNAMON TOAST TOFFEES

1 loaf bread, unsliced	1 tablespoon cinnamon
Softened butter	3 tablespoons confectioners' sugar

Remove crust from loaf of bread. Cut lengthwise in 2-inch slices, then cut slices into 3- or 4-inch pieces. Place under broiler and toast lightly on all sides. Remove, spread with butter, and roll in cinnamon and sugar. Place under very hot broiler on lowest rack. Continue turning until all sides are toasted and golden. Serve hot.

The "Toffees" are delectably "chewy." They are the perfect sweet with afternoon tea.

FRUIT CAPRICE

1 12-ounce package frozen peaches, defrosted
1 12-ounce package frozen raspberries, defrosted
3 tablespoons frozen lemonade, defrosted
2 tablespoons (2 envelopes) unflavored gelatin

½ cup cold water
1 cup boiling water
¼ teaspoon salt
2 teaspoons sugar
1 4-ounce can frozen orange juice, defrosted
1 large banana, diced
¾ cup seeded Tokay grapes
¼ cup walnut halves

Drain and reserve juice from defrosted peaches and raspberries. Combine lemonade with peaches. Soften gelatin in cold water for 5 minutes; dissolve in hot water. Add sugar, salt, peaches, orange, and raspberry juices to gelatin. Chill until consistency of unbeaten egg white. Carefully fold in fruit and nuts. Turn into well-oiled 6-cup mold; chill until firm. Remove to platter and center with bowl of whipped cream or Foamy Sauce.

Foamy Sauce:

4 eggs, separated
3 cups confectioners' sugar
Dash salt

1 tablespoon vanilla, *or* Grand Marnier

Beat yolks and sugar 10 minutes in electric mixer. Add stiffly beaten egg whites and beat 5 minutes longer. Add vanilla or liqueur. Serve at once.

Family Fare Skillet Brunch

(SERVES 6)

Shrimp Louisianne   Rye Toast   Golden Watercress Salad
Chocolate Streusel Coffee Cake
Coffee   Tea

Suggested wine: California Pinot Blanc or other California white

ADVANCE PREPARATION SCHEDULE

Previous Day	Early Morning
Cake	*Cook fresh shrimp*
	Grapefruit in orange dressing

SHRIMP LOUISIANNE
(For Skillet or Chafing Dish)

2 4½-ounce cans shrimp, *or* 1
   pound fresh *or* frozen shrimp,
   cooked and cleaned
3 tablespoons butter
¼ cup coarsely chopped onion

10 eggs
⅓ cup milk
Salt to taste
¼ teaspoon pepper
1 teaspoon oregano

Cook fresh or frozen shrimp (see Index). Heat butter in large skillet; add shrimp and onions; sauté for a few minutes until onions are golden brown. Combine eggs, milk, salt, pepper, and oregano; beat well and add to shrimp mixture. Cook slowly, stirring from outer edge of pan toward center until eggs are set. Serve immediately.

GOLDEN WATERCRESS SALAD

2 grapefruit, peeled and sectioned
  (see Index)

2 heads lettuce (hearts)
3 cups watercress, chopped

Pour Orange Dressing over grapefruit and chill several hours. Break lettuce hearts into small pieces and toss with watercress. Line a salad bowl with outer leaves of lettuce heads; fill with the watercress mixture. To serve, pour combined grapefruit and Orange Dressing over greens; toss lightly and serve on chilled salad plates.

Orange Dressing:

½ cup salad oil
⅓ cup tarragon vinegar

1 tablespoon orange marmalade
1 teaspoon salt

Combine all ingredients and blend well.

CHOCOLATE STREUSEL COFFEE CAKE

½ cup (¼ pound) butter	1 cup dairy sour cream
1 cup sugar	2 teaspoons vanilla
2 eggs, beaten	¾ cup chopped pecans
2 cups cake flour, sifted	1 tablespoon cinnamon .
1 teaspoon baking soda	1 tablespoon cocoa
1 teaspoon baking powder	3 tablespoons brown sugar

Cream butter and sugar until creamy; add eggs. Sift cake flour, baking soda, and baking powder together 3 times. Add sour cream and flour mixture alternately to creamed butter, sugar, and eggs. Beat well; add vanilla. Combine pecans, cinnamon, cocoa, and brown sugar. Butter a 9-inch spring form with tube; sprinkle with flour. Pour ½ batter in pan; add ½ nut mixture, then balance of batter and top with remaining nuts. Bake in a preheated 375° oven 35 minutes.

Family Fare Luncheon

(SERVES 6)

Tuna Lasagna   French Onion Bread

Pineapple Crème Brûlée   Yeast Butter Cookies

Coffee   Tea

Suggested wine: Rosé

ADVANCE PREPARATION SCHEDULE

Deep Freeze	**Previous Day**	**Early Morning**
Cookies	*Crème Brûlée*	*Prepare tuna*
		Spread bread

TUNA LASAGNA

2 6½-ounce cans tuna, drained
3 tablespoons lemon juice
1 #2½ can tomatoes
1 8-ounce can tomato sauce
1 1½-ounce envelope spaghetti
  sauce mix

1 8-ounce package Lasagna
  (wide noodles)
½ pound Mozzarella cheese, sliced
Grated Parmesan cheese
½ teaspoon salt
⅛ teaspoon pepper

Break tuna into large pieces and moisten with lemon juice. Combine tomatoes, tomato sauce, and spaghetti sauce; stir thoroughly and simmer for 30 minutes. Add salt and pepper; adjust to taste. Fold in tuna carefully. Cook noodles as directed on package; drain. Arrange noodles, tuna mixture, and cheese alternately in well-greased 1½-quart baking pan. Bake 25 minutes in a preheated 350° oven.

FRENCH ONION BREAD

½ cup Parmesan cheese
½ cup grated onion
1 cup mayonnaise

1 loaf French bread, cut
  in 12 1-inch slices

Combine cheese, onion, and mayonnaise. Spread on French bread slices; place under broiler for 2 or 3 minutes, or until browned and heated.

PINEAPPLE CREME BRULEE

1 3⅝-ounce package vanilla
  pudding
1¾ cups milk

1 cup heavy cream, whipped
1 teaspoon vanilla
⅓ cup brown sugar

Pineapple tidbits

Prepare a package of vanilla pudding according to package directions, using only 1¾ cups of milk as indicated; cool. Add vanilla to whipped cream and fold into cooled pudding. Pour into shallow heat-resistant 1½-quart casserole and sprinkle sugar evenly over the top; dot with pineapple tidbits. Set in a pan of ice, place 6 inches under broiler; broil about 5 minutes until sugar is melted and pineapple glazed. Return to refrigerator to set glaze.

YEAST BUTTER COOKIES

4 cups all-purpose flour
Pinch salt
1 2/3-ounce package compressed yeast
2 cups (1 pound) butter *or* margarine (*or* ½ and ½)

1 cup sugar
2 egg yolks
2 egg whites
½ cup chocolate shot decorations

Sift flour; resift with salt. Crumble yeast into butter and combine well. Add sugar and egg yolks to butter mixture and cream thoroughly. Mix in flour until a ball is formed. Wrap in wax paper and refrigerate 1 hour. Beat egg whites lightly.

Remove dough and roll into marble-sized balls. Flatten in palm of hand; dip top half of each into egg white, then in chocolate shots. Place undipped side on ungreased cooky sheet. Bake in a preheated 375° oven until lightly browned. Do not overbake. Makes 124 cookies.

Note: Dough is sticky and is more manageable if chilled in long rolls. Cookies can then be cut as for refrigerator cookies with a minimum of handling as dough softens quickly.

Suggestion: Unless you have a large cooky jar, half this recipe will suffice. Halve all ingredients except yeast. If you prepare the full recipe, the extra cookies will freeze well.

Family Fare
Low Calorie Luncheon

(SERVES 6)

Tomato Bouillon   Curry Coconut Lobster
Green Salad — Yogurt Dressing
Vanilla Blanc Mange *or* Apple Snow Pudding
Cinnamon Cookies

ADVANCE PREPARATION SCHEDULE

Previous Day	Early Morning
Bouillon	*Yogurt Dressing*
Vanilla or	*Prepare lobster*
Snow Pudding	

TOMATO BOUILLON

2 teaspoons butter *or* margarine
¾ cup chopped onion
6 cups tomato juice
1 bay leaf

½ cup celery, chopped with leaves
½ teaspoon oregano
¼ teaspoon seasoned salt
⅛ teaspoon pepper

Heat butter in medium saucepan; add onion and sauté, stirring, until golden, about 3 minutes. Add other ingredients; simmer 15 minutes, stirring occasionally. Strain and adjust seasoning. Serve hot or cold. Makes 6 servings: 1 cup, 63 calories.

CURRY COCONUT LOBSTER

6 large frozen rock-lobster tails
1 tablespoon butter
2 teaspoons curry powder
1 tablespoon fresh grated ginger
   root *or* 1 teaspoon grated
   preserved ginger
2 tablespoons grated onion
Juice of 2 oranges

Juice of 1 lemon
1 teaspoon brown sugar
¼ teaspoon salt
Pinch pepper
Pinch nutmeg
1 cup flaked coconut
Low-calorie ginger ale for
   basting

Boil lobster tails according to package directions. Cut away the under shell and remove vein. With a sharp knife, slice across the lobster meat at 1-inch intervals for bite-sized eating. Melt butter; add curry, ginger, onion, and sauté until onion is tender. Stir in all remaining ingredients except ginger ale; simmer, stirring, about 5 minutes. Place lobsters, meat side up, on a broiler pan, spoon the curry mixture over each, and broil 3 to 4 inches from the heat, about 8 minutes or until tails begin to brown lightly. Baste after 2 minutes of broiling with a little ginger ale, and then frequently with pan drippings. Serve with Fluffy Rice (see Index). Makes 6 servings: 170 calories per serving.

GREEN SALAD — YOGURT DRESSING

1 quart mixed greens

Toss with Yogurt Dressing.

YOGURT DRESSING

1 cup yogurt	1 tablespoon onion
2 tablespoons vinegar	Few grains freshly
¼ teaspoon salt	ground pepper
¼ teaspoon sugar	¼ teaspoon seasoned salt

Combine yogurt, vinegar, salt, sugar, onion, pepper, and seasoned salt. Blend well and refrigerate until serving time. Makes 1¼ cups: 10 calories per tablespoon.

VANILLA BLANC MANGE

2 envelopes (2 tablespoons) unflavored gelatin	1 teaspoon non-caloric liquid sweetener
3 cups skim milk	2 teaspoons vanilla
1 tablespoon sugar	1 1-pound can dietetic fruit cocktail, drained
¼ teaspoon salt	

Sprinkle gelatin over ½ cup milk in medium bowl to soften. Heat remaining milk slowly, just until bubbly around edge of pan. Pour over gelatin, stirring until dissolved. Add sugar, salt, sweetener, and vanilla. Refrigerate until consistency of raw egg white. Beat with rotary beater or electric mixer until very frothy and almost doubled in bulk. Pour into 6 individual molds or 8-inch (5½ cup) ring mold. Refrigerate several hours.

To serve, loosen edge with sharp knife; invert onto serving plates or platter. Spoon fruit cocktail over molds. Makes 6 servings: 1 individual mold with ¼ cup fruit cocktail, 81 calories per serving.

APPLE SNOW PUDDING

1 envelope (1 tablespoon) unflavored gelatin	3 tablespoons lemon juice
½ cup cold water	2 teaspoons non-caloric liquid sweetener
2 8½-ounce cans dietetic applesauce	¼ teaspoon cinnamon
1 tablespoon grated lemon peel	¼ teaspoon nutmeg
	2 egg whites
Pinch salt	

Sprinkle gelatin over cold water to soften. Combine applesauce, lemon peel and juice, sweetener, and spices in saucepan; bring to boil, stirring. Add softened gelatin, stirring until dissolved. Pour into bowl; refrigerate 1 hour. Beat egg whites with salt until stiff peaks form. Fold into gelatin mixture and pour into serving bowl. Refrigerate until set. Makes 6 servings: ⅔ cup, 48 calories.

CINNAMON COOKIES

5 tablespoons butter	1 tablespoon milk, fruit juice,
1 cup sifted all-purpose flour	or coffee
¼ teaspoon baking powder	2 teaspoons non-caloric liquid
2 teaspoons vanilla	sweetener
1 teaspoon cinnamon	

Cream butter until light and fluffy. Sift flour and baking powder together. Combine vanilla and milk; add and blend non-caloric liquid sweetener. Stir into flour mixture and blend thoroughly. Sprinkle cinnamon over dough and knead in so that there is a streaked appearance. Shape dough into balls, about ½ inch in diameter, and arrange on a cooky sheet. Flatten balls with a fork dipped in cold water. Bake in a preheated 375° oven 15 minutes, or until edges are browned. Makes 30 cookies: about 35 calories each.

Family Fare Dinner

(SERVES 6)

Beef Stew English Style Crusty French Bread
Love Apples — Juno Dressing
Eggless Lemon Pie
or
Cheeseless Cheese Pie
Coffee Milk

Suggested wine: red Burgundy or Bordeaux

BEEF STEW ENGLISH STYLE

2½ pounds lean beef
1 tablespoon shortening
1 tablespoon sugar
1 tablespoon flour
2 10-ounce cans beef bouillon
½ teaspoon salt
⅛ teaspoon pepper
Pinch thyme

1 sliced clove garlic
1 bunch carrots, about 6
12 small potatoes
12 small onions
½ green pepper
½ 10-ounce package green
beans, frozen
¼ cup dry red wine

Have beef cut in about 2-inch cubes. Heat shortening in large sauce-pan, add beef, and brown lightly. When just tinged, add sugar to glaze meat; complete browning. Sprinkle flour on meat and shake pot to spread it evenly. Add hot bouillon, all seasonings, garlic clove, and 3 carrots. Cover and simmer 2½ hours or until tender. Cook potatoes, onions, and remainder of carrots together for 15 minutes; drain and add to stew. Add green pepper and frozen beans, bring to a boil, simmer 5 minutes. Add wine and again simmer 5 minutes. Serve piping hot in large tureen and ladle into ample bowls. Enjoy this hearty stew with crusty French bread.

LOVE APPLES

6 medium tomatoes   Leaf lettuce
1 hard-cooked egg yolk, sieved

Spear tomatoes on a fork, one at a time. Dip into boiling water (or hold over lighted burner until skin cracks); peel. Place in refrigerator to chill thoroughly. Serve icy cold on a frill of lettuce leaves, sprinkled with egg yolk. Serve Juno Dressing separately.

JUNO DRESSING

1½ tablespoons lemon juice   ½ cup dairy sour cream
¾ teaspoon salt   ¼ cup chili sauce
½ cup mayonnaise   ¼ teaspoon paprika
1 teaspoon Worcestershire

Gently blend, and place in refrigerator several hours so flavors may "marry." Serve chilled.

Note: An especially fine dressing with a seafood salad.

EGGLESS LEMON PIE

Crust:

½ cup (¼ pound) butter   24 graham crackers,
½ cup confectioners' sugar, sifted   rolled fine

Melt butter, add sugar and graham crackers. Line 10-inch pie pan or spring form with crust mixture. Press firmly to sides and bottom. For spring form, line sides 1 inch high.

Filling:

1 15-ounce can condensed milk   Grated rind of 1 lemon
1 cup sugar   1 3-ounce package lemon gelatin
Juice of 3 lemons   ½ cup boiling water

Chill milk several hours or overnight. Pour into large chilled bowl; whip until stiff. Add sugar, lemon juice, and rind. Add lemon gelatin to boiling water and dissolve. Cool. Combine with lemon mixture. Place in refrigerator for 24 hours.

CHEESELESS CHEESE PIE

Crust:

¼ cup butter   10 graham crackers,
¼ cup sugar   rolled fine

Melt butter; add sugar and graham crackers and press into 8- or 9-inch pie pan. Reserve 2 tablespoons crumb mixture for topping. This is a thin crust.

Filling:

2 eggs, separated	½ cup sugar
1 pint half and half sour cream	1 teaspoon vanilla

Beat yolks until thick; combine with cream, sugar, and vanilla; blend well. Beat egg whites until very stiff and fold into yolk mixture. Pour into prepared shell. Sprinkle reserved crumbs around edge. Place in a preheated 325° oven; bake 30 minutes. Cool and refrigerate at least 3 hours.

Family Fare Sunday Dinner

(SERVES 6)

Baked Mushrooms Noix

Sweet-Sour Chicken   Broccoli — Browned Butter

A Crisp Salad   Hard Rolls

Ice Cream Bonbons   Poppy-Seed Cookies

Coffee

ADVANCE PREPARATION SCHEDULE

Deep Freeze	**Early Morning**
Cookies	*Broil chickens*
Bonbons	*Mushrooms for baking*

BAKED MUSHROOMS NOIX

1 pound (about 12) large fresh mushrooms	1 clove garlic, crushed
	¼ teaspoon thyme
1 cup pecans, chopped fine	½ teaspoon salt
3 tablespoons chopped parsley	⅛ teaspoon pepper
¼ cup butter, softened	½ cup heavy cream

Wash carefully and remove stems from the mushrooms. Wipe mushroom caps with a damp cloth. Place 2 caps, hollow side up, in each of 6 individual ramekins. Chop the stems (there will be about 1 cup) and combine with the pecans, parsley, butter, garlic, thyme, salt, and pepper. Mix well and heap into the mushroom caps. Pour cream proportionately over stuffed mushrooms; cover and bake in a preheated 350° oven 30 to 45 minutes, or until tender. Baste once or twice with the cream in the dish. Serve with fancy crackers.

SWEET-SOUR CHICKEN

1 #2 can pineapple chunks, drained
2 tablespoons cornstarch
1 cup vinegar
2 green peppers, cut in strips
1 2-ounce jar pimiento

3 tablespoons prepared mustard
1 tablespoon Worcestershire
Dashes Tabasco
2 2½-pound frying chickens, quartered
1 teaspoon salt

½ teaspoon seasoned salt

Drain pineapple and reserve juice. Mix cornstarch with vinegar and cook until clear; add green pepper, pimiento, mustard, Worcestershire, and pineapple chunks. Add juice from pineapple slowly, stirring constantly; add Tabasco and cook over low heat 15 minutes. Dry chicken and sprinkle with salt and seasoned salt; place on rack about 6 inches from heat. Broil chicken until well browned and tender, 20 to 30 minutes. Place in shallow baking dish; pour sauce over chicken, and bake in a preheated 350° oven ½ hour.

BROCCOLI — BROWNED BUTTER

2 10½-ounce packages frozen broccoli spears, *or* 3 pounds fresh broccoli

Cook frozen broccoli according to package directions. For fresh broccoli, trim or remove large leaves, make deep gashes in large stalks, up, through bottom. Tie stalks together. Place upright in lower part of double boiler, with sufficient boiling water to cover stems. Reverse top of double boiler for cover; steam 10 minutes over direct heat. Or broccoli may be placed flat in saucepan and cooked, covered, in 1 inch boiling water.

Remove carefully to serving platter. Sprinkle with salt and serve with Browned Butter.

BROWNED BUTTER

¼ cup butter 1 tablespoon lemon juice

Heat butter in saucepan until lightly brown, being careful not to burn. Stir in lemon juice before serving.

ICE CREAM BONBONS

1 quart ice cream 1 7½-ounce can peanuts,
chopped fine
Chocolate Dipping Sauce

Form firm ice cream into balls with melon ball cutter, roll quickly in chopped peanuts. Place on a tray and freeze for about 1 hour or until quite firm. Quickly dip balls into sauce and refreeze for about 1 hour longer (or for longer periods of time for future use). Serve in sherbet glasses or in orange shells.

Note: For longer periods store in plastic bags after refreezing. These are versatile little things; prepare them in quantities for the freezer. Spear on sticks or colored toothpicks and delight the youngsters.

Chocolate Dipping Sauce:

6 1-ounce squares unsweetened   1⅓ cups sugar
   chocolate   ¼ cup (⅛ pound) butter *or*
⅔ cup water   margarine

Melt chocolate with water in top of double boiler. Add sugar and boil gently over direct heat for 4 minutes, stirring constantly. Remove from heat and stir in butter. Keep warm over hot water while dipping. Makes about 2 cups.

POPPY-SEED COOKIES

3 cups all-purpose flour, unsifted 1½ cups (¾ pound) butter *or*
1 cup sugar plus 2 tablespoons   margarine, softened
¼ teaspoon cinnamon   ⅓ cup poppy seeds

Combine dry ingredients; blend thoroughly with softened butter. Press firmly into 12″ x 18″ ungreased jelly roll pan. Sprinkle evenly with poppy seeds. Refrigerate 1 to 2 hours. Bake in a preheated

325° oven about 45 minutes. Cut, while hot, into 1¾-inch squares. Makes approximately 60 cookies.

Family Fare Dinner

(SERVES 4 OR 5)

Marinated Flank Steak

Celery au Gratin   Baked Potato Variations

Poppy-Seed Rolls

Individual Chocolate Pies

Coffee   Tea   Milk

ADVANCE PREPARATION SCHEDULE

Previous Day

Marinate steak

Early Morning

Prepare celery
Pies
Poppy-Seed Rolls
(see Index)

MARINATED FLANK STEAK

½ cup salad oil
¼ cup soy sauce
3 tablespoons honey
½ teaspoon garlic powder
½ teaspoon ginger
1 tablespoon minced onion
1½ pounds flank steak

Mix oil, soy sauce, honey, garlic powder, ginger, and onion thoroughly; pour over steak, turning to glaze all sides. Prick steak with fork, turn, repeat. Refrigerate for 24 hours, turning and forking meat several times. Remove from marinade, place on pan under preheated broiler, and broil 6 minutes on each side. Slice in diagonal slices.

CELERY AU GRATIN

4 cups coarsely sliced celery	3 tablespoons cream cheese
¼ cup finely chopped onion	3 tablespoons blue cheese
¼ cup chopped green pepper	½ cup heavy cream
1 tablespoon butter	½ teaspoon salt
⅛ teaspoon pepper	

Wash and trim celery; cut into ½-inch pieces. Cook until tender in sufficient water to just cover. Drain, reserving ¾ cup celery broth.

In a skillet, sauté onion and green pepper in butter until tender. Cream blue cheese and cream cheese; add cream and then celery broth. Combine this with sautéed onion and pepper. Stir until blended. Season with salt and pepper. Place drained cooked celery in buttered 1½-quart casserole; pour cheese mixture over celery. Bake uncovered in a preheated 375° oven 20 minutes, or until surface is lightly browned.

BAKED POTATO VARIATIONS

Split open 4 or 5 hot baked potatoes. Crumble slightly and top with one of the following:

(1) Sprinkle with seasoned salt; add a pat of butter or margarine; then top with dairy sour cream, chopped chives, and crumbled bacon.

(2) Mix ½ cup dairy sour cream, ¼ cup finely chopped pared cucumber, and ⅛ teaspoon salt.

(3) Combine ½ cup dairy sour cream, ¼ cup minced green onions, ¼ teaspoon salt, and ⅛ teaspoon cayenne.

(4) Blend ½ cup dairy sour cream, 2 teaspoons prepared horseradish, and 1 teaspoon onion salt.

(5) Stir 1 tablespoon finely chopped fresh dill or 1 teaspoon crumbled dill weed into ½ cup dairy sour cream.

(6) Combine ½ cup dairy sour cream, 2 tablespoons vinegar, and 1½ teaspoons blue cheese salad dressing mix.

(7) Golden Mushrooms (see below).

GOLDEN MUSHROOMS FOR BAKED POTATOES

1 tablespoon butter *or* margarine	¼ teaspoon paprika
½ medium onion, chopped fine	1½ teaspoons flour
½ pound fresh mushrooms, sliced	¾ cup dairy sour cream
¼ teaspoon salt	1 teaspoon minced parsley

Heat butter in skillet, add onion and sauté until golden. Add mushrooms, seasonings, and cook 5 minutes. Sprinkle with flour, mixing well. Stir in sour cream, bring to a boil and simmer 10 minutes. Serve hot over potatoes. Garnish with parsley.

INDIVIDUAL CHOCOLATE PIES

2 tablespoons flour	1 tablespoon butter
1 cup sugar	Pinch salt
2 egg yolks, well beaten	1 teaspoon vanilla
2 1-ounce squares unsweetened chocolate, melted	8 flaky pastry shells, baked and cooled
1 cup boiling water	1 cup heavy cream, whipped
Nutmeg (optional)	

Mix flour with sugar; add egg yolks and melted chocolate. Mix well and place in double boiler; add 1 cup boiling water, mixing thoroughly. Stir mixture constantly over boiling water until it thickens. Remove from heat and add butter, salt, and vanilla. Beat long and hard, until very smooth. Chill. Pour chocolate filling into shells and top with sweetened whipped cream; sprinkle with nutmeg. Have leftover chocolate custard for tomorrow's lunch.

Never-Fail Pie Crust:

3 cups sifted all-purpose flour	1 egg
1 teaspoon salt	1 teaspoon vinegar
1 cup shortening	5 tablespoons cold water

Sift flour and salt together. Cut in shortening with pastry blender until mixture resembles small peas in size. Beat egg with vinegar and water. Mix thoroughly with flour mixture. Turn out on wax paper and press into ball. Roll out on floured pastry cloth to ⅛-inch thickness. Cut into 4½- or 5-inch rounds; invert pans and place dough over bottoms. Pinch edges to flute shells; prick with fork to keep shell from puffing. Bake in a preheated 500° oven 12 minutes.

Family Fare Dinner

(SERVES 6 TO 8)

Lemon Whitefish

Asparagus Soufflé   Boiled New Potatoes

Berliner Rolls

Applesauce Trifle

Coffee   Tea

ADVANCE PREPARATION SCHEDULE

Deep Freeze   **Early Morning**

Berliner Rolls   *Fish*

Trifle

LEMON WHITEFISH

¼ cup salad oil *or* butter	2 tomatoes, diced
2 cups sliced onions	2 lemons, sliced thin
6 slices whitefish	½ cup water
2 teaspoons salt	1 teaspoon cider vinegar
½ teaspoon pepper	2 teaspoons sugar

1 bay leaf

Heat the oil in a deep skillet; add onions and brown until golden. Arrange the fish over the onions and sprinkle with salt and pepper. Add the tomatoes, lemon slices, water, vinegar, sugar, and bay leaf; cover and simmer over low heat 20 minutes. Remove bay leaf. Serve hot or cold.

Note: 3 pounds of fish will serve 8.

ASPARAGUS SOUFFLE

1½ 10½-ounce cans cream of asparagus soup	1 cup grated Cheddar cheese
	6 egg yolks, well beaten

6 egg whites, beaten stiff

Heat soup and cheese in double boiler until cheese is melted. Stir a small amount of soup mixture into egg yolks and return to remaining mixture. Fold in beaten egg whites. Pour into ungreased 2-quart casserole; set into another pan of water. Bake in a preheated 300° oven 1 hour. To test, cut into soufflé with a knife; if clean when removed, the soufflé is done.

BOILED NEW POTATOES

3 pounds new potatoes   Salt   ¼ cup butter, melted

Select potatoes of uniform size. Scrub well, and scrape or peel lightly, removing eyes. Bring salted water to a boil (using ½ teaspoon salt for each cup of water); add potatoes and boil about 35 minutes or until done. Drain, return to pan and shake over heat to dry. Serve with melted butter.

Note: 3 to 3½ pounds serves 8, depending on your fondness for the popular potato.

BERLINER ROLLS

3½ cups all-purpose flour, sifted
1 teaspoon salt
½ cup (¼ pound) butter
½ cup margarine
1 ¼-ounce package active dry yeast
¼ cup warm water
¾ cup dairy sour cream
1 whole egg, well beaten
2 egg yolks, well beaten
1 teaspoon vanilla
1 cup sugar

Sift flour and salt into mixing bowl; cut in butter and margarine until it resembles small peas in size. Dissolve yeast in water. Stir into flour mixture with sour cream, eggs and vanilla and mix well with hands. Cover with damp cloth and refrigerate 2 hours. Roll half of dough on sugared board into an 8″ x 16″ oblong. Fold dough in 3 parts with ends toward center, overlapping. Sprinkle with sugar, roll again in same fashion. Repeat a third time. Roll about ¼ inch thick. Cut into strips 1″ x 4″. Twist ends in opposite directions, stretching dough slightly. Form in shape of horseshoe, and place on ungreased baking sheet, pressing ends to keep shape. Repeat with rest of dough. Bake in a preheated 375° oven about 15 minutes or until delicately browned. Take from baking sheet immediately. Makes about 5 dozen.

APPLESAUCE TRIFLE

2 #2 cans applesauce
2 8-ounce packages pound cake,
   sliced thin
¼ cup half and half cream
½ teaspoon cinnamon (optional)

Topping:
¼ cup currant jelly
1 #2 can applesauce
½ cup heavy cream, whipped
  (optional)

In a 5" x 9" buttered loaf pan arrange alternate layers of applesauce and cake, starting and topping with applesauce. There should
be 4 layers of cake. Moisten each cake layer with 1 tablespoon
half and half cream and sprinkle with cinnamon. Bake in a preheated 375° oven 30 minutes. Serve warm or cold. Cut from the
pan in ¾-inch slices. Top with spoonful of currant jelly and additional applesauce; for glamour add a dollop of whipped cream.

Family Fare Magyar Dinner

(SERVES 6)

Beef Consommé — Liver Dumplings
Hungarian Veal Paprika
Pickled Beets   Potato Pancakes
Royal Plum Jelly Cake
Coffee

ADVANCE PREPARATION SCHEDULE

Deep Freeze
Plum Jelly Cake

Previous Day
Consommé
Pickled Beets

Early Morning
Veal (without
sour cream)
Prepare dumplings
for cooking

BEEF CONSOMME

4 pounds beef shank *or* rump	4 cloves
1½ pounds beef bones	3 carrots, sliced
3 quarts water	½ green pepper
1½ teaspoons salt	4 stalks celery, sliced
1 teaspoon sugar	½ kohlrabi *or* parsnip
1 onion	3 sprigs parsley
1 bay leaf	½ cup tomato juice
Pinch nutmeg	2 beef bouillon cubes (optional)

Place beef, beef bones, water, salt, sugar, onion, bay leaf, nutmeg, and cloves in a large kettle; add 2 or 3 outer red leaves of onion for color. Cover and simmer slowly 1 hour. Add vegetables and tomato juice; simmer, covered, for 3½ hours more. The meat should be removed when tender, about 3 hours after vegetables are added. When soup is done, strain into a bowl, cool, and refrigerate several hours or overnight. When set, remove congealed fat from top. If a stronger stock is desired add 1 or 2 beef bouillon cubes before serving. To serve, reheat and add Liver Dumplings to each serving.

So many flavorful vegetables may be blended in consommé. Parsnips, leek, kohlrabi, celery, root or cabbage, all available at most times, may be added or subtracted. Chicken bones or leftover gravy will give a new flavor. This stock can be frozen and when in the quandary of what to serve take a quart of stock from the freezer; add cubed leftover beef and spark an embryo Pot au Feu. Add a package of frozen mixed vegetables and you have it. Use the beef for another menu by reheating it in soup stock; prepare a beef hash or slice it cold for sandwiches.

LIVER DUMPLINGS

5 slices dry white bread	1 tablespoon parsley
¼ pound beef *or* calves' liver	1 tablespoon butter
1 tablespoon chopped onion	1 egg

Soak bread in water; squeeze excess water out. Grind liver and bread together. Sauté onion and parsley in butter. Add onion and parsley to bread mixture; add the egg and mix well. Shape into about 12 medium-sized dumplings; dip hands in cold water while making each dumpling so that mixture does not stick. Test one dumpling; if slightly soft and falls apart in soup, add a few bread crumbs. Add dumplings to soup and boil for 15 minutes.

HUNGARIAN VEAL PAPRIKA

¼ cup flour	1 onion, sliced
1 teaspoon salt	2 teaspoons paprika
⅛ teaspoon pepper	1 cup hot water
3 pounds boneless veal, cut in 1-inch cubes	2 medium tomatoes, cut in small pieces
½ cup fat	1 cup dairy sour cream

Combine flour, salt, pepper, and dredge veal cubes. Heat fat in saucepan, add onion, and sauté with veal and paprika until meat is well browned, stirring frequently. Add hot water to tomatoes, rub through sieve, and add to meat. Cover, and simmer 1½ hours or until veal is fork-tender. Remove gravy and slowly pour into sour cream, stirring continually. Pour back over meat and simmer 10 minutes longer. Serve in casserole.

PICKLED BEETS

1 #2 can beets	½ teaspoon salt
¼ cup vinegar	1 onion, sliced
1 tablespoon sugar	1 bay leaf
2 cloves	

Drain beet liquid into bowl. Add remaining ingredients and blend well. Add beets. Refrigerate for 4 or more hours, blending flavors.

POTATO PANCAKES

5 medium potatoes, grated	2 eggs, well beaten
1 small onion, grated	3 tablespoons dairy sour cream
3 tablespoons flour	½ teaspoon salt
Vegetable shortening *or* chicken fat	

Drain potatoes thoroughly. Combine potatoes, onion, flour, eggs, sour cream, and salt; mix well. Heat shortening or chicken fat to ½-inch depth in skillet. Drop batter from tablespoon. Fry until golden brown on both sides. Drain on paper toweling.

' ROYAL PLUM JELLY CAKES

1½ cups (¾ pound) butter	4 ounces German sweet chocolate
3½ cups all-purpose flour	½ teaspoon cinnamon
1½ cups sugar	½ teaspoon ground cloves
3 eggs, beaten	1 cup plum preserves

Crumble butter into flour; add sugar and eggs. Melt chocolate over hot water and add to first mixture; blend in cinnamon and ground cloves. Chill in refrigerator ½ hour; remove and place half the dough in a 11″ x 16″ x 3″ pan. Press down to ¼-inch thickness and cover with plum preserves. Cut remaining dough in strips; roll in hands or on table into pencil-like lengths; and cross in lattice fashion over cake. Bake in a preheated 225° oven 30 to 35 minutes. Cut while warm in 2-inch squares.

Family Fare Dinner

(SERVES 6)

Tomato Vegetable Soup   Matzo Balls

Your choice of Hamburger Selections:

Country Pie   Barbecued Hamburger

Cheddar Cheeseburgers   Hamburgers with a Chinese Accent

Hamburger Noodle Casserole

Green Beans Country Style

Marble Cake

Coffee   Milk

Suggested wine: California Pinot Noir

ADVANCE PREPARATION SCHEDULE

Deep Freeze	Previous Day	Early Morning
Soup	*Soup*	*Dressing*
Cake	*Matzo Balls for boiling*	

TOMATO VEGETABLE SOUP

1 onion	3 sprigs parsley
3 carrots	3 #2 cans tomatoes
8 to 10 green beans	1½ pounds chuck
1 cup spinach	3 veal knuckles
1 cup cabbage	1 slice beef liver
2 potatoes	6 chicken wings
1 cup peas	Salt and pepper to taste
3 stalks celery	3 14½-ounce cans cream of
1 parsnip	tomato soup, undiluted

Dice vegetables and soup greens and place in a 6-quart kettle; add chuck, veal knuckles, liver, chicken wings, salt and pepper; cover with water. Cook over high heat for ½ hour. Lower heat and cover; simmer 5 to 6 hours. Cool and refrigerate overnight. Remove fat and pour through strainer to clear broth. Reheat to boiling point. Add tomato soup and bring to a boil again. Cook 5 minutes. Serve with Matzo Balls. (Serves 16. Freezes well.)

MATZO BALLS

2 tablespoons chicken fat	2 tablespoons finely chopped
1 cup matzo meal	parsley
1 egg	1 teaspoon salt
3 tablespoons finely diced white	½ teaspoon poultry seasoning
meat of chicken	½ cup water

Mix chicken fat and matzo meal. Add well-beaten egg, chicken, parsley and seasonings. Add water gradually and blend well. Chill for several hours or overnight. Roll into tiny balls about ½ inch in diameter. Drop into rapidly boiling tomato vegetable soup. Continue to boil until all balls are floating on top of soup.

Note: Delicious with chicken soup or broth, as well.

COUNTRY PIE

Crust:

½ cup tomato sauce	¼ cup chopped onion
(½ 8-ounce can)	½ cup chopped green pepper
½ cup bread crumbs	1½ teaspoons salt
(flavored may be used)	⅛ teaspoon oregano
1 pound ground beef	⅛ teaspoon pepper

Combine tomato sauce, bread crumbs, ground beef, onion, green pepper, salt, oregano, and pepper; mix well. Pat mixture into bottom of a deep 9-inch tin and pinch 1-inch flutings around edges. Set aside.

Filling:

1⅓ cups minute rice	½ teaspoon salt
1½ cups tomato sauce (use remaining half plus 1 8-ounce can)	1 cup water
	1 cup grated Cheddar cheese

Combine rice, tomato sauce, salt, water, and ¼ cup of cheese. Spoon rice mixture into meat shell. Cover with aluminum foil. Bake in a preheated 350° oven 25 minutes. Uncover and sprinkle top with remaining cheese. Return to oven and bake uncovered 10 to 15 minutes longer. Cut into pie-shaped pieces.

BARBECUED HAMBURGER

1½ pounds ground beef	1 tablespoon vinegar
1 cup chopped onion	1 tablespoon sugar
½ cup catsup	1 tablespoon Worcestershire
1 tablespoon prepared mustard	Salt and pepper
½ cup water	4 hamburger buns

Brown beef, stirring to keep crumbly. Add onion, catsup, mustard, water, vinegar, sugar, Worcestershire, salt and pepper. Cook ½ hour until onion is soft. Serve over buns.

CHEDDAR CHEESEBURGERS

2 pounds ground chuck	¼ teaspoon pepper
1 cup shredded Cheddar cheese	½ teaspoon salt
1 medium onion, grated	¼ teaspoon Worcestershire
½ cup chili sauce	8 large hamburger buns

Mix chuck, ¾ cup cheese, onion, chili sauce, pepper, salt, and Worcestershire lightly. Spread on hamburger buns; place on baking sheet. Sprinkle with ¼ cup cheese. Preheat oven to 475° and bake burgers approximately 10 minutes.

Suggestion: Use miniature buns and serve as appetizer.

HAMBURGERS WITH A CHINESE ACCENT

2 teaspoons soy sauce
½ teaspoon hickory salt
½ teaspoon cracked pepper
1 teaspoon monosodium glutamate
½ cup hot water
2 pounds ground chuck

In a large bowl, combine soy sauce, hickory salt, cracked pepper, monosodium glutamate, and water. Add meat and mix well. Shape into 6 patties. Broil about 4 minutes on each side for medium done. This taste treat brings the outdoor grill indoors. More hickory salt may be added for a more woodsy taste.

HAMBURGER NOODLE CASSEROLE

2 tablespoons butter
1 pound ground beef
1 clove garlic, crushed
1 teaspoon salt
Black pepper, to taste
1 teaspoon sugar
2 8-ounce cans tomato sauce
1 8-ounce package medium noodles
1 3-ounce package cream cheese, softened
1 cup dairy sour cream
1 cup creamed cottage cheese
6 scallions, or green onions, chopped
½ cup grated Cheddar cheese

Melt butter in a 10-inch skillet; add beef and sauté until brown, breaking it into small pieces as it cooks. Add garlic, salt, pepper, sugar, and tomato sauce; blend well, cover, and simmer 15 to 20 minutes. Cook noodles in boiling salted water (½ teaspoon salt for each cup water) for 10 minutes; drain. Blend cream cheese, sour cream, and cottage cheese in electric mixer until very smooth. Add scallions. Grease a 2-quart casserole well, place a layer of noodles in bottom; spread with a third of the cheese mixture, then a third of the meat and repeat twice. Sprinkle with Cheddar cheese and bake in a preheated 350° oven 30 to 40 minutes.

GREEN BEANS COUNTRY STYLE

2 #2 cans green beans
1 onion, sliced
1 tablespoon salad oil
1 tablespoon vinegar
Salt and cracked pepper

Drain green beans, add sliced onion, salad oil, and vinegar. Sprinkle with salt and cracked pepper. Let stand for 1 hour; drain. Serve with Spiced Sour Cream Dressing.

Variation:

Substitute fresh or frozen beans, approximately 4 cups.

Spiced Sour Cream Dressing:

1 cup dairy sour cream	1 tablespoon prepared
½ cup mayonnaise	horseradish
1 teaspoon lemon juice	¼ teaspoon onion juice
¼ teaspoon dry mustard	2 teaspoons chopped chives

Combine sour cream, mayonnaise, lemon juice, mustard, horseradish, onion juice, and chives. Refrigerate for 3 hours before serving.

MARBLE CAKE

4 eggs, separated	1 cup evaporated milk
½ pound butter *or* margarine	½ cup cocoa, mixed with
2½ cups sugar	⅓ cup warm coffee and
3 cups all-purpose flour	pinch of soda
1 tablespoon baking powder	Confectioners' sugar

Beat egg whites until stiff. Cream butter and sugar and add egg yolks; beat well. Sift flour and baking powder. Add flour and milk alternately, beating until creamy; fold in egg whites. Remove a third of the batter to another bowl and add cocoa mixture, stirring until well blended. Grease a 10-inch tube pan thoroughly and sprinkle with flour. Alternate spoonfuls of white and chocolate batter in pan. Slash through batter with a spatula to give marbled effect. Bake for 1 hour or longer in a preheated 350° oven. Test by sticking toothpick into center; if it comes out dry, cake is done. Cool on cake rack for 10 minutes before removing from pan. Dust with sugar.

Family Fare Dinner

(SERVES 8)

Savory Soup

Bombay Curry   Green Beans Marinara

Apples à la Mode   Pecan Rounds

Tea   Milk

Suggested wine: Chablis

ADVANCE PREPARATION SCHEDULE

Previous Day	Early Morning
Pecan rounds	*Partially cook curry*
	Apples for broiling
	Green beans
	Soup

SAVORY SOUP

4 cups tomato juice	4 teaspoons lemon juice
4 cups orange juice, strained	1 teaspoon celery salt

1 teaspoon chives *or* mint, minced

Combine tomato, orange, and lemon juices with celery salt. Simmer 10 minutes. Garnish with minced chives or mint. Serve piping hot or icy cold.

BOMBAY CURRY

6 tablespoons shortening	½ teaspoon sugar
2 onions, chopped fine	½ teaspoon chili powder
2 cloves garlic, minced (optional)	2 pounds stewing lamb *or* beef in 1-inch cubes
2 tart apples, chopped	
2 tablespoons curry powder	2 6-ounce cans tomato paste
1 teaspoon dry ginger	1 14-ounce package precooked rice
2 teaspoons paprika	

½ teaspoon powdered turmeric

Heat shortening in saucepan; add onion, garlic, and apple; sauté until golden brown. Add curry powder, ginger, paprika, sugar, and chili powder; cook until quite brown. Add meat and brown evenly; add tomato paste and enough water to cover. Cover and simmer about 30 minutes. Cook rice according to package directions; add turmeric to water to tint rice a deep yellow. Serve with side dishes, to be sprinkled on top.

Side Dishes: Small bowls of sliced banana with grated coconut and peanuts; chopped bacon; chopped egg yolks and whites; chopped onions; jam and chutney.

GREEN BEANS MARINARA

2 #2 cans French cut green beans	1 onion, sliced thin
½ cup Marinated Mushrooms (see Index)	1 8-ounce bottle Italian dressing

Combine beans, drained Marinated Mushrooms, thinly sliced onion, and cover with Italian dressing. Refrigerate. Serve cold in lettuce cups or over shredded lettuce.

APPLES A LA MODE

8 apples (Rome Beauties)	Red food coloring
½ cup brown sugar	1 quart vanilla ice cream
1 cup granulated sugar	Dairy sour cream
Brown sugar	

Core apples and peel halfway. Place in steamer or on rack in covered pan, using about ½ cup of water in the bottom, and steam until tender, about 20 minutes. Remove carefully and shape back into roundness. Add sugar to remaining water in pan (there should be ¾ cup) and dissolve. Pour over apples and place under broiler, basting continually until apples are thickly glazed. Broil for 10 to 15 minutes. Add red coloring to juice for bright color. Serve hot, with a scoop of vanilla ice cream; or serve warm or cold in compotes with sour cream and brown sugar.

Note: Though Rome Beauties cannot be surpassed, other varieties may be used.

PECAN ROUNDS

3 egg whites, unbeaten   4 cups pecans, finely ground
3 cups light brown sugar   1 teaspoon vanilla
                    Candied cherries

Mix egg whites and brown sugar; add nuts and vanilla. Form into
small balls and flatten, like a macaroon, on a buttered cooky sheet.
Decorate each with a small piece of candied cherry. Bake in a
preheated 350° oven about 10 minutes.

Family Fare Dinner

(SERVES 6 TO 8)

Honeydew Nova Scotia
Pork Chops Maui   Rizibizi
Celery Root Salad
Chocolate Shells   Ginger Crackles
Coffee   Tea   Milk

ADVANCE PREPARATION SCHEDULE

Deep Freeze	Previous Day	Early Morning
Ice cream balls	*Cook celery root*	*Pork chops to simmer*
Ginger Crackles		*Rice*
		Chocolate Shells

HONEYDEW NOVA SCOTIA

1 ripe honeydew melon   ½ pound smoked salmon
Curly endive   Freshly ground pepper

Chill melon thoroughly and quarter. Remove seeds and peel. Cut
into thin crescent-shaped slices. Arrange a bed of endive on each

plate; alternate 3 slices of melon with accompanying sized slices of salmon on each plate. Pass pepper grinder.

PORK CHOPS MAUI

2 tablespoons salad oil	½ clove garlic, minced
8 meaty pork chops	12 prunes, pitted
1 cup cubed pineapple	2 tablespoons soy sauce
1 onion, chopped	⅛ teaspoon marjoram
½ cup minced celery leaves	1 cup sliced celery

½ cup dried apricots

Heat oil in large skillet, add chops and brown evenly. Add pineapple, onion, celery leaves, garlic, prunes, soy sauce, and marjoram. Cover and simmer 20 minutes. Add sliced celery and dried apricots. Simmer 10 minutes more.

RIZIBIZI

1 pound fresh peas in pods	1 teaspoon salt
1 cup long-grained rice	2 tablespoons butter
2 cups boiling water	1 tablespoon chopped parsley

1 onion, chopped

Wash and shell peas; wash rice very thoroughly. Cook pods in water with salt. Discard pods, bring liquid to a boil, add rice and peas. Cover and cook slowly, about 20 minutes, or until rice is tender. Heat butter in saucepan, add parsley, onion, and sauté until lightly browned; add rice and peas slowly. Bring to a boil, reduce heat, and simmer 5 minutes.

Variation:

Use 1 10-ounce package frozen peas, defrosted and drained. Add with rice to butter and onion mixture. Cook 5 minutes.

CELERY ROOT SALAD

3 knobs celery root	⅛ teaspoon pepper
½ cup boiling water	¼ cup mayonnaise
Juice of ½ lemon	1 head Boston lettuce
2 tablespoons salad oil	3 tomatoes, quartered
½ teaspoon salt	1 green pepper, sliced

Peel knob celery and slice thin. Place in boiling water; add lemon juice, oil, salt, and pepper. Cover tightly and cook over low heat until barely tender, about 25 minutes. Remove cover and increase heat to boil away any water that is remaining. Drain and chill; mix with mayonnaise. Arrange lettuce cups on individual salad plates; fill with celery root and garnish with tomato and green pepper.

CHOCOLATE SHELLS

1 cup (6 ounces) semi-sweet chocolate pieces	2 cups sugar-coated puffed wheat
	1 quart ice cream

Melt chocolate over hot (not boiling) water. Remove from heat. Add cereal, stirring carefully until well coated with chocolate. Measure to overflowing ⅓ cup of mixture and set on wax paper. Using two forks, shape mixture into shells or nests. Let stand until hardened.

To serve, fill with scoop of ice cream of your choice. A great success, especially with the youngsters.

GINGER CRACKLES

1 cup sugar	½ teaspoon salt
¾ cup butter	2 cups all-purpose flour
1 egg	2 teaspoons soda
¼ cup molasses	1 teaspoon cinnamon
1 teaspoon ginger	¼ teaspoon cloves
Granulated sugar for coating	

Cream sugar and butter; mix in egg and molasses thoroughly until light and fluffy. Sift dry ingredients together and add, blending well. Form into balls, dip into sugar, coat well. Place on greased baking sheet, 3 inches apart, and bake in a preheated 375° oven 10 to 15 minutes.

Family Fare
Low Calorie Dinner

(SERVES 6)

Savory Soup   Rye-Krisps

Swiss Steak Provençale   Brown Rice Pilaf

Braised Cucumbers

Garden Salad

Peach Custard *or* Baked Pears Melba

Raisin Drops

Coffee

The minimum of calories is offered for stark contrast, as this is admittedly party fare. To share the dinner with the family, and for the slim ones, add dumplings to the soup, rolls with the steak and cake or cookies with the custard.

ADVANCE PREPARATION SCHEDULE

Previous Day	Early Morning
Garden salad	*Steak*
Peach Custard	*Rice Pilaf*
	Baked Pears
	Savory Soup
	(see Index)

SWISS STEAK PROVENCALE

¼ cup packaged dry bread crumbs
2 teaspoons salt
¼ teaspoon pepper
2 pounds round steak
2 tablespoons butter *or* margarine, melted

1 16-ounce can tomatoes, undrained
2 medium onions, sliced thin
¼ cup chopped celery
1 clove garlic, chopped fine
1 tablespoon Worcestershire

Combine bread crumbs, salt, and pepper. Trim fat from steak; wipe meat with damp cloth. Sprinkle one side with half of crumb mixture; pound into steak, using rim of saucer. Repeat on other side. Brush both sides with butter; place under broiler, turning once, until browned on both sides. Combine tomatoes, onions, celery, garlic, and Worcestershire in Dutch oven (or heavy skillet with tight-fitting cover); add steak and simmer, covered, 2 hours or until meat is tender. Makes 6 servings: 1 slice with 2 tablespoons pan juices, 311 calories.

BROWN RICE PILAF

1¼ cups boiling water
1 chicken bouillon cube
½ cup uncooked brown rice
½ cup chopped onion
1 3-ounce can sliced mushrooms, drained
1 teaspoon salt
¼ teaspoon pepper
Dash thyme
½ cup thinly sliced celery

Add water to bouillon cube in 1-quart casserole, stirring until dissolved. Add rice, onion, mushrooms, salt, pepper, and thyme. Bake in a preheated 350° oven, covered, 1 hour and 10 minutes. Stir in celery with fork; bake 10 minutes longer. Just before serving, fluff up rice with fork. Makes 6 servings: ½ cup, 66 calories.

BRAISED CUCUMBERS

4 cucumbers, pared and sliced thin (6 cups)
2 teaspoons salt
3 bacon slices, diced
1 teaspoon sugar
¼ teaspoon non-caloric liquid sweetener
⅛ teaspoon pepper
1 tablespoon cider vinegar

In small bowl, layer cucumbers, sprinkling with salt. Refrigerate 30 minutes, covered. Meanwhile, in large skillet, sauté bacon until crisp; drain well. Add cucumbers, thoroughly drained, sugar, sweetener, pepper, and vinegar; stir to mix well. Cook, covered, over low heat, 10 to 12 minutes. Makes 6 servings: ¾ cup, 35 calories.

GARDEN SALAD

1 10-ounce package mixed
frozen vegetables, cooked
1 tablespoon unflavored gelatin
3 tablespoons sugar *or* 1½ teaspoons non-caloric liquid
sweetener

½ teaspoon salt
½ teaspoon celery salt
1½ cups water
¼ cup lemon juice
½ cup grated carrots

Cook frozen vegetables according to package directions and chill. Mix gelatin with sugar (or sweetener), salt, and celery salt in a small saucepan; add ½ cup water. Heat slowly and stir until gelatin is dissolved. Remove from heat and add remaining cup of water and lemon juice. Set in refrigerator and chill until of jelly-like consistency. Fold in mixed vegetables and grated carrots. Pour into oiled 4-cup mold, or 6 to 8 individual molds.

Unmold on greens, garnish with radishes. Serve with commercial low-calorie dressing, or a dollop of yogurt. Makes 3½ cups. Using sugar in the recipe, each of 6 servings contains 60 calories.

PEACH CUSTARD

6 canned dietetic peach
halves, drained
2 cups skim milk

½ teaspoon almond extract
1 1½-ounce package vanilla
rennet custard

Nutmeg

Place the peach halves in 6 sherbet glasses.
Heat milk with extract to just lukewarm. Stir in custard until dissolved. Pour immediately into sherbet glasses; peaches will rise to top. Let stand 10 minutes; then refrigerate until well chilled. Sprinkle with nutmeg. Makes 6 servings: 58 calories each.

BAKED PEARS MELBA

3 fresh pears, halved, cored
and pared
1 cup canned unsweetened
pineapple juice
1 teaspoon non-caloric liquid
sweetener

¼ teaspoon dry ginger
2 tablespoons dietetic raspberry
preserve

Arrange pears in baking dish. Combine pineapple juice, sweetener, and ginger; pour over pears. Bake in a preheated 350° oven about 30 minutes, or until tender, basting frequently. Serve warm or cold in crystal compotes, with 1 teaspoon raspberry preserve over each pear. Makes 6 servings:

RAISIN DROPS
(Sugar-free cookies)

1¾ cups cake flour
½ teaspoon salt
1 teaspoon cinnamon
½ teaspoon nutmeg
½ teaspoon cloves
1 teaspoon baking soda
½ cup butter

1 tablespoon non-caloric liquid sweetener *or* 24 tablets, crushed
1 egg
1 cup dietetic applesauce
⅓ cup raisins
1 cup All-Bran

Sift together flour, salt, cinnamon, nutmeg, cloves and baking soda. Cream butter, non-caloric liquid sweetener and egg until light and fluffy. Add flour mixture and applesauce alternately, mixing well after each addition. Fold in raisins and All-Bran. Drop by level tablespoonfuls on greased cooky sheet, about 1 inch apart. Bake in a preheated 375° oven 20 minutes, or until golden brown. Makes approximately 48 cookies.

Family Fare Dinner
(SERVES 6)

Beef Vegetable Soup — Marrow Balls
Knife and Fork Sandwich
Potato Salad — Wine Dressing
Lemon Cloud Cake
Coffee   Milk

Suggested wine: Valpolicella or other Italian red wine

ADVANCE PREPARATION SCHEDULE

Deep Freeze	Previous Day	Early Morning
Cake	*Soup*	*Potato salad*
	Salad dressing	*Marrow Balls*

BEEF VEGETABLE SOUP

Large soup bone, halved
2 pounds beef brisket, cubed
3 quarts water
2 tablespoons salt
1 bay leaf
¼ teaspoon thyme
⅛ teaspoon pepper

½ green pepper, sliced in strips
¼ cup minced parsley
2 stalks of celery, diced with leaves
2 white turnips, diced
2 carrots, diced
1 #2 can tomatoes

¼ cup sherry (optional)

Place bones and beef in deep kettle and cover with water. Add salt, bay leaf, thyme, and pepper. Simmer about 4 hours, skimming occasionally, then strain through sieve; remove fat and add green pepper, parsley, celery, turnips and carrots. Cook slowly about 30 minutes or until vegetables are tender; add tomatoes and heat through. Drop tiny uncooked Marrow Balls on top of soup so that they rest on vegetables or meat; cover kettle and cook gently about 15 minutes. Add sherry. Makes about 2 quarts.

A good luncheon dish for another day. Stores well.

MARROW BALLS

¼ cup fresh marrow
2 tablespoons butter
3 eggs
¼ teaspoon salt

⅛ teaspoon paprika
2 tablespoons chopped parsley
½ cup cracker crumbs

Combine marrow and butter and beat until creamy. Add eggs, salt, paprika, parsley, and crumbs. Blend well and shape into balls the size of a marble. Drop into simmering beef soup; cook for 15 minutes.

Note: Use raw marrow from marrow bones.

KNIFE AND FORK SANDWICH

¼-inch round slice iceberg lettuce
1 slice rye bread
2 teaspoons sweet pickle relish
2 thin slices boiled ham

Potato Salad (see recipe below)
Tomato quarters
Celery
Olives

Place lettuce on plate. Butter the bread, spread with sweet pickle relish and place on lettuce slice. Fill each slice of ham with Potato Salad and roll the slice. Place 2 filled slices on top of bread and garnish with tomato, celery, and olives.

POTATO SALAD

6 medium-size potatoes, sliced
½ cup sauterne or Rhine wine
4 green onions and tops, chopped
1 cup chopped celery

¼ cup minced parsley
1 2-ounce jar pimiento
2 hard-cooked eggs, whites chopped, yolks grated

Parsley sprigs

Cook potatoes in their jackets; peel and slice while still warm. Add wine to potatoes and mix lightly. Combine onions, celery, parsley, pimiento, and whites of hard-cooked eggs. Add to potatoes; blend in dressing and toss lightly. Chill for several hours. Garnish with grated egg yolks and parsley sprigs. (The recipe serves 6 if used just as a salad.)

WINE DRESSING

⅓ cup salad oil
¼ cup tarragon vinegar
1 teaspoon dry mustard

1 tablespoon sugar
2 teaspoons salt
¼ teaspoon pepper

Combine all ingredients and blend thoroughly.

LEMON CLOUD CAKE

1 package yellow cake mix
1 package lemon-flavored gelatin

4 eggs
½ cup salad oil
¾ cup water

Combine cake mix, gelatin, and eggs. Beat on low speed in mixer for 2 minutes. Add oil and water; beat 2 additional minutes. The batter will be thin. Pour into greased and floured 9″ x 13″ pan, place in a preheated 350° oven, and bake 35 minutes or until done. Test with toothpick which will be dry when center of cake is pierced. Cake should spring back from touch of finger as well. When still hot, pour Lemon Icing over cake and sprinkle evenly with coconut.

Lemon Icing:

2 cups confectioners' sugar   1 lemon, juice and grated rind
1 cup flaked coconut

Combine confectioners' sugar with juice and rind of lemon; mix very well. Place over hot water until ready to ice cake. Pour over cake, then sprinkle with flaked coconut.

Family Fare Dinner

(SERVES 8)

Split Pea Soup
Salmon Noodle Bake
Cucumber Ring Mold   Bean Panache
Chocolate Mint Pie
Coffee   Milk

ADVANCE PREPARATION SCHEDULE

Previous Day	Early Morning
Soup	*Assemble salmon*
Pie	*casserole for baking*
Cucumber ring	

SPLIT PEA SOUP

2 cups dried green split peas
3 quarts cold water
1 cooked ham bone, *or* root
of smoked tongue
3 medium-size bay leaves
¼ cup diced celery

2 chicken bouillon cubes
2 tablespoons butter
1 medium onion, cut fine
1 teaspoon sugar
2 teaspoons salt
¼ teaspoon white pepper

2 tablespoons flour

Pick over and wash the peas. Soak them in cold water overnight, drain, and place in soup kettle with ham bone, or tongue; add the cold water and bay leaves. Simmer slowly, but steadily, 4 hours or more; add the celery and cook until peas and meat are tender. Remove ham bone. Skim fat off top of soup and add bouillon cubes. Heat butter in a skillet; add onions and brown; add sugar, salt, pepper, and flour. Gradually add a cup of soup to onion mixture, then return to remainder of soup. Adjust seasonings.

Note: This soup is actually a leftover recipe, as it utilizes the ham bone or tongue root of a previous dinner.

SALMON NOODLE BAKE

1 8-ounce package medium noodles
2 10½-ounce cans cream of
mushroom soup
1 cup water
1 cup grated Cheddar cheese

½ teaspoon Worcestershire
1 16-ounce can salmon
½ cup fine cracker crumbs
3 hard-cooked eggs, sliced
2 tablespoons butter

Cook noodles according to package instructions. Heat soup and water over medium heat; add cheese and Worcestershire; stir until smooth. Remove from heat. Add flaked salmon and noodles; blend well and pour into greased 1½-quart casserole. Sprinkle cracker crumbs over top, dot with butter, and garnish with egg slices. Bake in a preheated 350° oven 40 to 50 minutes.

CUCUMBER RING MOLD

1 envelope (1 tablespoon)
unflavored gelatin
¼ cup lemon juice
2 tablespoons cold water
½ cup boiling water
2 tablespoons sugar

¾ teaspoon salt
6 medium cucumbers, pared
1 8-ounce package cream cheese
1 cup mayonnaise
¼ cup minced onion
¼ cup minced parsley

Soften gelatin in lemon juice and cold water; dissolve in boiling water. Add sugar and salt. Halve cucumbers and scrape out seeds; put cucumber through food chopper, using fine blade. Drain and measure; 2 cups of drained, ground cucumbers are required. Soften cream cheese; add cucumber, mayonnaise, onion, and parsley, mixing well. Stir in gelatin mixture and pour into 8 greased individual molds; chill until firm. Unmold and serve on lettuce, topped with 1 teaspoon mayonnaise. Dust with a dash of paprika.

Note: For a more elaborate dinner, we suggest a 6-cup mold, garnished with overlapping cucumber slices and strips of pimiento.

BEAN PANACHE

1 pound green beans, cooked and drained	2 tablespoons butter
½ pound wax beans, cooked and drained	½ pound lima beans, fresh *or* dried, cooked and drained
1 onion, chopped	1 tablespoon chopped parsley
	Salt and pepper

Trim green and wax beans; French-cut them in strips. Sauté onion in butter for 10 minutes. Toss with the green, wax, and lima beans. Add salt and pepper to taste and sprinkle with parsley. Serve hot.

Note: Frozen vegetables do very well for this preparation.

CHOCOLATE MINT PIE

Filling:

6 2-ounce milk chocolate candy bars, without nuts	1 pint heavy cream, whipped
1 11-ounce package miniature marshmallows	1 teaspoon peppermint extract

Melt chocolate bars and marshmallows in top of double boiler and stir until blended. Fold whipped cream with peppermint extract, then fold in marshmallow mixture. Pour into Graham Cracker Crust.

Graham Cracker Crust:

20 graham crackers, crushed	¼ cup butter, melted
¼ cup sugar	

For top and bottom crust, combine graham crackers, butter, and sugar. Line a 9-inch pie pan with ⅔ of crumb mixture. Press in firmly. Pour chocolate filling into shell and cover with remaining ⅓ of crumb mixture. Refrigerate several hours until chilled.

Family Fare
Blue Danube Dinner

(SERVES 6 TO 8)

Barley Soup   Crackers
Wiener Schnitzel
Noodles and Cabbage   Beet Relish
Rye Bread
Viennese Walnut Torte *or* Apple Bremen — Fluffy Sauce
Coffee

Suggested wine: Rhine

ADVANCE PREPARATION SCHEDULE

Deep Freeze	Previous Day	Early Morning
Torte (without filling)	*Soup*	*Noodles*
		Beet Relish
		Torte, or
		prepare apples for baking
		Fluffy Sauce (without cream)

BARLEY SOUP

4 quarts cold water	1 #2 can tomatoes
3 carrots, diced	(2 cups)
4 pounds soup meat and bones	¾ cup barley
2 large onions, chopped	1 4-ounce can mushroom pieces
1 parsnip, diced	*or* 4 ounces dried mushrooms
1 parsley root, diced	2 tablespoons chopped parsley
Chopped parsley leaves	(for garnish)

Place all ingredients, except parsley for garnish, in a large kettle, bring to a boil; reduce heat, cover and simmer 2½ hours. Cool, refrigerate. To serve, remove fat, reheat, sprinkle each serving with chopped parsley.

If dried mushrooms are used, wash and soak 2 hours before cooking.

WIENER SCHNITZEL

6 veal steaks	1 teaspoon paprika
¼ cup flour	⅛ teaspoon pepper
1 teaspoon salt	4 tablespoons butter
1 cup dairy sour cream	

Dredge steaks with flour and pound with edge of saucer, so that flour remains and steaks are tenderized. Sprinkle with salt, paprika, and pepper. Heat butter in saucepan or Dutch oven; add meat; brown over medium heat until golden and even. Add sufficient water to cover meat. Bring to a boil, reduce heat, place lid on pan, and simmer 1 hour or until tender. Add sour cream. To serve, heat, but do not boil.

Instead of simmering on stove, veal may be baked, covered, in a preheated 325° oven 1 hour.

Variation:

Serve with buttered noodles, or rice.

NOODLES AND CABBAGE

1 tablespoon salt	1 teaspoon sugar
4 cups finely shredded cabbage	¼ teaspoon pepper
¼ cup butter *or* fat	3 cups broad noodles, washed and drained

Mix the salt and cabbage together and let stand 30 minutes. Squeeze out all the liquid. Heat the butter in a deep skillet. Add the cabbage, sugar, and pepper. Cook over low heat 25 to 35 minutes or until cabbage is browned. Stir very frequently. Add the noodles and toss to blend thoroughly.

BEET RELISH

2 cups grated cooked beets	1 teaspoon salt
1/4 cup prepared red horseradish	2 teaspoons vinegar
2 teaspoons sugar	2 tablespoons salad oil

Mix all the ingredients together, place in refrigerator, and chill for a few hours.

VIENNESE WALNUT TORTE

9 egg yolks, beaten	1 cup cake flour, sifted
1 cup sugar	9 egg whites, beaten stiff
1/2 pound walnuts, ground	1 cup heavy cream, whipped

Beat sugar and egg yolks until lemon colored and creamy; blend in walnuts, and beat in flour until smooth. Fold in stiffly beaten egg whites. Pour into greased 9-inch spring form; bake in a preheated 325° oven 1 hour. Remove sides of pan, cool cake, split in half and fill with whipped cream.

APPLES BREMEN

Crust:

| 1/2 pound graham crackers | 1/3 cup melted butter |
| 1/2 teaspoon cinnamon | |

Roll crackers between 2 sheets wax paper or in paper bag until fine, even crumbs result. Reserve 1/2 cup. Mix remaining crumbs with butter and cinnamon; line 9-inch spring form, both bottom and sides. Press firmly.

Filling:

3 pounds apples, Greenings *or* MacIntosh	1/2 teaspoon cinnamon
	1/4 cup raisins
1/4 cup (1/8 pound) butter	2 tablespoons confectioners' sugar
1 cup sugar	

Peel, core, and quarter apples; slice thin as for pie. Place in saucepan, add butter, cover tightly, and steam 20 minutes. Shake pan frequently, but do not stir. Add sugar, cinnamon, and raisins; mix gently. Pour into prepared spring form and sprinkle reserved 1/2 cup crumbs over top. Place in a preheated 450° oven for 5 minutes. Sprinkle with confectioners' sugar and serve with whipped cream or Fluffy Sauce.

FLUFFY SAUCE

2 egg yolks, well beaten	½ teaspoon vanilla
¾ cup confectioners' sugar	1 cup heavy cream, whipped

Beat egg yolks and sugar thoroughly; add vanilla and fold in whipped cream. Chill until ready to serve.

Family Fare Dinner

(SERVES 8)

Onion Soup Soupçon
Rolled Rump Roast
Pine-Pear Salad
Hot Fudge Cake Pudding
Coffee   Tea   Milk

ADVANCE PREPARATION SCHEDULE

Early Morning

Roast
Prepare casserole for slaw

ONION SOUP SOUPCON

2 tablespoons butter	¼ teaspoon nutmeg
3 onions, sliced	¼ teaspoon celery seed
4 cups water	1 cup Croutons
6 beef bouillon cubes	(see Index)

Heat butter in saucepan; add onions and sauté 3 minutes. Add water and bouillon cubes, bring to a boil, cover and simmer for 20 minutes. Stir in nutmeg and celery seed. Serve with croutons.

ROLLED RUMP ROAST

1 4- to 5-pound rump roast, rolled	2 tablespoons flour
1 onion, sliced	2 cups beef bouillon
2 carrots, quartered	1 teaspoon seasoned salt
6 whole potatoes	2 tablespoons bead molasses
¼ pound beef suet	1 10-ounce package frozen peas, or beans

Wipe roast with paper toweling, place in roasting pan with onion, carrots, potatoes, and suet. Roast, uncovered, in a preheated 375° oven 1 hour. Do not add water. Remove meat and vegetables from roaster. Stir flour into pan drippings until smooth; add bouillon and return meat and vegetables to pan. Sprinkle with salt and spread molasses on meat. Cover pan, reduce heat to 275°, and bake according to following schedule for total roasting time:

2½ to 3 pounds — 2¼ hours
3½ to 4 pounds — 2½ hours
4½ to 6 pounds — 3 hours

The last half hour of cooking, push vegetables to one side and add peas or string beans. To serve, slice roast, place on hot platter and arrange vegetables around it. Strain gravy and serve separately.

PINE-PEAR SALAD

Cinnamon Pears:

1 #2½ can pears, drained	1 #2½ can pineapple
⅓ cup red cinnamon candies	1 head leaf lettuce

Combine pear liquid and cinnamon candies in a saucepan. Bring to a boil. Remove from heat; place pears in hot liquid. Cool and chill. Drain pineapple and chill. To serve, arrange lettuce leaves on individual salad plates, place a pineapple slice on each, then a half pear, flat side down. Serve with Fruit Mayonnaise.

Fruit Mayonnaise:

1 cup mayonnaise   1 tablespoon lemon juice
1 tablespoon cinnamon pear liquid

Mix well.

HOT FUDGE CAKE PUDDING

1 cup sifted all-purpose flour	2 tablespoons butter, melted
2 teaspoons baking powder	½ cup half and half cream
½ teaspoon salt	1 teaspoon vanilla
⅔ cup sugar	1 cup sifted brown sugar
2 tablespoons cocoa	¼ cup cocoa

1¾ cups boiling water

Mix flour, baking powder, salt, sugar, 2 tablespoons cocoa, and sift
3 times. Combine butter, cream and vanilla. Add flour mixture and
blend lightly. Pour into 2-quart buttered casserole. Combine the
brown sugar with ¼ cup remaining cocoa and sprinkle over batter.
Pour boiling water slowly over mixture. Bake in a preheated 350°
oven 30 minutes. Serve hot.

Family Fare Dinner

(SERVES 4 TO 6)

Egg Timbales

Braised Lamb Shanks   Spinach Anna

Buffet Potatoes

Lemon Chiffon Bavarian

Coffee   Milk

Suggested *wine:* Pouilly-Fuissé or red Burgundy

ADVANCE PREPARATION SCHEDULE

Previous Day	Early Morning
Timbales	*Lamb Shanks*
Lemon Bavarian	*Cook spinach*
	Crisp potatoes

EGG TIMBALES

½ cup finely chopped parsley   1 teaspoon Worcestershire
4 hard-cooked eggs, riced   1½ teaspoons unflavored gelatin
½ cup mayonnaise   2 tablespoons cold water
¾ teaspoon salt   ⅓ cup boiling water
Thousand Island Dressing (see Index)

Combine parsley, eggs, mayonnaise, salt, and Worcestershire. Soak gelatin in cold water for 5 minutes; add boiling water and dissolve. Blend with first mixture. Pour into six 4-ounce molds. Place in refrigerator until set. Unmold and serve on sliced tomato with bowl of dressing served separately.

Note: For a luncheon entrée, double the recipe and pour into 6-cup ring mold. Fill center with lobster or crabmeat salad and serve with Thousand Island Dressing (see Index).

BRAISED LAMB SHANKS

6 lamb shanks   ¼ teaspoon pepper
1½ teaspoons salt   3 tablespoons butter *or* oil

Season lamb with salt and pepper. Melt butter in Dutch oven; add shanks, simmer and brown evenly. Pour Basting Sauce over shanks, cover and simmer, or bake in a preheated 300° oven 2 hours or until tender. Baste frequently with sauce in pan.

Basting Sauce:

¼ cup vinegar   ¼ teaspoon cayenne pepper
½ cup water   1 thick slice lemon
2 tablespoons sugar   1 cup onions, thinly sliced
1 tablespoon prepared mustard   ¼ cup (⅛ pound) butter *or*
½ teaspoon pepper   margarine
1½ teaspoons salt   ½ cup catsup
2 tablespoons Worcestershire

Combine all ingredients, mix well and bring to a boil, simmer 10 minutes. Makes 1¾ cups.

SPINACH ANNA

1 12-ounce package frozen chopped spinach	½ teaspoon seasoned salt (optional)
3 eggs	Salt and pepper to taste
¼ cup milk	2 tablespoons butter
⅛ teaspoon crushed rosemary (optional)	¼ cup bread crumbs

Cook spinach according to package directions; drain thoroughly; squeeze dry if necessary. Beat eggs and milk together and add rosemary, seasoned salt, salt and pepper; adjust to taste. Add spinach; melt butter in skillet and brown the bread crumbs. Add egg and spinach mixture and cook, stirring from sides of pan, until eggs are scrambled solidly.

BUFFET POTATOES

4 large baking potatoes	1 teaspoon pepper
¼ cup (⅛ pound) butter	1 teaspoon savory
½ pound Cheddar cheese	Paprika
1 cup minced onion	2½ cups half and half cream
½ cup minced parsley	(approx.)
1 tablespoon salt	

Wash, peel, slice potatoes thin; put into ice water for about ½ hour. Drain, arrange a layer of potatoes in well-buttered casserole, dot with butter. Sprinkle thickly with cheese, onion, parsley, and seasonings; repeat layers, reserving ¼ cup cheese for topping. Pour in sufficient cream to cover potatoes. Bake in a preheated 450° oven 10 minutes; reduce heat to 350° and sprinkle with the ¼ cup cheese. Continue baking for about 2 hours. Serve in casserole.

LEMON CHIFFON BAVARIAN

Line bottom and sides of 8-inch spring form with Vanilla Crumb Crust. Reserve ¼ cup of crumbs for topping.

Vanilla Crumb Crust:

1½ cups vanilla wafers, crushed   6 tablespoons butter, melted
¼ teaspoon cinnamon

Combine crumbs, butter, and cinnamon; press onto sides and bottom of pan.

Lemon Chiffon Filling:

4 eggs, separated	¼ cup cold water
Juice of 2 lemons	¼ cup hot water
Rind of 1 lemon	½ cup sugar
½ cup sugar	1 cup heavy cream, whipped
1 envelope unflavored gelatin	¼ cup crushed vanilla wafers

Beat egg yolks until thick and lemon colored. Add lemon juice, rind, and ½ cup sugar. Soften gelatin in cold water; dissolve in hot water. Combine the above ingredients in top of double boiler and cook until thick, stirring constantly. Cool; place in refrigerator until slightly congealed. Beat egg whites until very stiff; add second ½ cup sugar, 1 tablespoon at a time, until stiff and glossy. Remove egg custard mixture from refrigerator; fold in egg whites and whipped cream. Pour into pan lined with crumb crust and top with reserved crumbs. To serve, remove rim of pan; place on paper doily on cake plate.

Family Fare Dinner

(SERVES 4 TO 6)

Chicken Country Captain
Cooked Vegetable Salad — Relish French Dressing
French Bread
Peanut Butter Pie
Coffee

Suggested wine: Graves or other white Bordeaux

ADVANCE PREPARATION SCHEDULE

Early Morning

Chicken for baking
Bread for heating
Pie
Vegetable Salad

CHICKEN COUNTRY CAPTAIN

½ cup flour
1 teaspoon salt
¼ teaspoon pepper
2 teaspoons monosodium glutamate
2 2½-pound fryers, disjointed
½ cup salad oil
1 teaspoon seasoned salt
2 onions, chopped
2 green peppers, sliced

1 clove garlic, minced
¼ cup chopped parsley
1 #2½ can tomatoes
1 teaspoon mace (optional)
1 or 2 teaspoons curry (to taste)
⅛ teaspoon paprika
½ cup currants or raisins
½ cup toasted almonds, halved or slivered

Combine flour, salt, pepper, and monosodium glutamate in a paper bag. Place chicken pieces in the bag a few at a time and shake to coat well. Heat oil in skillet, add chickens, sprinkle with seasoned salt, and brown well. Remove to a 4-quart roaster or casserole. To oil in which chicken was browned, add onion, peppers, garlic, and parsley and sauté lightly. Add tomatoes, mace, curry, and paprika; simmer for 15 minutes. Pour over chicken in the casserole. Cover and place in a preheated 275° oven; bake for 1½ hours or until tender. Remove chicken to warm platter, add currants to sauce, heat and pour over the chicken; sprinkle with almonds. Serve with 6 cups of Fluffy Rice (see Index).

Note: This is a deliciously different chicken recipe.

COOKED VEGETABLE SALAD

1 package frozen mixed vegetables
½ cup diced celery

½ cup chopped green pepper
¾ cup Relish French Dressing, or Garlic Cheese Dressing

Cook vegetables according to package directions. Cool and chill. Combine with celery and green pepper; toss with Relish French Dressing and serve in lettuce cups.

Note: This is a great way to utilize leftover cooked vegetables, especially lima beans or green beans. If vegetables have been buttered, rinse them in hot water and chill.

RELISH FRENCH DRESSING

¼ cup salad oil	Dash freshly ground pepper
¼ cup vinegar	1 teaspoon finely chopped
½ teaspoon salt	green onions
1 teaspoon sugar	1 hard-cooked egg, finely
½ teaspoon paprika	chopped
¼ teaspoon dry mustard	1 teaspoon sweet pickle relish

Combine all ingredients in a jar and shake well. Shake before each use. Makes ¾ cup.

Garlic Cheese Dressing:

This dressing is exceptionally good with the Cooked Vegetable Salad. The recipe is in our *Thoughts for Buffets,* page 360.

FRENCH BREAD

1 extra-large loaf French bread   ¼ to ½ cup melted butter

Cut bread in 1-inch slices to, but not through, bottom crust. Brush each side of slice and entire crust generously with butter. Wrap in foil and heat for 15 minutes in a preheated 400° oven. Makes about 15 slices.

PEANUT BUTTER PIE

1 cup light *or* dark corn syrup	⅓ cup chunk-style peanut butter
1 cup sugar	1 9-inch unbaked Pastry Shell
3 eggs, slightly beaten	(see Index)
½ teaspoon vanilla	1 cup heavy cream, whipped

Combine corn syrup, sugar, eggs, vanilla, and peanut butter; mix until thoroughly blended. Pour into prepared Pastry Shell. Bake in a preheated 400° oven 15 minutes; reduce heat to 350°; bake 30 to 35 minutes longer. Filling should appear slightly less set in center. Cool, then chill. To serve, top with whipped cream.

Family Fare Dinner

(SERVES 4)

Paprika Huhn   Raised Dumplings
Guacamole Tomatoes
Candied · Applesauce   Pound Cake Mary
Coffee   Milk

ADVANCE PREPARATION SCHEDULE

Deep Freeze	Previous Day	Early Morning
Cake	*Dressing*	*Salad vegetables*
		Applesauce
		Chicken (before adding livers)

PAPRIKA HUHN

¼ pound bacon, diced
2 small onions, sliced
1 large green pepper, diced
1 tablespoon paprika
1 2½- to 3-pound broiler-fryer,
   cut up

1 teaspoon salt
½ cup chicken broth
8 to 10 chicken livers
1 4-ounce can sliced mushrooms
   (optional), drained
1 cup dairy sour cream

1 tablespoon flour

Pan-fry bacon in large skillet until crisp and place on paper toweling to drain. Reserve 3 tablespoons bacon fat and return to skillet. Add onion and green pepper to fat; sauté until soft; do not brown. Stir in paprika, add chicken, sprinkle with salt. Cook slowly until chicken is lightly and evenly browned, about 15 minutes. Pour in broth; bring to a boil, reduce heat, cover and simmer 30 to 40 minutes until almost tender. Add livers; cook about 5 minutes on each side, until pink disappears. Cover again and simmer 10 minutes. Add mushrooms. Blend sour cream with flour, add to chicken, crumble bacon into small bits, and stir into mixture. Heat. Serve with sour cream gravy over chicken and border platter with Raised Dumplings.

Variation:

Substitute soft noodles or Spaetzle (see Index) for the dumplings.

RAISED DUMPLINGS

1 ⅔-ounce cake compressed yeast	1 teaspoon salt
¼ cup lukewarm water	1 teaspoon sugar
1 cup milk	1 egg, beaten
1 tablespoon butter *or* margarine	4 cups sifted all-purpose flour
¼ cup butter, melted	

Soften yeast in lukewarm water. Scald milk in double boiler. Add 1 tablespoon butter, salt, sugar, and stir until well blended. Cool to lukewarm. Add yeast to milk mixture, then add beaten egg and flour to make a firm dough. Beat or knead until dough is smooth and satiny. Place in lightly greased bowl, cover, and let rise in warm place until dough is double in bulk, about 1 hour. Cut pieces from dough about the size of a large walnut, using scissors or sharp knife. Mold into smooth balls and place on a floured board to rise, about 1 hour. When again double in size, drop one at a time, into gently boiling water. Cover and cook 15 to 18 minutes. When done, lift from water, using slotted spoon or fork. To serve, place on heated platter, break apart with a fork, and pour remaining butter over dumplings. Makes 32 dumplings.

GUACAMOLE TOMATOES

2 large tomatoes	2 teaspoons grated onion
¼ teaspoon salad *or* olive oil	¼ teaspoon chili powder
¼ teaspoon lemon juice	⅛ teaspoon ground coriander
1 ripe avocado, peeled and mashed	⅛ teaspoon salt
	Shredded lettuce

Slice off top of tomatoes and scoop out pulp; reserve pulp but remove seeds. Sprinkle hollows with oil and lemon juice. Turn upside down on platter and chill in refrigerator 1 hour or more. Combine avocado, tomato pulp, onion, chili powder, coriander, and salt. Fill tomato shells and serve on shredded lettuce.

This recipe may be increased, but watch the chili powder and coriander, as well — seasoning is so personal a taste.

CANDIED APPLESAUCE

12 red cooking apples, medium size	¼ teaspoon cinnamon
1½ cups water	1 tablespoon lemon juice
¾ cup sugar	Rind of ½ lemon, sliced
4 cloves, whole	¼ inch thick

Peel, core, and slice apples in eighths. Reserve peelings of 2 apples. Combine water with remaining ingredients in a saucepan and add reserved strips of peelings; bring liquid to a boil. Add apples, arrange carefully so all are submerged in syrup; reduce heat and simmer until apples are translucent and tender. Do not overcook. Pour into a bowl, remove peelings, and cover with syrup. Cool, refrigerate, and serve with lemon rind in glass compotes or other deep dishes.

Note: This is especially good with roasts.

POUND CAKE MARY

1 cup (½ pound) butter, softened	6 eggs
1 cup margarine, softened	Sufficient flour to fill empty confectioners' sugar box
1 1-pound box confectioners' sugar (retain box)	1 teaspoon vanilla
½ teaspoon almond extract	

Cream butter, margarine, and sugar very thoroughly; add eggs and beat until thoroughly blended. Measure flour into empty sugar box, and sift into creamed egg mixture. Add vanilla and almond extract; combine thoroughly. Pour into well-greased angel food pan. Bake in a preheated 350° oven 1 hour and 15 minutes, or until cake draws away from sides of pan. Cool on cake rack for 15 minutes; loosen sides with a spatula and turn out on cake plate.

This freezes exceptionally well, and is a many-purpose cake to have on hand. Mary's quaint use of the sugar box as a measure was of such interest that we have given it to you as an intriguing bit of memorabilia.

Family Fare Dinner

(SERVES 6)

Cheese Halibut

Tomato Indienne   Potato Carrot Charlotte

Strawberry Rhubarb Pie

Coffee

ADVANCE PREPARATION SCHEDULE

Deep Freeze
Pie

Early Morning
Halibut to reheat

CHEESE HALIBUT

2 pounds halibut	2 cups milk
2 tablespoons lemon juice	1 cup grated American cheese
¼ cup (⅛ pound) butter	1 teaspoon salt
¼ cup flour	¼ teaspoon pepper
Parmesan cheese, grated	

Broil halibut on foil (no pan to clean), until opaque on both sides. Remove bones and break into medium-size pieces; pour lemon juice over halibut. Melt butter in saucepan; add flour, stirring until smooth, then add milk and blend until smooth and thickened. Stir in cheese, salt, and pepper; continue to stir until cheese is melted. Adjust seasonings. Fold in halibut lightly, and heat thoroughly. Serve with Parmesan cheese.

Variation:

Place in buttered ovenware casserole, spread with Parmesan cheese, place under broiler until browned. One-fourth cup wine may be substituted for ¼ cup of the milk.

TOMATO INDIENNE

1 #2½ can tomatoes	2 teaspoons sugar
1 tablespoon arrowroot *or* flour	¼ cup shortening
2 tablespoons water	1 small onion, diced
1 teaspoon salt	1 green pepper, diced

1 tablespoon curry powder

Pour tomatoes into saucepan. Make a thin paste by combining arrowroot with water; add to tomatoes. Stir in salt, sugar, and cook until thick. Melt shortening in a skillet, add onion and green pepper; sauté until well browned. Stir in curry powder, and add to tomato mixture; simmer 10 minutes.

Note: Curry is a matter of taste; a lesser amount may be sufficient.

POTATO CARROT CHARLOTTE

1 cup grated carrots (about 4)	1½ teaspoons salt
¾ cup water	1 teaspoon sugar
3 cups grated and drained potatoes (about 5)	½ teaspoon ginger
3 egg yolks, beaten	3 tablespoons shortening, melted
¼ cup cracker meal	3 egg whites, beaten stiff

Place carrots and water in a saucepan and cook at a medium boil 15 minutes. Let cool in the liquid. Do not drain. In a large bowl combine potatoes, egg yolks, cracker meal, salt, sugar, ginger, shortening and the undrained carrots. Fold in egg whites. Pour into a greased 2-quart baking dish and bake in a preheated 350° oven 30 to 45 minutes. Serve hot.

Note: The original recipe endorses chicken fat as the best shortening for this pudding.

STRAWBERRY RHUBARB PIE

1½ cups sifted all-purpose flour	½ cup shortening
¾ teaspoon salt	2 to 4 tablespoons cold water

Strawberry Rhubarb Filling

Sift flour and salt together into a large bowl. Cut or rub in shortening until mixture is crumbly. Sprinkle with water, mixing lightly until dough begins to hold together. Turn out on a floured board or pastry cloth and press dough into a ball. Cover or wrap in wax paper, and place in refrigerator while preparing Strawberry Rhubarb Filling.

Strawberry Rhubarb Filling:

1 cup sugar	¼ teaspoon salt
¼ cup all-purpose flour	3 cups fresh rhubarb, cut in
½ teaspoon cinnamon	1-inch slices
2 cups whole *or* sliced strawberries	

Combine sugar, flour, cinnamon, and salt. Add to rhubarb and strawberries; mix lightly. Turn into bottom crust.

To prepare crust:

Remove dough from refrigerator, place on floured board and roll to circle ⅛ inch thick, large enough to loosely fit into 9-inch pie pan. Trim edge. Roll remaining dough out to rectangle about ⅛ inch thick. Using a knife, cut 6 petal-shaped pieces of dough about 3 inches long. Cut remaining dough into strips ¾ inch wide. Turn filling into bottom crust. Arrange petals over pie filling to form "flower." Have one point of each petal adhere to rim of pastry. Brush rim with water. Place strips around the edge, pressing firmly to hold petals and strips. Flute with fingers or pie crust wheel. Bake in a preheated 425° oven 35 to 40 minutes.

Family Fare Dinner

(SERVES 8)

Cassoulet Provençal   Crusty French Bread

Beet Slaw

Frozen French Chocolate

Coffee   Milk

Suggested wine: St. Emilion or other red Bordeaux

ADVANCE PREPARATION SCHEDULE

Previous Day

Cassoulet
Beet Slaw
Frozen Chocolate

CASSOULET PROVENCAL

1 pound pork, cut in 1-inch cubes	1 6-ounce can tomato paste
1 pound lamb, cut in 1-inch cubes	1 beef bouillon cube
2 tablespoons oil	¾ cup boiling water
3 large onions, sliced thin	¼ cup vermouth (optional)
1 teaspoon salt	1 tablespoon chopped parsley
1 clove garlic, minced, *or*	1 1 pound, 4-ounce can kidney
¼ teaspoon powdered garlic	beans *or* white navy beans
1 bay leaf, crushed	3 slices bacon, cut in 1-inch
⅛ teaspoon thyme	pieces
¼ teaspoon pepper	6 country pork sausages

¼ pound garlic sausage, sliced

Wash and dry the meat. Heat oil in a 3-quart saucepan, brown pork and lamb, add onions, and brown; reduce heat and add salt, garlic, bay leaf, thyme, pepper, tomato paste, the bouillon cube (dissolved in boiling water), vermouth, and parsley. Cover and simmer about 1½ hours or until tender.

While meat is cooking, assemble bean ingredients. In a 2-quart saucepan, sauté bacon and pork sausages until sausages are lightly browned. Drain off the fat. Add beans and garlic sausage. Bring to a boil, reduce heat; simmer until well heated, so that flavors are blended. When meat is tender, add the bean mixture and enough liquid from meat and beans to cover contents of saucepan. Place in a preheated 325° oven and bake 1 hour.

Leftover meat may be used, poultry may be added or substitution of beef may be made for pork or lamb. If made the previous day, the flavor improves and the excess fat which covers the cassoulet may be removed.

Story has it that the thrifty French housewives of the provinces devised this dish to utilize leftovers. Today it is a specialty. Many versions are given, and we have taken the liberty of presenting ours for your pleasure. Your own individual touch, as well, will be appropriate with this recipe.

BEET SLAW

2 envelopes (2 tablespoons) unflavored gelatin
½ cup cold water
1½ cups hot beet liquid *or* boiling water
1 cup cider vinegar
Juice of 1 lemon
1 tablespoon prepared horseradish

½ cup sugar
Salt to taste
2 cups finely shredded cabbage
2 cups coarsely shredded *or* diced cooked beets, drained

Soften gelatin in cold water; add hot liquid to dissolve. Stir in vinegar, lemon juice, horseradish, sugar, and salt. Cool and refrigerate until thick and syrupy. Fold in cabbage and beets. Pour into 1½-quart greased mold, or 8 individual greased molds. Serve on beds of curly endive.

Zippy in flavor and colorful enough to brighten any meal — especially good with pork or chicken.

FROZEN FRENCH CHOCOLATE

1 2¼-ounce package custard-flavor dessert mix
1 14½-ounce can (1⅔ cups) evaporated milk
1 4-ounce package German sweet chocolate, broken in pieces

1 4-ounce package miniature marshmallows
1 cup heavy cream, whipped
1 cup toasted pecans, coarsely chopped

Combine custard-flavor dessert mix, milk, and chocolate. Cook over medium heat, stirring until mixture comes to a full boil. Remove from heat (mixture will be thin). Cool. Pour into refrigerator tray. Freeze until partially frozen. Turn into bowl. With electric or rotary beater, beat till fluffy. Add miniature marshmallows and pecan meats. Fold in whipped cream. Freeze until firm. Makes 1 quart.

Note: To toast pecans, place in pan with 1 teaspoon butter. Roast in 400° oven until slightly browned. Watch carefully that they do not burn.

Family Fare Dinner

(SERVES 4)

Chicken Broth *or* Canned Consommé

Kreplach *or* Cracker Balls

Tongue Creole

Spanish Chick Peas   Salad Valencia

Speedy Strudel

Coffee   Hot Chocolate

ADVANCE PREPARATION SCHEDULE

Previous Day	Early Morning
Cracker Balls	*Kreplach*
Tongue	
Soup (see Index)	
Strudel	

KREPLACH

Filling:

1¼ pounds lean chuck, boneless, cooked	1 egg, beaten
1 large onion	¾ teaspoon salt
	¼ teaspoon freshly ground pepper
2 tablespoons chopped parsley	

Grind meat and onion together; add egg, salt, pepper, and parsley. Boil water and salt; keep it boiling. Have a strip of floured wax paper next to your board.

Dough:

1 cup unsifted all-purpose flour	¼ cup water
¼ teaspoon salt	3½ quarts water (boiling)
1 egg, beaten	1 tablespoon salt

Sift the flour with the salt; add egg and water; mix and knead well until dough is smooth and soft. Roll into a piece about 12" x 12", approximately ⅛ inch thick. Cut into 4 strips, then cut each strip into 4 squares. Fill each square with a heaping tablespoon of ground beef. Makes 16 kreplach. Don't put any flour on the dough, just a little on the board and the rolling pin. Press the edges of each square together making a triangle or any shape. Place each one on the wax paper as you make it. When all 16 are made, drop them in the boiling water, to which a tablespoon of salt has been added; let boil about 8 to 10 minutes while you roll out and make another piece, etc., until all 4 parts are made. When each batch is finished take them out of the boiling water and put them in a bowl of cold water. When cool, ease lightly into a colander to drain. Serve with consommé or chicken broth.

CRACKER BALLS

4 eggs	¼ cup shortening, melted
½ cup cracker meal *or* matzo meal	½ teaspoon salt

Mix and place in refrigerator overnight. Form into 1-inch balls and drop into boiling soup; cook for about 15 minutes.

TONGUE CREOLE

1 4-pound to 5-pound tongue, fresh *or* lightly pickled	2 stalks celery, diced
1 large onion, diced	1 pound small fresh mushrooms
¼ cup (⅛ pound) butter	1 11-ounce bottle chili sauce
1 green pepper, sliced	1 cup tongue stock

To boil fresh tongue (if pickled tongue is used, do not season):

1 4-pound to 5-pound fresh tongue	1 bay leaf
2 medium onions	1 teaspoon pickling spices
3 stalks celery with leaves	1 teaspoon salt
1 garlic clove (optional)	

Place tongue in saucepan, add all ingredients and add water to cover tongue. Bring to a boil, reduce heat and simmer very slowly until tender, about 3 hours. To serve without further preparation, be certain tongue is fork tender. When not cooked sufficiently, it has a rubber-like texture. Well cooked, it is succulent.

For Tongue Creole, cook until almost tender, and reserve 1 cup of the stock. Remove skin while warm. Let cool and slice. Heat butter; add onions, celery, green pepper and mushrooms, and sauté gently until onion turns yellow. Add chili sauce and about ¾ cup of reserved stock; blend thoroughly. Lay slices of tongue in sauce and simmer gently for an hour. This is best if prepared in advance and then reheated.

SPANISH CHICK PEAS

2 cups (1 can) chick peas   ½ teaspoon salt
¼ cup olive oil   ⅛ teaspoon pepper
        1 tablespoon parsley, chopped

Drain peas, wash thoroughly under running water and drain again. Heat oil in saucepan and add peas. Sauté lightly until thoroughly heated. Dust with salt and pepper and sprinkle with parsley.

SALAD VALENCIA

½ cup orange juice   ½ cup heavy cream, whipped
½ cup water   ½ cup shredded coconut
 1 3-ounce package orange-   1 banana, sliced
   flavored gelatin   1 orange, segmented
½ cup Rosé wine (any fruit juice Leaf lettuce
   may be substituted for wine)

Combine orange juice and water; pour into saucepan; bring to a boil. Pour over gelatin; dissolve and refrigerate. Add wine. Cool until mixture drops in mounds from spoon. Beat with rotary beater until fluffy and fold in whipped cream. Blend in coconut, banana and orange. Pour into oiled 1-quart mold, refrigerate until firm. Unmold on lettuce-lined platter; garnish with sliced oranges.

SPEEDY STRUDEL

2 cups all-purpose flour   ⅓ cup shortening
2 tablespoons sugar   Dash salt
½ cup (¼ pound) butter   ¼ cup ice water

Combine flour and sugar, add butter, shortening, salt, and enough ice water (about ¼ cup) for pie dough. Form into a ball, wrap in wax paper and refrigerate overnight. Remove 1½ hours before rolling. Cut dough into 4 equal parts; roll each part on board as thin as possible. Spread with melted butter, and scatter a few bread crumbs over it. Spread with Filling, roll into long thin rolls, and bake in preheated 350° oven for 30 minutes.

Filling:

> 2 tablespoons sugar   ¼ cup grated nuts
> Jelly   2 tablespoons butter, melted
>   2 tablespoons bread crumbs

Use as directed.

Family Fare Dinner

(SERVES 4)

Beer Beef Ragout

Squaw Corn   Molded Fruit Compote

Sailor's Duff Pudding — Foamy Sauce *or* Brandy Sauce

Coffee   Tea

Suggested wine: Mountain Red Burgundy

ADVANCE PREPARATION SCHEDULE

Previous Day	Early Morning
Fruit Compote	*Beef Ragout*

BEER BEEF RAGOUT

> 2 pounds lean chuck, cut in   1 tablespoon sugar
>   1-inch cubes   ¾ teaspoon salt
> ½ cup flour   ½ teaspoon pepper
> ½ cup (¼ pound) butter   1 tablespoon tomato paste
> 1 medium onion, diced   5 carrots, quartered
> 1 12-ounce can beer   4 potatoes, quartered
> 1 bay leaf   2 tablespoons sherry *or*
> 5 sprigs parsley   Madeira
> ⅛ teaspoon thyme   1 tablespoon cognac

Dredge meat with flour until completely coated; heat butter in saucepan, add meat, and brown lightly but thoroughly; add onion as meat browns. Onion will brown lightly. Add beer, bay leaf, parsley, thyme, sugar, salt, pepper, and tomato paste. Simmer, covered, about 2 hours. Add sufficient water to keep liquid content at least an inch high. Add vegetables last hour of cooking. To serve, stir in cognac and Madeira or sherry; reheat. Remove bay leaf and parsley. Arrange meat and vegetables attractively on platter.

SQUAW CORN

5 slices bacon	¼ cup chopped onion
1 #1 can whole kernel corn	¼ cup diced green pepper

Sauté bacon in skillet until crisp; drain and set aside. Crumble when dry. Remove all but 2 tablespoons bacon drippings. Add onion and green peppers to drippings and sauté about 5 minutes; blend in corn and crumbled bacon. Heat and serve.

MOLDED FRUIT COMPOTE

1 #2 can crushed pineapple	1 15-ounce can raspberry
2½ cups pineapple liquid	applesauce
2 3-ounce packages raspberry	Lettuce
gelatin	

Drain pineapple. Add sufficient water to juice to make 2½ cups. Bring 1 cup to a boil; add gelatin and stir until dissolved. Add remaining liquid; chill. When mixture reaches jelly-like consistency, add combined raspberry applesauce and pineapple; blend well. Pour into oiled 6-cup mold and refrigerate until congealed. Serve on leaf lettuce.

Note: This mold is larger than needed for this menu. The recipe may be cut in half, or leftovers will refrigerate well for several days.

SAILOR'S DUFF PUDDING

1 egg	½ cup molasses
2 teaspoons sugar	1½ cups all-purpose flour
2 tablespoons butter	1 teaspoon baking soda
½ cup boiling water	

Dissolve soda in hot water. Beat remaining ingredients until light, combine with soda liquid, and pour into buttered covered mold. Place in steamer and steam 1 hour. Serve with Foamy Sauce — more to the young ones' taste (see Index) — or Brandy Sauce.

BRANDY SAUCE

1 egg yolk, beaten	3 tablespoons brandy
1 cup sugar	1 cup heavy cream, whipped

Cream egg yolk with sugar; add brandy, and fold in whipped cream. Makes 2 cups.

Hints to Help-Less Housewives

1. Read each recipe carefully; read it twice if completely new.
2. Always preheat oven to temperature indicated unless otherwise stated.
3. When measuring salt, hold container and pour it over sink. Salt is elusive and can prove disastrous if too much spills into the preparation.
4. Use the blender for making crumbs from stale bread or crackers.
5. The skillet or pan for an omelet or pancakes is heated sufficiently when water dropped on it sputters on the surface. Use a measuring cup with a spout or a pitcher when making pancakes and pour a sufficient amount onto the griddle.
6. Molds for salads should always be greased or oiled lightly. Turn upside down to drain excess oil.
7. When beating egg whites, have beaters clean and dry.
8. Beat the whites first; an unnecessary washing is thus eliminated, as the beaters can then be used for the yolks.
9. To clear beaters of electric mixer of as much of the bowl mixture as possible, reduce speed slowly, while slowly lifting the beaters. Turn off the motors just as beaters have completely emerged.
10. Deep Freeze: Previous day preparation is suggested as a helpful time-saver. It is for your convenience; if your preference is for immediate preparation, by all means do so.
11. The above is true of all preparations where you may prefer im-

mediate serving of foods rather than cooking in advance and reheating. Again, the advance preparation schedule is for your planning convenience.

12. If you question the freezing potential of a recipe, check with Advanced Preparation Schedule.

13. Save utensil washing by sifting flour or other dry ingredients on wax paper.

14. It is helpful to store flour sifters in a bag, thus eliminating flour dust in your cupboard. Washing sifters causes flour to adhere, and it is difficult to remove.

15. For easier beating or blending of shortenings such as butter, margarine, or cream cheese, allow them to soften to room temperature.

16. Coffee: Use 1 tablespoon to ¾ cup water. This is a general measurement. A clean pot is imperative for good flavor.

17. Have a memo pad at hand and as the last item of a category is removed from the shelf, list it for replacement on your next shopping tour.

18. Chop parsley in advance and store in transparent wrap or foil.

19. Foil containers are wonderful for reheating rolls.

20. Place a foil mat under the milk cartons to avoid possible leakage.

21. Cut a Sunshine, Angel Food, or similar textured cake with a sawing motion. A piece of silk thread cuts nicely.

22. To remove the white membrane more easily when peeling an orange (or a grapefruit), soak the unpeeled orange in hot water for a few minutes.

23. If a sauce or soup is too salty, add one or two small raw, peeled potatoes, let them boil about 5 minutes, then remove.

24. When measuring molasses, grease the cup and the molasses will not stick.

25. All measurements are level.

26. Color or flavor ice cubes; add fruit juice or coloring before freezing.

27. Lemon or vinegar in a fish kettle reduces odors.

28. For a tossed salad, the greens should never be cut, unless so specified. Tear them in bite-sized pieces.

29. To cut marshmallows, dip scissors in water to keep from sticking.

30. Store crackers in a warm, dry place. A cupboard near the stove (if you happen to have one) is a "self-crisping" device.
31. Cooky or pastry dough is much easier to roll if chilled beforehand.
32. The kitchen timer is a wonderful reminder of baking or cooking, especially if you have duties in other rooms.
33. Store foods in categories; a real time-saver in locating items.
34. Always date your frozen food packages so as to use them in time sequence.
35. The use of vegetable shortening is very effective to prevent preparations from sticking to baking pans.
36. Do not beat quick breads after adding dry ingredients; just stir.
37. Heavy cream doubles and often triples in volume when whipped.
38. One cup of raw rice becomes three when cooked.
39. Fresh tomatoes keep longer when placed with stem end down.

Food Hints

Fruit

Wash strawberries before hulling.

Drop peeled avocado or banana in lemon juice to prevent its turning dark.

When peeling citrus fruits or pineapple, do so over a bowl so as to catch the juices.

To ripen avocado or pineapple, place in a brown paper bag; seal and let stand in a warm, not hot, spot.

To store a ripe pineapple in a refrigerator, wrap well to prevent other foods from absorbing odor.

To prevent discoloration of fresh fruit, the juice of citrus fruits has been designated. There is, as well, a product with an ascorbic acid base available for this purpose.

Nuts

Be certain nutmeats are fresh before using, as they will spoil the flavor of baked products if at all rancid. Taste before using.

A broken nut is about a ⅓-inch piece; coarsely cut, ¼-inch; finely chopped is self-explanatory.

To blanch almonds, drop into boiling water, allow to stand 5 minutes until skins slip off.

To brown almonds, spread on pan in moderate oven and watch carefully. For salted nuts, add 1 teaspoon salad oil to each cupful in pan, stir often, drain and salt.

Eggs

When boiling eggs, remove from refrigerator, let stand at room temperature at least 20 minutes before using, to prevent cracking when dropped in hot water. Drop them into boiling water and start timing from the moment the water reboils.

Plunge hard-cooked eggs into cold water immediately upon removing from pan. To prevent yolks from turning dark, do not cook longer than 12 minutes. Roll them around while boiling, so that yolk is centered.

A sudden change of temperature from refrigerator to hot water may cause cracking. If the egg should crack, a dash of salt in the water will firm the seeping egg white.

The volume of beaten egg whites is increased when eggs are at room temperature.

When preparing meringue for desserts, add 2 tablespoons flavored gelatin to a four-egg recipe for color and flavor.

Recipes for Leftover Egg Whites   *Recipes for Leftover Egg Yolks*

Chocolate Meringue Bread	Lemon Sauce for Trout
Lemon Angel Cake	Zabaglione
Walnut Meringue	Gold Cake
White Cloud Angel Food Cake	Brandy Sauce
Meringue Glacée	Foamy Sauce
	Sauce Maxim

Egg whites may be frozen. Mark each container with the number stored, and have them ready for your next egg white recipe need.

Omelets: For successful preparation, do not make an omelet for a larger quantity than 6 eggs. If more is needed, make two omelets.

Use a rotary hand beater for best results.

Meats

A boned or rolled roast requires ten more minutes cooking time per pound than one cooked with bones.

Meats cooked in liquid should be simmered slowly. Fast cooking causes meat to become stringy.

When roasting meat, do not prick with a fork; if necessary to turn it, use tongs.

To avoid worry when roasting, use a meat thermometer.

Liver loses its flavor if stored longer than twenty-four hours.

Do not separate slices before placing bacon in pan, as they slide apart when warm.

To prevent steaks and chops from curling, slash through outside fat at 1-inch intervals.

When roasting, remember that ovens vary, also that meats and poultry vary in age and tenderness.

Freezing meats in conveniently planned amounts prevents waste and hastens thawing time.

Grind meat once for patties, but two or three times when making small meat balls or meat loaf.

When pounding raw meat, moisten it to prevent sticking to hammer.

For crisp bacon, pour off fat continually while frying.

Use undiluted canned consommé to baste poultry.

To store meat:

> Remove from market paper.
> Do not wash.
> Do not wrap airtight in refrigerator; cover loosely.
> Meat should lie as flat as possible.
> Store in coldest part of refrigerator.

Do not permit cooked meat to remain out of refrigerator longer than two hours. Cool cooked meat before refrigerating, but do not wait until it becomes cold. Store in tightly covered container.

Use leftover cooked meats within four days.

Proper care of meat before, during, and after cooking is important. Meat cuts may be divided into two classes, tender and less tender.

1. Tender:
   Tender cuts are best when cooked by dry heat — roasting, broiling, pan broiling, frying.
2. Less Tender:
   Less tender cuts are best when cooked by moist heat — braising or simmering. Roasting at a low temperature, about 325°, prevents shrinkage. The use of a meat thermometer to indicate proper degree of doneness is advised.

The rule of low heat is also indicated for cooking less tender cuts; always simmer over low heat.

Frozen Meats: To store, wrap airtight in freezer paper or foil. Separate meat into packages of serving size. For convenience in storing meat patties, wrap separately.

Cooking methods and degrees of doneness are the same for fresh and frozen meats; only the total cooking times vary.

Roasting: Hard-frozen oven roasts require approximately one-third to half again as much cooking time per pound as do the corresponding fresh roasts.

Broiling: Thicker cuts of hard-frozen steaks will require one-fourth more to two times as much broiling time as the corresponding fresh cuts.

To slice: It is easier to slice meat when slightly frozen, particularly thinly sliced tenderloin for pepper steak, Sukiyaki, etc.

To defrost: Allow meat to remain in refrigerator overnight or long enough to defrost. For quick thawing, place (wrapped) under running cold water. Do not defrost at room temperature, as it may spoil readily if allowed to stand too long.

Do not immerse unwrapped meat in water for thawing, unless it is to be cooked in that water.

Cheese

Cook cheese at a low temperature as it becomes stringy when subjected to high heat.

Do not freeze cheese. It becomes mealy.

Though cheese may mold in the refrigerator, it does not spoil. Cut off the mold and use the balance.

Vegetables

To remove kernels from a cob of corn, place ear in the funnel of an angel food pan and shave down on the cob; kernels will fall into the pan.

When boiling cabbage, add a piece of rye bread to the water to eliminate odor.

Work on paper when peeling vegetables; wrap and throw out the refuse at once; eliminates mess.

Noodles, Rice, and Barley

In Italian recipes, pastas are not rinsed in cold water. American recipes, as a rule, specify a cold bath for noodles, etc.

For especially good flavor, cook noodles, rice, barley, etc., in bouillon.

When cooking a starch, such as rice or noodles, grease the kettle before adding water, to prevent a ring from forming around the kettle.

Mushrooms

There are approximately 20 to 24 fresh mushrooms in a pound. A 6- to 8-ounce can equals 1 pound of fresh mushrooms. As substitution for ½ pound of fresh mushrooms, use a 4-ounce can.

Never soak mushrooms. Wash under running water, then pat them dry. Broiling mushrooms dries them; when sautéeing, use very little butter — just enough to keep surface coated. Cook them in a single layer. When preparing stews, add mushrooms during last part of cooking. Do not discard stems; use them for sauces, soups, and dips. A small amount of water added to the butter when sautéeing steams them deliciously plump. To store, cover with moist toweling; refrigerate. Toweling should be replaced often.

To release the full flavor of dried mushrooms, soak a minimum of 2 hours.

Bread, Pastry, and Yeast

We urge you to meet the challenge of yeast baking. In reality it is fun and a great convenience. Preparation may be done in advance; dough may be refrigerated for a short length of time. The advantage of yeast baking is the ability to plan ahead as the length of time required for cake or bread can be closely determined.

Yeast dough needs a temperature of about 85° to rise. It must not have extreme heat. Use a room thermometer to dispel worry.

For best results, soften active dry yeast in warm, not hot, water (105°).

For compressed yeast, use lukewarm water (85°).

If scalded liquid is an ingredient, be certain to cool it as heat produces coarse texture.

A small amount of sugar added to yeast dough acts as a leavening agent. It adds flavor and color to the texture, as well.

If there is any question as to the freshness of compressed yeast, combine the cake with one tablespoon sugar. The yeast is fresh if it dissolves in 2 or 3 minutes and you may proceed with your recipe.

Brush rolls and coffee cake before baking with melted butter or slightly beaten egg yolks for a browned, glazed result.

Yeast refrigerator dough should be frozen no longer than 2 weeks.

To hold up under refrigeration, dough must have a high proportion of sugar.

To refrigerate, cover closely with heavy duty aluminum foil. To further safeguard the dough, cover with a cold, damp towel. Do not permit it to dry. Punch dough down daily.

A dough made with milk should not be kept longer than three days.

As a general rule, dough should rise until doubled in bulk. To test, press two fingers deeply into dough and if holes remain when fingers are withdrawn, dough has risen sufficiently.

For freezing yeast rolls or bread, bake as directed, cook, wrap, seal, and freeze quickly. To thaw, bake in sealed wrapping in 300° oven for about 15 minutes.

Baked yeast dough when wrapped in airtight covering will keep for months without impairing quality.

Homemade "brown-and-serve" Rolls: Bake about 10 minutes and remove before browned; cool, wrap and freeze quickly. To serve, remove wrappings and let stand at room temperature 15 minutes; place in a preheated 450° oven for 5 to 10 minutes, or until brown. Serve at once.

To deep-freeze cakes: It is simpler to freeze unfrosted cakes. Defrost when needed and then ice.

To deep-freeze frosted cakes: Place frosted cakes in freezer without wrapping and allow to remain until completely frozen and frosting is firm; then wrap carefully.

Regarding details of advance preparation, there are many preliminaries and kitchen maneuvers, which we hope you will develop. E.g. to save time assemble as many of the needed ingredients as is possible, sift dry ingredients preparatory to their use, prepare basic sauces and those items which can be assembled to be ready for later preparation. Partially cook where indicated those items to be added later. Have at hand those ingredients used for last-minute addition. These are part of advance preparation, but too detailed to enumerate.

To ship cookies, use a 3-pound shortening can with a tight cover. Cover it with decorative paper and make it attractive as well as practical.

Pie Crust: The use of vinegar in a pie crust produces a tender crust. Brown the crust during baking by brushing top crust with milk.

If using double-acting baking powder, adjust according to can directions.

For a graham cracker crust, 15 crackers, crushed, equal 1 cup of crumbs.

Sauces and Seasonings

Bouquet Garni: A faggot or bouquet of herbs or plants used to season soups, stew, sauces, etc. The variety depends on the recipe.

When used with crumbled herbs, they may be tied into a sack made of cheesecloth or a comparable material. The bouquets are, as a rule, removed before serving.

A Garni for a stew might be a pouch of parsley, a bay leaf, a clove of garlic and ⅛ teaspoon of thyme.

For a soup, a faggot of carrots, parsnips, parsley, an onion and a turnip could be used.

There are endless combinations depending on taste and needs.

Fine Herbs Blend: To make one variety of Herb Blend use ½ teaspoon each of the following:

Tarragon	Chives
Parsley	Basil
Savory	

Add to salad bowl. Or try a bit in meat sauces, casseroles or omelets or on broiled meat or chicken. Good with cooked green beans or spinach.

Seasoned Flour:

1 tablespoon salt	½ cup flour
½ teaspoon pepper	1 teaspoon paprika

Combine in paper bag, add chicken or other ingredients to be coated; shake well. Sufficient for 2 chickens.

Other seasonings such as garlic salt, seasoning salt, or monosodium glutamate may be added.

Sauces: The two basic sauces are the White Sauce and the Brown Sauce. With the addition of curry, eggs, olives, dill, mushrooms, tomatoes, etc., they become an infinite variety.

Medium White Sauce:

⅓ cup butter	1 quart milk, heated
½ cup flour	½ teaspoon salt
⅛ teaspoon white pepper	

Melt butter in saucepan, add flour and heat until bubbly and smooth. Do not brown. Stir in milk slowly; blend in salt and pepper. Cook until heated and smooth.

Brown Sauce:

2 tablespoons butter	2 cups canned beef consommé
1 tablespoon flour	⅛ teaspoon pepper
2 tablespoons minced onion	1 tablespoon tomato paste
1 bay leaf (optional)	

Heat butter in saucepan, add flour, cook until bubbly. Blend in minced onion and cook, stirring until light brown. Add consommé gradually and bring to a boil; add pepper, tomato paste and bay leaf. Simmer 20 minutes, strain, cool and store.

Small quantities of soup stocks in the freezer are a great convenience when preparing sauces, gravies or chowders.

Dehydrated onion soup is excellent seasoning for stews, ground beef, etc.

Celery leaves are fine seasoners for soups or sauces.

A dash of sugar in soups or meat sauces heightens flavor.

Vanilla sugar gives a superb flavor where both vanilla and sugar are ingredients. To have it on hand, place a vanilla bean in a canister with ½ pound sugar; replenish the sugar when necessary and replace the bean every 6 months.

1 tablespoon vanilla sugar has the equivalent of ¼ teaspoon vanilla. Reduce amount of sugar in recipe accordingly.

Add a dash of salt to cake batters and dessert sauces.

Use 5 large marshmallows in the syrup when stewing fruit. They foam and act as self-basters; especially helpful when used with cinnamon drops or color.

Spices and Herbs. Herbs and spices add glamour to cooking as do cosmetics to women. Keep all spice containers airtight. Do not allow them to dry out in the usual storage disarray.

To have proper spices, divide them into categories:

1. Salads   2. Roasts and Stews   3. Sauces   4. Baking

Do use them and cultivate your own preferences.

Any sauce prepared with herbs, directed to be added to a partially cooked recipe, should be combined no sooner than the last hour of cooking. Generally add ¼ teaspoon of dried herbs for each four servings. When seasoning with herbs, experiment and use sparingly until you determine your taste for them.

Garlic: This powerful herb is deliciously aromatic when used with discretion and most fastidious cooks find it an essential, although a few diners find it disagreeable. In the majority of recipes, you may take the option of eliminating it.

Brief Notes about Wine

Wine is divided into seven categories:

1. Aperitif or appetizer wines; i.e., the driest or medium dry Sherry or Madeira, specialties like sweet or dry Vermouth, Dubonnet, Lillet.
2. White table wines.
3. Red table wines.
4. Rosé wines.
5. Crackling Rosé wines (a relatively new type).
6. Sparkling wines.
7. Dessert wines. I.e., medium sweet to sweet Sherry and Madeira; white, tawny, or ruby Port, Malaga, Marsala.

White wines should never be served so chilled that the bouquet and flavor are obscured. Any red wine should be served at room temperature and opened at least a half hour before use, so that the bouquet and flavor will develop because of aeration.

It is easier to cook *with* wines than without. Wine serves to enhance flavors that are present, supply flavor where flavor is lacking, tenderize and supply elements that assist general nourishment.

Planned Pantry

THESE lists have been assembled for your convenience in preparing the recipes in this cookbook. Those foodstuffs least frequently mentioned in the menus are marked with an asterisk. The entire listing becomes a handy staple guide for cooking and dining.

Refrigerator Foods

Dairy Products

Butter and margarine
Cheeses:
   American
   blue
   Cheddar
   cottage
   cream
   Swiss
Dairy sour cream
Eggs
Milk
Whipped cream dispenser*

Vegetables and Meat

Bacon
Carrots
Celery
Green pepper
Lettuce
Parsley
Tomatoes

Miscellaneous

Beef extract*
Fruit*
Horseradish (prepared)

Lemons
Mayonnaise
Mustard (Dijon style)

Yeast

Vegetable Bin

Garlic   Onions   Potatoes

Freezer Foods

Breads and rolls
Cakes and pies
Chives*
Cocktail rye
Coffee cake
Dessert shells*
Fruits, assorted frozen
Ice creams and sherbets
Ladyfingers

Lemonade and orange juice
Macaroons
Marrow bones*
Marshmallows
Meats, poultry and fish
Seafoods:
  Crabmeat
  Lobster
  Shrimp
Vegetables, assorted frozen

Canned Goods

Fish
  Anchovies (rolled & filleted)
  Caviar (red & black)
  Clams*
  Crabmeat
  Fish balls (bottled)*
  Lobster
  Oysters*
  Salmon
  Sardines
  Shrimp*
  Tuna

Juices and Beverages
  Apple*
  Apricot nectar
  Beer*
  Grape*
  Grapefruit*
  Lemon
  Pineapple*
  Soft drinks*
  Tomato

Fruits
  Applesauce*
  Apricots
  Cherries (white and red)*
  Cherries, Maraschino* (green
    and red)
  Crabapples, spiced*
  Cranberries, whole and sauce
  Fruit cocktail*
  Lingonberries*
  Mandarin oranges
  Peaches
  Pears
  Pineapple (slices and chunks)

Soups
  Beef bouillon and consommé
  Chicken bouillon and broth
  Consommé Madrilenè*
  Cream of mushroom
  Onion
  Tomato

Specialty
Anchovy paste*
Chopped dried beef*
Cocktail onions*
Cocktail sausages*
Deviled ham
Ice cream sauces (chocolate, etc.)
Kumquats
Marrons*
Olives:
  Green
  Pimiento-stuffed
  Pitted black
  Ripe
Pickles (sweet, sour, and dill)
Senf Gurkin*
Truffles*
Watermelon rind

Vegetables
Artichokes (hearts and bottoms)
Asparagus, white
Baked beans*
Beets (whole and sliced)
Carrots, baby*
Chick peas*
Corn (niblets and creamed)*
Hearts of palm
Kidney beans*
Peas
Potatoes, shoestring
Onions (tiny whole and fried)*
Tomatoes (whole and Italian)
Sauerkraut*

Miscellaneous

Capers
Chow mein noodles*
Milk (condensed and evaporated)
Mushrooms
Mushroom sauce*

Pimientos
Tomato paste
Tomato sauce
Water chestnuts
Wild rice

Condiments, dressings and spreads

Apple butter*
Barbecue sauce*
Blue cheese spread*
Catsup
Chili sauce
Chutney
Corn syrup (white and dark)*
Honey*
Jams, jellies, and preserves
Kitchen Bouquet (a gravy browner)*

Mayonnaise
Molasses (dark and bead)*
Mustards
Oils (olive and salad)
Peanut butter*
Pimiento cheese spread*
Salad dressings
Soy sauce
Steak sauce*
Sweet pickle relish*
Syrup, maple*

Tabasco Sauce
Vegetable shortening
Vinegars:
  Cider

Tarragon
White
Wine
Worcestershire sauce

Miscellaneous packaged goods

Barley*
Bouillon cubes (beef and chicken)
Bread and cracker crumbs
Buckwheat groats*
Cereals
Cheese-garlic dressing mix*
Coffee (ground and instant)
Cornflakes
Corn meal (white and yellow)*
Cornstarch
Cracked wheat (seasoned)*
Crackers, soda, etc.
Cream of wheat*
Croutons
Dried fruits:
  Apricots
  Dates
  Prunes
  Raisins
Dried mushrooms*
Egg barley*
Flour shaker
French dressing mix*

Gelatins (unflavored and fruit)
Gingersnaps*
Graham crackers and crumbs
Grated Parmesan cheese
Macaronis (pastas)
Matzos*
Matzo meal
Non-caloric sweetener*
Noodles (fine and broad)
Oatmeal*
Onion soup mix
Peas, beans and lentils (dried)*
Potato chips
Potato flour and starch*
Pudding mixes
Rices, brown, white and wild
Salad dressing mixes*
Soup mixes*
Spaghetti
Spaghetti sauce mix*
Tea (bags and bulk)
Vanilla wafers
Zwieback*

Baking Shelf

Baking powder
Baking soda
Biscuit, cake, and pie mix*
Candied fruits (cherries, citron, and ginger)*

Chocolate:
  semi-sweet bits
  sweet cooking
  unsweetened baking
Cocoa

Coconut (flaked and grated)
Cream of tartar
Extracts:
 Almond
 Lemon*
 Mint*
 Orange*
 Vanilla
Flavorings, brandy and rum*
Flours, all-purpose and cake
Food coloring
Nuts:
 Almonds, whole and slivered

Cashews*
Peanuts*
Pecans, whole and chopped
Pistachios*
Walnuts, whole and chopped
Sugars:
 Confectioners'
 Granulated
 Brown, light* and dark
Vanilla bean*

Herbs and Spices

Allspice*
Anise seeds*
Apple pie spice*
Basil
Bay leaves
Caraway seeds
Celery seeds and salt
Chervil*
Chili powder*
Cinnamon
Cloves, whole and ground
Coriander*
Curry powder
Dill weed and seed
Garlic, powder and salt
Ginger (dry and preserved)*
Hickory or smoked salt*
Mace*
Marjoram*
Monosodium glutamate
Mustard (dry English)
Mustard seed*

Nutmeg
Onions, instant minced*
Onion salt*
Oregano
Paprika
Parsley flakes*
Peppers:
 Black ground
 Cayenne*
 Coarse ground
 Crushed red*
 White
Peppercorns
Pickling spice*
Poppy seeds
Poultry seasoning*
Rosemary
Salt, savory* and seasoned
Sesame seeds
Tarragon leaves
Thyme
Turmeric*

Wines and Spirits

Banana Cordial
Beer
Benedictine
Bitters (Angostura)
Brandies:
    Apricot
    Blackberry
    Peach
    Plain
Burgundy
Chablis
Chianti
Claret
Cognac
Cointreau
Crème de menthe

Curaçao
Grand Marnier
Grape wine, sweet
Kahlua
Kirsch
Madeira
Marsala
Peach liqueur
Pernod
Port
Rosé
Rum, white and dark
Sauterne
Sherry
Vermouth, dry and sweet

Garnishes

Flower Garnishes

Cucumber flowers: Remove each end of cucumber so cucumber is 1½ inches long; hollow slightly and scallop cut end in harlequin points around edge to form 4 or 5 deep petals. Insert 1-inch strip of carrot for stamen. Place on greens.

Grapefruit roses: These are made from the peeling and can be included when grapefruit is being sectioned. There is an added operation, a double peeling. First, peel off the outer yellow skin (zest), leaving the white membrane. Next peel off the white membrane in a long strip about ¾ inch wide, leaving the pulp exposed as when making sections. Reroll the strip until desired size of "flower," fasten with toothpick, and place it so that the exposed pulp is on the underside. Place it in cold water, add a few drops of red coloring (green for St. Patrick's Day), keep it immersed for an hour or two, and you have a blushing pink to red "rose" depending on your color preference. Make two or three small flowers from one peeling or 1 large one. Set them at one end of the platter in a bunch of verdant, crisp parsley.

To section grapefruit: Peel grapefruit over bowl to catch juice. Starting at stem end peel grapefruit in spiral fashion, cutting through skin and membrane exposing pulp and thus removing all white substance. Slip a sharp knife between pulp and membrane in both sides of each section until all are released. Use care so they are not broken. (Note "To Make Roses")

Radish Roses: Using sharp paring knife, cut off tip of radish. If there are greens, leave an inch or two. Peel 4 or 5 petals from tip of radish ¾ of the way to stem. Place in ice water to crisp and petals will open.

Orange Roses: Peel them in a long ¾-inch strip as for grapefruit roses, but do not remove the zest. Roll them to desired size, and spear with a toothpick to hold their shape. They may be wrapped in clear plastic and stored in the refrigerator.

Carrot flowers: Cutters for carrots and turnip flowers are available in the household departments. Slice the carrot ¼ inch thick crosswise, then cut the flowers from the slice. Spear them on a toothpick, add a center of the contrasting vegetable and place about six in a large bunch of parsley. Have it decorate an end of the entrée platter.

A carrot flower or two on parsley tucked into the joints of a large fowl is attractive.

Tomato roses: Peel tomatoes with vegetable peeler, starting at top and peeling around and around to bottom of tomatoes. Roll peeling around itself into rose shapes. Use pulp for Sauce Aurore.

Easter ham daisies: Instead of pineapple slices, decorate ham with four 5-petaled daisies. Cut twenty 1-inch petals of candied orange peel and fasten each petal to ham with whole cloves. Center each "daisy" with a half of candied cherry.

Other Garnishes

Carrot curls: Using potato peeler, cut long, thin wide strips the length of carrot; roll around finger, fasten with toothpick and crisp. Drop in salted water and refrigerate overnight. Curls will hold.

Carrot sticks: Cut carrot into ¼" julienne strips. Crisp them in ice water.

Parsley and watercress: Though mentioned with the menus, lux-uriant parsley and crisped fresh watercress, both eye-appealing garnishes, are worth repetition. Use them with a lavish hand.

Use foods of contrasting texture and color.

A sprinkling of chopped parsley, grated carrots, or sieved eggs makes an interesting topping, separately or in contrast.

Try slices of lemon dipped in chopped parsley, slices of lemon dipped heavily in paprika, or green pepper rings.

Stuffed olives: Slip 1-inch length of julienne carrot through pitted black or green olives.

Pickle fans: Slice small sweet pickles in length to about ¼″ from bottom. Spread section fanlike.

Cut pimiento into strips or stars, or chop finely to sprinkle for color. Cut celery into 2-inch lengths. Fringe one end by making ¼-inch cuts through half the length. Chill in ice water.

Peel a cucumber with an apple corer and remove seeds. Fill with processed pimiento cheese. Chill and cut into ½-inch slices. Use for garnish or relish.

Make a chain of onion and green pepper rings. Use for garnish or relish. Cut a slit in the green pepper ring; slip it through the onion ring.

Feathered celery: Clean celery hearts, remove unnecessary leaves, leaving a few for a feathery top. Cut each stalk through the heart in 4 or 5 lengths; the heart holds it together. With a sharp knife make several thin 1-inch slashes lengthwise through peeling and edge of outside stalk. Place in ice water and refrigerate several hours. Slashes will curl and give celery a lacy look. One tablespoon of sugar may be added to ice water to enhance flavor.

When a pastry tube is not at hand for decorative writing for a cake, improvise one by snipping off one corner of a clean envelope, fill it with frosting and force it through the opening.

Glossary

OF SOME TERMS USED IN OUR RECIPES

Acidulated water	water, with lemon juice or vinegar added, at a ratio of 1 tablespoon to 2 or 3 cups water (as for cooking artichokes)
Adjust seasonings	check for taste and add salt, pepper, etc., as needed
Al dente	Italian term for pastas, spaghetti, noodles, etc., cooked until done, but firm
A la	in the manner of
Amandine	with almonds
Antipasto	appetizer assortment
Aspic	a molded gelatin used in molds and as a garnish for cold dishes
Au jus	served only with natural juices
Bar le duc	a french currant jelly
Bechamel	a rich white sauce
Bind	to hold a mixture together by adding eggs, flour, butter, etc.
Blanch	to immerse, briefly, in boiling water, removed from heat
Blaze	to pour warm liquor over food and ignite
Blend	to combine ingredients until smooth and well mixed
Bouillabaisse	a fish stew
Bouquet garni	a faggot or bouquet of herbs or plants used in variety for seasoning specific recipes
Capers	pickled flower buds, used for flavoring
Caramelize	to melt sugar over low heat until it becomes brown and syrupy
Chateaubriand	roast middle cut of tenderloin
Chaudfroid	a cold, jellied opaque sauce used for glazing
Choux paste	cream puff pastry
Coat spoon	the cooking stage when a liquid adheres to a spoon in a thin layer
Collop	an oyster-sized piece of meat, usually presented individually, rather than as a stew

Cook "short"	to simmer with very little liquid
Court bouillon	a simmered stock used for poaching meat, fish, or vegetables; composed of the proper combination of liquids for either one
Croûte	a pastry shell in which food is baked
Deglaze	to remove clinging particles from pan in which meat has been browned, usually by dissolving with liquid
Dollop	usually applied to a thick spoonful of heavy sauce dropped as a topping
Doneness	to particular taste or texture
En brochette	broiled on a skewer
En coquille	in a shell
En papillote	baked in paper; replaced in many instances by aluminum foil
Fillet or filet	a boned piece of meat or fish, or to remove bones from meat or fish
Fine herb	an aromatic mixture of chopped herbs and plants
Fines herbes	a mixture of fresh or dried herbes, usually tied in small bags and dropped into sauces as seasoning
Flavors "Marry"	a preparation is allowed to stand so that seasonings blend completely
Flambé(e)	French for flame
Foie gras	goose liver (Pâté de Fois Gras — goose liver paste)
Fork tender	tender when tested with a fork
Fold	to blend mixture in an overlapping, lifting motion, from one side of a bowl to the other
Fold in	to incorporate, to fold, a light mixture such as egg whites with a heavier one
Forcemeat	a seasoned stuffing of finely minced fish, meat or fowl
French cut	to cut with small knife with corrugated blade
Gâteau	a round flat cake
Gelée	a jellied mixture, or preparation in aspic (jelled) mixture
Glacé	iced or frozen foods

Glaze	a thin coating of syrup or aspic; or to brown a topping sauce by baking or boiling
Gnocchis	small Italian dumpling
Julienne	food cut in long thin strips; or pertaining to recipes with julienne garnish
Knead	to work a mixture with the hands, folding and pressing until smooth
Macedoine	a mixture of fruit or vegetables
Marinate	to soak in a marinade or French dressing
Mince	to chop finely
Mollet	a soft-cooked, peeled egg
Niçoise	as prepared in Nice
Noisette	a tidbit
Pâté	seasoned paste, used often for appetizer
Poach	to simmer in liquid just below boiling point
Poulet	chicken
Purée	to force through a sieve or mill to a pulp
Ragout	a thick stew
Ramekin	small individual baking dish
Reduce	to cook until mixture becomes diminished in quantity
Roe	fish eggs (caviar)
Roux	a mixture of heated butter and flour, mixed to a paste and used as a thickening agent with a liquid for sauce or gravy, etc.
Sauté	to brown in a little fat or oil
Scald	to heat until almost boiling; to pour boiling water over food
Score	to make gashes in surface
Sear	to brown meat quickly at high heat
Shallots	a mild bulbous onion
Shortening	cooking fat
Skewer	a long metal or wooden pin used to hold meat or fowl in place; used for threading pieces of meat for broiling or for lacing fowl to enclose stuffing
Slivered	cut into shreds
Spaetzle	a type of small dumpling
Steam	to cook as in a double boiler or in a steamer

Stock liquid strained from cooked meat, fish or vegetables

Toss to lift carefully with large fork and spoon, in order to mix lightly

Trim to cut away unwanted or unsightly parts of food

Truffles fleshy underground fungus found in France; similar in flavor to mushrooms

Truss to tie wings and legs of poultry close to body to hold it in shape

Velouté a rich, velvety white sauce

Water bath a shallow pan of water in which a mold or dish of food is baked

Work to mix or knead slowly

Zest colored, oily exterior skin of citrus fruit (rind)

Serving Ideas

Forethought in planning the serving needs correlates with the Advanced Preparation Schedule. Whether you have help or not, last minute confusion is avoided, and our hostess can remain relaxed and at ease.

After your menu is set, plan your accessories and have them in shining readiness by the previous day.

Arrange your flowers early in the day.

Have your candy and nuts at hand.

There are many auxiliary items conducive to organization.

Trays are an indispensable item. Arrange your accessories and your table appointments on them, to be brought to the dining room with a minimum of effort.

The tray runs the gamut from this labor-saving device to the dainty breakfast-in-bed service. Use it as a place setting before the fire, TV, or for buffet service. A tray makes a charming individual guest setting for informal gatherings. It carries, it contains, it dispenses. A space saver for use and for storage, as trays can be stacked compactly.

A good rule to follow: Serve hot foods very hot. Serve cold foods icy cold.

Serve salads, of course, on cold plates; add dressing just before using, unless otherwise mentioned.

Preheat your plates for hot food and chill for cold so that the preparations may retain the proper temperatures as long as possible.

The tea cart, too, has many time- and labor-saving uses. It may serve as a bar with the needed glasses and equipment. As an hors d'oeuvre table, the platters may be arranged on the upper shelf, the serving pieces and plates, conveniently on the lower tray.

For afternoon tea, the hostess may have all her service before her, and the cart becomes a tea table.

The cool refreshment on a warm day is doubly invigorating when wheeled attractively onto the veranda.

The cart may be arranged in advance for the late evening snack, with whatever foods can stand at room temperature.

It is helpful in organizing and planning a party. The service of the first course in the living room simplifies the dining room service. The cart can be an auxiliary table, an accessible shelf for clearing, and a pleasure to wheel away.

Buffet service is expedient for a large group and conducive to informal fun.

Plate service, with the dinner courses served individually to each guest is simple and quick. With the appetizers served in the living room, there remains only the service of the dessert.

Family service with the host serving at the table is another comfortable, informal method. The tea cart can again become the serving table if more room is needed.

Doilies and place mats are lovely and simple to launder. The plastic mats are a great innovation and some of the more beautiful can be used for semi-formal entertaining.

Try using squares of colored wall tile for hot pads. They are colorful and smart.

Wineglasses make delightful cigarette holders for the dining table.

For a change, serve soup in a goblet.

Oversized Old-Fashioned glasses are lovely low containers for the table flowers. Use three or four in a row, depending upon the length of the table.

For informal dining for lunch or dinner, have your coffeepot and cups at hand, to serve as wanted and accessible for "seconds."

Snack tables are delightful for the buffet service.

Mugs are great for the sandwich and soup menu — even for that coffee refresher to accompany the routine telephone calls.

The Hibachi is a delightful Japanese adaptation. It makes the cocktail hour a busy "pre-course" to the dinner, and gives the hostess time for the last-minute touches. Light the charcoal about an hour in advance to have it burned to a glowing bed of coals. Have the food on trays, the skewers available, and sauces nearby. The guests will spear their selection and cook it to taste. Serve little ribs, barbecued in advance, to be reheated. Prepare Tartar Balls, to be speared and cooked, as well as marinated beef tenderloin, cocktail sausages, Shrimp Ramaki and many others which are indexed. Our *Thoughts for Buffets* has a delicious selection.

When entertaining guests from other parts of the country, or even other countries, serve them your regional specialties.

Table Decor

FOR interesting table arrangement, secure three birds of paradise of different lengths at one side of a low container. Arrange lemon leaves to extend from base of flowers to opposite end of container and onto the table. Scatter orange and green-pointed fresh peppers on the leaves, to follow contour of the arrangement.

Construct a palette of heavy cardboard for an artistic occasion, making holes for paint containers; place a small bouquet in each hole to represent paint color, and extend long stalks of another variety for brushes. Place palette over shallow bowl filled with water, to keep flowers fresh.

Use a gay cloth with a potted plant for the centerpiece. For a simple party cut flowers added to the plant greens are easily arranged and lovely.

The specialty departments in most stores have long-stemmed, multicolored glasses of various heights. Each glass is solidly filled with a candle. Lighted and grouped on the table with a simple arrangement of flowers, they make a charming centerpiece.

For a kitchen shower luncheon fasten a circle of Styrafoam in center of large, flat bowl. Into it, spear a shocking-pink feather duster, a plastic, rose-decorated flyswatter, a varicolored sponge dish mop and a flower-adorned bottle brush. Edge the base with gold or colored doilies and make fill-ins of colored kitchen sponges.

Conversation is stimulated by adding colored measuring spoons, a cooking-spoon holder and whatever your imagination dictates. Present it to the bride as her gift for the day.

The centerpiece at an engagement party may be individual pink corsages, formed into one large arrangement with lace doily backing and a wide pink satin ribbon attached to each bouquet, leading to each place setting. Pink mints and pink-dipped fondant almonds in a pair of compotes may be placed at either end of the table.

For a graduation party, roll up a ten-inch sheet of paper like a diploma and tie it with one-inch ribbons of school colors. Slip appropriate flowers and greens through ribbon and place on cake or on platter with cake. Paper mortarboards may be purchased or made for centerpiece and place cards. Use a base of greens with class flowers for center.

At a party for pre-schoolers, a musical carousel as a centerpiece will set the tune. Circle it with cake clowns, one for each guest, as decoration, and to be served with the dessert ice-cream clowns.

For the Christmas dinner centerpiece, plan a basket of beautiful fruit. Start the arrangement with a fresh pineapple standing upright just off center so that the frond rises above the arrangement. Spread stalks of frond apart and insert sprigs of bright holly between them. Bank fruit of your selection around pineapple and drape bunches of grapes gracefully and tuck kumquats and nuts in crevices. Use Christmas candles, of course.

The Thanksgiving dinner table can have as a centerpiece a large flat basket piled high with gold and bronze-sprayed seasonal fruit and gourds and small bouquets of bronze chrysanthemums tucked between fruit.

On Mother's Day, arrange a centerpiece composed of Mother's gifts, topped with a gold crown made by the children.

For New Year's Day supper a figure of the New Year baby, surrounded by good luck symbols — a gold paper horseshoe, a rabbit's foot, a four-leaf clover, for example — would be a centerpiece with significance.

Measurements and Weights

Dash or pinch = less than ⅛ teaspoon

3 teaspoons = 1 tablespoon	8 tablespoons = ½ cup
16 tablespoons = 1 cup	4 tablespoons = ¼ cup
4 ounces = ½ cup liquid	2 pints = 1 quart
8 ounces = 1 cup liquid	4 quarts = 1 gallon

2 cups = 1 pint

2 tablespoons equivalent to 1 fluid ounce

To Measure Raw Eggs:

5 whole eggs = 1 cup   8 to 9 egg whites = 1 cup

12 yolks = 1 cup

The packaging of butter has simplified measurement:

1 pound = 2 cups	¼ pound or 1 stick = ½ cup
½ pound or 2 sticks = 1 cup	⅛ pound or ½ stick = ¼ cup

With butter packaged in ¼ pound cubes or sticks, this convenience is assured. However, when using tub butter, or undivided pounds, the older method of measuring still has value. For example, to measure ½ cup butter (¼ pound) pour ½ cup cold water into a measuring cup, add sufficient cold butter to cause the water to rise to the 1-cup line, then drain and ½ cup butter remains.

Spoon amounts are level as with other measurements.

Flour: When directions call for measured sifted flour, in resifting, use wax paper for repeated operations.

Measurement of Shelled Nuts: Nuts vary in weight. A pound of shelled almonds equals about 3 cups. A pound of whole shelled walnuts or pecans equals about 4 cups. A pound of shelled peanuts equals 2¾ cups. One cup of unshelled nuts equals ⅞ cup finely chopped nuts.

Measurement of Chicken: One 2-pound cooked chicken will make about 2½ cups of diced chicken.

Brown Sugar: When measuring, be sure it is firmly packed.

Approximate Measurement of Cans in Terms of Cups:

#1 can	10½ ounces, or 1½ cups
#2 can	15 ounces or 2 cups
#2½ can	1 pound, 13 ounces or 2½ cups
#300 can	15 ounces or 2 cups
#303 can	1 pound or 2 cups

These are approximate sizes for fruit and vegetable measurement and we are listing reference to those measurements and products or ingredients which are used in this book. We do not attempt to cover the entire category. This is merely for the convenience and enjoyment of those of you who use these recipes.

Evaporated milk (approximate measurements):
small can = 6 ounces or ¾ cup
tall can = 14½ ounces or 1¾ cups
        sweetened condensed milk = 15 ounces or 2 cups

Soups: 10½ ounces = approximately 1¼ cups

Yeast
    active dry yeast   ¼-ounce package
    compressed yeast   ⅔-ounce cake
    household yeast   1-ounce cake

Pots, Pans, and Gadgets

SOME indispensable gadgets without which no kitchen is complete.

Bean slicer	To French-cut fresh string beans.
Kitchen tongs	To turn chicken; to remove hard-boiled eggs; for adjusting food portions when cooking in a roaster, and endless other uses.
Assorted wooden spoons	For blending pastries and various other kitchen uses.
Vegetable peeler	For use in peeling not only vegetables, but preparing cheese, chocolate, grating carrots and a variety of other uses.

Cutters for carrot and turnip flowers	To add the last touch to the entrée platter.
Rubber spatula	To scrape the last delicious drop of batter or other food from a bowl; used for folding the light ingredients, and for mixing the heavier (be certain it is pliable).
French cutter (cutter with a scalloped blade)	Makes a scalloped pat of an ordinary butter slice; makes scalloped edge of a slice of fruit or vegetable more attractive.
Cooking spoon rest	To catch the spoon drippings between bastings.
Melon ball cutter	Pile a high mound of melon balls on a fruit platter. Arrange a dish of butter balls for a buffet, or try potato balls as a garnish as well as a vegetable.
Memo pad and pencils	To jot down your shopping needs.
Ice-cream scoop	Use for portioning mashed potatoes or puréed vegetables.
2-cup flour sifter	Measures the flour into a cup as it sifts.
Clipboard	For messages to the family and memorandums.
Kitchen scissors	Indispensable for finely cut vegetables, slicing, and countless other operations.
Egg slicer	
Slotted spoon	
Vegetable brush	
Measuring cup with a spout	
Garlic press	Invaluable, as its use releases the minced garlic and gives subtle flavor, eliminating the too strong taste of the herb.
Cook and Serve Containers	Both attractive and convenient; most move from the refrigerator to the oven to the table and give ease to preparation.
Skillets	We have recommended the use of various sizes, from 6-inch for crêpes to the larger for oven pancakes. The electric skillet and the chafing dish are attractive for serving.

Saucepans	Various sizes are needed for the preparation of recipes.
Molds and dessert pans	Lovely molds are attractive when used for salads, desserts, etc. and come in various sizes. The following are recommended as those most frequently indicated in our recipes. *Fish:* 4 to 6 cups. *Heart:* 6 cups. *Ring:* 4 to 6 cups. *Individual:* 3 and 4 ounces. *Decorative:* square, star, high hat, about 4 to 6 cups. *Jelly roll pan:* 15″ x 18″. *Spring form:* 9″ or 10″. *Tube pan:* 9″ or 10″.
Sandwich cutter	The rim of a 4-ounce orange juice glass makes a convenient sandwich cutter; likewise the lid of a mason jar.
Food mill	The food mill has many uses and makes a simple operation of sieving or puréeing.
Cooky sheet liners	A parchment-like paper available in most stores. They come in various sizes, eliminate buttering the pan, and prevent the cookies from becoming too brown on the underside.
Deep fat frying	To test fat for proper heat, a thermometer is most reliable. To test without a thermometer: A one-inch cube of bread dropped into hot fat will brown in 90 seconds at 325° to 350° in 60 seconds at 360° to 375° in 40 seconds at 375° to 400°
Meat thermometer	The meat thermometer is an indispensable item for accuracy in roast preparation. It removes the worry of required doneness of a roast. Use care in inserting it as it must not touch any bone.
Candy thermometer	A candy thermometer is a great help, not only for candy making, but in the preparation of basic syrups.

Toothpicks	The colored toothpicks are attractive for serving the appetizers, the cheese nibblers, and the other bits, too small to handle. Natural wood picks are indispensable for fastening meats, stuffings, etc.
Paper goods	The paper or sheer plastic type doilies are practical, decorative, and indispensable for most every service.
Candles	Have birthday candles on hand for an emergency.
Foil-lined dishes	Foil-lined baking dishes are a real time-saver.
Cupcake liners	Have paper cupcake liners on hand.
Aluminum foil	Use aluminum foil to catch the drippings when roasting or broiling.

Recipes Adaptable For Leftovers

Poultry

Chicken Salad Supreme, p. 475
Chicken Almond Appetizers, p. 531
Indonesian Chicken Curry, p. 514

Lamb
Curried Lamb, p. 532
Bombay Curry, p. 577

Beef
Fillet of Beef Flambé (flame leftover thin, cooked beef slices), p. 22
Soy Steak Sauce (marinate and reheat leftover beef), p. 52
Pepper Steak Del Prado, p. 71
Eggs Gaxton, p. 80
Pizzaburgers, p. 104
Cantonese Beef, p. 123
Beef Bourguignon, p. 180
Cold Beef Fillet Marinara, p. 199
Chinese Beef and Vegetables, p. 350
Sukiyaki, p. 434

Veal
Bohemian Veal (reheat with combined sauce ingredients), p. 278

Ham
Ham à la Crème, p. 229
Curry Ham Sauce, p. 259
Split Pea Soup (use ham bone), p. 589

Vegetables
Duchess Potatoes Amandine, p. 270
Basque Potatoes, p. 299
Vegetable Chowder, p. 492
Cooked Vegetable Salad, p. 600

Eggs
Eggs à la Russe, p. 6
Deviled Eggs, p. 104   } Post-Easter leftovers
Eggs en Soufflé, p. 389

Pork
Oriental Pork, p. 523

Sandwiches
Use leftover chicken for
Hot Chicken Sandwiches, p. 118
Pyramid Sandwiches, p. 126
Use leftover ham for
Crusty Deviled Ham Sandwiches, p. 482
Chef's Sandwich, p. 519
Williamsburg Club Sandwich, p. 519
Jonathan Ham Sandwich, p. 519
Knife and Fork Sandwich, p. 587

Chowders and Soups
Use leftover shrimp and chicken for
Tureen of Mulligatawny, p. 148
Fish Chowder, p. 238
Chicken Shrimp Soup, p. 280
Chicken Sub Gum Soup, p. 358
Use leftover fish for
Cioppino Fisherman's Wharf, p. 304
Use leftover vegetables for
Vegetable Chowder, p. 492
Use leftover tongue root or ham bone for
Split Pea Soup, p. 589

Classified List of Menus

Index

The number of persons served is indicated at the beginning of each menu

The number of persons served is

indicated at the beginning of each menu

The number of persons served is

indicated at the beginning of each menu

The number of persons served is

indicated at the beginning of each menu

The number of persons served is

indicated at the beginning of each menu

The number of persons served is

indicated at the beginning of each menu

The number of persons served is

indicated at the beginning of each menu

The number of persons served is

indicated at the beginning of each menu

The number of persons served is

indicated at the beginning of each menu

The number of persons served is

indicated at the beginning of each menu

The number of persons served is

indicated at the beginning of each menu

The number of persons served is

indicated at the beginning of each menu

The number of persons served is

indicated at the beginning of each menu

The number of persons served is

indicated at the beginning of each menu

The number of persons served is

indicated at the beginning of each menu

The number of persons served is

indicated at the beginning of each menu

The number of persons served is

indicated at the beginning of each menu

The number of persons served is

indicated at the beginning of each menu